"Mr. McManus gives the reader a glimpse into the shrapnel and lead flying among desperate soldiers, and his pacing is impeccable. . . . *September Hope* describes the slow, unfolding train wreck in gripping detail. It is a testament to men assigned the impossible who, through sheer willpower, almost pulled it off."
—*The Wall Street Journal*

"In September 1944, the Allies' heady advances ground to a bloody halt all along the Western Front. John C. McManus's superb *September Hope* takes us to the heart of some of the most intense and dramatic combat of the entire war. A riveting and deeply moving story of uncommon courage."
—Alex Kershaw, *New York Times* bestselling author of *The Longest Winter*

"A fine account of one of the Second World War's most fraught and frustrating battles. John C. McManus's extensive research allows him to tell the story with verve and authority."
—Rick Atkinson, Pulitzer Prize–winning author of *An Army at Dawn*

"In *September Hope*, John McManus continues his mission to document the experiences of American GIs on the Western Front of World War II. Focusing on the U.S. Airborne operations in the Netherlands, McManus mines a rich and too-long-neglected vein of stories, many revealed here for the first time. *September Hope* details the valor of American soldiers—in this case Airborne forces— who routinely and decisively defeated the vaunted elite of the Wehrmacht, including SS and parachute troops."
—Mark Bando, author of *101st Airborne: The Screaming Eagles at Normandy*

"John C. McManus's *September Hope* is an absolutely riveting and vivid narrative that captures the full extent of the heroism of America's troops in Operation Market Garden. McManus weaves together the tense deliberations among Allied generals in their headquarters with the blow-by-blow experiences of soldiers battling their way through enemy territory. This is military history at its finest. "
—Andrew Carroll, Editor of the *New York Times* bestsellers *War Letters* and *Behind the Lines*

"McManus's crisply written book tells of the campaign as seen through the eyes of the privates, sergeants, and captains who jumped into the Netherlands and the air crews who got them their."
—*St. Louis Post-Dispatch*

Also by John C. McManus

Grunts:
Inside the American Infantry Combat Experience, World War II
Through Iraq

American Courage, American Carnage:
The 7th Infantry Regiment's Combat Experience, 1812
Through World War II

The 7th Infantry Regiment:
Combat in an Age of Terror, the Korean War Through the Present

U.S. Military History for Dummies

Alamo in the Ardennes:
The Untold Story of the American Soldiers Who Made the Defense of
Bastogne Possible

The Americans at Normandy:
The Summer of 1944—The American War from the Normandy Beaches
to Falaise

The Americans at D-Day:
The American Experience at the Normandy Invasion

Deadly Sky:
The American Combat Airman in World War II

The Deadly Brotherhood:
The American Combat Soldier in World War II

SEPTEMBER HOPE

The American Side of a Bridge Too Far

John C. McManus

CALIBER

Dutton Caliber
An imprint of Penguin Random House LLC
penguinrandomhouse.com

The Library of Congress has catalogued the hardcover edition of this title as follows:
McManus, John C., 1965–
September hope: the American side of a bridge too far/John C. McManus.
p. cm.
Includes bibliographical references and index.
ISBN 978-0-451-23706-4
1. Arnhem, Battle of, Arnhem, Netherlands, 1944. 2. World War, 1939–1945—Campaigns—Netherlands.
3. World War, 1939–1945—Aerial operations, American. 4. United States. Army. Airborne Division 82nd—
History. 5. United States. Army. Airborne Division 101st—History. I. Title.
D763.N42A7356 2012
940.54'219218—dc23 2011053222

PUBLISHING HISTORY
NAL Caliber hardcover edition: 2012
NAL Caliber trade paperback edition: 2013
First Dutton Caliber trade paperback edition: 2019
Dutton Caliber ISBN: 978-0-451-23989-1

Designed by Alissa Amell

146119709

CONTENTS

"In the years to come everyone will remember Arnhem, but no one will remember that two American divisions fought their hearts out in the Dutch canal country and whipped hell out of the Germans."

—Lieutenant General Lewis Brereton, First Allied Airborne
Army Commander, diary entry, November 21, 1944

For Nancy, with enduring love and gratitude

And for Cornelius Ryan and Charles B. MacDonald, who both made sure the American side of a bridge too far would never be forgotten

FOREWORD

A t the end of August 1944, the Allied world was filled with hope. The Allies had experienced what was, for them, the greatest month of the war. In the Pacific, the Americans had taken the Mariana Islands, and the Japanese were in full retreat throughout the theater. In Europe, Soviet armies had annihilated more than twenty German divisions and had pushed the hated enemy from Russian territory. Indeed, Soviet forces were deep inside Poland, at the edge of Warsaw. In the West, General Dwight D. Eisenhower's burgeoning armies had liberated Paris, along with the rest of France. Flush with victory and the possibility of an imminent end to the war, British, Canadian, and American armored columns plunged into Belgium, Holland, and Luxembourg. Rumors swirled among the troops that Germany would surrender any day now and that everyone would be home for Christmas. The Germans were supposedly in disarray, overwhelmed on all fronts. They were losing soldiers by the thousands, even as Allied bombers pulverized their cities. For the Third Reich, it seemed, the end was near. At least that was the hope. Then came September 1944 and Holland.

Beyond all the sunny talk of impending victory and white Christmases at home (as if the soldiers would not be needed for postwar occupation duty even if Germany did collapse) loomed a disturbing, gloomy reality, for those who chose to see it. That reality can be summed up in one word: logistics. By September, as Eisenhower's armies advanced closer to Ger-

1

many, their supply situation steadily worsened. The issue was not a lack of matériel. The Allies had plenty of fuel, food, ammunition, trucks, jeeps, tanks, and the like. But, three months after D-day, the vast majority of these supplies were still entering continental Europe over the Normandy beaches. This ungainly situation seriously limited how much matériel could be unloaded from the ships at any given time. The larger problem, though, was transporting it all from the beaches to the fighting fronts hundreds of miles to the east. Before the Normandy invasion, Allied planes had bombed French railroads, bridges, and highways, mainly to impede the movement of German reinforcements to the invasion beaches. Now these same transportation nodes had to be repaired and used to move cargo-laden locomotives and trucks to the front. All of this would take time. Nor did the Allies possess the airlift capacity to sustain their armies that way.

The solution to the entire mess was possession of deepwater harbors, especially Antwerp, the greatest port in northern Europe. Capable of handling at least ten thousand tons of freight per day, Antwerp alone could fill the supply needs of the majority of Eisenhower's armies. Incredibly, on September 4, soldiers from Britain's 11th Armoured Division captured most of the city and all of the extensive harbor facilities intact, with barely a fight. Yet this was only the first step in making use of Antwerp. They also needed to seize control of the Scheldt estuary, a sixty-mile waterway leading from the city to the English Channel. The Scheldt was studded with narrow islets, canals, and low-country islands, all of which could be fortified to prevent the passage of ships. Without control of the Scheldt estuary, Antwerp was useless. In the absence of any orders from higher command to cut off or begin clearing the estuary, the men of the 11th Armoured, who were desperately weary after many frenetic days of advancing, settled down for a well-earned rest. The estuary remained uncleared. With Germany ostensibly on the verge of collapse, though, few Allied commanders worried much about the Scheldt. It was a stunning oversight and one that was to have profound consequences.

In September 1944, Eisenhower wanted to advance into Germany on a broad front. Newly promoted field marshal Bernard Montgomery, his most contentious subordinate, favored a single-front advance into Germany, north of the Siegfried Line fortifications and the industrial Ruhr, with Berlin as the ultimate objective. Their differing concepts have been chronicled, and debated, by a legion of historians, for many decades, so there is no need to recapitulate them here in any sort of depth. It is fair to say, though, that their ideas grew from distinct national differences. Montgomery keenly understood that, by the end of 1944, Britain was nearing exhaustion, especially in relation to manpower. The longer the war continued, the weaker the British position would become in the Allied coalition. Humane and thoughtful, Montgomery had no wish to see his countrymen endure another hard winter of war, all the more so because, by September, the Germans were peppering British cities indiscriminately with V1 and V2 rockets. Because of all this, and the ugly supply situation, Montgomery believed that only a single thrust along his own northern front offered any hope of ending the war in 1944.

As an American, Eisenhower had a completely different perspective. Certainly he had no wish to see the war drag into 1945, but if it took a few months past Christmas to defeat Nazi Germany, he was perfectly willing to see that happen. To him, the broad-front advance emphasized all the advantages that material-rich America had endowed upon the Allied coalition—manpower, food, ammunition, and vehicles. Given these strengths, the Allies would then simply overwhelm the hard-pressed Germans with continuous attacks on all parts of the front.

Eisenhower did not speak of his broad-front strategy in historical terms but, interestingly, it harkened back to Lincoln's blueprint for victory in the Civil War. Like the Allies in World War II, the Union during the Civil War held distinct advantages over the Confederacy in manpower, war matériel, and transportation. As such, Lincoln chose to put maximum pressure on the rebels by blockading their ports, seizing control of their rivers, and launching constant attacks on their undersupplied armies. Obviously this worked. Montgomery's single-front thrust was predicated on the flawed notion that taking Berlin in 1944 would end the war. This presupposed a successful dash, against no substantial counterattacks, across the north German plains, followed by a bloodless fight for a major metropolitan area, and a "pack-it-in" mentality among the Nazi regime and the still-formidable German army. Eisenhower intuitively understood that just as Richmond was an overrated objective for the Union in 1864, Berlin was equally overrated for the Allies in 1944. The key to defeating Germany was to take the industrial Ruhr and to destroy the German army. This would deprive the Germans of the necessary matériel to continue fighting, and, more important, it would destroy their will to do so. Only a broad-front advance offered any realistic hope of achieving these objectives (as the subsequent course of the war demonstrated).

Yet, in September, the supreme commander repeatedly sent mixed signals to his subordinates on Berlin's importance. Worse, he strayed from his broad-front approach, authorizing a bold, visionary, but deeply flawed plan designed by Montgomery to execute his single thrust and end the war quickly. The plan was, of course, known as Operation Market Garden. It envisaged airborne drops to seize key bridges, combined with a lightning armored advance that would strike ultimately over the Rhine and into the vitals of Germany. In essence, the plan was based mainly on hope—hope that Nazi Germany was just about finished, hope that the weather would hold, hope that all bridges would be captured intact, hope that most of the German opposition would come from overaged invalids.

When Eisenhower gave Montgomery permission (and priority of supply) to launch Market Garden, he made his worst decision of the war. Market Garden was a bad idea because it took the Allied focus off Antwerp—and Antwerp was what mattered the most. Without the necessary supplies, the Allies had no chance of sustaining a victorious push into Germany. The reality in September 1944 was that only Antwerp could provide them with those supplies. In turning their attention from opening up this ideal supply port to unleashing the bold Market Garden, the commanders were basically pinning their hopes for success on the military equivalent of a Hail Mary pass.

This book, then, is about the consequences of Eisenhower's poor decision, mainly for those Americans who paid such a high price for it. The vast majority of books on Market Garden focus on the British 1st Airborne Division at Arnhem, to the point where there is little new to say on that aspect of the battle. Once the British were besieged at Arnhem, Market Garden's entire outcome depended not just on their ability to hold out, but on the success or failure of the two American airborne divisions. If the Americans could hang on to a narrow corridor of roads and capture key bridges, then British tanks could make it to Arnhem to rescue the British paratroopers and fulfill Market Garden's ultimate purpose of invading northern Germany. Truly, everything hinged on this. Yet there is no single book on the American experience in Market Garden. Because the U.S. role in the battle, and the ensuing stalemate and nightmarish slog to clear the Scheldt, were all quite significant, this is a real historical oversight. Indeed, even Cornelius Ryan in his classic account *A Bridge Too Far* gave relatively short shrift to the American aspect of the operation. My goal is to rectify that gap in the literature of Market Garden in such a way that perhaps Ryan would approve of it. The story is truly a dramatic human tale of euphoria, hope, and tragic disappointment. Those Americans who fought in Holland could never forget the experience—the courage and forbearance of the Dutch people, the rich, moist earth, the muddy canals and dikes, the tidy homes and streets, the sunshine of September hope giving way to the chilly rain of October disappointment.

Market Garden and Antwerp are, in my view, part of the same story. This book reflects that interpretation. Part I, "The Leap," chronicles the frenzied pace of Market Garden, when seconds counted and the Allies were optimistic that crossing Dutch rivers could end the war. Part II, "The Fall," covers the sad aftermath of Market Garden's abject failure when, in

October and November, troopers of the two airborne divisions manned static lines, battling the climate and the Germans, while newly arrived soldiers from the 104th Infantry Division (the Timberwolves) fought desperately to open the muddy, wet Scheldt estuary. My story is based on a rich blend of underutilized primary sources such as group combat interviews, unit journals, after-action reports, latter-day personal interviews, oral histories, unpublished memoirs, and even systematic, descriptive surveys from the remarkable Cornelius Ryan collection at Ohio University. The cast of personalities is extensive, from privates to generals. My personal hope is that this book will offer a new way to see and interpret these momentous events.

Together, the two parts of *September Hope* comprise a moving tale of pathos, tragedy, and squandered valor. It is, in my opinion, an epic human story—endlessly compelling and moving. And it all began on a late summer's day with a leap into the blue Dutch sky.

PART I

THE LEAP

Into the Blue Dutch Sky

Amid the vivid blue canopy of a late-summer sky, hundreds of bulbous, olive drab C-47 Skytrain aircraft flew in practiced formations. Planes literally filled the gentle heavens, almost as if they were multiplying their numbers while in midair. They comprised the most ambitious aerial armada in history. Inside one of the leading C-47s, Brigadier General James Gavin, commanding officer of the 82nd Airborne Division, stood near an open door scanning, with his piercing blue eyes, the skies outside and the ground some fifteen hundred feet below. He was a bit surprised by the deep green hue of the Dutch countryside. Here and there, clumps of red-tiled roofs jutted out of the green landscape, marking the location of villages, each of which looked alike to the youthful general. All around him, impossibly vast numbers of C-47s bobbed slightly up and down as they knifed through pockets of air, each one of them flying inexorably toward an unseen drop zone. The sound produced by this propeller-driven armada was immense, like the buzzing hum of several million bees. The drone of the engines mixed uneasily with the whipping of the wind plus the natural creaking and groaning of each plane's thin metal skin to produce a steady sound track of noise.

As the general gazed at the neighboring planes, he retreated into his own thoughts. Every aircraft contained a stick of paratroopers, between fourteen and eighteen of his men, each waiting for the order to stand up, attach a small hook to a static line, and then leap out of their planes into the void. To Gavin, each plane's cargo was so precious that it might as well have been hauling gold. These troopers were *his* men, in every meaning of the phrase. They were a mixture of hard-bitten veterans and apprehensive rookies. Many, including the general, were about to make their fourth combat jump. From Sicily to Normandy, they had formed a bond stronger than oak. Gavin was their leader, in both a physical sense as commander and an emotional sense as the ultimate kindred spirit. He was fond of welcoming new officers with an admonishment that, in the 82nd Airborne, they were expected to be "first out of the door of the airplane and last in the chow line." He embodied all the young airborne warriors—no matter the unit—in a way that nearly everyone inside those planes understood but few could define with any precision except to say, as one of them did, that "every man [was] a clone of the CO."

At a casual glance, an observer might mistake Gavin for one of his soldiers. At age thirty-seven, he was the youngest division commander in the United States Army. His chiseled baby face seemed to belong to a man in his early twenties, not his late thirties. The combination of close-cropped brown hair, narrow cheekbones, and a wide, sturdy Irish nose lent a sort of movie-star quality to his appearance. Tall, ramrod straight, lean and sinewy, he exuded athletic grace. Women found him irresistible. Men would follow him anywhere. Although experienced combat soldiers tended to be contemptuous and wary of their senior officers, most troopers of the 82nd Airborne openly idolized General Gavin. He was known for his hands-on leadership, seemingly always at the front, facing danger, brandishing his trusty M1 Garand rifle, fighting alongside his people, without ever losing sight of the bigger picture so necessary to senior command. The men affectionately called him "Slim Jim" for his physique, or "Jumping Jim" because of his obvious mania for parachuting out of airplanes.

Anyone in the outfit who cared to learn more about the general was impressed by the underdog quality of his life story. Orphaned to a New York City convent at age two, he was never able to pinpoint the identity of his birth parents, except that they had probably been Irish immigrants.

Martin and Mary Gavin, a dysfunctional Irish couple from the Pennsylvania coal town of Mount Carmel, adopted him in 1909. His boyhood was marked by a sad mix of family tension and shanty-Irish genteel poverty. At seventeen he was so eager to escape these unhappy circumstances that he absconded to New York and joined the army as an underage recruit. He quickly found that he was born to be a soldier. His performance as an enlisted man was so impressive that he earned an appointment to West Point, graduating in 1929 to become an infantry officer. As the United States entered World War II, Gavin was drawn, as a young major, to the newly created paratroopers. He was one of the early airborne pioneers, a military intellectual who helped create the new parachute culture out of whole cloth, devising training methods, testing equipment (sometimes with free-fall jumps), and perfecting combat tactics. He commanded the 505th Parachute Infantry Regiment in Sicily and Italy, where he earned his fearsome reputation for bravery and charismatic combat leadership. "He always wanted to be where 'the action' was," one of his officers commented. Highly impressed, the 82nd Airborne's commander, General Matthew Ridgway, had then promoted to him to brigadier general to serve as his assistant division commander in time for the jump into Normandy. After that campaign, when Ridgway was promoted to command the XVIII Airborne Corps, Gavin inherited command of his beloved 82nd Airborne. The young general's life was the military version of a rags-to-riches, Horatio Alger story.

Now, as Gavin stood in the doorway of that C-47, his unlikely rise from a disadvantaged urchin to a boy general was the last thing on his mind. He was deeply worried about this jump into Holland. His concern had begun practically the first moment he had learned, a week earlier, of this ambitious plan known as Market Garden. As a paratrooper, he was, of course, used to dropping behind enemy lines. But in this operation, he was not sure whether he had enough troops to carry out his orders, which, by now, he knew by heart: "The 82nd Airborne Division will seize and hold the bridges at Nijmegen and Grave (with sufficient bridgeheads to pass formations of the [British] Second Army through). The capture and retention of the high ground between Nijmegen and Groesbeek is imperative." Basically, he had to hold, until relieved by the British armor, a twenty-five-mile perimeter some fifty miles behind the German lines. Because of shortages in transport aircraft, he had to do this with only three-quarters of his infantry strength, at least for the initial jump. "Inevitably there would be huge gaps in the perimeter I was to seize and defend," he later wrote. On top of this, he and his men were, for the first time in the war, jumping in the daylight, presenting themselves as ideal targets for German antiaircraft gunners. While he was confident that his remarkable troopers could overwhelm their enemies and accomplish their herculean mission, he wondered how great the cost would be. "The flak in the area is terrific, the krauts many," he had confided to his diary three days earlier. "It looks very rough. If I get through this one, I will be very lucky. It will, I am afraid, do the airborne cause a lot of harm."

He was even more worried about the chances of success for the British 1st Airborne Division, slated to land a dozen miles to the north, even deeper behind enemy lines, with the objective of taking the Rhine road bridge at Arnhem. This was challenging enough, but they were actually jumping eight miles away from their objective, because they feared the presence of enemy flak batteries near the bridge. In effect, this meant they would probably have to fight their way to the bridge rather than jumping on or near it. The previous day, when Gavin had first heard about this during a briefing from the 1st Airborne commander, Major General Roy Urquhart, he was taken aback. Gavin had turned to Lieutenant Colonel Jack Norton, his twenty-six-year-old operations officer (G3) and blurted, "My God, he can't mean it." Norton, a fellow West Pointer from the class of 1941, had replied morosely, "He does, and he is going to try to do it." For Gavin, Market Garden fostered a sense of slippery foreboding. The drop, the timetable, the linkups, all left little margin for error, and Gavin knew it. Yet he was not the type to dwell on his misgivings or betray them to his subordinates. At one point, during the frenetic planning for the operation, the division chief of staff had complained that the 82nd's mission was more appropriate for two airborne divisions, not one. "There it is," Gavin had replied crisply, "and we're going to do it with one."

Now, as the general's plane flew inexorably north, toward the Groesbeek heights, he scanned the ground intently for familiar landmarks but saw none. Like every other man on the C-47, he was laden with at least seventy pounds of weapons and equipment. Most notably, the general had tucked his M1 Garand underneath his reserve chute, almost parallel to his crotch. At his right hip was a holster with a .45-caliber pistol. His main chute rested tightly over his shoulders. Clustered near the chute along his torso were musette bags full of ammunition, grenades, maps, and personal items. His star-adorned helmet was perched firmly on his head.

Flak boomed distantly outside, like slightly audible thunderclaps. At Gavin's order, the soldiers in his C-47 stood and hooked up to their static lines, getting into position to exit the plane quickly in case the flak grew more accurate and mortally wounded the bird. Standing to Gavin's right was Norton. Like Gavin, he too was laden with musette bags, but he also had a small SCR-536 radio, or "walkie-talkie," nestled on top of his reserve chute, almost at the top of his breastbone. He too was studying the countryside, trying to figure out where they were. Next to him was First Lieutenant Hugo Olson, Gavin's well-liked aide-de-camp, who also carried a walkie-talkie atop his reserve chute. Gavin could hardly see the faces of the other men standing behind Olson in the shadowy, oily-smelling interior of the C-47. The line of men looked more like a random procession of boots, helmets, parachutes, uniforms, and weapons than a powerful stick of flesh-and-blood paratroopers.

A minute passed, and then another. Still, Gavin could not pinpoint their position. He noticed, several hundred feet below, a large fleet of C-47s flying across the path of Gavin's flight. Paratroopers began disgorging from the planes, their chutes blossoming in the blue sky. He was surprised to see an unidentified unit jumping so close to his own. For a tense moment, Gavin wondered whether his plane had somehow veered far off course. He decided that these jumpers must be from the 101st Airborne Division, scheduled to jump just a few miles to the south of the 82nd's zone. Breathing a sigh of relief, he suddenly noticed the Grave bridge, the first of his division's objectives, immediately below. Now he knew where he was. More flak crackled outside, but it was distant and inaccurate. Gazing now at the horizon, General Gavin saw the Groesbeek heights, his intended drop zone. He glanced at Norton and saw that he too recognized where they were. The plane leveled off at four hundred feet, the planned altitude for the drop. In a minute or two—flak permitting—they would be on the ground. Gavin lowered his head slightly to study the ground and saw a freshly dug trench system just at the edge of the trees bordering their Groesbeek drop zone. "Small arms fire was coming up from it," he later wrote. "[A]s the ground rose, it seemed to be very close to us. The triangular patch of woods near where I was to jump appeared under us just as the [green] jump light went on."

For Gavin and his troopers, the moment of action had finally arrived. The general knew there was no more time now for rumination or doubts. He must propel himself through the door of the C-47, into the void beyond. For better or for worse, it was time to go, and, as the commander, he would lead the way. Without a second's hesitation, he shuffled through the open door and leaped into the blue Dutch sky.[1]

CHAPTER 1

A Big Idea

Seven days before Gavin made his leap, Field Marshal Bernard Montgomery, commander of Britain's Twenty-first Army Group, stood on the tarmac at Melsbroek airfield and peered into the distance, watching the supreme commander's C-47 prepare to land at this airfield just outside of Brussels. Montgomery had not seen Eisenhower in over two weeks and, to Montgomery's way of thinking, this lack of personal contact spoke volumes about how out of touch Eisenhower was with the battles raging many miles over the eastern horizon, all along the frontiers of Germany. Montgomery liked Eisenhower as a man, but he thought him ill suited for direct command of armies in the field. Ike, as nearly everyone called the commander of Supreme Headquarters Allied Expeditionary Forces (SHAEF), was a diplomat, an organizer, a big-picture strategic thinker who excelled at managing people. He was not, in the field marshal's opinion, a combat commander. Ike, throughout his long army career, had spent most of his time as a staff officer, and he had logged little combat time. By contrast, Monty, as most called the field marshal, had spent plenty of time in battle, commanding soldiers, from his days as a small-unit leader in World War I (when he was badly wounded) to this war, when, in four years, he had risen from division to army group command, mainly by winning battles.

Revered by the British public, he was the country's most famous general, and, it is fair to say, he reveled in the reputation he had built. Egotistical, vain, and abrasive, the diminutive Briton believed wholeheartedly in his own greatness. Yet he was perceptive enough to understand that his country was now the junior partner to the United States in the western Allied coalition, and that this necessitated serving under an American supreme commander. Monty supposed that this was inevitable, so he had long since reconciled himself to it. The problem, as Montgomery saw it, was Eisenhower's attempt to control the armies as a land force commander, but from a remote distance. Even now, on September 10, Ike's headquarters was located four hundred miles to the west in the Norman town of Granville on the western side of the Cotentin Peninsula. "This was possibly a suitable place for a Supreme Commander," Monty later wrote, "but it was useless for a land force commander who had to keep his finger on the pulse of his armies and give quick decisions in rapidly changing situations." In fact, since the latter part of August, communications between Eisenhower and his subordinates had been sketchy, at best. There were no telephone links from Granville to the army group commanders—Montgomery, Lieutenant General Omar Bradley of Twelfth Army Group, and Lieutenant General Jacob Devers of the Sixth Army Group. Radio contact between Ike and these men was almost nonexistent. To communicate with his commanders, Ike was almost totally dependent on cables, and even that medium was sometimes unreliable. For instance, Monty had sent a message to Ike nearly a week earlier, on September 4, outlining his proposal for a "powerful and full-blooded thrust towards Berlin." Eisenhower did not receive the message until the next day, when he quickly cabled a response. For some reason, this reply was fragmented into two parts, one of which reached Montgomery on September 7, the other on September 9. To make matters worse, the ending paragraphs were the first to arrive; the introductory material came only later. Obviously, this was a ridiculous and unacceptable situation under any circumstances, but especially now, when vital decisions needed to be made. Monty intended to tell Ike, in no uncertain terms, that communications must be improved and that he must agree to unleash Twenty-first Army Group's push for the enemy capital.

The Germans were reeling. The Allies had decimated their armies in Normandy and had followed up that victory with a powerful invasion of South France. Rather than lose whatever remained of their armies in France, the Germans began a headlong retreat to the east. Allied soldiers had liberated Paris on August 25. Now, more than two weeks later, the remnants of German units were still fleeing to the borders of their fatherland. Montgomery had come to believe that the German army was on the verge of total defeat. He knew as well as anyone that the Allied logistical situation was grave. But in spite of the supply problems, he believed the time was right for a major thrust into northern Germany, all the way to Berlin, to end the war in 1944. Only the Twenty-first Army Group was in a position to make such a thrust. To do it, Monty believed that he needed absolute priority of supply, at the expense of all the other Allied armies, which, of course, were primarily American.

Eisenhower apparently did not agree. He was reluctant to halt all of his armies so as to assign logistical priority to Monty for a Berlin move. "No reallocation of our present resources would be adequate to sustain a thrust to Berlin," Ike told Monty in the September 7 message. The two men had whiled away two vital weeks arguing at a distance through their garbled cables. All the while, Montgomery had pressed, nearly to the point of obnoxiousness, for a face-to-face meeting. Each time he had insisted that Eisenhower come see him, rather than the other way around. "It is difficult to explain things in a message like this," he had told Ike in one cable. "[W]ould it be possible for you to come and see me?" While some in Ike's headquarters might have viewed such a request as impertinent, the affable supreme commander did not. He was loath to pull his generals away from their commands just to come see him far behind the lines. As the senior officer, he believed it was his responsibility to visit his subordinates. So he had agreed to fly this morning from Paris, where he had been visiting Bradley, to meet now with Monty in Brussels.[1]

The plane descended to the runway and rolled to a stop. Inside, Eisenhower braced himself for what he knew was sure to be a difficult meeting with the prickly field marshal. In truth, Eisenhower had disliked Montgomery since they had first met in the spring of 1942, when Eisenhower, as a two-star general, was visiting Britain on a fact-finding mission. During a briefing on training exercises in southern England, Montgomery, then a three-star general, had interrupted his talk to ostentatiously remonstrate with Ike for smoking in his presence. Eisenhower amiably stubbed out his cigarette, but inside he seethed at the British general's rudeness. A subsequent two years of dealing with the insufferable Monty—even for most of that time as a superior—had hardly cultivated any fondness in Ike for the man.

To Eisenhower, the field marshal was amazingly obtuse for someone who had achieved such a celebrated reputation. He seemed not to understand that, as supreme commander, Ike could hardly halt the advance of American troops in order to give absolute priority for a decisive British drive on Berlin, even if such a move were possible, which Eisenhower seriously doubted. American public opinion would never accept this sort of leading role for the British, especially now that the United States was providing most of the troops, equipment, matériel, and financial muscle for this "crusade in Europe," as Ike termed it. More than that, it simply made good sense for the western Allies to exert maximum pressure on Germany, by advancing on a broad front. This would enhance the Allies' decisive manpower and matériel advantages. A single-front advance negated those advantages and invited defeat in detail from an enemy army that had demonstrated an incredible penchant for effective counterattacks. Moreover, Monty did not seem to comprehend that, whether the Allies advanced on a single or a broad front, they could not defeat Nazi Germany until the current supply situation had improved and, at that, rather dramatically. "He did not understand the impossible situation that would have developed along our great front when he, having outrun the possibility of maintenance, was forced to stop or withdraw," Eisenhower later wrote. The key to the supply situation was Antwerp. In his heart, the supreme commander knew that the Scheldt had to be cleared and the port facilities of Antwerp opened up quickly. He was not sure that Montgomery truly appreciated that.

So the supreme commander was not looking forward to this meeting. To make matters worse, his right knee was in a plaster cast, limiting his mobility so much that he could not comfortably leave the plane. About thirty years earlier, he had injured his left knee playing football at West Point, ending a promising career as a halfback. For many years since, he had thought of his right knee as his "good" knee. That had been true until a week ago. He and his pilot, Captain Tom Underwood, had been flying back to Granville in a small L-5 observation plane. Bad weather forced them to make an emergency landing on the beach. With the tides coming in, and fearing that the beach was mined, Underwood and Eisenhower began pushing the little plane to higher ground. Ike slipped on the wet sand and badly wrenched the right knee. Now, a week later, the knee had not improved all that much. In fact, he still could hardly bend it, especially while in the cast.[2]

Now, at Melsbroek airfield, no sooner did the plane roll to a stop than Montgomery strode toward it and hopped aboard, followed by Major General Miles Graham, his supply officer (G4). True to Montgomery's meticulous nature, he had thoroughly prepared for this meeting, honing his many arguments. Personal time with the supreme commander was at a premium, and he intended to use his productively. The C-47 was more plush than the usual fare. Instead of hard bucket seats or benches, Ike's plane was adorned with reasonably comfortable upholstered seats, each of which was bolted firmly to the deck. Montgomery sat down opposite Eisenhower and exchanged cordial greetings with him. Immediately, Monty noticed that Ike had two men with him—Air Chief Marshal Sir Arthur Tedder, the deputy supreme commander, and Lieutenant General

Sir Humfrey Gale, Ike's G4, both of whom were fellow Britons. Montgomery wanted the closest thing he could get to a one-on-one talk with Eisenhower. He asked the supreme commander to expel Gale from the meeting, even as he insisted that his own supply man, Graham, remain. Ike patiently acquiesced to the insulting request. Gale stood up and left. Monty probably would have loved to banish Tedder as well, because he realized that the air marshal loathed him, but he knew that Ike would never agree to this.

Nonetheless emboldened, Montgomery pulled from his pocket a bundle of Eisenhower's choppy communications from the previous week. In his nasal, singsong British cadence, Montgomery began to lecture Eisenhower, almost like a headmaster dressing down a naughty schoolboy. Referring to the communications in his hand, Montgomery exclaimed, "They're balls, sheer balls, rubbish!" According to Monty, the supreme commander had not explained what he meant by priority of supply. Further, his misguided broad-front policy was wrong and would end with "dire consequences." Ike's approach would lead only to continued "jerky and disjointed thrusts" against Germany, and these halfhearted attacks would inevitably fail. It was far better to concentrate all resources ("absolute priority," in Monty's parlance) on one full-blooded thrust into northern Germany. The harangue went on for several moments, with Monty recapitulating the same argument he had made for several weeks. He argued, as he later recalled, that "the quickest way to open up Antwerp was to back my plan of concentration on the left."

Eisenhower sat quietly, listening intently, struggling to keep his cool. As a boy, he had been prone to violent temper tantrums. After one particularly bad meltdown, he had learned the lesson that he must find a way to control himself. Ever since, his struggle to maintain an even keel had continued, by and large successfully. So instead of exploding at his rude, disrespectful subordinate, he waited for him to take a breath, then leaned forward, touched him firmly on the knee, and said: "Steady, Monty; you can't speak to me like that. I'm your boss." This steadfast but restrained gesture defused the tension perfectly. As if snapped out of a trance, the chastened Montgomery graciously replied, "I'm sorry, Ike."

Monty reiterated, much more politely, his same argument, asking once again for complete priority of supply. "Montgomery . . . made great play over the word 'priority,'" Tedder wrote in a postmeeting memo, "and insisted that his interpretation of the word implies absolute priority if necessary to exclusion of all other operations." When Montgomery finally finished, Ike replied that he never meant to give Monty, or anyone else, that sort of priority to the exclusion of everything else. "What you're proposing is this," Ike said. "If I give you all the supplies you want, you could go straight to Berlin. Monty, you're nuts. You can't do it. What the hell! If you try a long column like that in a single thrust you'd have to throw off division after division to protect your flanks from attack. Now, suppose you did get a bridge across the Rhine. You couldn't depend for long on that one bridge to supply your drive."

Montgomery assured Eisenhower that he could do exactly that, but only if the supreme commander would support him properly. "Just give me what I need and I'll reach Berlin and end the war."[3]

Eisenhower was unpersuaded. Having anticipated his boss's recalcitrance, Montgomery changed the subject to something more specific and, he expected, more compelling to Ike. Earlier this morning, the field marshal and his staff had, under a heavy veil of secrecy, put the finishing touches on a bold plan to realize Monty's vision. They proposed to drop three airborne divisions, plus an independent parachute brigade, anywhere from fifteen to sixty miles behind the German lines in Holland. The paratroopers would secure key bridges along the main highway from Eindhoven to Arnhem, over the Rhine into Germany. With the bridges secured, armor from Lieutenant General Brian Horrocks's British XXX Corps would link up with the airborne troopers and then lead the vanguard of a mighty thrust into northern Germany, toward Berlin. Each phase of the plan had a code name. The airborne drop would be called Market. The armored thrust was named Garden. In general, the plan would be known as Operation Market Garden.

The proposed operation had another added benefit. All summer long, the Germans had been hurling pilotless rockets, known as V1s, at Britain's cities. These early-generation missiles had killed more than six thousand people and wounded nearly eighteen thousand. Deadly though they were, the V1s were relatively easy to see, identify, and shoot down. On the ground, a person could hear when a V1 engine cut out, realize that an explosion was imminent, and prepare accordingly. By late summer, Allied planes and antiaircraft crews were shooting down one out of every two rockets the Germans launched into British airspace. Many more failed to reach their targets because of weather issues or navigational errors. The threat seemed to be in check.

However, just two days before this meeting, the Germans had unleashed a much more formidable missile, the V2. This new rocket carried more explosives than the V1. It also plunged to earth with no warning and was far too fast to be shot down by planes or flak guns. The V1 had already reprised unhappy memories of the blitz among the war-weary British public. With the launching of the V2s, Prime Minister Winston Churchill and the War Cabinet realized that the Germans could now bombard their cities at will. British intelligence knew that most of the V2 launching sites were in Holland, especially in the Rotterdam and Hague areas. On September 9, only a day before this meeting, they had asked Montgomery whether he might be able to cut off and destroy the launch sites. This had evolved Market Garden from a concept into a bona fide plan, one that Monty now viewed as an absolute necessity.

As Montgomery explained all this to Ike, the supreme commander's countenance began to change. He was intrigued by this Market Garden plan. Montgomery had a reputation for caution and stolidity, but Market Garden was bold and imaginative. Ike was impressed and a bit excited. He liked the idea of seizing a bridgehead over the Rhine at Arnhem. He obviously sympathized with the goal of neutralizing the V2 sites, but there was more to his attitude shift than all this. The Allies had built up, at great expense, a mighty airborne capability. Paratroopers and glidermen had more than proven their worth in Normandy. After that battle, the British and Americans had expanded their airborne capability by creating the First Allied Airborne Army, a formidable force containing three U.S. airborne divisions, two British divisions, and one Polish parachute brigade, along with an American troop carrier command and two British troop carrier groups. The airborne divisions were made up of picked men, the cream of the Allied crop. They were well trained, young, and aggressive. Ike knew they were underutilized, though. After Normandy, they had returned to England and had done little more than train and wait for new orders. In fact, since early August, Allied planners had devised no less than sixteen separate missions for the airborne, only to scrub them, mainly because the ground forces had already overrun the potential drop zones.

Like any commander, General Eisenhower wanted to employ all of the resources at his disposal. The airborne troopers comprised some of his best assets, yet they were sitting in England, effectively on the sidelines. He knew that this could not continue much longer. These men had to be used sooner rather than later. And he could not simply plug them into the line like regular infantry divisions. Otherwise, what was the point in training them, at such time and expense, to be paratroopers? They needed an actual airborne mission, and Market Garden fit that bill. Ever sensitive to political winds, Ike also knew that powerful voices in Washington, including his own mentor, General George Marshall, the army chief of staff, and General Henry "Hap" Arnold, chief of the Army Air Forces, were impatient to see the First Allied Airborne Army put to work.

As Eisenhower turned over Market Garden's potential in his mind, he convinced himself that, if he authorized Monty's plan, he would not be green-lighting the equivalent of the British field marshal's single-front thrust for Berlin. To Ike, Market Garden merely represented a limited effort to establish a bridgehead over the Rhine, to be used as one more springboard for a later broad-front advance into Germany, when the supply situation permitted. Market Garden need not mean a divergence from his intent to advance into Germany on all fronts. Nor would Market Garden, in Eisenhower's opinion, distract from the urgency of clearing the Scheldt and making immediate use of Antwerp. He believed that Montgomery could do both at the same time. All this in spite of the fact that German resistance on the western front was already stiffening, that even with the addition of the airborne, Twenty-first Army Group's manpower was stretched practically to the breaking point, and that Market Garden could not help but absorb most of SHAEF's limited resources. In reality, this would mean a weak single-front thrust at the expense of any momentum for the broad front. He was basically compromising between the two in such a way as to guarantee the failure of both. For someone of Eisenhower's incisive intellect, it was stunningly poor thinking.

He gazed at Montgomery. "I'll tell you what I'll do, Monty," he said. "I'll give you whatever you ask to get you over the Rhine, because I want a bridgehead . . . but let's get over the Rhine first before we discuss anything else." In uttering those words, he had made a fateful decision. Market Garden would become a reality. Many thousands of lives would never be the same because of it.

The supreme commander promised to do the best he could to supply the operation, but with the understanding that, once over the Rhine, Monty would turn his attention to clearing out the Scheldt. The two men agreed to September 17 as the launch date for the drop. The meeting broke up cordially on that note. It had lasted no more than an hour, but it would forever change the course of history.

Monty and Ike went their separate ways, each viewing Market Garden in his own manner, with his own preconceptions. Ike was still miffed at Monty's tirade, but he was pleased to have put him in his place while at the same time mollifying him, if only in a minor way. The American was also excited to see what the airborne could do in such a large operation. Antwerp, the broad front, and Market Garden, he was sure, could all coexist.

While Montgomery was pleased that Ike had authorized Market Garden, he was frustrated that the American general still stubbornly refused to see the merit in his single-front plan to seize Berlin and supply it accordingly. Perhaps, with the success of Market Garden, that might come later. For now, there was a major operation to plan and little time to do it.[4]

CHAPTER 2

Plans and Schemes

The Eisenhower-Montgomery meeting unleashed a flurry of activity in the First Allied Airborne Army. Colloquially known as the "First Triple A," the airborne elements of the army were organized into the U.S. XVIII Airborne Corps under Lieutenant General Matthew Ridgway, and the British I Airborne Corps, under Lieutenant General Frederick "Boy" Browning. The First Triple A was commanded by Lieutenant General Lewis Brereton, an American flier of World War I vintage. Bespectacled and high-strung, Brereton was actually a naval academy graduate who had transferred to the army in 1911 and served as a fighter pilot on the western front during the Great War. In the Second World War, he had held a series of commands in the Pacific, Mediterranean, and Europe, including, most recently, the Ninth Air Force. The middle-aged Brereton was competent but uninspiring. In 1941, as air commander for General Douglas MacArthur, he had lost the bulk of his planes on the ground under the weight of Japanese bombs. Brereton and MacArthur subsequently blamed each other for this fiasco. Both were canny political infighters who knew how to distance themselves from failure well enough to continue their careers unabated. Brereton's chief sponsor was his old friend "Hap" Arnold, who, as head of the Army Air Forces, had made sure to place his friend "Louie" in a series of key commands.

Even so, Brereton was hardly thrilled with his current job. Back in July, when he had found out that he was being transferred from command of the Ninth Air Force to the new airborne army, he wrote in his diary, "I 'took a dim view' of this new assignment." At the Ninth, he had been in his element, commanding waves of fighter planes—a real glamour post to the old fighter pilot. By contrast, his First Triple A kingdom consisted mainly of unruly airborne troopers and mundane troop carrier aviators. To Brereton, that was a bit of a comedown, but he had since grown used to it, and he, like so many others, was eager to see what his massive airborne force could do in combat.

His first whiff of Market Garden came on the afternoon of September 10, just a few hours after the Montgomery-Ike meeting. After a briefing from Montgomery, General Browning flew back to England and telephoned Brereton to inform him of the new operation. The two generals then organized a meeting of their commanders and key staff officers for that evening at 1800. They met at Sunninghill Park, an eighteenth-century country mansion about thirty miles west of London where Brereton had made his headquarters. Dark green ivy covered nearly all of the three-story house except for the windows and doors. At the appointed time, the American and British officers congregated in Brereton's expansive, map-lined office. In all, there were twenty-six of them, representing both the paratroopers and the fliers.

Brereton called the meeting to order and immediately turned the floor over to Browning, who was, at that point, the best versed on the Market Garden plan. The dapper Browning cut an impressive figure. Educated at Eton and Sandhurst, the forty-seven-year-old was cultured, well-spoken, refined, and charming—the very embodiment of an aristocratic British officer. In 1932, he had married Daphne du Maurier, a famous novelist. Since 1941, he had developed British airborne doctrine and had overseen the creation of the army's parachute divisions. Yet he had never actually led troopers in battle.

With a gleam in his eye, Browning told his colleagues, "The object is to lay a carpet of airborne troops down over which our ground forces can pass." This was to take place along "the British Second Army's main axis of advance from about Eindhoven to Arnhem inclusive." He outlined more about Montgomery's basic concept. The 101st Airborne would be dropped just beyond XXX Corps' front lines near the Belgian–Dutch border and seize seven water crossings along a thirty-mile sector, from south of Eindhoven to north of Uden. Immediately to the north, the 82nd Airborne Division would drop in the Grave–Nijmegen area, capture the modern bridge spans over the Maas and Waal rivers, and control the neighboring high ground around Groesbeek. The most challenging mission belonged to the British 1st Airborne Division and the 1st Polish Parachute Brigade. Their task was to drop more than sixty miles behind enemy lines and take the Arnhem bridge over the Rhine, which was, effectively, the gateway into northern Germany.[1]

As Browning spoke, Jim Gavin entered the room and took a seat as unobtrusively as he could. The young American general had spent the day in London with his British girlfriend, Valerie Porter, a slim, auburn-haired beauty who hailed from an upper-class family and spoke with the Oxbridge accent to prove it. Upon receiving a call from Brereton's headquarters about the meeting, Gavin had hopped in his car and driven as fast as he could to Sunninghill. Upon arriving, he was struck by Browning's reference to the ambitious operation as a "party." To Gavin, the use of this word to describe what would surely be a bitter battle reflected more than just the British penchant for ironic understatement. It revealed something about Browning's inexperience and his failure to appreciate the deadly realities of combat. "He unquestionably lacks the [steadying] influence and judgment that comes [sic] with a proper troop experience basis," Gavin had written in his diary about Browning only a few days before. "He is personable and impressive but completely and entirely impractical." Gavin personally liked him, but he felt he had much to learn.

As Browning finished outlining the operation, the commanders began planning and making decisions in a steady give-and-take discussion. Their task was monumental. They had to prepare a corps-size airborne operation, coordinate the appropriate air and ground forces, choose drop zones, arrange for the availability of suitable intelligence data (maps, photos, enemy order of battle, and the like), and decide how best to take and hold their respective objectives until they linked up with the British ground forces. This did not even take into account the question of resupply, which, Brereton assured everyone, would come partially from the air but mainly by ground, assuming, of course, that the ground troops succeeded in piercing the German lines and meeting up with the airborne troopers. "Many details for planning were considered," Brereton later wrote in an after-action report, "such as routes, photo coverage, disposition of forces, and time needed for preparation. Decisions had to be made immediately because of the shortness of time." In the recollection of one participant, there was much discussion of such details as "available lift, parachute and glider takeoff airfields, airborne division missions, troop-carrier missions, departure airfields and unit assignments to departure airfields, enemy flak and troop dispositions, flight routes . . . probable drop and landing zones."

Brereton designated Major General Paul Williams of the IX Troop Carrier Command to oversee all troop carrier units and whatever bomber formations might be used for resupply. Williams said that 220 of his aircraft were currently in France, airlifting supplies to frontline units. It would take a couple days to recall them to England and prepare for Market Garden. The assembled officers debated potential dates for the operation, eventually settling on September 17 as a tentative D-day.

They decided to fly the airborne divisions into Holland along two routes. The 1st Airborne and the 82nd Airborne would go in along the northern route. They would form up over East Anglia, fly directly across the Channel, continue over the Dutch islands and then to their respective objectives in the Arnhem and Nijmegen areas. In traversing this route, they would brave German flak boats and other guns for about eighty miles. The southern route, involving the 101st Airborne, was longer but, the planners expected, a bit safer. The planes would skirt around London, form up over Manston, avoid British antiaircraft batteries (and the possibility of friendly-fire incidents) along the coast, and then fly due east over Allied territory in Belgium. At the last minute, they would turn north, pass directly over German lines, and drop north of the Eindhoven area. The biggest danger for them would be fire from the enemy front lines. Along both routes, the planes and gliders would fly in carefully orchestrated "serials," in three parallel lanes about a mile and a half apart. The American parachute serials would fly at four-minute intervals, the glider serials at seven-minute intervals.

All of this, Brereton announced, was to take place in full daylight, a first for the Allies in the European war. The previous month, during the invasion of South France, the Allies had dropped paratroopers at dawn, but every other major drop, from Sicily to Normandy, had taken place in darkness, albeit with a full moon. Brereton knew that this no longer made sense. The Allies ruled the daytime air. Whereas German night fighters were still a substantial threat, the Luftwaffe was in no position to impede a daylight drop in any meaningful way. Nor did any of the potential drop dates in the next week offer the moon conditions that airborne commanders insisted upon for any night operation. At night, navigation over Holland might have been a problem. In the day, Williams's crews would have little problem finding their drop zones. The main issue with the daytime was the risk of greater accuracy from German flak batteries. The transport planes were slow, unarmed, with no armored protection, and no self-sealing fuel tanks. They could be sitting ducks for enemy antiaircraft gunners. But Brereton accepted this risk in the expectation that "a proper employment of the supporting air forces available could knock out flak positions in advance and beat them down during the airborne operations themselves." To the First Triple A commander and his subordinates, the advantages of going during the day clearly outweighed the risks.[2]

Given the sheer enormity of the task at hand, the three-hour meeting went smoothly. Still, some serious misgivings arose. As General Gavin recalled, "All commanders were concerned about the outcome of the operation." The 101st Airborne contingent, for instance, was appalled at the size of their thirty-mile drop zone. Brigadier General Anthony McAuliffe, the head of the division's artillery units, was standing in for Major General Maxwell Taylor, his commanding officer. McAuliffe spoke up and argued that the drop zone was far too large. The division could not hope to seize and hold seven major objectives from south of Eindhoven to north of Uden. If the Screamin' Eagles attempted this, McAuliffe asserted, they would end up fighting in scattered, isolated groups, similar to what had occurred in Normandy. Brereton initially demurred but eventually agreed. The planned dispersion of the 101st probably would create innumerable problems of tactical integrity and resupply. Not to mention how easy it might be for the Germans to cut off and annihilate the little bands of paratroopers. The problem was that Montgomery had specifically outlined the thirty-mile landing zone for the 101st, so any change in this plan would have to be approved by the field marshal. Brereton encouraged the 101st Airborne leaders to appeal directly to Twenty-first Army Group about this issue.

As the meeting neared its end, Brereton made one last major announcement. Browning would command all three airborne divisions. Pure and simple, this was a political decision. In addition to serving as commander of the British I Airborne Corps, the suave Browning was also Brereton's deputy. This implied seniority for Browning over General Ridgway, the other corps commander in First Allied Airborne Army. The British understood the need for an American commander of this army. But in the British-dominated Market Garden, Brereton—attuned as ever to the political winds—sensed that his allies expected one of their own to command the airborne side of the operation. Browning had waited his entire career for such an opportunity. What was more, he and Brereton had clashed, about a week before, over the wisdom of an operation that was eventually canceled by Montgomery. Browning had felt that the operation, known as Linnett II, was too hasty and poorly planned. Brereton did not agree. Browning had threatened to resign rather than lead such a flawed and badly conceived operation. With Linnett II canceled, the two generals made up and the resignation talk ceased. Now, a week later,

Brereton had no wish to antagonize his British colleague again. He was to command the airborne drop (generally referred to as Market) in spite of the fact that two of the three airborne divisions were American. In fact, this was the first time that U.S. paratroopers and glidermen would serve under foreign command.

When Brereton made this announcement, Gavin immediately thought of General Ridgway, who was not present at the meeting. Gavin knew that his mentor Ridgway would not be pleased. In terms of pure credentials, no one was more qualified to command Market than Ridgway. He had plenty of combat experience. He was an airborne innovator and pioneer. For two years, he had known nothing but success. According to Gavin, "[Ridgway's] great courage, integrity, and aggressiveness in combat all made a lasting impression" on everyone who served under him. Very simply, he was the best choice for command. Ridgway was indeed deeply disappointed when he later found out about Brereton's decision, mainly because he thought he and his staff were much better qualified for the job than Browning and his people. Ridgway especially disliked the idea that he would have little or no role in Market while someone else controlled his men. He later admitted to harboring "a sense of deep disappointment, if not of resentment" at Brereton's choice of Browning over him. Already an uneasy tone was set for Market Garden.[3]

The meeting at Sunninghill ended at about 2100. Now it was time for planners at a lower level to work out innumerable details. Fortunately, much of the planning for previously canceled operations was useful for Market Garden. Operation Comet, the most recently scrubbed mission, equated quite closely to this operation, so staff officers employed much of the same information in their current deliberations. Gavin, for instance, went directly to nearby Moor Park, the palatial headquarters of I Airborne Corps, where he studied maps, terrain analyses, drop zones, and lift plans assembled by the British for previous operations. After spending most of

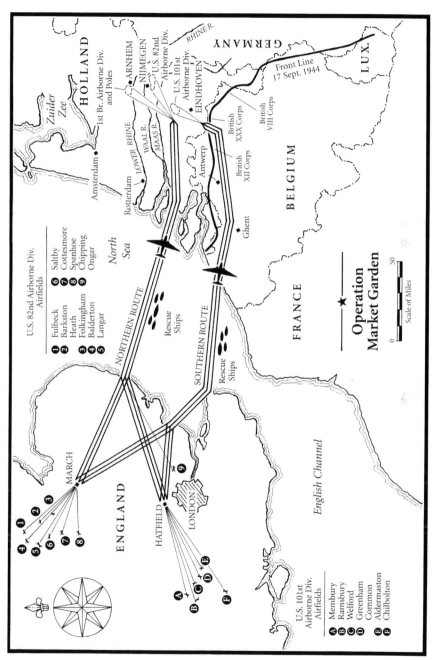

the night analyzing this information along with reconnaissance photos and intelligence on German troop dispositions, the American airborne staff officers huddled with their troop carrier counterparts at Eastcote, the troop carrier headquarters, on the morning of September 11. "The principal items on the agenda were selection of routes, selection of [drop] zones, and preliminary discussions on the loading plans," the Army Air Forces official historian wrote.

The challenge was to coordinate the logistical requirements and movements of the massive air flotilla with the needs of the ground troops. This required a slew of decisions to assign specific troop carrier squadrons to carry specific ground units. The airborne officers had to figure out how to transport their people from their training areas to their respective airfields. Once the paratroopers and glidermen were sealed into their airfields, the airmen promised to provide them shelter and sustenance. The paratroopers insisted upon absolute unit integrity. Platoons, companies, and battalions needed to be dropped together. This required minute planning among the aviation staff to figure, down to the squad level, how best to utilize the available aircraft to carry the necessary troops. "The Air Commander and the Airborne Commander decided, in conjunction with each other, on Drop Zones and Landing Zones [for gliders] after a careful examination of terrain estimates and enemy defense overprints," the IX Troop Carrier Command's after-action report stated. The airmen were mainly concerned with flak and the flying routes to the zones. The airborne commanders, in the recollection of one staff officer, chose zones based on "location of bridges, the dominating terrain in the vicinity of these bridges, the likely avenues of approach of the enemy, the terrain compartments dictated by waterways, the location of flak, the flight of the aircraft and finally the physical obstacles on the ground surface."

Once they made these decisions, they selected takeoff times and a tentative schedule on the order of arrival at the drop and landing zones, unit by unit. By and large, the two sides worked well together, but there was some frustration among the paratroopers at what they perceived as the inflexible attitude of their aviation colleagues. "They were unable to shift aircraft from one airfield to another," Lieutenant Colonel Norton wrote in near exasperation, "to change serials and their order of arrival over DZs [drop zones], to the extent that the ground plan became secondary to the air plan. Only by the most careful and tedious planning and the juggling of troops, trucks, aircraft loads, air corps supplies, and airfield billeting accommodations was the plan made at all workable." In criticizing the troop carrier reluctance to move planes from airfield to airfield, Norton did not seem to grasp that unit integrity was just as important to the airmen as to the ground soldiers.

The soldiers were also slightly disappointed with a few other hard-and-fast stipulations from the troop carrier commanders. General Williams insisted that his C-47 crews fly only one mission per day (in spite of subtle pressure from Brereton for more). Williams believed that any attempt to fly multiple missions would exhaust the crews and lead to accidents. If crewmen were flying more than one mission, they would inevitably run out of daylight by the time they returned to England, loaded their aircraft with more soldiers and supplies, and then flew back to Holland. Many of his pilots were new to combat. He doubted that these rookies could pull off such a daunting task. Moreover, he did not have enough maintenance capacity or ground crewmen to support such fever-pitch operations. So one mission per day would be the rule for Market Garden. General Williams also rejected the idea of flying two or more gliders per C-47 tow plane as overly dangerous and unwieldy. Not enough of his glider pilots and C-47 pilots were trained for such a tricky endeavor. All of this meant that the airborne divisions could not be dropped in their entirety on September 17. Generals Gavin, Taylor, and Urquhart had to prioritize which of their assets to drop on the first day and which could be earmarked for landing on subsequent days. This left the Allies at the mercy of potential bad weather and strong enemy opposition once the surprise of the initial drops wore off and the Germans responded with reinforced counterattacks, as they inevitably would.

After all the give-and-take, the planners finally agreed on tentative drop zones. In Gavin's division, the 504th Parachute Infantry Regiment would land at Overasselt, north of Grave and the Maas River. Their mission was to seize the main bridge over the Maas at Grave along with a series of canal bridges that led into Nijmegen. Later, at the behest of Colonel Reuben Tucker, the regimental commander, Gavin agreed to drop elements of the 504th south of the Maas as well. The general's other two parachute regiments, the 505th and the 508th, would land in drop zones just east of the Groesbeek heights, a prominent ridge spur that brooded over the eastern and southern approaches to Nijmegen. They would hold a perimeter against potential counterattacks coming from the German border, only a few hundred yards to the east. Browning's staff was especially concerned about the possibility of armored counterattacks out of the Reichswald, a heavily wooded area just over the border, in Germany. The troopers of the 505th and 508th were also, in Gavin's words, supposed to "mop up toward the Maas–Waal [River] Canal and Nijmegen." He then hoped to fly in his 325th Glider Infantry Regiment as soon as possible to reinforce the Groesbeek heights and push for Nijmegen. In all, the 82nd Airborne Division was responsible for a ten-mile sector and the capture of six major bridges, including the ultimate objective—the highway bridge over the Waal River at Nijmegen.

In the 101st, General Taylor elected to drop his 501st Parachute Infantry Regiment near Veghel and, in the words of his field orders, "secure the canal and stream crossings in the . . . area." His 502nd Parachute Infantry Regiment was to land near St. Oedenrode to secure the main highway and the Wilhelmina Canal crossings at Best. The 506th Parachute Infantry Regiment would drop near Son, north of Eindhoven. Taylor ordered them to take "the three crossings of the Wilhelmina Canal at Zon [Son] immediately upon landing. Be prepared to move on Eindhoven within two hours after landing for the purpose of securing the stream and canal crossings at that point." All of this amounted to two canal crossings and nine highway and railroad bridges. Like Gavin, Taylor chose to bring his glider regiment, the 327th, in as reinforcements within a couple days of the parachute drops.

His intended drop zones were based on a considerably smaller area of responsibility for the 101st than originally envisioned in Montgomery's Market Garden plan. Rather than the thirty-mile perimeter earmarked by Monty, Taylor wanted responsibility for half of that. Montgomery's plan would force Taylor to drop his troopers in small, scattered groups, thus increasing their vulnerability to strong enemy counterattacks and weakening their overall effectiveness. Brereton had already taken up Taylor's cause with the field marshal and, after some debate, persuaded him to reconsider his orders. Montgomery agreed to let General Taylor discuss the matter with Lieutenant General Miles Dempsey, commander of the British Second Army. Since XXX Corps was part of Dempsey's army, he was in the best position to determine the validity of Taylor's proposed amendments. Dempsey and Taylor met on September 12 at Montgomery's headquarters, and the British general readily agreed to Taylor's requests. The 101st Airborne commander and his staff officers collectively breathed a huge sigh of relief.[4]

As Taylor and Dempsey worked out their agreement, Field Marshal Montgomery was causing some consternation among his superiors at SHAEF. Even though Eisenhower had given him the go-ahead for Market Garden, Montgomery was still dissatisfied with their meeting in Brussels. To Monty, there was little purpose to the Arnhem thrust without proper priority of supply. He still wanted Ike to halt all other Allied moves and invest everything in Twenty-first Army Group's attempt to breach the Rhine. So he shrewdly attempted to force the supreme commander's hand. He cabled Ike and contended that his decision to continue advancing on a broad front while simultaneously agreeing to unleash Market Garden had "certain repercussions which you should know." Monty claimed that, without more supplies and transport vehicles, he could not launch Market

Garden on September 17. Now he would need until September 23 at the earliest or perhaps even as late as September 26. "This delay," Monty explained, "will give the enemy time to organise better defensive arrangements and we must expect heavier resistance and slower progress." The problem was not a paucity of supply for the airborne but for Dempsey's ground formations. Dempsey did not have enough truck transport to launch the operation, especially for his XII and VIII corps, the two units that would attack on either side of Horrocks's XXX Corps to protect his flanks and those of the airborne troopers.

When Eisenhower received this message, he was a bit nonplussed, but he knew he had to act immediately upon it. In a sense, the supreme commander was coming face-to-face with the consequences of his decision to authorize Market Garden. Whether Eisenhower liked it or not, the operation meant launching a single thrust, and a single thrust required priority of supply for Montgomery. Montgomery was absolutely right about this. It also made no sense to delay it for the better part of two weeks, since one of the avowed purposes of the operation was to take advantage of the Germans' chaotic eastward retreat. No one wanted to give them more time to settle down, reorganize, and prepare new defenses in Holland or elsewhere.

Montgomery knew this all too well. Ordinarily he was rather obtuse about how best to influence superiors. But this time he pressed the perfect button. In his recollection, "This message produced results which were almost electric." Eisenhower immediately dispatched Major General Bedell Smith, his powerful chief of staff, to Montgomery's headquarters. With Ike's permission, Smith promised to provide one thousand tons of supplies per day, by road and air, to the Twenty-first Army Group. Planes that had been shuttling fuel and freight to Bradley's Twelfth Army Group would now support Montgomery. In addition, three U.S. infantry divisions, the 26th, the 95th, and the 104th, all newly arrived in Normandy, would be stripped of their vehicles and held in place. Their trucks would now go to Dempsey's units. Bradley had been scheduled to receive these three divisions as reinforcements, so Ike's decision was coming at his expense and would thus seriously dampen the operational pace of U.S. operations along the expanse of what had been a broad-front advance. Needless to say, Bradley was livid. "It was strategy by subterfuge," he later wrote, "dangerously foolhardy—the wrong plan at the wrong time and the wrong place." Some of the U.S. airmen were angry at Ike's order to cease airlifting supplies to Bradley in favor of Montgomery and Market Garden. "The entire Holland operation smacked of a political move and one of aggrandizement for Montgomery, a perfect ass as a man and a commander," Colonel James Duke, the IX Troop Carrier Command chief of staff, wrote bitterly some years later. Montgomery, of course, saw it all much differently. The promise of more trucks and supplies immediately mollified him. "Most grateful to you personally and to Beetle for all you are doing for us," he cabled Ike. Monty once again promised to launch Market Garden on September 17.[5]

No sooner was the supply situation resolved in Montgomery's favor than another wrinkle emerged. By September 15, just two days before the scheduled start of the operation, disquieting intelligence about the Arnhem area had come to light. Dutch resistance groups and Ultra intelligence had detected elements of the enemy's 9th and 10th SS panzer divisions in Arnhem, not far away from the planned British drop zones. This disturbing information had found its way, via Dutch army liaison officers and top secret Ultra briefings, to Dempsey and Browning. One of Browning's intelligence specialists, twenty-five-year-old Major Brian Urquhart (no relation to the commander of the 1st Airborne) was greatly alarmed at the reports. In truth, he already thought that Market Garden was, at best, a bold gamble, or at worst, sheer madness. He was adamantly opposed to it. Similar to General Gavin, he detested the propensity of his colleagues to refer to the operation as a party. He was also disgusted by the exaggerated mood of ignorant optimism he sensed around I Airborne

Corps headquarters. "I was quite frankly horrified by the plan," he said. "Even if we should capture all the bridges intact, I just couldn't see how we were going to get to Arnhem in time to relieve those troops." Even if all went as planned, he doubted that the capture of the Arnhem bridge over the Rhine would lead to any sort of triumphant advance, as if XXX Corps could somehow "walk into Germany like a bride into a church. This concept was asinine."

He sensed that many of his elders believed, as in 1918, that Germany was about to collapse altogether. Young Urquhart, of course, was born after World War I, so he had no recollection of the kaiser's demise. He knew only that, based on the information he was analyzing each day, Hitler's Germany was anything but finished. "This total misappreciation of German fighting efficiency and morale was particularly worrying in an operation where lightly armed troops were going to be dropped a long way forward from supporting ground troops and asked to sit and hold an objective until relieved."

In hopes of finding concrete evidence of the two German armored divisions' presence in Arnhem, he had requested, on September 12, low-level reconnaissance flights from Royal Air Force Spitfires. The result was vindicating but troubling beyond description for Major Urquhart. The Dutch agents and the Ultra intercepts were correct. The photographs revealed the presence of camouflaged enemy tanks and self-propelled guns in the wooded areas near Arnhem. When Urquhart showed the photos to Browning, the general dismissed the notion that the armor posed enough of a threat to Market Garden to warrant cancellation. Browning further wondered whether the tanks were even serviceable. Urquhart replied that, even if they were not, "they were still tanks and they had guns." As it sank into Urquhart that the photographic evidence would not dissuade anyone at a more senior level from launching Market Garden, he came unglued. By his own admission, he became "rather hysterical about the whole thing." As a result, General Browning decided that he could no longer stomach the worried young major. He quickly dispatched him on convalescent leave. The dramatic photographs had no substantial effect on the I Airborne Corps' plan for the pending operation.

Even if Urquhart had succeeded in persuading Browning to reconsider Market Garden, the airborne commander hardly had the power to cancel the operation. That kind of decision needed to be made at a higher level, perhaps with Brereton but more likely with Montgomery himself. There is no evidence that Monty ever saw the reconnaissance photographs, but, by the time Urquhart showed them to Browning, Monty too knew about the presence of the two panzer divisions in Arnhem. On September 15, Major General Kenneth Strong, Ike's intelligence chief, related his latest estimate to Bedell Smith. In it, he determined that not only were the remnants of the 9th and 10th SS panzer divisions now in Arnhem, but they would soon be replenished with new tanks and equipment.

The news staggered Smith. Already skeptical of Market Garden, he now thought that, in light of this new information, two airborne divisions should be dropped at Arnhem instead of one. This would mean dropping the 82nd Airborne Division farther to the north, closer to Arnhem, or perhaps employing the British 6th Airborne Division, which, as First Allied Airborne Army's reserve, was currently refitting after fighting in Normandy. He took this idea directly to Eisenhower. Ever the politician, Eisenhower refused to intercede directly with Montgomery; yet he still found a way to keep his options open. "He said he could not tell Monty how to dispose his troops," Smith recalled, "but he gave me permission to fly to his HQ and give him an argument." Eisenhower must certainly have agreed with Smith's concerns, or else he never would have sent him to Montgomery's headquarters. The supreme commander knew he had to proceed very carefully, though. Ike understood that if he personally attempted to interfere in the field marshal's tactical planning, he would risk another divisive confrontation with him. Smith, though, could effectively run interference. It was a long shot, but perhaps he would succeed in persuading Montgomery to make the necessary changes. Of course, Ike could have decided to cancel the operation altogether, but this would have been even more politically explosive. Only bad weather or obvious logistical shortfalls would provide him with an excuse to cancel the operation in any harmonious way.

On the same day as the briefing from General Strong, Smith flew to see Monty. He related Strong's information and pleaded with Montgomery to amend his plans—all to no avail. Montgomery appreciated that the location of the enemy armor was not exactly welcome news, but, in his opinion, it hardly changed anything. The 1st Airborne Division, he assured Smith, was strong enough to hold off the Germans until relieved by XXX Corps. "He waved my objections airily aside," Smith said. "He was quite confident that the thing would go all right as set." To Smith, the British commander actually seemed more concerned with the terrain than with the Germans. Of course, Smith, as a nonairborne type, had no appreciation for the myriad problems his proposed changes would cause. The 6th Airborne was not ready for combat. It would effectively be thrown to the wolves. Nor was there anywhere near enough air transport to drop four full divisions at one time. The idea of changing, at the last minute, the 82nd Airborne's drop zones and mission was completely untenable—as demonstrated by the intricate planning process that Lieutenant Colonel Norton discussed—unless SHAEF was willing to agree to a postponement of the operation. Even if the 82nd was to drop at Arnhem, Smith offered no thoughts as to how this unit, or the 6th Airborne or whoever, would maintain contact with the 101st Airborne at Eindhoven. Given these practical concerns, one could hardly expect Montgomery to be persuaded in any way by Smith's eleventh-hour vagaries.[6]

The sad truth was that Market Garden could not be changed or amended into a better concept. It stood as what it was—a deeply flawed plan, based mainly on hope, stemming from the faulty premise that a single thrust into northern Germany could magically spell doom for Hitler. It was a zero-defect plan that could succeed only if everything, or at least most things, went right. The airborne troopers had to take all, or most, of their assigned bridges. The XXX Corps tanks had to advance fast, with no major delays. Together the tanks and troopers had to hold a narrow highway corridor behind enemy lines. The soldiers of VIII Corps and XII Corps had to move just as quickly to prevent the Germans from cutting the highway and counterattacking the vulnerable paratroopers. The weather had to be good enough for repeated resupply-and-reinforcement drops, not to mention effective close air support. Most important, German opposition had to be just as light and disoriented as the optimistic planners expected, because even the slightest enemy reaction could upset Market Garden's delicate balance.

The only way to address Market Garden's many deficiencies was to cancel it, and none of the senior Allied officers were willing to do that, all for their own reasons. Brereton wanted to prove the relevance of airborne forces. Monty wanted to pursue his dream of knifing into northern Germany, taking Berlin and ending the war in 1944. Browning, having sat on the sidelines for years, wanted to lead a great airborne operation. Eisenhower, the man most responsible for Market Garden, wanted so badly to forge compromise and harmony among his multinational command that he was willing to detract from a broad-front concept he knew would succeed in favor of a single-front concept he suspected would fail. Thus, no one was willing to do what must be done—kill Market Garden in its cradle.

CHAPTER 3

Foreboding

While Bedell Smith argued with Monty in Brussels, back in England a group of young American paratroopers sat casually around the desk of Major Oliver Horton in his austere Ramsbury headquarters. The little village served as a base for Horton's 3rd Battalion, 506th Parachute Infantry Regiment. During the long months of training that preceded the Normandy invasion, his troopers had forged deep bonds of friendship with the locals. Back in July, when the Normandy survivors had returned to the village aboard buses, the entire village turned out to enthusiastically welcome them back. For the paratroopers, parties and revelry soon followed, along with practice jumps and intensive training. The men were enjoying their break from the war, but they all knew that more combat awaited them, and they had grown cynical at the many anticlimactic dry runs they had experienced throughout August and early September, as operation after operation was canceled.

Thus, the body language of the staff officers and company commanders who ringed Horton's desk betrayed a bored expectancy of the sort that inevitably follows false alarms. But this time Captain Derwood Cann, the battalion intelligence officer (S2), noticed something different. Major Horton had spent the morning in conference with his superior, Colonel Robert Sink, commander of the 506th Parachute Infantry Regiment, a few miles away at Littlecote House, Sink's headquarters. To Captain Cann, the major's handsome features now seemed drawn and serious, as if he were almost too tired to contemplate the consequences of whatever he was about to tell his people. In an instant, everyone else also noticed Horton's grave demeanor. "After a few seconds the atmosphere of the room changed," Cann wrote, "and we knew another airborne mission had been born."

Horton glanced around the room. "Gentlemen," he said slowly in his precise Southern accent, "this battalion has been alerted for an airborne mission and must be prepared to clear this camp," no later than 0800 the following morning. With calm thoroughness, Horton proceeded to dispense orders to each of his staff officers. Lieutenant Alex Bobuck, his personnel officer (S1), was to provide him with a list of all able-bodied men in the battalion. "I want every physically fit jumper to make this operation," Horton drawled. He ordered Captain John Kiley, his operations officer (S3), to make arrangements to load the battalion aboard trucks the next morning and move them south to an airfield called Chilbolton, home of the 442nd Troop Carrier Group. Captain Cann, as the intelligence officer, was to visit regimental headquarters for a full briefing on the operation. "You will also be furnished maps, photos, and overlays," Major Horton told him. "Take that equipment and set up a briefing room in the marshaling area. Make the room large enough to accommodate a platoon."

Major Horton turned his gaze to his four company commanders. "All leaves and passes are canceled. No one will leave this base without a special pass." Those troopers who were off base would be found by military police or sergeants and brought back. Every man was to pack his gear and get ready to move out. "Remember, the battalion will take nothing with them except combat clothing and weapons." Everything else would be loaded into duffel bags and locked in a unit warehouse. For now, the specifics of their mission would remain a mystery. Horton would provide those details once everyone was sealed into the airfield at Chilbolton.

The meeting broke up and the word of the impending movement and airborne mission went forth, prompting a flurry of activity. Men spread rumors about the unit's ultimate destination. Sergeants ordered privates to shut up and pack. "The air surrounding us seemed to get close and tense," Captain Cann recalled. "The entire battalion was steaming with excitement, not the wild kind, but the kind of quick action and efficiency. Each soldier seemed to know exactly what to do. Men were hurrying everywhere, some turning in equipment and others drawing equipment. Vehicles were coming in and going out of the area."

At airborne bases all over England, the same process was taking place. Battalion commanders briefed staff officers and company commanders. Company commanders briefed platoon leaders. Platoon leaders briefed squad leaders. Squad leaders briefed their soldiers. Each company area swarmed with activity, not unlike a recently disturbed anthill. All the while, anticipation hung in the air like a dense blanket of humidity. "Somehow it was different this time," one rifleman remembered. "We all felt that we would be going in."

Staff officers worked through the night, attending to a dizzying array of details. They arranged for buses and trucks to transport the troops to the airfields. Once there, the troops had to be quartered somewhere, so the planners assigned hutments, tents, and hangars to each company, right down to the squad level. Intelligence officers and their section sergeants immersed themselves in the details of their respective missions and then prepared detailed sand tables of their objectives. "Overlays were drawn, photos put together, and the sand tables brought to life," Captain Cann wrote. "Every wall was lined with squares of paper and maps with neat red and blue lines on them. The sand tables had changed from just a box full of dry sand into a quiet country-side studded with green fields, canals, roads, bridges and towns." All of this required detailed artistry, under a serious time crunch. In some cases it even required midnight requisitioning to acquire the necessary wood, maps, aerial photo interpreting kits, rolls of acetate, and draftsman kits so necessary to produce such detailed, accurate sand tables.

By midday on September 15, the frenetic movement process was complete. The ground troops were sequestered inside their airfields. Barbed-wire fences ringed the air bases. White-helmeted military policemen patrolled the fence lines. As the gates snapped shut, sealing off the troopers from the outside world, anyone who still harbored doubts that a real operation was in the offing soon changed his mind. "Outgoing letters were held back at the post office," the historian of the 440th Troop Carrier Group wrote. "Telephone facilities were cut off and only official urgency could bring permission to leave the confines of the base."[1]

At airfield after airfield, a panorama of human drama unfolded as the reality set in among the troops that this operation—whatever it entailed—was for real. At Cottesmore, Sergeant Ross Carter and the members of his squad were already pining away for the girls they had met in Leicester and the English Midlands. Their unit, the 504th Parachute Infantry Regiment of the 82nd Airborne Division, had fought hard (and brilliantly) in Sicily and Italy, but because they had suffered such terrible losses, they had missed out on the Normandy jump. All summer long, when they were not training, they were carousing. On the front lines in Italy, they had picked up scabies. They quickly passed them on to the girls, who then passed them on to everyone else. Soon, the entire population of Leicester seemed to be scratching red welts. Sergeant Carter and the other young troopers were so determined to enjoy their limited time in England that they hardly cared. "The truth of the matter is that we conducted ourselves like uncouth barbarians," he said. Months of combat had "dissolved most of the thin veneer that civilization spreads over the instincts. The boys simply went wild in England and didn't give two hoots in hell what they said or did."

The amorous liaisons had more consequences than a simple outbreak of scabies. By the middle of the summer, pregnant women began flocking to regimental headquarters, asking to see the likely fathers. They wanted marriage or restitution, whichever was more convenient. But weddings were few and compensation slim. In Carter's recollection, "The erring lovers roared and bellowed at the thought of being penalized financially . . . for what they regarded as a trifling matter." Now, as they sat in this veritable equivalent of a holding pen, all of that seemed very distant, as if only part of a rollicking dream.

Many miles to the south, at Greenham Common, Corporal Charles Vest of the 502nd Parachute Infantry Regiment, 101st Airborne Division, felt a similar sense of confinement. "I had the feeling my freedom was really gone. Guards were everywhere." In addition to the military policemen who patrolled the wire, his own unit posted guards at such places as briefing and headquarters tents. "It was like a tent city within a tent city." Indeed, the days of freedom were over, and Captain Abner Blatt, the surgeon for the regiment's 3rd Battalion, knew that all too well. When the word came to move to Greenham Common, he had been planning a "really big prop blast" of a party to welcome new officers to the unit. Instead of ordering liquor and party favors, he was now making sure his medical section had enough bandages, morphine, and surgical instruments.

If the soldiers could not enjoy the delights of alcohol or women in the marshaling areas, they could at least still indulge in their other traditional pleasure—gambling. Dice and card games broke out all over the place. Soldiers huddled together in small groups amid clouds of cigarette smoke, peering intently at the roll of the dice or the dealing of the cards. Private Delbert Jones of the 502nd Parachute Infantry Regiment's demolition platoon sat in on one such card game. As it turned out, this was his lucky day. Everything went right for him. "I know I won over a thousand dollars," he said. The problem was that, cut off from the outside world as they were, he had nowhere to spend the money and no way to send it home. "I only wish I could have gotten a pass to London," he said. "Man, would I have had a ball." Obviously no such passes were forthcoming. He ended up losing all the money when his luck ran out.

When they were not gambling or gabbing, the soldiers spent much of their time preparing their weapons and equipment. In the recollection of one officer, the men "were going about their duties in a most cheerful and determined manner. They were cleaning their rifles, sharpening knives and bayonets; machine gunners were filling their ammunition belts, and mortarmen were uncasing round after round of mortar ammunition. Other riflemen were stripping grenades from their cartons and adjusting pins. Everyone was busy."[2]

As each man occupied himself with these necessary tasks, he struggled internally with his own emotions about going into combat. For anyone who let himself think about the imminent danger he was facing, there was a queasy feeling in the stomach at the idea that, within a few days or even a few hours, he could cease to exist. Most of the veterans were resigned to the inevitability of seeing battle again. Some of the 82nd Airborne stalwarts would actually be making their fourth jump. They could not help but wonder whether their luck would run out this time. General Gavin believed that "courage, for every man, is like a bank account—it can be overdrawn." He knew all of these survivors personally. In spite of his own misgivings about Market Garden, whenever he encountered these men, he reassured them that the plan would work and they could overwhelm the Germans without heavy losses. Replacements, for their part, were usually apprehensive but excited.

Among neophytes and old hands alike, the attitudes ran the gamut from the reluctant to the eager. Private Donald Lassen was decidedly reluctant. "I was scared," he said. "Nobody looks forward to dying." Sergeant Bill Tucker, who had seen heavy combat in Normandy with I Company of the 505th Parachute Infantry, was still hoping that the operation might be canceled. "I don't think I was in a good frame of mind. I was extremely nervous about the daylight aspect of the operation—and I was really bugged about flak." After braving intense flak during the night jump in Normandy, Tucker figured he and the members of his airborne stick would be even more vulnerable to enemy antiaircraft fire during the day. Another Normandy veteran, Sergeant James Corcoran, felt nothing but fear at the notion of one more combat jump. He began to calm down only when, by pure chance, he bumped into his brother, who was a captain in a quartermaster unit that was moving supplies into Corcoran's marshaling area. He visited with his brother for a few hours and caught up on family news. "That did bring some relief," Corcoran later admitted. First Lieutenant James Baugh, a highly experienced combat soldier who was now serving as executive officer of D Battery, 80th Airborne Antiaircraft Battalion, felt "quite cynically fatalistic" at the thought of yet another operation. He could see no end to the combat jumps "until Tokyo had capitulated." Private First Class Frank Castilione was so frightened that he "started to sweat." He could hardly sleep. After fighting in Normandy, he knew that combat "was no game—they were out to kill me." Private First Class John Cipolla, a rifleman in C Company, 501st Parachute Infantry, had also fought in Normandy, so he had no illusions about what awaited him in Holland. "Jumping into combat was not exactly my way of having fun," he deadpanned.

Among the thousands of men in the two American airborne divisions, inevitably a few were so apprehensive that they went to extreme measures to avoid the mission. First Sergeant Frank Taylor of A Company, 508th Parachute Infantry, claimed that, in his unit's marshaling area at Langar, several able-bodied men came to him and begged "to be left behind on the operation." Corporal Richard Klein, a radioman in Headquarters Company, 3rd Battalion of the 501st Parachute Infantry, personally witnessed two veteran members of his company deliberately shoot themselves in the foot rather than jump. To Klein, these sad incidents were stark evidence of "what lengths a man will go to to avoid jumping into combat after once having experienced it."[3]

In the vast majority of cases, the troopers—whether rookie or veteran—were eager to jump, if only to be with their buddies and hasten the end of the war. "I was a little concerned for myself, but if all the rest of these dummies were gonna go, I was too," Private Tom Moseley of F Company, 504th Parachute Infantry Regiment, quipped. Quite a few soldiers who were still recuperating in various hospitals from Normandy wounds hastened back to their units when they found out that a jump was imminent. First Lieutenant William Mastrangelo, a platoon leader in G Company, 505th Parachute Infantry, still had forty-four stitches in his leg and right wrist from the effects of a German grenade. Upon hearing about the new mission, he repeatedly begged his doctor to discharge him and send him back to G Company. The doctor, who originally planned to send the lieutenant home to the United States, finally relented. "Okay, if that is what you want," he said, "you're discharged." First Sergeant Dan Zapalski of I Company, 502nd Parachute Infantry, was nursing a leg wound from the Normandy campaign, but he could not imagine this new operation taking place without him. To Zapalski, "That was a prospect worse than death." But his battalion commander, Lieutenant Colonel Robert Cole, did not think he was fit for action. The fiery and charismatic Cole was fast becoming a legend among his men. He had led a near-suicidal bayonet charge against German positions north of Carentan, a feat that would eventually earn him the Medal of Honor.

When Cole asked Zapalski who would be a good choice to fill in for him as I Company's first sergeant for the jump, the horrified NCO lobbied for permission to go. This sparked a torturous, half-hour-long argument between the two willful men. Zapalski claimed that there was nothing wrong with his leg and that he "had a nice, healthy scab to prove it." Cole knew that Zapalski's immigrant mother was a widow, so he prevailed upon to him to think of how his potential death could affect her. "I pointed out that my widowed mother was proof of why I was obligated to go," Zapalski recalled, "the principal reason being the debt to my country for taking care of her and giving her the opportunity to raise three kids without much trouble." Cole replied that he knew of no mothers who were "willing to lose their sons in a senseless war." This had no effect on Zapalski. The two continued bickering and the argument grew quite heated. Finally Cole, in near-total exasperation, conceded that the sergeant could go if the regimental surgeon approved—in writing. He accused Zapalski of being a "fatheaded Pollock . . . typical of all stupid, emotional, first-generation Americans—impractical, burdensome, and unreasonable." With that, Lieutenant Colonel Cole stalked off. Zapalski immediately hustled over to the surgeon and, after another protracted argument, won his reluctant approval to go. "Don't come crying to me when the leg begins to bother you," the doctor admonished as he signed the permission slip. "I'm not responsible for your suicide."

Many of the able-bodied troopers were as eager to jump as Zapalski. Second Lieutenant Robert O'Connell, a brand-new assistant platoon leader in D Company, 501st Parachute Infantry, had actually been itching to liberate Holland ever since, at Fort Benning, he had seen propaganda films showing the German terror bombing of Rotterdam. "[I] thought to myself at the time, 'We're not going to let them get away with it.'" Technician Fourth Grade Frank Carpenter had grown weary of the seemingly endless training routine in England. "Combat was easier than training, training, training. I was glad to be going back." He was absolutely convinced he would survive. Private Melvin Iseneker, a new replacement in C Company, 506th Parachute Infantry, was, like many other rookies, very excited at the prospect of going into combat. In fact, his biggest fear was that somehow this operation would be scrubbed like the previous dry runs. "I don't think any one of us wanted to be held back," he wrote. In his tent at Membury, he dropped a match into an oil burner he was using to heat water and peeked over the rim to make sure it had lit properly. At that exact moment, it exploded with a flash. For several long seconds, he could not see anything. He was so eager to go on the jump that, instead of worrying about his vision, his first thought was, "Now I have done it; I'll be held back." He need not have worried. His sight soon returned and he made the jump, albeit without eyebrows. Captain Jack Isaacs and many of the troopers in his G Company, 505th Parachute Infantry, had been fighting since the previous year in Sicily. They were not so much eager to return to combat as they were determined and confident. "We had begun to develop a methodical, calculating, cunning" state of mind, he later explained.[4]

At the airfields, after commanders and their staff officers put the finishing touches on field orders, plans, and the like, they began their briefings, usually speaking to officers first and then enlisted men. They outlined the big picture of Market Garden, the objectives of neighboring units—General Gavin, for instance, made sure that all of his battalion command-ers knew the missions of their colleagues—and then finally focused on their own specific missions. They also issued maps, Dutch money, am-munition, and rations to their men. In some cases, Dutch army liaison officers dispensed valuable information on terrain, weather, local resis-tance groups, and German troop locations.

The briefings took place in special tents or conference rooms that were adorned with sand tables, maps, and reconnaissance photographs. At Chilbolton, Captain Derwood Cann's intelligence section set up all their equipment in a Nissen hut. Map boards, illuminated by bright, reflective lamps, lined the walls. In the center of the hut, elevated sand tables por-trayed, down to the most minute detail, the 3rd Battalion, 506th Para-chute Infantry Regiment's landing zone north of Son. The battalion officers crowded into the room and listened quietly as Captain John Kiley, the unit's highly respected operations officer, outlined their mission: "This battalion will land on DZ [Drop Zone] 'C' at thirteen thirty hours, sev-enteen September. The planes will fly over the DZ at a hundred and ten miles per hour with an altitude of one thousand to eight hundred feet. The red light will come on at thirteen twenty-five hours, five minutes be-fore the green light. All troops will jump on the green light. A series of white panels [placed by pathfinders] will mark the DZ. Immediately upon landing on the DZ, the battalion will assemble on the green smoke signal, reorganize, and secure DZ 'C.'" From there they would move south, capture the Son bridge over the Wilhelmina Canal, and then keep going to Eindhoven. After the briefing, company commanders and platoon leaders circulated around the room, studying the maps, photos, overlays, and sand tables. Then, one by one, the companies rotated through the hut while their newly enlightened commanders relayed everything they had just learned.

At every airfield, men learned such specifics about their drop zones, objectives, and timetables (aircraft assignments came later, on the day of the operation). At Spanhoe, when Lieutenant Stuart "Flash" McCash, a theatrical platoon leader in F Company, 504th Parachute Infantry, briefed his men, he threw back the cover of a sand table and pointed to a sign labeled, "Grave," for the town and bridge they were to capture. "Men," he said dramatically, "this is our destination."

Without missing a beat, Private Philip Nadler wisecracked, "Yeah, we know that, but what country are we dropping into?"

Soon, everyone in the unit began referring to the town as "Gravy" instead of the Dutch pronunciation, "Grav-uh." To Corporal George "Mickey" Graves, "It seemed a good omen that the name of the town where we were supposed to jump was so identical to my own name." When Private First Class Warren Purcell learned that his unit, G Company, 501st Parachute Infantry, would drop near Veghel, he and his buddies were a bit concerned about the ambitious nature of Market Garden as a whole, but excited to drop in Holland. "Maybe it was because of the pictures of windmills, tulips, canals, wooden shoes, etc., that we had in our minds. If we had to make a jump, we were glad it was here." Corporal James Blue and the members of his platoon felt the same way. When Lieutenant John Foley, the platoon leader, told them they were dropping near Groesbeek, a sergeant of Dutch ancestry exclaimed, "We're heading for the land of wooden shoes and windmills." As Private First Class James Allardyce, a new replacement in B Company, 508th Parachute Infantry, listened to his briefing and scanned his eyes over the sand table, he could hardly contain his excitement. He could not wait to "ride the [XXX Corps] tanks . . . all the way to Berlin!"

After several days of hearing wild rumors, many of the soldiers were just happy to know where they were going and what the new mission entailed, even if it promised to be dangerous. At Greenham Common, the men of H Company, 502nd Parachute Infantry, found out that they were to take two bridges over the Wilhelmina Canal in the vicinity of Best and hold off any German reinforcements that threatened the narrow corridor from Eindhoven to Grave. Even though intelligence indicated that there were few enemy troops in the area, the task was still daunting (events would prove it to be a bigger challenge than anyone imagined). Lieutenant Ed Wierzbowski's 2nd Platoon drew the most difficult aspect of the mission—to seize and hold the two bridges. In spite of the danger, he and his men were just glad to finally be going back into action. According to Wierzbowski, their spirits were very high now that they knew where they were going. To release some pent-up excitement, they decided to play a game of football. "I was invited to join," the lieutenant later wrote. "Right off I was handed the ball and both sides tackled me [with] all of the men piling on. This was to happen each time I carried the ball, which was 90 percent of the time. I must admit it did relieve any tensions at the expense of a number of bruises for me."[5]

Some of the troops were anything but excited about the ambitious Market Garden plan and their place in it. To Private First Class August Duva, who had seen combat in Normandy, the idea of breaching the Rhine and riding all the way to Berlin against minimal opposition was little more than "a Montgomery day dream." First Lieutenant Patrick Mulloy, a platoon leader in C Company of the 307th Airborne Engineer Battalion, nursed "serious doubts about the success of such a bold invasion." The experienced officers of the 504th Parachute Infantry, world-weary after so much fighting in Italy, were skeptical that the promised waves of British tanks would actually link up with them in any acceptable amount of time. At their briefing, Colonel Reuben Tucker, their commander, said facetiously, "I'm supposed to tell you—and I'll quote—'We will have the world's greatest concentration of armor with us on this operation.'" His officers actually burst out laughing, as did he. One of his company commanders, Captain Carl Kappel, thought cynically to himself, "One Bren gun carrier might show up."

Across the Channel, at XXX Corps headquarters, Lieutenant Colonel Curtis Renfro, the 101st Airborne Division's liaison officer, was equally skeptical. After listening to XXX Corps commander Lieutenant General Brian Horrocks brief his officers in a theater at the Belgian town of Bourg-Léopold (a meeting made famous by the movie *A Bridge Too Far*), he had some serious concerns. Renfro could not shake the feeling that German opposition would be more formidable than the British anticipated. After the briefing, when Horrocks asked Renfro what he thought of the Market Garden plan, he gave a noncommittal shrug and said, "It's all right." Knowing this lukewarm response was tantamount to outright skepticism, the good-natured Horrocks chuckled. Renfro took this as an indicator that Horrocks too had his own reservations about the plan.

Troop carrier commanders were also briefing their crews, and many of the fliers were just as worried about the operation as the ground troops. Aviators were concerned about flak, the daylight drop, and the possibility of enemy fighter opposition, not to mention the difficulty of shuttling and landing gliders deep behind enemy lines. At Saltby, Tech Sergeant W. E. Wood, a C-47 crew chief in the 314th Troop Carrier Group, worked long hours refitting his plane to accommodate British troopers of the 1st Airborne Division's 3rd Parachute Battalion. Because British jump procedures were different from American, Tech Sergeant Wood had to install special parabuckets, jump mats, and static lines. With this accomplished, he and the members of his crew attended a squadron briefing. "Our faces fell when we learned that we were to drop at Arnhem," Wood confided to his diary. "[T]hat meant a long run over enemy territory in broad daylight." Many miles to the south, at Chilbolton, Flight Officer William Richmond, a glider pilot in the 442nd Troop Carrier Group, found out that he would fly a resupply mission on the second day of the operation. He had mixed emotions about this. "While I wasn't exactly jumping for joy, I wasn't about to go on sick call either," he said.

At Fulbeck, fliers from the 440th Troop Carrier Group packed into a stuffy, warm RAF gym to hear the news that they would drop elements of the 376th Parachute Field Artillery Battalion and the 3rd Battalion, 508th Parachute Infantry Regiment, over the Groesbeek heights. Decked out in khaki trousers, leather flying jackets, and misshapen fifty-mission crush hats, they listened attentively to briefing officers who, one by one, strode onto the gym stage to address them. "The commanding officer, the operations officer, the weather and radar specialists, each presented his topic in a short, fact-loaded talk that was strictly battle-pointed," one crewman recalled. Instead of engaging in the good-natured banter typical of group gatherings, most of the aviators sat quietly, jotting copious notes, somber expressions on their faces.

The serious, resolute mood only deepened when Lieutenant Colonel Louis Mendez, the 3rd Battalion's commander, ascended the stage and stared wordlessly for two long minutes at the fliers. An absolute hush descended over the gym as the aviators stared back at Mendez. West Point trained, emotional, and inspirational, Mendez had earned the Distinguished Service Cross for his conspicuous bravery at Normandy. Similar to General Gavin, Mendez had a knack for demanding excellence out of his young officers but doing it with a sense of humor. One time, in a leaders' meeting, he put a new officer on the spot by handing the young lieutenant a pencil and ordering him to talk about it for five minutes. Whenever he saw one of his men commit the military faux pas of failing to remove his hat while indoors, he was fond of asking, "Is your head cold?"

Through valor, professionalism, and impeccable integrity, Mendez had cemented a strong attachment to his paratroopers, enlisted and officers alike. In Normandy, he had seen them scattered all over the place in the chaotic night drop. Some had even been mistakenly dropped in flooded areas, where they subsequently drowned. He held the airmen most responsible for the scattered drop, and he was determined to see that it would not happen again. After two minutes of stony silence, when he was sure he had their attention, he finally spoke: "When I brought my battalion to the briefing prior to Normandy, I had the finest combat ready force of its size that will ever be known," he told the fliers. "Gentlemen, by the time I had gathered them together in Normandy, one-half of them were gone!" Tears began streaming down the colonel's cheeks. "I charge you all—put us down in Holland or put us down in hell, but put us down *all in one place* or I will hound you to your graves." Without another word, he turned and walked off the stage.[6]

By the afternoon of September 16, most of the preparations were finished. Transport planes and gliders were lined up on their runways. Equipment bundles containing such items as radios, machine guns, communication wire, food, medical supplies, antitank mines, ammunition, mortar tubes, and even components of artillery pieces were neatly packed and affixed to the belly cargo racks of planes. Most every soldier had cleaned and oiled his personal weapon (some nervous souls cleaned their rifles as many as a dozen times) and laid out all of his equipment for the next day's jump. Squad leaders had quizzed their troopers on drop zones, rally points, and unit objectives. Pilots and navigators had studied their maps and photographs, memorizing takeoff times, rendezvous points, flight routes, drop times, and flak concentrations. Crew chiefs had tinkered with their planes, making sure they were prepared to haul paratroopers or gliders. Radiomen had familiarized themselves with important frequencies and call signs.

There was little to do now except wait, fritter away the final hours, and think about what lay ahead. Quite a few men immersed themselves in letter writing or in reading books. Several units gathered in hangars or tents to watch movies. Some, like the soldiers of F Company, 508th Parachute Infantry, enjoyed an impromptu concert played by their unit band. "Some troopers were dancing, and others clapped their hands in time to the music," Private Dwayne Burns recalled. In another unit, several hundred men gathered in a hangar to hear a swing band. "Feet were stamping and arms were flailing as tune after tune rebounded off the soundboards of the hangar walls," one eyewitness later wrote. Church services of all denominations were common and well attended. In one typical instance at Spanhoe, troopers from the headquarters section of the 504th Parachute Infantry Regiment gathered around their chaplain, Captain Delbert Kuehl, for a brief, informal service. In low voices, they sang "Jesus Calls Us," "In the Garden," and "God Be with You Till We Meet Again," each of which addresses the notion of life after death. In the recollection of Corporal Mickey Graves, a clerk in the S1 section, every man fervently hoped that the hymns would not be "appropriate for our particular cases." The young, irreverent paratroopers had a reputation for drinking, chasing women, and fighting like wildcats. But, with the possibility of violent death lurking, all of a sudden religion seemed worthwhile. Captain Cann, the intelligence officer, was struck by the especially large turnout for his battalion's church services. "Strange, but I had never before noticed as many of the troopers attending church," he wrote with tongue firmly in cheek.

The food, excellent and plentiful, was a nice distraction for the troops. For the briefest of moments, the paratroopers, who so often ate prepackaged rations, had the opportunity to eat what the air force ate. What was more, they did not have to worry about kitchen police duty. "We had large steaks for almost every meal and plenty of ice cream," Cann said. Second Lieutenant Robert Neill's company also enjoyed beef at each meal, prompting the typical jokes about "fattening us up for the kill" and final meals for condemned men. At Membury, Private Donald Burgett's eyes practically bugged out of his skull when he entered a large mess tent and saw generous portions of "fried chicken, mashed potatoes, gravy, and vegetables" served by a long line of cooks. He and his friends happily filed through the line, filled their mess kits, and proceeded to gorge themselves.

A few men felt such deep foreboding that they could hardly concentrate on such things. At Spanhoe, Staff Sergeant Clark Fuller, the communications NCO for H Company, 504th Parachute Infantry, struck up a conversation about the operation with Staff Sergeant Jimmy Allen, an old friend. As they talked, Allen shared his belief that each man in combat had only so much luck. When his allotment of luck ran out, he was dead. Simple as that. In a matter-of-fact but definite tone, as if discussing the weather, Staff Sergeant Allen told his friend, "I've used up my luck. This mission will be my last one. I won't be coming back." The stunned Fuller did not know what to say, but his buddy was right. He would indeed lose his life in a few days, during the combat crossing of the Waal River, one of the most dramatic battles of the entire war. Not far away, in the same marshaling area, Captain Walter Van Poyck, commander of E Company, 504th Parachute Infantry, experienced the same feeling as Allen. As the captain mulled over the company's mission to seize the Grave bridge, he was nearly overwhelmed with a personal sense of impending doom. "I had a strong premonition I wasn't going to make it back," he later wrote. Troubling though this was, he knew that, as commander, he could not dwell on such feelings. He forced the grim reaper thoughts from his mind. Fortunately, his premonition was wrong.

Many miles to the south, at Greenham Common, after Lieutenant Ed Wierzbowski's platoon was finished playing their spirited game of football, his platoon sergeant, John White, took him aside for a private talk. "Lieutenant, I've got a feeling I'm not coming back from this one," Staff Sergeant White said. His expression was serious and self-assured. Wierzbowski was uncomfortable with such a premonition of death. He attempted to crack a few jokes in hopes of snapping the sergeant out of his reverie, but to no avail. No matter what Lieutenant Wierzbowski said, the sergeant simply repeated that Market Garden would be the end for him. What especially struck Wierzbowski was how serene and peaceful the sergeant seemed, as if he had come to terms with his own death. "He seemed calm & relaxed," Wierzbowski later wrote, "with a deep conviction in his mind that showed in his eyes." When the two finished talking and the lieutenant returned to his tent, he had trouble sleeping that night. All he could think about was Staff Sergeant White's premonition, especially "the look in his eyes & . . . the smile on his lips." He wondered how Staff Sergeant White could be so certain of his own demise and yet so calm about it. The lieutenant had no way of knowing that his trusted NCO was exactly right. He would not survive the coming battle. Nor could Wierzbowski know the ordeal that he and the rest of his platoon would soon face at Best.

The young officer was not the only one who could not sleep. An eerie silence settled over the marshaling areas as men tossed and turned on their cots, wondering what the next day might bring. Lying on one such cot in a tent at Cottesmore, Sergeant Ross Carter wondered to himself: "Tomorrow night at this hour some of us will be dead. Who will it be?" Thousands of others pondered the same question.[7]

Even as the troops seethed with anticipation at the airfields, their generals met one last time at Browning's Moor Park headquarters for a final review of the Market Garden plan. Each division commander briefed the others on his own plans. When it was General Gavin's turn to speak, he explained, with a map and pointer, his intention to seize the vital bridges from Grave to Nijmegen, while at the same time holding the Groesbeek heights. For the young general, the last few days had been "a blur of checking troop units, reexamining the details of our tactical plans, flying a light plane to various units to check their planning and . . . poring over aerial photographs of the area in which we were to land and fight, searching for signs of enemy weapons or enemy activity."

All of this now boiled down to one fundamental question on the mind of everyone in that room: Did the 82nd Airborne have enough combat

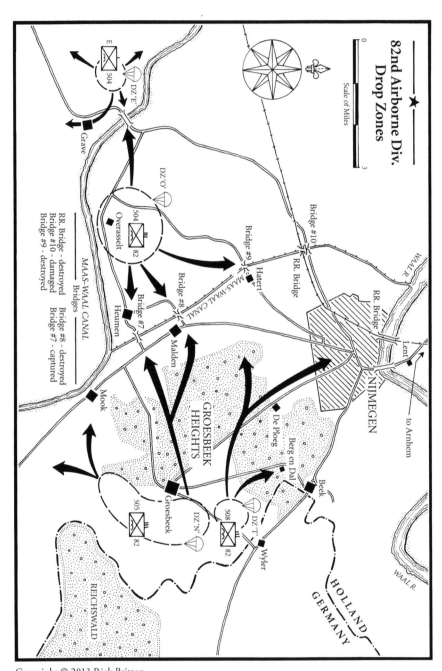

82nd Airborne Div.
Drop Zones

Scale of Miles

0
3

DZ 'E'
504
E

Grave

DZ 'O'
504
82
Overasselt

Heumen

Bridge #7

Bridge #8

Malden

MAAS-WAAL CANAL

Bridge #9

Hatert

Bridge #10

RR. Bridge

RR. Bridge

NIJMEGEN

Lent

to Arnhem

WAAL R.

WAAL R.

GROESBEEK HEIGHTS

De Ploeg

Berg en Dal

Beek

Mook

Groesbeek

505
82

DZ 'N'

508
82

DZ 'T'

Wyler

HOLLAND

GERMANY

REICHSWALD

MAAS-WAAL CANAL
Bridges

RR. Bridge - destroyed
Bridge #10 - damaged
Bridge #9 - destroyed
Bridge #8 - destroyed
Bridge #7 - captured

Copyright © 2013 Rick Britton

power to simultaneously take the bridges and hold the high ground? Gavin was worried that circumstances might force him to choose between the two vital objectives, particularly during the first couple days, before his entire division was on the ground. "The Nijmegen–Grosbeek [sic] high ground was the only high ground in all of the Netherlands," he later wrote. "With it in German hands, physical possession of the bridges would be absolutely worthless." From those Groesbeek hills, German artillery could pound the bridges, particularly at Nijmegen, and perhaps even destroy them. At the very least, they could impede or inhibit Allied movement along the roads and across the bridges. Moreover, the general knew that he needed to maintain control of the landing zones at Groesbeek to bring in supplies and reinforcements by glider. Because of this, he believed that control of this high ground was "the key to the accomplishment of the entire mission."

Browning agreed. As Gavin finished his briefing, the British general cautioned him: "Although every effort should be made to effect the capture of the Grave and Nijmegen bridges, it is essential that you capture the Groesbeek ridge and hold it." Gavin nodded his understanding and sat down.

General Browning's order, of course, made perfect sense. It was of paramount importance to hold the high ground. Any commander worth his salt understood that. Even so, the purpose of Market Garden was to seize *the bridges* in order to speedily unleash a major armored thrust into northern Germany, toward Berlin. High ground notwithstanding, the only way for the Allies to accomplish this ambitious objective was to take the bridges, and these were, after all, perishable assets, because the Germans could destroy them (and might well be likely to do so the longer it took the Allies to take the bridges). By contrast, the Groesbeek ridge spur wasn't going anywhere. If the 82nd had trouble holding it, and German artillery or counterattacks became a problem, the Allies could always employ air strikes and artillery of their own to parry such enemy harassment. Also, ground troops from Dempsey's Second Army could join with the paratroopers to retake Groesbeek from the Germans. So, in other words, given the unpleasant choice between the bridges and the hills, the bridges had to come first.

General Gavin did have some appreciation of this. At an earlier meeting with his regimental commanders, he had told Colonel Roy Lindquist of the 508th Parachute Infantry that even though his primary mission was to hold the high ground at Berg en Dal near Groesbeek, he was also to send his 1st Battalion into Nijmegen to take the key road bridge. Gavin told Lindquist to push for the bridge via "the flatland to the east of the city and approach it over the farms without going through the built-up area." Gavin considered this so important that he stood with Lindquist over a map and showed him this route of advance. If the 1st Battalion made the mistake of straying into the narrow streets of Nijmegen, the troopers would probably get bogged down in a house-to-house fight where, in Gavin's estimation, "one Kraut with a machine gun can hold up a battalion." Gavin had seen this happen in Sicily, Italy, and Normandy. He did not wish to repeat the experience in Holland. Nonetheless, within twenty-four hours, circumstances would conspire to spoil Gavin's good intentions and history would repeat itself.

At the same time, Colonel Lindquist had trouble reconciling Gavin's priorities for the two ambitious objectives of holding Berg en Dal and grabbing the bridge. He believed that Gavin wanted him to push for the bridge only when he had secured the critical glider landing zones and other high ground. According to Lindquist, his impression was that "we must first accomplish our main mission before sending any sizable force to the bridge." Actually, General Gavin wanted the 508th to do both at the same time, but somehow this did not sink into the 508th's leadership. "If General Gavin wanted Col Lindquist to send a battalion for the bridge immediately after the drop, he certainly did not make that clear to him," Lieutenant Colonel Thomas Shanley, the executive officer of the 508th, later wrote.

Perhaps this was a miscommunication on Gavin's part, but probably not. Lieutenant Colonel Norton, the G3, was present for this conversation (Shanley was not) and recorded Gavin's clear instructions to Lindquist: "Seize the high ground in the vicinity of Berg en Dal as his primary mission and . . . attempt to seize the Nijmegen bridge with a small force, not to exceed a battalion." Regardless of what Gavin said and how Lindquist perceived it, the real problem was that the Market Garden plan required the 82nd Airborne to do too much too quickly. Just as Bedell Smith had envisioned, there were not enough airborne troops to accomplish Montgomery's short-term objectives. In that context, Lindquist's confusion over mission priorities was quite understandable. The troopers of the 82nd Airborne Division were about to pay a steep price for these flaws in Market Garden's DNA.

Something even worse was brewing in relation to Arnhem. At the Moor Park meeting, when Gavin finished talking, Major General Roy Urquhart explained the 1st Airborne Division plan. When Urquhart told his American colleagues that the bulk of his division was scheduled to drop six to eight miles away from their prime objective, the Arnhem bridge over the Rhine, they were astounded. At this point, Gavin made his "he can't mean it" comment (described in the prologue) to Lieutenant Colonel Norton. Reflecting on this moment many years later, Gavin was to say, "I couldn't believe my ears." The 1st Airborne Division's job was, after all, the most important of the entire operation. Without control of the Arnhem bridge, Market Garden had no purpose. If the British failed, then everyone would fail.

General Urquhart shared Gavin's concern, but he had little choice in the matter. The RAF was so worried about flak over Arnhem that this was the closest they would agree to drop Urquhart's troopers. What was more, the planners believed that the open ground south of the Rhine near the bridge was too marshy for airborne landings. Actually, this was probably not true, at least according to Captain Arie Bestebreurtje, a Dutch army officer from Nijmegen who assisted the British in their deliberations. "I argued and argued that they could drop their troops and land their gliders practically on top of the bridge by making use of the Rhine 'winter bed,'" he later said. The winter bed was the flatland on either side of the river. In the spring, after the snow and ice of winter melted, the ground was indeed marshy. But in the fall, the river receded back into its original canal, and the winter bed ground hardened to form a perfect landing zone. "I don't think they believed me," Bestebreurtje commented. No one at the Moor Park meeting gave any indication that they knew of Bestebreurtje's claims about the winter bed.

While the ground near the Arnhem bridge may have been suitable for the landings, there was no doubt that heavy flak could pose a real danger to this or any other airborne drop, especially in the daylight. But there was a larger question that perhaps the planners had not considered sufficiently: Was it worse to suffer casualties while dropping on a heavily defended objective or risk never getting there in any real strength? Gavin, based on his experience, felt that it was much better to drop as near the objective as possible, even if it meant taking substantial casualties in the initial stages of the battle. To him, this was much better than "trying to wander around the countryside," absorbing even more casualties, and risking ultimate failure. The manpower-impoverished British were not willing to take the chance of absorbing heavy casualties by dropping near the bridge. Gavin kept his mouth shut and simply hoped that the British, with their long experience at war, knew what they were doing. General Taylor, commander of the 101st, probably harbored similar misgivings, but he too kept silent. Browning adjourned the meeting.[8]

Ten miles to the southwest, at Sunninghill, shadows were creeping along the ivy-covered walls of General Brereton's headquarters as late afternoon gave way to early evening. In Brereton's office, the commander was presiding over one last meeting with his meteorologists. The weathermen liked what they saw for September 17. They predicted minimum cloud cover, negligible winds, and mild temperatures. A slight smile crossed Brereton's tan face. This was exactly the news he wanted to hear. Everything was all set now. At exactly 1900 hours, he turned to Brigadier General Floyd Parks, his chief of staff, and said: "Lay the operation on." Parks nodded, went to his own office, picked up his phone, and sent the word out: Market Garden was officially on.[9]

CHAPTER 4

Rumblings

Over the clear eastern horizon, the sun slowly ascended, evaporating layers of fog from the bogs of England to the polders of Holland. A resplendent day beckoned, the sort that occurs when late summer meets early autumn. Twenty thousand feet over the Dutch coast, amid a hazy blue sky, 872 B-17 Flying Fortress bombers were dispersed into practiced formations of four or six aircraft. Each of the four-engine monsters flew inexorably eastward, like an avenging angel. Each carried a full complement of 260-pound fragmentation bombs, designed to kill enemy soldiers and destroy their antiaircraft guns. Usually the B-17s bombed industrial targets deep inside Germany, reflecting the strategic bombing vision of senior Army Air Forces leaders. Today was different. The bomber boys of the Eighth Air Force were charged with the mission of destroying German flak batteries along the corridors where the airborne armada would soon fly. The B-17s were also supposed to bomb enemy troop concentrations near the drop zones. In all, they were to hit 117 targets from the Rhine River to Eindhoven. The air planners hoped that the bombers would do so much damage to enemy antiaircraft positions in the corridors that the vulnerable C-47s and gliders would then have a smooth run to their drop zones.

Very few of the bomber crewmen knew the full scope of Market Garden. In predawn briefings at their bases all over East Anglia, they were simply told that their day's mission was to support Allied ground troops by bombing "tactical targets." Many of the airmen knew nothing of the planned airborne drops. What they did know was that missions to support ground troops tended to be safer than the longer hauls into Germany, where flak opposition was more formidable. "Their job is to get you out of the game, fair means or foul—usually the latter," one pilot wrote that fall to his brother on the topic of German flak gunners. "They aren't satisfied till you're out of the game forever." Beyond the fact that tactical targets were safer, the fliers liked these missions for two reasons. First, they were enthusiastic about aiding ground troops, whom they generally admired. Second, they enjoyed the idea of striking back directly at their antiaircraft tormentors. Ordinarily, the flak amounted to a dangerous obstacle to negotiate for the greater purpose of hitting a target, which meant that the bomber crews had little choice but to fly through it passively and hope to avoid getting hit. "It's a helpless sort of feeling," Lieutenant John Albanese, a bombardier in the 486th Bomb Group, wrote, "maybe like being used as a target for duck hunters on a spree. You just have to pray a little and sweat it out." By contrast, the flak *was* the target today.

The chance to mete out this sort of payback on what promised to be a comparatively safe raid ("milk run," in pilot parlance) meant that everyone wanted to fly this mission. When Tech Sergeant John Dornick, a top turret gunner in the 388th Bomb Group, found out that his crew was off flight status for several days of ground school, he raged to his diary: "G— dammit, the rest of the boys had a 'Milk Run.' Mad as hell that we didn't go." He bitterly surmised that "the bastards will schedule [more] 'milk runs'" while he and his crew completed ground school. Lieutenant John Angier was so miffed at being left off the flight roster that he attempted to change the schedule. He made such a nuisance of himself that Colonel James Luper, the group commander, personally grounded him. "So on the greatest day of the 8th Air Force, I sat on the ground," Angier fumed.

Now, as the fleet of bombers crossed the Dutch coast, they rendezvoused with 147 P-51 Mustangs, whose job was to protect the B-17s from enemy fighters. They were the sleek bodyguards, charged with the task of escorting their "big friends" to the target and back. Flying in tight formations of four aircraft, the bubble-canopied Mustangs danced to and fro at the edges of the bomber stream, looking for trouble, but there was none to be had. During the night, a force of 282 RAF bombers had raided enemy airfields, suppressing German fighter opposition. Moreover, Allied air superiority was such that no German fighters dared challenge this thousand-plane host. So the bombers proceeded unmolested deeper into Holland, with literally no enemy aerial opposition.[1]

Beginning at 0930, the B-17s began to make runs on their respective targets. Twenty-one thousand feet over Nijmegen, Lieutenant J. A. Dombrowski, a lead bombardier in the 94th Bomb Group, was huddled over his Norden bombsight, in the Plexiglas-encased nose of the plane. As he peered through the eyepiece, he noticed that his primary target, an antiaircraft gun in the northern part of town, near the Waal River, was silent. "But another battery was active, and I changed my aiming point in order to lay the pattern of bombs across this battery." When he was about five hundred feet short of the target, he salvoed his bombs. Immediately the rest of the planes in his formation did the same. Elsewhere in the group's formation, Flight Officer John Paulussen, another lead bombardier, was aiming for the same gun position. "We encountered barrage-type flak," he recalled, "but inaccurate and did not affect [the] run." As he released his bombs, and the other aircraft behind him followed, he stared below, trying to determine the results. "A number of buildings and installations appear to have been hit. An explosion took place about five hundred feet west of the target." Nearby, the 92nd Bomb Group pasted the same area. In postmission interrogations, crewmen reported that "about three-quarters of bursts hit south of [the Waal] river and about one-quarter in and across river . . . pattern about six hundred yards long."

The bombs were hitting more than just the German gun positions. They damaged the PGEM power plant near the river and set a nearby rayon factory ablaze. Several houses around town were hit, and an air raid shelter collapsed. Three people were dead. One eyewitness described in his diary "the heavy drone of air squadrons coming and going, the staccato noise of machine guns and the fierce bark of the ack ack. A red glow hangs against the black sky. The crackling of the fires can be heard from afar." The city fire brigade took to the streets with heavy extinguishing equipment, fighting the numerous fires. A Catholic community center served as an impromptu aid station for evacuees and casualties.

On the second floor of an apartment building within sight of the road bridge over the Waal River, Johanna Bremen, a nurse, was enjoying Sunday morning coffee with friends when she heard the explosions. They looked out the window and saw wounded, ragged-looking German soldiers making their way north toward the bridge. Sensing that liberation was at hand, they stood and danced for joy. As they all cried and laughed with delight, Bremen thought to herself, "What a beautiful view of the battle we shall have from here." It was far too good a view. The walls began to shake. Dishes fell to the floor. In a matter of moments, their joy turned to fear. They left the apartment and went, along with the other residents, downstairs to the building's main hallway. Outside, the explosions continued. They all began to pray. "I can still see an old lady," Bremen recalled, "standing there in the hall saying prayers. We were all saying them, answering her." Outside, at the Hunner Park, in the shadow of the bridge, German soldiers were busily digging foxholes. The explosions tapered off and then ceased altogether.

Fourteen miles to the north, three bomb groups hit German flak towers and likely bivouac areas at Deelen, just outside of Arnhem. As one of the groups, the 388th, made its bomb run through a patch of clouds, the lead bombardier, Lieutenant Harry Montevideo, was searching intently for the enemy guns. The bomb bay doors of the B-17 were open, reducing airspeed. The bombs were armed. The plane was flying in a straight line. At last the clouds dissipated and he spotted the area he had been briefed to attack. "The target was not exactly in the briefed spot but a few hundred yards to the right." He put the crosshairs of his sight on the target area and pulled the release lever. Bombs cascaded from the bay, and, freed from the weight of the explosives, the plane immediately surged upward. In a neighboring squadron, just as the lead plane was preparing to drop, it got caught in the prop wash of another plane and violently jerked around for fifteen terrifying seconds. The plane finally came under control and the bombardier loosed the bombs. In another B-17, Lieutenant William Duane, another bombardier, pulled the release lever of his Norden bombsight and watched the 260-pounders inexorably fall, each with a slight wiggle, to the green earth below. With a series of flashes, they exploded "in an excellent pattern on the flak sites . . . we encountered no opposition. For us this was a milk run."

With hardly any flak in the sky, the three groups turned and headed back for the coast. Lieutenant Jim O'Connor, a copilot, was helping his pilot descend to a cruising altitude over the Channel when a report came over the intercom that a bomb was still hung up in the bay. One of the crewmen worked his way to the bomb bay to get rid of it. This was serious business. The bay was too narrow for a man to wear a parachute, so this meant he would have to work the armed bomb free of its rack manually while hanging on to something firm. Before he even made it there, though, something odd happened. "The bomb suddenly let go and crashed through the closed bomb bay doors," O'Connor recalled, "narrowly missing a ship flying in formation beneath us." The near miss "triggered a serious cussing-out from the pilot below."[2]

Meanwhile, many miles to the southeast, the leading B-17s of the 401st Bomb Group were in the middle of their bomb run. Their job was to hit the Reichswald forest near Groesbeek, where the Allied airborne generals feared the Germans were amassing large numbers of tanks and self-propelled guns. Generals Browning and Gavin were especially concerned that armored units would emerge from the Reichswald to launch powerful counterattacks on the landing zones around Groesbeek. The airmen were supposed to prevent that. During their briefings in the small hours of the morning, they had been told that the woods were full of "tiger tanks," the generic American term for practically any German tank. The mission was, in the view of one airman, "a singular opportunity to help our ground friends."

As a long line of 401st Bomb Group B-17s approached the Groesbeek heights, Lieutenant Bob Grilley, a navigator in the leading low squadron, huddled over his plotting table, concentrating intently on finding the target. He had memorized photographs of the Reichswald, but he knew that several other nearby stands of woods looked very similar from the air. He glanced back and forth from the maps and photos atop his table to the scenery down below. Outside, about one hundred yards away, a few flak bursts dotted the sky. For Grilley and the other experienced aviators of the 401st, the bursts were almost laughable, even amateurish. They were, after all, used to flying through flak so thick that the skies outside were nearly coated black with the oily smoke of their explosions. By comparison, this run was child's play. Now Lieutenant Grilley looked through the Plexiglas window and saw trees a few miles ahead. "Goddamn, there was the woods up ahead right where it should be," he later recalled with a bit of wonderment. "The shape was a perfect match, and the target area, a long rectangle on the south edge, was all but marked out with a pencil." Grilley confirmed to the bombardier, Lieutenant G. R. Lewis, who was leaning motionless over his Norden bombsight, that this was indeed the correct target. At the appointed moment, Lewis tripped the release lever. The two men immediately lunged to either side of the bombsight to observe their handiwork. With noses almost pressed against the glass, they were reminiscent of kids peering through a candy store window. "The strike rippled through the narrow target to perfection," Grilley wrote. He leaned back and thought to himself, "Tiger! Tiger! Burning bright in the forests of the night." Lewis looked at Grilley. The bombardier was, of course, wearing his oxygen mask, but Grilley could see by the twinkle of his eyes that he was grinning. "Got the bastards," Lewis said with satisfaction.

Other lead crewmen were also having no problem finding the Reichswald and hitting it. In most cases, they dropped their loads at the edge of the woods and watched as the trail of bombs detonated in long strings, deeper and deeper into the forest. "Results were observed to be excellent," one of them later wrote. Indeed, they were. The group commander, Colonel Harold Bowman, later commended his crews for a perfect strike. However, he and his crews could not have known that, at this point, the Germans actually had no tanks in the Reichswald, only some antiaircraft guns and a few troops.

Twenty-five miles to the southwest, several other groups were bombing flak and troop positions in the Eindhoven and 's-Hertogenbosch areas. As at Groesbeek, the airmen tried to drop their bombs in the wooded areas where they believed the enemy was taking shelter. "Results were reported as good to excellent," the 381st Bomb Group war diary declared. The reality was substantially different. Although visibility was good, some of the crews had trouble finding their targets. "We searched several times for the target," Lieutenant Bill Frankhouser, a navigator in the 398th Bomb Group, recalled. The lead navigator, Lieutenant Steve Devlin, finally found the proper spot on the third run over the area, but then his bomb bay doors would not open. His plane and several others ended up returning to England with their bomb loads. "Steve took a lot of ribbing . . . about that misadventure," Frankhouser said. In honor of the occasion, they later named their barracks dog Stevie. Lieutenant Leo Leahy, a bombardier in the 384th Bomb Group, had no trouble with his bomb bay doors, but he found it difficult to determine the exact location of the flak guns he was supposed to bomb. "The pilot map I had was so out-of-date we had a little trouble determining our exact position." He spotted the target but dropped his bombs too short. Another lead bombardier, Lieutenant Harold Rarick, and his navigator, Lieutenant William Singer, were also working from obsolete maps. By the time they entered their bomb run, they did not really know where they were. "We picked up what we thought was the target," Rarick recalled. "I wasn't sure that it was the correct area but I thought I was in the vicinity." The potential target looked like the area they were briefed to bomb, so Rarick and Singer decided to hit it. Rarick released the bombs, and the other planes around him followed his lead. As Rarick's B-17 turned for home, he realized he had not bombed the correct place. "I blame the whole mission on the mistaken identity on my part and also on that of the navigator." Another bombardier in the group mistakenly released his bombs early because of an equipment malfunction. As was the case at Groesbeek, the bombing did not do much damage to German ground forces around Eindhoven.

In the main, antiaircraft opposition in this area was desultory at best, but there was one exception. In this instance, a railroad flak gun poured accurate fire at several B-17s of the 384th Bomb Group. A burst ripped into the number two engine of a bomber flown by Captain Omar Kelsay, a squadron commander. "The burst . . . also punctured the wing fuel tanks," he said. "[T]hen another shell riddled the cockpit, knocking the top off the upper gun turret, shattering the instrument panel and setting the bomber on fire." Knowing now that the plane was going down, Kelsay and his crewmen bailed out. The ball turret gunner, Staff Sergeant Thomas Schmeller, had no parachute. He fell to his death. The others parachuted. Three of them landed within the German lines and were captured. Captain Kelsay and the rest of the crew landed close enough to the XXX Corps lines to avoid capture. With the help of their British friends, they returned to their base at Grafton Underwood within two days.[3]

By 1145, the Eighth Air Force planes had bombed their targets and were well on their way back to their bases in East Anglia. They had dropped 2,917 tons of bombs. Forty-five percent of those bombs had landed within a thousand feet of their targets. Analysts claimed "good" results on 43 of the 117 targets. In addition to Captain Kelsay's plane, one other B-17 was lost (ironically enough, it was the one that John Angier would have flown had he not been left off the flight roster). Another plane in the 401st Bomb Group had crashed and exploded on takeoff, killing the entire crew. These men were probably the first casualties of Market Garden.

Now, as morning neared its end, the B-17s approached the English coast in loose streams of six or a dozen bombers. They were flying low enough that the crewmen were free of their oxygen masks. Many were chatting amiably about the milk run they had just made. In the nose of one B-17, Lieutenant James Talley was looking forward to returning to his base at Thurleigh when one of his comrades exclaimed, "My God! Look up ahead!" Talley looked out the window and did a double take. "I had never seen so many C-47s . . . all the way back to England." The sight was staggering. The sky seemed to be coated with planes. In total, there were 1,544 transport planes and 478 gliders in the air. They were carrying over twenty thousand troops. Most of the planes and gliders were flying only a few thousand feet below the bombers. Like many of the other airmen, Talley had not even known there was to be an airborne invasion of Holland. Now he was witnessing the great aerial armada of three airborne divisions. It was an armada that was so overwhelming, so thunderous that it practically brought life in southeastern England to a halt. Traffic jams piled up as people exited their cars and gawked at the planes. Church services stopped as curious parishioners sneaked outside to watch. Farmers paused from milking cows or tending farm animals to stare in amazement at the mighty host. Train passengers crowded against windows to catch a glimpse. A band playing a concert in north London was so overwhelmed by the noise that it had to stop playing. Phone conversations became impossible amid the cacophony.

High above all this, in the cockpit of one B-17, Lieutenant Charles Mellis stared in absolute amazement at all the planes. "Boy, I never saw such an air fleet before," he said. "They were all over the sky." Lieutenant John Albanese gaped: "I had never seen anything like it before—or since," he said. As he watched, he contemplated the struggle that the airborne troopers would soon face. Albanese decided that he would not trade places with them for anything in the world. In some cases, the bombers and the troop carrier planes were dangerously close together, on a veritable collision course as they flew in opposite directions. Fortunately, visibility was good enough for the bomber pilots to carefully negotiate their way around the airborne serials and make it safely to their bases. "I doubt that we shall ever see such diversified air might and movement of this nature again," one B-17 gunner later recorded in his diary.[4]

It was as if the bomber crewmen were passing a baton to their troop carrier brethren. In carefully choreographed formations, the troop carrier planes flew eastward toward the sea. Most were adorned with colorful nose art, sporting such nicknames as the *Wabbit Expwess, Idiot's Delight, Channel Ferry, Sleepy Time Gal, Bouncin' Babe, Ramp Tramp, Scotch Lass, My Shattered Nerves, Miss Behavin, Damn Yankee, Soiled Dove, Terror of the Ozarks, Flak Bait,* and *Ready Betty.* The nicknames, like the men who invented them, reflected the anxiety, the self-deprecating humor, and the sexual edginess of World War II–era American culture.

In staggered serials, the mighty armada rumbled by the white cliffs of Dover and proceeded to fly over the English Channel. "From time to time, a friendly flashing beacon or a radio signal from anchored Allied ships gave check points, identifying and confirming the air course," one C-47 pilot later wrote. Royal Navy sailors, riding in motor launches and torpedo boats, patrolled the waves below the aerial route, waiting to rescue the survivors of any plane that went down in the sea. Twin-engine Royal Air Force Hudsons and Warwicks functioned as the eyes and ears for the rescue crews. These specially fitted reconnaissance aircraft flew at the edges of the serials. Their pilots were poised to immediately report the location of any downed aircraft to the navy rescue crews.

Inside the C-47s, crowded rows of paratroopers sat in aluminum bucket seats "like grim steel-trap-jawed automatons," in the recollection of one trooper. Early that morning, they had eaten yet another lavish meal of fried chicken with all the trimmings, potatoes, thick slices of bacon, pancakes with syrup, apple pie, eggs, toast, jelly, fruit, all washed down with copious amounts of steaming, fresh coffee. After a final round of briefings (and the odd pep talk), they had loaded up and boarded their planes. The men were burdened with a tremendous amount of equipment and weaponry. One staff officer estimated that each soldier, with his full load, weighed three hundred pounds. Some of the more diminutive troopers were actually carrying more than their body weight. Private First Class John Cipolla, a rifleman, carried a typical load: a raincoat; a blanket; a three-day supply of K rations; a Gammon grenade; his main chute, fitted in a harness over his shoulders and torso; his reserve chute, slung just above his abdomen; extra bandoliers of rifle ammunition; ammo belts for a .30-caliber machine gun; hand grenades; a Mae West life preserver; a fighting knife; a shovel; leather gloves; a knapsack full of personal items, such as extra clothes, candy bars, and shaving gear; plus, of course, his loaded M1 Garand rifle. He and the members of his stick (the airborne term for a planeload of troopers) were so encumbered that they could not even reach into their pockets for cigarettes. The air force crew chief had to "pass out cigarettes and light them for us," Cipolla said. Lieutenant James Megellas, a platoon leader, elected to carry multiple weapons, including a Thompson submachine gun, a sniper rifle, a Colt .45 pistol, and two anti-tank mines. In addition, he and almost every other man in both divisions carried first-aid kits with plenty of morphine syrettes. Radiomen, machine gunners, and bazooka men, of course, had to carry their own heavy weapons in addition to all the other gear.[5]

Aboard General Gavin's plane, Captain Arie Bestebreurtje was thinking about his home and family. For him, this day was the culmination of a long odyssey. The twenty-eight-year-old officer had spent much of his youth in Nijmegen, so he knew the area quite well, and he was eager to get back there. Lithe and athletic, the six-foot-three Bestebreurtje was a former speed skater who was good enough to have made the Dutch Olympic team in 1936. In 1940, he had earned a law degree from the University of Zurich, and soon after married a woman he met there. In the wake of the German conquest of his country, he and his wife, Gertrude, left Switzerland and traveled to England by way of Spain. Gertrude eventually went to New York. Arie stayed in England, joined the exiled Dutch army, and even attended Sandhurst, the British military academy.

After years of training, he was now in charge of a multinational Jedburgh commando team, under the control of the American Office of Strategic Services (OSS). His two team members, Lieutenant George Verhaeghe and Tech Sergeant Willard "Bud" Beynon, were Americans. Their job was to mobilize the support of local Dutch resistance cells in and around Nijmegen. Bestebreurtje, in particular, had even more responsibilities as a Dutch army liaison to the 82nd Airborne Division. During the Market Garden planning process, he had initially worked with the British, but, only a few days before, he had suddenly been transferred to the 82nd. Even though he had known Gavin and his staff only a short time, they felt like old friends. He was highly impressed with what he called "American efficiency," and comfortable with the easygoing comradeship of the 82nd Airborne Division officers, who referred to him as "Captain Harry." The young Dutchman spoke excellent English with only a slight Dutch accent—the propensity to say "vuz" instead of "was," for instance—so he fit right in. He especially admired Gavin. "He had a feeling, a compassion for his soldiers," Bestebreurtje once said of his commander, "a basic kindness."

Before boarding this plane, Captain Bestebreurtje had written Gertrude a letter and enclosed a special note for his toddler daughter to read only in the event of his death. "I went to Holland," he told his little girl, "because it was my duty to do so." Now, awash in the drone of the plane's two powerful engines, he sat contemplating his wife and daughter, hoping they would somehow be okay if he did not survive the coming battle. Among the Americans around him, he stood out because he was the only one wearing British battle dress and a green beret. One of his sleeves was adorned with an orange lion and the word "Nederland." He fixed his gaze on Lieutenant Colonel Walter Winton, the G2, and Lieutenant Colonel

Norton, both of whom looked rather glum. Bestebreurtje smiled and shouted above the din, "I know you're feeling pretty miserable, and I understand, but I feel pretty good because I'm going home." The two Americans smiled wanly and nodded.

A couple seats away, closer to the door, First Lieutenant Hugo Olson, Gavin's aide-de-camp, was much more blasé. To him, the weather was so beautiful that this almost seemed like a lazy Sunday back home, "quiet and peaceful, with couples strolling along the streets." Olson casually reclined in his little seat and read an overseas edition of *Time* magazine. Aboard other planes, many troopers also calmly took refuge in reading material of one sort or another. On Private First Class Leonard Tremble's plane, one man read the Bible while another perused a comic book. "I am sure each with his own personal thoughts," Tremble later wrote. On a plane carrying a stick from Headquarters Company, 1st Battalion, 505th Parachute Infantry, Lieutenant Thomas Furey, the commanding officer, read the Sunday edition of the *Daily Express*, a paper owned by Lord Beaverbrook. Private David Kenyon Webster, a Harvard English literature graduate who was now serving as a rifleman in E Company, 506th Parachute Infantry, tried to lose himself in a copy of *We Jumped to Fight*, a book about paratroopers in the North Africa campaign. "I was very disappointed in both the writing and the story," he later commented, "but the title was appropriate."[6]

Others engaged in similarly nonchalant pursuits. Captain Mac Shelley, the operations officer of the 504th Parachute Infantry, passed a pint of Black & White Scotch around to all seventeen men on his plane. In a matter of minutes, the bottle was empty (Shelley later flung it at an antiaircraft gun near his drop zone). Lieutenant Jack Carroll, a twenty-six-year-old platoon leader in F Company, 505th Parachute Infantry, talked baseball with the men on his plane. "We had men from all over the country, so we had lots of opinions on who would be in the World Series." In Serial A-20, carrying the 2nd Battalion, 502nd Parachute Infantry, Lieutenant Samuel Carp and a few buddies overturned a box and played a friendly game of bridge. Inside another plane carrying troopers from the 502nd, Private First Class Francis DeVasto sang his way through most of the journey. Elsewhere, Private First Class George Hurtack, another young rifleman, eased back in his seat, closed his eyes, and thought of the beautiful Dutch girls he expected to meet once he was on the ground. In the leading aircraft carrying the 505th Parachute Infantry, Captain Bob Piper, the regimental personnel officer, was slated to be the first man out of the plane. He was sitting next to his commander, Colonel William Ekman, taking in the view, when the colonel leaned over to him and, with a slight twinkle in his eye, said, "Bob, we made out fine when I had you lead our jumpers into Normandy, so I'll ride your back again." Quite a few men slept, most notably General Taylor, who dozed off for the duration of the flight, waking only long enough to munch on a K ration meal.

The mood on many other C-47s was one of deep concern and fearful anticipation. For Lieutenant Megellas and his men, the flight was a "serious, somber event." Lieutenant Ernest Murphy, a member of the same company, noticed that, "The men who had been in combat were quiet and reserved. They understood what was about to happen in a very short time." Many, like Sergeant Ross Carter, were churning inside, trying to control their fear. He had been fighting since Sicily, so he knew exactly what to expect. He sat quietly, smoking cigarette after cigarette, trying to calm himself. "I let myself think of being *shot at* but not of being *shot and hit*. Imagination given free play could ruin a man under such tensions; therefore I kept tight reins on mine."[7]

Under such grim circumstances, quite a few found refuge in doing anything and everything to distract their worries. Some fidgeted with their equipment and, in high voices that betrayed their nervousness, asked the next man: "Hey, Joe, look an' see if my reserve [chute] is fastened, will ya?" Lieutenant John Foley, a platoon leader in A Company, 508th Parachute Infantry, let each of his men take a turn standing or lying in the door to absorb the breathtaking sight of the aerial fleet of planes. "It seemed to have a relaxing or comforting effect," he later commented. Another platoon leader, Lieutenant John Holabird, believed that part of his job was to be inspirational during difficult times. To distract and perhaps even entertain his men, he "did acrobatics in the open door of the plane to show the devil-may-care attitude," swinging his arms in and out of the open space. At any moment, the plane could have shifted slightly and pitched him out over the sea. Years later, when thinking about the chances he had taken, he began to have nightmares and could not bring himself to get on a plane. Sergeant Burt Christenson, like many NCOs, maintained a stern, impassive face in front of his men. "Your composure in the eyes of the new men will . . . let them see the efficiency of a leader emerge from that face if you are going to command the respect of your men." He was determined not to show the slightest hint of fear, "even though it's there in your gut." Behind the veneer, he was full of anxiety, worrying about nearly every aspect of the jump. He sat near the door and felt a surge of fear-induced adrenaline pumping through his body.

For some, there was no way to mask the fright. The steady rocking of the planes, the oily gasoline stench so prevalent in the C-47 cabins, and the stabbing, gut-wrenching effects of fear produced a wave of uncontrollable nausea. Second Lieutenant Robert O'Connell, a new assistant platoon leader in D Company, 501st Parachute Infantry, was contemplating the overwhelming might of the air fleet beyond the open door of his C-47 when he suddenly felt sick and sweaty. "I distinguished myself by vomiting in my helmet," he quipped. A nervous bazooka man in Private First Class John Allardyce's stick leaned over and spewed his half-digested breakfast onto the floor of their C-47, leaving it slippery with a thin coat of vomit. Somehow no one else on the plane threw up. As one plane carrying Private James Cadden's stick began to buffet from air pockets, he and those around him got sick. "Many of us [regurgitated] in the bucket on the floor which had been supplied by the crew chief."

The air force crew chiefs provided those buckets not just for nauseous stomachs, but also for troopers to relieve their nervous bladders. The C-47s were equipped with a toilet, but they were far too small and cramped for the heavily laden paratroopers to use. Even the relief buckets presented a challenge for the overburdened troopers. Some had trouble keeping their footing inside the trembling planes. They ended up spraying the floor and even the boots of their unfortunate neighbors. Several hapless soldiers on Private Dwayne Burns's plane did exactly this, and soon there was an overwhelming stench of vomit and urine in the air. Burns somberly watched as a thin layer of the liquid detritus ran back and forth on the floor when the plane nosed upward and downward. "Thank God I'm sitting by the door!" he thought. As one trooper in Staff Sergeant Charles Mitchell's squad finished his business, he attempted to empty the bucket's contents out of the doorway. "My position was just to the rear of the open door," Mitchell recalled, "and the prop blast blew [the contents] back all over me." Everyone had a good laugh at the poor sergeant's expense.[8]

As morning turned to afternoon, the serials began to make landfall on the European coast. Soon after this, they linked up with a fleet of 548 Allied fighters whose job was to ward off German fighters and suppress enemy flak batteries. On the southern route, the planes carrying the 101st Airborne Division overflew the Belgian coast at Ostend. On the northern route, the transports carrying the 82nd and 1st Airborne Divisions crossed the Dutch coast near Schouwen Island in the Scheldt estuary. As a precaution against a potential amphibious invasion, the Germans had flooded much of northern Holland, and the sight of so much inundated land saddened many troopers. "We could see where the Nazis had broken the dikes to let the sea roll over the land," Private First Class Ernest Blanchard said. "It looked to us . . . that all of Holland was underwater." Sergeant Ross Carter could make out the tops of houses and windmills jutting above the flood but "no evidence of life . . . in the desolate expanse of sad waters." Tech Sergeant W. E. Wood, a C-47 crew chief flying in one of the 1st Airborne serials, stared, with a mixture of sadness and revulsion, at the display of flooded towns and farms. "It was a pitiful sight. At a few places

cattle or other livestock could be seen marooned on higher ground." Staff
Sergeant Russell O'Neal, a veteran about to make his fourth combat jump,
gazed down and wondered whether his stick would end up dropping in
the waters, as some of the 82nd Airborne Division troopers had at Normandy. As if reading his thoughts, O'Neal's platoon leader turned to him
and asked cynically, "Where do these fools think we are going to jump?
This whole goddamned country is flooded."

In addition to flooded lowlands, some of the 101st Airborne Division
troopers witnessed the stirring sight of the XXX Corps vehicles lined up
near the front lines, at the Belgian–Dutch border. "It was exactly like a
line drawn on a map," Captain Thomas Wilder, commander of the division's reconnaissance platoon, wrote. "The column of vehicles, tanks etc.
stopped . . . from there on the roads were clear, nothing moved in this
area, not a single sign of life." The notional dividing line was just north of
the Maas-Schelde Canal, where the British had carved out a bridgehead
and now stood ready to unleash the ground-attack aspect of the Market
Garden plan.

Opaque clouds of orange smoke wafted over the British lines, ensuring
that every aviator knew the location of friendly positions. On the ground,
the XXX Corps host was immense. Hundreds of jeeps, tanks, half-tracks,
personnel carriers, and trucks were lined up in neat rows along every pass-
able road and trail. Thousands of khaki-clad soldiers stood on or near their
vehicles, gazing upward, many of them shielding their eyes from the sun,
waving amiably at their airborne comrades. Not far from the canal, atop
the flat roof of a factory, Lieutenant General Horrocks was also marveling
at the sight of the planes overhead. "Hundreds of transport planes in perfect formation, many towing gliders, droned steadily northwards, protected on all sides by fighters, like little angry gnats, which filled the sky."
The affable Briton smiled to himself. The sight of the armada was comforting. He liked the idea that thousands of men would soon disgorge from
those planes and make trouble for the Germans beyond the horizon,
somewhere ahead of his own lines. He raised a pair of binoculars to his

eyes, looked to the rear, and studied his own positions. "I could see, carefully camouflaged and hidden in the woods and farms, some of the three hundred guns which were waiting for my word to open fire." As planes continued to drone overhead, General Horrocks felt a keen sense of anticipation. He lowered his binoculars and watched the planes fade into the distance. Zero hour was near.[9]

CHAPTER 5

Drop Day

For the Allies, the fighter planes fired the first shots. Like aerial sheepdogs protecting their flock, they roamed the skies in packs, looking for trouble. Many of the young men who flew those planes had become fighter pilots for the supposed glamour of flying hot planes and earning the rarefied status of an ace. For most, though, the reality was different. Theirs was actually a self-sacrificial job—a monotonous, dangerous grind of escorting the less glamorous heavy bombers or transport planes and strafing ground targets. Much the same way a bodyguard lays down his life for his charge, the fighter pilots learned that they were expected to do the same for their bomber and troop carrier brethren. On a bombing mission, what mattered most was the bombers' job of placing ordnance on target. Today, on drop day, the main priority was the troop carrier mission of dropping troops on their designated landing zones. The fighter jocks knew their task was to destroy any impediment to that objective, whether enemy fighters or flak. If necessary, they were to place themselves directly into the line of fire to shield the vulnerable C-47s and gliders.

As the serials overflew German-controlled territory, some of the fighters stayed near the transport planes, ready to ward off enemy aircraft (there were none). "A fighter would zoom under us and about the same time a fighter would roar over us," Private Thomas Steger, a rifleman in the 504th Parachute Infantry, recalled. "The roar of their engines added to the roar of our own and . . . made a noise I shall never forget." One of these fighter pilots playfully thumbed his nose at Sergeant Peter Dispenza as he buzzed past his C-47. "He was a real comedian!" the sergeant deadpanned. More commonly, the two sides exchanged smiles, friendly waves, or casual thumbs-up.

Other fighters were flying closer to the deck, searching for German antiaircraft positions. Before long, enemy flak began to pepper the skies. The pilots could tell the size of the enemy flak shells simply by looking at the smoke puffs. Gray or white meant twenty-millimeter rounds. Dark gray and off-black indicated thirty-seven- or forty-millimeter flak. Mushroom clouds of oily, greasy-looking black smoke were the telltale signs of the infamous eighty-eight-millimeter gun. By and large, the German gunners were sending up smaller stuff right now. Even so, all of it could be deadly to the low-flying troop carrier planes and fighters. At altitudes of one thousand feet and below, the fighter pilots circled in groups of four, each man covering the others, each of them searching for the exact location of enemy gun positions before diving to the attack. "At that altitude we were perfect targets," Captain Marvin Bledsoe, a P-47 pilot, wrote. "I visualized the gunners licking their chops."

At one point, flak exploded dangerously close to Bledsoe's plane. He could sense that small fragments were lacing into the fuselage. The natural inclination was to climb out of range. Instead, he and the others kept circling at low altitude, trying to spot their tormentors. In essence, they were playing a game of chicken with the enemy gunners. The more the Germans fired, the better the chances they might score a hit, but also the better the chances the Americans would spot them and retaliate. "That was the only way we could find them and knock them out," Bledsoe commented. He heard the welcome sound of another pilot's voice over the radio. "I've got the bastards spotted. Follow me!" Bledsoe and the others nosed over and dived, strafing the enemy gunners with a powerful array of wing-mounted .50-caliber machine guns. Each round had the capability of blowing a man's head off—every plane was capable of firing hundreds of such rounds in a matter of a few seconds. When Bledsoe and the other pilots finished their quick pass and flew away, the German guns were silent. In another instance, a squadron of P-51s spotted a pair of eighty-eight-millimeter guns and a pair of half-tracks mounting twenty-millimeter flak guns and dive-bombed them. "The two half tracks were set on fire," the unit after-action report claimed. "[W]e killed ten-plus enemy personnel manning the guns."

Whether the pilots were dropping five-hundred-pound bombs, strafing, or firing rockets, these runs were extremely dangerous. They required consummate courage and skill. "In the first place, the aircraft doesn't go where you are looking because its flight path depends on the angle of attack on the wing, which varies with your airspeed," an experienced fighter pilot wrote, "and in the second place, your bomb won't go where the airplane is going unless you are in a vertical dive because gravity starts pulling the bomb down as soon as it is released." The pilots had to be extremely careful not to dive too steeply, because the resulting g-forces could cause them to lose consciousness. Or even if they did remain conscious, they might have trouble pulling out of the dive. If they were too low when they released their bombs, the explosion could destroy their own plane or that of their wingman.

As they strafed, they were so low that, in effect, they and the enemy gunners were firing at one another point-blank. This made evasive maneuvers a must. Knowing that gunners fired at spots where they thought the plane would soon fly, they sought to evade them by outthinking them. "Use every bush and blade of grass for protection," one pilot advised. "Pull sharply up and gain altitude rapidly, making sharp turns . . . always do the unexpected in choosing your flight path." In doing this, though, they had to be careful not to collide with other aircraft. What was more, it was easy to become disoriented at such low altitudes and lose track of buildings, hills, or power lines, with predictably catastrophic results.[1]

The closer the armada got to the respective drop zones, the heavier the flak became, and the more the fighters unleashed their fury. To Captain

Henry Keep, they seemed like "a bunch of wasps. A flak tower would open up from the incongruously peaceful-looking Dutch countryside, and hardly before the first burst had died away, out of the sky would sweep one of the fighters, spitting fire as it rushed at the kraut gun." In another serial, Captain Robert Franco, a surgeon, watched as a flak tower opened fire. "Two RAF [Royal Air Force] Typhoons dove on it, hit it with rockets, and the explosion was impressive." The Typhoons, flown mainly by British or Canadian pilots, were especially known for their accuracy in destroying tanks and artillery pieces. In another plane, Corporal James Blue saw one dive straight at a concealed gun position. "Smoke flew from the Typhoon; we thought it had been hit. The plane was loaded with rockets, and I think the pilot fired all rockets, because the gun positions went up in smoke. The pilot very gracefully took his plane out of the dive and was on his merry way."

At nearly the same time, Lieutenant Charles Santasiero, a platoon leader in I Company, 506th Parachute Infantry Regiment, looked down and saw a group of Germans slowly pulling the camouflage cover from an eighty-eight-millimeter gun. To the lieutenant, it seemed as if the gun were pointed not just directly at his plane, but at him personally. "It is a hell of a feeling to see them about to blast you out of the sky," he later said. As he stood helplessly watching the crew load the gun, he heard a roar overhead. He glanced up and saw a fighter dive, in a blur, past his plane, right at the gun. "He hit it with a five-hundred-pound bomb dead center. Boy, what a ringside seat." Santasiero only wished he knew the pilot so he could thank him.

Several miles to the north, Private Steger, who had watched the fighters buzz around his C-47, now saw them plunge downward, straight at a flak boat and a fortified house that were firing at his serial. Every time the German gunners fired, the gun muzzle winked with red flashes. Below Steger's feet were equipment bundles loaded with some eighteen hundred pounds of explosives. All he could think about was what would happen if even one of those shells hit the bundles and set them off. Tracer rounds spit from the wings of one fighter and tore into the roof of the house, sending shingles flying in all directions. Another plane attacked the boat "like a hawk after a mouse. He . . . released a bomb. I could see the bomb going through the [air] like a football. It took the tugboat dead center . . . a flash of fire and then the black smoke." The enemy fire petered out. Near Arnhem, Tech Sergeant Wood, the C-47 crew chief, saw a Typhoon swoop along the water and unleash two rockets at an enemy flak boat. "The boat blew up with a blinding flash of flame and smoke." Wood doubted that the German crew ever saw the plane that killed them.[2]

The ubiquitous fighter planes, effective though they were, could not possibly destroy all of the antiaircraft guns. There were, after all, dozens of flak positions along the corridors and near the drop zones. The fighters did tremendous damage to those they could see, but they made little headway against guns that were concealed in wooded areas. The German gunners knew that unless they fled their posts altogether, their best chance of survival was to shoot down the paratroopers before they reached the ground. There was great incentive, then, for the gunners to loose heavy streams of fire at the planes, even at the risk of retaliation from Allied fighters. For those men whose aircraft were in the path of such active flak positions, the experience was terrifying. As flak peppered one C-47, a frightened radio operator leaned over to the navigator and asked how much longer they would have to fly through "that crap." The navigator did not even raise his eyes from the map he was studying. "Only a few more minutes," he replied tensely. But every minute under such fire felt like hours.

Most of the paratroopers had come to terms with the possibility that they might get killed while fighting on the ground. Dying in the air was something different altogether. Nearly all of the soldiers had an abject fear of being consumed in a ball of fire or plunging to the earth in a colossal crash. On the ground they could dish out plenty of punishment to the enemy. In the air they could do little else besides sit passively and hope to survive. "I had an intense horror of dying a futile death," Sergeant Ross

Carter said, summing up the attitude of nearly all of the aggressive para-troopers. "If I had to go in this war, I wanted to go giving a good account of myself." As flak bursts rocked Staff Sergeant Otis Sampson's plane, he looked out the door and noticed several German soldiers a few hundred feet below, running for shelter. "It won't be long now, you bastards," he yelled, "and I'll be down there among you!" As another C-47 overflew the Grave bridge and took fire from a twenty-millimeter antiaircraft gun, a sergeant shook his fist at the gunners and screamed, "You dirty krauts! You just wait a minute and we'll be down there to get you!" Some of the troopers on Captain Jack Isaacs's plane even threw grenades at a group of Germans. The grenades were, in Isaacs's recollection, "inaccurate and inef-fectual." Throwing them probably made the soldiers feel a bit better, though.

By now, nearly everyone was ready to jump, if only to get the hell out of their planes. Some yelled, "Let's go!" while others simply muttered the encouragement to themselves. On some planes, jumpmasters ordered their sticks to stand, hook up to their static lines, and be ready to jump in case the aircraft got shot down. Others simply remained seated, watching for the red light that was the signal to prepare. In either case, there was little else the troopers could do besides wait for their planes to arrive over the proper drop zone (provided they made it that far). Fortunately, amid all the engine noise, it was difficult to hear the unique *karumph* sound of nearby explosions. The noise of the explosions was generally faint but dis-tinctive, at least for those who knew what they were hearing. Many of the new men did not. One rookie in Private First Class August Duva's stick kept asking him whether the distant bursts were flak. Even though Duva could see clouds of oily black smoke outside, he kept responding, "No, not yet, you'll know when it comes," to the new man. Illogical or not, it seemed to placate him. A new man on another plane pointed out the door and innocently said, "Look at the black clouds below," to a group of silent veterans.[3]

The C-47s consisted of little more than a thin skin of aluminum with no self-sealing fuel tanks (the nylon-skinned gliders were even more vulnerable). When flak fragments collided with Lieutenant Winston Carter's C-47, it sounded "like hail." Others thought the sound was more like pebbles or rocks smashing into a car. On one plane, Private First Class Lawrence Dunlop was terrified that a burst of flak would knife through the floor of the plane and that he might "get it in the rear any second." The crew chief on Captain William Best's plane apparently had the same fear. He removed his flak vest, placed it under his backside, glanced at Best, and said: "At least I'm not going to get shot from below."

On another plane, Lieutenant James Megellas stood in the door watching tracer rounds whiz in every direction and had "a very naked feeling . . . with no place to hide. It appeared as though every tracer bullet was heading for me." The fire was indeed close enough that it wounded two men in his stick. He ordered one of his sergeants to unhook them from their static lines "so as not to impede the exit of the others." On a nearby C-47 in the same serial, Captain Delbert Kuehl, the chaplain of the 504th Parachute Infantry Regiment, was standing at the door next to Captain Moffatt Burriss, the commander of I Company, when a line of tracers arced up toward them. To the chaplain it seemed as if "we were going to swallow them." He and the captain both scrambled away from the door and took shelter behind the dubious protection of the thin aluminum fuselage, "which afforded us no more protection than the open door." Realizing this, he and Burriss glanced at each other and laughed.

This reaction was by no means unusual. As Lieutenant Jack Tallerday's plane was closing in on his unit's drop zone near Groesbeek, he saw a heavy machine gun open fire, seemingly at his plane. The line of tracers seemed to lead right into the open doorway where Tallerday was standing. "I did take a giant step backward as if to avoid them." The bullets passed under the plane's belly and fell harmlessly to the earth. The plane flew well out of range before the enemy machine gunners could adjust their aim. On a neighboring C-47, Lieutenant William Meddaugh was also standing in the doorway when a burst of flak exploded uncomfortably close. "It was so close that I automatically reacted by throwing an arm up in front of my face as if to ward off any fragments. Immediately afterward I felt sort of foolish."

There was no need to feel foolish. Enemy antiaircraft fire was hitting many planes, setting some on fire. Aboard the ominously named *Clay Pigeon*, Private First Class George Doxzen's stick was standing up, waiting for the word to jump, when huge hunks of flak smashed into the plane's belly. Fragments hit his jumpmaster, Lieutenant Tom Seibel, in the chest, tore a hole the size of a bass drum in the fuselage, and set the cabin on fire. The lieutenant tumbled out of the door and the rest of the stick followed, except for Doxzen. "The . . . flak burst had knocked me down and I was dazed," he said. In a matter of seconds, the fire spread, the engines shut down, and the plane began to dive. Doxzen contemplated going down with it, but he managed to stagger to the door and jump alongside the plane's radio operator, Staff Sergeant Harry Tinkcom. "Both he and I left the plane at almost the same time," Tinkcom said. The two were momentarily tangled together, but both landed safely, as did the plane's crew chief, Tech Sergeant Joseph Curreri. Six of the men in Doxzen's stick died. "The plane's trailing flames reached them like a giant fiery hand," Curreri said. "I watched in horror as their chutes ignited like torches." The rest of the paratroopers landed safely but were taken prisoner. The two pilots rode the plane all the way down and managed to survive the crash, although one of them broke both his legs. The airmen and Doxzen eventually made it to British lines.

In another instance, a concealed twenty-millimeter gun fired an accurate burst at a plane that was carrying a stick from Lieutenant Isidore Rynkiewicz's platoon in H Company, 504th Parachute Infantry. The shells smashed into the equipment bundles in the belly of the plane, one of which contained composition C explosives that quickly caught fire. "Yellow and red streamers of flame appeared in the inky black smoke," said Captain Arthur Ferguson, who was riding aboard a nearby C-47 in the same serial.

Technician Fourth Grade Paul Mullan, a radio operator, watched as the flames spread quickly through the bundles, and he knew it was only a matter of time before they engulfed the plane itself. He asked his platoon leader why someone on a neighboring plane did not radio the stricken aircraft and tell them to drop the bundles. "Radio silence," the lieutenant replied.

"They know we are here," Mullan replied incredulously. "They are shooting at us."

In fact, the pilot of at least one neighboring plane was indeed radioing the stricken aircraft to warn the crew about the fire, but Mullan had no way of knowing that. The blaze soon filled the cabin with acrid smoke. Private George Willoughby, an eighteen-year-old rifleman, saw that Lieutenant Rynkiewicz was wounded, as was the stick's BAR man. "Within seconds, the plane was so full of smoke you could not see anything," Willoughby later wrote. The flames ate through the bottom of the plane. Fortunately, Willoughby and the other troopers were hooked to their static lines and thus in a position to exit quickly. "At that time, others and I fell through the floor of the plane. I could smell flesh and see the skin hanging from my face and hand. I . . . released my rifle when the flames burned my hands." Lieutenant Virgil "Hoagie" Carmichael, the battalion intelligence officer, stood in the door of another C-47 and watched as Willoughby and the others bailed out. "Their parachutes were camouflaged . . . and the Air Corps [chutes] were white nylon." The plane then nose-dived and crashed, at a forty-five-degree angle, into a tract of flooded land. Only one of the airmen survived. Every member of the stick lived. All but two were captured (including Willoughby, who spent the rest of the war as a POW).

In all, the German gunners succeeded in destroying thirty-five C-47s, most of which were shot down over or near their drop zones (fourteen gliders failed to make their landing zones). Almost all of the C-47s disgorged their troopers before going down. In several instances, pilots stayed with burning planes to deliver troopers accurately. Lieutenant Herbert Schulman was at the controls of one such flaming plane. "Don't worry about me," he told his flight leader. "I'm going to drop these troops in the DZ." Schulman disgorged his troopers and then went down with his plane near the town of Veghel. Major Dan Elam, Lieutenant John Gurecki, and Lieutenant Robert Stoddardt all did the same. All of them could have prematurely dropped their troopers to save their own skins. Instead they sacrificed their lives for the sake of the mission. By 1300, H-hour for Market Garden, the aviators were in position to make the most accurate airborne drop of the war, just as Lieutenant Colonel Mendez had so emotionally requested back in England.[4]

Specially trained pathfinders—two planeloads per drop zone—jumped twenty minutes ahead of the main serials and marked targeted areas with smoke, colored panels, radio, and navigational aids. Their work, in addition to the high visibility of a clear day and the courage of the aviators, meant that most serials had little trouble finding their drop zones. A few minutes after 1300, the troop carrier planes began making their final runs. In many cases, the Americans caught glimpses of Dutch civilians standing in groups, gaping in amazement, cheering and waving. The Americans returned the greetings with almost as much enthusiasm. "I actually waved to some people directly and got a 'V' [for victory] sign in return," Lieutenant Neal Beaver recalled.

Several hundred feet above Drop Zone C, not far from St. Oedenrode, Colonel Frank MacNees was flying the lead plane of his 435th Troop Carrier Group through heavy flak. Black clouds boiled and drifted through the sky. Behind him, almost as far as the eye could see, the sixty-four planes of his group were fanned out in correct vee formations. All at once, a shell burst alongside the tail of his C-47. The crew chief rushed forward to the cockpit and exclaimed, "The tail is gone!" The plane continued to fly normally, though, so Colonel MacNees knew he was wrong. With his eyes still trained forward, scanning the approaching drop zone, the colonel replied sarcastically, "Sergeant, you are the only man I know of who has

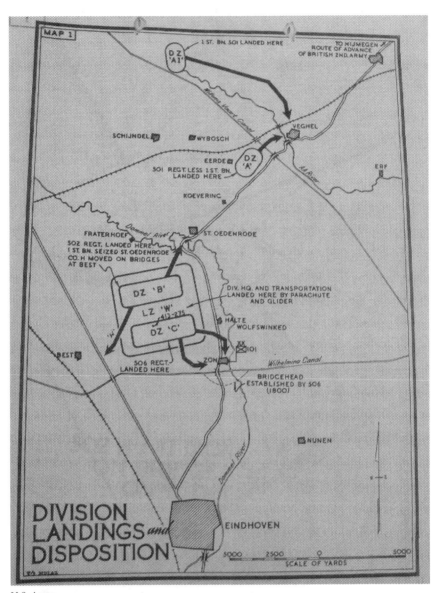

DIVISION LANDINGS *and* DISPOSITION

U.S. Army

actually flown in a C-47 with no tail." Everyone exchanged sickly, relieved grins.

In the cabin of the same aircraft, Lieutenant Colonel Patrick Cassidy, commander of the 1st Battalion, 502nd Parachute Infantry Regiment, was waiting for the signal to jump, all the while watching flak score hits on planes all around them. A C-47 carrying a stick from his A Company was soon engulfed in flames. Cassidy counted seven camouflaged airborne chutes before the descending aircraft slipped out of view. Even closer, a plane carrying Lieutenant Colonel Raymond "Bud" Millener, the division chief of staff, also caught fire. This was the aircraft piloted so bravely by Major Elam. As Elam held the controls in a cockpit filling up with smoke, Millener and the other troopers hurled themselves out the door. Colonel MacNees caught a glimpse of Elam's copilot struggling to control the plane amid the smoke. "[His] face was ghastly and he obviously was choking for breath." At that moment, MacNees ordered his own copilot to turn on the green light. Several feet to the rear, Lieutenant Colonel Cassidy was still transfixed, watching Elam's dying plane, hoping everyone would get out. General Taylor was standing next to the young battalion commander. The general noticed the green light, leaned over, and said, "Cassidy, the green light is on." Cassidy acknowledged the general's admonition, hesitated a moment, and then shuffled through the door, followed by everyone else. Close by, the plane carrying Private James Cadden's stick sustained several hits, caught fire, and began to rock back and forth as the pilots lost control. Only moments earlier, he and his buddies had taken turns vomiting in a relief bucket. Now as they scrambled to eject from their burning plane, the man ahead of Cadden hastily stepped into the bucket, where his boot stuck. Unable to dislodge it, he jumped. As Cadden followed him out the door, he saw the bucket "for an instant on his foot with its contents strewn out through the air."

About a thousand yards to the south, the 506th serials were arriving over Drop Zone B, closer to Son. One serial disgorged its troopers relatively unscathed before the antiaircraft fire intensified. "Heavy flak was received by the formation," the regimental after-action report stated. "[R]egtl. Hq planes were the heaviest hit." In fact, the plane carrying Colonel Robert Sink, the regimental commander, sustained major damage to one of its wings. Seeing pieces of the wing dangling in the breeze, Sink turned and said, to no one in particular, "Well, there goes the wing." The plane stayed airborne, though, and everyone got out alive.

Aboard another plane, Private John Lindberg was hooked up, standing just behind the cockpit, next to the radio operator. Lindberg was the push man, the last in his stick of sixteen troopers slated to jump. The flak suddenly grew more accurate. *Thug! Thug! Thug!* Several pieces of steel tore into the plane. Private Lindberg glanced down and saw black smoke curling through the floor. Up and down the stick, the troopers hollered for the green light. Lindberg repeatedly tried to get the radioman's attention and alert him to the fact that the plane was in flames. In total exasperation, he screamed, "You stupid bastard, the plane is on fire!" In fact, the pilot probably knew this but was bravely holding his course until he arrived at the exact spot where he was supposed to drop the stick. At last the green light winked on and everyone charged through the door.

In spite of the flak, the 506th drops were highly successful. Out of 135 planes, only two crashed on the drop zone and two others elsewhere. "The Air Corps should receive a great deal of credit for the excellent dropping of the parachutists," the regimental after-action report asserted, with the additional claim that this was the best jump the unit ever had, including practice jumps.

Miles to the north, the 504th Parachute Infantry was having little trouble with flak at Overasselt, but several concealed batteries in the woods around the Groesbeek heights harassed other 82nd Airborne serials as they arrived over the drop zones in that area. "During the last five minutes, we were under continual fire," an officer in the 505th Parachute Infantry wrote. "[M]any planes were hit and parts of them shot off, but our regiment was lucky in that none of our planes were shot down before everybody jumped. The air force did a good job in dropping us in the right place."

At the same time, Lieutenant Colonel Charles Young and his 439th Troop Carrier Group prepared to drop their troopers from an altitude of just over five hundred feet, with an airspeed of 120 miles per hour, as was typical. He looked down and saw a twenty-millimeter gun crew scrambling to their weapon. "We could see whitish yellow flames at the gun muzzles, and the tracers went by our cockpit on both sides at the same time." Several of the rounds impacted against the side of the plane. It sounded, in Young's estimation, as if someone were hitting the aircraft with a sledgehammer. Fear gnawed away at him and he wondered how much of this he could stand. "You want to duck, but there's no place to duck. You get mad but you don't have anything to hit back with." Somehow his plane and the others negotiated the fire and dropped their troopers.

In a neighboring group, Captain Donald Orcutt was under "a hail of enemy fire" trying to safely deliver soldiers from the 508th Parachute Infantry onto Drop Zone T just northeast of Groesbeek. "My eyes were glued to the image of my squadron commander's airplane as I tried to hold position relative to him. Sweat streamed off my forehead, down my nose, and dripped from my left hand onto the knees of my trousers. I dared not take my right hand off the throttles in order to wipe my eyes." Finally, the green light flashed from the astrodome of the commander's plane. Orcutt's copilot illuminated their own aircraft's green light and dropped several equipment bundles. To Orcutt, the paratroopers seemed to take forever to jump. When they were finally all gone, he banked the plane and barely escaped a point-blank shot from a flak gun that was close enough for Orcutt to make out the facial features of the crewmen. Away from the drop zone, when he was finally out of danger, he realized that he was absolutely soaked in perspiration.

In spite of the heavy pockets of flak, the C-47s over the American drop zones had a survival rate of nearly 96 percent, dropping 14,109 paratroopers, the vast majority within a mile of their intended drop zones. "We could not have landed under better circumstances," Lieutenant Colonel Mendez later wrote to his air force counterpart, Lieutenant Colonel Frank Krebs, whose 440th Troop Carrier Group had dropped Mendez's battalion. Ironically, after Krebs dropped Mendez's stick, his plane was shot down (the only one in his serial) and he spent forty days being hidden by the Dutch resistance before returning to Allied control. A handful of troopers—a few dozen at most—refused to jump or could not do so because of equipment mishaps, wounds, or illness. They returned to England in their planes to face a court-martial or receive medical care, whichever was appropriate. In one case, a trooper pulled out his pistol and shot himself in the foot, but then jumped anyway. In another bizarre instance, a soldier in B Company, 504th Parachute Infantry, "went out of his mind," according to the crewmen of the C-47 on which he was a passenger. The man's jumpmaster persuaded the pilot to make an emergency landing at a field in England, where the man "was removed and taken to a hospital." With this done, the plane took off and rejoined its serial.[5]

Meanwhile, in the sunlight of early afternoon, paratroopers descended to the earth all over the various drop zones. The skies were literally full of men in chutes (resembling "khaki dolls," in the recollection of one distant observer), padded green bundles in multicolored chutes, and, of course, olive drab C-47s. The planes were almost like aerial clown cars, belching forth a seemingly endless stream of troopers into the blue sky. Silverwinged fighter planes buzzed above it all, still looking for trouble. This mighty host was an impressive demonstration of Allied power—the financial resources that made it possible, the industrial might that created it, and, most of all, the human beings who took the leading role in fulfilling its purpose.

Above Drop Zone O at Overasselt, one of those human beings, Private Thomas Steger, was attempting to follow his squad leader out of the plane when Steger fell down in the doorway. Instead of standing up again, he dived out. The opening shock of his chute was considerable, somewhat like "being on the paper end of a twenty-foot black snap whip." The sky around him was a colorful panoply of parachutes, from the camouflaged green chutes of individual troopers to the blue, orange, and forest green chutes of the equipment bundles. The descent seemed to take forever. Steger cursed the pilot, quite erroneously, for dropping his stick too high. Finally, he landed next to a house. "I came in real nice. My knees buckled and I was in Holland." Nearby, Private Philip Nadler, who had wise-cracked to his lieutenant about the Grave bridge, was looking upward at his deployed chute, checking for defects, as paratroopers were trained to do. For some reason, three panels were missing, "like a cut of pie." Because of these tears, he was falling fast. He looked around, trying to get his bearings and see where he might land. He spotted the Grave bridge, and, before he knew it, he landed heavily somewhere nearby. It took Nadler several minutes to untangle himself from the shroud lines of his chute and secure his rifle. To make matters worse, his ankle was badly sprained by his heavy landing.

Several miles to the northeast, over Drop Zone T, Major Benjamin Delamater, the executive officer of 1st Battalion, 508th Parachute Infantry, was cursing himself for not securing his M1 carbine better when the rifle bumped into his chin. As he descended, a myriad of thoughts flashed through his mind that were typical of nearly every trooper who jumped that day. "That must be our bundle. Who are those men running down there? Nobody should be ahead of us on this field. Is that a tommy gun or a Schmeiser? Too slow for a Schmeiser. There's Frigo. Hope Krixer and that aid man got down okay. Will we never get down? Just give us thirty minutes, Lord, thirty minutes, and then let them come after us. What a hell of a jolt! I know I'll never get out of this harness." With the assistance of red smoke and red cloth markers, Delamater helped assemble the battalion.

Descending northwest of Son, Private Don Burgett marveled at the sheer number of jumpers and planes in the air around him, more than he had ever seen before. Below, many soldiers from his battalion were already on the ground, freeing themselves from their harnesses, assembling on the drop zone. He looked back up and froze. "A C-47 was coming straight at me. Its port engine was aflame, trailing smoke." There were so many jumpers still in the air that Burgett wondered how the plane could possibly avoid them. As the aircraft bore through the sky, troopers disgorged from the door. At the same time, Burgett could clearly see the pilot in the cockpit. "His eyes were wide and round as he was being shaken by the controls. I was going to be killed; I just knew it." But Burgett was lucky. He drew his legs up and the plane buzzed underneath them, missing him by a matter of a few feet. In that instant, as the aircraft sailed by, Burgett stared at the stricken pilot. "His gaze was riveted straight ahead. He *knew* the fate that awaited him and his crew." A few horrifying seconds later, the aircraft hit two unsuspecting troopers, the propellers cutting them to pieces. After that, the plane hit the ground, "flipped up on its right wing, did a somersault, and disintegrated into a pile of wreckage."

Here and there, groups of German soldiers fired at the paratroopers as they dropped, right when they were most vulnerable (the men deeply feared and resented this). One of the Germans, Master Sergeant Jakob Moll, was in the village of Mook, organizing the soldiers of his company into cohesive fire teams to shoot at paratroopers from the 505th Parachute Infantry. Moll gazed upward and watched as hundreds of Americans flung themselves out of their C-47s. "It was an imposing picture," he later wrote, "although dreadful for us." He and the others "started active fire from rifles and MGs at aircraft and paratroopers who were still hanging in the sky." The machine gunners actually supported their weapons by draping them over the shoulders of their comrades. The heat of the guns and the noise of the shooting were nearly unbearable for those who served as impromptu platforms, but the firing continued unabated. Elsewhere another German soldier studied the panorama of chutes and, for the briefest of moments, thought they were snowflakes: "That cannot be. It never snows in September," he thought. The realization soon set in, for this man and so many others, that paratroopers were falling from the sky, not snowflakes. As one German soldier watched the troopers descend, he turned to his sergeant and quipped in a voice dripping with dark humor, "They're dropping from the heavens, and it won't be long before we're up there and join them!"

Private First Class Ernest Blanchard of F Company, 505th Parachute Infantry, was on the other side of that fire, trying to make himself as small a target as possible. "I could hear sounds of flak and small-arms fire coming up at me; some came awful close." He looked down and saw a German antiaircraft position not far below, shooting upward. "It looked to me as if . . . this gun was firing right at me." Another man in the same company, Sergeant Spencer Wurst, saw the same gun "positioned only four or five hundred yards from where many of us were landing." Just before Blanchard hit the ground, he saw the German gunners attempt to run away. "Other troopers on the ground took care of them," Blanchard said cryptically. The troopers all had orders to make a special effort to destroy antiaircraft crews, and they did exactly that.[6]

Not far away, Lieutenant James Coyle, a platoon leader in E Company of the 505th, was floating to earth over a large tent. He saw several enemy soldiers come out of the tent and begin to man what looked like twenty-millimeter guns affixed to large posts. He had always worried that he might drop right on top of alerted enemy soldiers. He knew that he was so laden with gear that he would be at their mercy. Now that nightmare seemed to be coming true. For the Market Garden drop, some of the soldiers packed their rifles in padded containers known as Griswold bags. Others, particularly the veterans, secured their weapons in place, usually just below their reserve chutes, so they would be ready to fight immediately upon landing. Lieutenant Coyle had a holstered pistol strapped where he could get to it. He worked his .45-caliber pistol free, but his chute was oscillating so much that "one second I'd be pointing the pistol at the ground and the next I'd be aiming at the sky." He gradually floated away from the tent, but one enemy soldier was running in his direction. Coyle holstered his pistol "so I wouldn't drop it or shoot myself when I hit." He landed, grabbed the gun again, worked his way through his shroud lines, and drew a bead on the German. But the enemy soldier had no interest in him. He was running away as fast as he could. To Coyle, he looked all of eighteen years old. The lieutenant let him go. "I hope he made it," he said of the young German.

As Captain LeGrand "Legs" Johnson, commander of F Company, 502nd Parachute Infantry, floated down to Drop Zone C, he glimpsed black-clad figures running around below. He figured that they must be enemy soldiers. Like Coyle, he extracted his .45-caliber pistol and tried to aim it at them, but his chute was oscillating too vigorously. "I hit the ground like a sack of potatoes and tumbled backward, head over heels." The gun popped out of his hand and the parachute covered his head. He flailed around, desperately trying to free himself from the chute and find his pistol. In Normandy, Captain Johnson had seen helpless paratroopers disemboweled. He was sure that the Germans were about to do the same to him when he felt a pair of arms grab him by the shoulders. A Dutch resistance fighter freed him from his chute and helped him find his company. "God, what wonderful people," Johnson later commented.

Wherever enemy fire materialized, it was far deadlier to the planes than to the men jumping out of them. Paratroopers made small moving targets. It was extremely difficult for German gunners, most of whom fired weapons designed to hit ground targets, to find the range and trajectory necessary to score hits on men falling through the air. Indeed, it is doubtful that ground fire killed any descending troopers in the American drop zones. In fact, there was probably more to fear from crashing planes, as well as the legions of falling equipment bundles and troopers. One man, for instance, lost his life when a bundle hit him in the head. Another fell three hundred feet and broke his back after his chute became tangled with a container and failed to open properly. He was lucky to survive.

In the vast majority of cases, troopers dropped and landed unmolested at or near their intended drop zones. Lieutenant Hanz "Harry" Druener hit the ground right next to a curious cow, "which kept sniffing me while I was trying to get out of my harness." Anxious to get out of his chute and rally his platoon, he was initially annoyed by his bovine companion. Once free and on his way, though, he was amused "that a cow should greet me on my first day in combat." As Private John McElfrish neared the ground, he realized that he was going to land on either a barbed-wire fence or a cow, so he chose the latter. "When I dropped on the cow, with the [parachute] canopy above its head, it bawled." McElfrish was concerned that the bawling would alert the enemy, but there were no Germans around. Sergeant Wurst landed in a plowed field and sank up to his ankles. "It was the best landing I ever made." Sergeant Guy Sessions, a squad leader in C Company, 501st Parachute Infantry, landed between a farmhouse and an apple tree. "I picked an apple from a heavily laden tree and began eating it as I might've done under more normal conditions." He continued munching on the apple as he assembled his squad. Private David Webster landed on a nice, flat field, alongside hundreds of other soldiers. "My risers had untwisted by the time I was ready to land. I reached up, grasped all four, pulled down hard, and landed standing up." There was almost a carnival atmosphere as he and the others began to assemble. First Sergeant Daniel Zapalski of I Company, 502nd Parachute Infantry, enjoyed one of his easiest landings ever, and he was rather pleased, since his Normandy leg wound had not quite healed. Back in England he had, of course, argued vociferously with his battalion commander, Lieutenant Colonel Robert Cole, to make sure he did not miss out on this operation. One of the characteristics that endeared Cole to his men was that his hard-charging demeanor was offset by a wry sense of humor. A few minutes after landing, Cole saw Zapalski, grinned, and asked, "How the hell ya doing, Gimpy?" Zapalski grinned back and assured his colonel that he was just fine.

Other landings were not quite as smooth. General Gavin had no sooner jumped from his plane and felt his chute deploy than it seemed the ground was rushing up at him. He came down heavily in a turnip field. "I really bumped my ass like it never had been hit before," he said. Pain jolted down his back. He and the many other soldiers around him began taking small-arms fire from a stand of woods in the distance. Adrenaline pumping, Gavin removed his pistol from its holster and placed it within reach on the ground. "I quickly began to take my rifle out from under the reserve chute, and I got out of the parachute harness while I lay on the ground." With this accomplished, he placed his pistol back in the holster, stood up, grabbed his rifle, and, in typical fashion, took off for the woods, in the direction of the fire. He had no idea that he had just broken two vertebrae.

Like General Gavin, Lieutenant Megellas jumped from a low altitude (probably less than four hundred feet). This, in combination with the over-size load of weaponry he was carrying, led to a heavy landing. "[It] jarred every bone in my body and broke the chin strap on my helmet, with the tip hitting hard on my nose but not breaking it." Corporal James Blue narrowly missed hitting a small house on Drop Zone T, but a replacement in his stick was not so fortunate. "As his boots struck the slate shingles, several of them tore loose; his chute collapsed and he came sliding off. He hit the ground very hard." Fortunately, he was okay. He got up, smiled at Blue, and said, in a thick Hispanic accent, "Damned if a man couldn't get hurt if he did this many times." Captain Louis Hauptfleisch, the 3rd Battalion, 504th Parachute Infantry Regiment's personnel officer (S1), landed right on the roof of a house in the village of Overasselt. "I crashed through the tiled rooftop and suffered leg injuries as a result." In spite of his wounds, he was able to hobble around and do his job.[7]

Within the first hour, the paratroopers had landed, secured their drop zones, and cleared them for the arrival of the gliders. Ferried by the 437th Troop Carrier Group, the 101st Airborne Division glider component consisted of two serials, totaling seventy Waco gliders, carrying jeeps and trailers, along with 311 signalmen, reconnaissance troopers, medics, and headquarters types, to LZ W north of Son. This cargo revealed something about General Taylor's expectations for a quick linkup with General Horrocks's XXX Corps. Taylor figured that his initial artillery and antitank support would come from the British, so he opted for the mobility of jeeps, reconnaissance troopers, and the communications of his signal people. By contrast, General Gavin opted for more guns, since his division was dropping farther behind enemy lines, and might take longer to link up with the British (not to mention the planners' concern for the possibility that the Germans had armor in the Reichswald forest). The 82nd's glider serial, consisting of fifty Wacos from the 439th Troop Carrier group, carried eight fifty-seven-millimeter guns from the 80th Airborne Antitank Battalion, plus jeeps, ammunition trailers, and a similar complement of signalmen, reconnaissance troopers, and headquarters personnel, to a spot near the 505th drop zones. Also, Gavin had elected to parachute the entire 376th Parachute Field Artillery Battalion at Drop Zone N south of Groesbeek (the first such artillery drop in history). "I was an infantryman, and I used parachute field artillery, and Taylor was an artilleryman and he didn't take his artillery in," Gavin later commented ironically. The 376th got down with ten of its twelve seventy-five-millimeter pack howitzers in condition to fire (one more would be operational by nightfall). The unit's only fatality was a lieutenant who was killed when, upon landing heavily, a grenade in his right pocket exploded, "tearing away the right side of his body chest down," in the recollection of one fellow officer.

Now the gliders of both divisions were approaching their respective landing zones. Over LZ W, at the controls of one Waco, Flight Officer William Fasking was scanning the ground, looking for a good landing spot, when the Germans opened up on him with flak and small-arms fire.

"My tow plane was hit and gasoline kept spraying back over my wind-shield, making it difficult to see," he recalled. At any moment, a tracer round could set the fuel on fire. Fasking knew it was time to cut loose. He reached overhead, grabbed the release handle, and let the tow rope go. Wind hummed over the wings as the glider gracefully banked for a land-ing. "The approach . . . was perfect and I had no trouble in picking my spot." He and his troopers landed, briefly took cover from small-arms fire, and then unloaded the glider. Flight Officer Arthur Johnson released, circled, found a spot, and then "landed in soft dirt which broke [the] glider's skids but no one was hurt." Not long after the pilot of Captain Thomas Wilder's glider released the tow rope, the aircraft came under intense fire. The captain's first reaction was to duck, "but I soon realized with something less than an eighth of an inch of canvas between me and the ground didn't make for very good protection." He stole a glance down and spotted several German soldiers "shooting . . . with rifles, machine guns, pistols, anything and everything." Other gliders were hit but not his own. His group landed safely. Close by, Lieutenant Kenneth Weber man-aged to land his glider on an ideal spot in the open field that was LZ W, but the job exhausted him. "The trip in its entirety was very tiring and would have been better if I had a copilot."

Nearly all of the glider pilots had to deal with the same issue. They were supposed to choose one person among those they were carrying and give him a quick overview on how to fly the glider, a dubious plan at best. Flight Officer Jack Whipple had many people to choose from on his glider. He was carrying two surgeons, a medical aide, a jeep driver, and a medical administrative officer. For some reason he chose the administration officer. The others rode in the jeep while the administrative officer sat in the co-pilot's seat. "I showed him the instrument panel . . . the airspeed indicator, and how to release the tow rope and then fly straight ahead at 75 MPH if I was hit and unable to fly the glider," he later wrote. Fortunately, that did not happen and he was able to release normally over the zone. "The LZ was very large and very flat with only a few low barbed wire fences. At about 25 feet . . . I started to flair the glider for landing and a frightened cow started to run toward the glider, then turned off just before we touched-down. The landing was very soft and we rolled to a stop just before a wooded area along the south side of the landing zone." The ground troops easily drove the jeep off the glider.

In one of the few gliders that had both a pilot and copilot, a burst of flak ripped through the floor of the cockpit, tore the copilot's left calf in two, severing his artery, and then hit the pilot in the right thigh. Both men slumped over and blacked out, and the glider immediately began to nose over, out of control. Corporal Jim Evans was perched on an ammunition cart right behind the cockpit and caught some of the shrapnel himself, but he hardly flinched. Captain John Harrell, sitting behind the cart, saw Evans lean over, grab the controls, and steady the aircraft. "He slapped the face of the pilot until he came around and was able to fly it." With the pilot now steering the glider, Evans turned his attention to the unconscious copilot. He pulled the man's muscles and tendons back in place, applied a tourniquet, and bandaged the leg. "[He] saved his life by using the tourniquet," Harrell asserted. If not for Evans, the copilot would have bled to death right there in the cockpit. The glider might well have crashed. Instead, the pilot landed the glider, knocking over a few fences but otherwise bringing them in safely.

With so many gliders flying around in such constricted airspace, collisions were a real concern. The closer a plane got to the ground, the more difficult it was for pilots to see other aircraft. Above a field where troopers from the 506th Parachute Infantry were assembling, the law of averages caught up with two of the gliders. Private Burgett happened to look up and see them collide about fifty to one hundred feet above the ground. "The impact sent both gliders into violent spins to their right," Burgett recalled. Inside one, Flight Officer Thornton Schofield was shocked by the sudden impact with another glider. There was little he could do to control his craft. "My glider shuddered violently . . . hovered momentarily, then nosed over and plunged toward the earth at an angle of seventy degrees."

When the glider hit the ground, Schofield felt "a terrific shock—enveloping my entire body—when the jeep we were carrying slammed down on my back." The jeep propelled him forward, through the windshield, and out of the craft. The other glider slammed straight into the ground and killed the pilot. Five men were injured but somehow everyone else on the two gliders was alive. "Considering the force of the impact," Schofield commented, "I am not hesitant in calling it a miracle." The paratroopers worked the survivors free of the wreckage and dispensed medical care to those who needed it.

To the north, at nearly the same time, the 82nd Airborne gliders were also coasting to the earth. In one glider, Sergeant John McNally, a member of an artillery forward observation team, was sitting in the copilot's seat, peering at a map, comparing it with a field that looked like their landing zone. The glider pilot glanced over at him and said, "Here goes nothing!" and released the tow rope. It skittered into the wind and they began gliding downward. "The pilot picked a large field near a farmhouse," McNally later wrote. "Just as we were ready to land, an innocent-looking haystack seemed to disintegrate, revealing a Heinie gun." Four bright red tracer rounds zipped past them, and machine gun bullets ripped through one of the wings. "The glider, like a wounded bird, twisted and turned in the air." Everyone aboard began yelling excitedly, but the pilot kept his cool and struggled fiercely to control the glider. He did a remarkable job, somehow managing to maneuver the reluctant aircraft over a different field. "With a stomach-dropping thud, we were on the ground, plowing up the dirt like a ship in a heavy sea." Meanwhile, the pilot of Lieutenant James "Buck" Dawson's glider shouted, "Get ready; we're cuttin' loose!" and reached over his head to release the tow rope. "We banked for an into-the-wind landing," Dawson wrote, "speed 140 . . . 120 . . . 90 . . . 60 miles an hour. [The pilot] nosed her into the soft dirt for an unexpectedly quick but perfect stop." They grabbed their weapons, exited the glider, and, expecting to take fire, flopped into a ditch. But there was no opposition.

For the 82nd, two of the gliders never made it to the landing zone; thirty-six landed in fields around Knapheide, in the 505th drop zone; the other twelve came down farther to the north, near the Wylerbaan, where the 508th had landed. In addition to the vital fifty-seven-millimeter guns, they brought in twenty-seven jeeps and 216 soldiers. Of the seventy gliders that comprised the two 101st Airborne serials, fifty-three made it to the landing zone; three aborted over England; one ditched in the Channel; two went down in Belgium; the rest were shot down or released in various spots before the landing zone. The fifty-three gliders that made the landing zone unloaded thirty-two jeeps, thirteen trailers, and 252 troopers. The better part of two American airborne divisions were now on the ground.[8]

General Gavin was moving north through the woods, along a sunken dirt road, heading for the little crossroads north of Groesbeek where he planned to establish his command post. Moments earlier, he and the men who landed around him had taken small-arms fire from this pine forest. Captain William Johnson, one of his engineers, had already killed a pair of German soldiers among the trees and had warned Gavin that more were probably lurking in here. Nonetheless, Gavin was eager to get to his command post, and this was the most direct route. Now the general was walking, rifle at the ready, along the right side of the road. Five yards ahead of him and slightly to the left, Captain Bestebreurtje, the Dutch OSS operative, was on point. Behind Bestebreurtje and Gavin were several of Captain Johnson's engineers. The road was flanked on both sides by seven-foot-high embankments that prevented any of them from seeing beyond the narrow corridor of the dirt road and the trees that surrounded it.

Sure enough, a German machine gun opened up from just to the right of General Gavin. Bullets whizzed past Gavin and Bestebreurtje as both hit the ground. Somehow, the gun had missed them from only a few yards away. Both of them knew that, in a matter of moments, the Germans would spot them and rake the dirt road with deadly fire. The general began crawling up the embankment, attempting to spot and shoot at the gun crew. At the same time, several yards up the road, Captain Bestebreurtje was crawling up another part of the embankment, thinking to himself, "Now I've got to apply what I've learned." For him, years of training had finally led to this moment, when he had to fight the Germans face-to-face, to liberate his own country. He was an expert marksman who could shatter the stem of a champagne glass at two hundred yards. As Bestebreurtje crawled up the embankment, he spotted movement and looked up. "I saw the German machine gunner stick his head up, looking." The man's white face contrasted drastically with the earthy darkness of the woods. With no hesitation, Bestebreurtje swung his carbine into place and snapped off a shot. "My shot hit him right in the center of the forehead." The bullet blew the top of his head off, killing him instantly. His lifeless body tumbled over the machine gun.

At this point, General Gavin reached the top of the embankment and saw one of the other gunners running away. He raised his rifle and tried to line up a good shot, but then decided to let the man go. "I probably would have ricocheted shots off the trees and wounded some of my own people if they were in the vicinity." He glanced to his left and saw the dead gunner. The machine gun was still there, resting in a small pit that the crew had hastily dug into the embankment. Bestebreurtje had meantime captured another survivor who was trembling with fear. The Dutchman whooped with joy. He was experiencing the adrenaline rush that comes with killing an armed enemy and living to tell the tale. General Gavin was impressed with Bestebreurtje's handiwork. He glanced at the tall Dutchman and said, "Whatever your role with this division, you're a mighty handy man to have around." Bestebreurtje smiled. He had just saved the division commander's life.

In this instance, fortune was smiling rather kindly on the Allies, and not just because Gavin was a uniquely charismatic, inspirational general who would have been sorely missed. Gavin had made a major mistake in failing to designate an assistant division commander, someone who would be a clear successor in the event of his death (something that, given Gavin's proclivities for risk taking, was a reasonable possibility). Had Gavin been killed on that wooded lane outside of Groesbeek, the 82nd Airborne Division would have been paralyzed with command chaos. His regimental commanders, and possibly even a couple members of his staff, would have claimed seniority for succession. In the short term, only General Browning, as commander of this operation, could have settled the issue. Yet Browning was, at the moment, quite busy organizing his own I Airborne Corps headquarters, much of which had just been set down by glider on Landing Zone N outside of Groesbeek. It probably would have taken him many hours, perhaps even a day or two, to decide on a replacement for Gavin. In fact, during Market Garden, Major General Roy Urquhart, the 1st Airborne Division commander, was cut off from his command, and presumed by many of his men dead or captured, for the better part of two days. Like Gavin, he had no assistant division commander, although he had at least orally dictated an order of succession to his chief of staff before takeoff. Even so, his absence prompted a messy, counterproductive quarrel for succession between two of his brigadiers. There is every reason to believe that the same sort of situation would have developed in the 82nd Airborne Division.

In any event, Gavin was lucky. After dispatching the German machine gun, he and the others proceeded unhindered to Groesbeek, although Bestebreurtje did shoot and wound another German who was attempting to flee on a bike. The Dutchman captured a briefcase from the wounded soldier that revealed the names and addresses of many Germans in the Groesbeek area. Gavin made it to his headquarters about half a mile west of the town. The command post was delineated by a sign, nailed to a tree, that read, "Champion C.P." The division's code name was Champion. "I at once went to work with the staff," Gavin wrote, "getting in touch with the parachute regiments and the other troops."

Bestebreurtje, meanwhile, met up with local Dutch resistance members in Groesbeek and found out that the forest contained an ammunition dump. Until only this morning, about two hundred German soldiers had been guarding the ammo. Apparently the bombing raids had scared many of them off. By the time the Americans had landed, only a few dozen scattered holdouts were left, and many of those elected to surrender. Bestebreurtje passed this information along to the general and began to establish communication, by phone, with other Dutch resistance fighters in Nijmegen and even Arnhem. Some of the Americans were so impressed with the ease of telephone communication that they jokingly asked Captain Bestebreurtje if he could place a call to Berlin and get Hitler on the line.[9]

In fact, while the captain made his phone calls and organized a nice intelligence network, Dutch citizens, whether resistance members or not, were joyously welcoming the Allied troopers in every landing area. "They were overwhelmed with happiness," the 505th Parachute Infantry Regiment's after-action report said. "[A]t once they came out of their well kept houses with beer, milk, fruit, etc. in their hands to share with us what they had." In the recollection of another American at Groesbeek, the Dutch "lined the streets and it was like a parade—flowers in helmets and some beer passed out." Troopers responded by distributing candy, gum, cigarettes, and K rations. Maria Josef van Onstein, the town burgomaster, proudly donned his official chain of office and greeted the Americans, many of whom were busy looking for Germans and local Nazi sympathizers. Although his English was limited, he struck up a conversation with an American officer. "I really admire the way you work," he told the officer. "It all seems to go so perfect; what a wonderful organization!" The American replied with a straight face, "We didn't do too bad, but it wasn't entirely perfect. We had planned to land at fourteen hundred hours but didn't jump until fourteen-oh-two . . . two minutes after the schedule." The town was full of Americans, in jeeps and on foot. Dr. A. J.

Henneman, a fifty-one-year-old physician, hastened to shake hands with as many soldiers as he could. "They seemed to carry literally everything on their person," he recalled, "and their numerous pockets were bulging. They were calm and friendly though very much on the alert."

A couple miles away, at Berg en Dal, Wilhelmus Fischer emerged from his house when saw the Americans enter his town and welcomed troopers from the 508th Parachute Infantry Regiment. The paratroopers gave him cigarettes and chatted until suddenly they spotted danger. "With lightning speed they threw themselves to the ground and started firing at an armed man, killing him instantly," Fischer said. The man was a hated Dutch Nazi "who had been pretty good at terrorizing the population and stealing food, but who had no chance whatsoever against real pros like these Americans." In another instance, a group of civilians corralled a local Nazi who was, in the memory of one airborne sergeant, "wearing civilian riding boots, breeches, shirt, and a brown jacket. As my men led him away he received several sound kicks in the rear end from the townspeople." In most cases, Dutch resistance members took their Nazi countrymen and other accused collaborators into custody. Eventually, they rounded up women who had dated or slept with German soldiers and shaved their heads in public.

Many Dutch were so excited to see the Americans, and so eager for liberation, that they did whatever they could to help them. Quite a few circulated around the drop zones in wagons or on foot, gathering supply bundles for the Americans. They also found other ways to assist the troopers. Outside of the town, Private First Class Thomas Horne was in the process of digging a foxhole when a Catholic priest materialized and motioned for him to stop. After a few minutes, the priest returned with a teenager who was, according to Horne, "wearing a Boy Scout uniform that he had outgrown years before. The priest told the young boy to dig." The kid finished the foxhole. When Horne started to get into it, the priest again told him to hold off. He left and came back with a small mattress and pillow. He gestured that it was now okay for Horne to occupy the hole. After that, the priest left one final time and later came back with a "big pot of stew which was very good! These people were very nice."

In the middle of town, Private First Class Henry McLean was watching bazooka teams set up positions along the main road when he noticed the nearby Hotel de Groot, an upscale inn. He wandered inside and began to investigate. "In the dining room I discovered that the German officers had been ready to sit down and eat their Sunday dinner when they were surprised by the parachute drop. They had fled across the flats, leaving their dinners untouched. The tables, row upon row of them, were a pretty sight, with white linens, silverware, and goblets." McLean sat down and feasted on two plates of food. Later, after he finished, he left the hotel and entered a café across the street. Inside, several people were sitting around drinking and talking. The barmaid offered him a beer and he happily accepted. When he took a sip, he was shocked that it was cold. For two full years while overseas, warm beer had been the norm, so this was a huge treat. "I will never forget how good that *cold* beer tasted," he later commented wistfully. The moment was too good to last. An officer came in, chewed him out, and ordered him to return to his unit.

Thirty miles to the southwest, in Schijndel, Mattheas van Oorschot was relaxing after high mass, enjoying a glass of beer and playing a game of billiards with a friend, when he heard the loud humming of aircraft. Van Oorschot, his friend, and several family members rushed outside and gaped, in awe, as hundreds of troopers from the 501st Parachute Infantry Regiment descended in the distance. Before long, other people came out of their homes. In groups they stood together silently, staring at the spectacle. Second by second, their excitement built. Van Oorschot's brother brandished a Dutch national flag and proudly displayed it from their home. Other people produced forbidden radios and bicycles. Music began to play. "People started to jump and dance," Van Oorschot later wrote in his diary. "[W]e were free. We ran like madmen up and down the house, shook hands. Some people stood silently sobbing, others kept staring at the sky, with tears in their eyes. There was laughing and crying. People kissed one another . . . others patted each other on the back, and many were very silent."

As the American soldiers landed and began moving around, Van Oorschot and the other Dutch civilians happily mixed with them, trying out English phrases such as, "How are you?" or, "You come make us free?" Girls danced around and hugged the paratroopers tightly, something the Americans obviously enjoyed. The Americans handed out the usual array of goodies. Van Oorschot was excited to get biscuits, chocolate, cigarettes, and a bandage. To him, the troopers seemed very serious and determined. "It struck us that the soldiers were not so very exuberant . . . they still had to fight. But to us they were angels."

A few miles to the southeast, near St. Oedenrode, Staff Sergeant Roy Nickrent and the other soldiers of the 1st Battalion, 502nd Parachute Infantry Regiment, landed a couple miles south of their objective. As they gathered their weapons and equipment and assembled to move out, happy Dutch civilians "of all ages, sizes and sexes" converged on the Americans, "giving us fresh fruit, food, cheese, milk, & cider. They were generous beyond imagination. Their liberation seemed the greatest event of their lives, whether they were young or old." Nickrent was deeply moved by this wonderful welcome, as were many other paratroopers. Lieutenant Colonel Hank Hannah, the 101st Airborne Division's operations officer, and the men around him were nearly overwhelmed with "ovations, cheers, offers of food, smiles, and an acceptance so wholehearted and unrestrained—so unlike our reception in Normandy—that it nearly brought tears to my eyes."

In some cases, the first contact was more restrained but no less warm. Wilhemina Ouweneel-Coppens, a twenty-four-year-old housewife in St. Oedenrode, saw the 502nd troopers land and heard a bit of shooting as they engaged in brief firefights with the few Germans who were near their drop zones. Ouweneel-Coppens and several of her neighbors wisely stayed inside her house while all this was happening. Then they heard a sharp knock at the door. "We opened the door and there was an enormous paratrooper, bayonet on his rifle." Before anyone could speak, the trooper brushed past them and ran upstairs, searching for German soldiers. Seeing that the house was clear, he came back downstairs. He glanced around, reached down to his boot, retrieved a pack of Camel cigarettes, and passed them around to the Dutch. Then he left. "Not a word was spoken," Ouweneel-Coppens recalled. "The entire episode, I think, lasted three minutes."

Not far away, Private James Howell and his buddy Private Clayton Kent were on a contact patrol, looking for another company. Both were deeply worried that they might find the Germans instead. They came to a barn and decided to investigate. Inside, they found German equipment strewn around, a discovery that only heightened their apprehension. They quietly left the barn and advanced toward an adjacent farmhouse. When they were about twenty feet away, the door of the house opened a few inches. Both Howell and Kent were fully alert, expecting the worst. Instead, in Howell's recollection, "A young woman and a very small girl (probably about three years old) came out. The woman had a pitcher of milk and the little girl held out an apple as an offering. The tension left and my heart went out to the Dutch people at that moment."

Five miles to the north, at Erp, a little suburb of Veghel, Gerardus Otten, a member of the local resistance cell, could hardly contain his exhilaration as he watched troopers of the 501st Parachute Infantry Regiment land all around the area. He and several other resistance members sat in a garden and happily observed the spectacle. "For us the liberation actually came falling from the skies," he later commented. After one American plane caught fire and crashed about half a mile away, Otten and many others ran to the site. The burning aircraft had partially settled in the Aa River. The heat of the fire was too intense for them to investigate the C-47, but in a nearby field, they found the body of Lieutenant Herbert Schulman (mentioned on page 94) who had bravely decided to stay with the dying plane so that he could drop his troopers on target. After some deliberation, they decided to bury Schulman's body in the local cemetery. "This was the only act of friendship which we could offer him. How deeply we realized that this supreme sacrifice of life had been brought for our freedom, in order to let us really live."

After burying Schulman's body, Otten and his cohorts hopped on their bikes and rode into Veghel, where the excitement over the landings was at a fever pitch. "An exuberant, festive spirit prevailed in the streets of Veghel. The red, white and blue Dutch flags, which had been enforcedly hidden those four years, were waving once more. Children and youngsters, decorated with orange or with the Dutch national colors, danced to accordeon [sic] music." Orange, the prevalent color of all things Dutch, was everywhere—sashes, placards, curtains, flags, sheets, and garments. When Otten first spotted U.S. soldiers, he was nearly overcome with emotion. "Their friendly grinning faces showed how pleased they were with the friendship showed to them by the Dutch." Groups of people stood around them talking, gesticulating, and laughing. The heavily laden troopers did not understand what the Dutch were saying, but they knew they were overjoyed. "They distributed cigarettes and chocolate generously. We acted like fools from sheer happiness."

About a mile to the south, in the little village of Erde, Adrianus Marinus, an eighteen-year-old local kid, was also ebullient. As the troopers of the 501st Parachute Infantry Regiment landed all over the fields outside Erde, he ran out there and began loading ammunition and other supplies onto carts. He was one of the few in his town who spoke English, so he functioned as an impromptu interpreter. "I was busy the whole afternoon with talking and translating." Several months before, one of his pro-German neighbors had said that he was so confident the Allies would never come to Holland, he would eat any British or Americans who dared to do so. As the Americans roamed the town, another neighbor said to the pro-German person, "Come quickly . . . because you can't keep up with eating them all!" Marinus and the others enjoyed a good laugh at the collaborator's expense. As the laughter died down, the Americans began to organize themselves into loose patrol formations ("tactical columns," in military parlance) and move out. The battle, after all, was only beginning.[10]

CHAPTER 6

Objectives

Time was important. In fact, it was crucial. The entire operation depended on seizing bridges and other objectives with the utmost speed. The more time the Germans had to figure out what was going on, the better chance they would blow up bridges, take high ground, and launch disruptive counterattacks to foil Market Garden. Thus, every paratrooper was infused with a kind of ants-in-the-pants urgency. Companies assembled and moved out in a matter of minutes, not hours, regardless of whether commanders could account for all of their men. Sergeants communicated this urgency in their own inimitable way, through a range of colorful phrases—"Come on, hubba, hubba, one time! Move out!" or, more commonly, "Come on, guys, move up. Don't you know there's a war on?"

In the midafternoon, with the sun high in the sky, 112 troopers from C Company, 504th Parachute Infantry Regiment, were spread out in disciplined columns along a country road, steadily moving to within a thousand yards of a small span over the Maas-Waal Canal near Malden. Code-named Bridge Number 8 by division planners, the bridge traversed one of the main routes into Nijmegen from the west. Number 8 was one of four such bridges over the canal (numbered sequentially from south to north, 7, 8, 9, and 10) that General Gavin hoped to take. Bridges 7 and 8 were closest to the 504th drop zones, so it made the most sense to grab them first.

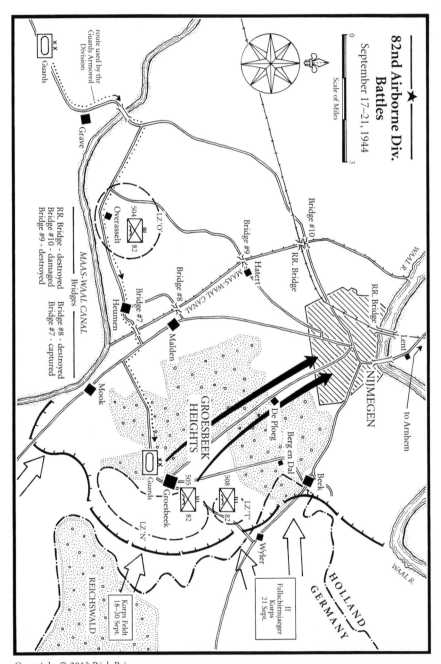

82nd Airborne Div.
Battles
September 17–21, 1944

Scale of Miles

0
3

Guards

route used by the
Guards Armored
Division

Grave

Overasselt

504
82

LZ 'O'

MAAS-WAAL CANAL
Bridges

RR. Bridge - destroyed
Bridge #10 - damaged
Bridge #9 - destroyed

Bridge #8 - destroyed
Bridge #7 - captured

Bridge #9

Bridge #10

RR. Bridge

Hatert

MAAS-WAAL CANAL

Bridge #8

Bridge #7

Heumen

Malden

Mook

GROESBEEK
HEIGHTS

De Ploeg

Guards

Groesbeek

505
82

508
82

LZ 'T'

Guards

LZ 'N'

REICHSWALD

Korps Feldt
18–20 Sept.

Wyler

Korps Feldt
Fallschirmjaeger
Korps
21 Sept.

HOLLAND
GERMANY

WAAL R.

Beek

Berg en Dal

to Arnhem

Lent

RR. Bridge

NIJMEGEN

WAAL R.

Copyright © 2013 Rick Britton

The plan was for C Company to take the bridge while a platoon from A Company set up positions nearby and laid down covering fire with machine guns, mortars, and rifles. But at this very moment, eight soldiers from A Company were actually already in sight of the bridge. Covered by three comrades, Lieutenant Richard Mills, Corporal George Smith, Private George Andoniade, Private Thomas Morgan, and Private George Brown made a rush for the bridge. Enemy small-arms fire erupted from either side of the bridge, sweeping up and down the road where the soldiers of C Company were approaching. Many dived for cover in the ditches, while others tried to work their way forward, in the direction of the bridge. Farther back in the column, Private Thomas Steger saw an eager new man get hit in the chest and lie down by the side of the road. "[The bullet] . . . entered about three inches below the collarbone and came out about two inches above his belt. It must have hit his lung, because every time he would breathe, a blood bubble would rise from his lips." A medic worked to bandage the wound. To Steger, the new man's brown eyes looked sad, as if he expected to die.

At the same time, machine gunners and sixty-millimeter mortar men set up their weapons and began laying down fire wherever they thought the Germans might be concealed. Somehow the five intrepid A Company men made it to the bridge, under fire all the way. Just as they got there, the Germans blew it up. "A tremendous explosion lifted the bridge high in the air and scattered it over a wide area," Sergeant Ross Carter of C Company later wrote. Although his squad was about five hundred yards away, "a few of us got bruised by the flying debris." The five men who rushed the bridge were fortunate that they were not instantly killed, although Lieutenant Mills and Private Andoniade were badly wounded. The three others were somehow unscathed. But Bridge Number 8 was gone.

A mile to the south, just outside of Heumen, well-armed troopers from B Company were moving east along a paved road, closing in on Bridge Number 7. The company had recovered most of its weapons and equipment from the drop zone—nine light machine guns, seven Browning automatic rifles, a pair of sixty-millimeter mortars, six bazookas, and several radios. The men were spread into two columns, with at least three feet between each soldier. About one hundred yards in front of the main body, a pair of scouts, Private First Class Harris Duke and Private First Class Herman Wagner, carefully walked the road, scanning ahead, covering each other every bit of the way. Alongside them, in the fields on either side of the road, flanking soldiers covered the two scouts and made sure that no enemy soldiers ambushed them from the shelter of gently sloping ditches that bordered the pavement. Duke and Wagner could tell the canal was up ahead, but it was hard to actually see the bridge, because it was obscured by apple orchards. Plus, the road at this point rose slightly in elevation, creating blind spots among the various dips and swales.

German small-arms fire rang out. All up and down the line, the paratroopers rolled into the ditches and began scanning the ground ahead for targets. Groups of them began low-crawling and low-running along the ditches, firing in support of one another, gradually edging closer to the waterline. One man, Sergeant Lawrence Blazzini, was killed as he moved along slightly elevated ground and into the kill zone of enemy weapons. The canal was about seventy-five feet wide. A dike, or raised causeway, ran the length of about three hundred feet, including the bridge, over the water and adjoining fields. The bridge itself was actually a lock that could be raised up to accommodate barge traffic. In the canal, just across a small sliver of water from the lock, was an island with a power plant and a house. Much of the German fire was originating from that house. Every trooper understood that the Germans had rigged up the bridge for demolition, so they cut any wires they saw. Quite probably, the Germans inside the house or the power plant had detonators that would allow them to blow the bridge.

Lieutenant Maurice Marcus and a handful of men from his platoon made it to the dike. Two of his men, Privates Charles Piazza and Shelton Dustin, set up a .30-caliber machine gun atop the dike, behind a strand of barbed wire. From there they could cover the house and any approach to the bridge from the other side of the canal. A bazooka team fired several shots at the house, but none of their rockets exploded. They followed up with rifle grenades and smoke grenades, the latter of which malfunctioned. Marcus wanted, of course, to rush the bridge, and he hoped to cover his men with this barrage or conceal them in the smoke. In spite of the malfunctioning rockets and grenades, he decided to go for the bridge. He knew that every minute he hesitated gave the Germans more time to blow it up. As Piazza and Dustin opened fire, Marcus and nine of his men took off. "They ran down the . . . side of the dike and across the two hundred yards separating the dike from the bridge proper," another member of the company later recalled. The dike sloped downward about five feet, affording the men some semblance of cover from the enemy small-arms fire (the army called this sort of slope a "defilade"). "Near the bridge was a flight of eight concrete steps leading up to the main road and bridge. Corporal William Nau was first up the steps and across the bridge." Nau and the others were under fire all the way.

When Nau reached the end of the bridge, Lieutenant Marcus followed and made it. Next came his assistant platoon leader, Lieutenant William Cummings, with Technician Fourth Grade Orie Burnett, their radioman. As they made it to the end of the bridge, Burnett took a round in the neck. Because of the wound, the young radioman was not thinking clearly. He handed his SCR-536 "walkie-talkie" radio to Lieutenant Marcus and attempted to run back across the bridge. It was one thing to get through that kill zone the first time, when the Germans were off balance. It was quite another to try it again, when they were alerted and firing all along the dike. Before Burnett could make it back, he got hit again and fell dead. Lieutenant Marcus, meanwhile, got hit as he attempted to take cover behind a sandpile. Wounded and in pain, he rolled into a dip that afforded him some defilade cover, but he was pinned down. At the same time, a few more soldiers got up and ran across the bridge. One of them, Sergeant Jerry Murphy, was shot and killed just as he reached the far end of the bridge. Seven others found a boat and safely rowed across the canal to join their friends. Together, those who made it to the far end of the bridge unleashed accurate machine gun, rifle, and bazooka fire on the German-held house.

By now, the company commander, Captain Thomas Helgeson, had advanced the bulk of B Company to the edge of the dike and the orchard to lay down even more fire. These men worked the Germans over with machine guns and mortars. The Germans were far too busy fighting for their lives now to even think of blowing up the bridge. The vital objective remained intact. It took the Americans most of the night to capture the little island and subdue German resistance (they eventually took about forty prisoners). Most important, though, Bridge Number 7 was firmly in Allied hands. Six B Company men had paid the ultimate price to secure it.[1]

Lieutenant John "Jocko" Thompson and his stick landed in open fields seven hundred yards southwest of the Grave bridge. In civilian life, the twenty-seven-year-old Massachusetts native had been a professional baseball player, pitching in the minor-league system of his hometown Boston Red Sox. In 1941, the year before the war started and the army beckoned him, he had notched an 8–13 record and a 3.56 earned run average as a hard-throwing left-hander for the Greenville Red Sox. Now, three years later, all of that seemed so far away. As a platoon leader in E Company, 504th Parachute Infantry Regiment, his mission was to take the southern end of the Grave bridge over the Maas River. At fifteen hundred feet long, with nine spans, the bridge was the largest and most modern in all of Europe. It was also, of course, one of Market Garden's most vital objectives. Without control of the bridge, the entire 82nd Airborne Division would be cut off behind enemy lines. XXX Corps would be stymied south of the Maas. In fact, the bridge was so important that Colonel Reuben Tucker, commander of the 504th, had decided to envelop it by dropping two companies from his 2nd Battalion to the north of it and the other company to the south. Back in England, the battalion's three company commanders had drawn straws to see whose company would get the especially dangerous assignment of taking the bridge from the south. Company E was the "winner," much to the chagrin of the commander, Captain Walter Van Poyck, who viewed the mission as, at best, "a sticky one." He immediately began having terrible premonitions that he would not survive.

Lieutenant Thompson had no such forebodings, only a strong urgency to get to the bridge. Upon landing, as he gathered his stick of fifteen men, he realized that they had not landed with the rest of the company. As a matter of fact, the bulk of E (or Easy) Company had jumped too soon and were now landing in and around the tiny village of De Elft, about a mile from the bridge. He tried to contact Captain Van Poyck by radio but could not get through. With no communications link to his commander, Lieutenant Thompson knew he had a decision to make. He could either lie low and wait for the rest of the company to join up with him, or he could go for the bridge with his small force to face potentially superior numbers of enemy defenders. In Thompson's opinion, there was no time to lose. He and his men had to push for the bridge, regardless of the losses they might take. Perhaps the decision was the result of a pitcher's do-it-yourself mentality; perhaps it simply stemmed from the mission-first culture of the airborne, or the fact that every man in the company understood the vital importance of the bridge. Regardless, Thompson made his choice with alacrity, almost by instinct. "I sent a messenger, Corporal Hugh Perry, back to where the company was assembling and told the company commander [Van Poyck] that we were proceeding toward the bridge," Thompson said.

As quietly as possible, the little group slipped into one of several small drainage canals that led to the river and began to wade north in hopes of evading detection. The water ranged from thigh-high to armpit-high. Soon, enemy machine gun and rifle fire began coming from the direction of Grave, to the southeast, and, in Thompson's recollection, "There was now fire coming from a camouflaged flak tower on the southern approach to the bridge." In addition to their rifles, the Americans had one light machine gun, one BAR, and two bazookas. They shot back with their rifles and continued their watery advance. The banks of the canal provided enough cover from the enemy fire that the paratroopers could keep moving unscathed.

A few hundred yards in the distance, they could see a rectangular stone building with a crenellated tile roof, and then, just beyond it, the bridge. The Americans figured that the building was a power plant and might contain the mechanism to blow up the bridge. Small groups of Germans soldiers were running back and forth from the plant to the bridge, gathering unseen items in their arms. Aiming low, Thompson's machine gun team began to "rake the ground between the bridge and the power plant." Near the bridge was a bend in the highway and then a straightaway that led southeast for about three-quarters of a mile to the town of Grave. A pair of motorcycles, followed by two trucks, rounded the bend and headed for the bridge. The bikes sped over the structure, out of range before the Americans could react. Not so for the trucks. Sergeant Roy Tidd took aim at the driver of the lead truck, shot, and killed him. The truck swerved to a stop. German soldiers began hopping out, hastily taking cover and returning fire with rifles. The occupants of the second truck did the same. "They had rifles and one or two LMGs [light machine guns]," the men of Thompson's stick told a postcombat interviewer. "There were between forty and fifty Germans. They were all on the east side of the road, placing the road between them and us." The two sides were about five hundred yards apart.

The Germans, firing from a slightly elevated position at soldiers who were enmeshed in shoulder-high water, outnumbered Thompson's group by a factor of three to one. Yet they were apparently leaderless and had no stomach for a fight. Some were overaged ethnic Germans from the area who had been pressed into army service but who had little inclination to die for their fatherland. "Under their uniforms some of them wore civvies, such as overalls," a Dutch resident of Grave later recalled. It was actually unfortunate that Tidd had opened fire on them, because their greatest desire was to escape. Now their mere presence delayed Easy Company's push for the bridge, albeit not for long. Over the course of ten noisy minutes, Thompson's men raked them over with BAR and machine gun fire. In groups of two and three, the Germans began disengaging and running across the fields in the direction of Grave, or across the bridge, where they would soon run into members of D and F companies, who were approaching the span from the northern side of the Maas River.

As the recalcitrant enemy soldiers bugged out, their fire naturally tapered off, freeing the aggressive American troopers to resume their advance. They emerged from the canal, flanked the power station on either side, and overran it. Inside, according to Thompson, they found "four dead German soldiers and one wounded; all they had been carrying was their personal equipment and blankets." They also found discarded weapons, boots, and even some food on a stove. The Americans had imagined that the frenzied Germans they had seen running around this building were searching for a detonator or carrying demolitions charges to the bridge, but their cargo was obviously more mundane. Even so, troopers found wires, which they cut. The American soldiers were wet and uncomfortable, but they were fully immersed in the necessary combat mentality, almost single-minded in their lust to take the bridge.

The power station was only fifty yards away from the southern end of the bridge, but just to the west (American) side of the road stood a concrete pillbox with a twenty-millimeter flak gun mounted on top. At various times during the advance, the Americans had taken inaccurate fire from this potentially devastating weapon. They could not get to the bridge without taking it out. Fortunately, they were so close to the pillbox that the enemy gunners could not depress their barrels low enough to hit the troopers. The bazookaman, Private Robert McGraw, edged around the power plant and worked his way close enough to the pillbox to line up a good shot. He fired three times. Two of his rockets sailed through a vent and exploded; the other missed. Enemy fire immediately ceased. The Americans bolted for the pillbox, overran it, and found the gun intact, with two dead crewmen and a wounded man lying nearby. Wisely, they took control of the gun. When another flak-mounted pillbox north of the bridge opened fire, Thompson's men answered with their own fire, staving off this threat. At the same time, the rest of the group seized control of the southern end of the bridge and fired a green flare to indicate that they had taken their side of the objective.

With that accomplished, they set up a roadblock consisting of several riflemen, McGraw's bazooka, the machine gun, and the BAR man. "About this time we were surprised to see two automobiles tearing down the highway toward the bridge from Grave," Lieutenant Thompson recalled. "As they neared the bridge, my BAR man . . . fired directly through the windshield of the leading vehicle, killing the driver." The passenger hopped out and tried to run away, but the Americans shot him down. The second vehicle attempted to turn around and head back toward Grave, but never made it. American bullets riddled the car, killing all three German soldiers inside. As the smoke from the massacre cleared, Thompson breathed a sigh of relief. For now, he controlled the southern approach to the bridge, and the rest of Easy Company was on the way (in fact, one squad had already linked up with Thompson at the power station, and many other soldiers from the company were making their way through the same canal that Thompson's men had traversed). As he surveyed the situation, he knew he had made the right call in pushing immediately to take his objective. He had absolutely no idea what was happening across the Maas River, on the northern side of the bridge.[2]

Even as that discomfiting thought flashed through the former pitcher's mind, groups of D and F company troopers were pushing for the northern end of the bridge with the same sort of urgency Thompson's men had displayed. In general, they attacked from the northeast along a raised embankment, or "dike," as they called it, that paralleled the river. As with Easy Company on the southern end, their main obstacles were twenty-millimeter flak guns on and around the bridge. The twenty-millimeter rounds were designed to tear aircraft apart, so the damage they could do to the vulnerable infantrymen was profound—shatter bones, blow heads off, or cause massive internal bleeding. For example, in one disquieting incident, Private Clarence Corbin, a medic, took a round right in the face, tearing off his nose and destroying his right eye. Clearly such fearsome weapons had to be respected, but they had one major vulnerability: Because they were antiaircraft weapons, they were far deadlier at long range than short range. In fact, as Lieutenant Thompson had found out, the twenty-millimeter crewmen could scarcely depress their barrels low enough to hit anyone or anything on the ground inside of about two hundred yards. The key, then, was to get inside that cone of fire and destroy them at close range.

Ditches and buildings along the northern approaches to the Grave bridge provided the necessary cover for the American paratroopers. By and large, they fought as cohesive teams, employing fire and maneuver tactics that overwhelmed the stationary Germans. In one instance, three volunteers from F Company armed themselves with Thompson submachine guns and crawled through a series of ditches to within grenade-throwing distance of one enemy gun. They pitched Gammon grenades and regular fragmentation grenades at the gun crew, forcing them to take cover in adjacent foxholes. The enemy soldiers responded with grenades of their own and ineffective rifle fire. When the three Americans exhausted their grenade supply, another group of five men crawled through the same ditches to provide them with more. A bazooka-wielding lieutenant fired two rockets into the gun position. All three men kept pitching grenades. The combination wrecked the gun. One of the three volunteers, Private

First Class Willard Tess, was wounded in thirty-two places by a German grenade, but refused to leave until the gun was destroyed. "They took no prisoners," an F Company after-action interview ominously declared.

Elsewhere, Lieutenant Richard Harris and seventeen men worked their way along the dike until they came to a thousand-yard stretch of flat ground. At the end of the long stretch was a nice house that could provide some good cover. At Harris's command, they began to run across the field, maintaining a fifteen-yard interval between each man. They would run about twenty-five yards and then hit the ground. "When most of the men had reached the middle of the open space, a twenty-millimeter in a shed . . . and three light machine guns opened up, pinning them flat and making it impossible to answer the fire," a group of soldiers recalled in a postcombat interview. The men flattened themselves as best they could and very gingerly crawled to the dubious shelter of a fence. "While the men were crawling, a horse and two cows walked along the fence, heads over the fence, following the men as they crawled, watching them." The Germans needed only to follow the path of the animals to know where the Americans were crawling. They intensified their fire accordingly. One bullet nicked Lieutenant Harris's chin but caused only a minor wound. Somehow no one else was hit, though the experience was terrifying. The men hugged the earth, the whiff of mud, manure, and grass in their nostrils. Each heard the supersonic snap of bullets whizzing overhead. Six of the soldiers found a ditch and, unwilling to continue the advance, took shelter there. Six others, including Lieutenant Harris, made it to the house and laid down a blistering wave of fire on the Germans. The enemy fire soon ceased.

Other groups were even closer to the bridge. One overran a twenty-millimeter pillbox at the north end of the span, while another, under Lieutenant Stuart "Flash" McCash, approached along the main road. "Some poor German soldier came riding down the dike . . . in a bike," Private Tom Moseley recalled. "Someone shot him right in the face and we just kept right on going." McCash's group began to take fire from another twenty-millimeter gun located farther along the riverbank, in the flats. A combination of bazookas and rifle grenades plus an assault from a cluster of D Company soldiers silenced the gun. It is also possible that Lieutenant Harris and his men contributed to the destruction of this twenty-millimeter gun. In the fog of combat, separate groups can often shoot at the same target or attempt to take the same objective while having no knowledge of their neighbors' actions.

In any case, McCash yelled that the time was ripe to cross the bridge. He took a few men, including Moseley, and cautiously started across. "I kept watching for each girder as we were going across because I figured they were gonna shoot us right off the bridge," Moseley said. Instead nothing happened. They made contact with Lieutenant Thompson at the south end and then went back. The fact that there were no friendly-fire incidents is either remarkable or incredibly lucky, since, in fighting toward the bridge, both American forces had been firing in the general direction of the other for quite some time.

The linkup of McCash's patrol with Thompson hardly meant that the Americans controlled the bridge. At any moment, the Germans might still blow it (in hopes of preventing this, D and F company soldiers used their shovels to cut any wires they saw). There were still groups of isolated enemy soldiers along the northern banks of the Maas and in some of the houses near the river. Moreover, the Germans still controlled Grave, and they began laying down fire on the bridge from that direction, making any movement in its vicinity rather perilous. Private Philip Nadler, a man whose personality was marked by a dry sense of humor, was bemused to see one of his buddies, Private Henry Cavello, jump up and urge everyone to cross the bridge. "We had all fought hard and wanted to move in," Nadler said. But as long as the enemy bullets kept pinging around the bridge girders and the ditches where the Americans were taking shelter, most of the men were content to sit and wait for an order to secure the span. "I wasn't getting up to cross the bridge," Nadler commented. "Besides, I figured some idiot with a plunger might be lurking around somewhere, just waiting for his chance."

Cavello stood at the entrance to the bridge, waving his rifle, urging the men to get moving. Everyone shouted at him to get down. Cavello's antics struck Nadler as funny because he was a physically small man who had proven to be anything but a gung ho combat soldier. Yet now, for some reason, Cavello seemed transformed. Smoke wafted from the barrel of his rifle as he paced back and forth, attempting to persuade his friends to get up. "Come on!" he shouted. "Let's go! Let's get across the bridge!" Finally, Nadler's lieutenant ordered him to go and get Cavello back under cover. Nadler had sprained his ankle due to a rough landing, but now as he stood up, the young private recalled a story he had once read about a Roman named Horatio, who had supposedly fought single-handedly for hours to defend a footbridge against hundreds of barbarians. Nadler hobbled to Cavello, took him by the arm, and led him back. "Come on, Horatio," he said. "We'll name the bridge after you." The nickname stuck. From then on, everyone in F Company referred to Cavello as Horatio.

Misguided or not, Cavello was in sync with Major Edward Wellems, the commander of the 2nd Battalion. When Wellems heard about the success of McCash's patrol, he ordered his whole battalion to cross. Not only did he want the bridge, but he also wanted his battalion in position to take the town of Grave. During the fight along the bridge approaches, Private Leo Hart had followed his platoon leader's lead at every turn. Hart thought of Lieutenant Martin Middleton as "a wonderful person and true leader . . . not in the least flamboyant . . . just quietly determined." Middleton hollered at his soldiers to get moving, and Hart followed him onto the first of the nine spans. The bridge reminded Private Hart of the Port Ewen Bridge across the Hudson River in his hometown of Kingston, New York. He and the rest of Middleton's platoon entered the walkway on the western side of the bridge, a bit farther away from the enemy fire originating from Grave. "We started to cross in ones and twos," Hart recalled. "I went over in one run, crouching as low as I could and zigzagging back and forth." Bullets clanked off the girders and whipped overhead or alongside with a distinctive buzzing-bee sound.

Nearby, Private First Class Joe Watts thought he saw a pair of German snipers who had tied themselves high atop the girders (one wonders where these enemy riflemen were when McCash's group was crossing a few minutes before). Watts pointed his tommy gun upward and sprayed the girders. Using the lower girders as shelter, he ran across in rushes. "As we jogged and dodged across the last of the nine spans, we were running out of places to hide," he said. He reached the south end and made contact with one of Lieutenant Thompson's men, who helped steer him away from mines by the side of the road. Dozens and then hundreds of other soldiers crossed the same way, braving intermittent fire with nearly every step. Some never thought about the possibility that the Germans might blow the bridge beneath them. Some thought of little else. The Germans were in a position to do nothing of the kind, partially owing to the fact that they had no orders to blow the bridge, but mainly because of the rapid nature of the American assault from both sides of the Maas. "Five hundred men crossed in twenty minutes and had only one man wounded," Major Wellems later said. Company F had lost four men wounded during the fight to the bridge and had taken fifteen prisoners. The Americans later found several specially fitted boxes of explosives inside the girders that had been painted over to resemble the rest of the respective spans. Engineers removed the explosives.

To solidify control of the Grave bridge, Wellems placed roadblocks on both ends. The blocks generally consisted of Hawkins antitank mines emplaced on the road, covered by dug-in riflemen and bazooka and machine gun teams on either side. Periodically, wayward Germans bumped into the block. In one instance, a tank emerging from Grave encountered an Easy Company roadblock a few hundred yards to the south of the bridge. The armored vehicle was covered with netting and tree branches, the commander standing obtrusively in the turret. Just as the troopers were about to open fire, some optimistic soul yelled, "Don't shoot! It's a Limey!" Hearing this, a relieved Captain Van Poyck stood up and began casually walking toward the tank. As he approached, he began to study the vehicle more closely and his eyes widened. "Simultaneously, as he realized I wasn't German, I realized he wasn't British," Van Poyck recalled. "He fired one cannon round at me, which passed close to me and shattered a tree at my right rear." Van Poyck dropped and rolled into a ditch. The tank sprayed the road with .50-caliber machine gun rounds and snapped off four more cannon shots. Then it turned around and started to leave. Several soldiers who had ventured into the open were hit and went down. With surprised shouts, the Americans fired two bazooka shots at the retreating tank (which conflicting eyewitness accounts described as a Mark III or a Mark IV). One rocket missed. The other clanked off the rear of the tank and failed to explode. The armored vehicle disappeared around a bend in the road and escaped. The brief attack wounded thirteen Americans and killed Lieutenant Hanford Files, the company's executive officer. Later, a staff car blundered into the roadblock and tripped off a mine, blowing the car into the air, killing all four passengers. From the German point of view, access to the bridge and across it was basically at a standstill, and this pointed to one indisputable fact: The Grave bridge—one of Market Garden's most important prizes—now belonged to the Americans.[3]

Twenty-five miles to the south, at Son, all was quiet, at least for the moment. Within an hour and a half of landing, the soldiers of Colonel Bob Sink's 506th Parachute Infantry Regiment (the "Currahees") were on the move, headed for the Son bridge, a small, two-lane span over the Wilhelmina Canal. Sink's task was to capture this bridge and two smaller ones on either flank and then continue a few more miles into Eindhoven, where he expected to join forces with the leading tanks of XXX Corps. His 2nd Battalion was marching down the main road into Son. Behind them, the 3rd Battalion was in reserve. A few hundred yards to the west, the 1st Battalion was on the flank, plunging into a stand of woods known as the Zonsche Forest.

Colonel Sink sat in a jeep on the main road outside of Son, watching

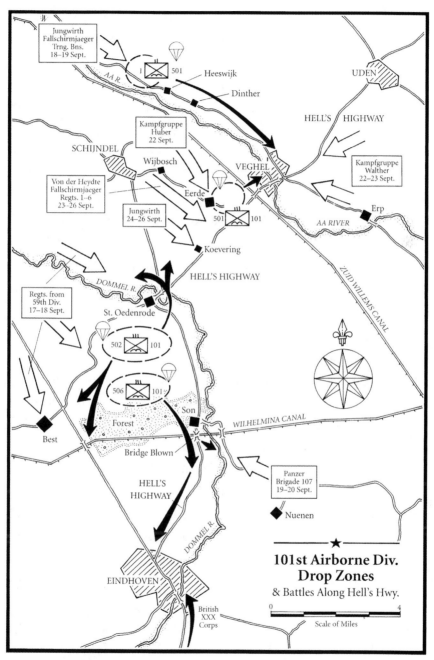

Jungwirth
Fallschirmjaeger
Trng. Bns.
18–19 Sept.

AA R.

1 | 501

Heeswijk

Dinther

UDEN

HELL'S HIGHWAY

Kampfgruppe
Huber
22 Sept.

SCHIJNDEL

Wijbosch

VEGHEL

Von der Heydte
Fallschirmjaeger
Regts. 1–6
23–26 Sept.

Eerde

Kampfgruppe
Walther
22–23 Sept.

Erp

Jungwirth
24–26 Sept.

501 | 101

AA RIVER

Koevering

HELL'S HIGHWAY

DOMMEL R.

ZUID WILLEMS CANAL

Regts. from
59th Div.
17–18 Sept.

St. Oedenrode

502 | 101

506 | 101

Son

Forest

WILHELMINA CANAL

Best

Bridge Blown

Panzer
Brigade 107
19–20 Sept.

HELL'S
HIGHWAY

Nuenen

DOMMEL R.

★

**101st Airborne Div.
Drop Zones**
& Battles Along Hell's Hwy.

EINDHOVEN

British
XXX
Corps

0 _____ 4

Scale of Miles

his soldiers file past. Someone told him that enemy tanks (identified as both Mark IIIs and Mark IVs) had been spotted half a mile to the east in the village of Wolfswinkel. He ordered a patrol to check this out, but before they could get there, a flight of P-51 Mustangs materialized overhead, spotted the tanks, and strafed them. The fighters destroyed three of the armored vehicles and forced the other to flee north. Black smoke billowed from the carcasses of the dead tanks. With the job done, the planes pulled up and began to fly away. "I watched them go with a sinking feeling in my heart," a wistful Private David Kenyon Webster said, "for we needed their firepower."

As the planes warded off the enemy armor, a Dutch civilian approached Lieutenant Norman Dike, the assistant S2 of the 506th, and told him that, a day or two earlier, the Germans had blown up the two smaller flanking bridges. Dike passed the message on to Sink. The colonel now knew that, if this report was correct, his mission depended on taking the main bridge at Son. He summoned a runner and told him to pass a message on to his battalion commanders: "Think flank bridges are out; concentrate on center bridge but reconnoiter others." As the man circulated among the battalion commanders, he amended the message to "get center bridge; pay no attention to others." This friendly bit of editing hardly mattered, because the Dutchman's report was correct. The two smaller bridges were gone. Only the center bridge in Son remained.

Up ahead, at the vanguard of the 2nd Battalion advance, a fire team from D Company was moving into the northern edges of Son. The rest of D Company and then E Company soon followed. The village was little more than a cluster of houses and cobblestone sidewalks bisected by the main road. People drifted out of their homes to welcome the soldiers. The local priest, Father Van Hussen, greeted the Americans with a smile and handed out cigars he had saved for just this sort of special occasion. The troopers thanked him and clasped hands with other people lining the road, but otherwise maintained a steady pace. They all understood the urgency of grabbing the bridge before the Germans could destroy it. Ever so steadily, they kept moving up the street.

All at once, a German soldier on a bicycle rode in among the point element, nearly colliding with them. He was so shocked that he fell from the bike and threw his arms in the air, wailing *"Kamerad!"*—the anthem of any German soldier who wished to surrender. The Americans bent over, picked him up, and began to question him. In the next instant, they heard the distinctive—and quite unwelcome—crack of an eighty-eight-millimeter gun. Two shells somehow missed them and smashed into nearby buildings. That quickly, the Americans turned their heads and looked a couple blocks up the street, deeper into Son. There, dug into the side of the road, alongside a boys' school, was a self-propelled eighty-eight-millimeter gun, with a crew of seven clustered around it. Immediately, the D Company troopers ran to the right, where a line of buildings offered protection.

A few hundred yards away, at nearly the same moment, Captain Melvin Davis and the soldiers of A Company were deep inside the Zonsche Forest, amid quiet stillness, leading the way for the 1st Battalion. Among the point element was an upbeat replacement who loved to crack jokes and sing Irish ballads. He glanced at Sergeant Don Brinninstool, a combat-hardened NCO, and wisecracked, "If this is combat, there's nothing to it." Brinninstool looked at him and replied darkly, "Just wait a while." *Crack!* An eighty-eight-millimeter shell streaked into the branches overhead, exploded, and spread deadly fragments in all directions. One of the fragments tore into the new man, killing him instantly.

More explosions ripped into the trees, sending bark, limbs, and fragments—metal and wooden—all over the place. The eighty-eight was a fiendishly versatile artillery piece, deadly to planes, tanks, and people alike. At ground targets, it could fire its ordnance with the parabola of a howitzer or the flat trajectory of a rifle. In this case, the German crewmen, who were well-schooled members of the Hermann Göring Training Regiment, lowered their barrels and fired their eighty-eights as veritable rifles.

When the shells detonated in the treetops, it only magnified their destructiveness. The captain was hit badly and went down. Another officer, Lieutenant George Retan, was killed. Several other men were wounded. The Americans were in a kill zone, under attack from more eighty-eights that were dug in along the canal, covering the avenue of approach from the forest to the bridge. Enemy machine gun fire only added to the mess. Many of the men tried to take cover behind the tree trunks, but they offered no real safety from the bursts, which were, after all, originating from overhead. Others tried to crawl forward to the edge of the forest, where they might be able to lay down fire at their tormentors, wherever they were.

A medic hunched over Captain Davis and began to bandage his wound. A shell exploded overhead. As it did so, the medic threw his body over the captain's, attempting to shield him. Fragments tore into the medic's left arm and into Davis as well. "Go on; help yourself," Davis said. "Go work on yourself and someone else."

"No, sir," the medic replied, "we'll get you fixed up. Don't worry about me."

Another shell exploded. More fragments tore into the captain's left side and the medic's left leg. The medic calmly pulled out more bandages and tried to place them on the commander's fresh wounds. Davis looked at him, smiled weakly, and said, "You'd better hurry, boy; they're gaining on you."

A few yards away, Sergeant Joe Powers stood up to move forward. "I was flattened by an explosion and took a hunk of shrapnel in my elbow, shattering it." He crawled backward and found a medic, who bandaged his arm and gave him a swig of whiskey and a shot of morphine. Nearby, Private First Class Nelson McFaul was running from tree to tree, dodging the explosions and the bullets. "I stopped to nudge someone when I was hit in the leg by a tree burst." Like so many others, he drifted back in search of medical attention. Corporal Charles Shoemaker saw one sergeant rise slightly up and immediately catch a machine gun burst in both legs, just below his crotch. "The way he spun around, throwing out his arms, and went down looked for all the world like an actor simulating being hit." It was all too real, though.

Sergeant Brinninstool, meanwhile, led a machine gun team to the edge of the forest. From here they could see one of the eighty-eights, and Brinninstool ordered the gunner, Private Paul Carter, to open fire. Private Donald Burgett, who had only a couple hours earlier seen two troopers killed by a dying C-47 during the jump, was just a few yards away from the machine gun team. As Burgett watched in dismay, "The [German] gun crew evidently saw the machine gun and fired a high-velocity shell at it point-blank." The explosion literally tore Carter and his assistant gunner, Private Prentice Hundley, apart. One of the ammo bearers, Private Don Liddle, "had his arm nearly torn from his body by a shell fragment that ripped the underside of his forearm, passed through the elbow, and tore open a large portion of his biceps muscle." The other ammo bearer, Private Earl Borchers, stumbled past Burgett, glassy-eyed, until his shattered legs gave out and he went down in a heap with his legs bent at odd angles. Not only were his bones broken, but a K ration tin and a flashlight were deeply embedded in his torn muscles. Sergeant Brinninstool was in shock, wondering whether he was about to die. "I thought half my face was blown off," he said. "I felt my face, which was bleeding from the nose and both ears and covered with sand, but still in one piece." In fact, he had facial burns and a concussion.

By this time, soldiers from B and C companies had entered the forest to bolster the battered remnants of A Company. Nearly every man knew now that the trees were the worst place to be. The only way to nullify the deadly enemy firepower was to rush through the forest and launch a point-blank attack on the eighty-eights. The American soldiers knew that the closer they got to these dreaded weapons, the less effective the guns would be, and the better the chances the paratroopers could kill or drive off the crewmen. They needed no leaders to tell them this. They understood it by instinct. The men emerged from the forest in small groups and rushed for the canal, generally by way of a brick sanatorium that offered some semblance of cover. Still, the Germans poured point-blank eighty-eight fire at the onrushing paratroopers. Shattered glass and masonry cascaded all over the place, adding to the terrifying fragmentation effect of the eighty-eight-millimeter shells.

As Private Gene Cook ran for the cover of the sanatorium walls, he glanced over and saw "the man near me, [Private First Class] Joe Gendreau, hit by an eighty-eight and still running several steps without a head." Private Burgett dived for shelter behind the bricks and came to a stop next to another paratrooper. "A quick glance told me he was dead. His head had been cut in two by a large shell splinter that sliced through the middle of his face as cleanly as a saw. Half of his head was missing." Burgett rolled him over and recognized Private George Newport. As more shells exploded, Burgett took a few minutes to catch his breath and process what he had just seen. He happened to look up and was staggered by yet another ghastly sight. "Staring at me and with one eye still intact and wide-open was the other half of George Newport's head. Hanging in a tree limb." Burgett reached up, carefully retrieved it, and placed it with the body.

All around him, men were screaming at the top of their lungs, running as fast as they could at the guns. Burgett fixed a bayonet to the end of his rifle, got up, and joined them. The eighty-eights kept firing. "I felt the invisible wall of the muzzle blast as a hot, heavy concussion hitting me with terrific force." The blasts made him stumble, but only temporarily. He and the others kept going. Burgett kept thinking, "If I get hit, make it quick." He and several other soldiers made it to one position and leaped over the sandbags, right at the German crewmen. Someone shot and killed one of them. Another fell back against the sandbags, thrust his hands over his head, and began to cry. Burgett aimed right for his chest. There was death in the young American's eyes. "My intent was to kill him and he knew it. Somehow I stopped. I don't know how or why, but I did. The bayonet point was just a fraction of an inch from his chest." The German sobbed and pleaded for his life. "*Nein, nein, bitte,*" he implored. Burgett lowered his rifle and gestured for him to get out of the pit. The sobbing prisoner was so frightened that he could not move. Two of Burgett's buddies had to drag him by the armpits over the sandbags and plop him next to several other prisoners.

Nearby, while attacking another eighty-eight, Private Cook "could see and feel the hot orange muzzle blasts as, charging low, we reached the sandbags around [a] gun pit, hurdling them." His group killed one crewman and took four prisoners. Corporal Shoemaker noticed a wounded German lying near the gun. "His belly had been opened from side to side. Another one was standing there wringing his hands. He told one of our people who spoke German that they had grown up together in the same village and were very close." The prisoner begged his captors to put his old friend out of his misery. They refused. The two enemy soldiers looked to be all of sixteen years old. The eighty-eights along the canal were now out of commission.

In Son, as a group of troopers from D Company maneuvered along a block of buildings to the right of the eighty-eight that was positioned near the boys' school, the enemy crewmen kept snapping off shots. One shell smashed through the picture window of a vacant department store. "The glass blew out, and the pressure blew me into the center of the street and knocked me unconscious," Private Edward "Babe" Heffron, a machine gunner in E Company, recalled. After a few seconds, he awoke, and, although he felt dizzy, he managed to hoist his rifle to his shoulder. "I felt something warm running down my arm, and I looked and I was bleeding." He inspected the arm and was relieved to see that his wound was only a minor cut from glass shards.

Machine gun fire also ricocheted down the street. Seeing this, Sergeant Hugh Pritchard edged onto the sidewalk, away from the fire. Sergeant Allen Westphal stayed in the middle of the street, running hard, yelling at the other soldiers to follow him. A bullet ripped through Westphal's calf. He went down, crawled over to the sidewalk, and said to Pritchard, "You know, that was stupid of me, wasn't it?" Pritchard had to agree.

In the meantime, the group from D Company kept moving and made it to within fifty yards of the eighty-eight. The Germans apparently had put out no flank protection for this valuable weapon (because they were either foolish or simply did not have enough soldiers). Private Thomas Glen Lindsey, a skilled bazookaman, crawled into position and took aim at the gun. "The crew still had not seen him," a soldier testified in a post-combat interview. "The rocket hit the gun near the elevating mechanism, and finished the gun. One German was killed by the blast and six others fled toward the bridge." The Americans had no intention of letting them escape. Sergeant John Rice, toting a tommy gun, raised that powerful weapon to his shoulder and shot them down, killing all.

The approaches to the bridge were now wide-open. In Son and outside of town, along the canal, soldiers from both battalions began to run for the vital objective. They took small-arms fire from German soldiers in a building across the canal, but this hardly deterred them. While some paratroopers laid down suppressive fire on the building, others raced for the bridge. They got within one hundred yards of it, and then fifty. They were almost there. Then, with a colossal roar, the bridge exploded, showering the area with debris. Anyone nearby hurled himself to the ground or was thrown down by the concussion. Sergeant Philip Carney was close enough that he "got splinters in my face from the flying debris." As Captain Richard Winters, commander of E Company, huddled under cover and watched the stone and timber remnants of the bridge fly through the air, he thought, "What a hell of a way to die in combat!" Private Cook saw flames and black smoke. One of the bridge's main beams "came tumbling down about thirty feet away, burying end-first into the ground." Not far away, Private Burgett was lying still, sheltering himself from debris, when he noticed an object turning in the air. Transfixed, he watched it twist and turn, trying to figure out what it was and how close it might hit, until it finally landed about fifty feet away. "A shock wave jolted through the ground; we got up to investigate. It was one of the main beams of the bridge . . . made of wood and about two feet square and maybe forty feet long. It had buried itself . . . into the ground."

At last, the debris dissipated and the smoke cleared. Fortunately, no one was seriously hurt. But the bridge was destroyed (though the central support pillar was still in place). Several soldiers, including Major James LaPrade, the 1st Battalion's commander, hopped into the water. The canal was only about eighty feet long and not very deep, an impediment to armored vehicles, but not to individual soldiers. Winters was amused at the sight of LaPrade "tiptoeing from rock to rock, trying to make his way across the canal without getting wet. He had a forty-five-caliber pistol in one hand as he tried to maintain his balance." Winters wondered why the major was not carrying a rifle, instead of a pistol. With a pistol in his hand, LaPrade looked the very embodiment of an officer and thus made a perfect target for enemy snipers.

In fact, the canal was still under fire from enemy soldiers in a pair of buildings on the opposite bank. On the American side, troopers began laying down a withering curtain of cover fire for LaPrade and his cohorts until the Germans faded away. "They established a bit of a beachhead area on the other side of the bridge, and cleared it out," Lieutenant Albert Hassenzahl, a platoon leader in C Company, recalled. "Several guys swam to the other side," Private Cook said. "Others got planks and ropes and built an unstable footbridge." They also found a pair of rowboats. First Lieutenant Harold Young and his platoon from C Company, 326th Airborne Engineer Battalion, had dropped with the 506th. He and his engineers now came up and began to improve upon the footbridge. "We had trained for many kinds of improvisations, but not this," he later said. "I sent men to find hammers, nails, boards, planks, et cetera." Soldiers fanned out all over town, appropriating barn doors, timbers, and anything else they could scrounge, all with the assistance of the Dutch, who helped them find some black-market lumber that a local contractor had been hiding. "Somebody located two boats, which we placed midway from shore to pier. Then we made a rickety bridge that worked, provided my men helped steady the infantry as they moved across."

Colonel Sink drove up in his jeep, dismounted, and studied the make-shift bridge as the engineers worked and other troopers hurried to and fro with armloads of building material. He understood immediately that his men would have to cross single file, with painstaking slowness. The whole 506th could pass over the canal on this rickety bridge, but it was going to take many hours. The push for Eindhoven, and the planned linkup with XXX Corps, would have to wait for tomorrow. Beyond that, who knew how much longer it would take the British columns to reach Son with their own engineers and the necessary materials and equipment to build a temporary bridge that was sturdy enough to hold armor? Market Garden had just experienced its first major setback.[4]

During the harried run-up to Market Garden, General Taylor had devised an alternate plan to deal with this very situation. On the chance that the Germans succeeded in blowing the main bridge at Son, he had earmarked H Company of the 502nd Parachute Infantry Regiment to grab the sturdy road and railroad bridges four miles to the west, near the little village of Best. In the absence of the Son bridge, the Best bridges could provide XXX Corps with an alternate route up the corridor. Based on the intelligence Taylor had received from corps and army sources, the general believed that H Company would encounter only token resistance at Best. The landings did nothing to change that expectation. Within a few hours, troopers from the 502nd seized the bridges at nearby St. Oedenrode with relative ease. The same was true of the 501st Parachute Infantry Regiment at Veghel, a few miles farther to the north.

The commander of H Company, Captain Robert Jones, assembled his company, plus a platoon of engineers, and set out for the bridges at Best. The route from their landing area at Drop Zone B to the bridges called for them to skirt through the western edges of the Zonsche Forest. The

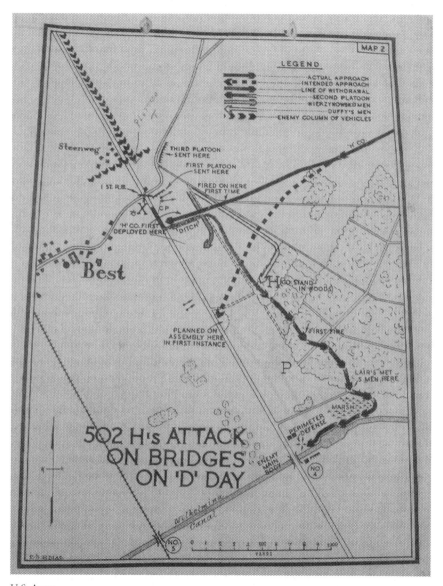

U.S. Army

column of paratroopers was bathed in afternoon sunlight. Temperatures hovered only in the low eighties, but the sunshine, in addition to the heavy clothing and equipment load of the troopers, made the weather feel downright tropical to some of the men. A few of the replacements made the inexcusable rookie mistake of discarding boxes of machine gun ammunition. "I don't believe any ammo bearer who had been in combat would ever do this," Captain Jones later commented.

There were other mistakes. Jones's lead scouts were supposed to navigate through the woods by using the steeple of the Best church as a reference point. Amid the trees, though, they lost sight of the steeple and led the company too far north. They had planned to exit the woods at a point on the main road south out of Best, where they would be in position for a quick march to the bridge. Instead they were six hundred yards too far to the north, near a crossroads just east of Best. To make matters worse, they soon came under intense small-arms fire from Germans in and around the town. Jones estimated that he was now facing a force of about one hundred Germans. Instead of dashing for the bridge, H Company found itself in a brawl among the outlying buildings of Best, the crossroads, and the edges of the forest. This was a machine gun, rifle, and grenade fight with little, if any, supporting fire on either side. Men bellowed in confusion, attempted to spot targets, and fired at anything that looked suspicious. The Americans were in the fields and ditches, or moving along the side of buildings. Many of the Germans were in the houses, firing from the windows.

Amid the buildings that comprised the outskirts of Best, Lieutenant William Craig, the executive officer of H Company, sized up the situation, desperately trying to reach his company commander by radio, but to no avail. As he ran from one house to another, attempting to contact the leading soldiers, an unseen enemy rifleman shot him in the left arm, near his shoulder. He went down immediately. A medic slid alongside him and began to give him first aid, when he "was shot thru his Red Cross arm band . . . [the] bullet going into his side." The medic slumped over Craig. "We both lay in [the] field like that until [the] sniper pulled out."

Lieutenant Ed Wierzbowski, the 2nd Platoon leader who had played football with his men in the marshaling area, came up with several of his soldiers to help the two wounded men. When Craig insisted on staying with the company, Wierzbowski would not hear of it. He ordered his runner to take the executive officer back to the battalion aid station and stay with him every minute to make sure he did not return. The runner did exactly as he was told, even accompanying Craig all the way back to England.

In the meantime, Wierzbowski and his group took cover behind a house, but they were taking heavy small-arms fire from another one around the corner. Wierzbowski's second in command, Staff Sergeant John White, worked his way around the side of the structure, into the open, and raised his rifle to shoot at an enemy soldier in a second-story window of the German-controlled house. As Lieutenant Wierzbowski watched in stricken horror, "The sniper hiding their [sic] beat him to it & caught him right between the eyes." In the next awful moment, White collapsed. He went down with the rubbery knees so typical of those who have been killed instantly. As Wierzbowski watched his beloved sergeant fall dead, all the lieutenant could think of was White's prediction, just the night before, that he would not survive this battle. Somehow, some way, the man had just known, and yet he had been so calm. "Needless to say, his loss was a great one," Wierzbowski reflected.

The young lieutenant had little time to dwell on the tragedy of White's death. He gathered his men and began to supervise a flanking movement just to the left, hoping to make it to the nice cover of a hedgerow. Then he and many others in the company noticed movement on the road. A long enemy column of twelve trucks, led by a lone motorcyclist, was traveling south, probably bound for the bridge. More important, they were heading straight for the ragged American positions on either side of the road. At least two of the trucks were towing twenty-millimeter guns. Captain Jones figured that, in the chaos of the moment, the Germans he was fighting would have trouble warning their motorized comrades of the American presence. He hoped to spring a perfect ambush. He told his men to hold their fire until the column made it past the crossroads and right into the thick of the American lines, if such a thing could even be said to exist. Inevitably, considering the circumstances, some of the Americans did not get the message. Someone, apparently from the headquarters element, opened up on the motorcyclist, killing him. "His body seemed to halt in midair as the cycle continued on," Wierzbowski later wrote.

From the German point of view, the man on the cycle did not die in vain, for his death alerted the rest of the column to the danger ahead. The trucks braked to a halt, and enemy soldiers jumped out and spread into the ditches and fields, well short of the crossroads. Instead of dying in the American kill zone, they now functioned as a vital reinforcement to those Germans who were already pouring out such blistering small-arms fire. As the men left their trucks, some unhooked the twenty-millimeter guns and opened fire at the Americans. At this point, an eighty-eight-millimeter gun, located in a gas station in Best, added its fire to the mess. The shells from this gun and the twenty millimeters began to explode among the trees and along the road, causing casualties. Private William Hammond was watching the enemy soldiers hop from their trucks and crawl into position. "There are two hundred more Germans coming this way," he yelled to the line of troopers around him (actually there were three hundred). In any small-unit action, fire superiority is of paramount importance, and the Germans now had it.

Closer to the woods, about one hundred yards east of the road, Captain Jones knew he had a serious problem. The intelligence types had claimed that the German presence in Best was negligible, but they were clearly wrong. The enemy was here in strength, and they were properly trained, well-armed infantrymen, not overaged rear-echelon types with no stomach for battle.

It was even worse than Jones knew. Intelligence clearly had no idea of the presence of these enemy soldiers, nor of the fact that General Kurt Student's First Parachute Army was headquartered only a few miles away at Villa Bergen in Vught. This army, commanded by one of Germany's airborne pioneers, consisted of parachute training battalions plus whatever Student could appropriate from a bevy of units that had been retreating from the Allied onslaught in France and Belgium.

Only a few hours earlier, a Horsa glider from General Browning's I Airborne Corps headquarters had crash-landed in Student's area. His soldiers had overrun the glider, killed one of the Allied soldiers inside, and captured ten others. In searching the craft, the German soldiers had found a copy of the 101st Airborne Division's operational plan and sent it immediately to General Student. Contrary to popular myth, this document pertained only to the 101st Airborne's area of operations. It was not some sort of magical Market Garden grand plan, yet it hardly needed to be. The 101st Airborne plans, in tandem with the landings around Nijmegen and Arnhem, alerted any German commander with even a lick of sense to the fact that the Allies intended to capture the bridges and smash over the Rhine into Germany. Student had led the German airborne invasion of Holland in 1940, so he especially appreciated the importance of the bridges from Eindhoven to Arnhem. He unleashed counterattacks against the 101st as quickly as he could.

What this meant for Jones and his men was that they were actually facing the leading elements of the 59th Infantry Division, a unit that had escaped from the Scheldt area and was now moving into position to attack the western side of the Market Garden corridor. Their presence was a direct consequence of Field Marshal Montgomery's failure to clear out, or even seal off, the Scheldt.

Throughout this firefight, Captain Jones had been in contact with his battalion commander, the fiery Lieutenant Colonel Robert Cole, apprising him of the worsening situation. Mindful of the reason Jones's H Company was on this mission in the first place, Lieutenant Colonel Cole told the captain to make a push for the bridges. As originally planned, the job was to go to Wierzbowski's platoon, plus a platoon of attached engineers and some machine gunners. Jones was not happy about losing a third of his combat strength in the middle of such a fierce battle. The order, in his opinion, put him "between the devil and the deep blue sea." But orders were orders. Sending messages largely by valorous runners who braved all manner of enemy fire to convey information, he ordered his people to pull back from the road and into the forest, about one thousand yards away. Somehow most of them made it and set up a makeshift perimeter about seventy-five yards long and fifty yards deep. The Germans continued to launch powerful probing attacks against H Company's shaky perimeter. Cole was not the type to leave a subordinate twisting in the wind. Knowing that H Company was in a serious battle, he made arrangements to bring up the rest of the battalion in support of them.[5]

In the meantime, as the sun began to set, Wierzbowski's group set off through the woods. By the lieutenant's own estimate, he had eighteen of his own men and twenty-six engineers. The trees were mostly young pines, planted in even rows, with firebreaks every twenty-five yards (in the short experience of the men, everything seemed to be neat and orderly in Holland). "The Germans had [the] fire lanes covered by machine guns, which continually cut the line of march," Lieutenant Charles Moore, the engineer platoon leader, said. Wierzbowski and Moore sent their soldiers across each fire lane in three-man rushes. Every third or fourth lane, German machine guns opened fire, but no one was hit, perhaps because of the gathering darkness. At last, after many such arduous and tense crossings, they made it to the edge of the woods. Here a few H Company stragglers, who had been separated in the confused withdrawal to the perimeter, joined Wierzbowski. The challenge now for the young lieutenant from Chicago was to move his group in the open, along the raised road, or dike, that led to the first bridge. Because the Germans were all over the woods, he knew they must have outposts, or even stronger positions, between his location and the bridge. Perhaps the darkness would shield them well enough to make it there.

A soft rain began to fall. The wet earth was pungent and dank. Droplets of water tumbled from pine needles onto shoulders and necks, adding to the apprehension and discomfort the soldiers felt at being so clearly behind enemy lines. The patter of the rain, though, helped obscure the noise of their movement. Wierzbowski knew it was time to leave the woods and head for the bridges. He sent his lead scouts, Privates Joe Mann and James Hoyle, ahead at a crawl. Mann was first. Hoyle was his slack man, maintaining a distance of about ten yards. Everyone else followed at a discreet distance. Crawling along in this fashion was exhausting and difficult. Uniforms became disheveled; pants got muddy and soaked. Each man had to make sure to keep his weapon atop his arms, shielded from mud and moisture.

Mann and Hoyle successfully led the group around a marsh to the paved road atop the dike paralleling the canal. "By crawling and under cover of the rain and darkness, we were able to infiltrate past [the German] outpost line of resistance," Lieutenant Wierzbowski said. They were still about five hundred yards from the road bridge. After they'd crawled through the muck from the forest to this spot, it was tempting to move along the road, but Wierzbowski understood that this was out of the question. On the road, they would silhouette themselves into perfect targets. Nor was it a good idea to move on the forest side of the dike, where there were obviously so many Germans. As was so often the case, the best route was the most difficult route—on the canal side of the dike, in the mud. They resumed their muddy crawl. Minute by tense minute, they neared the bridge, expecting at every second to bump into the Germans. At one point, the Americans heard a few rounds of enemy rifle fire, but this petered out. They still had not been discovered.

Lieutenant Wierzbowski, feeling that they must be close to the bridge, whispered orders for the men to remain in place while he and Mann scouted ahead. They slithered forward for a few moments and then finally saw, about fifteen yards in front of them, the stone archway of the road bridge. "Looking up, we saw two Germans who were just in the process of changing guard, for in the next instant one came down the embankment toward us," Wierzbowski recalled. "We set ourselves to jump the guard if necessary. He began walking his post all around us. As he worked his way back to the bridge we watched his boots pass within inches of our faces. All he had to do was look down and we would have been discovered."

Wierzbowski and Mann lay perfectly still, both attempting to control the pounding heart and rapid breathing that came with intense fear. Back at the main column, the men were growing restive and uneasy. The darkness, the rain, the danger of the mission, their lack of knowledge as to what in the world was going on, and concern for their two comrades made each minute seem like an hour. This purgatory lasted for thirty long minutes. By that time, the uneasiness of the group was such that they began to whisper to one another, loudly enough that Wierzbowski could hear them, and undoubtedly the Germans too. When the sentry was at his farthest point away, Wierzbowski sent Mann back to the column to shut them up. The lieutenant remained in place to eyeball the German bridge defenses, planning an assault. This was the mark of a good leader. He was thinking of his mission more than his personal safety.

Even as the voices grew louder, Mann managed to work his way back to his lieutenant. As he did so, German sentries on the other side of the canal began calling to the guard near Mann and Wierzbowski. They also snapped off a few confused rifle shots in the direction of the column. Then all was silent for a few pregnant moments, until a shower of potato masher grenades flew from the other side of the canal and onto the dike above the column of Americans who were huddling near the water. The explosions of these grenades did no physical damage to the men, but they broke their will to remain in place. Two of the men got up and scrambled up the dike, away from the bridge and the canal. Many others soon followed in what one soldier later described as "a stampede." Enemy machine gun, rifle, and twenty-millimeter fire tore through the night. A bullet hit Private Joseph Perkins in the shoulder and he went down. Amazingly, this was the only casualty.

The shooting created a diversion for Mann and Wierzbowski to escape. They ran along the canal, right in the line of fire. As Lieutenant Wierzbowski ran, he counted five enemy machine guns and one twenty-millimeter gun firing in all directions. He gathered up those men who remained in the original spot where he had left them and led them several dozen yards away to higher ground, atop the dike, where they pulled out their entrenching tools and began to dig in. The other soldiers who had scrambled over the dike disappeared, in small groups, into the night. The lieutenant never knew what happened to them. He now had eighteen men with him, two of whom were officers, and three of whom were wounded. For now, they were reasonably secure, but who knew how long that would last? In addition to their rifles, they had one machine gun, with five hundred rounds, a mortar with six rounds, and a bazooka with five rounds. The lieutenant now discovered the cruelest blow of all: A hunk of shrapnel had destroyed the platoon radio. Wierzbowski and his little group were now out of touch with the rest of the company and, for that matter, the entire outside world.

Even as that sickening realization sank into the twenty-two-year-old lieutenant, his captain was sending out patrols, in vain, to find him. Three separate times, patrols from H Company attempted to sally forth from their Zonsche Forest perimeter, in the direction of the bridge. Each time, they were driven back by heavy enemy fire. Captain Jones and his people were doing well just to hang on where they were. They were in no position to save Wierzbowski.

At the same time, Lieutenant Colonel Cole and the rest of the 3rd Battalion were making their way through the night, in a long column, from the drop zone to the forest, in hopes of linking up with H Company. "The column began to stop-start-stop—the invariable sign that the head of the column isn't sure just where it is going," Captain Abner Blatt, the battalion surgeon, later wrote to his wife. The soldiers began to bunch up in the accordion effect so typical of such situations. "It was very dark now—clear and with stars, but no moon." Frustrated and impatient, Cole halted the column and ordered a patrol to go forward and find H Company, but to no avail. German artillery and mortar fire were shrieking into the forest, mainly exploding in the vicinity of H Company's positions. When Cole's leading soldiers ran into German machine gun outposts, the colonel decided to halt near the edge of the woods, facing toward Best, set up a perimeter, and dig in. Patrols still tried to make physical contact with H Company but failed. Cole was in touch with Captain Jones by radio. When Jones told him that his own patrols had not found Wierzbowski, Lieutenant Colonel Cole turned to Major John Stopka, his executive officer, and said, "They've been annihilated beyond a doubt." Fortunately, the colonel was wrong, at least for now.[6]

Forty-five miles to the northeast, the streets of Nijmegen were quiet. Since the morning bombing raids, the city had been tranquil. Some residents still did not even know about the airborne landings. Most did. Throughout the day, they had expected the Allies to appear in force and liberate the town. Instead nothing had happened. A mixed mood of anticlimactic apprehension and curious excitement had descended over the city. Exacerbated by wartime blackout conditions, darkness was now settling over Nijmegen's venerable streets.

A couple miles outside of town, along the main Groesbeek–Nijmegen road, Lieutenant Colonel Shields Warren, commander of the 1st Battalion, 508th Parachute Infantry Regiment, was settling his unit into defensive positions for the night. The battalion had easily captured its objective at De Ploeg, along the Groesbeek heights, and Warren was preparing to defend it against possible enemy counterattacks. Instead, his superior, Colonel Roy Lindquist, commander of the 508th, came to him with a different mission. The battalion was to seize the Nijmegen road bridge over the Waal River. The previous evening, during a final briefing, Lindquist had told Warren that he might get this assignment. Tonight, when General Gavin had realized that the Groesbeek heights were secure, he told Lindquist "to delay not a second longer" in pushing for the bridge. As always, time was the vital factor. Gavin wanted the bridge before the Germans had the chance to defend it in force or blow it up.

At the 1st Battalion command post, Colonel Lindquist told Warren that, according to reports from the Dutch resistance, the bridge was defended by only eighteen unenthusiastic Germans. The colonel introduced Warren to Geert van Hees, a local who offered to guide Warren's men to the bridge. Together the men huddled over a map and chose the route. Warren suggested a quick move to the bridge from the east, along what he considered the most direct approach "on the concept that speed was important." Van Hees told him that this area was covered by an eighty-eight-millimeter gun and that the street was too narrow—in other words, it would be a kill zone. "He suggested a route nearly as short which followed a broad boulevard [the Groesbeek Weg] into town, and then swung east onto the bridge area from the flank," Warren later wrote. Van Hees added that this approach would take them past the resistance headquarters, where he could obtain updated information on the German dispositions. Warren knew that a local man like Van Hees knew more about Nijmegen than he could ever hope to understand. If van Hees was a bona fide Dutch resistance fighter, and everyone in the regiment seemed to think he was, then he could be trusted. To the battalion commander, it simply made good sense to do what he said. Moreover, Lieutenant Colonel Warren knew that a platoon-size reconnaissance patrol from C Company and the battalion intelligence section (under the command of Lieutenant Robert Weaver, a platoon leader in C Company) had, only an hour or two before, proceeded into Nijmegen along the most direct route to the bridge. If that pathway to the bridge was open, surely Weaver's patrol would have found it, and he could always link up with them. "The two were not so far apart that the movement could not be changed en route," Lieutenant Colonel Warren explained.

Van Hees's report of an eighty-eight-millimeter gun covering the main approach to the bridge does not seem to have struck the two American colonels as incongruous with his other claim that only eighteen men were guarding the structure. An eighty-eight indicated the presence of a flak or artillery unit, not a bare-bones skeleton crew of rear guards. Moreover, the Dutchman's suggested route of advance to the bridge was going to take Warren's people into the heart of the city. This was diametrically opposite General Gavin's premission admonition to avoid the built-up areas and go for the bridge via the flatlands along the riverbanks. Warren either did not know about Gavin's preference or felt that the promise of excellent guidance from a local negated the general's concerns about getting bogged down in the narrow streets of Nijmegen. Lindquist, for his part, later disingenuously claimed to have "no recollection of any prejump instruction to this effect." In fact, Gavin had, just the previous day, stood over a map with Lindquist, pointing out his desired route of advance. Lieutenant Colonel Norton, the G3, had witnessed and recorded the conversation in his planning notes. Captain Chester Graham, who served as the liaison officer between the 508th and division headquarters, was also an eyewitness to the meeting. He vividly remembered General Gavin telling Colonel Lindquist "to stay out of the city and to avoid the city streets. He told Lindquist to use the west farm area to get to the bridge as quickly as possible." In any case, the die was cast. The 1st Battalion was going into Nijmegen along the route chosen by Van Hees.

Neither Warren nor Lindquist knew that, even as they conferred with Van Hees, Lieutenant Weaver and most of his men were only a few miles away, making no headway. In fact, they were struggling just to find their way to the bridge. They wandered among a series of backyards in the heart of Nijmegen, hoping in vain to find a familiar landmark. At a complete loss, they finally knocked on the door of a house and asked whether anyone in the neighborhood could guide them to the bridge. They settled in to wait while the home owners went to fetch a guide. Weaver had an SCR-300 radioman from battalion headquarters, but the set did not work. He was completely out of communication with Warren and Lindquist.

Weaver had also lost touch with his three-man point element, led by Private First Class Joe Atkins, and that was a shame, because after somehow getting separated from the platoon, they had found their way to the bridge. They captured seven Germans who were undoubtedly members of the eighteen-man defense force referred to in the Dutch resistance reports. Atkins and his two friends guarded the prisoners and waited at the southern entrance to the bridge for the rest of the patrol to catch up with them, but they never did. "We decided to pull away from the bridge, knowing we could not hold off a German attack," Atkins said. Their German prisoners asked to come with them but, "having no way to guard them," they told them to stay put. On their way back, Atkins and the other two men promptly got lost themselves. They never hooked up with Weaver and the main group.

Once the lieutenant obtained a guide, he resumed the search for the bridge. Before they had even gone a block, they encountered two Germans and captured them. At the end of the next block, a German voice challenged them. One of Weaver's machine gunners opened fire, killing him. No sooner had the echoes of the shooting died out than they heard a truck approaching. "The men lay flat on the sidewalk, unobserved, and fired with machine guns, BARs, bazooka, and grenades, stopping the truck and setting it afire," an after-action report stated. Out of the darkness somewhere to the right, they began to take heavy machine gun fire. Bullets ricocheted off the pavement, wounding fifteen of the soldiers. The patrol's greatest asset, surprise, was gone. They were compromised. They responded with enough fire to disengage and retreat. All of the wounded men were ambulatory. The guide led the patrol through several dark side streets, all the way to the traffic circle, known locally as Keizer Lodewijk Plein, that led to the bridge (nowadays the circle is known as Keizer Traianius Plein).

With German strength in Nijmegen clearly building, and his patrol's presence revealed to the enemy, Weaver decided that there was no sense in moving on the bridge itself. To do so would invite slaughter. His job was reconnaissance, not assault. He gathered up his men and started back to the battalion.[7]

Meanwhile, outside of town on the Groesbeek–Nijmegen road, the 1st Battalion began to move out. Company A, under Captain Jonathan "Jock" Adams, was in the lead. First Lieutenant Woodrow Millsaps's B Company was not quite ready yet. They would catch up as soon as possible. The remainder of C Company plus mortarmen and machine gunners would stay behind to hold the De Ploeg high ground. Lieutenant Colonel Warren would go with A Company's leading troops. Van Hees hopped on a bicycle and pedaled ahead of Private First Class Walter Dikoon, the lead scout of A Company, to reconnoiter the blocks ahead of the company. In the recollection of Corporal James Blue, who was at the point of the advance, Van Hees would "ride forward to the next block, report back to Dikoon that all was clear; in turn Dikoon would inform the point and we moved forward." To Blue and the other soldiers on point, the Dutchman's knowledge was indispensable, his courage impressive.

In loose columns, the Americans made their way warily down Groesbeek Weg (Way) in this fashion. On and on they went in the cool black night. The troopers stayed close enough to one another to maintain visual contact, which in the dark meant about four or five yards, if that far. As their eyes adjusted to the darkness, they took in the sights around them. Stately trees lined the street in the precise, organized manner so typical of Dutch roads. Neat brick homes, set back behind black and gray wrought-iron fences, lined the way.

The troopers covered several uneventful miles. Then Van Hees pedaled back with a warning that a German machine gun was just ahead, pointed at the column's route of advance. The Americans thanked him and told him to step aside. Van Hees said he would ride ahead to the resistance headquarters and make contact with his comrades. The Americans, in the meantime, searched for the enemy machine gun. "Our squad . . . was broken down into two groups," Blue explained, "each group moving along opposite sides of the street, staying very close to the houses and picket fence."

Enemy machine gun fire rang out. Tracer bullets bounced off the pavement and swung in crazy circles. One officer was wounded; another was killed. Private First Class Dikoon spotted the enemy gun and killed the crew with a burst from his BAR (first scouts rarely carried this automatic weapon, but he seems to have been an exception). Lieutenant Colonel Warren and Captain Adams came up to the point to size up the situation. "Good work, men," Warren said. "Let's keep the ball rolling." The advance resumed with Dikoon once again in the lead. Van Hees reported that the way was clear to Keizer Karelplein, a large traffic circle located roughly a mile from the bridge. From here, the Americans planned to swing east and cover the last few blocks to the coveted objective. Van Hees pedaled off for the Dutch resistance headquarters. They never saw him again.

Dikoon turned right on Saint Anna Street and led the way to the traffic circle. The street was so dark that the men were now within touching distance of one another so as not to lose contact. As Private First Class Dikoon approached the circle, an unmistakable German voice yelled, "Halt!" An instant later, a machine gun opened up from the direction of the circle. Dikoon slumped over and fell dead onto the street. The night lit up with muzzle flashes and tracers as confused shooting rang back and forth. Men on both sides, frightened and confused, scattered in search of cover. The two sides intermixed as soldiers ran in every direction. Many of the A Company soldiers clustered behind the fences that lined the street.

From the German side of the roundabout, the Americans heard the sound of trucks halting and hobnailed boots hitting the pavement as soldiers jumped from truck fenders to the street. A half-track pulled out of a side street and rumbled slowly around the circle. Lieutenant George Lamm, Adams's 2nd Platoon leader, yelled for a bazooka team. Private

Van Walker, an assistant gunner, loaded a rocket into his gunner's bazooka. The gunner crept forward and snapped off a shot that hit the half-track squarely in the side and disabled it. "Our bazooka was disabled by the blast," Walker said, "and the gunner was wounded in the shoulder."

Enemy soldiers poured out of the half-track and ran in all directions. To the veteran paratroopers who caught glimpses of them, they appeared to be wearing the spotted camouflage uniforms typical of the SS. In fact, they were members of an SS reconnaissance battalion, probably from the 9th SS Panzer Division, and they had traveled from Arnhem to Nijmegen to buttress the bridge defenses. They were arriving just in the nick of time. Unbeknownst to the Americans, they were joining a 750-man Kampfgruppe (roughly analogous to an American battalion) made up of reservists, NCOs, antiaircraft men, and parachute trainees, under a colonel named Henke and named for him. Only a few hours earlier, Henke had placed the bulk of his force in fortified pockets defending the railroad bridge and the road bridge. These were the actual defenders of the Nijmegen bridges, not the paltry squad of misfits portrayed in the Dutch resistance reports. Henke had placed outposts at the traffic circles that led to the bridges. These were the defenders of the Keizer Karelplein who had originally opened fire on A Company. At almost that exact moment, their SS reinforcements arrived. Collectively, these enemy soldiers now stood between the Americans and the bridges.

The paratroopers grappled with this mixed force in the blocks around the Keizer Karelplein. To conserve ammunition and to guard against revealing their positions in the dark, officers ordered their men to use knives and bayonets instead of bullets in close combat. As the two sides struggled at close quarters in the nighttime confusion, actual hand-to-hand fighting—the rarest form of combat in modern history—took place. In one instance, a rifleman slipped into a German-occupied foxhole and stabbed an enemy soldier to death with a trench knife, a weapon that is a cross between brass knuckles and a dagger. Elsewhere, Corporal Blue and Private First Class Ray Johnson found themselves in an alley between two houses when an SS officer materialized and tried to run right past them. Blue told Johnson to bayonet him. "As he comes between us, Johnson gives him a long thrust and completely misses him," Blue explained. Johnson's rifle clattered to the ground. The officer brushed past and tried to climb over a wooden fence to get away. Blue fumbled with his trench knife and contemplated stabbing him in the back before deciding that his blade was way too short for such grisly work. He raised his tommy gun and fired a three-round burst that killed the officer.

"Who in the hell's firing that tommy gun?!" Lieutenant John Foley, Blue's platoon leader, exclaimed.

"It's me!" Corporal Blue replied. Foley knew the corporal well enough to realize that he must have had a good reason to fire the gun, so he let the matter drop.

By now, B Company had arrived to reinforce the scattered soldiers of A Company, and the battle settled into a stalemate. There were no lines to speak of, just strongpoints and scattered groups among the streets and buildings. In the estimation of one B Company trooper, "There [was] a lot of confusion in the darkness now—the enlisted men don't know where they are and the officers can't see anyone to command, so everyone starts shouting to find one another and get organized." A wounded German soldier, out there somewhere in the night, whimpered and cried for his mother and God. *"Mutter, mutter, helfen mir. Gott, helfen mir. . . ."* After a few minutes of this, a brusque American voice, probably an officer, commanded, "Someone shut that SOB up!" A short machine gun burst rang out and the whimpering ceased forever.

Martijn Deinum, a Dutch civilian who lived in a nearby house, heard a cacophony of English-speaking voices and then shooting. "To and fro, on the street and in the garden came a fusillade. With a loud clatter the first of our windows crashed down due to hand grenades that were thrown from the street into the garden. Then we heard the first death rattle of a human being—horrible." He and his family huddled under cover as best they could on the ground floor of their home. Soldiers of both sides were entering houses, looking for shelter and good vantage points to lay down fire. In one case, two Americans entered a house and, in the recollection of the owner, "One went on shooting all by himself; the other was slightly intoxicated."

Corporal Blue thought he saw movement along the German-held side of the circle and wondered whether the enemy was about to launch an attack against the thinly held American positions. He took Private First Class Johnson and another man named MacMillan to the northern side of the circle, close to where Dikoon had been killed. The three Americans stood next to an empty foxhole, listening and watching for German soldiers. From across the street, they heard the ominous sound of a bolt cocking on a German MG42 machine gun. As all three of them attempted to dive in the hole, the gun opened fire. MacMillan got in the hole first, with Blue close behind. Johnson was last and it cost him dearly. Blue looked up to see tracer rounds smash into Johnson. Mortally wounded, he collapsed onto Blue and died. "The Germans [had] spotted us and [were] throwing . . . grenades trying to hit the hole." They were coming uncomfortably close to plopping one of those grenades into the hole. "Blue, do something," MacMillan implored. Corporal Blue carefully pushed Johnson's body aside, grabbed a white phosphorous grenade, and hurled it in the direction of the German machine gun. The enemy crew broke the gun down and retreated. Under covering fire from an American machine gun, Blue and MacMillan retreated, but they had to leave their buddy's body behind.

Back on the southern approaches to the traffic circle, Lieutenant Colonel Warren had set up his command post in a nearby house. The colonel knew now that he was up against a force of equal or greater size than his own. Amid the ebb and flow of the fighting, he had tried to launch several attacks to push through German resistance at the circle. All of them failed. The realization was sinking in that he could not possibly make it to the bridge this evening. Van Hees had told him that the demolition controls for the road bridge were in the local post office, just a few blocks away. In an effort to confirm this information, Lieutenant Lamm had already led a patrol out in search of the Dutch resistance headquarters, but with no luck. Van Hees had, of course, disappeared during the fighting, giving rise to the suspicion among the Americans that he was a German sympathizer who deliberately led them into an ambush. Though this notion persisted for many years thereafter, even with General Gavin, it was not true. Van Hees was actually a loyal Dutch patriot who was either temporarily captured by the arriving SS men or simply became separated from the Americans in the confusion of the fighting (accounts differ).

Now, as the clock neared midnight, Warren ordered Captain Adams to send a patrol to the post office and destroy the demolition controls. Adams selected Lamm's 2nd Platoon for the mission and decided, much to the chagrin of his battalion commander, to tag along, mainly because he did not have confidence in Lamm's ability to follow the directions the captain had given him on his map. The patrol sidestepped around the traffic circle, carefully negotiated the neighboring streets, and found their way to the post office, where they began taking machine gun fire. "There was grazing fire coming down the street between us and the building," Adams later wrote. Lieutenant Lamm, Sergeant Charles Gushue, Sergeant Alvin Henderson, and a few other stalwarts immediately attacked. Gushue charged a machine gun, throwing grenades all the way, and then bayoneted the crew, hacking and stabbing them to death. At least two had their throats cut. Their gurgling screams were truly gruesome. Another soldier thought Gushue's actions were "very brave but foolhardy." Lamm and the others threw Gammon grenades to blast open the door of the post office. "Germans within the house used small arms and concussion grenades to hold off the patrol," an after-action report stated, "but the patrol, firing as it moved, drove into the building and fired on its occupants, most of whom . . . were leaving by every possible exit." The Americans destroyed four machine guns and an antiaircraft gun and killed an undetermined number of German soldiers.

They seized control of the building and destroyed anything that looked remotely useful for demolitions, from wires to switches. When they left the post office and started taking more fire from inside, they promptly set the building ablaze with thermite and white phosphorous grenades. They had also heard from Dutch sources that demolition controls could be in the Belvedere, a castlelike structure located immediately adjacent to the bridge. Somehow the patrol made it there. They engaged in a short firefight and lost one man killed, but found nothing to indicate the presence of the controls. In fact, Captain Adams personally doubted that either building housed any sort of demolition controls. In his view, the destroyed equipment "could very well have been just ordinary light switches." He was right. The post office building and the Belvedere almost certainly did not house the demolition controls for the Nijmegen road bridge. In fact, postwar investigation showed that those controls were located in one of two pillboxes north of the Waal River, near the bridge. What was more, it made absolutely no sense for the Germans to place their demolition controls south of the river, where they would then be trapped after detonating the bridge.

Be that as it may, Captain Adams had accomplished his mission, such as it was. He had lost one man killed and he had two others severely wounded. He and his men tried to make it back to the American positions around the traffic circle, but the German presence between the post office and that area was too strong. Seemingly everywhere they went, they ran into enemy soldiers. About six hundred yards away from the post office, Lamm found an empty two-story shop at the corner of Hezelstraat and Jodenberg—the building seemed like a barn to some of the men, while others described it as a warehouse—and they took shelter inside. They were safe for the moment, but they were cut off deep in Nijmegen. They would remain that way for two more days.

Back at the Keizer Karelplein, the fighting still raged inconclusively for most of the night. Warren was in no position to launch any more concerted attacks. He was stymied among the urban sprawl, exactly as General Gavin had envisioned. Had Warren entered Nijmegen from the flatlands along the river, he might have had a chance to grab the road bridge, but it probably would have been difficult to hold both ends against the combined might of Kampfgruppe Henke, the SS reconnaissance battalion, and other reinforcements from the 10th SS Panzer Division that were soon to arrive. In that sense, his mission was somewhat unreasonable. It reflected the unrelenting problem that the 82nd Airborne faced in Market Garden: namely, how it was to hold the Groesbeek heights while at the same time capturing the Nijmegen bridges, especially with only part of the division on the ground. This was truly one of the great flaws in the Market Garden design, and Warren's soldiers paid the price for it. The sad reality was that the first American push for the bridge had failed, and that it was almost preordained to do so.[8]

CHAPTER 7

Frenzy

As the first hours of September 18 ticktocked on clocks all over Holland, this was the situation: All three Allied airborne divisions were firmly on the ground with minimal losses from the first day's fighting. None of the three divisions were at full strength yet; all depended on follow-up glider drops for reinforcement. The airborne landings had caught the Germans by surprise and they were still off balance, even in some level of disarray. The 101st Airborne Division was firmly in control of the bridges at Veghel and St. Oedenrode. The Germans had blown the Son bridge in their faces. Colonel Sink was in the process of moving his regiment over an improvised footbridge in preparation for a postdawn push for Eindhoven. Lieutenant Wierzbowski and his little hard-core platoon were cut off a few hundred yards from the Best bridges. Nearby, a major battle was looming between German reinforcements of the 59th Infantry Division and the bulk of the 502nd Parachute Infantry Regiment. The 101st was basically in control of a narrow corridor, stretching from just south of Son all the way to the north of Veghel; whether the Screamin' Eagles could keep that corridor open against enemy counterattacks was an open question. General Horrocks's XXX Corps had not linked up with the 101st. In spite of a massive artillery bombardment of the German positions near the Meuse-Escaut Canal, the British tanks had run into bitter resistance from German antitank guns and paratroopers.

The British had made it only as far as Valkenswaard, four miles south of Eindhoven.

To the north, the 82nd Airborne Division was in control of a fluid pocket from the Grave bridge to the Groesbeek heights. General Gavin's men had succeeded in capturing only two of their desired bridges—the ones at Grave and Heumen. The Nijmegen bridges, of course, were still beyond their reach. The Germans had blown two others, bridges 8 and 9, in the faces of the all-American troopers. The 82nd Airborne had, as yet, made no attempt to capture Bridge Number 10 at Honinghutje, though they soon would. As with the 101st, the 82nd's ability to hold its fragile pocket against enemy counterattacks was in question. Farther to the north, at Arnhem, the British 1st Airborne Division was already in trouble. Only one battalion, under the command of Lieutenant Colonel John Frost, had made it to the Arnhem bridge, and they were essentially cut off, clinging only to the northern end of that vital objective, while warding off unexpectedly intense attacks from elements of the 9th SS Panzer Division. The rest of the 1st Airborne Division was attempting to link up with Frost, but was stymied by the German presence in Arnhem. Ever so steadily, German counterattacks from the west and the east were wedging the 1st Airborne into a perimeter at Oosterbeek, an elegant upper-middle-class suburb three miles west of Arnhem. To make matters worse, the division's radio sets had failed, so the British paratroopers were largely out of communication with General Browning and the Americans. In short, Market Garden was off to a mixed start.

The sounds of singing, barely audible in the nighttime air, were emanating from somewhere within the darkened town of Grave. On the outskirts of the town, patrolling troopers from F Company, 504th Parachute Infantry Regiment, listened intently, wondering whether their ears were playing tricks on them. The soldiers were walking silently along the main road into

Grave, working their way past a string of brick houses. The lead scouts halted and peered into the darkness, searching for danger, but there was none, only the sounds of distant, muffled singing. The melody sounded strangely like "It's a Long Way to Tipperary," and then it tapered off. Private Tom Moseley did not know what to think. "I kept looking for any-place to jump the minute the guns started going off," he later said. "I figured that place was full of Germans." Instead of shooting or the yells of Germans, he heard the sound of a piano playing "way off in the distance somewhere." He listened carefully, recognized the song, and smiled. Someone was playing "Het Wilhelmus," the Dutch national anthem. That could mean only one thing—the Germans were gone. To the young private, the moment was marvelous.

At nearly the same time relieved paratroopers began to understand that the Germans had retreated from Grave, the town's population realized the Americans had come. In twos and threes, and then by the dozens, they poured into the narrow streets to welcome the troopers. Singing full-throated versions of "Tipperary" and the national anthem, they shook hands with the Americans and patted them on the back. Groups of school-children stood together in lines and danced on the cobblestone. At the door of the town church, a mixed crowd of adults and children stretched out a parachute recovered from one of the drop zones, marveling at its size. Over their shoulders, severe German proclamations, contemptuously ig-nored by everyone, were still posted on the door.

Few of the Dutch could speak English. Many simply smiled at Private Philip Nadler, pointed to themselves, and said, "*Ich Hollander.*" Nadler's mother was Dutch, so he fancied himself an honorary Dutchman. He smiled back and replied in Dutch, "Me too." He wandered into an empty house, found a bed, and went to sleep. Other soldiers found a few wounded Germans still in town and took them prisoner.

Petrus Nefkens, a fifty-year-old resident of Grave, had known that liberation was imminent since the first parachute landings the day before. He had spent much of his Sunday at the nearby village of Velp, drinking with his friends. Back at his home in Grave now, he was amused that the American soldiers kept asking the locals for beer. To him, the GIs were "sturdy chaps . . . smartly dressed and generous with cigarettes and chocolate . . . you could never hear them coming because of their rubber soles." Nefkens's impression was typical. Nearly every other Dutchman, in Grave and elsewhere, was deeply impressed by the paratrooper's jump boots. Their silent rubber soles contrasted sharply with the noisy rapping of German hobnailed boots that had become such a hallmark of the Nazi occupation.

The Americans and the Dutch mingled, shared food or drink, and tried to converse in broken Dutch, German, or English. Resistance fighters returned several downed American aviators whom they had been hiding. Many of the Dutch, particularly the teenagers, lobbied hard to join the Americans in the struggle against the Germans. The Americans equipped them with German weapons and told them to carry out patrols and gather information on the common enemy. Captain Van Poyck's Easy Company even adopted one sixteen-year-old whom they affectionately nicknamed "Charlie." The captain later referred to him as "a constant inspiration."

The Dutch resistance fighters also gave the paratroopers a list of every collaborator in Grave. At one point, the Dutch rounded up three local women who had dated German soldiers. Led by a trio of boys who were beating drums, the Dutch led the women through the town in a vengeful parade. "It was the goddamnedest thing I've ever seen," Private Moseley recalled. "They . . . shaved their heads and painted black swastikas . . . on the top of their bald heads. The whole town came out to see it." He and other Americans were astonished to witness this sort of humiliating reprisal, but they hardly cared as long as no one was shooting at them.

Major Wellems, commander of the 2nd Battalion, 504th Parachute Infantry, laid out his command post in the town hall, and ordered his men to set up roadblock defenses on every approach to Grave. With the town and the bridge both under their control, he and his people settled down to wait for the British tanks of XXX Corps.[1]

Three miles away, on the northeast side of the Maas-Waal Canal, Lieutenant Lloyd Polette and a platoon of twenty-five paratroopers from E Company, 508th Parachute Infantry, were scuttling through the early-morning darkness, heading for Bridge Number 10 at Honinghutje. In this location, there were actually two spans, a railroad bridge and a road bridge, right next to each other. The Americans simply referred to both of them as Number 10.

As Polette's men advanced, the canal was at their left shoulders. They worked their way to within three hundred yards of the bridges before the Germans opened fire with machine guns, mortars, and burp guns. Polette and his men immediately took cover in ditches and kept edging closer as the enemy fire sailed overhead. They made it to within one hundred fifty yards of the bridge. Then the sun began to rise. Although the early-morning rays shone in the eyes of the Germans, they could still see their attackers far better than in the darkness. They began to lay down accurate mortar and machine gun fire on Polette's platoon. "I had set up all my BARs and machine guns to return the fire," Polette later said, "but after firing only a few rounds the machine guns were knocked out by mortar [fire]." Unlike some of the other bridges along the Market Garden corridor, these were heavily defended. The German defenses consisted of eight pillboxes, augmented by mortars and machine guns, manned by well-motivated NCO trainees along with a mixture of Wehrmacht infantry and engineers.

The Americans were pinned down, forced to hug the ground for dear life, and they were taking casualties. Eight paratroopers were already dead and four others wounded, mainly from the deadly accurate enemy mortar fire. Polette knew he would need help if he was to take the bridge. He sent

two runners to company and battalion, asking for help; one runner requested reinforcement, the other for supporting eighty-one-millimeter
mortar fire. Two of Polette's fellow E Company platoon leaders, Lieutenant Thomas Thomlinson and Lieutenant David Liebmann, answered the
call. Thomlinson's machine guns and sixty-millimeter mortars laid down
fire on the Germans around the bridge while Liebmann and twelve riflemen tried to work their way forward and add their own fire. In the meantime, Polette managed to withdraw with his survivors to a nearby house
and regroup before another push for the bridges. "The situation looked
entirely hopeless to me," his assistant platoon leader later commented. "No
one but a guy like Polette would even consider trying to take the bridge
with such a small force." This was indeed the ethos of the airborne. They
were self-starters, trained and inculcated to think of themselves as special,
steeped in the notion that small groups of dedicated soldiers could accomplish great things against superior numbers and firepower.

Under an umbrella of mortar fire, Polette's soldiers worked their way
forward for another attack. Several men from the Thomlinson and Liebmann groups were doing the same. German return fire remained intense.
"We could observe Germans walking, or attempting to get on the bridge,"
Polette said. "We kept them at a disadvantage with rifle fire. It was apparent that the enemy was attempting to destroy the bridge [Polette and most
of the other sources had a tendency to refer to both bridges in the singu-
lar]." Because the enemy fire was so thick, the Americans could not make
a rush for the bridges. The best they could do was to use their own fire to
prevent the Germans from moving around sufficiently to blow the structures. This was not good enough. As the paratroopers watched in frustration, the Germans blew their demolition charges, and the railroad bridge
disintegrated. The road bridge, on the other hand, remained in place, although obviously damaged.

On the heels of this break for the Americans came another. Several
hundred yards to the rear, a section of eighty-one-millimeter mortars, under Sergeant George Fairman, began to lay down devastating fire on the

Germans who were still near the road bridge. In all, the mortarmen unleashed seventy-five rounds, each of which left their tubes with a distinctive, and menacing, *thunk!* Each explosion spread deadly fragments in
every direction. The Germans no longer had any wish to hang around.
From their perspective they had carried out their mission of blowing the
bridges. They fled to the north, toward the Waal River. In one rush, Polette and several other men seized the damaged road bridge. A few minutes
later, a patrol from C Company, 504th Parachute Infantry, approached
from the west and linked up with Polette. The troopers had no idea
whether the bridge was still suitable for vehicle traffic. Only the Royal
Engineers could determine that, and they were still far away, at Valkenswaard. For now, the Americans knew their task was to hang on to Bridge
Number 10. Lieutenant Polette earned the Distinguished Service Cross for
his actions in this battle.

The paratroopers set up defenses around the wounded bridge. As they
worked, Dutch civilians emerged from the nearby village of Honinghutje
to welcome the Americans. "Oldsters, youngsters, fat women, and plump
girls formed a queue to greet us," Sergeant Ross Carter remembered. "We
would pause in our defense arrangements, shake hands all around, and start
back to work." They could hardly get anything done, though, because so
many people came out to greet them. Civilians pressed apples, pears, sandwiches, cakes, beer, and milk into the hands of the American soldiers.

One dour soldier in Sergeant Carter's squad who was interrupted several times finally turned to Carter and exclaimed, "These people ought to
go away and leave us be. If they don't quit handshaking, I'm gonna start
kissing the women. That'll break it up!"

Sure enough, the sourpuss, who was nicknamed Duke, spotted beautiful blond twins in the queue and decided to plant a kiss on both of them.
"Here's where I put a stop to Dutch cordiality," he said. As he shook hands
with the first twin, he pulled her close to him and laid a big kiss on her.
Everyone laughed and applauded. As he finished, the second twin sidled
up to him and puckered up. He pulled her close and kissed her the same

way. By the time he finally released her, the first twin was standing right next to him, waiting for seconds. "The strategy had backfired," Carter quipped, "to Duke's satisfaction."[2]

Early-morning shadows crept across the street corners of Nijmegen. Ragged plumes of smoke floated over the blocks around Keizer Karelplein, where, in a continuation of the nighttime stalemate, the 1st Battalion, 508th Parachute Infantry Regiment, was still trading shots with Germans across the traffic circle. Lieutenant Colonel Warren hoped to reorganize his embattled battalion and make another try for the bridge, but that would probably take many hours, and he worried that the Germans would blow the structure in the meantime. As Warren contemplated his options, he thought about the original report he had received the previous evening that only eighteen Germans were holding the bridge. This incorrect estimate, as much as anything else, had led him into this mess. "What a remarkable group of men," he thought, with bitter sarcasm.

Ten blocks to the northeast, another group of Americans from G Company, 3rd Battalion, 508th Parachute Infantry, were actually on their way to the road bridge. The previous evening, Lieutenant Colonel Mendez, commander of the 3rd Battalion, had ordered the company to reconnoiter the bridge. They had made it as far as Hengstdal, on the outskirts of the city, where they bivouacked on a patch of high ground, in a spot where they could actually peer over the maze of rooftops well enough to see their objective. In the early-morning daylight, Captain Russell Wilde, the commander, ordered his company to resume the advance. They moved through the streets in column, with five yards between each man. The first few streets they traversed were quiet. Then, at the head of the column, Private Angel Romero noticed a pair of Dutch civilians approaching, apparently heading for work, as they probably did every Monday morning. Both carried sack lunches. When they noticed the Americans, they stopped and stared, thunderstruck, and studied them quietly for a few moments.

"Americans," one of them said, more in explanation to his friend than as a question. The troopers nodded. The man strode over to them and kissed the American flag patch on their uniforms. "He let out a loud yell, threw his lunch in the air, and ran back to some nearby houses," Romero recalled.

People poured out of the houses and began to celebrate with Wilde's men. Some civilians were still dressed in their pajamas. They patted the Americans on the back and gave them flowers, apples, and milk. Orange banners and Dutch flags materialized out of windows and over awnings. Inside a nearby house, Agardus Leegsma, a twenty-year-old member of the Dutch resistance, heard the buzz and walked outside with his brother John, who was also a partisan. Agardus knew all about the parachute landings of the previous day, and he was eager, to the point of extreme excitement, about the prospect of Allied troops entering Nijmegen. In fact, he was so keyed up that he had laid out a uniform for himself and prepared a street map to assist the liberating soldiers. He had slept fitfully during the night, tossing and turning to the sounds of the distant shooting around Keizer Karelplein. Now Agardus and John caught sight of Wilde's soldiers and approached them. Both brothers spoke fluent English, and they showed their street map to the Americans. The map included careful notations representing locations of artillery pieces, machine gun posts, and the like. "They were very happy to have it and they asked me if we had seen any Germans around," Agardus recalled. In fact, the Leegsma brothers did have a good knowledge of German dispositions around Nijmegen. The two brothers and one of their neighbors, Gerrit Peinenburg, offered to assist the Americans as guides, and the troopers readily accepted. The Americans had trouble pronouncing Agardus's name, so they began calling him "Gas." The nickname stuck.

Together the Dutch guides and Wilde's soldiers eased through the cheering crowds and resumed their quest for the bridge along Berg en Dalseweg. They briefly skirmished with a small group of Germans at Canisius College, and hid out while an enemy half-track drove by, but otherwise maintained a steady pace. They took a right turn on Huygensweg and then a left turn on Praetoriumstraat. The guidance of the Dutch, especially Gas, was invaluable. They knew the best shortcuts, and had a good sense of where the Germans were. "We traveled through back yards, through houses, over high fences (8 or 10 ft.) that separated the back yards," Sergeant Glen Vantrease, a squad leader, later wrote. "The homes were representative of high income families most of whom were very concerned over our trespass." At times during their odyssey, they were under small-arms fire.

They reached the end of Barbarossastraat, almost within sight of the Keizer Lodewijk Plein, which was, in effect, at the foot of the large overpass that led to the bridge. One of the platoons, under Lieutenant Howard Greenawalt, killed seven Germans who were manning a roadblock near the circle. Gas and Captain Wilde climbed to the fourth floor of an apartment building that overlooked the bridge. The captain had been worried that the Germans would blow the bridge, so he was relieved to see it was still standing. He got on the radio and reported this to Lieutenant Colonel Mendez. In the streets below, Wilde's platoons began assaulting the circle and ran into a veritable wall of fire. One after-action report described it as "a barrage of 88s, 47s, 20s, MG, grenades and rifle fire." They had unknowingly run into the Kampfgruppe Henke defenders, plus other Germans who had been reinforcing them all morning. The fire was devastating. The Americans blazed back with a heavy volume of rifle and machine gun fire, but they were overmatched. The enemy fire stopped G Company right in its tracks. Bullets ricocheted along the pavement. Shells of every caliber smashed into buildings and rooftops, setting them afire. "We would go to one side of the bridge and then the other," Private Romero recalled, "and it was the same heavy fireworks. The Germans were everywhere." Sergeant John Hargrave, a radioman, heard the snap of a bullet near his head, looked around, and saw that the antenna of his radio was gone. He immediately hit the ground, as did everyone around him.

As Sergeant Vantrease tried to run for cover, a fragment tore into the small of his back, hitting him with such force ("like a sledgehammer," in his recollection) that he flew ten feet and fell heavily onto the street. Stunned and in pain, he could hardly move. A few feet away, Private Romero happened to look back and see Sergeant Vantrease lying helplessly, writhing in agony. Romero ran back, slung the sergeant over his shoulder, and hauled him to the shelter of a nearby house. "Some of the residents came to offer help," Romero said. "He was given first aid." Under the supervision of the Dutch, the soldiers put Vantrease in a basement, where he hid for several days under the care of the civilians. Other wounded Americans drifted back to St. Canisius Hospital, where a Dutch physician, Dr. C. H. ten Horn, cared for them (essentially right under the noses of the Germans).

The Americans tried one last time to rush past the traffic circle and get to the bridge, but it was no use. The German defenses were just too strong. "Our own infantry, now reinforced from the rear and supported by further artillery fire, were able to force the enemy well back to the south," a German officer later wrote. Wilde's men retreated to the streets near the traffic circle and took cover in houses. German artillery battered the homes all up and down these streets, setting some of them afire, forcing the Americans to take to the basements or move to other houses. Some could still catch glimpses of the bridge through windows, but, for all their chances of getting there, they might as well have been on the other side of the English Channel.[3]

Three miles away, at the 508th command post just outside of town, General Gavin's face fell as he listened to a briefing on the abortive efforts to take the bridge. During the night, erroneous reports had filtered up the chain of command, claiming that Lieutenant Colonel Warren's patrols had captured the structure. Now the young general found out that those reports were dead wrong. The Germans still controlled the bridge, and there was clearly no immediate prospect of taking it from them. Colonel Lindquist knew the location of Warren's command post near the Keizer

Karelplein, but he could not pinpoint the positions of Warren's companies within the city, and with good reason, because their situation was so chaotic. To make matters worse, Gavin was receiving reports of German counterattacks on his other flank, out of the Reichswald, along the Groesbeek heights. This was the very spot, from Kamp to Wyler to Beek, that he had weakened for the 508th's unsuccessful foray into Nijmegen. Only elements of that regiment's 2nd and 3rd battalions, along with parts of the 505th Parachute Infantry Regiment, were in place to defend this thinly held sector against what was shaping up as a major German attack. Even now, at Voxhill, the Germans were putting serious pressure on D Company of the 508th, threatening to overrun them. If the Germans seized this vital terrain, they could collapse the entire division front, or at least force Gavin to take it all back with costly counterattacks of his own. The enemy would also be in possession of the landing zones where, on this very afternoon, hundreds of gliders were scheduled to bring in the better part of his division's artillery. Gavin could well imagine the disaster that would ensue if the vulnerable gliders landed right on top of the Germans. They would be shot to pieces, probably even annihilated.

Almost as if he were trapped in a vise, Gavin was thus torn between the two major tasks that the Market Garden plan had laid at his feet—simultaneously take the Nijmegen bridges and hold the Groesbeek heights. For the time being, he had to choose between them. Given the situation, the bridge had to wait. He had to secure those landing zones before the gliders arrived. He told Lindquist to prepare plans to disengage his troops from Nijmegen and counterattack the landing zones. "It was a big order," Gavin later wrote. "[They] had been moving and fighting most of the night, and now they had to march six or seven miles back to Wyler, attack and destroy Germans in the woods, and travel on to clear the drop zone beyond." Truly, this was why he had trained them to such a fever pitch, precisely to carry out such strenuous orders.

As was typical for Gavin, he decided to check on Warren's situation himself. With only his driver and his aide in tow, he climbed into his jeep and headed for embattled Nijmegen. Like any other man, the general knew plenty of fear, but he seldom worried about the dangers he might face on such expeditions. He was somehow able to combine the tactical valor of a squad leader with the big-picture thinking of a division commander. It scarcely seemed to occur to him—or perhaps he was too courageous to care—how vulnerable he was, roaming around such contested areas in his jeep, with little personal protection (and no clear successor). In any case, this hands-on quality was what made Gavin a special leader in the eyes of his men.

On the way into Nijmegen, he stopped at the Sionshof Hotel, where Captain Bestebreurtje, the intrepid Dutch Jedburgh team leader, had established a headquarters for the Dutch resistance. About six hundred "Dutch underground" men, as the Americans often called them, were milling around inside and outside the nice two-story building. They were almost all dressed in civilian clothes, but some wore orange armbands.

Since parting ways with General Gavin the day before, Bestebreurtje had been busy. With the help of Lieutenant Verhaeghe, one of his Jedburgh team members, he had gathered these men together, while successfully sidestepping the personal, political, tactical, and petty differences that existed among some of them. Bestebreurtje had also worked the phones to gather information on German troop movements. In fact, from talking to phone operators in the Arnhem area, he probably knew more at this point about the dicey situation of the 1st Airborne Division than General Browning. Bestebreurtje and Verhaeghe had even been involved in the previous evening's fighting around the Keizer Karelplein. An enemy machine gun had opened up on them, wounding Verhaeghe in the left thigh and killing a teenage resistance fighter who was assisting them. Bestebreurtje was hit in the left hand and the left elbow. Another bullet shattered the bones of his right index finger. Several others had ricocheted off a pair of binoculars he had strapped across his chest. A few more deflected off the magazine of his M1 carbine. The former speed skater was clearly lucky to be alive.

Yet he had not even sought medical attention, and as he reported to General Gavin, he made no mention of his own wounds. The young captain told Gavin that the resistance men were eager to acquire weapons and join the fight. Many of them gathered around and nodded their agreement with Bestebreurtje's request. Gavin knew that fighters not in uniform had no claim to Geneva Convention protection. The Germans might well shoot them outright as spies or saboteurs. "I pointed out . . . the dangers of fighting in civilian clothes and the fact that if they were captured they would be killed," the general later wrote. The Dutchmen did not care. They had waited for many years to liberate their country, and the time was at hand. General Gavin relented and agreed to give them discarded weapons from his own wounded and dead soldiers. "I told them that there was only one mission I wanted them to carry out and it absolutely had to be accomplished: They had to save the Nijmegen bridge from German demolition." He asked them to infiltrate the buildings overlooking the bridge, cut any wires they saw, and hinder German movement by sniping at them. They readily agreed and set off on their mission.

Gavin climbed back into his jeep and resumed his journey into Nijmegen. He made it to Warren's headquarters, parked his jeep, and met with the battalion commander. Warren briefed the general on the intense battle still raging in the area around the circle and indicated that he was thinking about making another attempt for the bridge. "It was quite clear, due to the nature of the fighting and the degree and quality of the opposition, that he would need added means before he could advance to the point of seizing the bridge," Gavin said. The general told Warren to forget about any attempt to take the bridge on this day. The division commander ordered him to pull back and reorganize as best he could for a potential retreat out of Nijmegen to help the rest of the regiment secure the landing zone. Gavin then left the command post, got back in his jeep, and left Nijmegen to manage the emerging crisis along the Groesbeek heights.

At 1030, not long after his meeting with the general, Warren received the official order to pull out. He understood now that there was little time to lose. The race was on for the landing zone. He left the details of his battalion's disengagement and withdrawal to Captain James Dietrich, his S3, while Warren, in his own recollection, "double-timed most of the way with a small command party to the line of departure to reconnoiter." The battered survivors of A and B companies soon followed. With a sense of urgency, they marched back the same way they had come the night before. German artillery shells exploded all around them. Happy civilians, oblivious to the dire situation, emerged from houses along the route and crowded around the Americans, greeting them with smiles and food. "When the shells would come in, we would flatten out," Private James Allardyce said, "but the people just stood there." A nearby woman was hit and killed by fragments, but this did not seem to dampen the mood of the crowd. Lieutenant Woodrow Millsaps, commander of B Company, strode past several people who were dancing, singing, and pressing fruit into the hands of his soldiers. They clearly had no idea that the Americans were leaving Nijmegen, ceding it, at least for now, back to the Germans. "We dared not tell them, even if we could have spoken their language," Millsaps later wrote. For the young company commander, the encounter was "one of the saddest, and most touching experiences for me." The Americans scarcely exchanged a word among themselves. They just trudged on, past the people and out of town.[4]

Lieutenant Colonel John Michaelis, commander of the 502nd Parachute Infantry Regiment, knew he had a problem at Best. What had started out as a company-size mission to grab an auxiliary bridge had turned into a brutal contest of wills against a growing number of German reinforcements. The widening battle was not just about the bridge anymore. It was about holding off enemy attacks against the 502nd's section of the Market Garden corridor. Michaelis knew that Lieutenant Colonel Robert Cole's 3rd Battalion was pinned down in the Zonsche Forest, so, on the morning of September 18, he decided to send him some help. Michaelis ordered his

2nd Battalion, under Lieutenant Colonel Steve Chappuis (pronounced "Sha-pooey") to Cole's aid. When Cole heard of this, he radioed Chappuis, "I'll be glad to see you when you get here." Michaelis maintained his 1st Battalion in and around St. Oedenrode, where they held on to the bridges over the Dommel River and fended off halfhearted German attacks.

Chappuis avoided the woods. He intended to sweep through Best itself (roughly to the right of Cole's embattled force) and then drive for the bridges. Chappuis expected that, by smashing into the Germans, he would relieve pressure on Cole. The 2nd Battalion troopers attacked with the morning sun over their shoulders. Company D was on the left, E in the middle, and F on the right. "The fields ahead were covered by . . . small piles of uncollected hay," one officer recalled. "That was the only cover. From left to right, the line rippled forward in perfect order, and with perfect discipline, each group of two or three men dashing to the next hay pile as it came their time." In concentrated rushes, covering one another at every step, they pressed forward. The Germans opened up with a devastating mixture of machine gun, rifle, burp gun, mortar, artillery, and small-caliber cannon fire. Men tried to take cover behind the haystacks, but they offered little protection. Bullets and shrapnel penetrated them with impunity, set them afire, and hit anyone who attempted to take such false shelter. "You would get up and run ten paces and then hit the dirt, then up again," Corporal Robert Gryder explained. "People were getting killed and wounded all around." He took a bullet to the leg and went down.

In no time, two officers in Corporal Charles Vest's D Company got hit. He followed a machine gun sergeant who was trying to get his gunners to the shelter of a ditch. "I moved forward and layed [sic] down a heavy burst of fire into the woods to my immediate front. A sniper from my left front caught me in . . . my right calf." The bullet went through the muscle without hitting any bone. As Vest studied his leg, another bullet barely missed hitting the same spot. Then another came in and clipped his nose. He lay down and used a handkerchief to stop the bleeding in two spots. Not far away, Private Guy Whidden was attempting to take cover behind a small hedgerow, talking to his buddy, Private Chuck Schmollinger, when a mortar round exploded only a few feet away. Whidden was momentarily stunned and then began to look around. "As I looked up at Chuck, he continued to look down at me as he knelt; then blood appeared from his nose and ears." Schmollinger keeled over dead, apparently killed by concussion. Another nearby soldier was also dead. Whidden became aware that he was bleeding and glanced down at his right leg. "My boot was shattered above the ankle and dropped off, partly exposing bones in my lower leg." He sprinkled sulfa powder on the wound, tried to bandage it, and crawled back to the safest spot he could find.

Still, the Americans pressed ahead, returning fire as best they could. Private Lud Labutka was yelling at everyone around him, telling them to spread out. "Some of our guys were bunched up," he said. "You're never supposed to get close to the next guy. Then a mortar shell hit three of them. One guy was hit right in the lap. Another one of them was dying. He had me recite the Act of Contrition to him. He died right there in my arms." Not far away, First Lieutenant Bernard McKearney, a platoon leader in E Company, tried to comfort Private First Class Al Pontecorvo, a taciturn New Yorker who was badly wounded. The lieutenant kept telling Pontecorvo he would be okay, but the New Yorker shook his head. When McKearney persisted, Pontecorvo blurted angrily, "You think you know everything!" In fact, this time the lieutenant was wrong. Pontecorvo died. McKearney moved on, made it to some trees, and slid into a ditch. He peered through the trees and saw a pair of parked trucks with eighty-eight-millimeter guns hitched to them. German soldiers were standing around talking. He opened fire on them. "They were confused and tried to get out of action." Another group jumped into their truck and began to drive away when two more of McKearney's men arrived and poured accurate fire into the vehicle. They hit the driver, who crashed the truck and destroyed the gun.

A few dozen yards away, on the right flank of the whole assault, Captain LeGrand "Legs" Johnson's F Company soldiers were desperately trying to maintain the advance, shooting at any Germans they saw. "My company made a beautiful flanking attack," he later wrote, "but we were up against such great odds, the company was cut off. We killed Germans as they attacked us over the flat ground until we ran out of ammunition." In truth, they were more isolated than cut off, but the situation was perilous nonetheless. Captain Hank Plitt, a regimental staff officer, braved heavy fire to replenish the company with ammunition. "Hank had two jeeps shot out from under him," Captain Johnson said. Plitt ended up employing Dutch volunteers, who loaded ammo and other supplies aboard two-wheeled carts and hauled them to the Americans, all the while under fire.

Private First Class Paul Dely was at the leading edge of the F Company attack, and got pinned down in front of his platoon. He lay behind a haystack, about forty yards from the Germans who were sheltered at the edge of a dirt road. "[He] stepped from his behind his cover and threw a grenade into the road and announced it was for Hitler," Dely's platoon leader, Lieutenant James Tolar, recalled. The rest of the platoon tossed their grenades to Dely and he uncorked them, one by one, "designating each time a different member of Hitler's staff as the intended recipient." Later, as the platoon kept attacking, Tolar took a bullet in the leg and went down in a wet, muddy barnyard. He kept yelling for help, but the enemy fire around him was so thick that no one could get to him. "So he crawled out, cussing us," Captain Johnson said. "He did the breaststroke, flat on the ground. His chin made rivulets like the prow of a boat." With every stroke, Lieutenant Tolar cussed out his fellow soldiers until he made it to relative safety.

Private First Class Emmert Parmley was a runner for one of Johnson's other platoon leaders, Lieutenant Nick Schiltz. The young officer kept a photo of his toddler son inside his helmet so that he could easily access it and look at it. As the lieutenant attempted to keep up the momentum of his platoon's attack, he sent Parmley to the rear of the advance to police up stragglers. "I should have been with him," Parmley lamented, although "being assigned to rear guard saved my life." Schiltz's platoon ran straight into the German defensive line, within small-arms range of seemingly every German in the area. Men went down killed or wounded. Others hit the ground and froze. Lieutenant Schiltz circulated around, trying to keep everyone moving. "He rose up . . . cussing and screaming," Captain Johnson, who was watching him through field glasses, later said. "The Germans caught him in the open and concentrated rifle and machine gun fire on him. It sounded like nothing I have ever heard. He must have been hit a hundred times. Bullets, passing through his body, as well as a haystack, set the haystack on fire—and him." Parmley was shocked and deeply saddened by the death of his lieutenant. As he saw him die, he felt a terrible sense of guilt that he had survived and the lieutenant had not. "He was a fine, brave officer," Parmley said. Later, when the shooting died down, Parmley made a point of retrieving the photo of Schiltz's son from the dead lieutenant's helmet.

The Americans had no supporting artillery—a direct consequence of General Taylor's reliance on the distant British for such fire support—and little in the way of mortar fire. The attack was bound to fail, and it did. Chappuis's battalion suffered more than 25 percent casualties. He knew that if he did not break off the attack and withdraw, he would lose his entire force. There was just too much German opposition for them to make it to the bridge. He pulled his companies back and reorganized as best he could.[5]

Cole's 3rd Battalion, in the meantime, remained under intense fire. His main force made contact with Captain Jones and H Company early in the morning, but the best they could do was form an embattled perimeter. Everything from artillery to small arms raked their positions. Enemy twenty- and forty-millimeter fire was so intense that it began to defoliate the treetops, the *quack-quack* noise of antiaircraft guns mixing with the fluttering sounds of falling branches and leaves. In some cases, the guns even set the trees ablaze. By twos and threes, German soldiers infiltrated through the gaps that separated the various companies, working their way in for close shots at the Americans. This sniper fire, and the shelling, restricted the mobility of the paratroopers. In one clearing, Private First Class Harry Johnson's mortar team ran out of high-explosive sixty-millimeter mortar shells, so they resorted to using white phosphorous marking rounds on the Germans. "[They] were strung out among the cabbages in a patch and, as they were hit by the phosphorous, they were jumping up and screaming like hell." Once a soldier is hit by a phosphorous round, the only way to extinguish it is to deprive it of oxygen, usually by packing the wound with mud. Water only makes it burn brighter. One glob of white phosphorous can eat through skin and muscle all the way to the bone. When the wounded Germans jumped up and ran, they only made their injuries worse. One screaming soldier, crazed with pain, raised his arms in surrender and ran toward the American foxholes. As he did so, he took a direct hit from an eighty-eight-millimeter shell, which, in Johnson's recollection, "disintegrated him."

In one of several deep foxholes that served as the battalion command post, Lieutenant Colonel Cole was frustrated. His companies were clearly taking a beating. He had no idea what had become of Wierzbowski's platoon at the bridge, since he was still out of communication with Captain Jones and all of H Company. Cole's radioman, Technician Fifth Grade Robert Doran, was having difficulty maintaining contact with the companies and with his regiment. Cole sensed that Chappuis's battalion was similarly bogged down, fighting a surprisingly large number of Germans around Best. The colonel decided to call for air support, and told Doran to send the request. In an effort to improve reception, the young radioman left his own hole and tried to find a good spot where he might establish regular contact. "With complete disregard for his own safety, he was constantly exposing himself, until he was completely without cover," Private First Class John Fitzgerald, a runner for Cole, later said. "[Doran] knew what had to be done and just did it. That was the way Bob did everything."

The colonel, Doran, and Fitzgerald had formed a strong bond in the many months they had served together. The West Point–trained Cole was a demanding and exacting commander, the sort who was not afraid to chew men out if need be. Profanity came as naturally to him as breathing and eating. His cussing was so creative that he achieved a sort of artistic level of expression with it. "Many times he would give me messages for the company commanders that would make a stevedore blush," Fitzgerald said. The young runner was an oxymoron in that he possessed a poor sense of direction but somehow always found a way to deliver his messages and make it back to the command post. Cole liked to needle him. "Goddamn it, Fitzgerald," he would say with a twinkle in his eye, "what took you so long? You're the only soldier I know who can get lost between his barracks and the PX."

The colonel was a colorful disciplinarian and highly courageous leader in the George Patton mold. But he also possessed an innate kindness, good humor, and warmth. At twenty-nine, he was only seven or eight years older than most of his men, so he could relate to them. It was not at all unusual for him to bawl out a sentry for giving the wrong password and then give him the raincoat off his own back. The welfare of his soldiers was his highest priority, not his own glory or aggrandizement, and his troopers sensed that. This very morning, he had given a can of sliced grapefruit to Doran and Fitzgerald, an item so precious that, in Fitzgerald's estimation, it "had the equivilant [sic] value of a five carat diamond." It is no exaggeration to say that the soldiers of the 3rd Battalion revered Cole, not just for his charismatic valor, but also for his human touch. "He was probably the greatest man I ever knew," Charles Olson, his operations sergeant, once commented.

Now, as Technician Fifth Grade Doran paced around, looking for the right spot to get good radio reception, Cole and Fitzgerald urged him to take cover, but the radioman stayed in the open, heedless of the danger. A heavy burst of machine gun and small-arms fire came in, and Doran caught a burst in the head. He fell dead to the forest floor, pieces of his skull and brains splashed onto his radio. Cole scrambled from his foxhole, wiped the gore from the radio, and saw that it was still working. His executive officer, Major John Stopka, ran up and told him that a P-47 air strike was on the way. Cole turned to Fitzgerald and ordered him to find his driver, Private J. C. Conners, who was supposed to bring up a jeepload of ammunition. Fitzgerald took off.

To mark their own positions for the fighter pilots, troopers popped orange smoke and laid out orange recognition panels (or, according to some accounts, simple orange flags) at the edge of the forest, where enemy fire was most intense. The P-47s, in the recollection of one witness, "came low to strafe, and their bullet fire began to hit the battalion positions." Major Stopka ran among the men, supervising the laying of recognition panels beyond the trees, where he hoped the pilots would see them. Someone told Stopka that Cole wanted to see him. The major ran back to the command post, where he found Cole wiping Doran's blood from his uniform and the radio. The colonel directed Stopka to deal with the radio while he checked on the recognition panels. After Cole finished placing them, the planes circled back and made another strafing run. This one was much more effective, and enemy fire noticeably slackened. Taking advantage of the respite, Lieutenant Colonel Cole walked beyond the woods into the open field that constituted no-man's-land, to make sure the panels were firmly in place for another effective run. He stopped, put a hand up to shield his eyes from the sun, and watched a circling plane for a few moments. From across the field, a shot rang out from a house only a couple hundred yards away. Staff Sergeant Olson, from the vantage point of the trees, watched as a bullet tore through "the rim of [Cole's] helmet and through the head" at his temple. The colonel immediately went down.

Cries rang out for a medic. Captain Blatt, the battalion surgeon, had been treating men under fire all morning. When he heard that the colonel was hit and needed his help immediately, he was stunned. Cole was such a larger-than-life figure, and he had defied the odds so many times (mainly in Normandy) that, to the young doctor, he "seemed to have a charmed life." Blatt regained his composure and, with the help of two other men, dragged Cole back into the forest. The young doctor examined the colonel's wound and saw immediately that he had no chance of surviving. "Although he was still breathing, it was obvious that he would be dead in a minute or two."

Just then, Private First Class Fitzgerald returned from his errand and saw what was going on. He knelt down, took Cole's shattered head in his hands, looked at Blatt, and said: "Why don't you do something for him?"

Blatt shook his head sadly. "I'm sorry, John; there is nothing I can do for him now."

The doctor was right. Cole was dead in a matter of seconds. The men carefully placed his body in a foxhole and covered it with a parachute. With the battle still raging, they had little time to dwell on their grief, but it was there. "Part of myself went with him," Sergeant Olson later said. Lieutenant Ralph Watson, who had also watched the colonel die, was in a veritable state of denial. He got in touch with Major Stopka and, instead of telling him outright that Cole was dead, he said to the major: "You are in command of the battalion." Stopka initially thought this was only temporary, a routine matter while Cole attended to some pressing detail. A full hour passed before he learned the terrible truth that Cole was gone. Blatt believed that, had he lived, he would have become "one of our outstanding general officers." Fitzgerald, who knew the colonel like few others, was devastated. "His complete devotion to duty, a warm sense of humor, and the ability for combining strict discipline with human understanding were the qualities that made him an outstanding officer among outstanding men."

As the news circulated among the men, a veil of enraged grief descended over the battalion. When someone spotted a German running from the house where the shot had come from, a machine gun opened up and mercilessly cut the enemy soldier down. Sergeant John Brandt subsequently led a squad to clean any remaining Germans out of the house. "After a brief battle, the Germans gave up." Brandt and the others were almost reckless in their aggressiveness. "No one was hurt, fortunately, but in our haste and desire to avenge Colonel Cole's death, we almost met our end." The 3rd Battalion soldiers consoled themselves that, by killing the running German and clearing the house, they had gotten the sniper who killed Cole. But no one could ever be sure.[6]

Half a mile away, spread among a motley series of foxholes overlooking the Best bridge, Lieutenant Wierzbowski and his battered group heard the sounds of shooting from the forest. They hoped that this meant the battalion was on the way to relieve them, but this was, of course, not to be. Cut off from the outside world, they could not know that the shooting was from the abortive 2nd Battalion attack as well as the 3rd Battalion's struggle to survive in the forest. In the daylight, they had an excellent view of the stone bridge, only sixty yards in the distance, and the railroad bridge about three hundred yards farther away, yet they were frustratingly out of reach. The area was crawling with Germans. Enemy soldiers were dug into positions around a barracks that stood just twenty yards away from the south side of the bridge. Another sizable group was about seventy-five yards away, on the other side of the road that led to the bridge. To Wierzbowski's rear was the forest, and that area, of course, was hardly secure. The Americans understood all too well that they were surrounded. "The raising of our heads alone would draw heavy fire," Wierzbowski later wrote. "It was truly exasperating to look up and see the object of our mission just seconds away . . . and still be unable to move." The lieutenant decided he had no choice but to sit tight, wait for darkness or reinforcements (whichever came first), and then make a rush for the bridge.

Although Wierzbowski's group was in no position to attack, they still comprised a mortal danger to any Germans who strayed anywhere near their holes. At one point, a group of enemy soldiers, apparently retreating from the 2nd Battalion attack, approached Wierzbowski's position. His machine gunner slaughtered them. "We saw about thirty-five of the enemy fall, thereby causing the remainder to flee in the general direction from which they came." German fire tore into the platoon foxholes, causing more

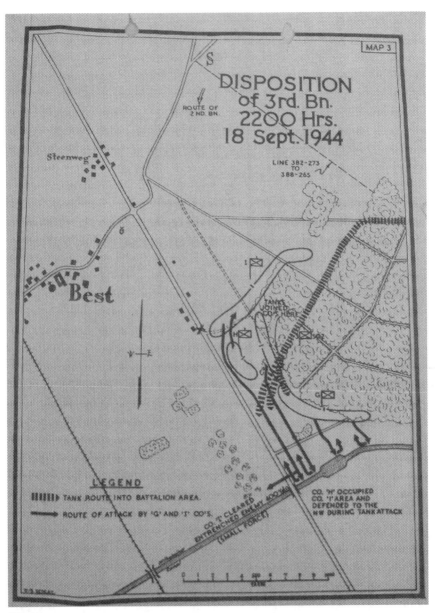

casualties among Wierzbowski's dwindling force. His medic, Private First Class James Oravec, moved around, helping the many wounded soldiers.

When things quieted down, the Americans saw a civilian car pull up to the bridge. A civilian and a German officer got out, spoke for several minutes to the soldiers around the bridge, and then left. A few minutes later, as the Americans watched, the bridge exploded with such force that it lifted them bodily in their holes. Concrete and bits of steel rained down around them. They crouched low and waited for the debris to dissipate. Lieutenant Wierzbowski's mission had just changed from a quest for the bridge to a stark odyssey for survival.

The same P-47s that had strafed in support of the 3rd Battalion overflew the canal and unleashed .50-caliber rounds all along the banks. The fire came so close to Wierzbowski that he literally scrambled away as bullets kicked up dirt alongside him. When the planes were gone, he authorized sorties from small groups of soldiers. Private Lawrence Koller, Private Tony Waldt, and Technician Fifth Grade Vincent Laino volunteered to go to the battalion command post and tell them about the bridge's demise and the platoon's predicament. "They soon returned, having run into an ambush," Wierzbowski recounted. They had not made it far, but they managed to capture three Germans, including an officer and two medics. Wierzbowski immediately ordered the medics to assist Oravec any way they could.

As the hours unfolded, eighty-eight-millimeter shells exploded distressingly close to the little group. Mann and Hoyle, the intrepid scouts, grabbed the bazooka and went on a quest to destroy the guns. They found an ammo dump and blew it up with a bazooka rocket. Hoyle then managed to destroy an actual gun with one shot at a distance of one hundred fifty yards. The two men also killed six Germans with their rifles, though Mann was hit twice in the upper torso by enemy rifle bullets. The two men managed to crawl back to the platoon, where Oravec treated Mann and the latter begged the lieutenant to keep him in action. "Where could anyone find braver men?" the lieutenant later wrote in admiration. In addition to the exploits of the two scouts, a machine gun team crawled forward several dozen yards, placed their gun over a rise in the ground, and shot up an enemy ammunition truck, setting it on fire.

The Germans had seemingly been willing to maintain a wary distance from the surrounded platoon, but, after absorbing such damage, they began to put pressure on the Americans. "We thought we were under heavy fire before, but now they really poured it in," Wierzbowski said. A shell fragment tore into Private Onroe Luther's head, killing him. Private First Class Jacob Northrup caught a hunk in the base of his spine and bled to death. Lieutenant James Watson, an engineer officer, was with the machine gun team, spotting targets. He got shot in the abdomen, right at the top of his crotch. He doubled over in shock and then lay back, rolling around, writhing in pain. Private First Class Oravec, the courageous medic, crawled out to treat him. He administered one of the platoon's last remaining morphine syrettes and called back to Wierzbowski for help. The young Chicagoan crawled to them. Watson was in such shock and pain that he was convinced his testicles had been shot off. He was desperately trying to unholster his .45-caliber pistol to shoot himself. "I . . . had to fight him to take away his forty-five automatic," Wierzbowski said. "I attempted to assure him his privates were intact by telling him he was hit in the upper thigh." Wierzbowski managed to subdue his fellow lieutenant, though he was hardly able to calm him down. Watson still believed he had been emasculated. Wierzbowski hoisted the wounded man over his shoulder and ran all the way back to a foxhole on the reverse slope of the platoon position, where the medics were treating the wounded men. Oravec made it back too. Wierzbowski and Oravec looked Watson's wound over carefully and happily informed him that his testicles were intact. Watson finally calmed himself, but he was in no less pain for the welcome knowledge.

The firefight died down. A short time later, the men heard the sound of approaching engines. "Now what?" Wierzbowksi thought in exasperation. He and the others looked across the canal and could hardly believe what they saw. A British armored car and scout car from the 2nd Household Cavalry Regiment materialized on the other side and drove the Germans off with machine gun fire. XXX Corps had been on the move since sunrise, and, for Wierzbowski's group, this was the first indication that they were progressing toward a linkup with the 101st Airborne. The British scouts knew that the Son bridge had been blown, so they were searching for the Best road bridge. They were, of course, disappointed to see that it too was gone, but surprised to find Wierzbowski's group. The presence of British scouts raised the hopes of the lieutenant and his men that they were about to be relieved. The Americans conversed with their allies by shouting back and forth across the canal. They asked the British scouts to radio the 3rd Battalion and inform them that the bridge was gone. The British tried, but could not get through (their radios were probably on a different frequency), so they relayed the message to their higher command in hopes they would pass it on to the 502nd's commanders.

Corporal Daniel Corman found an abandoned rowboat and a piece of timber, using them to row across the canal to the British. They gave him badly needed medical supplies—the Americans were down to their last bandages, sulfa packets, and morphine syrettes—and whatever ammunition they could spare. When Wierzbowski saw Corman row back and forth, it occurred to the lieutenant that he could withdraw his wounded men in that fashion. Perhaps the British could then evacuate them. But the two scout vehicles were in no position to take on such a demanding task (the wounded numbered in double figures); nor, quite frankly, was this kind of thing part of their mission. When Wierzbowski called across and asked them to take his wounded men, they replied, "Stay where you are; I'm sure that help will be here very soon. Until it does, we will cover you." The lieutenant was disappointed, but he understood. Under the protective muzzles of the British scouts, they relaxed and settled down to wait. "We felt our troubles would soon end." Help, after all, had to be on the way. But he had no idea that the regiment was in little position to do much of anything for him. Another long night of isolation beckoned.[7]

Two miles away, on the other side of the Wilhelmina Canal, the entire 506th Parachute Infantry Regiment was on the move, heading south down the main road into Eindhoven. Colonel Sink had used the hours of darkness to shift most of his troops across the improvised footbridge that the engineers had constructed at Son. There was no more time to lose, though. The colonel knew he had to take Eindhoven—a major city of 130,000 people—and link up with XXX Corps immediately, if not sooner. In Eindhoven, there were four bridges he needed to capture. The Market Garden timetable was already behind. He was, after all, supposed to have linked up with the British the day before. Instead they had stalled at Valkenswaard, four miles south of Eindhoven, and he had been stymied by the destruction of the Son bridge. So the sooner his paratroopers cleared the Germans out of Eindhoven and joined hands with the British, the better. Sink even instructed his battalion commanders that they were to move with such haste that they were not to "waste any time killing Germans."

In long columns with proper flank protection, the 3rd Battalion led the way, followed by the 2nd and the 1st. The terrain along the northern approaches to the city was flat, with open fields and a few hedgerows. Houses and other buildings, including a church, were visible in the distance. This was the northern suburb of Woensel. Morning fog had given way to brilliant sunlight. As the Americans approached Woensel, they began taking small-arms, mortar, and machine gun fire. They spread out along the ditches and fields and returned fire as best they could. Along the eastern side of the road, Captain Derwood Cann, the intelligence officer who had constructed detailed sand tables for his battalion back in England, was leading a six-man patrol to locate enemy positions when one of his soldiers was hit. Everyone took cover in a ditch just east of the road. Cann crawled over to one of the men who carried an SCR-300 radio and contacted the battalion commander, Major Oliver Horton, reporting that they were facing, in his estimation, "an enemy platoon armed with machine guns and rifles." Cann listened to the shooting and peered across the road, where he saw "the assault companies deployed . . . and ready for more action."

The Americans returned fire and advanced in rushes, driving the surviving Germans back to the buildings. As Private Jack Grace and a buddy moved toward the buildings, they came upon a wounded German soldier. Grace turned to call for a medic. His friend had other intentions. "Before I knew what was going on he shot the German dead." Grace was disgusted and dismayed. Not only was it wrong, in his estimation, to execute a wounded man; it tempted fate. Death, after all, stalked these infantrymen at all times. Grace believed that God would be more likely to spare the lives of those who were merciful than those who committed heinous acts. As Private Grace and the other soldier stood over the dead German soldier, Grace told his friend "he was wrong and he would get his someday—he did."

On the other side of the road, Lieutenant Charles "Sandy" Santasiero, an experienced platoon leader in I Company, was at the point of the advance, as was customary for him. To Santasiero, leading meant that he should always be in front. He even regularly functioned as his own first scout. He happened to glance back and saw Captain John Kiley, the battalion's respected operations officer, approaching him. The two men were good friends who had been through a lot of combat together. Santasiero immediately noticed that Kiley had a map case and a pair of binoculars slung over his torso, prominently on display, as were his silver captain's bars. "Goddamn, Kiley," Santasiero said, "what in hell are you doing up here? You shine like a fucking officer. You know the krauts are waiting to kill officers. Please get your ass to the rear."

Kiley smiled at his friend. "Sandy, not many of us old-timers are left. I worry about you every time a mission bogs down and you end up leading the attack for us."

Santasiero was right. The German fire was definitely accurate enough to pinpoint officers. The conversation between the two men was over for only a few seconds when a bullet ripped through Captain Kiley's throat, killing him instantly. Santasiero, to assuage his grief, turned around and cursed at the dead body of his friend for his carelessness. Nearby paratroopers, believing that the shooter was in the tower of the church, known locally as Vlokhoven, peppered the structure with rifle and bazooka fire. The sniper may actually have been at the base of the tower, in the Vlokhoven church garden, at least according to one postwar investigation. Regardless, Kiley was dead.

Another officer, Lieutenant Mickey Panovich, who had once played basketball at UCLA, caught a sniper round that grazed his right ankle and tore through his left leg, chipping the tibia bone. One of his troopers dragged him inside a house belonging to Helena Wolfensberger, a twenty-seven-year-old housewife. She laid him on her carpet, gave him milk and applesauce, and cared for him as best she could. "I tied off [his] leg because I saw that his whole calf had been shot away," she said. "After a little I loosened the bandage 'round his leg a bit and took the [morphine] syringe from his pocket and emptied it into his leg."

He lapsed in and out of consciousness. In spite of her care, Panovich's legs were soaked with blood by the time the medics got to him. They were able to save him, though. In a separate incident, made famous by the book and miniseries *Band of Brothers*, Lieutenant Bob Brewer was also in full view of the Germans, looking the part of an officer, when a German sniper opened fire on him. The bullet traveled through his throat, just below the right jawline and out the left side of his neck. He collapsed in a heap. "Blood flowed from my mouth like a fountain," Brewer later said. His men gave him up for dead, but somehow he held on long enough for a medic to save his life (and subsequently get hit himself). Brewer and Kiley had both been shot in the throat. One was fortunate. The other was not.

In the meantime, the attack into the northern suburbs proceeded well until the Germans began to open fire with a pair of eighty-eight-millimeter guns they had set up at the intersection of Kloosterdreef and Woenselse streets. The guns belonged to Flak Brigade 18 and had arrived in town only the night before. Private Bill Galbraith was in a doorway, dodging machine gun fire, when the shells started coming in. "An eighty-eight shell hit the building across the street. It blew out the whole front of the building. The second one damned near tore my left leg off at the knee and put me on my butt in the street. I crawled back to the doorway. Another round came in with shrapnel hitting me in the shoulder." He decided that if he stayed in this spot much longer, he would get killed. He began hobbling to the rear and had made it only a short way when Pete Klompmaker, a Dutch civilian, opened the door to his home and dragged him inside.

The eighty-eights were so close that the German crewmen could see their targets, a rarity for artillerymen. They fired their powerful weapons like rifles, sometimes even at individual men. Lieutenant Santasiero's platoon shot back at the Germans with everything they had, including rifle grenades and bazookas. Explosions shattered windows and sent bricks flying. Major Horton's jeep rolled to a stop near Santasiero and the battalion commander hopped out. "Charlie, the Dutch are on our side," the major drawled, "and I think you are destroying too many buildings."

Santasiero was in no mood for such recriminations. He had already seen his good friend Captain Kiley die, and a member of his platoon was lying dead in the street only a few yards away. Three others were wounded, buried in rubble. "Major, what you are looking at was done by an eighty-eight," Santasiero replied angrily. "Now tell it to the dead trooper in the street. I will destroy a building anytime to save one of my men." Without a word, the major got back in his jeep and left.

As the fighting raged, Colonel Sink wandered around, taking note of the situation. He sensed that, though German resistance in Woensel was sharp, there was little depth in the enemy's Eindhoven defenses. Deciding that it made no sense to keep pushing 3rd Battalion into town, straight into the muzzles of the eighty-eights, he told them to stay where they were while the 2nd Battalion swung east, looped around, and attacked the guns from the flank. With the guidance of Dutch civilians, the 2nd Platoon of

F Company took the lead. They negotiated their way from east to west, along Pastorie Street and then slightly north along the Kloosterdreef into an advantageous attack position. The Germans had no idea they were there until it was too late. Thanks to a warning from Coby van Luyt, a Dutchwoman, they captured two enemy soldiers who were so close to the paratroopers that they almost collided with them. "They didn't seem to know we were in the vicinity," Staff Sergeant John Taylor, one of the squad leaders, related.

The woman's fiancé, Bert Pulles, had already pointed out the location of the German guns to the Americans, and Private Robert Sherwood fired several rifle grenades at one of the gun crews. Staff Sergeant Taylor leaned into street, perched himself on a curb, and fired an entire eight-round M1 Garand clip at them. Two of the Germans were wounded and fell down. His stripper clip failed to eject from the breech of his rifle, so he and Sherwood ducked behind a pair of steps while Taylor cleared his weapon. The other German crewmen swung the gun around to shoot at the attacking Americans. "When the big gun finally fired, it knocked the side of the house out just above our heads," Taylor said. "It sounded like every building in that part of town was coming down." For a few moments, the dust and debris obscured their view of the gun. When it cleared, they saw the muzzle pointed straight at them. To Taylor, "That gun . . . looked like it was ten feet wide!" The eighty-eight snapped off more shots. More bricks and debris collapsed around them.

The rest of the squad had begun to pour fire on the eighty-eight crew. Mortarmen, with only the tube and a few shells at their disposal, balanced their weapon between their legs and laid down effective fire. Sergeant George Martin opened up with a machine gun. Sherwood resumed firing his rifle grenades. One of them scored a direct hit on the eighty-eight. The German crewmen began to scatter into the nearby buildings. A rifle grenade hit one of the German-held houses, wounding ten enemy soldiers. Taylor shot an officer in the leg. The first gun was out of action. The second gun went even more quickly. When the American rifle, mortar, and machine gun fire intensified, the enemy crewmen destroyed their eighty-eight by blowing the breech and then tried to escape. The Americans rounded them up and took them prisoner. In the short battle, the 2nd Platoon killed thirteen enemy soldiers and took forty-one prisoners. The platoon lost two men wounded, one of whom was Sergeant Martin. A bullet had ricocheted off the jacket of his machine gun, sending a shard into one eye and inflicting major damage. He ended up losing the eye.[8]

With the guns neutralized, German resistance in Eindhoven effectively collapsed. The Americans hunted down and killed or captured a few remaining pockets of enemy soldiers (intelligence estimated that only a couple hundred of them were defending the town). In one spot, the troopers disarmed their foes, questioned them, and forced them to lie down in the street, under guard, while locals gawked at them. The 2nd Battalion easily moved south and grabbed the bridges. "We hold the center of town and we are sitting on the four bridges," an elated Lieutenant Colonel Robert Strayer, the battalion commander, radioed regimental headquarters.

Colonel Sink's soldiers began to spread out all over Eindhoven. All along, Dutch civilians had been part of the battle, helping the Americans by providing information on the Germans and guidance through the city. But these were individual helpers—people who happened to be in the right place at the right time or were simply courageous and especially committed to the liberation of their city. Now, as the shooting died down and the Americans took over, the population as a whole spilled onto the streets. The mood was joyful, even frenzied. People jammed the streets, hugging soldiers, blowing kisses at them, shaking their hands, patting them on the back, even asking for autographs. Soldiers passed out cigarettes, chocolate, and K rations. In many cases, local girls held hands or engaged in passionate kissing sessions with them. "Imagine all the spectators at an inaugural parade to suddenly swarm into, over and under the ranks—carrying fruit, pitchers of beer, sandwiches of dark bread or just waving Dutch flags or bits of orange cloth, or just running, trying to touch you, everyone happily yelling at the tops of their lungs, begging for a souvenir," Captain Robert

Harwick, executive officer of the 3rd Battalion, wrote. Sergeant Taylor, fresh from his duel with an eighty-eight, now found himself engulfed by well-wishers. "We were mobbed by happy people, just like in a parade. I never ate so many apples and pears in my life." Nearby, Private John Lindberg took in the wonderful sight of "people shouting, laughing, taking pictures, some with tears in their eyes, throwing kisses and offering beer . . . barbers giving troopers free shaves . . . it was crazy!" Soldiers and locals mixed together in happy groups, posing for pictures taken by whoever happened to have a camera handy.

To the Dutch children, the American soldiers seemed larger than life. Thirteen-year-old Joop Muselaars stood and gawked. "To my eyes these soldiers seemed to be enormously big fellows." Like many other boys, he was fascinated to study, and even touch, their rifles, machine guns, bazookas, boots, helmets, and uniforms. In his memory, "Nearly all of them wore big, flashy rings." At one street corner, a group of kids asked Private First Class Lawrence Davidson where he was from. "Kentucky," he replied. They immediately launched into an impromptu version of "My Old Kentucky Home." For Davidson, their singing "made tears come to my eyes and I felt very homesick." Private Don Burgett told several people that his hometown was Detroit. Each time, someone would respond by saying, "Henry Ford." When another trooper said he came from Chicago, the civilians pantomimed shooting with a tommy gun and said, "Gangsters, brrrrrrrrrrrrrrrrrrrrrrp!" Maria Van Dijk, a forty-four-year-old housewife, eagerly asked one trooper where he was from. "Wyoming, beautiful country," he replied. She excitedly showed this man and his buddies some defaced photographs of Hitler that she had hung from a lamppost. "These boys of the 101st looked on rather 'foolishly,'" she later wrote, "for they could not realize what all this meant to us, to be free at last." On another street corner, a Dutchman struck up a conversation with Sergeant Bill Guarnere, a street-smart cynic from south Philadelphia, and asked him, "Can you define freedom? You can't because you don't know what freedom is until you lose it." The young sergeant never forgot the conversation.

Private David Kenyon Webster, whose literary intellectualism practically mandated cynicism, was nearly moved to tears by the joyful reception. "It was the most incredible thanksgiving demonstration that any of us had ever witnessed, and it fixed Holland forever in our hearts."

The Dutch police took to the streets, helping with crowd control, but also joining in the celebration. To the Americans, their dark helmets and black uniforms looked eerily similar to SS outfits, and there were several near-shooting incidents. Fortunately, so many of the Eindhoven residents spoke English that they were able to explain to the Americans who the police were. Jan Peter Boyens, a forty-three-year-old, English-speaking history teacher, defused one such potential tragedy. When Boyens asked the paratrooper what would have happened if he had not interceded, the American replied, "Oh, nothing much, just a little hole . . . between the eyes. I'm a very good shot, you know." This soldier and another trooper were sitting against a monastery wall and, in Boyens's recollection, they were "surrounded by six extremely affectionate Eindhoven girls." None of the girls spoke English, so, with Boyens acting as the translator, they set up dates for that night with two of the girls.

At the same time, members of the Dutch resistance, wearing armbands and brandishing whatever weapons they could scrounge, began circulating around. They got in touch with U.S. commanders, acted as guides, and briefed them on German troop movements (apparently a major force had been in Eindhoven the night before but had since marched, under cover of darkness, to Best, where they were fighting the 502nd). Some of the partisans exacted reprisals against collaborators. "The air seemed to reek with hate for the Germans," one staff officer later said. As was the case in so many other places around newly liberated Holland, they singled out women who had slept with Germans for especially humiliating treatment. They shaved their heads, confiscated their possessions, and paraded them through the streets while people stood and jeered. The Americans felt a mixture of revulsion and satisfaction when observing such spectacles. They figured that this was something for the Dutch to settle, and they generally remained aloof. Lieutenant Santasiero observed one such newly bald woman, whose clothes had been torn off, trotting under armed guard, clutching a black handbag. "It was a sad sight but funny the way she clung to her purse, since all she had on was a pair of high-heeled shoes." In another instance, Sergeant Elmer Gilbertson's squad watched in fascination as a crowd descended on three women and shaved their heads. The women looked at Gilbertson's group "and appealed to us for help, but we just stood and watched the show." The hatred in the air was so palpable that Gilbertson almost had the feeling that the people would have turned on his squad if they had interceded on behalf of the collaborators.

As Eindhoven celebrated, and the paratroopers prepared to spend the night in the city, regimental headquarters of the 506th made radio contact with the British. They found out that tanks of the Guards Armoured Division—the most powerful element of Horrocks's XXX Corps—were heavily engaged against well-placed eighty-eight-millimeter guns at Aalst, in the southern suburbs of Eindhoven. The British would need several more hours to destroy these resistance nests. In the meantime, a troop of five British reconnaissance vehicles under the command of Lieutenant Michael Palmer took a circuitous route to the west around Eindhoven, entered the town from the north, and made contact with Colonel Sink's command post in Woensel at 1215. This was the first linkup between XXX Corps and the 101st Airborne. The excitement was high on both sides. Sink and Brigadier General Gerald Higgins, the assistant division commander, personally greeted the British soldiers. The troop radioed back to their division: "Stable boys have contacted our feathered friends." In all likelihood, two of the vehicles of this troop continued on to Best, where they encountered Lieutenant Wierzbowski's platoon.

An hour later, an even more substantial communication link became available. With the Germans gone, Joke Lathouwers, an Eindhoven telephone operator, had the free run of the Dutch phone exchange. She called the Son police station (Son 244 was the number) to see if she could get in touch with the Americans. To her delight, an American voice answered.

She immediately patched the American-controlled line at Son through to British-controlled phone numbers in Aalst and Valkenswaard. "The telephone exchange between the troops had become a fact," she wrote in her diary. The Americans told the British about the capture of Eindhoven and, more important, about the blown bridge at Son. The British immediately made arrangements to move Bailey bridge equipment and their engineers to the head of their column so that, whenever XXX Corps made it through Eindhoven, the bridge builders would be in good position to reach Son first. All the while, Lathouwers listened proudly. "I can hardly describe what went through me all those hours," she said.

Later in the afternoon, the tanks at last subdued the resistance at Aalst and entered Eindhoven from the south amid delirious crowds. The vehicles crawled slowly through the humanity-lined streets. The celebration was raucous—people routinely climbed aboard the vehicles and hung on for the ride. The British soldiers enjoyed the welcome as much as their American partners. Eventually, the armor made contact with their "feathered friends" of the 101st Airborne Division. The first linkup of Market Garden had finally happened.[9]

CHAPTER 8

Landing Zones

Hundreds of feet above the struggle on the ground, just over the western horizon, a magisterial procession of aircraft was approaching. The long column stretched for miles over Holland. To observers on the ground, it almost seemed as if the sky were black with planes. In total, there were 1,336 American troop carrier aircraft, 340 British Stirlings, and 1,250 gliders. Some of the gliders were huge British-made Hamilcars, others British Horsas. The majority were American Wacos. They all traveled in carefully planned corridors along the previous day's northern route. About 1,100 of the planes contained British paratroopers or were towing gliders to reinforce the 1st Airborne Division at Arnhem. Some 450 Wacos, plus their C-47 tow planes, were headed for Drop Zone W (now dubbed Landing Zone W) in the 101st Airborne sector. Another 454 Wacos and an equal number of C-47s were on the way to the 82nd Airborne landing zones. A few miles behind them, 252 B-24 Liberators of the Eighth Air Force were in trail. Their task was to drop badly needed supplies to the two American airborne divisions. Above, below, and along the perimeter of this breathtaking aerial fleet, nearly four hundred fighters buzzed around, functioning in their normal role as bodyguards. If the sight of all these planes bordered on overwhelming, the noise of their engines was all-encompassing, like a steady, massive drone or even a protracted sonic boom.

Unlike the previous day, the Luftwaffe was not a no-show this time. In fact, the previous evening, in reaction to the news of the Market Garden landings, Hitler had met with his staff and ordered full-blown counterattacks on the ground and in the air. Nearly a hundred enemy fighters, one of which was an ME-262 jet, attempted to molest the great air fleet. The friendly fighters kept them at bay. Dogfights raged to the northeast of Arnhem and the east of Eindhoven. American pilots claimed to have shot down twenty-nine German fighters for the loss of four of their own. These lopsided assertions may or may not have been accurate, but that hardly mattered. What did matter was that no German fighter made it anywhere near the troop carrier armada.

Beyond the security concerns, the job of towing and flying so many gliders within such a tight air corridor was arduous for the aviators. "When you towed a glider, you went very slow," Captain Abe Friedman, a navigator on a C-47 crew, said, "so you'd rather not tow a glider. [They] have a lot of drag on your engines. The engines have to go full power. The pilots had to watch out for a lot of stuff." C-47 pilots had to concentrate on flying straight and level so as not to upset the attitude and flight path of their gliders. Glider pilots had to wrestle with their own craft to stay in proper position behind the tow plane. If they strayed too far above, below, or to the side of the C-47, they could lose control or stray into the plane's prop wash. "There is a steady physical pressure . . . required to keep the glider in level flight," one pilot later wrote. The fog and clouds were so thick along the fleet's flight path that it was not unusual for glider pilots to lose visual contact with their tow planes.

The gliders themselves were packed with cargo, vehicles, equipment, and troops, often to the point of overload. The unarmed Waco consisted of little more than a metal frame coated with a thin skin of nylon fabric. The floor was made of plywood. A pair of tires, sticking out from the belly, comprised the landing gear. The majority of the glider pilots had no communication with the crewmen of the tow planes. For the minority, coiled telephone wire wrapped around the nylon towing cord served as a crude form of communication.

As with the previous day's mission, few of the glider pilots had trained copilots with them. They simply chose a competent-looking airborne soldier, put him in the right seat, and quickly briefed him on how to fly the glider. Aboard one Waco, Lieutenant James Fox, a glider pilot in the 441st Troop Carrier Group, selected a sergeant who was in charge of a bazooka team. The aircraft was loaded with a jeep and accompanying supplies. "There's nothing to it," he told the skeptical sergeant. "It's just like driving a truck." Private Ralph Smith, a sniper in the 101st Airborne Division, had been chosen by his commander to accompany a jeep and its driver into LZ W. As paratroopers, Smith and the driver were already leery of riding in the rickety glider. As they flew along, the pilot turned and dispensed complicated instructions on how to land the Waco if he got hit. Smith and the jeep driver glanced at each other apprehensively and then looked at the pilot. "Sir, you can do the three of us one big favor," the jeep driver said. "Don't get hit!" By contrast, aboard another glider, the trooper whom Flight Officer Jack Merrick chose as a copilot was bragging that he could fly the plane with no problem. Merrick turned over the controls to him. "Within seconds he had the glider too low from the tow plane and off to the right," Merrick recalled. "I quickly swung the controls back to my side and got the glider back into position."

For the glider pilots, there was literally no such thing as a routine flight. The job required unbroken concentration and considerable stamina. "I would liken [it] to running the distance races . . . in the Olympics," Lieutenant Paul Tisdale, a glider pilot in the 437th Troop Carrier Group, said. In fact, by the time his glider was over Holland, he was already fighting exhaustion. "Every muscle ached from keeping that SOB in position . . . flying was like a wrestling match with the wheel & pedals. I was sopping wet from the effort." He had no copilot. Nor was there even anyone else aboard his glider. He was on his own. The turbulence created by so many hundreds of aircraft in such close proximity to one another only added to the strain. Flight Officer James Hopkins was also alone, carrying a seventy-five-millimeter howitzer and one hundred shells. "I passed the time by chewing an unlit cigar," he said. In practically no time, the cigar was only an inch long, "and I didn't spit once."

Flight Officer Frederick Gilliam was nervous himself, but he could tell that the troopers aboard his glider were even more tense. "I suggested that everyone should empty his bladder to increase his chances of survival should he be hit," Gilliam wrote. "The youngster in the copilot's seat told me in a strained voice that he couldn't get rid of a drop!!" Private First Class Don Rich and his squad mates from G Company of the 327th Glider Infantry Regiment had no such trouble. They carefully passed a latrine bucket along the long line of men sitting inside the glider. "We all chuckled as the young soldier who dumped the contents out the door was hit by them when the wind caused them to blow back into the glider," he later wrote. Turbulence soon buffeted the fragile glider, and several men retched into the empty bucket. On another Waco, Lieutenant Gale Ammerman began singing the first part of "Swinging on a Star," a song made popular by Bing Crosby. Although the buffeting of the glider and the whipping of the wind made it hard to hear, several of the troopers immediately behind him soon joined in. They finished this song and then launched into a rendition of "G.I. Jive," another popular song. "All of a sudden [this] seemed a little less dangerous place," Ammerman commented.

Elsewhere in the formation, Flight Officer Fred Lunde was flying a Waco with the words "Miss Iffy," chalked just below his pilot's window, in honor of his girlfriend. The glider was loaded with mines and several troopers from the 307th Airborne Engineer Battalion. In an effort to calm the engineers, who he could tell were uncomfortable, he affected a confident persona. However, when he retrieved a cigar from his jacket and put it to his lips, his hands shook. He glanced at the airborne corporal who was sitting in the copilot's seat and said, "Don't worry; I'll get you in and on the ground safely, and then you can help take care of me." If the corporal was impressed, he didn't show it. Other glider pilots were even more worried about surviving once they got on the ground. Farther along in the column, the pilot of Captain Adam Komosa's glider kept saying, "Captain, protect us against the krauts when we get there, will you?" After enough of this, Komosa, in exasperation, replied, "Look . . . land us in the right spot and you have my word, we will take good care of you. You're the boss in the air. I'll take over after we hit the ground."

There were 4,555 men aboard the planes and gliders heading for the American landing zones. Because there were no radio links between the aerial serials and the ground units, not one of them could communicate with the ground troopers below. As a result, those who were headed for the 82nd Airborne zones had no idea that some of them were in German hands. If that did not change—and in a hurry—they would be shot down in droves. Yet no one in the planes knew what might lie in store for them. Perhaps, just this once, ignorance really was bliss.[1]

On the ground, at the 82nd Airborne Division command post, General Gavin was listening to situation reports, feeling worried and frustrated. "With two battalions, the 505th was attempting to hold from Mook on its right to Kamp on its left a front of six or seven miles," he wrote. "It did this by establishing strong road blocks at key road intersections and small villages where the Germans would be expected to appear. The gaps were kept under surveillance by patrols." General Gavin was thankful that the Germans had not realized how shaky this front truly was. All morning long, the 505th troopers had staved off attacks on the various roadblocks, but the enemy made no serious attempts to rush through the gaps between the blocks. In one instance, artillery crewmen warded off an attack from a dozen self-propelled guns, destroying five of them. To the north, the 508th was also hanging on, but Gavin had had to reinforce them with two companies of engineers. To him, the German attacks seemed ad hoc, more typical of units hastily assembled and thrown into battle, rather than a well-planned, all-out push. This was correct. The attacking enemy unit, the 406th Infantry Division, consisted of paratroopers, middle-aged replacements, and Austrian Luftwaffe men who were training to be infantrymen, under the leadership of some experienced officers and NCOs, supported by a formidable mixture of antiaircraft guns and artillery pieces. They were not a threat to collapse the entire eastern flank of the 82nd Airborne Division, but many of them were on the landing zones, and it would take little effort for them to wreak havoc on the vulnerable gliders. Basically, Gavin knew that he had to clear them out of there or the gliders would face disaster. There was little time to lose. He ordered immediate counterattacks. The 505th would take back Landing Zone N near Groesbeek, and the 508th was to recapture Landing Zone T close to Wyler. Pathfinders had marked both drop zones with oversize signs of the appropriate letter.

With Lieutenant Hugo Olson, his aide, Gavin left the command post and set out on foot through the woods for Groesbeek to watch the counterattack. On the way there, they heard distant Germans yelling for them to halt. Instead of complying, Gavin and Olson simply picked up the pace and kept moving. When they were out of danger, a few silent moments passed as both men processed what had just happened. At last, the general broke the tension by saying, "You know, Olson, that would have been a hell of a thing if they captured us back there."

They made it safely to Groesbeek, where they took up station on the upper floor of a building to watch the fighting. As the general studied the beautiful open fields that comprised Landing Zone N, he could already hear shooting. "As I watched, I wished there were some way I could get word to the gliders so that they would not be surprised by the German fire immediately upon landing. I experienced a terrible feeling of helplessness." For Gavin, there was one bright spot, though. The original plan had called for the planes to arrive over the zones late in the morning, but weather had forced them to postpone takeoff by a few hours. Now, in the early afternoon, that proved to be a fortunate break. They were going to need every extra minute. Even as the general watched and worried, the troopers were moving through the woods, racing for the landing zones. Colonel William Ekman, commander of the 505th, had carefully timed his attack so as to seize the landing zone from the Germans to coincide almost exactly with the arrival of the planes. "We knew what we were going to do, when we were going to do it, and what was coming," he later said. "The enemy did not." Company C, under the command of Captain Anthony Stefanich, assumed the lead role of assaulting the landing zone. With sheer boldness, or perhaps reckless bravery, the troopers emerged from the woods and advanced right at the Germans over the flat fields. "The C Company troopers were firing and the Germans were running away from us," Lieutenant Jack Tallerday, the company executive officer, recalled. "It looked like a line of hunters in a rabbit drive, and the Germans looked like rabbits running in no particular direction." The sheer audacity of the attack scattered the Germans and pushed them east, toward the trees of the Reichswald and away from the vital landing zone. The Americans chased them away, killing some and capturing several others. One of the frightened prisoners raised his hands and said, "Me Austrian! No shoot!"

Not far away, a retreating German rifleman turned and fired a shot that hit Captain Stefanich in the chest, a couple inches from his heart. He had served with the outfit since North Africa. By all accounts, he was one of the most beloved officers in the entire division, a man who commanded universal respect. He was a champion boxer within the division, the sort of officer who led with a mixture of compassion and empathy. "Captain Stef," as the men called him, had proven his bravery in combat many times over. "It is difficult to put into words the love we felt for this man," Private Arthur "Dutch" Schultz, a BAR man, commented. "He was not only a symbol of leadership . . . he was a symbol of innocence." Stefanich was a PR person's dream come true. He did not drink, smoke, or chase women, and in garrison, he attended mass every morning. Badly wounded in Normandy, he had made it back to the company in time for Market Garden. During his convalescence, he had become engaged to a nurse named Mary Ann.

Now, as the attack wound to a conclusion, he lay seriously wounded, going into shock, with his lifeblood draining into the rich Dutch soil. Several of his platoon leaders and a medic clustered around him. They knew he was dying. Lieutenant Tallerday knelt down, grabbed the captain's hand, and leaned over him. The two men had gone to Officer Candidate School together and they were close friends. Stefanich looked at Tallerday and said, "Jack, take care of my troopers and the company; we've come a long way together and you are the best friend and officer I know. Give my love to my family and tell them I did my best. Tell Mary Ann I love her." Stefanich weakly squeezed Tallerday's hand, smiled slightly, and died. The medic, in tears, turned away, and raged, "He's gone. I couldn't help him." The scene was like something out of a war film, but it was all too genuine. "It happens in real life sometimes," Lieutenant Richard Brownlee, one of the platoon leaders, said.

Landing Zone N was now cleared. Company C had achieved its mission, but at a cost the men could never forget. It forced them, in the estimation of one sergeant, "to accept the hardly believable—that the Germans could kill such a capable, energetic, devout company commander." The bitter truth was that the captain's death brought each man face-to-face with his own vulnerability.[2]

Even as Stefanich breathed his last, the troopers of the 508th were carrying out a similar attack several hundred yards to the north, at Drop Zone T. The lead actors in this drama were the hardworking troopers of Lieutenant Colonel Warren's 1st Battalion. In a matter of a few hours, they had disengaged from their hard fight around the Keizer Karelplein and had hightailed it—not quite at a run, but almost at a trot—some five miles from inner Nijmegen, through the Berg en Dal woods, toward the open fields of the landing zone. In spite of the fatigue and disorientation of his soldiers, Warren was able to deploy his battalion into an attacking formation. He placed B Company on the left, C Company on the right. The battalion headquarters element trailed a few hundred yards behind them, followed by A Company, the unit that had absorbed the worst of the previous night's fighting in Nijmegen (recall that Captain Adams and an entire platoon were still cut off in the city). "The urgent need for speed and the promise of new action breathed spirit into the tired unit," Major Ben Delamater, the battalion executive officer, later wrote. "To be late would be tragic for the glierists soon to come in." The men experienced the sort of adrenaline surge that goes with combat, and this, at least for the time being, "dissipated the fatigue of the previous thirty hours' almost continual mental and physical strain." This was the purpose behind the grueling, physically exhausting training of the airborne. All of these paratroopers had endured similar fatigue and deprivation in their training, so the feeling was not new to them. They were prepared and programmed for just this sort of situation.

At the edge of the woods, they tore gaps through a heavy wire fence. From here they erupted out of the trees, into the clearing. All was quiet as they worked their way up to a slight rise. Beyond the little rise, along the many dips, swales, and gullies that peppered the fields, German soldiers were clustered around antiaircraft guns and machine guns. Some of these men had fought in World War I. One of the middle-aged men called out to an officer of the same age, "Captain, we've already stormed the Craoneer Heights in 1914!"

The officer replied, "Can't you see it's up to us old boys to run the whole show again; and we will do it exactly as we did then."

As the young paratroopers—many of whom were half the age of their adversaries—crested the rise and kept advancing, the Germans opened fire. The quacking of their twenty-millimeter guns mixed with the ripping sound of MG42s. Now began a free-for-all as the troopers closed in, at a dead run, on the enemy soldiers. "They moved across the fields firing at every possible target," an eyewitness later recalled. Some of the Americans shot from the hip, or paused to spot targets, or to take cover. Many simply descended on their enemies and shot them at point-blank range. "Col. Warren told me later that the attack looked like one of the Battalion field problems at the Infantry School, Fort Benning, Georgia," First Lieutenant

Woodrow Millsaps, the commander of B Company, wrote. One of Millsaps's men, Private First Class James Allardyce, was near the leading edge of the advance. "Everyone spread out in a skirmish line and soon we were all shooting and being shot at," he recalled. "I remember hearing the bullets whistle by and kick up the dust. A machine gun peppered the ground just in front of my face as I tried to squeeze into an obviously too small wagon rut to get cover." He got up and dashed over a slight rise, into a field of sugar beets. "Just as I slowed down, I got it in the right upper arm by a sniper." A medic dressed his wound and he drifted to the rear. Nearby, Private First Class Milton Mackney could distinctly hear machine gun bullets crack as they flew past his head. He dived for cover and then, after a moment, raised his head slightly to look around. "I . . . saw other troopers charging across the field; bullets were kicking up dirt among them, with some troopers hitting the ground and then rising to go forward," he recalled. "To me, it looked like a classic infantry charge they would have in the movies."

At the very point of the advance, Sergeant Jim Kurz was doing what an NCO should do—leading by example. When he and a few other soldiers reached a line of German-occupied foxholes, he positioned a machine gunner, Corporal Tony Mrozinski, to lay down cover fire while Kurz and his BAR man, Private First Class Chester Stanley, directly assaulted the holes. Stanley sprayed each hole with BAR fire. The Germans shot back with machine guns, rifles, and even a twenty-millimeter gun, but somehow none of the Americans were hit. Sergeant Kurz blasted them with single shots from his Colt .45 pistol. As he fired and moved, he kept wondering to himself, "How the hell can they keep missing?" Kurz and the two others destroyed two machine guns, killed several Germans, and prompted the survivors to surrender. Elsewhere, First Sergeant Leonard Funk of C Company was herding another group of prisoners through a cabbage patch when several enemy soldiers popped up several yards away. Some had their hands raised in surrender. Others opened fire. Funk swung his tommy gun and fired several bursts at them. "I heard the bullets from Funk's tommy gun ping on their helmets," Private Bob Mills said. "That only lasted a few seconds and then he had more prisoners."

In another spot, Lieutenant Millsaps and his men cornered a group of Germans in the cellar of a farm building. When they refused to surrender, Millsaps threw a Gammon grenade into the building. "Falling debris and the concussion knocked him flat but unhurt to the ground," Major Delamater related. "About ten Germans came running out, almost trampling him in their haste." Other paratroopers hurled more Gammon grenades inside. The rest of the enemy soldiers, about sixty in all, surrendered.

Warren's troopers, quite simply, overwhelmed the enemy soldiers with sheer aggressiveness and bloodlust. Only well-trained and well-led men, in peak physical condition, imbued with an intense fighting spirit, could have pulled this off, even against such a scratch force of enemy who had little armor or artillery support. The paratroopers destroyed or captured some sixteen antiaircraft guns, each one of which could have blown innumerable gliders out of the sky. The surviving Germans either surrendered or fled in panic. The 1st Battalion killed fifty enemy soldiers and captured 149 others. The battalion lost five men killed and ten wounded. The area was still under some German antiaircraft, machine gun, mortar, and artillery fire, but the paratroopers had done their job. The landing zones were under American control, and just in the nick of time. As the troopers cleared out the last of the enemy positions, they looked up and, in the recollection of one man, saw "the movie-thriller sight" of the gliders descending on the landing zone. Sergeant Kurz sat down and watched the incoming gliders with intense satisfaction. As the aircraft got closer, he took a moment and "thanked God we had cleared the field in time."[3]

A few hundred feet above Kurz, the men in the gliders had no idea that they had escaped disaster by such a slender margin. One by one, they cut themselves loose from their tow planes and began to descend, dodging enemy tracer rounds all the way. According to one aviator, the C-47s, after disgorging their gliders, "swept sharply upward and leftward to evacuate the flak-ridden area as quickly as possible." The enemy fire was thick and accurate enough to shoot down two C-47s after they released their Wacos. Fighters prowled on the fringes, ready as always to deal with the flak positions at a moment's notice. Lieutenant J. W. McAlister, a P-51 Mustang pilot, "came awful close to getting shot down by flak—got in the damned stuff and couldn't get out." At the same time, Captain Marvin Bledsoe, an experienced P-47 pilot in the 353rd Fighter Group, was zooming in at a low level, helping his wingman strafe a German truck, when he suddenly noticed the snout of a twenty-millimeter gun poke through a haystack and open fire at him.

Bledsoe had actually come to dread such encounters with flak gunners. His squadron had lost several pilots while supporting the landings the day before. He had spent much of the night tossing and turning, reflecting on those losses, worrying about the perils of strafing. Upon learning earlier this morning that he would fly cover for the glider landings, he had felt physically ill from fear, and had spent a full hour in the latrine trying to calm his queasy stomach. Now, his fear forgotten in the chaos of the moment, he glanced back, spotted the gun, and circled into position for a bomb run. "It was going to be difficult to drop our bombs without getting our fannies busted," he said. "I kept my dive as shallow as possible, and as I released my bombs I gave the ship full power." The concussion of the five-hundred-pound bomb was tremendous. He thought of a fellow pilot who had, the day before, dropped a bomb only to destroy the tail of his own plane and go down. Captain Bledsoe's plane held together, though he had no idea whether he'd destroyed the gun.

In direct contrast to Bledsoe's majestic P-47, the Wacos were rudimentary aircraft, designed for the most basic of tasks. But as they circled and swooped downward, there was a curious sort of grace about them. Theirs was the purest form of flight—no engine power, just wings and the wind. In that sense, they were like birds. When Flight Officer Frederick Gilliam released, "a solid wall" of tracers was belching upward from the landing zone below. "My glider had shrapnel and bullet holes but my landing was perfect." Flight Officer Morris Johnson maneuvered his Waco "through an opening in the trees that was about a city block wide. I figured I was in for a little trouble, because the field had been plowed recently and it was still rough. I landed as slow as I could manage and really had very little damage to the glider."

All of the glider pilots had been trained to land into the wind. This would make it easier to land with the nose upward, and the wind itself acted as a brake of sorts (all pilots worried about crashing into trees, buildings, fences, and ditches). Mindful of this, Flight Officer Fred Lunde turned his Waco into the wind and found a nice, sandy spot near a farmhouse, where he set the aircraft down quite easily. "The Germans were firing their 88 millimeter cannons onto the field as the gliders were landing," he later wrote. "[O]ne hit nearby causing our very quick exit from the glider." Typically, the sensation of landing felt like riding in a car, at full speed, over a bumpy field.

All around Landing Zones T and N, hundreds of gliders were touching down. "Some land on grass, others in a cloud of dust on freshly plowed fields," Lieutenant James "Buck" Dawson, an airborne officer, related in a present-tense account. "Some straight at a tree, a house, or a hill. Will they clear it? Some don't, but most of them do, some how lifting suddenly, almost miraculously, and then pointing down for a landing. Many nose over in a cloud of flying dirt and their heavy jeep, trailer or artillery piece tears loose in the crash to plow through the side of the flimsy glider." Lieutenant Dawson saw one glider cartwheel into a mass of twisted wreckage. Cases of artillery shells flew from the mess, landing twenty yards away. In his recollection, the fuselage was "twisted like a bar rag being wrung out." Yet, somehow, no one was hurt.

General Gavin, from his vantage point in Groesbeek, also watched the gliders cut loose, circle, and touch down. "As they landed, they raised tremendous clouds of dust, and the weapons fire increased over the area.

Some spun on one wing; others ended up on their noses or tipped over as they dug the glider nose in the earth in their desire to bring them to a quick stop." The general saw men emerge from the gliders. Some joined the paratroopers in shooting at unseen Germans, who were harassing the landings from a relatively ineffective distance. Others began to unload jeeps, trailers, artillery pieces, and cargo from the gliders. The men on the ground had to keep a sharp eye upward, lest they be hit by a landing glider. In one spot, a Waco smashed into a haystack, right above a foxhole occupied by Corporals Ted Johnson and Fritz Roggan. Fortunately for them, they were deep enough in their foxhole to avoid getting hit. They had to dig their way out, though. Private Herbert Smith, an artilleryman in D Battery, 376th Parachute Field Artillery Battalion, was not so lucky. The wing of one glider hit him in the back of the head and broke his neck, killing him instantly.[4]

Twenty-five miles to the southwest, at nearly the same moment, the first glider serials carrying 101st Airborne Division reinforcements were approaching Landing Zone W from the west. Like their comrades in the 82nd Airborne serials, they were under intermittent antiaircraft fire (and had been for much of the trip over Holland). In some spots, individual German soldiers lined up and fired at the planes with their rifles and machine guns. Seeing this, Colonel Joseph Harper, commander of the 327th Glider Infantry Regiment, and his jeep driver poked their personal weapons through a window of their glider and returned fire.

Serial A-35, leading the entire procession, took the brunt of the enemy fire. Brigadier General Anthony McAuliffe, the division artillery commander, was in the first glider, behind the lead C-47. "The flak was nerve wracking," McAuliffe later wrote to his wife, "got holes thru my jeep and my tug plane had its right engine shot out." The pilot of the C-47 tow plane was Colonel Bill Whitacre, commander of the 434th Troop Carrier Group. In an effort to save his own plane, Whitacre could have cast McAuliffe's glider loose over enemy territory. "I had visions of landing in a real hot spot," McAuliffe later admitted. Instead,

Colonel Whitacre hung on all the way into the landing zone before finally cutting him loose. Whitacre also managed to keep his own plane in the air.

Farther back in the same serial, Private First Class Don Rich was "scared for my life as the explosions continued to pound angrily around us, resulting in the glider being violently tossed around." The shooting sounded like the popping of popcorn. Airsickness was a problem aboard many similarly buffeting gliders. The airborne "copilot" on one Waco left his seat, went behind the trailer they were hauling, and retched his guts out. Then, without a word, he returned to his seat in the cockpit. "He was gritty and by willpower kept himself in shape," the pilot later told a debriefing officer. To combat such airsickness, antinausea pills had been issued. Because they could cause drowsiness or even dull the senses, General McAuliffe avoided them. His aide, on the other hand, took three and, according to the general, "went out of his head . . . he had to be knocked out."

Aboard another glider, Sergeant Robert Bowen could hear bullets tearing through the nylon fabric that covered the wings. A couple of rounds came up through the floor and glanced harmlessly off a pair of cloverleaves containing eighty-one-millimeter mortar ammunition. "Then there was a loud crack beside my head," Sergeant Bowen recalled. "I flinched and looked at Frank McFadden, one of my scouts, who was jammed against me. The bullet had torn through the fabric on the side of the glider, whistled between our heads, and exited out the roof." Bowen and McFadden exchanged weak, relieved grins. On another glider, a bullet hit a passel of mortar shells and started a fire. In case of such perils, each Waco was equipped with a fire extinguisher—the soldiers quickly grabbed it and put the fire out.

Farther back, in another serial, Flight Officer Shelton Rimer was wrestling so hard to keep his Waco under control that he felt like his arms might fall off. He could hear and see the enemy fire. To his right, the airborne soldier who was functioning as a nominal copilot put his hands over his face. "I'd like to have done the same," Rimer later deadpanned. As they neared the landing zone and prepared to cut loose, he saw a nearby glider "with its left wing shot off. Right before me I saw it come to pieces in midair and then crash. I was scared stiff." Lieutenant Paul Tisdale, who was flying his glider all alone, and using every bit of strength in his body to keep it flying straight, suddenly took a big hit at the tip of his right wing. The flak tore off a four-foot section of the wing and left his aileron dangling wildly in the wind. The glider rolled to the right and began to nose over. "I had to 'stand on' the left rudder with all my reserve strength and hold the wheel completely over to the right with brute effort to retain some semblance of upright flight."

Although the Germans were scoring hits on many of the C-47s and Wacos, their fire was nowhere near accurate or heavy enough to truly impede the landings. In successive waves, the gliders cut loose and began descending. Along the two-mile expanse of Landing Zone W, they made landfall in groups large and small. Rimer picked out what he considered to be a perfect field, saw it was already inundated with several other gliders, and chose another one nearby. "I landed in a potato patch beside a Dutch farmer's house," he wrote his wife. "The ground was so soft I didn't roll a hundred feet and my skids threw potatoes in all directions. The airborne was so tickled to be on the ground alive, I thought they'd beat my back in." Civilians came out of the house and greeted them warmly. Flight Officer Jack Merrick landed his Waco safely and brought it to a stop against a barbed-wire fence. Merrick was carrying a jeep and an airborne soldier. Together with the other soldier, he drove the jeep off the glider to an adjacent house. "I remember seeing a Dutch girl carrying a pail of milk to soldiers and she was dressed just like in pictures: big hat, baggy pants and wooden shoes," Merrick later wrote. General McAuliffe's Waco landed in a nice, flat field. As the glider skidded along the ground, the wheels came up through the floor. At last the plane came to a stop. No one was hurt. McAuliffe was a qualified paratrooper who had elected to land in the glider to demonstrate his support for the glider troopers. He later told General Taylor that, in future operations, he intended to jump into combat—he had had enough of riding gliders!

As Private First Class Rich's glider neared the ground, his entire squad of troopers looked at the floor and quietly prayed to themselves. "As the glider slowed down, each bump seemed bigger than the last as we bounced along in the air," he wrote. "The glider touched down and bumpily skidded through the field and after what seemed like minutes (but in fact was . . . not much over ten seconds) [it] came to a stop, right at the edge of a waterway." Rich and the others, including the pilot, breathed a big sigh of relief. When the glider carrying Technician Fourth Grade Alvin Karges, a radioman, landed on a beet field, he noticed that beets actually came right up through the flimsy floor of the rickety craft. The pilot fought to decrease their speed. As Karges stared, transfixed, at the pilot, he saw that he "was covered with beets and crap, right up through the floor." Somehow no one was hurt.

Not far away, Lieutenant Tisdale, through sheer strength and skill, managed to shepherd his wounded glider to the ground. At just the right moment, he pulled the wheel back, all the way into his gut, and set the bird down on an open field. "The force of the landing was great—like hitting the bottom of an elevator shaft out of control—and the radio jeep broke through the floor of the cargo compartment, not forward through the cockpit. The cargo was intact! And, oh, yes, I did pray en route. Like mad." The landing zone was under some small-arms and mortar fire, but this began to taper off as more and more gliders landed. The troops unloaded cargo and vehicles, assembled their squads as best they could, and began to converge on their rallying points. German opposition to the 101st landings was nowhere near as threatening as in the 82nd zones. The entire process took about two hours.[5]

The glider landings in both areas were remarkably successful. Out of 450 gliders, 428 reached Landing Zone W and its immediate environs. They safely disgorged 2,579 troops, including two full infantry battalions from the 327th Glider Infantry, 151 jeeps, 109 trailers (plus supplies), and two bulldozers. General Taylor now had most of his infantry on the ground, plus medics, engineers, artillerymen, signalmen, ordnance, and quartermaster specialists. Ten gliders never made it out of England—five disintegrated in flight; the others crashed for various reasons. Three more went down in the Channel; British air-sea rescue saved everyone aboard them. The rest crashed elsewhere in Holland or returned to England attached to damaged tow planes. The Germans shot down a pair of C-47s in the first serial—this group of planes faced the heaviest fire of all—and damaged another twenty-one others. Among the following eleven serials, two C-47s were shot down.

In the 82nd Airborne sector, where the opposition was more formidable, the results were no less remarkable. Some 385 gliders landed within the division's lines. Of the 212 bound for Landing Zone N, 150 landed within a half mile of their target. Ninety came down right on the recently contested Landing Zone T; seventy-one others landed a mile to the west. A few actually made landfall at Drop Zone O, on the 504th Parachute Infantry Regiment's drop zone of the previous day. Nineteen gliders set down in German-controlled territory; eight of these actually flew right over Landing Zone T and, much to the frustration of the watching paratroopers, kept going, right into Germany. Most of the men aboard those gliders made it back to the American lines, though. A handful of gliders went down in the Channel; the men inside were rescued by the ubiquitous air-sea crews. The Americans lost nine C-47s to flak on the approaches to the landing zones and above them. More than 90 percent of the returning aircraft were still operational. The other 10 percent were heavily damaged and needed extensive repairs, but all of them would fly again. Very few, if any, glider pilots were killed in the landings.

When General Gavin found out how much cargo and reinforcements the contested landings had brought his division, he was thrilled. "The courage of your pilots in the face of hostile fire was magnificent," he later told General Paul Williams, the troop carrier commander. Thanks to this courage, about fifteen hundred of Gavin's troopers were safely on the ground. The 319th Glider Field Artillery Battalion recovered all of its howitzers and twenty-six out of thirty-three jeeps. The 320th found eight out of twelve howitzers, along with twenty-nine out of thirty-nine jeeps. The 456th Parachute Field Artillery retrieved ten of its twelve guns, and twenty-three out of thirty-three jeeps. Battery B of the 80th Airborne Antiaircraft Battalion claimed all eight of its antitank guns. The engineers safely brought in every man, plus all of their jeeps. The Signals Company recovered eight out of ten jeeps and all of its soldiers. Gavin was later to comment that the successful landings "seemed almost a miracle."

Once on the ground, the duties of the American glider pilots were unclear. The British, who could scarcely afford to underutilize any manpower source, routinely cross-trained their glider pilots as infantrymen. Even now, these men were reinforcing the Arnhem perimeter. American glider jockeys labored under a completely different set of expectations. They were aviators first, last, and always. Their job was to fly, and they did it well. On land, they were proverbial fish out of water. Most had some weapons training, but few had any experience with infantry tactics or appreciation for ground warfare. Upon landing, they had standing orders to make their way back to airfields in Belgium and return to their groups in England. For the majority, this was difficult, especially in the 82nd Airborne sector, where the troopers had not yet even linked up with XXX Corps. It would take some as long as a week to drift back to Brussels and then to England.

In the meantime, many began drifting around, under loose command arrangements, trying to find ways to help their airborne brothers. They were courageous, well intentioned, and, at times, very helpful. Some fought as impromptu riflemen. Some helped out the medics. In many cases, the paratroopers put them to work guarding prisoners. Lieutenant Tisdale, who had laboriously piloted his wounded glider to a safe landing, joined nine other pilots in guarding several hundred German prisoners. The enemy soldiers were packed together in a small soccer field. The pilots wielded submachine guns. "Of course, the prisoners could have broken out at any time by swamping us with sheer numbers, so we cowed them as much as possible psychologically." They made the prisoners sit down close together with their heads down. Tisdale and the other pilots threatened to shoot anyone who raised his head more than a few feet. The rookie guards did not have enough food, water, or latrine facilities to properly care for the POWs. Nor did they have the necessary training to keep them under control. They were fortunate indeed that the prisoners did not try to escape en masse.

Mindful of perilous situations like this, some of the ground commanders, such as General Gavin, came to believe that the glider pilots were more of a hindrance than a help. "One thing in most urgent need of correction," he wrote a few days after the initial landings, "is the method of handling our glider pilots. I do not believe there is anyone in the combat area more eager and anxious to do the correct thing and yet so completely, individually and collectively, incapable of doing it than our glider pilots. Many of them arrived without blankets, some without rations and water, and a few improperly armed and equipped." Because they were members of the troop carrier command, they did not necessarily answer to ground commanders like Gavin, and that was a source of great frustration to him. "They frequently became involved in small unit actions to the extent that satisfied their passing curiosity, or [they] simply left to visit nearby towns. Glider pilots without unit assignment and improperly trained, aimlessly wandering about cause confusion and generally get in the way and have to be taken care of. I feel keenly that the glider pilot problem at the moment is one of our greatest unsolved problems. . . . Glider pilots must be well trained ground soldiers or they will not live long."

Gavin recommended that the pilots be assigned to specific ground units and go through training with them. Like the British, Gavin wanted to prepare them for a bona fide dual role as infantrymen and pilots. This did not happen during Market Garden or anytime thereafter. Here, in fact, was a conflict between the Army Air Forces—yearning for independence as a new branch of the service—and the ground army. The glider pilots came from the air force. They were autonomous from the ground units, and that was exactly the way their leaders wanted it. Troop carrier commanders would not hear of using their valuable pilots as infantrymen. A 52nd Troop Carrier Wing report, written about the same time as Gavin's, conceded that the pilots needed better weaponry and preparation to survive on the ground. But the airmen said nothing about using their pilots as infantry. Their greatest point of emphasis was that "a definite plan for the evacuation of glider pilots should be known by all concerned and should be carried out at once unless an emergency exists." There was no such plan during Market Garden.

Even had Gavin gotten what he wanted, it is doubtful that the glider pilots would have submitted to airborne-style discipline. They tended to be defiant, independent-minded daredevils. In the words of one pilot, "They were all mavericks. All glider pilots had been rejected somewhere and volunteered for this. [They] *chose* the most demanding and dangerous (as far as they knew) service available" in order to prove that they were as tough as anyone else. Lieutenant Tisdale, for instance, had been rejected from other flying jobs because he had 20/100 vision. He wore contact lenses while flying. He knew many others who had been washed out of fighter, bomber, or transport pilot training for disciplinary problems. They saw themselves as underdogs. "We were very close to one another emotionally," Tisdale said. "We had that 'go for broke' attitude, to an extraordinary degree. Glider pilots were . . . like jailbirds suddenly allowed to become astronauts. They simply would not play the Boy Scout, tin soldier game. They had a superb contempt for fatuous regulations and their handmaidens. They were like brothers should be—one for all and all against any 'outsider.'" As potential airborne infantry trainees, they would not have had a problem with courage. They had plenty of that. They would have had trouble, though, with the group-first mentality of the infantry, along with the requisite group cohesiveness and harsh, peer pressure–enforced internal discipline. The glider pilots were individuals, supremely self-confident. They were used to working in an environment of virtual autonomy. Even a rifle squad would have seemed like a big group to them. Perhaps it was for the best that they did not become more heavily involved in the ground fighting.[6]

Within minutes of the glider landings, the B-24s appeared over the landing zones in both divisional sectors. Instead of dropping bombs on the enemy, they were to drop supplies on the landing zones. A screen of fighter planes, acting as bodyguards, covered the heavies above and along the flanks of their supply runs. The planners had specifically chosen the B-24 groups because their Liberator bombers could, if stripped down properly, carry more cargo than the B-17s. Ground crewmen removed the ball turrets to create an opening from which to drop supplies. They then loaded the bomb bays and waists with twenty supply bundles containing such items as ammunition, K rations, medical supplies, and rifles. The average load on each plane totaled two tons. "The packages had static lines on them attached to the planes so that when they dropped, the static lines would open parachutes to help break their fall," Staff Sergeant Warren McPherson, a waist gunner in the 44th Bomb Group, explained. While bombardiers salvoed packages from the bomb bay, McPherson and several other crewmen were supposed to drop all their cargo through the hole where the ball turret had been. To supervise the drops, one drop master from the 2nd Quartermaster Battalion accompanied each B-24.

The previous day, the surprised bomber crewmen had been hastily trained to drop these cargo loads from low altitude, a brand-new experience for nearly all of them (quite a few of the youthful bomber boys had delighted in buzzing the farms of East Anglia from such low levels). The Liberator crewmen were used to flying over their targets at twenty thousand feet and upward. Now, as they overflew the landing zones, most were under five hundred feet. Some were as low as one hundred feet. "The silver giants with the multicolored names and mascots painted on their sides leisurely buzzed the men below as they confidently roared past," Lieutenant

Dawson said. The noise was deafening, like a wave of thunderclaps. The racket of high-performance engines echoed along the canals and dikes. Frightened farm animals scattered in every direction.

From here the war became very personal for the bomber crewmen, strikingly different from the psychological distance of high-altitude warfare. "All along our course, the Dutch people gather in groups to wave at us," one pilot related to a debriefer. "We're so low we can almost shake hands with them." Lieutenant F. C. "Hap" Chandler, a navigator in the 489th Bomb Group, had a good view of them from his perch in the nose of the plane. "The Dutch were all out in the middle of the street waving flags and cheering us on. I started seeing these pretty Dutch girls waving at us, so I took off my helmet." Another crewman looked down and saw half a dozen Dutchmen holding a flag with one hand and waving with their free hands. "It was a very moving sight and made me realize what we were fighting for," he said. "We were so low that we could see the expressions on their faces," Lieutenant E. T. Beniarian of the 93rd Bomb Group recalled. To Lieutenant Daniel Budd, a pilot in the 491st Bomb Group, it seemed as if everyone in Holland had taken to the streets to wave and cheer. "I could hardly speak from emotion," he later confided to his diary. "[W]hole towns were out in the yards waving. Old men and women and small kids, everyone waving their shirts, sticks with cloths on the ends, overjoyed people." In some cases, American ground troops looked up at the planes, waved, and cheered. Another aviator saw troopers "calmly smoking cigarettes, and going about their job in a businesslike manner." Lieutenant Samuel Syracuse, a bombardier in the 489th, peered through the nose of his B-24 and saw "our troops wildly waving to us. The entire area was jammed with gliders, some cracked up in landing. There were also hundreds of parachutes dotting the countryside."

The Germans, of course, were nowhere near as elated to see the low-flying fleet of bombers. Even as civilians and Allied soldiers cheered their arrival, the Germans began to shoot at them from practically every direction with everything from eighty-eight-millimeter flak guns to rifles. Because of range and accuracy factors, the most dangerous weapons were twenty-millimeter guns and machine guns. The airspeed of the bombers was slow, 150 miles per hour at the most, and they flew in straight vee formations, making perfect targets. The Germans could scarcely miss them. Flak began exploding uncomfortably close to many of the birds. Machine gun and rifle bullets clanked off the skin of numerous B-24s. The bullets made a curious sound, almost like gravel hitting sheet metal. Lieutenant Chandler, who had taken off his helmet to show off his looks to the cheering Dutch girls, now felt "like a jackass. Holes started coming in the airplane. I tried to crawl back in that damned helmet." He saw a line of Germans firing at his plane from the cover of some trees. An American .50-caliber machine gun, mounted on a jeep somewhere below, drove them off. For the first and only time in Lieutenant Manny Abrams's experience, he could actually see the men who were shooting at him. "I saw German soldiers with submachine guns, crouching on the ground, kneeling in the belfries, all firing away at the bomber stream," he said. "In turn, our waist and tail gunners were returning the fire with .50-caliber machine guns." The gunners had to be careful, though, not to hit the Dutch or friendly soldiers with their answering fire. "The Germans threw everything they had at us," one airman wisecracked. "Some of us were convinced they shot arrows and threw knives."

Few of the B-24s escaped damage. Wings were shot up. Fuel tanks were punctured. Hydraulic lines were severed. Turrets were damaged. Men were wounded by flying shards and small-caliber bullets alike. A concentrated string of machine gun fire nearly severed the rudder and elevator cables of one plane from the 491st flown by Lieutenant Eugene Scamahorn. "We had to leave the formation as we had considerable difficulty keeping up with the others," he later wrote in his diary. They dropped their load and limped away. A burst of flak exploded near the nose of another B-24, shattering the Plexiglas and wounding the navigator, Lieutenant Harold Clark. "Ned, I'm hit," he called over the intercom to the pilot, Lieutenant Edward "Ned" Twining. "Where are you hit?" Twining asked. "They shot me in the ass," Clark replied. Another crewman went to the nose, told Clark to drop his trousers, and tended to his wounds, even as the plane absorbed more hits.

Elsewhere, a major fusillade of fire raked through the entire expanse of Staff Sergeant Wilson Pitts's B-24. The waist section was riddled with bullets. The intercom and the hydraulics were shot away. Several men were wounded, including the quartermaster sergeant, who was standing right next to Pitts in the waist. "[He] had leg wounds and was bleeding profusely. I split his pant leg and applied a tourniquet to keep him from bleeding to death. I applied sulphur [*sic*] powder to the flesh torn badly by machine gun bullets." Outside, the wings of the plane were heavily damaged. A twenty-millimeter shell tore a hole through one of the flaps. Somehow the plane did not go down. Others did, though. During the drops, the Germans shot down nine B-24s. One of these planes, piloted by Lieutenant Wade Sewell, absorbed several major flak hits in the waist and the wings. "When the bomb bay doors failed to open, I knew something was probably seriously wrong," Lieutenant Adolph Bremer, the bombardier, later said. For a few moments, as they dropped their supply containers and pulled away for the trip home, it seemed as if the plane might be okay. Instead, one of their engines soon burst into flames. Sewell ordered everyone to bail out as the plane went down in enemy territory. Bremer, Sewell, and three others evaded capture. Three became prisoners. Three others were killed, including Corporal Nevin Johnson, a soldier from a ground unit in England who, against orders, had stowed away on the plane. Lieutenant James Gerow's B-24 was shot up so badly that he was soon down to two engines. He tried to fly the wounded plane to Brussels, but another enemy antiaircraft battery scored a hit on them and the plane caught fire. "I called the crew over the interphone to bail out," Gerow later said, "and pressed the warning bell." Two of the crewmen were killed while bailing out. Only two made it back to the Allied lines. The rest, including Gerow, became prisoners.

Amid the thick enemy fire, the B-24 crewmen began dropping their cargo. Bombardiers salvoed the supply canisters just as they would bombs. Quartermasters and waist gunners manhandled the bundles through ball turret holes. Tech Sergeant Frank Hostetter and his friend Staff Sergeant Boleslaw Gusciora (whom he simply called "Gus") were responsible for throwing out boxes of ammunition from the bomb bay catwalk. "The hydraulic reservoir in the bomb bay was hit by small-arms fire," Hostetter said. "The oil was about to drown poor Gus. He would take a swipe to clear his eye, then look to see if the supplies were still hanging on the bomb shackles." They dropped the ammunition and then plugged the hole with chewing gum. Obviously this was dangerous business. In one plane, a loadmaster was attempting to dislodge a stubborn bundle when he lost his footing. Captain Adam Komosa, safely on the ground now, watched in horror as the loadmaster "slipped through the bomb bay and plunged to his death." Nearby, Flight Officer Frederick Gilliam also watched the unfortunate man fall. "His screams never ceased until he hit the ground," Gilliam wrote sadly. Corporal Mickey Graves and a group of soldiers in the 504th Parachute Infantry Regiment headquarters watched grimly as the man's "squashed body was brought into the CP and covered with a chute."

All over the skies, parachutes blossomed from other B-24s and gently floated to the ground. The noise, the number of heavy bombers flying at such low altitude, and the panoply of chutes were all awe-inspiring, especially to the airborne troopers. "Colored nylon chutes . . . blue, orange, and white, float down with the much-needed food and ammunition bundles tied on," Lieutenant Dawson recounted. "Collapsing on the ground like huge mushrooms in Technicolor, these parachutes, along with those of the day before and the abundance of gliders, literally blanketed the fields."

Some crews had trouble finding the correct release points. Colonel Ezekiel Napier, for instance, took his 489th Bomb Group on three separate runs in an effort to locate the right place. "We got the hell shot out of us," Lieutenant Chandler said. "We were scared to death." This was especially true for the pilot of his plane, whom he thought of as a coward and a drunkard. The frightened pilot did not even bother to confirm that they were over the right spot. He ordered the bombardier and loadmaster to drop the load. "I don't think he gave a damn," Chandler said. "He just wanted to get out of there." Others were better-intentioned, but they were hopelessly disoriented or diverted by the ferocity of the German fire. Only half of the tonnage intended for the 101st Airborne Division was ever recovered by the soldiers of that outfit, and the majority of it was outside of Landing Zone W, the intended drop spot. The Germans helped themselves to the rest. The supply drop in the 82nd Airborne landing zone was more accurate. About 80 percent of the 258 tons was recovered by Gavin's men. The general considered these supplies "vital to our continued combat existence."

With their loads dropped, the B-24s turned away, gained altitude, and disappeared over the western horizon. Dozens were damaged, some so badly that they made crash landings at emergency fields. Four of these were no longer fit to fly. Ground crews managed to salvage the rest, in their usual industrious fashion. Many of the planes had wounded men aboard who required hospitalization. For the bomber crewmen, the mission was unforgettable—an oddly emotional glimpse into the world of ground combat, and one they would just as soon not revisit again. "I think the air crews all heaved a sigh of relief, leaving this kind of personal war behind," Lieutenant Abrams commented. Indeed, they did. The ground troops, on the other hand, had no such option. Their struggle continued.[7]

CHAPTER 9

Euphoria and Desperation

With the dawn came new hope. At Son, excited whoops could be heard as sappers of the 14th Field Squadron, Royal Engineers, put the finishing touches on a Bailey bridge over the Wilhelmina Canal on the morning of September 19. South of the canal, a column of reconnaissance cars, tanks, trucks, Bren carriers, and other vehicles were strung out in a long line along the N69 highway, where they had waited all night for the hardworking, bleary-eyed sappers to complete the bridge. Now crewmen shouted eagerly back and forth, urging one another to mount up and get ready to resume the advance. Engines turned over. The stench of gasoline fumes permeated the air. Dutch civilians stood alongside soldiers, American and British, watching the XXX Corps column spring to life. The scout cars led the way across the bridge; tanks soon followed, then the rest. One by one, each vehicle rolled over the bridge's slight incline, onto the cobblestone road, and then on to the north.

They roared through town after town in the 101st Airborne sector—Son, St. Oedenrode, Eerde, Veghel, and Uden. At each place, they were cheered and urged on by groups of Screamin' Eagle paratroopers, most of whom had spent over two days wondering when the XXX Corps tanks would reach them. Civilians also lined the road, excitedly waving and shouting at the British soldiers. The column moved at a brisk pace, sometimes as fast as thirty miles per hour, with the very dash Field Marshal

Montgomery had envisioned only a week and a half before, when he first conceived of Market Garden. The operation was a day and a half behind schedule, so there wasn't a moment to lose.

With drivers maintaining a prudent twenty to thirty yards' distance between vehicles, the column spanned well over two miles from start to finish. In a mere two hours, they reached Grave, where the welcoming crowds were especially large. Friars from the nearby St. Henricus Institute for the Blind clustered along the side of the road, waving and gesturing happily. Girls in long skirts, high socks, and button-down coats raised their arms in salute (to American eyes, the gesture almost resembled the touchdown symbol). Finally, at approximately 0830, the British guardsmen met up with their comrades from the 82nd Airborne Division. The all-American paratroopers were, of course, especially happy to see the British. To the troopers, the mighty fleet of vehicles represented two good developments. First, they were no longer cut off behind enemy lines, dependent solely on aerial resupply. Second, they now had friendly armor to help them deal with potential German counterattacks, armored or otherwise. As Lieutenant James Megellas stood alongside the road and watched the vehicles roar past him, he could scarcely imagine how any German force could hope to stop them. "Tanks, armored vehicles, half-tracks, mounted artillery pieces, mechanized vehicles of all types and sizes, and accompanying infantry paraded in a steady stream," he wrote. The veteran platoon leader had been fighting for nearly two years. The impressive column made him feel, for the first time, as though the end of the war was in sight.

Half a mile away, just outside of Overasselt, Generals Browning and Gavin regarded the approaching XXX Corps vehicles with similar excitement. They stood together at the edge of the road, poring over maps, chatting easily, and smiling like old friends. Yet somehow they were a study in contrasts. Browning wore a beret and an airborne smock with a small pair of binoculars draped over his chest. So impeccable was his battle dress that he wore a perfectly knotted tie at his throat. Periodically he puffed on a rapidly burning cigarette he was clutching between the index and middle fingers of his right hand. Gavin, the nonsmoker, held a pen and a map in his right hand. Like any other trooper, he wore Corcoran jump boots, parachute trousers, web gear, a jump jacket, and a helmet. Only the star on the front of his helmet and another on the shoulder of his jacket betrayed his rank. Gavin looked at the XXX Corps vehicles and beamed. "It is difficult to describe my feeling of elation at that moment," Gavin later wrote. With the British armor now at his disposal, he felt he could deal with anything the Germans might throw at him. "I was really living," he said.

Gavin and Browning soon organized a conference with Major General Allan Adair, commander of the Guards Armored Division, and two of his key commanders from the Grenadier Guards, Lieutenant Colonel Edward Goulburn of the 1st Motor Battalion (infantry) and Lieutenant Colonel Rodney Moore of the 2nd Armored Battalion. Goulburn, who had been fighting hard for two days while battling a deep, racking cough, was struck by Browning's immaculate countenance, "a contrast to our filthy appearance." General Browning, in his steady, articulate cadence, briefed the guard officers on the situation: "The 82nd Airborne Division holds the high ground southeast of Nijmegen. Their patrols have entered Nijmegen but they don't control the bridges there yet. Those bridges are still intact. There are quite a few Germans about and we're going to have to winkle them out with something stronger. The bridges must be taken today . . . at the latest tomorrow."

Everyone understood that "something stronger" meant tanks. Browning told them that he knew little about the 1st Airborne Division's situation at Arnhem—in fact, because of the radio problems, he had received only three nondescript communications from them—but it was clear that the sooner they linked up with the 1st Airborne, the better. General Adair was surprised that the paratroopers had not already captured the Nijmegen bridges. "I just assumed the bridge would be in airborne hands and when we arrived, we would sweep through." Gavin knew that the capture of the two Nijmegen bridges rested "squarely on my shoulders." The sketchy communications out of Arnhem could mean only that General Urquhart and the 1st Airborne were in trouble and needed help. With the arrival of XXX Corps, he now felt he could make a major push for the bridges. He proposed to attach the 2nd Battalion of the 505th Parachute Infantry to the two Grenadier Guards battalions for a thrust into Nijmegen. Gavin had supreme confidence in the 2nd Battalion and its commander, Lieutenant Colonel Ben Vandervoort. In fact, he thought of Vandervoort's outfit as the best in his division. For two days, he had held the battalion in reserve for just this kind of situation. He knew that his division was short of infantry, but he expected the 325th Glider Infantry Regiment to arrive the following day. In the meantime, he proposed to place one of Adair's other battalions from the Coldstream Guards to cover the sector previously held by Vandervoort. The British agreed with Gavin's concept. Now it was just a matter of working out the details.

As the commanders conferred, armored cars from the 2nd Household Cavalry Regiment continued north, along the planned Nijmegen route. They reached the damaged Honinghutje Bridge over the Maas-Waal Canal (or Bridge Number 10, as the Americans called it), which Lieutenant Lloyd Polette and other troopers from the 508th Parachute Infantry had captured the day before. Because this span was ideally located close enough to Nijmegen for a quick push through the city's western suburbs, the Market Garden planners had earmarked it as the main route of advance for XXX Corps. However, a contingent of Royal Engineers inspected the damaged girders of the steel bridge and determined that, although it could probably handle truck traffic, it was too heavily damaged to accommodate heavy armor. This superb reconnaissance and engineering work saved the main XXX Corps column much time and trouble. Instead of proceeding due north on the original route over Bridge Number 10, the column turned due east, through Overasselt, and crossed the Maas-Waal Canal over the Heumen bridge (Number 7 in American parlance), which B Company of the 504th Parachute Infantry had seized in the early hours of the first day. Once across the Heumen bridge, the vehicles turned left and headed north, along a route that led directly into Nijmegen. As they reached the little suburb of De Kluis, they began to slow down and reassemble for the big push. Through the trees, they could just make out the rooftops of the city. Beyond them, unseen, the bridges beckoned.[1]

Many miles to the south, in a dingy trench overlooking the carcass of the Best bridge at the Wilhelmina Canal, Lieutenant Ed Wierzbowski awoke to the sounds of shooting and yelling. It took the exhausted young platoon leader a few moments to shake the cobwebs of sleep from his brain. The previous night had been another long one for Wierzbowski and the survivors of his platoon, cut off behind the German lines in the Zonsche Forest. There had been one pleasant development, though: A platoon-size group under the leadership of Lieutenant Nick Mottola had broken through to them. Mottola and his men had dug themselves positions covering one of Wierzbowski's flanks. Wierzbowski and his people were so tired from their ordeal that, with Mottola's group standing watch over them, they had immediately gone to sleep. Now, as Wierzbowski looked around and began to focus on his surroundings, he realized that Mottola's platoon was under heavy attack. "I . . . saw men running, some of them jumping into the canal and crossing over to the other side, others just running off," Wierzbowski wrote, "some swimming and the others crawling along the wrecked bridge, the remainder running along the canal bank."

Then, just like that, they were all gone. Wierzbowski and his men were once again on their own. He reorganized them as best he could into makeshift fighting positions. The majority were wounded, some to the point where they could no longer even hold a rifle. They had almost no ammunition left. They had virtually no food and very little in the way of medical supplies. Their situation appeared hopeless, yet the able-bodied never even contemplated abandoning their wounded to make good their own escape. It was probably for the best that they did not know of two other cruel breaks they had suffered. The British armored cars that had spent most of the previous day covering them were gone. Their crews had seen Mottola's group arrive and, forming the impression that Wierzbowski was no longer cut off, they had left. In addition, another airborne patrol from E Company of the 2nd Battalion had made contact with them and promised to carry word of their plight to Lieutenant Colonel Chappuis at 2nd Battalion headquarters. Instead these men had spent most of the night wandering lost in the woods. By the time they got to Chappuis, they conveyed only the message that the Best bridge was gone. They mentioned nothing about Wierzbowski's situation.

Now, a thick morning mist hung over Wierzbowski's position. In that mist, he saw movement and then vague forms no more than twenty yards away. "More and more appeared until I knew we were completely surrounded," he recalled. "Yelling a warning to the men, I redied [sic] a grenade as were the others also doing." As Wierzbowski and Sergeant Thomas Betras tossed outgoing grenades, several German potato masher stick grenades landed all around them. Two of them rolled into a foxhole. Betras and another man grabbed them and threw them back. Another exploded harmlessly. Still another exploded next to a machine gun, right in the face of Technician Fifth Grade Vincent Laino. "It blew his eye out and blinded his other eye," Wierzbowski recalled, "leaving his face a bloody pulp." Laino called out to the lieutenant, asking whether his remaining eye was destroyed. "No, it's fine," Lieutenant Wierzbowski lied. "You can't see because there's blood in your eye." Nearby, a bullet ripped through Private Lawrence Koller's temple. He groaned, slumped over, and died. Another potato masher sailed over Wierzbowski's head and hit Laino in the knee. The blind trooper groped desperately for it, found it, and threw it back just before it exploded.

A second later, a potato masher landed in the trench, only a foot away from Wierzbowski, right next to Private First Class Joe Mann. The intrepid Mann still had his arms immobilized in slings, owing to the bullet wounds he had received the day before. Alongside Mann were several other wounded soldiers. He yelled, "Grenade!" As Wierzbowski turned to look, he saw Mann "deliberately slide his back on the grenade, covering it with his back. In that instant the grenade exploded into his back." Small fragments inflicted minor wounds on the lieutenant and two other men, but Mann absorbed the brunt of the blast. Wierzbowski took Mann by the shoulders. The young private looked at his platoon leader and said, "Lieutenant, my back's gone." He eased back, closed his eyes, and died. Mann had laid down his life so that those men around him could live. "I can think of no words to aptly describe his sacrifice or heroism," Wierzbowski later commented. Mann earned the Medal of Honor, not just for jumping on the grenade, but for his conspicuous bravery during the platoon's entire three-day ordeal.

In the meantime, the Germans were closing in and the Americans were out of ammo. They now faced annihilation or captivity. The men called to Wierzbowski, asking whether they should keep fighting or give up. At last, the lieutenant reluctantly gave the order to give up. "Okay, this is the time," he said. Private Tony Waldt placed a dirty white handkerchief on the end of his empty carbine and waved it as a sign of surrender. The shooting stopped and the Germans descended on them. The two enemy medics, who had shared the platoon's ordeal for more than a day, pleaded with their countrymen to spare the lives of Wierzbowski's survivors and they complied. The lieutenant and his men raised their hands, climbed out of their holes, and began, under the watchful eyes of their captors, to troop away. In the distance, from the direction of the forest, they heard much shooting, as if a major firefight were going on. They put their heads down and walked in the other direction.

As the Wierzbowski platoon trudged away with their captors, a massive 101st Airborne attack was already under way to clear the Germans from the Zonsche Forest and Best area. General Taylor ordered two battalions from the 327th Glider Infantry, along with both of the 502nd battalions already fighting in the forest, to attack. They were supported by newly arrived Cromwell tanks from the 15/19 Hussars. For the paratroopers, the presence of the tanks was electrifying. Many of the 502nd men had been fighting amid the trees since the afternoon of drop day. They had yearned for the support of heavier weaponry and now they had it. "It seemed everyone leaped out of their holes as if ejected by some force at the same time," said Private First Class Emmert Parmley, who had lost his highly regarded platoon leader the day before. "We were all yelling and were going to charge." Instead the British tank commander calmly told them to stay put while his Cromwells hosed down the German positions. As they fired round after round, white flags appeared, seemingly out of nowhere. German soldiers began surrendering in droves. Soon there were so many that, in Parmley's recollection, "we just motioned them to the rear."

In fact, after nearly two days of hard fighting, the German 59th Infantry Division was ready to crack. Throughout the morning and early afternoon of September 19, the paratroopers, glider infantry soldiers, and British tankers bashed through the collapsing German front. Here and there sharp firefights raged but, in the main, the enemy soldiers were in no mood to fight. Most gave up at the first opportunity. At the same time, more American reinforcements arrived by glider on Landing Zone W. This glider lift consisted of the 1st Battalion of the 327th Glider Infantry, plus the artillery and antitank battalions that Taylor had eschewed in favor of his infantry. Dense fog and poor weather severely hindered the landings (far more so than enemy opposition), and only 209 out of 385 gliders made it to the landing zone. Even so, these reinforcements, combined with the division's powerful attack, were simply too much for the makeshift 59th Infantry Division. German resistance around Best petered out and then died altogether. "They came in groups of fifty to sixty from all directions," Corporal Pete Santini of the 502nd recalled. "We held our fire and allowed as many to surrender as wanted. They were lined up and thoroughly searched for concealed weapons. I estimate there were between five and six hundred of them." At the height of the surrenders, Major John Stopka, who had taken over command of the 3rd Battalion, 502nd Parachute Infantry, after Lieutenant Colonel Cole's death, excitedly radioed regiment, "Send us all the MPs [Military Police] available," to deal with the droves of prisoners. Private First Class Don Rich's G Company of the 327th Glider Infantry alone captured 159 enemy soldiers. One of them, a middle-aged conscript, walked up to Rich, sobbed, and began pleading with him. "He didn't want to fight. Through the blubbering tears, it was clear he thought I would kill him." Instead, Rich walked him to the rear and turned him over to troopers who were guarding a group of POWs.

In all, the 101st Airborne captured some fifteen hundred German soldiers and shattered the offensive effectiveness of the 59th Infantry Division. In pondering the sudden capitulation of soldiers who had fought quite well for nearly two days, the 101st Airborne historian theorized that "most of these men, battle-weary and confused, had just retreated across France and Belgium. Initial success cheered them. But they were queasy about fighting paratroopers. And when they heard the tanks as well, it was just too much." At Best, the Americans had hoped to capture a nice alternate crossing route over the Wilhelmina Canal. Instead they had become enmeshed in an ancillary fight to hold the western flank of their corridor. In the process, they chewed up the better part of an enemy division whose soldiers, in the view of one airborne officer, "had to be defeated somewhere" before they could make trouble in another sector.

One happy by-product of the division's victory on September 19 was the liberation of Lieutenant Wierzbowski and the remnants of his platoon. After they were captured, the Germans had taken them to a field hospital. From there, they could hear the approaching sounds of the battle. The booming of tank guns from very close range made it very clear to the captors and prisoners alike that Allied forces were close. Through subterfuge, Wierzbowski and a few of his men got their hands on some German weapons and took their former captors prisoner. The Wierzbowski platoon was still holding these prisoners when American troops arrived and officially liberated their fellow paratroopers. "Just as we went in," Lieutenant Wierzbowski later recounted with pride, "we came out, strictly on our own." Back in England a few days before, when the platoon had playfully engaged in a pickup football game, they had had enough players to fill out three complete teams. Now, as they returned to the American lines, there were six members of the platoon left, and three of them were wounded.[2]

With the XXX Corps–airborne linkups, a distinct Allied salient now knifed north for nearly fifty miles along the main Dutch roads, from the Belgian border to the Nijmegen suburbs. For the Germans, the bad news was that their forces along the corridor were now cut in two, making communication and coordination on either side of the divide quite difficult (plus they were soon to come under pressure from British VIII and XII corps attacks that were designed to protect the flanks of XXX Corps). The good news for the Germans was that they enjoyed significant freedom of movement along either side of the Allied-controlled salient and could attack it from any direction. Moreover, the salient was so thin and, in some spots, so lightly held that it was quite vulnerable to being cut by German attacks.

In the afternoon of September 19, the first of many such German attempts to sever the corridor—or "Hell's Highway," as the Americans were already calling it—unfolded. The 107th Panzer Brigade, under the command of Major Freiherr von Maltzahn, was a powerful formation. It consisted of thirty-six Mark V Panther tanks, eleven Panzerjäger IVs, a battalion of panzer grenadiers in half-tracks, a self-propelled assault gun company, and several antiaircraft guns, along with some engineers and support troops. Originally, the German high command planned to use the brigade to stave off American attempts to take the western German city of Aachen. Instead, in fulfillment of Hitler's order to snuff out Market Garden with all available strength, the brigade was rerouted by train to Holland, where they off-loaded their vehicles on September 18. Under cover of fog, the 107th spent most of September 19 rumbling noisily and tortuously through the narrow streets of villages, from Venlo to Helmond. At Helmond, six miles to the east of Son, they were reinforced by a battalion of German paratroopers. Von Maltzahn's plan was to capture and destroy the new Allied Bailey bridge at Son, and thus choke off the entire Market

Garden operation. He expected help from the 59th Infantry Division on the other side of the corridor, but, after their debacle at Best, they were obviously in no position to do anything.

The terrain between Helmond and Son was not well suited for armor. The ground was honeycombed with canals, dikes, and marshes. Because of this, Major von Maltzahn could not spread his brigade out for an all-out assault on the bridge, the road, and the town. Instead, he was forced to lead his attack with only a few tanks and some dismounted panzer grenadiers over a narrow spit of ground alongside the Wilhelmina Canal. Basically, this amounted to a reconnaissance in force. The lead Panthers crept out of the trees, just a few hundred yards east of the bridge, on the south side of the canal, and opened fire. Only a small force, consisting of a platoon from A Company, 506th Parachute Infantry Regiment, and some engineers, was holding the bridge. Division headquarters was situated in a schoolhouse at the eastern edge of Son. The division hospital was on the other side of town, just west of the road.

A shell hit a British supply truck on the bridge, setting it on fire. Oily smoke billowed from the wrecked truck. Other shells screamed into the town, scoring several direct hits on the division CP. Technician Fourth Grade George Koskimaki, a radioman for General Taylor, saw the tanks and ran inside to warn the command group. "As soon as I got into the building, a shell crashed through the tile roof as I handed the message to an aide," he later wrote in his diary. "[T]hey also fired on the observer who was in the tower beside the headquarters building. He came down in a hurry." Technician Fourth Grade Robert Schmitz, another radioman, was outside in the schoolyard eating when the shells came in. He took off for any cover he could find and ended up with a group of engineers. Near the bridge, Corporal Charles Shoemaker of A Company could actually see the leading Panther a couple hundred yards away. "He looked about the size of a house!" From the schoolhouse to the bridge, the Americans shot back with machine guns and rifles, forcing the enemy infantrymen to take cover at a distance from their tanks. Bullets bounced off several houses in Son, pockmarking them and kicking up dust. Tracer rounds skipped along the road.

As many as five tank shells hit the schoolhouse. In the midst of this, General Taylor emerged from the building to see for himself what was going on. Not long before the shooting started, he had actually received reports from Dutch resistance sources and his own reconnaissance platoon that armor was approaching from the east. He had wondered whether the tanks were from the British VIII Corps, advancing on the eastern flank of the Allied corridor. Taylor's own eyes confirmed that the tanks were not British. He had little at hand with which to defend his command post, so he used anyone he could grab. In addition to headquarters troops, he had some glider pilots and staff officers, including Lieutenant Frederick "Ted" Starrett, General McAuliffe's aide who had taken too many antiair-sickness pills the day before. Taylor sent Starrett, Lieutenant Colonel Ned Moore, the division personnel officer, a Dutch liaison officer, a few other men, and a bazooka team on an expedition to take out the German tanks. They crossed the bridge and roamed the trees on the south side of the canal, engaging in close encounters with the Germans, to very little effect. At one point, a soldier from A Company was in danger of being overrun by the panzer grenadiers. He ducked down and threw a half-eaten apple at them in hopes they would think it was a grenade. The Germans halted and dived for cover, long enough for him to make his getaway.

In the meantime, General Taylor went to Landing Zone W and retrieved some men from the 1st Battalion, 327th Glider Infantry Regiment, along with a fifty-seven-millimeter antitank gun and crewmen from B Battery, 81st Airborne Antitank Battalion, all of whom were fresh from a glider landing only a couple hours earlier. The crew, under the supervision of Captain Alphonse Gueymard, the battery commander, rolled the gun into position behind a house near the bridge and opened fire on the lead tank. All the while, they were under small-arms fire. Some of the crewmen returned fire with their carbines while their comrades loaded the gun. "Our first round disabled the tank and the crew jumped out and disappeared," Gueymard recalled. "Several other rounds were fired for good measure." The lead tank soon caught fire. Not long after this, a bazooka team hit and disabled another tank. It too brewed up. Flames licked at the turret. Ammo began to cook off. Major von Maltzahn ordered a retreat, lest he lose any more tanks.

The Germans had missed an opportunity to choke off the Son bridge-head while it was still weakly defended. In the hours following the German retreat, Taylor reinforced the bridge defenses with most of the 1st Battalion, 327th Glider Infantry, several more guns from the 81st, and the 1st Battalion, 506th Parachute Infantry (he also made arrangements to relocate his command post to a more secure spot). Even though the Americans had turned back von Maltzahn's attack, it sounded an ominous note for any Allied soldier who cared to ponder the full implications of it. The attack on the Son bridge was the first indicator that the Germans could attack the corridor, in practically any spot of their choosing, and with relative surprise. It meant they could cut Hell's Highway and choke off the entire Market Garden advance.[3]

Thirty miles north of Son, outside the Sionshof Hotel, Nijmegen's streets were filled with the sounds of clanking treads, roaring engines, and high-spirited shouts. Morning fog and clouds had given way to a warm layer of late-afternoon sunshine. Groups of ten or a dozen paratroopers were clustered atop British tanks. Other American troopers were dismounted, milling around the vehicles. Interspersed among the tanks were Bren carriers, each of them filled with British infantrymen. British and American commanders had spent much of the day organizing their push for the Nijmegen bridges. There were two mixed columns of Grenadier Guardsmen and 505th Parachute Infantry paratroopers. In one column, the troopers of D Company, 505th, joined a troop of five Sherman tanks from the 2nd Armored Battalion, and a platoon of motorized infantrymen from Lieutenant Colonel Goulburn's 1st Motor Battalion. Commanded by

Captain John Neville, a British officer, the column's mission was to seize the railroad bridge. The other column was larger, consisting of about twenty British tanks, an understrength company of motorized infantry, and the balance of Lieutenant Colonel Vandervoort's 2nd Battalion of the 505th, including his Headquarters Company, weapons platoons, as well as E and F companies. Vandervoort put E Company in the lead, with F Company trailing. The job of this group, of course, was to capture the main objective—the Nijmegen road bridge. Because Dutch resistance operatives still insisted that the bridge's demolition controls were in the post office, and no one had any idea that Captain Jonathan Adams's group from A Company, 508th Parachute Infantry, had already overrun the building, the commanders earmarked a portion of this column to take the post office. A troop of tanks plus three infantry platoons (two British and one American) received this task. They would all start out as one column and then split up once they moved deeper into the city.

Inside the Sionshof, Captain Arie "Harry" Bestebreurtje, the Dutch Jedburgh leader, chose several resistance men to act as guides for the various columns. One of the guides was the ubiquitous Geert van Hees, who had led Lieutenant Colonel Shields Warren's 1st Battalion, 508th Parachute Infantry Regiment, into Nijmegen on the first night of Market Garden. In the confusion of that first night's fighting, Van Hees had become separated from the 508th troopers (prompting years of unfounded suspicion among some of them that he was a traitor). Now he was back in action with the 505th. Truly the columns represented not just a combined arms effort, but an Allied undertaking. The Dutch functioned as the eyes and ears. The British, with their heavy armor, were the powerful fists. The Americans comprised the legs and sinews of the effort.

After an abortive strafing attack from a single German fighter plane, the column rumbled away from the Sionshof along tree-lined Groesbeekseweg, the same route Warren's men had taken. Each vehicle maintained a distance of thirty or forty yards from its nearest neighbor. The pace was slow, no more than five or ten miles per hour. Some of the paratroopers spread out and walked along the flanks, looking for trouble. In some instances, they employed horses and carts to carry machine gun or mortar ammunition. At times, the column halted while the crewmen of leading vehicles verified directions or paratroopers checked for enemy soldiers in suspicious-looking buildings. They did not know that they were unlikely to encounter much opposition until they approached to within a half mile of the bridges, where the Germans had concentrated their defenses. The Dutch had provided good information to the commanders on the German dispositions. The road bridge alone was defended by somewhere between five and seven hundred SS men who were dug in along its approaches. They were equipped with machine guns and mortars and supported by antitank guns, armor, and even some artillery on the north side of the river. This information did not seep down to the soldiers. "We went into the city cold," Sergeant Spencer Wurst, a squad leader in F Company, recalled. "We were absolutely ignorant. We had no information whatsoever on the situation." In his case, he had not even seen a map of the city. Nor did he know anything about the bridge defenses. "We were going into urban street fighting . . . with no idea as to the size or layout of the streets."

Inside one of the British tanks, Robbert Smulders, a Dutch guide, heard "a cacophony of sounds, music, voices, and information broadcasts." When the music started up, "the men in the tank would join in and hum the tune." The three lead tanks were named after the Three Musketeers—*d'Artagnan*, *Porthos*, and *Aramis*. As was practically standard by now around the areas of Holland affected by Market Garden, excited civilians emerged from homes to greet the Allied soldiers. The tank crewmen and infantrymen shook hands and engaged in a few pleasant conversations but they kept moving. On one street corner, when the column temporarily halted, a group of civilians celebrated the Allied presence by clumsily playing out-of-tune brass instruments. Captain Robert Franco, Vandervoort's battalion surgeon, sat in the passenger seat of his jeep, glumly listening to their sorry sounds. They seemed so enthusiastic that Franco did not want to risk offending them by telling them to cease and desist. Yet he wondered how much more of their screeching he could take. From a Bren carrier just in front of his jeep, a tall British soldier caught his eye and said, "A bit grim, isn't it?" Franco could only laugh and agree wholeheartedly.

The advance resumed and continued past the Krayenhoff barracks. German artillery, accurate enough to wound several men and kill at least one, began to rain down. The column kept moving. At a vee in the road, the vehicles split into the three preplanned columns—the main column turned right, or eastward, onto Groesbeeksedwarsweg; another swung west toward the railroad bridge; the smallest group bore left and headed for the post office. The latter column easily made it to the objective. The only opposition came from a small antitank gun, which the tanks quickly destroyed. When the infantrymen stormed the post office, they found, in a repeat of Captain Adams's experience on the evening of September 17, no obvious demolition controls (for good reason, because there were none there). Major George Thorne, the British officer in command, tried to push east, toward the Keizer Lodewijk Plein, the roundabout that led to the road bridge. But his vehicles were halted by intense eighty-eight-millimeter fire. The shells set several houses on fire and inflicted nine casualties on Thorne's force. He and his men retreated to the vicinity of the post office, where the tanks set up at street corners and the infantrymen fanned out into surrounding buildings. Gerardus Groothuijsse, a Dutch resistance fighter, joined with a group of British soldiers to capture several drunk SS men, one of whom was an officer, in a nearby building. When the officer realized that Groothuijsse was a partisan, he called him a terrorist and hinted that, when the Germans regained control of Nijmegen, he and his fellow terrorists would "be taken care of good and proper" by the returning SS. A British guardsman, whom Groothuijsse knew only as "George," overheard these threats and ordered the SS officer to come with him. After a while, George returned with a German watch and offered it to Groothuijsse as a souvenir. "I then went out to take a look at where George had gone with the German," the Dutchman later wrote. "I found [him] in Julianapark. He was dead."

Meanwhile, to the west, Captain Neville's column was rolling along Oude Heselaan, to within striking distance of the railroad bridge. The troopers were dismounted and, in the recollection of one soldier, "staying on the sides of the street in order to give the tanks fields of fire." The tanks were situated in the middle of the street. At one corner, an elderly Dutchman stood in the doorway of his house with a coffeepot in one hand and a cup in the other, offering drinks to the soldiers. Several soldiers took sips and thanked him. As they neared the railroad overpass, or embankment, that led to the bridge, they began to take small-arms and machine gun fire from German soldiers who were dug in around the railroad tracks or hiding in boxcars. Up ahead, at an intersection, the soldiers spotted what they thought was a tank but was probably a self-propelled gun.

Captain Neville, mindful of his mission, ordered an all-out push for the bridge. "The plan was simple, if unimaginative," he later wrote. "Three tanks were to charge the opening in the embankment while the other two gave covering fire. At the same time the Americans, aided by the infantry carriers, were to gain the embankment from the south, and drive out the machine gunners from the flank." The problem was that the enemy's defenses were nearly impenetrable for Neville's small force of five tanks, three carriers, and just over a company of infantry. An entire Kampfgruppe—battalion size, by Allied standards—of 750 to a thousand soldiers was deployed in the blocks that led to the bridge. Interestingly, many of these German soldiers had participated in the defense of the Honinghutje bridge the day before against Lieutenant Lloyd Polette and his partners. Now, in Nijmegen, these Germans were supported by several antitank guns, flak guns, and a pair of self-propelled guns, plus presighted artillery from across the river.

As the tanks attempted to charge through the underpass, they came under withering artillery fire. "The leading tank was hit and destroyed immediately," Neville recalled, "and the next was hit immediately afterward. All but one of the crew in the leading tank were killed, and my own driver, contrary to orders and with misplaced bravery, jumped out of my tank and went to the rescue of those trapped." He saved several crewmen but sustained serious burns. More artillery, combined with shells from the flak guns, only added to the crisis.

While the surviving tanks backed up to escape the kill zone, the infantry brawled with groups of enemy soldiers in the area around the overpass and the nearby Kronenburger Park. The fighting was more akin to a small-unit struggle for survival rather than any cohesive attempt to seize the bridge. Staff Sergeant Paul Nunan remembered that the park suddenly came alive with "tracer slugs . . . there seemed to be three colors of tracer, red, orange, and light greenish color." A machine gun opened up from somewhere on the left. Around another corner, a twenty-millimeter crew added their shells to the mix. Sniper fire came from surrounding buildings. Lieutenant Russ Parker popped into the open and sprayed the rooftops with Thompson submachine gun fire. As he fired, he chewed heavily on a cigar. Nunan and another NCO, Sergeant Herbert Buffalo Boy, a Sioux tribesman from one of the Dakota states, added fire of their own. Nunan spotted the twenty-millimeter gun and a saw a German huddling for cover behind a nearby utility pole. He loosed a burst of Thompson fire at the pole but could not tell whether he hit the enemy soldier. A few yards to his left, he saw Private First Class Robert Robinson, a .30-caliber machine gunner, caught in the open as he displaced. Robinson actually swung the gun around and fired it from the hip, mowing down five German soldiers who were probably crewing the twenty-millimeter gun. A bazooka team fired a rocket that exploded near the twenty-millimeter gun. Soon after, Nunan sneaked up close to the gun and pitched a Gammon grenade at it. "It exploded on the gun with a roar. I turned to rejoin my platoon and felt a blow at the back of my left knee as though I had been struck with a club. I went down on the sidewalk and quickly got up." A bullet had nicked a tendon behind his knee. He limped back to platoon headquarters in the yard of a house about a block away. As German artillery shells roared in, a medic cut off his trousers and bandaged up Nunan's knee. The sergeant began to shake violently from the shock of his wound, the ferocity of the fighting, and the sudden chill of the air.

By the time Nunan lay wounded, shaking with the trauma of a combat wound, Captain Neville had already sensed the enemy's strength around the railroad bridge. He ordered the group to pull back and consolidate into a defensive position. "We placed our three remaining tanks in strategic places and everyone else took cover in the adjoining houses," he said. "There were about six seriously wounded men who probably would not have survived without medical treatment [whom] I decided to send back in a carrier."

Near the railroad tracks, as Lieutenant Waverly Wray, the executive officer of D Company, was pulling back with a group of a half dozen soldiers, a sniper opened fire, killing him and another soldier. Wray had been with the division since North Africa and was so brave, and such a larger-than-life personality, that he had become something of a legend among the troops. He had earned the Distinguished Service Cross for conspicuous bravery at Ste.-Mère-Église in Normandy. General Gavin and Lieutenant Colonel Vandervoort both thought of him as one of the very best lieutenants in the entire division. He was one of the few airborne types who did not drink, smoke, or even curse. The strongest epithet the deeply religious Mississippian would utter was "John Brown!"—the name of the famous abolitionist who had attempted to incite a slave uprising in 1859. Brown's name may have been reviled to Southerners like Wray, but it hardly compared with the usual four-letter fare so common among the paratroopers. Wray had a reputation as a true killer in combat, but one who somehow never lost sight of the enemy's humanity. Once, in Normandy, he had personally crawled into no-man's-land to bury the body of a dead German. Lieutenant Wray, upon returning to his own foxhole, had pulled out his Bible and said a prayer for the dead German soldier. Like everyone else in D Company, when Sergeant Nunan heard of Wray's death, he was devastated. Nunan, who had been fighting with the outfit

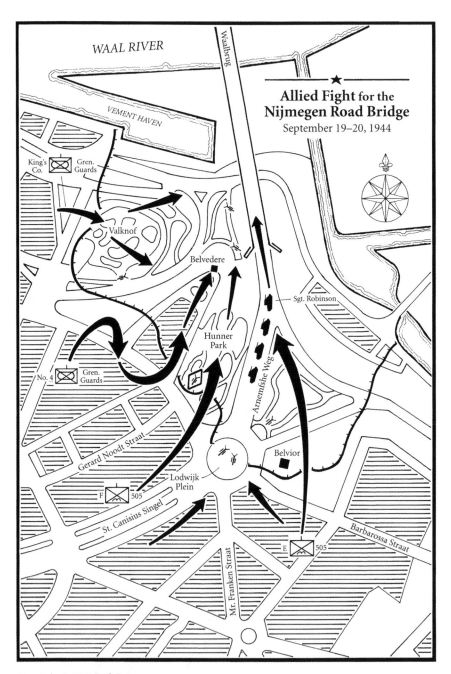

WAAL RIVER

Waalbrug

VEMENT HAVEN

★

**Allied Fight for the
Nijmegen Road Bridge**
September 19–20, 1944

King's
Co. ⊠ Gren.
Guards

Valknof

Belvedere

Sgt. Robinson

Hunner
Park

Arnemtshe Weg

No. 4 ⊠ Gren.
Guards

Gerard Noodt Straat

Belvior

Lodwijk
Plein

F ⊠ 505

St. Canisius Singel

Barbarossa Straat

Mr. Franken Straat

E ⊠ 505

for two years, believed Wray was "one of the finest small-unit combat leaders I have ever known. Coupled with a sense of fairness and justice, he was respected and admired by everyone who knew him."

Tinged with the gloom of mission failure and irreplaceable loss, the paratroopers and British guardsmen settled for the night into a wary, unhappy perimeter, well short of the railroad bridge.[4]

About fifteen hundred yards to the east, the main column made it to within a few hundred yards of the road bridge before running into a network of wickedly effective German defensive positions. The approaches to the road bridge made for ideal defensive terrain. Dense blocks of two- and three-story homes, shops, and apartment buildings gave way to the wide-open vistas of the Keizer Lodewijk Plein roundabout. The open boulevards converged at the roundabout and led, in a gently rising embankment, to the bridge. A large, rambling house known as the Villa Belvoir sat atop a patch of high ground overlooking the roundabout. A company of German paratroopers were in and around the Villa Belvoir. SS engineers had sown mines and strung barbed wire around the house (and in the Hunner Park too). The Germans could fire from the Belvoir's windows, along with slit trenches they had dug in the picturesque garden outside the house. Other enemy soldiers were spread out inside sturdy buildings along the blocks that led to the bridge.

On the left (from the attacker's perspective) was the Hunner Park, a tree-covered grassy landscape, situated atop higher ground than the approaching streets. Within the Hunner Park was a ruined castle known as the Valkhof, which had once represented Charlemagne's seat of power in Holland. Under the skilled leadership of two SS captains, Karl-Heinz Euling and Leo Hermann Reinhold, the SS defenders had turned the bridge approaches into a formidable defensive network. A self-propelled eighty-eight-millimeter gun, poised to fire in any direction, defended the roundabout.

The Hunner Park was especially formidable. A pair of antitank guns, along with four Mark IV self-propelled guns, were cleverly concealed among the maze of trees. Euling's men had dug a mutually supporting series of trenches from which they could defend the park against attacks from any direction. The ruins of the Valkhof, along with another neighboring castle tower known as the Belvedere (which Captain Jonathan Adams and his patrol had attacked on the first night's fighting in Nijmegen), comprised perfect observation posts and headquarters sites. Some of the German soldiers took effective cover in air raid shelters. Regardless of the impact on civilians, the engineers methodically laid waste to anything that might aid the attackers. "Even church towers had to be blown because they were pointers for enemy artillery fire stuck right in front of our noses," Captain Albert Brandt, the engineer commander, said. The defenders were supported by eighty-eight-millimeter guns in the village of Lent across the river and by soldiers of Kampfgruppe Henke, many of whom had moved from the bridge approaches in Nijmegen across the river to a prewar rampart known as Fort Hof van Holland.

The lead Sherman was tank number fifty-one under the command of Lieutenant John Moller. When it rolled past the corner of Dr. Claes Noorduynstraat and Graadt van Roggenstraat, toward the open vista of the roundabout, the Germans opened up from nearly every direction. An eighty-eight-millimeter shell slammed into the turret of Moller's tank, killing him. Molten flames spread inexorably around the turret; plumes of white smoke belched upward; ammo began to cook off. Corporal Earl Boling and several other nearby paratroopers tried to save the stricken crew. "We attempted to rescue [them] but it was too late." In a matter of seconds, the enemy gunners located the two trailing tanks and hit them as well. One of the tanks burned fiercely; the other managed to back up and make it to the cover of a house. All the while, machine gun and rifle fire swept along the dangerous streets. "The extent to which the enemy had prepared the defense of the bridge soon became evident," Lieutenant John Phillips, a platoon leader in E Company, later wrote. "Anti-tank guns covered every street approach." Automatic weapons only added to the danger. Men hollered to one another in confusion and fear. "It soon became obvious that a direct advance down this street was impossible," Lieutenant Colonel Goulburn wrote. The last thing he wanted was to get involved in a house-to-house fight, "as our main idea . . . was to get on over the bridge."

Goulburn and Vandervoort coordinated two armored flanking attacks on the roundabout, but they ran into the same wall of fire and made no headway. The American commander ordered his eighty-one-millimeter mortar crews to set up in the town cemetery, about half a mile from the bridge, and lay down fire. In his recollection, they were "walking high-explosive shells up and down the roadbed of the massive stone-piered and steel-arch bridge. They hoped to get lucky and cut any exposed wires leading to demolition charges." They probably did not cut any wires, but they did succeed in limiting German movement back and forth across the river. British artillery, firing from positions outside of Nijmegen, pounded Lent and the area around Fort Hof van Holland, pinning down Kampfgruppe Henke.

As much as the commanders wished to avoid a house-to-house struggle, they could not. The approaches to the bridges were so heavily defended that the mobility of the armor was limited. The natural place for the infantrymen to take shelter was the buildings. Moreover, the Americans and the British soon realized that they could not even capture the Hunner Park, much less the bridge, without controlling the surrounding blocks. Thus, much to Goulburn's chagrin, the battle degenerated into a time-consuming room-to-room struggle. The tanks provided as much support as they could, but it was up to the paratroopers to take the buildings. "By far the most dangerous part of driving the Germans back fell to our rifle squads," Lieutenant Colonel Vandervoort said. "In the labyrinth of houses and brick-walled gardens, the fighting deteriorated into confusing face-to-face, kill-or-be-killed showdowns between small, momentarily isolated groups and individuals. Friend and foe mixed in deadly proximity. Germans would appear where you least expected them. You fired fast and straight or you were dead."

One block along Reinhold Straat was comprised of, according to several troopers, "a maze of small yards, each separated . . . by shoulder-high spiked iron fences or by walls into whose tops pieces of broken glass had been imbedded; to go from door to door it was necessary to go through the street gates." As Lieutenant Phillips remembered it, "The troops moved through houses and buildings . . . hurling hand grenades into the windows and firing as they entered. Groups of three or four would close in hand-to-hand fighting with nests of Germans found in the rooms." Hand-to-hand combat meant duels to the death with knives, bayonets, pistols, rifles, tommy guns, or, as the term indicates, bare hands. It was highly traumatic and physically exhausting. Private First Class James Keenan's squad made liberal use of bazookas. "We went from building to building by blowing holes in the walls and thus clearing street by street in this ingenious fashion." As Private Patrick O'Hagan's squad entered the backyard of one burning house, he noticed several rabbit hutches stacked atop one another in the yard. A lifelong animal lover, O'Hagan stopped and gazed at the plump, healthy-looking rabbits. Nearby was a box of carrot tops and greenery. He grabbed handfuls of the food and carefully placed them in each hutch. Then he moved on.

In the main, the atmosphere was hellish and surreal. Fire raged in many of the houses. Dense clouds of gray and black smoke billowed over the various blocks, obscuring an otherwise sunny late afternoon. Curtains fluttered in the breeze through shattered windows. Snipers of both sides lurked behind the curtains, searching for victims. Bodies lay in the streets and in bedrooms alike. Among the alleys and yards, soldiers could seldom see more than a few feet in front of them. The blocks were so closely packed with buildings that even windows offered limited lines of sight. Under the cover of smoke grenades, Lieutenant James Coyle's platoon ran across an open street and made it into a two-story building overlooking the roundabout and the Hunner Park. They were the very lead element of the entire advance, but they were so far forward that they found it difficult to maintain contact with the rest of the column. From the second story of the building, they poked their weapons through open windows and unleashed deadly fire on the crew of one antitank gun. Predictably, they soon came under accurate artillery fire. One eighty-eight-millimeter round bounced off a windowsill, sailed through a room, and exploded near a machine gun team. "Private Carl Beck received a very bad face wound at this time," Lieutenant Coyle related. In fact, a large fragment flew through his mouth and tore out, in the recollection of one man, "most of the side of his face, including his eye." Beck fell down. Several others rushed to his aid. "We pulled him from the debris and got an aide man, who attempted to evacuate him," Corporal Boling recalled. Beck was unconscious from concussion. Lieutenant Coyle gave him first aid and helped carry him to the back of the house to the medic. Another soldier, who was not quite as badly wounded, also went with the medic. "I'll be back just as soon as I can," he told his squad mates.

Along some of the blocks, the SS men had painted defiant, militant messages on walls. On one wall they wrote, "We Black Ones Trust the Führer; our faith is loyalty"; on another they said, "Rather Dead Than Tyranny"; still another contained a threat of, "Death to the Murderers of Our Fatherland" and a profession that, "We Believe in Adolf Hitler and Our Victory." Fortunately, few of the American and British soldiers could read German well enough to understand these delightful proclamations.

As the fighting raged, the streets remained very dangerous. In one spot, Private Donald Lassen hurled himself into a doorway and took cover during one particularly intense artillery barrage. He glanced up and saw a nearby tank get hit. "I saw one English tanker bail out of his tank with a teacup in his hand & run like hell for the tank behind him." The British passion for tea made a deep impression on the Americans. In another spot, Captain Franco, the doctor, saw a pair of British tankers, wearing black berets, brewing tea over a fire, seemingly in the pathway of enemy fire. "The flame was several feet high and the tracers appeared to go right through it." Somehow the two soldiers remained unscathed.

The constricted cityscape was a nightmare for the tankers. Death lurked everywhere, and this made the crewmen understandably jumpy.

Sergeant Spencer Wurst dashed across one intersection ahead of a Sherman and took cover alongside a house. The tank's turret swiveled to the right and the driver gunned the engine to cross the open intersection. As the gunner snapped off a shot, the tank crossed the street and rolled past Wurst and three other members of his squad. All of a sudden, the tank gun hit a tree, spun around, and pointed right at Wurst's group, from only fifteen feet away. "When the muzzle hit the tree, I think it pushed the gunner forward against the firing mechanism," Wurst later wrote. "The last thing I remembered, the gun was coming on line with me when the damn thing fired. The detonation was close enough to stun me. I couldn't hear much for the next few hours." The armor-piercing shot disintegrated a newly arrived replacement whom Wurst did not really know. Another man was badly wounded, and Sergeant Wurst, wobbled though he was by concussion, managed to give him first aid. Oblivious, the tank rolled on. Wurst and the wounded soldier were fortunate. If the shell had been high-explosive, instead of armor-piercing, they would almost certainly have been killed by the fragmentation effect at such close range.

By the time dusk began to settle over the boiling streets of Nijmegen, the combined Allied force had managed to occupy the blocks overlooking the Hunner Park, the roundabout, and the bridge. It had taken several hours of hard fighting, with considerable casualties, just to make it this far. The Germans were still firmly ensconced in the Hunner Park, the Valkhof, and along every approach to the bridge. They were busily setting fire to buildings, in hopes of touching off a massive conflagration to flame out the Allied soldiers who were in the blocks overlooking the entire area around the bridge.

Lieutenant Colonel Vandervoort was not the type to worry about such obstacles, only results. He believed that, in spite of the ferocity of German resistance, his battalion and the British tanks were in position to make a final assault on the bridge. "The momentum was ours all afternoon," he commented. "We wanted to continue while we held the upper hand." His dedication was commendable but misplaced. The hard afternoon of urban combat had spread out his companies among the various blocks, diluting their combat power and eroding the vital tank-infantry cooperation so necessary for a bridge assault. The tank formations were also spread into ineffective small groups, often out of contact with the infantry. Among the intersections and alleyways, they were preoccupied with a cat-and-mouse game of survival with the German antitank gunners. In short, it would be very difficult for Vandervoort and Goulburn to reorganize their task force and launch the sort of coordinated attack necessary to overrun the Hunner Park and other formidable positions around the bridge.[5]

In fact, even as Vandervoort contemplated a bridge assault, General Gavin had already decided to order him to halt for the night. From the general's perspective, the efforts to seize the Nijmegen rail and road bridges had clearly failed. Given the level of enemy resistance around the bridges, the casualties, the confusion, and the onset of darkness, there was little reason to continue the attacks. "If I did nothing more than pour infantry and British armor into the battle at our end of the bridge," Gavin wrote, "we could be fighting there for days." He decided something else was necessary to dislodge the enemy from Nijmegen and secure the bridges.

At Malden, only a few miles from where the fighting was raging along Nijmegen's riverfront, Gavin met with generals Adair, Browning, and Horrocks. The latter had established his forward command post in a Malden schoolhouse. The generals stood together on the sidewalk outside the schoolhouse and absentmindedly scuffed the pavement with their boots as they conferred. The genial Horrocks looked at Gavin and said, "Jim, never try to fight a corps off a single road." He was referring to the difficulties XXX Corps was already encountering in keeping the tenuous Market Garden corridor secure from German counterattacks (such as the Son bridge attack). His long column of tanks, trucks, and other vehicles was already proving to be highly vulnerable, not just to direct attacks, but to long-range enemy artillery fire. The situation was unique in that XXX Corps' highway supply line was also its front line. The American general smiled and nodded his appreciation of Horrocks's dilemma.

The casual exchange between the two men belied the serious mood that was descending over the senior officers. Without knowing many of the specific details, all of them understood that General Urquhart's 1st Airborne Division was in serious trouble at Arnhem. In low murmurs, they discussed the gravity of 1st Airborne's predicament. "Jim, we've got to get to the other side of the Waal and get to Arnhem right away," Horrocks said.

Browning admitted that he did not know as much about the situation in Arnhem as he would have liked, but he knew that time was running out. "We know they are in real trouble and we have got to get there within twenty-four hours."

This confirmed what Gavin already suspected. At best, he figured Urquhart's people could hold on for another two days, but only that. Every hour they were cut off and under German attack meant more men killed, wounded, or captured. He thought of the British paratroopers as his brothers. Their lives were as important to him as those of his own men. So he proposed a bold idea that had been forming in his mind over the course of the day. The bridges, he believed, could be taken only by double envelopment. He had to seize both ends more or less at the same time, not just to outflank the Germans, but to prevent them from blowing the bridges up. While Vandervoort and Goulburn resumed their push for the bridges, Gavin proposed to move elements of his 504th Parachute Infantry Regiment to the water's edge, put them in boats, assault across the river, and take the bridges from the north end. He planned to launch this bold gambit just after dawn the next morning.

A brief moment passed as the British generals digested Gavin's idea. To the American, Horrocks appeared "quite skeptical . . . Allan Adair noncommittal, and Browning somewhat of an observer." Gavin underscored the point that he had to capture the bridge as soon as possible and that this was the best way. There was one problem, though. The Germans had cleared most of the boats out of the Nijmegen area. In fact, at Gavin's behest, Lieutenant Adrian Finlayson had spent the day scouring the area for boats, but had not found enough to accommodate a sizable river crossing. So Gavin asked Horrocks whether XXX Corps had any boats. After some discussion, Horrocks's staff officers told Gavin that they had thirty-three boats in trucks somewhere in their long column. They did not know where they were; nor could they say how long it would take to get them forward, but they promised to retrieve them as quickly as possible.

Gavin turned to Horrocks. "If you can get those boats to me, I'll move the 504th Parachute Infantry to the riverbank and make the crossing as rapidly as possible."

Horrocks nodded his assent. "Okay, Jim, do it."

The river crossing was on. In the twilight sky above the tidy homes of Malden, the sun slowly drooped below the western horizon.[6]

CHAPTER 10

Resolve

From the troubled, hard-pressed British-held perimeters at Oosterbeek and Arnhem to the combat-scarred streets of Nijmegen, and
even as far south as Eindhoven, the night was forbidding. Joyous
celebrations of liberation had given way to the dreadful calculus of modern
war—explosions, firefights, destruction, anguished cries of the wounded
and the stricken. In Eindhoven, the onset of darkness brought with it the
droning sounds of approaching aircraft. Seventy-six German bombers,
crewed largely by airmen who had once been stationed at the Eindhoven
airfield during the occupation, arrived over the middle of the city. First
they dropped flares. Then, from altitudes as low as four hundred feet, they
dropped bombs among the narrow streets and densely packed supply vehicles of XXX Corps. "It was really very easy for the Luftwaffe," Alan
Moorehead, a British war correspondent who was with the XXX Corps
column, later wrote. "The British had not yet had time to move up their
antiaircraft guns. Half a dozen trucks carrying shells were hit directly
and at once the shells were detonated and began to add a spasmodic stream
of horizontal fire to the bombs which were now falling at a steady rhythm
every minute. A number of petrol lorries took fire as well and these
flames, billowing loudly, reached across to other parts of the convoy which
was just then passing through the town, notably the lorries with small
arms ammunition. These bullets exploded and now it seemed that the city
was being engulfed by every sort of explosion at once."

The crackling of exploding bullets combined with the windy howls of gasoline fires and the menacing crash of falling masonry. The flames ate the trucks so voraciously that they left behind nothing except skeletal metal frames. In all, eighteen trucks were destroyed and the column sent into disarray. Flames roasted buildings and people alike. "It was the most terrifying night of our lives," Fie-Blaauw Baghuis, a thirty-two-year-old housewife, said. As was true for many other residents, the cellar of her house offered the only shelter from the relentless bombs. "Every few minutes . . . we could hear the scream of bombs." Somehow, none of them hit her house, but others were not so fortunate. The bombing destroyed 228 buildings and damaged 8,940 others. Some 227 Eindhoven residents were killed—including forty-one when a bomb scored a direct hit on an air raid shelter—and eight hundred were wounded. Generals Brereton and Ridgway were both in the area during the bombing and were quite fortunate to escape unhurt. The Germans got away with no losses. They had managed to take advantage of a rare lapse in the Allied air umbrella, something that would not be repeated again during the Market Garden operation. The raid was yet another disquieting example of the Allied corridor's vulnerability. For the Dutch, it was a harbinger—the joy of liberation was giving way to the grimness of total war.

To the north, the horizon over downtown Nijmegen glowed orange with the flames of numerous fires, many of which had been deliberately set by the Germans to drive the Allies away from the bridges. Artillery shells exploded all along the urban landscape. Flares burst in the night sky, adding to the eerie pyrotechnic half-light. White phosphorous shells touched off fires in many buildings. The flames ate up bedding, furniture, carpet, curtains, and woodwork. Brick exteriors were coated with black scorch marks. Combat raged among the parlors and cellars of many homes. "Artillery, mortars and high-velocity guns were working us over, and the town was coming down around us," the diary of E Company, 505th Parachute Infantry, recorded.

The once picturesque river town was becoming, minute by minute, a field of ruins. To Sister Symons Disithee, a nun who was treating the many wounded who were pouring into St. Canisius Hospital, the combination of the fires and the din of battle comprised "a terrifying spectacle against the dark evening sky. The rattle of machine guns and thud of hand grenades and cannon were constantly heard . . . looking out, one saw the city ablaze." She treated more wounded Americans, Germans, and local civilians than she could count. She and the rest of the hospital staff worked themselves to the brink of exhaustion. Captain Robert Steele, Goulburn's adjutant, was a couple blocks closer to the river, in a house that served as battalion headquarters. The home was owned by "a rather frosty old Dutchwoman who was very oblivious to the reasons which brought us there." Captain Steele circulated around, relaying the colonel's orders to the scattered Grenadier Guards units. As he moved about, he paused every now and again to take in the sight of "burning houses and roads blocked by fallen trees or a burning vehicle." To Steele, the sounds of battle were more overwhelming in the constricted city than in the open countryside.

In another house overlooking the roundabout, Martijn Deinum, a local, and one of his friends were trying to prepare a meal when they smelled smoke. At first they thought the smoke came from a neighboring building, but they soon realized that their house was on fire. They grabbed fire extinguishers and battled the flames, but the blaze kept spreading. "It was all rather enervating!" he exclaimed in his diary. "The flames crackled, a mortar burst . . . blasted in a large window, a shower of tracer munition and mortar bombs was coming down and bullets were flying through the foyer. Wherever we looked out, the city was burning like a torch." They finally doused the flames with fire hoses, but the charred ruins continued to smolder. Outside, the streets themselves were, in the recollection of another civilian, "littered with glass, wood of windows and doors, tree branches, stones, and roof tiles."

Refugees fled from the fires and the fighting. In tattered groups, they made their way south and west, away from the riverfront. Many converged on the Albertinum, a convent located many blocks away from the road bridge and thus the worst of the fighting. Within the convent walls, the cries of children mixed with the groans of the elderly and the disabled. Albertus Uijen, a civil servant and resistance member, helped them get as comfortable as possible. "A place is sought for each of them in the spacious building," he paused and wrote in his diary. "Already the ground floor is almost full up, many have even found accommodation in the chapel." The power was out in the building (and indeed in much of the city) so "people have to make do with candles and batteries [flashlights]."

Meanwhile, in the blocks around the riverfront, groups of soldiers maintained a wary vigil throughout the long night. The front lines, such as they even existed, were fluid at best. Patrols clashed at the edges of the Hunner Park. A few American soldiers managed to infiltrate a line of German foxholes. With knives and bayonets, they moved from hole to hole, killing several Germans and capturing a few more. German soldiers patrolled around the Allied-controlled blocks. Some of the Germans were lost or had become separated from their units during the afternoon fighting; some were looking for trouble or gathering information on the location of their enemies; some were simply searching for food or loot. On the first floor of a house overlooking the roundabout, Corporal Earl Boling and two of his buddies heard the sound of hobnailed boots approaching on the pavement outside. Knowing that both the British and Germans wore boots with hobnails, they held their fire for a few moments. At last, as they peered through the window of their house, they saw five German soldiers coming straight for them. Boling opened up with a BAR. Another man, Private First Class John Keller, threw a grenade at them. The third man, Private First Class George Wood, fired his Garand. The grenade explosion wounded one German. The others charged at the American-held house. "I fired on them," Boling said, "dropping two between the curb and the building; the other two fell outside the window. I attempted to fire over the window edge and realized the clip of the BAR was empty." Boling crouched down to change magazines. As he did so, a wounded German grabbed at the windowsill and pointed his pistol at the Americans. The adrenaline of self-preservation surged through Boling's veins. He fumbled for a bayonet that he had attached to his boot. Wood said, "I'll get him." The private had captured an Italian pistol during the previous year's campaign in that country. He grabbed the gun and, in Boling's memory, "fired five shots at about a three-foot range. We could see the German's head bounce with each impact, but he did not release the windowsill and drop until the fifth shot."

At another block, closer to the Hunner Park, Lieutenant Jack Carroll and his platoon were quietly holed up in a burning apartment building, cut off from the rest of their native F Company. "A whole [German] platoon marched right down the street by our hiding place but never looked inside!" In this case, the flames probably dissuaded the Germans from investigating the building. One of Carroll's squad leaders, Sergeant Spencer Wurst, heard a bloodcurdling scream emanate from a house across the street. "It lasted for thirty seconds, but seemed like it would never stop. Someone must have been bayoneted or knifed in the lower extremities, because no one could have screamed that long if the wound had been to the chest cavity. The sound cut through the silence, annihilating our morale." He and his men had no idea whether the screamer was German, American, British, or Dutch, but it hardly mattered. "Screams have no nationality," Wurst later said. In another house not far from the railroad bridge, Private William McMandon was standing guard with a buddy, peering through a window, when they sensed movement outside. "Nine or ten German soldiers sauntered down the street—passing within four yards of us—one round of ammunition and there would have been none," he recalled. "Fearing the holocaust this might have created along that street, we permitted them to pass unmolested." During the long night, many others on both sides chose to prudently avoid opening fire if it was not absolutely necessary. A sense of anticipation hung over the boiling city blocks, as if by some sort of tacit agreement the two sides were marshaling their strength for a great struggle in the daylight.[1]

At the division command post in the woods outside of Nijmegen, General Gavin and his staff spent the night studying maps, planning the river crossing. Mindful that time was a crucial factor for the survival of the British paratroopers at Arnhem, the general hoped to launch the crossing shortly after sunrise. For that to happen, though, the 504th's advance to the riverbank needed to go smoothly, with little German interference. Plus, the XXX Corps engineers needed to get the boats to them in time. Gavin planned to load the regiment's 3rd Battalion aboard the boats and launch them right where the Maas-Waal Canal intersected with the Waal River, about a mile north of the railroad bridge (in essence flanking the Germans who were now fighting Vandervoort's men and the Grenadier Guards). Fire support for the crossing would come from the 2nd Battalion, along with two battalions of tanks from the Irish Guards, and a blend of British and 82nd Airborne artillery.

Troopers from C Company, 307th Airborne Engineer Battalion, would operate the boats and ferry their infantry brothers to the enemy-held north shore. When they had disgorged the 3rd Battalion, they were to turn around, row back to the south side, and ferry the reinforcing 1st Battalion, plus headquarters and supporting personnel, to the north side. The engineers were hardly well prepared for their daunting job. They had no training in the handling of boats and, like everyone else in the 82nd Airborne, no experience whatsoever with amphibious operations. Yet now Gavin planned to place them center stage for Market Garden's greatest drama. To Lieutenant John Holabird, one of the engineer platoon leaders, the choice "was flattering . . . and at the same time a little fantastic." He and his men had always felt distinctly different, and a bit scorned, by the rough-hewn men of the rifle companies. "We were always somewhat of a joke—effete and a little precious. We usually followed people around, not led them." They did not need to match the riflemen for sheer toughness. That was beside the point. Gavin chose them for their creativity, innovation, and ingenuity.

While the engineers focused on ferrying the assault troops and clearing mines from the riverbank, everyone else was supposed to destroy all German resistance and seize the northern ends of both bridges. The terrain would not be easy. "The north bank on which the landing was to be made had sloping edges and insecure footing," a unit after-action report stated. "Beyond the water's edge stretched flat ground for approximately 800 yards at which distance runs a 30 foot high dike with a 20 foot road on top." As the 504th captured this ground and the bridges, Vandervoort's 2nd Battalion, 505th, and Goulburn's Grenadier Guards would resume their urban push for the southern end of the bridges. Gavin knew full well that his plan was risky, but he believed it was the only hope of taking the bridges quickly enough to save the 1st Airborne and Market Garden itself. "Something had to be done," he later wrote. "I could not conceive of sitting on the southern bank . . . while Urquhart was destroyed eleven miles away."

All night long, the orders filtered from Gavin's command post to the affected units. At one point, the general visited the 3rd Battalion to personally speak with the commander, Major Julian Cook, who would lead the first wave across the river. The twenty-seven-year-old West Pointer had always been known by his middle name of Aaron to his devout Roman Catholic family. But in the army he was called Julian. He had been with the regiment since Sicily, serving much of that time as Colonel Tucker's supply officer. This was his first operation in command of the 3rd Battalion. Since drop day, the unit had seen very little combat, and Cook was still not sure that his soldiers, particularly his NCOs, believed in his leadership. He had taken over the battalion in England after the bitter Anzio campaign. Fresh from this hellish Italian battlefield, the battalion had experienced a slew of discipline problems. The new commander came down hard on the wayward soldiers, canceling leaves and putting everyone through intense training. The men resented such martinet treatment from a fresh-faced commander who had not been with them at Anzio, and whose fighting qualities they did not know. The sergeants especially begrudged an admonition he had given them one day that their indiscipline might be okay in garrison where he could always supervise them, "but in combat I'm not going to be there to kick your tail." This implied that he would not face dangers alongside his men and gave rise to the notion among his sergeants that he was just a rear-echelon administrator, not a fighting soldier.

The meeting between Gavin and Cook was hardly the stuff of story-books (perhaps that is why Gavin never discussed it any of his writings). Cook was one of the few soldiers in the 82nd Airborne Division who was not particularly enamored of the general. The young major felt more loy-alty toward Colonel Tucker, his old boss, and he came to believe that Gavin was jealous of the inspirational regimental commander. When Gavin informed Cook of his mission, the battalion commander reacted angrily. To Cook, the mission amounted to suicide or, at best, sheer reck-lessness. He had no idea how many boats he would receive, nor when they would arrive. Even if he and his men succeeded in making it across the river, he found it hard to believe they could fight their way over eight hundred yards of open ground, capture the dike road, and still make it to the bridges, more than a mile away.

Under the stress of such imminent danger, Cook was in no mood to hold his tongue with his superior. "Well, General, if you wanted men on the north bank of the river," he said, "it would have been very simple to have dropped them in the beginning." In the recollection of Lieutenant Virgil "Hoagy" Carmichael, the 3rd Battalion's intelligence officer, Cook "was fuming mad at General Gavin." Cook did not know that, during the planning for Market Garden, Gavin had considered and rejected this very idea, deeming it too risky. If he had dropped troopers north of the bridges, they probably would have been besieged and destroyed by the same enemy soldiers who were defending the structures now (similar to Lieutenant Colonel Frost's battalion at Arnhem). The general took Cook's imperti-nence in stride—perhaps because he was prone to such prickly honesty with his own superiors—focusing only on the task at hand. In no uncer-tain terms, he ordered Cook to be ready for a morning river crossing. "He told us that we had to get the bridge so as to relieve the troops at Arnhem and they were hurting," Cook later said.[2]

That night, Gavin caught a few hours of fitful sleep. By daylight, when the general visited Colonel Tucker at his command post, the boats still had not arrived. According to XXX Corps, they were on their way, but no one could say when they would arrive. Both officers sensed that the crossing would be delayed, but neither could decide yet how long. Gavin was anxious to see the crossing site for himself. With Lieutenant Hugo Olson, Sergeant Walker Wood, and a driver in tow, he hopped in his jeep and took off.

The streets of northern Nijmegen were eerily quiet, so much so that the general was suspicious of impending danger. About a mile from the river, he ordered the driver to stop the jeep while he, Olson, and Wood reconned on foot. As the three men spread out and cautiously proceeded, they saw movement in the distance. About four hundred yards away, in an open field, a German patrol of about sixteen men, with rifles at high port, was heading toward them. "I stood behind the corner of a brick building and began to fire at them rapidly and they hit the ground," Gavin said. Sergeant Wood took cover at another corner and added his own fire. As Gavin fired, he aimed his M1 Garand from man to man, "Since I wanted to impress them with the amount of fire that was coming from us." The confused Germans were more interested in self-preservation than in shooting back at the three Americans. Gavin and his two charges took advantage of that confusion to take off. They made it back to the jeep and returned to Tucker's headquarters. Gavin told Tucker, "We do not even have the site yet where we launch the boats." The colonel vowed to clear the blocks all the way to the crossing site. It took much of the morning for 504th patrols to flush out snipers and shoo German patrols from the area.

Gavin's carefully laid plans were unraveling practically by the moment. "It was a nice schoolbook solution, but it didn't work out," he later said. Even as Tucker waited in vain for the boats, he told the general that the men could not stage their crossing in the Maas-Waal Canal, whose banks were right in the open, under the guns of the Germans on the railroad bridge. Moreover, the current was too swift. The men would labor just to paddle from the canal to the river, much less across the river to the north bank. Instead the commanders chose to stage from a spot a few hundred yards to the east, between the city's electrical power plant and the Nyma silk factory. The chosen spot offered defilade cover for the troops behind a raised dike, "thus hiding them from view from the north bank," according to a postbattle report, "and the buildings of the factory and the powerhouse obstructed view from the east, especially the railroad and highway bridges across the Waal." However, the new launch point also meant that the troopers would have to manhandle their heavy boats over the raised dike and down a slippery, muddy slope to the river's edge, all in plain view of the Germans.

In the meantime, for want of the boats' arrival, Gavin was forced to postpone the crossing to 1100, then 1330, and finally 1500. Every lost hour enhanced the probability of extinction for Urquhart's 1st Airborne Division, especially for Frost's surrounded battalion at the Arnhem bridge. Even now, that defiant force was on the verge of total destruction. The four trucks carrying the boats were dealing with two problems—miles of traffic and persistent enemy attacks on the narrow Market Garden corridor. They had been impeded, for instance, by the enemy bombing of Eindhoven during the night. As the morning unfolded, they were delayed by a renewed 107th Panzer Brigade attack on the Son bridge (barely and courageously rebuffed by the 101st Airborne Division and ten British tanks). In addition, during the journey, a German shell hit one of the trucks, setting it afire. Just that quickly, the number of available boats went from thirty-three to twenty-six.[3]

Knowing none of this, the 504th troopers, almost all of whom understood the urgency of their mission, spent much of the day waiting in abject frustration, wondering when the boats would arrive. The delay did give the officers and NCOs time to take a look at the crossing site and conduct briefings. Major Cook and a group of his leaders entered the power station through an opening in the corrugated sheets that comprised the north wall and climbed to one of the top floors, where a sizable window offered a panoramic view. A few artillery shells exploded here and there on either side of the river. Together, they took in the daunting sight of the crossing area. "[We] had a perfect view of the north bank of the river . . . [and] the railroad bridge on the right," Lieutenant Carmichael wrote.

Staff Sergeant Robert Tallon, the battalion operations sergeant, decided to take the elevator to the upper floors, but it got stuck. "I was scared to death," he said. He had visions of being abandoned and forgotten, or, even worse, he worried that the elevator would break loose and plummet to the ground. Frantically, he pushed buttons and levers until the elevator began to work again. At the first possible stop, he exited, climbed the stairs, and joined the others. He peered intently at the north bank, looking for German movement. "I could pick out several camouflaged German emplacements. It was an eerie feeling. I couldn't see anybody, but I knew they were there." A few feet away from Tallon, Captain Moffatt Burriss, whose I Company was scheduled to go over in the first wave, raised a pair of binoculars to his eyes and was practically dumbfounded by what he saw. He estimated that the river in this spot was at least three hundred yards wide. The angry waters looked forbidding indeed. "We could tell by the swirling, foamy waters that the current was strong," he said. "This was no ancient, meandering river. It flowed straight and deep and swiftly." Moving his binoculars slowly to the left and right, he studied the flat terrain on the north bank and the dike road. He and his men would have to move very fast to make it through that kill zone. He could even see some of the German defenses, most notably a twenty-millimeter gun on the railroad bridge and Fort Hof van Holland, the moated strongpoint that covered the entire expanse of the open ground from the road to the river's edge. Standing nearby, Captain Carl Kappel, the commander of H Company—another first-wave unit—took in the same sights. In his recollection, he "wasn't too happy about a daylight crossing." To Kappel, the best way to attempt such a bold assault was under cover of darkness, but he knew, much to his chagrin, that they could not afford to wait until nightfall.

Before entering the power station, all of them had known intellectually that this mission would be extremely dangerous, at best an iffy proposition. Now the sight of the wide, unforgiving river, the bridges, the flatness of the north bank, and the ubiquitous German weapons made the reality of what they were about to attempt sink into each man. This was a suicide mission! They were expendable! A silence descended over the group as each soldier wrestled with these unhappy thoughts. "We are being asked to make an Omaha beach landing all by ourselves," Cook thought to himself. At the same time, Sergeant Tallon thought, "We're really crazy to try such a fool stunt." Captain Henry Keep, the battalion operations officer, enjoyed a reputation for irrepressible fearlessness among his comrades, but even he was speechless. "I had a strange feeling inside," he later wrote to his mother. "I think everyone else did too because no one said a word. We just looked." Cook briefly reviewed the plan with them and they left. As they descended the stairs—Tallon, for his part, was only too happy to avoid the elevator—they remained silent but determined. In the main, they were experienced combat soldiers. They understood better than anyone the unhappy probabilities they would soon face. But they were convinced that the crossing was necessary for the larger purpose of saving 1st Airborne and, for that matter, Market Garden as a whole. This was what the mission represented in their minds.

As the afternoon wore on, the senior officers made their own reconnaissance of the site. At various times, Horrocks, Gavin, Browning, and Tucker all visited the power station or its environs. Tucker spent much of his time coordinating communications and fire support with Lieutenant Colonel Giles Vandeleur, the commander of the two supporting British tank battalions. The British commander formed an impression of Tucker as "a fine soldier, one who knew his job thoroughly and was keenly anxious to get on with it." At Tucker's request, Vandeleur stationed himself in the power station, where he could effectively spot targets and relay firing orders to his tanks near the riverbank. In addition to studying the crossing site from the vantage point of the power station, General Horrocks mingled with the waiting American paratroopers. "My God, look at 'em," he exclaimed to Tucker. "They make an assault river crossing in a very short time . . . here they lay some of 'em fast asleep! What wonderful troops." Tucker nodded and beamed with pride.[4]

The troops may have looked outwardly calm, but, as the waiting continued, they grew increasingly nervous and impatient. By 1400, Cook's entire battalion was congregated behind the cover of the dike between the power station and the Nyma factory. There was still no sign of the boats. No one had any idea when they would arrive. Many of the troopers took off their packs, lay down, and dozed off. Some cleaned their weapons. Others chatted with their buddies or smoked absentmindedly. Officers used the idle time to organize the men into boat teams. They planned to put a squad of thirteen men aboard each boat, plus two or three engineers to serve as makeshift coxswains. A team of forward observers from the 376th Parachute Field Artillery Battalion would also go along. In all, the first wave consisted of some 260 soldiers. Major Cook dealt with his nervous anger by circulating among the troops, exchanging wisecracks. At one point, he joked that he was planning to cross the Waal like George Washington over the Delaware River, standing on the prow, right fist clenched, shouting, "Onward men, onward!"

Among the troopers, there was a mood of grim determination mixed with impending doom. Most had gotten at least a glimpse of the wide river, the flat north bank, and the bridges in the distance. They needed no extensive briefing to understand the extreme danger of making a daylight river crossing in the face of such difficult terrain and a determined enemy. "I doubt if there was one man who didn't consider this a suicide mission," Captain Delbert Kuehl, the regimental chaplain, later wrote, "but I heard not a word from any trooper that they weren't ready to go." Kuehl himself understood the danger quite well, but he decided to go with the first wave.

He figured that if there was ever a time when the men would need him, it was now. For the young Protestant clergyman, it was the hardest decision he had ever had to make, and it reflected his unbending faith in God.

Most everyone else, of course, had no other option but to go. They knew that these inactive moments of waiting might be their last on earth, but instead of savoring them, they were oddly eager to get on with the mission. It was as if the anticipation of death were somehow worse than the real thing. "As we grouped behind the protected dike along the river prior to the assault, we prepared in our own way to meet our maker," Lieutenant James Megellas said. "It did not seem militarily or humanly possible to accomplish such a mission." Megellas turned to one of his best friends, Lieutenant Richard LaRiviere (whom everyone called Rivers) and asked him to contact his mother in the event that he did not survive the crossing. LaRiviere assented and asked Megellas to do the same.

At least two men had premonitions of death. Lieutenant Harry "Pappy" Busby, a platoon leader in I Company, confided to Megellas. "I'm going to get it today," he said. Busby felt that the odds of survival were too long. The law of averages was bound to catch up with him. While Busby seemed resigned to his own death, Lieutenant Steve Seyebe experienced a similar premonition and reacted angrily to it. He took out a Camel cigarette and lit it up with a Zippo lighter. In total disgust, he turned to Chaplain Kuehl and said, "I have no chance of getting across." With a flourish, he flung the highly prized pack of Camels and the Zippo to the ground. Lieutenant Carmichael, who was sitting nearby, retrieved the items and gave them to someone else.

In another spot, Private Louie Holt said to his sergeant, Clement Haas, "This is suicide; we will all get killed." Haas and two other men reassured Holt that they would be okay, "as we would have plenty of support in the form of artillery, tanks, and aircraft firing on the Germans before and during our attack." Lieutenant Tom MacLeod, one of the engineer platoon leaders, crawled to the edge of the dike and peered at the river. For a long moment, he shuddered at how wide it looked. As he descended the embankment to the spot where his men were waiting to go, he locked eyes with Corporal Louis Gentile. MacLeod smiled and asked, "Ready to go, Gentile?" Gentile, who was probably just as frightened as his lieutenant, smiled back. "I guess so, sir." Neither man wanted to betray evidence of his own silent fears to the other, and in that way they reassured each other. This was all too common among the clumps of waiting men.

It did not help morale that, a couple hundred yards farther north along the riverbank, a popular officer from D Company was lying wounded, calling for help. Lieutenant Edward Wisniewski was known affectionately to his friend Megellas and many other regimental officers as "Polack." He and Megellas had gone through jump school together and had served side by side since North Africa. "He was an outstanding officer and combat leader, highly respected by officers and enlisted men alike." The job of Wisniewski's D Company was to set up just north of the power station and provide fire support for the crossing. As Wisniewski led a patrol into position, he was hit by German small-arms fire from the other side of the river. He lay pinned down on the other side of the dike, crying for help. Medics waved a Red Cross flag and tried to retrieve him, but the Germans shot at them. The rest of D Company was on the other side of the dike, pinned down themselves by the same enemy fire. For at least an hour, he lay helplessly in the open, under the eyes of the enemy, too badly wounded to move himself, begging for someone to rescue him. His cries could be heard by many of the 3rd Battalion men who were waiting for the boats to arrive. "Some of his good friends were almost frantic with despair that they could not help him," Lieutenant Carmichael wrote. Megellas felt nothing but anger and frustration as he heard his good friend's wounded voice in the distance. Medics eventually did get to Wisniewski, but he ended up dying in a field hospital.

Not all was so serious. When Lieutenant Colonel Vandeleur's tanks began maneuvering into position along the riverbank, one of the crewmen leaned out of his turret, proffered a bottle of Scotch, and said to Private First Class Lawrence Dunlop, "Blimey . . . have a snort . . . you fellows can use it worse than we can." Dunlop, a machine gunner in H Company, was only too happy to take a long pull from the bottle.[5]

....

As the assault troops waited for their terrifying moment of truth, General Gavin finalized his own preparations. He coordinated the air, artillery, and tank support for the Waal crossing, as well as the renewed push by the Vandervoort-Goulburn task force for the road bridge. With these tasks completed, he sat down against the trunk of a pear tree to watch the crossing. He had badly wrenched his back a few days earlier, during the landing, and it was beginning to act up. His extremities felt numb and listless. Just as he finally got comfortable, sitting with his back against the tree, he received an urgent radio call from Lieutenant Colonel Robert Wienecke, the division chief of staff. Wienecke was very frustrated and more than a bit agitated. For much of the day, he had been receiving reports of strong German attacks on the 508th and 505th parachute infantry regiments' positions along the Groesbeek heights. "I gave them my deepest sympathy and began to get nervous," he later said. He knew as well as anyone how thinly spread out the 82nd Airborne Division truly was. As the reports of enemy attacks intensified and the calls for help became more insistent, Wienecke worried that the Germans might actually succeed in collapsing the entire northeastern flank of the division front before Cook's river crossing could even get started.

Like any good chief of staff, Wienecke enjoyed a close, trusting relationship with his division commander (in fact, they commonly referred to each other as "Jim" and "Bob" during their radio conversations). Lieutenant Colonel Wienecke knew Gavin well enough to understand that he liked to be in the thick of the action rather than sitting in his command post. "General Jim didn't like to be called back to the CP for 'insignificant' problems," Wienecke explained. Thus, as the alarming reports had poured in to Wienecke, he had deliberated as to whether the situation was important enough to require the general's full attention. By midday, he had decided that the answer was yes. Then, when he radioed the general, he could not get through to him. The general's radio was in his jeep. He and his small group had left the jeep unattended on a road behind the power station while Gavin made his many arrangements. Repeatedly, Wienecke transmitted, "Jim from Bob, over . . ." and got no response. As each fruitless minute passed, Wienecke grew more frantic. Where exactly was the general and just why in hell was his radio unattended? the chief of staff wondered. At last, after nearly thirty minutes of this, he got through to Sergeant Walker Wood. Immediately Wienecke vented his considerable frustration on Wood. "For reasons of good taste, I'll not tell you what I told Wood . . . but the essence was . . . *never* leave the radio unattended."

Meanwhile, General Gavin stood up, stretched his aching back, and got on the radio. "This is Jim, over."

"This is Bob, sir. You'd better get the hell back here or you won't have any division left, over."

"What's up, over?" the alarmed general replied.

"Well, there is a major German attack coming in from the north. You have got to decide what to do with whatever we have in reserve." Wienecke explained what he knew about the enemy push and urged the general to return to the command post. The Germans were apparently attacking in three prongs—one against the 508th at Beek and Wyler; one in the middle at Groesbeek; and, most ominously, one against Mook, near the vital Heumen bridge over the Maas-Waal Canal. Neither the general nor his chief of staff knew that the attackers were recently arrived paratroopers of the II Fallschirmjäger Corps. In response to the Market Garden landings, they had been transferred from their training area in Cologne to the Reichswald and thrown into the battle alongside several Mark V Panther tanks and supporting antiaircraft guns. The German commanders had divided this force of some two thousand soldiers into three distinct Kampfgruppen with orders to break through to Nijmegen and the Heumen bridge.

Gavin may not have known these particulars yet, but he immediately understood the seriousness of the enemy threat. The idea of their fighting their way into Nijmegen was bad enough. But if they took Mook, they might well seize the Heumen bridge. This was the only Allied-controlled bridge in the Nijmegen area. It was also the main XXX Corps supply route. If the Germans controlled the bridge, they could strangle the entire 82nd Airborne Division and its British partners north of the Maas-Waal Canal. Without this bridge, the Waal crossing—indeed, the entire effort to take the Nijmegen bridges—was pointless. The general also knew that, at least for today, he could not count on any reinforcement from the 325th Glider Infantry Regiment. Once again, they were impatiently sitting in England, socked in by fog. Thus, his reserves were limited to small elements of the 505th and 508th, along with tanks from the Coldstream Guards.

Gavin weighed all this in his mind. He had been in combat long enough to know that sometimes local commanders bearing the brunt of enemy counterattacks tended to overblow their significance. That did not seem to be the case here. He trusted Wienecke enough to believe that these German attacks were very serious and required his personal attention. The general knew that only he could decide whether to use the division reserves to deal with this threat, and how to employ them. "You can't make a decision off a map ten miles from the battle," he later said. "You really have to get out there where you smell it, and taste it, and talk to people." Gavin realized that he must decide between going to the command post to deal with the enemy attacks along the Groesbeek heights or staying put to supervise the Waal crossing. From the beginning of this operation, his division had been torn between these two major areas of responsibility, and now this had presented the commanding general with a serious conundrum. He hated the idea of leaving the 504th troopers as they prepared to embark on such a daunting task. But he also knew that he could not sit idly by while the German attackers threatened to seize the vital bridge in his sector and collapse his entire divisional front. Here was a moment when Gavin's failure to employ an assistant division commander really mattered. Both situations called for the attention of a general officer, yet there was only Gavin. Reflecting on this many years later, he admitted that this was a real mistake. "I would have been better off . . . if I had had an assistant division commander," he conceded. After mulling over his unhappy choices, he decided to go back to the command post. "There seemed to be no question that my proper place was back where the decisive fighting was then taking place," he wrote. He gathered Olson and Wood and took off in his jeep for the command post.[6]

Even as the general sped out of Nijmegen, bitter fighting raged in the pathway of the German advance. Tank-infantry attacks by Kampfgruppe Hermann in and around Mook were especially menacing due to the threat they posed to the critical Heumen bridge. They smashed into the 1st Battalion, 505th Parachute Infantry, whose companies were spread thinly into squad- and platoon-size outposts. "It was an amazing sight looking down and watching Germans, four abreast, marching toward you," Staff Sergeant Elmo Jones recalled.

At the little hamlet of Plasmolen, roughly a mile east of Mook, a squad from B Company, armed only with machine guns and a bazooka, attempted to hold off a Mark V tank and an infantry assault. The men did at least have the protection of log-reinforced dugouts. The machine gun team opened up, forcing the German infantrymen to take cover, but also attracting the attention of the Mark V. "It began firing 75's and 20mm over the entire area," American survivors related to an after-action interviewer. "The fire cut the dirt away from the top of the dugout position of the MG's . . . immediately in front and knocked out the gun positions, setting on fire ammunition in the positions." The tank fired again and destroyed one of the machine guns, splitting it in two. Private First Class Abraham "Abie" Mallis, the gunner, aimed his carbine and futilely emptied an entire clip at the tank as it fired directly at him, tearing up the logs over his head. A bazooka gunner crawled up and scored at least four hits on the tank. This did no damage to the Mark V, but the enemy crew wisely pulled back and unleashed devastating fire on the American dugouts, forcing the paratroopers to take cover or retreat. At another outpost, Private First Class Robert Yeiter and a buddy watched in terror as German soldiers closed in from all sides. The Americans retreated as fast as they could. "I remember diving over a chicken wire fence. I swear it was seven feet high. [We] hit the top with our belly and flipped over on our feet on a dead run for fifty yards to a stone wall, with bullets skipping all around us."

Soon, the Germans overran much of Mook itself, cutting off stubborn groups of American defenders, many of whom took shelter in cellars. "The platoons were surrounded by the enemy," the regimental after-action report said. "They wouldn't give up, but continued the fight with the help of battalion mortars and supporting artillery." The artillery support came from the 456th Parachute Field Artillery, and it slowed the German advance considerably. In Mook, the fighting raged from house to house, which basically meant that small, isolated groups of men on both sides fought personal battles to the death. High-powered rifles, submachine guns, and grenades did tremendous damage to the human body in such enclosed spaces. This lethal cat-and-mouse game methodically destroyed the quaint little town in a matter of hours. The environment was unforgiving and ruthless. Private First Class Kenneth Truax's sixty-millimeter mortar team was so desperate that they were using a captured German helmet as a makeshift baseplate. "I aimed and held it with my hands while a fellow by the name of [Private] Julius Wyngart dropped the shells into its tube." A nearby machine gunner, who had joined the unit in England as a replacement, was firing his .30-caliber gun at the attacking Germans when he got hit and died. "He fell over the top of the machine gun with his hand still on the trigger and the round of fire was completed."

Colonel William Ekman, the commander of the 505th, knew how important it was to hang on to Mook. At the height of the fighting, he scraped together a squadron of British tanks, plus a platoon of paratroopers, and personally led them into a counterattack. They fought their way to a cut-off platoon, but ran into intense Panzerfaust fire from Germans who had taken shelter in the basement of a bakery. One of the Panzerfaust rounds blew the track off a Sherman tank. The British tank commander refused to abandon his tank until he had expended every round. The courage of this man and many others involved in the counterattack bogged the Germans down into an unproductive struggle for the ruins of the town.

As the harrowing fighting raged in Mook, General Gavin finally arrived at the tent in the woods that served as his command post. Immediately, he could tell that the situation was every bit as troubling as Wienecke had described. As Gavin studied the division situation map and weighed what to do next, he noticed that his superior, Major General Matthew Ridgway, commander of the XVIII Airborne Corps, was also in the tent, about fifteen yards away, discussing the situation with members of the division staff. The two men had served together for nearly two years and they enjoyed a deep mutual respect. Gavin knew that military courtesy called for him to brief Ridgway on the unfolding battle. But with the crisis at Mook bubbling, he had little time to spare on such niceties—as always Gavin yearned to be in the thick of the action. Nor did he really know enough details for any sort of coherent report to Ridgway. "I . . . weighed carefully . . . whether to interrupt you or go to Mook as quickly as possible and then return," Gavin wrote to Ridgway about two weeks later. "The situation at Mook appeared none too good, and I was sure you would want the correct picture when I talked to you." The young general asked Wienecke to convey his apologies to Ridgway and left for Mook.

Ridgway did not react well to his subordinate's lack of communication. The corps commander was already in a sour mood. He was angry that his divisions were under Browning's command. He felt practically useless without the command responsibility that he believed rightfully belonged to him. He had been pinned down during the Eindhoven bombing raid and had spent much of the previous twenty-four hours seething with anger over what he perceived as XXX Corps' inexcusably slow, apathetic advance. Under other circumstances, he probably would have sloughed off Gavin's abruptness, but today, it rubbed him decidedly the wrong way.

"I do recall some annoyance . . . the result of his more or less ignoring me," Ridgway later wrote. Ridgway already felt like something of an insignificant third wheel, and this only stoked those feelings. Gavin's impudence also struck Ridgway as disrespectful and downright rude, perhaps even humiliating. He left the CP in a huff, bound for more ineffectual wanderings.

He was not willing to let the matter drop. In October, he sent a chilly letter to Gavin, requesting a formal explanation of the incident. The letter struck Gavin as inordinately petty and useless, especially in the context of ongoing operations. "Such a lack of trust and confidence between his and my command can only do us both and our units harm," Gavin opined in his diary. Gavin wrote a carefully worded mea culpa to Ridgway, but he was so put out with the general's formal letter that he asked to be relieved. In truth, neither general really wanted this. Ridgway believed that his young charge was "as fine a combat commander as any in our service in WWII." Gavin could not truly imagine leaving his beloved 82nd Airborne. Ridgway refused the request. Gavin assured his commander that he had never meant any disrespect. The two men smoothed over the tension and restored their formerly solid relationship (indeed, in later years, a regretful Ridgway was to say that, given the intensity of the 82nd Airborne's battle that day, "Gavin had plenty of justification for his brusqueness toward me").[7]

In the meantime, Gavin and his two aides hopped into the general's jeep and drove as far as a railroad overpass north of Mook, where they ran into intense fire. "The bullets were whining over my head like hornets," Gavin recalled. "I remember seeing a cow come up over a rise, and when the bullets hit it, it shuddered and dropped to its forelegs and then just rolled over and died." The general's party managed to make contact with a lonely bazookaman who was cowering in a foxhole about twenty yards away. Ahead of him, a string of mines adorned the road. "He seemed to think that the Germans were about to overrun his foxhole and he was quite frightened." The soldier was so scared that he was shaking involuntarily. Gavin reassured him that help was on the way and this calmed him down a bit. A little farther up the road, in the direction of Mook, a lone British tank was in position. In reaction to the heavy small-arms fire, the tank backed up and inadvertently ran over one of the mines, damaging the tank. The crewmen hopped out and took off for the rear. As Sergeant Wood and Lieutenant Olson laid down cover fire, Gavin sent the jeep driver back to division headquarters with orders to send up a reserve battalion from the Coldstream Guards. Before these reinforcements could arrive, though, the firing in Mook died down dramatically, thanks to the success of Colonel Ekman's counterattack.

A trooper delivered an apple-cheeked, teenage enemy prisoner to Gavin. "He was part of a combat team that had the mission of driving through Mook . . . capturing the bridge over the canal, and joining up with an attack through Beek, four or five miles to the north." This information confirmed what Gavin had surmised about the German attacks on the Groesbeek heights. He made contact with Ekman, who confirmed that the 505th had the situation under control in Mook. As the senior officers talked, Lieutenant Olson, who had once served as a platoon leader in B Company, saw the survivors of his old outfit. The young lieutenant felt very guilty that he had not been with them for the worst of the fighting in Mook. He hardly knew what to say. He felt even worse when he saw the bodies of several platoon members. "I remember staring at one kid . . . called 'Rocky,'" he later said, "a friendly teenage boy with a crew cut, dead beside his machine gun. His machine gun was empty and his rifle was empty." Waves of revulsion, regret, and guilt came over Olson. He turned away in disgust.

Gavin was now satisfied that the Germans were not going to take the Heumen bridge, so he turned his attention to the German attacks in the 508th sector, where a battalion-size German force, under Major Karl-Heinz Becker, had been attacking all day. As before, Gavin wanted to see the battle with his own eyes. After a quick stop at division headquarters, he and his companions motored to Berg en Dal. When they got there, they found themselves right in the middle of the battle. "We came to the road crossing near the DeGroot Hotel in Berg-en-dahl," the general wrote. "From there the road down to Beek was steep and curved in several places. The entire place was under very heavy fire."

They dismounted the jeep and took cover. Gavin crawled on his belly across the paved road to the shelter of a nearby stand of woods. Bullets zipped several feet over his head. He found the sound strangely comforting. The zipping noises, as opposed to sharp cracks, meant the bullets were too high to do any damage. He made it to the trees, where he was more or less safe from enemy fire, and met up with a group of weary-looking 508th troopers who were digging foxholes. "They told me that the Germans had half-tracks firing twenty-millimeter antiaircraft weapons as ground weapons. They were nasty to deal with, since the twenty-millimeter round exploded in the air and inflicted severe casualties." The enemy also had tanks. Perhaps Gavin's greatest strength as a commander was the ability to inspire his soldiers. "The general had a kind of sixth sense," Olson once said. "He seemed to know instinctively where he should be." In the forest, he assured the exhausted men that the situation would soon be under control. The ridgeline near Berg en Dal was good defensible ground, and he insisted that the Germans would have trouble dislodging the Americans from it. In such instances, soldiers are usually concerned mainly for their own safety. If a senior officer can assure them that all is not lost, it creates hope for survival, which, in turn, generates a willingness to fight. This was exactly what Gavin did in the woods and all around the 508th sector.

At one point, he encountered Lieutenant Colonel Louis Mendez, commander of the 3rd Battalion. Mendez, who was an equally charismatic leader, briefed the general. Mendez told him that the Germans had overrun Beek and Wyler, but that he had held them off at Berg en Dal by shifting platoons around to various trouble spots. Gavin was pleasantly surprised that the Germans had not found the gaps between such tenuous strongpoints and bulled their way into Nijmegen. The fact that they hadn't indicated poor leadership, poor training, or, most likely, sheer exhaustion on their part. Gavin promised Mendez to increase his artillery support and expressed the hope that he might be reinforced by the 325th the next day. Regardless, Gavin planned to counterattack, as soon as possible, to regain the lost ground. Both officers believed—correctly, as it turned out—that the German attack was already dwindling and would lose all momentum when darkness set in.

Gavin also learned that the remnants of the regiment's A Company were behind enemy lines at Hill 75.9 (nicknamed Devil's Hill by the men), holding the highest ground in the entire Nijmegen region. These were the same men who had fought so hard in the original attempt to take the Nijmegen road bridge and the subsequent attack to clear the glider landing zones. They had taken Devil's Hill in a bold, daring assault against German paratroopers on September 19. Aided by a protective screen of friendly artillery, they had held out all day on September 20 against ferocious enemy attempts to regain the hill. "We were surrounded by the German troops in this area," Lieutenant John Foley, the commander, later wrote. "We were shelled and attacked by a superior force but held our ground." During one firefight, the Germans had stopped shooting and demanded their surrender. Foley had shouted back, "If you want me, come and get me!" and ordered his men to open fire. Company A, or what remained of it, continued to hold out.

In the bigger picture, Gavin was confident by late afternoon that the II Fallschirmjäger Corps attacks would not collapse his division front. He still controlled the Heumen bridge, and he believed he would, during the night or perhaps the next day, recover all the lost ground. It would be an overstatement to say, as Lieutenant Colonel Wienecke did, that Gavin, "by his own personal 'command presence' . . . turned the tide" at the Groesbeek heights. The soldiers themselves, and smaller unit leaders, accomplished that. Moreover, the enemy Kampfgruppen were not quite strong enough to accomplish the ambitious missions assigned to them, at least against a first-class formation like the 82nd Airborne Division. There is little question, though, that Gavin's decision to leave Nijmegen and assume direct control of the battle on the flanks solidified the situation there. He turned chaos into confusion, fear into resolute calm. He was clearly an inspirational figure to any soldier who saw him, and this injected much-needed life into the American defensive battle. In that sense, his personal presence was a substantial asset, expended wisely for the greater purpose of holding the divisional flanks. But it also meant that the main push for the Nijmegen bridges would go on without him.[8]

CHAPTER 11

Resolution

The once picturesque riverfront was now a ghastly wreck. Half-destroyed, fire-scorched homes scarred by collapsed roofs, piles of masonry, and jagged shell holes lined the urban lanes near the Nijmegen bridges. Plumes of slate-colored smoke billowed malevolently upward, blotting out the sun. German artillery periodically pounded the ruins. "We heard houses crashing down and the shriek of shells was incessant," Martijn Deinum jotted in his diary. "Glass shattered at each burst and we felt the air pressure acutely." Like many other Dutch civilians, he huddled alongside a small group of people in a basement, with no water, no power, and little food. City hospitals were choked with the wounded, both civilian and military. Refugees were still fleeing from the city. German planes periodically buzzed the tormented streets, strafing vehicles and people alike.

All around the Hunner Park, from the Valkhof to the Belvedere tower to the Keizer Lodewijk Plein roundabout, battle-hardened German soldiers waited in foxholes, dugouts, and trenches or behind antitank guns for the Allied attack they all knew was imminent. They had strung barbed wire all over the Hunner Park. Their trenches and fighting holes gashed through the greenery, creating a pockmarked landscape. Many of the young Germans were prepared to defend the bridge approaches to the last. Some of their comrades were still sprinkled among the houses that brooded over the park. All day long the blocks around the park had echoed with the sounds of small firefights. Tanks shot up German-controlled houses. Bazooka-wielding paratroopers blasted holes in the walls of some houses, opening the way for their buddies to charge through the newly made openings and kill the German defenders. In a few cases, troopers hopped from rooftop to rooftop, assaulting their enemies from what amounted to the high ground of the cityscape. "Jolly sight, seeing those chaps jump from rooftop to rooftop," one British officer jauntily commented. Methodically, the combined arms Allied force reduced the German presence in the area. At some point, the British reached the two-story building where Captain Jonathan "Jock" Adams and his survivors from A Company, 508th Parachute Infantry Regiment, had been holed up since the original American attempt for the bridges on Market Garden's first night. Adams and his newly rescued group left Nijmegen and managed to reunite with their A Company comrades on Devil's Hill, where fighting still raged.

Among the dense Nijmegen blocks, close encounters between the two sides were all too common. During one patrol, Lieutenant Robert Dwyer, who headed up the regimental demolitions platoon, peeked through a hedge and found himself face-to-face with a German soldier. As both men blinked in surprise, the German sputtered, *"Heil Hitler!"* Dwyer and the other members of his patrol backed off and opened fire. "It turned out to be a . . . machine gun crew digging in," Dwyer related. In the brief firefight, the Americans killed one of the gunners. The others fled. A photograph of the dead man's family fell out of his pocket onto the street. It lay flapping in the breeze, as if bearing mute testimony to those in Germany who would soon mourn the fallen soldier.

The close-quarters tension was especially high in the blocks loosely held by E Company of the 505th, immediately overlooking the roundabout. The smoke and glare from multiple fires made visibility tricky. Lieutenant James Coyle and Sergeant Ben Popilsky were standing in a doorway when they saw two men walking along a nearby sidewalk. The sergeant had seen the men a few minutes earlier and realized that their uniforms were unfamiliar, but he had assumed that they were British tankers. Now Coyle immediately recognized them as enemy soldiers. "I could see in the light of [a] burning building that they wore the helmets and smocks of German paratroopers." Coyle and Popilsky opened fire. One of the German soldiers fell down and lay groaning on the sidewalk. The other scrambled away and took cover behind a tree. He shouted to the Americans for permission to take care of his wounded comrade (Popilsky understood German, so he translated for Lieutenant Coyle). The lieutenant refused. "I wanted the wounded German soldier as a prisoner," Coyle said, "and I was not about to let the other man come back and pick us off." Popilsky and the German carried on an animated conversation in Yiddish. Exasperated, the German paratrooper broke off negotiations. "*Verdammte Amerikanische Schweinhunds!*" he yelled, and took off. The two Americans yelled, "Kraut bastard!" By the time Coyle and Popilsky got to the wounded man, he was dead.

There were still quite a few other enemy soldiers lurking in the area. They took to attics or basements and sniped at the Americans. Not long after this incident, one of these snipers shot and killed Popilsky. As several other men, including Private Earl Boling, assaulted the house where the shooting came from, they were driven back by intense submachine gun fire and several grenades. The fire mortally wounded Corporal Thomas Burke. "We were pinned down between the walls of the backyard by intense fire from the second floor," Boling later wrote. As Boling looked at Burke's body, he thought of a conversation they had once had. "If anything happens to me," Burke had said, "let my mother know how it happened so she won't think I got shot getting away." Boling resolved to do just that. All at once, a grenade flew out of the house and exploded near him, wounding him in the legs and killing Corporal James Crouse. Lieutenant Coyle brought up Private Martin Carpenter, a bazookaman, and ordered him to blast the house. His potent rounds shattered the back wall of the house. Under the cover of this fire, Coyle ordered everyone to withdraw.

Some of the German interlopers were mortar or artillery observers who found the houses to be perfect hiding places from which to call down destruction upon the Americans. One such observer found a perfect target in Staff Sergeant Otis Sampson's sixty-millimeter mortar section. An artillery shell burst above him, showering fragments downward. "A sharp, red-hot pain shot into me as if someone had hit me with a sledgehammer," Sampson wrote. "Everything started to go black and I was going along with it." He was badly wounded in the back and the leg. The veteran Sampson, who was an original member of the 505th, thought of his men and his mother. "I was ready to die and was excepting [sic] it willingly." Instead he staggered to his feet and tried to give himself first aid. Private First Class Dennis O'Laughlin got to him and dragged him into a cellar to wait while he retrieved a jeep and some medical assistance. O'Laughlin personally drove Sergeant Sampson to a hospital.

As Sampson's drama was playing out, the rest of the company methodically hunted down and killed off most of the remaining enemy in their midst. Thinking the Germans were all dead or gone, Lieutenant James Smith, the company commander, and Lieutenant William Meddaugh, his executive officer, were walking together single file through a backyard, on their way to visit one of the platoons, when they saw two men approaching them. Smith was in the lead, Meddaugh right behind him. Meddaugh recognized immediately that the two strangers were German soldiers. "My reaction when I saw them was that they were *prisoners* and I expected to see one or more of our own men following close behind. But it suddenly dawned on me that they were both armed with machine pistols." For a couple of pregnant moments, the two pairs of men stopped short and stared at one another as each man processed in his mind that he was face-to-face with an enemy and not just an innocuous stranger. The two German soldiers turned and ran, out of the yard, through an alleyway, around a corner. Smith and Meddaugh took off after them. "[Smith] was able to get off a couple fast shots with his pistol and I got off a burst with my Thompson," Meddaugh said. One of the Germans dropped dead. The other got away from the two officers but ran right into another small group of Americans. He wisely surrendered.[1]

By the time midafternoon shadows began dancing along the ruined blocks of downtown Nijmegen, the houses overlooking the bridges were under Anglo-American control. Goulburn and Vandervoort were now ready to unleash their all-out assault for the southern end of the bridges. The British commander assigned the left-flank objectives of the Valkhof and the Belvedere tower to two of his infantry companies. On the right flank, the Americans were to push across the roundabout into the Hunner Park—E Company would be on the right of the roundabout, along the Belvoir, while F Company plunged straight across the open boulevard into the park. "There was no concealment and fire power would be the only cover when we moved," Vandervoort later wrote. Tanks would support the infantry, as would Vandervoort's eighty-one-millimeter mortar teams from their ghoulish positions half a mile away in the town cemetery. Once the assault force had trapped and destroyed the Germans in this pincer attack, they could capture the road bridge. Goulburn ordered the same group that had attempted to take the railroad bridge the day before to simply renew their assault.

At 1500, the bold attacks began. "The Grenadier Guards tanks—four abreast—converged from avenues on both flanks," Vandervoort said. "The troopers stormed the German positions, shooting as they came. The assault was met by a blast of bullets from the bunkers and trenches." In fact, the F Company attack began a bit too early, without proper fire support from machine gun teams and tanks. Captain Robert Rosen, an inexperienced officer who had just taken command of the company, swung his Thompson submachine gun over his head and shouted, "Let's go! Follow me!" He bravely took off, with several other men in trail. In another context, this act of leadership would have been seen by the troopers (and historians) as heroic. Instead, it came off as foolhardy, perhaps even amateurish, because it was premature and improperly supported. Amid the confusion, not all of the F Company men left cover to follow the captain.

At best, parts of two platoons joined in the attack. Sergeant Spencer Wurst, a squad leader, was one man who did. The Pennsylvania native took off across a sidewalk, running as fast as he could for the park, hoping his own men would follow him. "We got to the street and started into the park under direct small-arms, grenade, and machine gun fire at ranges of fifteen to seventy-five yards," he recalled. "The enemy was well dug in, fighting from foxholes and trenches located between the sidewalk on back to a hundred yards into the park."

As they ran, Wurst and the others formed a ragged line of sorts. Out of the corner of his eye, Wurst saw an unarmed German soldier, his arms up, pop out of a foxhole and run for the sidewalk. The man clearly wanted to surrender, but the Americans were so keyed up for close-quarters fighting that they shot him down. Most of the German defenders were SS soldiers and thus not inclined to surrender. But when the Americans killed one of the few who did wish to give up, any others who might have leaned in that direction probably thought they did not have the option. Sergeant Wurst formed the opinion that "this incident . . . resulted in many needless casualties." In any event, the German fire was so intense that the attackers made little headway. According to one after-action report, the troopers "were met by heavy grazing fire from MG's, automatic weapons, rifles, grenades and 20mm and were soon pinned down." Captain Rosen caught a bullet in the face. Sergeant Wurst saw him holding his hands over his bleeding mouth, sprinting for the rear. The rookie captain soon died of his wounds. The abortive attack cost the lives of four other men. Two more were badly wounded.

Within half an hour, Lieutenant Joe Holcomb, the new company commander, had reorganized the company, extracted previously pinned-down soldiers like Wurst, and renewed the assault with plenty of fire support, particularly from machine gunners. What followed was not so much a conventional, incremental battle as a bloody free-for-all. From a myriad of different directions, the British and Americans converged on the formidable German defenses. The fighting was intimate and personal. "No-quarter combat became the order of the day throughout that quarter-mile area," Vandervoort recalled. "The Germans seemed indifferent to death; the paratroopers retaliated with ice-cold ruthlessness."

With urgency that could be born only of mortal fear, Vandervoort's paratroopers flung themselves across the open blocks, past the Belvoir, through the roundabout, and over the sidewalk ramparts in the middle of the park. Near the roundabout, Lieutenant Peter Prescott, a tank troop commander in the Grenadier Guards, was trailing behind one of his Shermans when the tank absorbed a direct hit from a Panzerfaust and caught fire. In the turret, his platoon sergeant was killed instantly. Enemy machine gunners slaughtered all but one of the vacating crewmen. "[He] was very severely wounded in the abdomen and took cover beside the tank," Prescott recalled. An American medic braved intense fire to treat the wounded man, but he could not save him. The medic was lucky to make it back, under cover of smoke grenades, to Prescott's tank.

Just then, a German soldier leaned out of a second-story window and fired a Panzerfaust at Prescott's Sherman. The round glanced off the deck of the tank but did not set it afire. As the lieutenant tried to maneuver away from the enemy soldier's kill zone, he found himself looking squarely at a partially concealed antitank gun in the park shrubbery. "We fired at each other almost simultaneously." Prescott missed. The enemy did not— the armor-piercing shell wrecked Prescott's Sherman, and he and his crew bailed out. After initially taking shelter in a house, Prescott took command of the last remaining tank in his troop.

From the vantage point of a basement across the street, Captain Arie Bestebreurtje, the Dutch Jedburgh leader, watched the tanks burn. Beyond them, the bridge loomed large over the area—impossible to miss. It struck the young operative as "a monumental thing that completely dominated the scene. The road split up into several large avenues at the circle and a long ramp . . . up onto the bridge." As he watched, he noticed that his hands were shaking. To take his mind off his own fear, he slung his submachine gun and began hauling ammo to anyone who needed it.

Initially, at least, the surviving tanks stood on the edges of the park and sprayed the German holes while the infantrymen plunged right into middle of them. There was no order, no rationality, no plan to the assault. It amounted to small groups of desperate men fighting for sheer survival. A twenty-millimeter round laced into the torso of Lieutenant John Dodd, one of the key officers who was leading the attack. The lieutenant had a gaping hole in his side. He collapsed to the ground. A medic, with tears welling up in his eyes, could see that he was beyond any hope. He took out a morphine ampule and injected it into Dodd's leg. Sergeant Vernon Francisco was so enraged by the impending death of his lieutenant that he stood in the open, pitching grenades at the enemy crew until he either killed them or drove them away. Nearby, Private Wayne Galvin had no sooner taken in the sight of the angry sergeant than a mortar shell exploded a few yards away. "My left wrist was shattered," he said. "I also was hit in the left thigh." He hobbled around and kept fighting until the leg collapsed. A mortar shell burst right above Private Harold Peterman, showering him with deadly fragments. He fell down and died on Oranjesingel, the wide avenue that led to the roundabout.

Sergeant Wurst and his squad were in the middle of the confusion, right among the German holes, fighting the enemy face-to-face. As the young squad leader huddled behind a tree, he could scarcely believe the intensity of the enemy fire. Such venerable trees restricted visibility in the park, but they offered life-sustaining cover. "It appeared to me that I could reach out and grab the bullets as they flew," Wurst wrote. "I took cover in the prone position behind a very large tree. I fired as fast as I could, and many rounds of enemy fire burrowed into that tree trunk." Enemy fire ripped into the tree anywhere from six inches to a foot too high. The noise of all the weapons—machine guns, rifles, grenades, antitank guns, tanks, mortars—was absolutely deafening. Men who were right next to each other had to shout in each other's ears to be heard.

Several yards away from Wurst, his assistant squad leader, Corporal Howard Krueger, physically dragged a German soldier out of one hole and forced him to surrender. As the German crawled to the rear, he paused to bandage a wounded American. A burst of German fire inadvertently hit and killed him. Off to the right was a staggered line of men that comprised E Company's assault. In the recollection of Lieutenant Smith, they "had to literally drive the Germans from their holes with grenades and cold steel." Machine gunners actually fired their weapons from the hip, a rarity in World War II. Riflemen pitched grenades into foxholes. Soldiers huddled momentarily behind the shelter of trees or embankments to catch their breath before forcing themselves to assault the next hole or dugout. Everyone struggled to stay out of the barbed wire or cut holes through it. In more than a few instances, troopers traded shots with their German enemies from only a few feet away. Some even fought them with bayonets or fists.

The British infantrymen were engaged in vicious fights around the grounds of the Valkhof amid the ruins of Charlemagne's castle and an old chapel. "In front of us for about 100-150 yards was a big sunken garden bounded on the left by houses [near the river], on the right this high bank and wall, and in front of a very big house," Major H. F. Stanley, the infantry battalion commander, wrote. The British used white phosphorous grenades and submachine gun fire to kill enemy soldiers in the house and surrounding dugouts. The house was the site of Captain Karl-Heinz Euling's headquarters. The German commander managed to escape with about sixty soldiers and evade the onrushing Allied troops. The house itself went up in flames, killing dozens of Germans. In the wake of this, the British captured the Belvedere tower. Glancing to the right, Major Stanley could just begin to see the American paratroopers overrunning the Hunner Park. The sight excited the young major. "They are splendid individual fighters and know no fear," he said. He was right that they were formidable soldiers, but wrong in his assumption that they had no fear. Every man in the Hunner Park was immersed in fear, but most kept going, even as men around them fell dead or wounded. There was little time to think or reflect. The assault was based on pure animal instinct. "The Nazis could not withstand the combined assault of [the British] and the Americans," Lieutenant Colonel Goulburn wrote, "and were forced back yard by yard through their trenches."

Some of the German infantry soldiers began fleeing from their positions, in hopes of sprinting over the road bridge to the German-held north bank. From a captured enemy trench, Sergeant Wurst's squad was in perfect position to unload on one such retreating group. As the enemy soldiers rushed from girder to girder, Wurst and his men shot them down in droves. "As soon as they dashed to the next girder, we had them. There were thirty or so at the start but I don't believe a single one got across." The park itself was still under intense mortar and artillery fire. This had the effect of limiting Allied movement. Isolated German soldiers held out to the end, forcing the British and the Americans to carefully check every single position. Slowly, the Allies were gaining control of the Valkhof and the Hunner Park. Just beyond those objectives, the road bridge beckoned.[2]

At precisely 1440, three British trucks rolled to a stop on the road behind the southwest corner of the Nyma factory. The drivers hopped out, opened up their cargo beds, and began to unload the much-anticipated boats. Lounging nearby, Major Cook's 3rd Battalion troopers eagerly stood up and descended on the trucks to help the British unload them. Curiously, although the 3rd Battalion soldiers were no more than a mile away from the Valkhof, they could not even hear the fight for the southern end of the bridges, which was even then still raging. Cook and his men were shocked at the flimsiness of the canvas boats. They had expected substantial watercraft, maybe even with outboard engines and some armor, not these glorified tubs. "They looked like pieces of plywood with canvas wrapped around them and a few extra boards piled on top," Captain Moffatt Burriss said. To the South Carolinian, they looked like "they wouldn't make it across a swimming pool," much less one of Europe's largest rivers. The boats were nineteen feet long and no more than thirty inches high. The

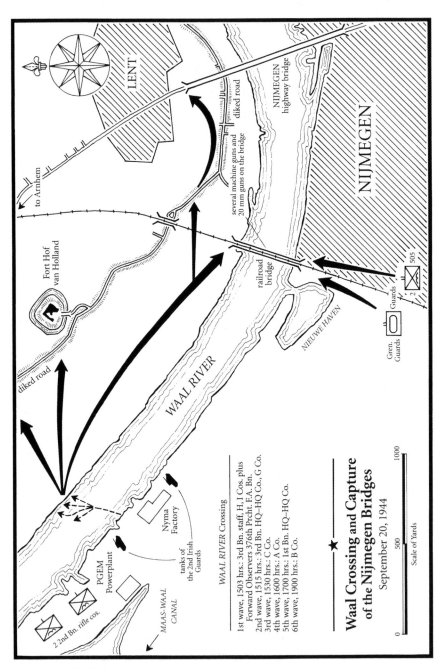

LENT

to Arnhem

NIJMEGEN highway bridge

diked road

several machine guns and
20 mm guns on the bridge

NIJMEGEN

Fort Hof
van Holland

railroad
bridge

diked road

NIEUWE HAVEN

WAAL RIVER

505

Gren. Guards

Gren.
Guards

2 2

Nyma
Factory

tanks of
the 2nd Irish
Guards

PGEM
Powerplant

MAAS-WAAL
CANAL

2 2nd Bn. rifle cos.

WAAL RIVER Crossing

1st wave, 1503 hrs.: 3rd Bn. staff, H, I Cos. plus
Forward Observers 376th Prcht. F.A. Bn.
2nd wave, 1515 hrs.: 3rd Bn. HQ–HQ Co., G Co.
3rd wave, 1530 hrs.: C Co.
4th wave, 1600 hrs.: A Co.
5th wave, 1700 hrs.: 1st Bn. HQ–HQ Co.
6th wave, 1900 hrs.: B Co.

★

**Waal Crossing and Capture
of the Nijmegen Bridges**
September 20, 1944

0   500   1000

Scale of Yards

canvas skin of each boat wrapped around a skeletal, flat, grated plywood bottom and wooden pegs that held up the gunwales. A wooden tiller at the rear served as a rudder. Chaplain Kuehl asked how the boats were propelled. "Canoe paddles," someone replied. The young clergyman felt a sinking feeling in his stomach. Each boat was supposed to come with eight paddles. In fact, some had as few as two. When Cook's men asked him how they could row with only two paddles, he told them to use their rifle butts. Each boat weighed almost four hundred pounds, but, with weapons and ammo, they would probably weigh twice that during the crossing.

Lieutenant Mike Sabia, one of the engineer officers, had the job of supervising assembly of the boats. He had discussed how to do so with the British, but, in truth, the engineers simply learned on the fly. The boats were fairly easy to put together. Engineers quickly snapped the wooden pegs into the proper places. Some infantrymen helped. Others crowded around to watch or, when boats were ready, piled their gear into them. Lieutenant Tom MacLeod, one of the engineer officers, thought ruefully as he worked, "What in the world are we going to do with boats made out of cloth?" To Captain Henry Keep, who hailed from a wealthy Pennsylvania family, the boats were "smaller than Daddy's tin ducking boat." Private Walter Hughes had frequently sailed the Hudson River during his youth, so he, more than anyone, knew how unsuited the boats were for the task at hand. His heart began to race with nervousness and fear. "I knew boats, and these things didn't look like they belonged in a duck pond, let alone a wide river like the Waal," he said. He thought about loosening his bootlaces so that he would be able to swim the river barefoot when his boat sank. "My fear was not the enemy; it was surviving the crossing." Lieutenant James Megellas, who had spent many days fishing on Wisconsin lakes, had similar thoughts. To him, the boats looked rather similar to the little fishing craft he had often employed. At most, four or five people had been able to pack together to cast their lines. He knew that each boat team would consist of as many as sixteen men, plus their ammo and weapons.

"By any standard the boats would be dangerously overloaded," Magellas wrote. "I wondered if we could stay afloat even without enemy resistance."

To Captain Burriss, there was an element of ridiculousness about the whole thing, "like a Laurel and Hardy movie, only with real lives at stake." While he kept such thoughts to himself, many of the troopers, particularly the enlisted men, kept up a stinging commentary as they watched their comrades assemble the boats. "Where are the Boy Scouts to go with these toys?" one of them wisecracked. "You mean I'm trusting my life to that thing?" another mused. Still another exclaimed, "I can't even swim. Oh, shit, I'm in big trouble." Sergeant Clement Haas, who also could not swim, dearly wished he had a life vest.

As the boatbuilders worked, eight British Typhoons swooped in along the river and shot up the German-held north bank, with little effect. The Germans unleashed a stunning volume of antiaircraft fire, although none of the planes were hit. Almost as quickly as they appeared, they were gone. The thick antiaircraft fire, though, provided a troubling preview for the troopers of what they would soon face.

At 1450, the supporting fire began in earnest. Artillery, mortars, and tanks opened up on the German positions across the river. For nearly ten minutes the Allied crewmen hurled high-explosive shells at the enemy before switching to white phosphorous smoke shells. The ensuing smoke screen looked wispy and thin to the paratroopers. Plus, the wind was blowing it back in their direction. In their hearts, the men knew that German visibility would barely be impaired.

Then, at last, it was time to go. At 1503, Major Cook blew a whistle and ordered everyone to move out. Officers yelled, "Let's go!" Each boat team—twenty-six in all—stood and hoisted their awkward, heavy boats to their shoulders. "They were . . . rather clumsy . . . to handle . . . especially on a hot day when you were trying to get them into the water as quickly as you could," Lieutenant John Holabird recalled. "There was the usual groaning and grumbling and slipping and everybody snapping at everybody else." Arduously, each group ascended the dike and ran as best they could under such heavy loads. They stumbled over the road, toward the river some one hundred fifty yards away. When the men were slowed by a wire fence that stood along the route to the river, tanks had to overrun parts of it, while soldiers blew more holes in the impediment with Gammon grenades. Major Cook, whose men had once doubted that he would share any danger with them in combat, was in the lead. He stood next to one opening in the fence, holding it down, personally wishing each man luck. "I stood trying to hustle them up and I spoke to just about every man in the battalion," Cook said. As the heavily laden troopers edged past the major, he made eye contact with as many men as he could, calling each person by name or rank. "Hi, there, Sarge," he typically said. "Come on; get going." Everyone responded with a greeting or a wisecrack, the most typical of which was, "Hey, Major, do you have a cup of coffee or a drink?" Cook just smiled and gestured toward the river. Later, one of the NCOs, in recalling the moment, said, "He fooled us completely. He turned into a real good leader and a good soldier."[3]

Once past the wire fence, they descended the steep embankment, then stumbled across fifty yards of open, muddy ground that led to the riverbank. Under the weight of the heavy boats, many of the soldiers sank ankle-deep into the mud. Already the smoke screen was dissipating. Awkwardly, the men began to heave their boats onto the sandy soil at the river's edge and board them as best they could. Some of the boats edged into the water smoothly, while others were bogged down in the mud. A few even sank and had to be pulled laboriously out of the water by frantic paratroopers. "The footing was not solid," the survivors later told an army historian. "The shoal went off gradually and many . . . thinking they had the boat fully afloat, had to jump out again, float the boat more fully, and then jump in again."

At some point (accounts differ as to when), the Germans spotted the crossing force and opened fire. A terrifying blend of mortar shells, twenty-millimeter fire, eighty-eight-millimeter fire, machine gun fire, and small-arms fire began coming in. Most of it was coming from enemy positions on the railroad bridge, the dike road, and Fort Hof van Holland. The combination of the friendly-fire support and the enemy fire was deafening. The shooting echoed off the water and the urban landscape. "An ear-shattering noise began," Jan van Gent, a Dutch resistance man who was with the British tanks, later related. "The two- and four-centimeter flak, stationed somewhere near the railroad bridge, fired like mad." This fire was so intense that, according to Van Gent, it sawed two concrete poles in half along the dike road. "As if in a rage at our trying anything so dangerous, he was throwing everything he owned at us," Captain Keep wrote. He himself felt naked in the wake of such fierce enemy opposition. He was right to feel that way. They were out in the open, on the low riverbank, with no cover of any kind. Behind them, the Irish Guards' tanks continued to hurl shells at the Germans, while the 2nd Battalion soldiers were laying down reasonably accurate mortar and machine gun fire. The drifting clouds of smoke offered little, if any, real concealment. Other than that, they were pretty much on their own. Keep looked around and was amazed to see that, in spite of all this, no one was wavering.

Amid the chaos of dodging the enemy fire, the men desperately set about the task of boarding the boats. Lieutenant Megellas, like many of the other officers, had a difficult time maintaining any semblance of organization. "Trying to coordinate the efforts of men getting in the boats and crossing a river with a fast-moving current was next to impossible." As a private named Legacie attempted to get his team's boat moving, he actually got bogged down in the mud and was stuck underwater. His commanding officer, Captain Carl Kappel, hurriedly stripped off his gear (he was not wearing a helmet) and went in after Legacie. Kappel was confident in his strong swimming skills, but he was surprised at the swiftness of the current. He reached Legacie, grabbed him, and dragged him back to the river's edge. "I was worn out by the time I got him back," Kappel said, "huffing and puffing like an old man. I was so tired I couldn't get him out of the water." Legacie was okay. Kappel had little time to recover. He put his gear back on and hopped into the first boat he could see.

By now, most of the men had climbed aboard their boats and were shoving off from the fire-swept south bank. Each man jostled for a place in his boat. Some sat; some knelt; some leaned over the sides—no one stood. The men along the sides paddled as vigorously as they could. Many used their rifle butts, while a few even used their hands. On the roof of the power station, Staff Sergeant Kenneth Nicoll, whose eighty-one-millimeter mortar section was firing in support of the crossing, watched them struggle against the swift current. "With the bullets flying everywhere and when the current hit those boats, you oughta have seen those boys," he later marveled. On the road that paralleled the river, Corporal Bill Chennell of the 2nd Household Cavalry Regiment stood atop his armored car and strained his eyes for a look at the boats. "I could hear the machine guns fire from the opposite bank," he recalled. "Then the American paratroopers seemed to be swallowed up in the smoke. You could . . . see the tracers from the machine guns, but not the Americans. It was obvious that no one would get through that blanket of fire unhurt." The young British scout was filled with admiration for the Yanks.

Closer to the riverbank, Lieutenant John Gorman, an Irish Guards tank commander, was pumping shells at the north bank as fast his crewmen could unleash them. The little American armada struck him as almost pathetically small against the formidable backdrop of the river, the opposite bank, and the hulking bridges looming a couple miles to the right. The German fire appeared to be overwhelming. "It seemed to me the Germans must have had their guns firing two or three feet above the water level, catching the Americans across the chests," he later said. "In the water, the Americans seemed to be moving very slowly." Gorman's commander, Major Edward Tyler, was worried about the safety of his own tanks. They were, after all, perched out in the open, along the dike road, on the river side of the power station. "We were wide-open. Sixteen tanks silhouetted against the skyline." Tyler's tanks blasted away with their main guns and their machine guns. They also fired some smoke shells to make up for the huge gaps that were forming between the clouds of drifting smoke. At one point, as Tyler studied the opposite bank through his binoculars, he was amazed to see one of his tanks score a direct hit on a horse-drawn German antitank gun, without harming the horse. "I learned later the gunner had purposely tried to avoid killing the horse because he was genuinely fond of them and a dedicated horseman himself." In the power station, Colonel Tucker and General Browning watched, awestruck, as the boats muddled through the swift current and the wall of enemy fire. Browning turned to Tucker and said, "What magnificent troops to move forward like that. Any nation should be proud of them."

In the boats, the men were feeling terrified, not proud. Incoming enemy fire was so intense that it seemed as if the water were churning. To Captain Burriss, it was like being in the middle of a sudden rainstorm, with "the sky actually hailing bullets; they kicked up little spouts of water everywhere; it was like a hailstorm on the water." So many mortar shells exploded and so many machine gun bullets skipped along the water that to Staff Sergeant Clark Fuller, it "made the water around us look like it was raining." For Private First Class Everett Trefethern it was "like a school of mackerel on the feed." In the recollection of Private First Class Lawrence Dunlop, the river became "like a boiling pan of water." The water around Lieutenant Megellas's boat was swirling and splashing so much that it reminded him "of a school of piranha in a feeding frenzy."

The engineers intended to instill a rhythm into the desperate paddling of each boat team. But, in the chaos of the moment, most of the men frantically gouged their paddles, rifle butts, or, in a few cases, their hands into the water with little coordination. Everyone was soon soaked to the skin. Grunting, groaning, and shouting "Heave ho!" they simply rowed as best they could. The job was at once exhausting and terrifying. Men rowed until they felt their arms would fall off. Then they handed their paddles to someone else, rested a few moments, and resumed their efforts. Staff Sergeant Fuller's boat actually circled randomly for a few moments before the soldiers figured out that they were rowing at cross-purposes. At last, they established enough of a rhythm to get back on course. "Finally, we started moving out toward the middle of the river," he recalled. To the young NCO, their progress was so excruciatingly slow that the river seemed to be more than a mile wide.

Aboard a nearby boat, Captain Keep, the operations officer, flashed back to his rowing days at Princeton. Amid the stress of the moment, he vividly remembered the days of old, when his coxswain would bellow a steady cadence as he rowed fiercely on Lake Carnegie. Now, in this very different place, Keep began to sound off just like him—"One, two, three, four!"—in an effort to regulate the strokes of the soldiers around him. It wasn't much, but it made him feel a little better. "By now the broad surface of the Waal was covered with our small canvas craft," he later wrote, "all crammed with frantically paddling men. Set to the deafening roar of omnipresent firing, this scene of defenseless, frail canvas boats, all jammed to overflowing with humanity, all striving desperately to cross the Waal as quickly as possible and get to a place where at least they could fight—this was fiendish and dreadful. We looked like a bunch of animals, void of dignity and normalcy." They were like single-minded automatons, obsessed with making it across the river.

Many were so frightened that they could hardly command themselves to move or even raise their torsos above the gunwales of their respective boats. They had to, though, because anyone who wasn't helping to row or steer was simply deadweight. Some men cursed and roared. Others prayed fervently. Major Cook, in a trance of fear, kept repeating, "Hail Mary, full of grace . . . hail Mary, full of grace . . ." as he paddled vigorously. For earnest Catholics like Cook, the Hail Mary is a prominent crisis prayer, so it was not surprising that it would be foremost in his mind during the most frightening moments of his life. All thoughts—joking or otherwise— of standing up like George Washington were long gone now. Behind Cook, on the same boat, Chaplain Kuehl prayed aloud, over and over, "Lord, thy will be done!" The courageous clergyman seriously doubted that anyone would make it to the north bank.

To say they were all sitting ducks would be an understatement. Ducks, after all, are comfortable in the water; not so for paratroopers. With each desperate stroke, they found themselves in closer range of the enemy weapons. Firing from the railroad bridge, Fort Hof van Holland, and the north-bank dike, the Germans could scarcely miss. Their fire swept mercilessly through water, canvas, and flesh alike. The man sitting shoulder to shoulder with Chaplain Kuehl had his head blown completely off. Alongside him, Lieutenant Hyman Shapiro, the battalion's assistant surgeon, "saw his head disappear." Several other men in the boat were hit. As Kuehl leaned over to help one of the wounded, he was hit "with a . . . fragment in the back which knocked me over on top of the very man I was treating." Fatal head shots were distressingly common (an indicator of the deadly accuracy of German fire). At the stern of Captain Burriss's boat, he was sitting next to the engineer who was manipulating the wooden rudder, guiding the boat. All at once, the captain saw the man's wrist turn red as he got hit. He turned to Burriss and asked him to take the rudder. "Just as I reached for the rudder, he leaned forward and caught a twenty-millimeter high-explosive shell through his head, a round that was meant for me," Burriss said. Blood and brains splattered all over Burriss's right shoulder, helmet, and neck. The captain also caught some shrapnel, but he was okay. The dead engineer keeled over the side of the boat. With his torso and head in the water but his feet caught inside the boat, he became, in effect, a second rudder, steering the boat off course. As Captain Burriss tried to steer with the real rudder, he reached down, disengaged the dead man's feet, and pushed him into the river. "As I watched his body float downstream, I could see the red blood streaming from what was left of his head." Private John Schultz, a mortarman, happened to glance up and see a bullet tear through the head of Sergeant Wilford Dixon. "[He]. . . was right beside me. He . . . died immediately."

Staff Sergeant Tallon was paddling intently when he heard a thud next to him. "The kid on my right groaned and slumped over in my lap," Tallon recalled. "I looked down at him and knew that he had been hit and pushed him over onto the floor of the boat. I could see that he had been hit in the chest." The bullet gashed a hole in his upper body and exited between his shoulder blades. "He was dead . . . very dead." Just then, to the left, a mortar shell scored a direct hit on a neighboring boat, sending up a geyser of water, and then the boat vanished from his line of vision. Those who survived the blast splashed into the river. None of the troopers in the remaining boats could do anything to help them. Several drowned. Private Louie Holt, who had feared that the Waal crossing was tantamount to suicide, went down with that boat. Rowing earnestly in a nearby vessel, Technician Fourth Grade Albert Tarbell, a radioman, happened to see Holt at that terrible moment. "To this day I can still see the look on [his] face as our eyes met." Holt did not survive.

On another boat, Lieutenant Harry "Pappy" Busby got hit and died, just as he had predicted to his buddy Lieutenant Megellas. Upon climbing into his boat, he had argued with Private First Class Matthew Kantala about where to sit. "He took the seat and he got killed," Kantala said. "He was the old goat of the company," one of the officers said of him. Shortly after Busby's death, Kantala himself was badly wounded with fragments to the face and hands. "Lead was flying at us from all directions," Lieutenant Megellas later wrote. "In other boats, bullets opened gaping holes in the canvas sides. The men were frantically trying to keep their boats afloat, bailing with their helmets." Some stricken vessels were so full of dead and wounded that they drifted aimlessly downstream, away from the intended landing spot.

Lieutenant Patrick Mulloy, an engineer platoon leader who had fought at Anzio, thought the fire was the thickest he had ever experienced. He carried a .45-caliber pistol holstered across his torso, and at one point, "something smacked into my side." At first he thought he was hit, but instead the bullet had torn away his holster and left him only grazed. "I had a pretty good-size bruise across my stomach and hip." A few seconds later, a mortar shell exploded close by, badly wounding Corporal Lou Gentile, who was sitting close to Mulloy. "He was pretty well torn up . . . he was conscious, but only briefly." Gentile soon lost consciousness and died. As Private First Class Leonard Tremble's boat neared the shore, a burst of small-arms and mortar fire swept through his vessel, hitting several men and badly wounding him. "I was hit in the face, left shoulder, left leg, and compound fracture of the right arm," he said. All he could think about was bleeding to death. He lay down in the now drifting boat and waited for help. Nearby, Private First Class Herbert Keith, an engineer, was paddling when he saw his buddy Private Herbert Wendland get hit, slump over, and die. Keith, who had planned to sit in that very spot but had found a different place instead, was now consumed with guilt. "I kept thinking that would have been me sitting there," Keith later said. "Before we got to the beach [north bank] this thing whacked me on the back and sent me sprawling to the bottom of the boat." A twenty-millimeter shell had clipped his back and gashed it open, but, through some phenomenal piece of luck, the round had not exploded.

About twenty yards away from the north bank, another boat was hit by a mortar shell, pitching everyone aboard forward, capsizing it. Cursing, spitting, and dog-paddling, the wet troopers made it to shore as best they could. Private Joseph Jedlicka, loaded down with a BAR and two belts of oversize magazines, sank to the bottom of the river, underneath about eight feet of water. Instead of trying to swim, he simply held his breath and walked on all fours to the north bank. His commanding officer, Lieutenant Ernest Murphy, was in the process of accounting for everyone on the sunken boat when he saw Jedlicka emerge from the water. To Murphy, the BAR man seemed like a wayward child. "Get out of the water," Murphy said. "This is no time to be playing around."

"Well, L-T," Jedlicka replied, "I can't swim and I had to crawl on the bottom." In spite of the seriousness of the situation, the lieutenant and the other soaked members of the boat team laughed.

By the most generous estimate, only thirteen of the boats were still in usable condition by the time they made it to the shore (several never made it). Needless to say, the boats landed unevenly, in chaotic clumps. Fortunately, the muddy, sandy soil led to a small embankment that offered some

semblance of welcome cover, at least from those Germans who were shooting from the positions along the dike and the fort. The exhausted troopers
hopped out of their boats, gathered their weapons, and staggered up the
beach to the embankment. "Every man, on getting out of the boat, knew
his job," a postbattle report said. "There was much vomiting from exhaustion." Quite a few of the men had had nothing to eat for the better part of
a day, so they had very little to vomit. In most cases, they simply retched
nervous bile and river water out of their nauseous stomachs.[4]

Enemy fire swept along the lip of the embankment, but the troopers
were at least able to take cover and gather themselves for a few moments
of surcease. Lieutenant Shapiro, the doctor, set up an impromptu aid
station in the dunes. "I had a couple of calls and administered . . . a few
injections of morphine," he recalled. "Most of the [wounded] men were in
the boats still and I told the engineers to take them back with them [to the
south bank]." Many did make it back across the river, where they received
more elaborate first aid than Shapiro could offer. Wounded men began
pouring into the regiment's forward collecting point in the basement of
the Nyma factory building. "All the wounded were soaking wet and covered with the sticky red mud of the river bank which added greatly to the
misery and wretchedness of the scene," Corporal Mickey Graves later
wrote in his diary. He and several other men from the S1 section assisted
the medics by placing wounded men in jeeps and driving them from the
Nyma factory basement to hospitals around Nijmegen. In the basement,
he saw a wounded Chaplain Kuehl circulating around to give whatever
relief he could to the many stricken soldiers. "Covered from head to toe
with red mud . . . with no consideration of his own condition, he was
comforting the most seriously wounded." The sight only deepened Graves's
admiration for the chaplain.

Later, after delivering one load of casualties to a hospital, Corporal
Graves witnessed even more of the grim results of the crossing. "There was
no electricity or heat. Dutch girls and nuns were helping the overworked
medics. The wounded were operated on as soon as their turn came on

improvised tables—some died before that turn." When that happened, the bloodstained medics simply sighed and covered the bodies with blankets. "Long rows of stretchers covered all the halls and hallways of the ground floor of the hospital. Blood was splotched over the floor, and blood-clotted clothing was scattered about. The smell of alcohol and ether filled one's nostrils. I was filled with both a heart-wrenching feeling of dejection and a warm sense of appreciation [for] the medical profession." As Graves watched sadly, a soldier with a gaping chest wound drooped over and, without emitting a sound, died on the spot. Elsewhere, Graves found a badly wounded buddy with whom he had served in Italy. "It was a nightmare, Mickey, a nightmare," the man said of the Waal crossing. Graves shook his head and wished he could do more to help his old friend.

In the meantime, within only a minute or two of landing, groups of unscathed soldiers—along with men who were hit but could still fight—got up and began moving over the embankment to the open ground that led to the dike. Here and there they encountered German trenches and killed a few enemy soldiers. "[We] continued through the trenches on the run, finding them generally deserted except for a few Germans who were killed, most of whom were huddled in dugouts seeking protection from the heavy [supporting] fire from the south bank," Captain Kappel wrote. Staff Sergeant James Allen, one of Kappel's squad leaders, turned to him and said, "Well, our luck is still holding out." The captain nodded.

From up ahead, the fire originating from the dike road was withering. Anyone who lingered, even for a moment, risked getting riddled with bullets. Everyone was intent now, to the point of obsession, on traversing the deadly open ground and overwhelming the Germans at the dike. "The only thing to do was head for the dike, because there wasn't a goddamned bit of cover anywhere else or anything," Lieutenant Thomas Pitt, the battalion personnel officer, later said. Almost as one, they rose up and ran along the open ground. They advanced in rushes, by leaps and bounds. One ragged group would go to ground and fire support for another that was running straight at the Germans. Then that group would flop down and support the next one and so on, just as they had been trained. "You have seen in movies pictures of infantry troops attacking across open terrain, employing fire and movement," Captain Keep wrote. "Well, this made any Hollywood version pale into insignificance." The men howled, cursed, and fired their weapons from the hip. To Lieutenant John Gorman, a British tank commander who was standing in his turret on the other side of the river, firing in support of them, they looked "terribly slow; I found myself . . . mentally urging them on faster and faster . . . we were trying to direct our fire just above their heads."

Private First Class Dunlop, the machine gunner, supported the audacious attack by practically leaning on the trigger of his .30-caliber machine gun. "I think I was actually gleaming, licking my chops," he later admitted. "We were a bloodthirsty bunch." Indeed they were. All the pent-up fear and frustration of the river crossing—helplessness, really—now vented itself in a bloodlust for killing. The average trooper was not thinking so much of the group mission as a hunger for revenge against the enemy soldiers who had shot at them so mercilessly while they were vulnerable in their boats. For them it was payback time. "All of the fear of the last fifteen or twenty minutes seemed to leave me," Staff Sergeant Fuller said, "to be replaced by a surge of reckless abandon. I felt as though I could lick the whole German army." Most of the others felt the same way. As paratroopers, they were inclined to be aggressive, perhaps even reckless. Now, under the extreme stress of the situation, they had become ruthless killing machines. Captain Keep later described them as "fanatics rendered crazy by rage and the lust for killing, men who temporarily forgot the meaning of fear. It is in such moments that great feats of history occur."

There was no cover to be had, no middle course of action to take. They would either make it forward and kill their enemies or they would die. Leading one group, Captain Burriss somehow kept going unscathed in the face of intense machine gun fire. "Men began to drop on both sides of me," he wrote, "some grabbing their legs or shoulders and others falling like sacks of sand." Those who were wounded crawled back to the river's edge. Others kept moving. Most made it across the open ground in a matter of a few minutes. Burriss and a few others got to the leeward side of the dike and hit the ground. From here the Germans on the other side could only fire over their heads. The Americans pitched grenades at the German-held side. After the grenades exploded, the troopers stood up, leaned over the dike, and shot anyone they could see. Some of the enemy soldiers raised their hands and attempted to surrender. The Americans did not let them. "It was too late. Our men, in a frenzy of the wholesale slaughter of their buddies, continued to fire until every German on the dike lay dead or dying," Burriss admitted. In another spot, Lieutenant LaRiviere and several men encountered a group of thirty or forty who tried to give up ("ordinary run-of-the-mill soldiers" in the lieutenant's recollection). The Americans simply shot them all down.

In most cases, though, the Germans resisted to the end. The fighting was at close range, so close that the antagonists could clearly see the facial features of their enemies. Just as Lieutenant Carmichael made it to the dike, a BAR man alongside of him was crossing the dike road. A nearby German machine gunner spotted him and opened up. The burst of bullets swept through the BAR man's helmet "and he came turning back with his brains shot out." The Americans pitched grenades into the machine gunner's hole, killing him. Sergeant Ted Finkbeiner was more fortunate. He stuck his head over the German-held side of the dike and found himself face-to-face with a machine gun. "I ducked, but the muzzle blast blew my cap off."

Elsewhere, Lieutenant Megellas's platoon sergeant, Staff Sergeant Marvin Hirsh, caught a round in the arm, just above the wrist. "I bandaged his wound with gauze that I had strapped to the side of my boots," Megellas said. The sergeant kept fighting. Not far away, Staff Sergeant William White charged over the dike and fired at a group of fleeing Germans. "There go those sons of bitches!" he roared. "After them, men!" Other soldiers ran along the road and shot at the fleeing enemy. All along the dike, such personal battles raged. "Everyone was shooting and running, shooting and running," Private Walter Hughes later said. The Americans made liberal use of grenades, then shot the hapless Germans from only a few yards away. In Hughes's latter-year estimation, "It was a terrible thing for an eighteen-year-old to have to experience." The German soldiers were anything but elite fighters. In fact, the best German soldiers were in Nij- megen, fighting Goulburn and Vandervoort. These men at the dike, and in Fort Hof van Holland, were the leftovers, a mishmash of flak-battery crewmen, Kampfgruppe Henke survivors, engineers, and artillerymen. Many were underage or overage. They had fired so heavily at the para- troopers while they were in the water, not just because this was their job as soldiers, but because this was when the Americans were vulnerable. All of them had understood what deadly adversaries the paratroopers would become upon reaching the north bank. Now they were finding this out firsthand as they died in droves at the hands of these avenging angels in jumpsuits. "Not proudly, I tell you, I killed boys over 15 & men over 65 in their foxholes," one of the Americans wrote sadly many years later. "I did see old men grab our M1's and beg for mercy—they were shot point blank."

Gradually, as German resistance along the dike petered out, the surviv- ing groups of Americans turned right and began making their way along the road, toward the bridges. "The attack . . . developed into a series of daring small-unit actions of individuals from different squads and pla- toons," Megellas commented. "Ahead of my men and me were open fields, orchards, and a scattering of farmhouses and barns," and then Fort Hof van Holland.

As Megellas and his cohorts fought against scattered groups of Ger- mans throughout this area, the engineers were back at the river, evacuating wounded men and ferrying reinforcements to the north bank. Only eleven boats now were still operational, and many of them had bullet or shrapnel holes. With typical hasty improvisation, men stuffed handkerchiefs, gloves, wool caps, and odd bits of discarded uniforms into the holes. This was hardly ideal, but it plugged the gaps well enough for the boats to at least stay afloat. At least one boat team used their entrenching tools as paddles. All the while, they were under heavy fire from Fort Hof van Holland and especially the railroad bridge. "Launching of the boats was made more difficult by the stretch of mud and shallow water through which the boats had to be pushed in order to get them off," one group later told an army historian. "During the crossing, five men were hit during a terrific barrage of artillery. Sniper and twenty-millimeter fire continued all the way across. Bullets skipped along the waves, passed through boats, and skipped along the other side."

In the power station, General Browning was still watching. Awestruck, he turned to General Horrocks, who had just joined him, and said, "I have never seen a more gallant action." On the river, aboard one of the boats, Tech Sergeant Frank Dietrich was crouching low, dodging incoming fire, when he heard singing in the distance. He peeked over the gunwale and was amazed to recognize the voice of Sergeant Ross Carter, an old buddy, singing the "Song of the Volga Boatmen." "Volga, Volga, mother stream! O, thou river, broad and deep!" the irrepressible Carter bellowed in the lowest baritone voice he could manage.

Because the smoke screen had dissipated and the Germans knew exactly where to shoot on the river, the initial reinforcement trips were perilous, but not quite as much as the first wave's assault had been. Eventually, as the Americans overran German defenses on the north bank, fire on the river slackened. Over the course of two hectic hours, the engineers made five separate circuits. They brought with them Major Cook's G Company, followed by elements of his battalion headquarters, followed by the 1st Battalion's A, C, and B companies (in that order), plus the battalion headquarters. These reinforcements added vitality to the push for the bridges. By the time they were all across, only five boats were usable. The engineers, who many of the infantrymen thought were the unsung heroes of the crossing, suffered eight killed and twenty-six wounded.[5]

In a ditch on the far side of the dike road, Lieutenant Megellas and the eleven men in his group were under cover, taking in the odd sight of German-controlled Fort Hof van Holland. The place was like something out of the nineteenth century, not the twentieth. "It was . . . moat encircled, with a drawbridge on the north side," Megellas said. "It resembled an inverted bowl, with the sides sloping at about a forty-five-degree incline from the edge of the moat to the top of the fort, a distance of about fifty feet." The Germans had placed their machine guns and a twenty-millimeter antiaircraft gun atop the parapet, and periodically they would pop up and fire bursts along the dike road and at the river. Megellas and the other men poured heavy fire on those enemy emplacements, prompting the Germans to hop down from the parapet and take shelter in bunkers they had built inside the walls of the fort. Seeing this, one of Megellas's squad leaders, Sergeant Leroy Richmond, stripped off his harness and gear, jumped into the water, and swam to the edge of the incline. He climbed the wall and peeked into the fort. Megellas and the others began to circle around toward the drawbridge. From one of the bunkers, a rifle shot rang out. Richmond felt a sharp pain in his neck. He ducked down behind the incline and saw, to his immense relief, that the rifle bullet had only grazed him. "He must have been wearing a rabbit's foot," Megellas quipped.

The lieutenant and several others, including Private First Class Dunlop and two other men who just happened to reach the fort at the same time, began pitching grenades (including Gammon grenades) and firing into the fort. Friendly artillery and mortar fire, called in by forward observers from the 376th Parachute Field Artillery Battalion who had participated in the river crossing, was also still pounding the fort. After another brief exchange of fire, the Germans made no further attempt to emerge from their bunkers. Megellas was mindful that his mission was to take the bridges, not the fort. "I didn't know how many Germans were inside the fort, but as long as they didn't constitute a threat to our forces still crossing the river or impede our attack on the bridges, I was not concerned." He ordered the group to set out for the highway bridge. Later, other soldiers from A Company of the 1st Battalion overwhelmed the remaining enemy defenders, took eighteen prisoners, and secured the fort.

By late afternoon, as the sun began descending over the husks of Nijmegen's ruined buildings on the other side of the river, groups of paratroopers were closing in on the prized bridges. Confused firefights raged, and in many instances, they were costly to the Americans. In one spot, Private First Class John Rigapoulos, a well-liked Anzio veteran, plopped down next to Technician Fourth Grade Albert Tarbell. The two men had gone through jump school together. Tarbell saw that a machine gun bullet had taken off the tip of Rigapoulos's left thumb. He waved the mangled thumb at Tarbell and said airily, "Well, here's another Purple Heart." Instead of going back to the riverbank for medical attention, he stayed with a group that was moving on the railroad bridge. A burst of machine gun fire caught him in the chest and sent him flying backward about twenty feet. He was dead by the time his quivering body rolled to a stop.

Nearby, Staff Sergeant Allen, who had commented to Captain Kappel about their luck in making it across the river, got hit in the thigh by shell fragments as he attempted to take several prisoners. At first the wound did not seem very serious. "I remember chuckling and telling him he had a good one, meaning it was bad enough to get him out of action for a while, but not a serious or fatal wound," Captain Kappel said. In fact, Allen was hit in the femoral artery and he soon bled to death. Closer to the railroad bridge, behind an embankment, Staff Sergeant Tallon and a new man who had joined the unit as a replacement in England were under fire from an unseen machine gun. "I'm going to have a look," the new man said to Tallon. The experienced sergeant screamed, "No!" and tried to grab him as he started crawling up the embankment. "He peeped over the top and instantly fell back with a nice, neat black hole square in the middle of his forehead," Tallon mournfully recalled. Lieutenant Steve Seyebe, who only hours before had bitterly predicted his own death, was killed leading an assault over the dike road, near the railroad bridge. "Just as he got to the top [of the road], they had a machine gun setting there and they hit him," Technician Fourth Grade Paul Mullan, a radioman who was with him, later said.

The Germans were suffering much worse, though. The heavily armed group defending the three-span railroad bridge now found themselves between determined attacking forces on both sides of the river. In an attempt to drive both Allied forces away from the bridge, they pinballed back and forth. As paratroopers began to climb the concrete stanchions and work their way along the open railroad bed that led to the spans, they engaged in sharp, wicked firefights with the hard-pressed Germans. Men from both sides hurled grenades back and forth. Some Germans had tied themselves to the bridge girders, and they fired downward at the troopers. Others turned their heavy weapons on the advancing Americans. "Many machine guns, including 20mm, fired grazing fire along the top of the railway embankment," Captain Kappel wrote. The captain himself hurled several Gammon grenades at the Germans in response to the fire. In the midst of the fighting, the Americans cut any wires they saw, in hopes of preventing their enemies from blowing the bridge.

The German soldiers, meanwhile, were now taking heavy fire from Goulburn's tanks in Nijmegen and concentrated fire from the attacking paratroopers. They were effectively trapped. By the dozens and then the hundreds, they panicked and ran for the north end of the bridge. "German troops were coming, en masse, toward our position," Lieutenant Edward Sims recalled. "We let them come within range, then opened fire and continued to fire until all enemy movement stopped." The Americans mercilessly blazed away with machine guns, BARs, rifles, and grenades, stopping the Germans in their tracks. Lieutenant LaRiviere, who did much of the shooting, remembered it as a complete slaughter. A few fortunate soldiers managed to surrender successfully, but they were the minority. Most either could not, or would not, give up. "We neither offered nor gave any quarter to the Germans on the railroad bridge," one of the American participants later said.

Watching from the vantage point of the south bank about a mile away, Lieutenant Gorman, the British tanker, was practically transfixed by the macabre sight of the swirling mass of desperate humanity. "There seemed to be hundreds of them on the bridge, scrambling across, stumbling and getting up and stumbling again. They seemed confused and panic-stricken." He dearly wished to add his own fire to their misery, but his commander would not let him for fear of hitting the nearby Americans. The bullets laced into the trapped Germans, tearing holes in uniforms and bodies alike. Gouts of blood spraying from the stricken enemy soldiers looked, at a distance, almost like puffs of smoke. Some of the Germans went down immediately. Others stumbled around until they were hit many more times. Quite a few were wounded. They lay on the tracks or under the girders, writhing in agony. Those who were in the girders had no chance. Their lifeless forms dangled in their harnesses. A few of the Germans had legs, arms, or even heads blown off.

Panicked survivors now attempted to jump off the bridge into the river or onto the muddy flats some eighty feet below. "The men were shooting them in the air until stopped by [me] due to the shortage of ammunition," Captain Kappel later wrote. One German officer, who was not at the bridge, later claimed in his diary that "the Americans acted cruelly, throwing the wounded from the bridge into the Waal and shooting . . . captured riflemen." This may well have been true, but it is not corroborated in any other German record or American account (perhaps for obvious reasons). What is clear is that, after the horrendous river crossing, the paratroopers were in no mood for mercy. These enemy soldiers were, after all, the same men who had shot at them so relentlessly when they were in the boats (most American accounts describe the fire emanating from the railroad bridge as the heaviest and deadliest). Now it was time for payback. Such was the ruthless, dehumanizing environment of close combat. "At the time of this action, my men and myself were tense and angry because of the strenuous fighting and the loss of many of our own men during the crossing," Lieutenant Sims wrote. In the heat of the moment, the Germans were targets, not men, to Sims and the others. Only later did the reality of war's tragic waste hit home to him. Reflecting upon what he did, Sims concluded that "this terrible slaughter of humans is not something to be proud of or brag about. It continues to bother me that I had to make the hasty decision that led to the death of so many young men." Lieutenant Allan McClain, who also participated in the slaughter, contended that "not one [German] made it" across the bridge. He found himself sickened by it all and claimed that he later counted 267 dead enemy soldiers on the bridge. The number of Germans who fell to their deaths or drowned in the river will never be known.

By now, Captain Kappel was in contact with Major Cook and Captain Keep. Collectively, they hoped that British tanks from Nijmegen would now cross the railroad bridge, link up with them, and push together for the road bridge. Cook radioed Colonel Tucker with this request. "They are going to act on the bridge," Tucker vaguely replied. At almost the same time, Major Tyler, who had watched the American fight at the railroad bridge, exclaimed excitedly, and equally vaguely, into his own radio, "They're on the bridge! They've got the bridge!" In the confusion, the commanders in Nijmegen thought Tyler and the others meant the road bridge, so, instead of sending their tanks onto the railroad bridge, they made preparations to send tanks to the road bridge.[6]

At the same time, Captain Burriss and another group of about fifteen paratroopers were actually fighting for the northern approaches to the road bridge. They charged up the concrete stairs that led to the highway embankment, past heavy concrete roadblocks—each painted with distinct white vertical stripes—and a pair of wooden guard towers. They skirted along the bridge railings, peering through the smoky mist that hung over the bridge span. For a moment, all was quiet. Then Burriss encountered a German soldier who quickly surrendered to him. The captain turned to Lieutenant LaRiviere and ordered him to take several men across the bridge and cut any wires they discovered. Several of the men found wires coiled along the beams and piers, and severed them with their fighting knives. The eerie quiet soon ended, though. "A German hiding high in the girders shot and killed the enlisted man standing between us," Burriss wrote. LaRiviere whirled around, raised his rifle, and shot the enemy soldier to death. One of the dead German's harness straps caught in a girder and he hung limply several dozen feet above the pavement.

The sound of small arms crackled as the Americans on the bridge traded shots with Germans who were underneath the bridge's main span or tied to the girders (the latter were apparently demolition engineers, not snipers). As Sergeant Jimmie Shields carefully walked toward the bridge span, he took fire from several of the engineers in the girders. He returned fire with his BAR and killed one who he swore was a woman. "The helmet fell off . . . revealing long, flowing hair," he said. More Germans emerged on foot from the dusky shadows with their hands held high in surrender. The mood here was different than at the rail bridge. Burriss's group was only too happy to accept. "It was now getting darker and the shooting was sporadic," Private First Class Dunlop said. Captain Burriss, standing near the main span, took stock of the situation. His group was small. The situation was still in flux. But he was confident that he was in control of the northern end of the bridge. What he didn't know was whether the Germans were about to blow it or, for that matter, what was happening with the Allied attack from the southern end of the bridge.

Half a mile away, in an open field along a quiet block of houses on the Nijmegen side of the river, Sergeant Peter Robinson was sitting in the turret of his Sherman tank, waiting. He and his troop of four tanks had been in reserve all day, doing little more than lounging around their Shermans, waiting for orders. To the grizzled, twenty-nine-year-old Dunkirk veteran, being in reserve usually meant trouble, especially on a day like today, when most everyone else was fighting so hard along the riverfront. Robinson figured the higher-ups had to have something serious in mind for his troop.

Sure enough, at 1800, an order came to report to Major John Trotter, his squadron commander. Robinson hopped into a scout car and drove to the major's command post, some five hundred yards away from the road bridge. Flames raged through the adjacent blocks. Somewhere in the distance, closer to the river, he could hear shooting. The major greeted him abruptly with an order to take the road bridge. "You've got to get across at all costs," he said. "Don't stop for anything." The plan was for Robinson's four tanks to go first, fight across the bridge, and link up with the Americans. Lieutenant Tony Jones, in an armored car, would follow behind and defuse all demolitions on the bridge. Behind Jones, Captain Peter Carrington, Trotter's second in command, was to protect the rear. There was no time to lose.

As Robinson turned to leave, Major Trotter shook his hand and said, "Don't worry; I know where you live and I'll let your wife know if anything happens to you."

"Well, you're bloody cheerful, aren't you, sir?" the no-nonsense NCO replied. As he drove back to his troop, he caught his first glimpse of the bridge. "It's bloody big," he thought. The gloomy idea that he was about to lead a suicide mission nagged at him. For all he knew, the Germans would simply blow the bridge once Robinson's tanks got onto it, tumbling all of them into the river below. At the very least, the enemy probably had the bridge covered with multiple antitank guns.

Minutes later, with these troubling thoughts set aside, Robinson and the others were off. Lieutenant Jones glanced at Captain Carrington and never forgot the indelible expression on the face of the young aristocrat as he looked blankly into the distance. "He was frowning worriedly, and frankly . . . I didn't blame him one bit." They rolled carefully through Nijmegen's tortured streets at fifteen miles per hour, edging to the Keizer Lodewijk Plein roundabout, and began to ascend the bridge embankment. The sergeant huddled in his turret, clutching a pistol and his radio handset. "It seemed to me the whole town was burning down," Robinson said. "Buildings were on fire to my left and right. It was just beginning to get dark. Visibility was limited." Tracer rounds were coming from the north side of the bridge, in his general direction (possibly these were from the American firefights on the north end). Robinson had a direct radio communication link with division headquarters. He pressed the transmitter. "We are approaching the bridge and preparing to cross it."

As they ascended the embankment and approached the bridge span, they began taking eighty-eight-millimeter antitank fire from a German gun crew concealed somewhere among the burning buildings on the northern side of the Waal. A sharp but short gunfight ensued. An eighty-eight shell ricocheted off the pavement and struck Robinson's tank, knocking out his radio but otherwise leaving the Sherman intact. The sergeant threw a couple of smoke grenades and ordered his driver to back up. He dismounted and ordered the commander of the tank behind him, a lance sergeant named Billingham, to get out and take over Robinson's old tank. "The sergeant didn't want to give me his tank," Robinson later said, "and he argued with me for several seconds. Finally, I told him I was ordering him out and damn quick. He got out and I got in." They regrouped and resumed their advance, with Sergeant Charles Pacey's tank in the lead. Once more, the British traded shots with the enemy gun crew. "[They] exchanged about six rounds apiece with the [tanks] spitting 30 cal tracers all the while," Lieutenant Colonel Vandervoort, who was watching the whole scene from a building in Nijmegen, later wrote. To him, the firefight comprised "quite a show in the gathering dusk." The .30-caliber fire destroyed the firing mechanism of the German gun and chased the crew away. The tanks kept rolling onto the bridge.

Atop a concrete pillbox on the north side of the Waal, General Heinz Harmel, commander of the 10th SS Panzer Division, was holding a pair of binoculars tightly to his eyes, studying the bridge amid the twilight. Pacey's tank came into view, then Robinson's, then Billingham's, steadily creeping over the bridge. The orders from Harmel's corps commander,

Lieutenant General Wilhelm Bittrich, and his superior, Field Marshal Walter Model, commander of Army Group B, were very clear: The bridge must not be destroyed. Model felt he would need it to counterattack the Allied-held pockets along Hell's Highway. Harmel had argued, in vain, for the destruction of the bridge. A few hours earlier, when the Americans had launched their reckless river crossing, he had never imagined that it could succeed. Somehow it had. Now, with the paratroopers making trouble on the northern side of the river, and the British tanks rolling onto the bridge, his worst nightmare was coming to fruition. If this continued, the Allies might actually punch through thinly held Lent—the north-bank suburb of Nijmegen—and make a real push for the embattled British perimeter in the Arnhem area.

Model's orders had not kept Harmel from preparing the bridge for demolition, just in case. Now, as he watched the British tanks roll under the bridge span, his mind was racing. "What shall I do?" he wondered. "What is most urgent, most important?" The more he thought, the more he convinced himself that, if Model were here and could see for himself what was unfolding, he too would agree that the bridge had to be destroyed. The thirty-eight-year-old Harmel was an experienced combat leader who had fought in France, Yugoslavia, and Russia. He knew that sometimes a commander on the scene must make a difficult decision—even one that contravenes orders. Harmel knew that, right here, right now, the bridge had to go. There was really no other choice.

On the ground beside him, a soldier was huddling over a plunger, looking at Harmel, eagerly awaiting his orders. The general lowered his binoculars and looked at the man. "Okay, let it blow," he said. The man lowered the plunger. Nothing happened. He tried again. Still nothing happened. For some reason, the charges did not work. There was no more time to fix them. Harmel's eyes widened as this uncomfortable reality sank in. "I could no longer afford to worry about the bridge," Harmel later said. "It was too late. I expected to see the bridge collapse and the tanks to be plunged into the river. But instead I could see the tanks moving forward relentlessly. They got bigger and bigger, came closer and closer." Harmel fled the scene and focused on reorganizing his scattered units to stop an expected Allied push for Arnhem. He especially made sure to block every possible route of advance to Arnhem with whatever antitank guns and artillery pieces he had left.

Back on the bridge, the tanks were charging across, blazing away at several SS engineers still hanging from the girders. "We . . . opened up on them with our Brownings [machine guns] and played merry hell with them," Guardsman Leslie Johnson, the gunner on Robinson's tank, recalled. "They were falling out like ninepins." Shots clanged off the girders. The incoming fire was heavy enough that Johnson later opined, "I swear to this day that Jesus Christ rode on the front of our tank."

The Shermans edged their way past the concrete roadblocks. As Pacey covered, Robinson's tank kept going, down the northern embankment and into a confrontation with yet another antitank gun. "Johnson pumped three or four shells into it and blew it to pieces," Robinson remembered. As they moved forward, they found themselves in a running battle against more guns and German infantrymen. "They were so close I didn't bother to look through my sights," Johnson said. "I only needed the periscope and that was enough. We could feel the tracks going over them as we shot them down, and there was blood and gore all over the tank." He could actually feel the Sherman bumping over bodies on the road. Robinson called the rest of his troop on the radio, ordered them to close up with him, and then resumed his advance. Before long, he saw figures in a ditch to the left of the road. At first, he thought they were Germans. For a few moments, they shot at him and he shot back before he realized they were Americans, not Germans. "Cease fire, those are our feathered friends," he told his crew.

At nearly the same time, the Americans, led by Captain Burriss, realized that the tank in front of them was British. Burriss and the other troopers excitedly converged on Robinson's Sherman. "We're Americans," they yelled. Robinson smiled and waved. Captain Burriss, who still had blood and viscera on his uniform from the Waal crossing, was so elated that he climbed the turret, grabbed Robinson's neck, and said, "You're the sweetest guys I've seen in months." Other men leaned over and smooched the tank itself. Robinson was amused at the American behavior. "It was the first time I had ever seen a tank kissed," Robinson quipped, "whilst frankly, I felt like kissing them."[7]

This linkup notwithstanding, the area around the bridge was still dangerous. German antitank guns and Panzerfausts actually destroyed two of Robinson's tanks as they left the bridge, and most of the evacuating crewmen were captured. The surviving Shermans, and Carrington, did succeed in joining up with Robinson. On the bridge itself, Lieutenant Jones, the engineer, hopped out of his scout car and searched for the German demolitions. "The first thing I saw were six or eight wires coming over the railing and laying on the footpath." Jones snipped them with his wire cutters. He was so intent on his work that, at first, he hardly realized there were still enemy soldiers on the bridge. He personally captured several— eventually he and his team rounded up eighty-one—including one who showed him where the explosive charges were placed. Each charge had been carefully packed in a green-painted tin box that perfectly matched the color of the bridge. The boxes were prefabricated to fit the exact bridge girder spot where German engineers had placed them. Each box even had a serial number. The lieutenant removed the detonators and threw them into the river. In all, he estimated that the Germans had wired the bridge with at least five hundred pounds of TNT. "It was a really remarkable piece of engineering, one hundred percent efficient, a thoroughly good job," he said—which was why Jones had no idea why the charges had not detonated.

After the war, a notion took hold, particularly among the Dutch, that a twenty-two-year-old Nijmegen resistance fighter named Jan van Hoof had sneaked onto the bridge on September 18 and cut the demolition wires right under the noses of the Germans. Van Hoof was a student at the University of Nijmegen. University officials and a priest who ran the university were, in the recollection of Captain Bestebreurtje, "principally responsible for generating and perpetuating the story." The main evidence for Van Hoof's exploit was testimony by his family to the effect that he had excitedly told them, with a certainty apparently born of direct knowledge, that the bridge was safe from German destruction. They had also found wire cutters in his overalls. While this hardly comprised incontestable proof of such an amazing feat of sabotage, Van Hoof was indeed a courageous member of the resistance. At significant risk to his own life, he had gathered, over the course of several months, much useful intelligence on German dispositions in Nijmegen. He was one of the resistance men who congregated at the Sionshof Hotel after the initial Market Garden drops. He had also functioned as a guide for Allied units in the city, a job that cost him his life on September 19. He was riding on the bumper of a British scout car that was headed for the railroad bridge when the car got hit by a German antitank gun and set afire. The two British soldiers with Van Hoof fell out of the scout car and burned to death on the sidewalk. Van Hoof, who was wearing the telltale orange armband of the Dutch resistance as well as a helmet, was beaten up and executed on the spot by German soldiers.

In 1946, the Dutch government conferred the Militaire Willemsorde, its highest military decoration, on the fallen resistance man. A subsequent government investigation found no conclusive evidence that Van Hoof sabotaged the German demolitions. Nor did they find otherwise. In the absence of undisputed proof that he did not thwart the Germans, his legend grew as a national hero in Holland (in fact, on the northern end of the bridge, there is a stone relief that depicts him cutting the wires).

In the broader view, though, many Allied soldiers, and postwar historians, did not accept the Van Hoof story. Lieutenant Jones, the engineer who was probably in the best position to determine what happened to the German demolitions, found it highly unlikely that anyone had previously tampered with them. "There was no evidence of any sort to convince me that anyone had removed any of the charges," he wrote. "Everything was perfectly in order." In fact, the German presence on the bridge was such that it is difficult to imagine that anyone, much less a young civilian untrained in demolitions, could have sneaked onto the bridge and severed the key wires right under their noses, especially in daylight hours. Even if he had done so, the Germans would have had nearly two days to discover what had happened and make repairs. Indeed, Jones himself may have done more than any other individual to thwart Harmel's plan to blow the bridge.

General Gavin put no stock in the idea that Van Hoof had sabotaged the demolitions. "I do not think that he saved the bridge," the general once wrote quite bluntly. Gavin had trained his troopers to cut wires whenever they took a bridge. For him, this was almost a point of pride. He and many other Americans, including Captain Burriss, came to believe that the troopers of the 3rd Battalion cut the key wires during their fight for the northern end of the bridge. This was a plausible, but debatable contention. For instance, Captain Kappel, who was a trained demolitions specialist, said that all the severed wires he saw on the bridge were for communications, not demolitions. General Hans Albin Rauter, the SS police chief in Holland who was the chief architect of Nazi terror throughout the country, was involved with the planning to demolish bridges at Nijmegen and elsewhere. He claimed that SS engineers removed the charges from the Nijmegen bridge "in order to prevent an accidental explosion through artillery fire, which had happened elsewhere." His implication was that the charges were never put back in place, a contention that, in light of Lieutenant Jones's testimony about the apparent readiness of all German demolitions, is hard to believe. Another possible explanation, and perhaps the most likely one, is that the bridge was under such intense, protracted shell fire that fragments cut the crucial wires or damaged the detonating mechanisms. This might explain why so many German engineers were in the girders, apparently working on the wires when the Allies took the bridge.

Few of these engineers survived the battle. Those who did never provided any public explanation. Thus, the mystery of why the explosives failed to detonate has never subsided and probably never will.[8]

Regardless of why the bridge did not blow, what mattered the most was that the Allies were in control of it by sunset on September 20. The carnage around the bridge was revolting. Bodies hung from girders. Several dead Germans lay on the concrete in great pools of their own blood. Bullet-pocked vehicles reposed sadly along the railings. Fires raged along the riverfront. A pall of evil-smelling smoke hung over the bridge and adjacent buildings alike. Groups of German soldiers fearfully roamed in the darkness, looking to escape or surrender (according to American accounts, several hundred surrendered in the course of the evening). Wounded men of both sides cried for help. "It was there that I saw precisely what war signifies," Father William Peterse, a local priest who hastened to the scene to help the wounded, later commented. "Mutilated bodies. Severely wounded and dying soldiers. The road was littered with hand grenades. Stolen bicycles had been shot to pieces."

The American survivors of the "Waal regatta," as many of them sardonically called the river crossing, joined forces with a few British tanks to carve out a shaky bridgehead in Lent that evening. The exhausted paratroopers believed they had accomplished the most dangerous task in crossing the river and seizing the northern end of both bridges. For them, the crossing and subsequent fighting had been hell on earth. "I don't think that any man that went across that river . . . and [was] fortunate enough to make the other side will ever in his life forget it," Lieutenant Pitt said. Another participant, Corporal Jack Bommer, referred to it as "the most vivid show of courage, patriotism, and love for one's way of life I have ever seen." Cook's battalion alone had lost twenty-eight men killed, one missing, and seventy-eight wounded. Companies H and I were nearly decimated.

The Americans had been willing to make this terrible sacrifice because they believed it would save their airborne brothers at Arnhem and Market

Garden as a whole. Now it was the turn of their British allies from XXX Corps to roll over the bridges with tanks and reinforcements, fight their way to Arnhem, capture the bridge there, relieve their embattled countrymen from the 1st Airborne Division, and press on into Germany. There wasn't a second to lose. In the American view, the time to attack was right now, while the Germans were in disarray and General Urquhart's troopers were still holding on in the Arnhem area. Instead XXX Corps halted for the night, prompting a bitter dispute between the Americans and the British that has never really abated.

During the evening of September 20–21, as the realization sank into the Americans that the British tankers were staying put, ugly confrontations ensued. In one spot, an outraged Lieutenant LaRiviere argued with a British tank commander to get moving. When he refused, the headstrong LaRiviere bitterly threatened, "I'll blow your head off and take the tanks myself." Fortunately, he did not follow through on the threat. Captain Burriss had a protracted argument with Captain Carrington, the ranking British officer in Lent, and urged him to attack. Carrington calmly explained that he had no orders to do so; moreover, he was concerned about continued opposition from a nearby enemy antitank gun. Burriss was having none of it. He was nursing a minor wound from the crossing and grieving over the loss of so many of his men. Indeed, his uniform was still badly stained with the blood of the soldier who had been killed right next to him during the crossing. The American captain lost his temper. "You mean to tell me you're going to sit here on your ass while your own British paratroopers are being cut to shreds, and all because of one gun?"

"I can't go without orders," Carrington replied evenly.

"You yellow-bellied son of a bitch," Burriss said angrily. "I've just sacrificed half of my company in the face of dozens of guns, and you won't move because of *one* gun." Burriss cocked his tommy gun and held it to Carrington's head. "You get this tank moving or I'll blow your damn head off!" Carrington ducked into his turret, closed the hatch, and locked it.

Colonel Tucker, who had crossed the river in the final wave, did not resort to threatening violence against his British colleagues, but he was among the angriest. Lieutenant A. D. Demetras, a communications officer, overheard him arguing with a British officer. "Your boys are hurting up there," Tucker implored. "You'd better go! It is only eight miles." By the time General Gavin encountered him the next morning at the command post he had set up in Fort Hof van Holland, the colonel was so beside himself he could hardly speak. "I have never seen him so angry," Gavin recalled.

The American cussing and raging was to no avail. The British tank men refused to push for Arnhem that evening. What especially irked the troopers was the sight of British tank crews brewing and drinking tea. "It left a very bad taste with us," Lieutenant Megellas said, "and a poor impression of the British military man." To the British, tea breaks amounted to little more than a temporary diversion, an ingrained part of any day, as natural as snacking or napping while they waited for new orders. But to the Americans, the tea breaks indicated nonchalance, as if the British soldiers did not really care about the plight of their airborne countrymen at Arnhem. The American paratroopers felt a deep camaraderie with General Urquhart's men as fellow airborne soldiers. In many cases, they had trained with the British troopers, gotten drunk with them, eaten with them, picked up women with them, and, at times, they had brawled with them in bars. Plus, they knew what it was like to be cut off in enemy territory, dependent upon relief from land forces. "Much of our motivation to make that river crossing was because of our own past jump combat experience and our feeling for the position Urquhart was in," Gavin said. He had conceived of the crossing because he was under the impression that every moment counted in the drive for Arnhem. Otherwise, he and his men would have been only too happy to have waited until nightfall to make the crossing. "It would have been much less costly and easier." The Americans had crossed the river with the greatest of urgency. Fair or not, the fact that the British soldiers sat and slurped tea during such crucial hours gave the troopers the impression that their own urgency (and sacrifices) had been for naught. It also seemed to indicate that the British tank crewmen cared more for their own safety and comfort than for the lives of the 1st Airborne troopers at Arnhem. "How could they not keep going?" Private Hughes later plaintively wrote, summing up the feelings of all his comrades. "How could they leave them without even trying to get through? For years these thoughts have haunted me."

As always in combat, though, the average soldier's perspective was limited, perhaps even distorted. Tucker's troopers had no idea of the bigger picture. They had crossed the river and captured the bridges under the flawed impression that mass waves of armored reinforcements were ready and waiting to press on to Arnhem. In truth, XXX Corps' situation was a mess. General Horrocks had few tanks and troops at his disposal for such an attack. Thousands of vehicles were strung out along a tenuous forty-mile corridor and beyond, all the way to the Dutch–Belgian border. The two supporting corps on the flanks of the corridor, VIII and XII, had not been able to prevent the Germans from launching powerful attacks that wreaked havoc on the mobility and supply of XXX Corps units. In many spots, the Allies controlled only the roads and the ditches alongside them. Even places where the Allies were strong, such as Son, Veghel, and St. Oedenrode, were under enemy artillery fire. The Allies were expending vital resources and men just to keep the road open. Because the Allied route of advance was so constricted, and so slender, any German counterattack was disruptive, no matter how strong or weak. Truck drivers were spending as much time taking cover in ditches as driving their vehicles. Instead of roaring north to Arnhem, tankers and infantrymen were absorbed in pushing the Germans away from the vital road. Moreover, one of Horrocks's key units that he might have rushed to Arnhem, the Grenadier Guards, was still snuffing out the remnants of German resistance along the Nijmegen waterfront (Vandervoort's battalion was similarly involved).

As a result of all these problems, ammunition, food, and gasoline were running dangerously low for Horrocks's frontline units, as well as in the

82nd Airborne. The amiable Horrocks was beginning to realize he was actually fighting three distinct battles: one to keep the corridor open, one to hold the Groesbeek heights, and one to make it to Arnhem. Obviously this was too much, and it was a direct result of Market Garden's overly ambitious nature, not to mention that nearly everything had to go right for the operation to succeed.

Plus, there was another problem. The terrain between Nijmegen and Arnhem was hardly suited for tanks. "It was a dike embankment with a road running along the top," Lieutenant Colonel Giles Vandeleur, whose 2nd Battalion, Irish Guards, had supported the river assault, later said. "It was a ridiculous place to operate tanks." The road had wide ditches on either side. The adjacent country was flat but honeycombed with orchards that could—and eventually did—hide German antitank guns. "Any vehicle on [the] embankment was a sitting duck for the German anti-tank gunners," General Horrocks wrote in his memoirs. "[O]ne knocked-out vehicle could block a road for hours . . . it was infantry country." Against any sort of significant opposition, tanks could not survive on their own in this terrain. They would need large numbers of accompanying infantrymen and, most likely, plenty of air support. British infantrymen in the Nijmegen area were scarce. Horrocks ordered the 43rd (Wessex) Infantry Division to hasten to the scene, but this unit was a long way off on the evening of September 20–21. Of course, Tucker's troopers were more than happy to go forward with any willing tankers that evening, but their ranks were badly depleted, and, frankly, this was not their mission. The 82nd Airborne Division was already badly overextended. An Arnhem junket would only exacerbate that problem. If the 1st Airborne was to be saved, the British had to do it. With only a few well-worn tanks on the north side of the Waal, they were in a very weak position to do so on that fateful evening. Robinson, Pacey, and Carrington hardly comprised a suitable force to establish a strong linkup with General Urquhart's division. "By the time the English tanks arrived," General Harmel later contended, "the matter was already decided."

It is true that Horrocks might well have pushed for Arnhem with Giles Vandeleur's 2nd Armored Battalion of the Irish Guards that night. They had spent the day near the southern bank of the river, supporting the American paratroopers. They certainly could have left those positions, driven past the embers of the fighting around the Valkhof, crossed the bridge, gone through Lent, and taken their chances along the main road. But they were low on ammo and, even though the Germans were fractured and confused that night, Vandeleur's battalion probably did not have enough infantry to make it all the way to Arnhem in the dark. Even if they had, they would have run into strong resistance from the 9th SS Panzer Division, which was ever so steadily destroying Urquhart's perimeter at Oosterbeek, and Lieutenant Colonel Frost's intrepid 2nd Battalion survivors three miles to the east on the northern end of the Arnhem bridge. Indeed, Frost's battalion was already on the verge of complete annihilation by the early-morning hours of September 21. Only the most overweening optimist could envision a scenario in which the Irish Guards would have fought their way to Urquhart in Oosterbeek and Frost at Arnhem (or, for that matter, either one of them) and gone on to fulfill the strategic purpose of Market Garden.

Even so, it was absolutely inexcusable that the British commanders did not at least try. As long as there was any remote possibility of saving the British paratroopers, Horrocks and Browning should have attempted to do so, regardless of circumstances. If they were not willing to do that, then they should never have allowed the 82nd Airborne Division troopers to make the perilous Waal crossing. These men paddled their way into hell, and captured their objectives in spite of the considerable odds arrayed against them. In the opinion of one trooper, they "didn't know the meaning of quitting." Their senior leaders should have had the same attitude. The valor of the troopers who carried out the crossing, and the British tankers who risked all to fight their way across the road bridge, defies description. What they accomplished, at such great cost, was significant, but it should have meant so much more, if not necessarily for the outcome of

Market Garden, then perhaps for the fortunes of their airborne brothers at Arnhem. Moreover, every minute did indeed count on the evening of September 20–21. There is no question that the British delay that night afforded the Germans the opportunity to regroup and strengthen their defenses between Nijmegen and Arnhem. This, in turn, enhanced the probability of the 1st Airborne Division's annihilation.

The cold, hard reality was that, as the sun set on September 20, Market Garden had become less about forcing a single-front northern gateway into Germany and much more about an effort to rescue the 1st Airborne. The abortive British efforts to reach Urquhart's embattled division in the days after September 20 proved this point beyond much doubt. "We [went] from great elation to morbid despair," one British soldier dejectedly said. The Market Garden leap had failed. Now only the gloomy fall remained.[9]

PART II

THE FALL

CHAPTER 12

Self-Deception

G eneral Dwight Eisenhower glanced around the expansive SHAEF war room inside the Trianon Palace Hotel at Versailles. Located near the venerable palace of French kings, the beautiful Trianon was one of the finest hotels in Paris. Indeed, with its white stucco facade, elegant balconies, oversize windows, and sumptuous gardens, a casual observer might mistake the five-story hotel itself for a palace. The sprawling building was an ideal home for Eisenhower's enormous headquarters. Only two days earlier, on September 20, he had finally moved that headquarters here from isolated Granville. To the supreme commander, though, the Trianon was opulent almost to the point of extravagance. He had never really been comfortable amid such princely surroundings. Perhaps it was a product of his Midwestern, lower-middle-class upbringing. For his personal quarters, he had actually passed on a luxurious villa in favor of a modest house fifteen minutes away in St. Germain. Ike found it highly ironic that Field Marshal Gerd von Rundstedt, his opposite on the German side, had once lived in the same house during the German occupation.

Now, on September 22, Eisenhower was sitting at the head of a large conference table in the war room. Assembled before him were most of his key subordinates—Arthur Tedder, his deputy, Trafford Leigh-Mallory, his air chief, Bertram Ramsay, his naval chief, plus two of his army group commanders, Jacob Devers and Omar Bradley. His other army group commander, Bernard Montgomery, was conspicuously absent. In fact, earlier this morning, several members of Ike's staff had cynically placed bets on whether the abrasive British field marshal would bother making the trip from his headquarters east of Brussels to this meeting. As the winners collected their spoils from the losers, they generally agreed on one thing: In their opinion, Monty's absence was a calculated insult, a power play, a rude rebuff of Ike's status as supreme commander. Most of the men around the conference table, including Bradley, perceived the absence of Montgomery the same way. In later years, Montgomery adamantly disputed this notion, claiming that the Market Garden operation required his full attention. "I decided that I could not leave the battle front," he explained. Yet there was no escaping the fact that, as the operation unfolded, Montgomery had become oddly distant from it. Browning, Horrocks, and the division commanders were the key decision makers. Perhaps this was the nature of an airborne operation, but the reality was that, as of September 17, Monty had not been intimately involved in the battle. This was odd for a commander who had conceived of the operation and was investing such great hope in its outcome. A liaison officer with Monty's headquarters told Major Chet Hansen, Bradley's aide, that the field marshal "did nothing that day—there was no reason in the world why he could not attend except that he did not wish to defer to Ike." Hansen, who disliked Montgomery, concluded that "anyone else would probably be fired for such an attitude."

In another passage from his memoirs, the field marshal perhaps touched upon the real reason for his absence. "I knew I was not popular at either Supreme Headquarters, or with the American generals, because of my arguments about the conduct of the war; I thought it best to keep away while the matter was being further argued." So he instead sent his affable, well-liked chief of staff, Major General Freddie de Guingand, to represent him. De Guinand had spent much of the summer defusing the tension between Montgomery and his colleagues, so the field marshal's explanation made some sense.

Even so, it was a very poor decision on Montgomery's part and demonstrated his complete lack of political savvy. He did not understand how his colleagues would perceive his absence. Whether Monty meant to or not, they assumed he was boycotting the meeting for his own selfish reasons. What was more, he had spent much of the late summer seething with frustration over Eisenhower's remoteness from his commanders. He had particularly chafed over the lack of face-to-face communication. Today's meeting was the perfect opportunity to press his arguments over the future conduct of the war, not just to Ike himself, but to Monty's own fellow army group commanders. It was the very thing he had demanded so adamantly only a few weeks earlier. In that sense, his failure to attend the meeting was hypocritical. It also revealed a troubling lack of good judgment on his part. Bradley later summed up the attitude of nearly everyone at the Trianon that day: "I do believe the war could have spared Monty for a few hours that one afternoon."

Bradley and the others sensed that today's meeting would set the tone for the entire fall campaign in Europe. "This was the most important gathering of the Allied brass since the final Overlord review on May fifteen at St. Paul's School in London," Bradley said. Yet without Montgomery, there was little chance that the commanders would come up with a cohesive plan. De Guingand was empowered to make his boss's arguments, but he could not make commitments on behalf of his chief.

A faint whiff of Market Garden's failure permeated that august room, but all of those in attendance were too distant from the fighting to fully appreciate the completeness of the impending Allied strategic defeat in Holland. As Eisenhower presided, the meeting developed into anything but a give-and-take airing of arguments (needless to say, the mood would have been decidedly different had Montgomery been there). Ike asked everyone to agree with the notion that "possession of an additional deepwater port on our north flank was an indispensable prerequisite for the final drive into Germany." Basically, that meant Antwerp. No one dissented. In fact, the day before, Bradley had written presciently to Eisenhower that "all plans for future operations always lead back to the fact that in order to supply an operation of any size beyond the Rhine the port of Antwerp is essential." The Allies, of course, controlled the city and its port facilities, but they had yet to clear the Scheldt estuary, without which Antwerp was useless. Market Garden was only distracting them from this vital task. The supply situation had grown even more problematic in the two weeks since Market Garden was conceived. The Allies desperately needed Antwerp's supply capacity, and there was little time to lose. Even now, the Germans were strengthening their numbers and their defenses in the Scheldt. Equally ominous, thousands of German soldiers who would have been cut off if the Allies had grabbed the Scheldt in early September were escaping deeper into Holland, where they were putting intense pressure on the northern flank of the Market Garden corridor.

In spite of all this, de Guingand relayed his commander's request to continue his operation to push into northern Germany. Monty's wishes had not changed since August. In spite of the setbacks in Holland, he wanted full priority of supply to breach the Rhine, envelop the industrial Ruhr, and drive for Berlin. The field marshal seemed to think that the understrength Canadian First Army could handle the task of opening up Antwerp (almost as if it were an afterthought) while his other army, the British Second, drove into Germany.

At this point, Eisenhower could have—and probably should have—insisted that Montgomery concentrate primarily on clearing the Scheldt as a prerequisite for any advance into Germany. Instead, he authorized more of the same, effectively giving Monty what he wanted. "The envelopment of the Ruhr from the north by Twenty-first Army Group, supported by First Army, is the main effort of the present phase of operations," he said. Indeed, after the meeting, an exultant de Guingand wired to his chief that Ike had pledged "one hundred percent support" for the field marshal's concepts.

Ike's statement, whether he intended or not, gave Montgomery the green light to continue sidetracking the Scheldt in favor of Market Garden. At various times, Eisenhower had stressed the importance of Berlin, the Ruhr, and Antwerp to Montgomery. Given these mixed signals, it is not surprising that the field marshal would interpret his orders in whatever manner he wished. In that respect, his absence from the conference actually worked to his advantage. Until he received clear, unambiguous instructions from Ike that he was to devote first priority to clearing the Scheldt (something an exasperated Eisenhower eventually did in a cable on October 9), Monty would continue chasing the Berlin dream at the expense of Antwerp. Moreover, Ike's new instructions compelled Bradley to assume control of the British VIII Corps sector, just east of Hell's Highway. In effect, this meant that two more American divisions would be earmarked to help Montgomery. Eisenhower's decision to maintain priority for Monty also consigned Lieutenant General George Patton's Third Army to the back burner of the war. "We're putting a lot of money into an unprofitable stock," one of Bradley's staff officers opined when he heard about Ike's instructions.

To be fair, Ike did give Bradley permission to make a limited push for the Ruhr through the Aachen corridor, in the hope that he and Montgomery would envelop this vital industrial area from the south and north respectively. The supreme commander also told Devers that his Sixth Army Group could launch an offensive to capture Mulhouse and Strasbourg, as long as his operations did not divert supplies needed for the northern armies.

To Ike, his instructions represented a nice compromise among the many competing interests of his subordinates. He ended the meeting in an upbeat mood, feeling as though he had defused tension with Montgomery and maintained the momentum of a broad-front advance into Germany. "We have obtained complete understanding that should hold all the way from here to the completion of our present bid for the capture of the Ruhr," he happily cabled Montgomery in the wake of the meeting.

"I regard it as a great pity that all of us cannot keep in closer touch with each other because I find, without exception, when all of us can get together and look the various features of our problems squarely in the face, the answers usually become obvious." The trouble was that all of them had not, in actuality, gotten together at the Trianon; nor had they formed common understandings. Even if Monty had shared Eisenhower's assumption that the field marshal's Twenty-first Army Group must concentrate on clearing the Scheldt with as much gusto as he afforded the push for the Ruhr, Monty had nowhere near the strength for such multitasking. Bradley, for his part, was bitterly disappointed with the meeting. Major Hansen, sensing his chief's letdown, noted in his diary that "he is beginning to look tired." Bradley resented what he thought of as Eisenhower's favoritism toward Montgomery, but his disagreement with Ike's instructions that day went much deeper. He would later write that the supreme commander had made "yet another poor decision. Giving the Ruhr attack first priority inevitably meant further delay in opening Antwerp, which was the key to any victory."

In Eisenhower's mind, Market Garden still represented nothing more than a bridgehead across the Rhine, while other armies continued to push east, into Germany. He still did not grasp the fact that he could no longer afford the luxury of Market Garden. Nor did he seem to understand that Market Garden was coming at the expense of all other operations, ultimately for no good purpose. Every day the operation continued only sapped the vitality of an already tenuous Allied advance. Though Montgomery was not receiving the absolute priority of supply he wanted, he was still getting the majority of what Ike could give him, at the inevitable expense of Bradley. Yet Monty was producing no results with this comparative abundance.

The logistics were unforgiving and immutable. Only Antwerp could feed an Allied advance into Germany, whether on a single front, as Montgomery envisioned, or a broad front, as Ike preferred. By choosing to double down on troubled Market Garden, Ike was essentially guaranteeing the failure of all Allied operations that fall, at least if defeating Germany in 1944 was the ultimate objective. Eisenhower's original choice on September 10 to give the go-ahead for Market Garden had been a poor decision, but this one, taken twelve days later, might well have been even worse. He had violated an old military maxim—never reinforce failure.[1]

CHAPTER 13

Road Killing and Ridge Holding

I n the little village of Erp, predawn fog had given way to midmorning sunshine. Inside a modest two-story brick home, Gerardus Otten, a Dutch resistance fighter, carefully peered through the window at the street outside. What he saw and heard took his breath away. "German infantry, armored cars and tanks streamed by," he later wrote in his diary. The hoarse shouts of the German soldiers mixed with the deafening rumble of the tanks. Otten and the other resistance men in the room with him observed dozens of armored vehicles. As each moment passed, they worried that German soldiers might enter the house or open fire on it. Several times, tanks pointed their main guns at the house, but instead of firing, they simply drove by. Otten's group counted the vehicles and, in excited tones, relayed the numbers to a harried telephone operator who was on the line with a U.S. officer in Veghel, a couple miles to the west. "Another large tank is passing . . . and another one . . . and another one," she intoned. The Germans were clearly in a hurry. This had to mean they were about to launch an attack. The Dutch patriots knew their target must be Veghel, and they expressed this opinion to their American friend. When the column finally petered out and the reports tapered off, the American said, "I would like to pass along special gratitude on behalf of American headquarters for the wonderful work." A moment later, the line went dead.

Otten did not know that similar reports had been filtering from other

344

Dutch resistance operatives to the 101st Airborne Division chain of command throughout the evening of September 21–22. In fact, the Germans were coming from the west and the east. The western force was comprised of Kampfgruppe Huber of the 59th Infantry Division. It was a blend of two infantry battalions, supported by self-propelled artillery and tank destroyers. The eastern force was more powerful. It included Major Freiherr von Maltzahn's 107th Panzer Brigade, which had made two serious attempts to take the Bailey bridge at Son on September 19 and 20. Von Maltzahn alone had between two and four hundred vehicles, many of which Otten's group spotted at Erp. When combined with self-propelled assault guns, infantrymen, and engineers, he had about three SS battalions. The enemy target was indeed Veghel, which Colonel Howard "Jumpy" Johnson's 501st Parachute Infantry Regiment had defended since the first day of Market Garden. Their intention was to cut Hell's Highway and seize the Veghel bridges over the Aa River and the Zuid-Willems Vaart Canal in hopes of strangling the entire Allied corridor in Holland.

For nearly three days, Major General Maxwell Taylor, the 101st Airborne commander, had resigned himself to the fact that, after initially seizing most of the bridges in his sector, his mission was now defensive in nature. He later compared the Screamin' Eagles' role to that of nineteenth-century frontier cavalrymen who had guarded railroads and settlements against the mounted attacks of Native American tribes. Taylor was planning to use the corridor as a base from which to launch small attacks to keep the Germans off balance. Now, though, on the morning of September 22, he was concerned enough about the oncoming German onslaught to order as many reinforcements as he could spare to the Veghel area. Unfortunately, during the night, Colonel Johnson had sent two of his battalions, with several British tanks, to assault Schijndel, a town five miles to the west of Veghel and on the opposite side of the canal. They were now enmeshed in a battle at Schijndel, and it would take them several hours to disengage and move back to the Veghel area. Only the 2nd Battalion, under the command of Lieutenant Colonel Robert Ballard, was still in

Veghel. These men were dispersed in foxholes and buildings along the edges of the town. Taylor ordered the 327th Glider Infantry Regiment and the 2nd Battalion, 506th Parachute Infantry Regiment, to make haste for Veghel. The general himself was at Son, effectively isolated from the impending battle. Brigadier General Anthony McAuliffe, his division artillery commander, happened to be looking for a good spot for the division headquarters in Veghel, so Taylor put him in charge of defending the town and keeping the vital road open.

For miles along the road on either side of Veghel, British trucks, troop carriers, supply trailers, and other vulnerable vehicles were spread out in various clumps, making ideal targets. "There was a great line of stalled traffic, waiting for the way to be cleared," one paratrooper said. In one spot, an American patrol from the 501st intelligence section came upon four lonely trucks, with antiaircraft guns in tow. The crews were resting, drinking tea. One of the patrol members, Private First Class Carl Cartledge, paused to tell the British commander that the trucks were so visible on the road that he and the other patrol members had seen them from half a mile away. The young paratrooper suggested that the British move their vehicles. "The British captain told this American private how presumptuous I was to tell him what to do," Cartledge later said. The private shrugged and left. He and the four other men on the patrol were happy to put some distance between themselves and the four trucks.

Within mere moments, the German columns arrived half a mile away, just over the eastern horizon. They unleashed a hellish fury on these trucks, along with any other targets they saw in and around Veghel. Tank and self-propelled artillery shells peppered the area. The intensity of the shelling was almost beyond description. The center of town was especially hard hit. Only a few days earlier, crowds of jubilant civilians had celebrated with their American liberators among the narrow streets. Now, almost in the blink of an eye, the place turned into a kill zone. The mood of the locals changed from jubilation to horror. "The orange cloth that people were waving and hanging out of upstairs windows sure went out of sight," Lieutenant Robert Neill commented. People scurried for the cover of basements, even as their homes and shops went up in flames. "In the space of minutes the whole . . . town had become gray . . . and deserted, like a town abandoned for a hurricane," Lieutenant Laurence Critchell later wrote.

The shells shrieked in mercilessly, shattering trees, smashing through roofs and walls, exploding against the concrete, sending masonry flying in every direction. "The ground rocked with successive explosions that shook the area," Private First Class Don Rich recalled. "Three at a time, boom, boom, boom, one salvo after another. Men were screaming between explosions from fear and pain." Some ran desperately for the cover of a drainage ditch. Others, like Rich, dug holes as frantically as they could. Alongside Veghel's venerable multistory Catholic church, he scooped out shallow grooves in the earth as shells smashed into the roof of the church and even skipped off it. With every scoop, he recited prayers through thin, white, fear-ridden lips. "The barrage was utterly terrifying. There was no way to fight back. We were so helpless." He could feel the concussion of the nearby explosions, so close and so potent that they caused physical pain. Somewhere nearby, a soldier was crying for help. Private First Class Henry Sherman, a medic, got up and ran to the man. A trio of shells exploded near Sherman. He went down in a heap, probably dead before he hit the ground. Nearby, another shell exploded near Sergeant Joe Slish and sliced him in half at the waist. The sergeant's bodybuilder physique had once been the envy of everyone in the company. Now what remained of him lay in two bloody, lifeless pieces.

Not far away, Technician Fifth Grade Darwin Clippinger, a radioman, spotted an open field with a shed that might offer some shelter from the accurate barrage. He sprinted for the shed. On the way there, he saw a lieutenant who was badly wounded in the groin and stopped to help him. "I cut off his pants and put some sulfa powder and a bandage on him." He resumed his trek but, instead of going to the shed, he found a shell hole. He crowded together in the hole with several other soldiers, two of whom were wounded, and waited out the barrage. Private David Kenyon Webster found a partially safe spot in the entrance to a shelter crowded with civilians. "Clutching their children as the shells bammed into their neat homes, they wept and wailed, shrieked and moaned, and sang dismal old Dutch hymns," he later wrote. Gloomy though the mood was, he figured it was better than chancing the shells somewhere in the open. The shelling hit the town convent so hard that it killed five nuns and wounded three others.[1]

Intense though the German fire was, Ballard's 2nd Battalion troopers managed to stymie the enemy assault on the town. Instead of trying to overrun the American-held foxholes and buildings, the German vehicles began, by about midday, to gravitate to the north, where they cut the road about four hundred yards outside of Veghel. Some of the enemy vehicles turned south and attempted to get into Veghel from that direction. By this time, American reinforcements from the 327th Glider Infantry, F Company, of the 506th Parachute Infantry and the 81st Airborne Antitank Battalion, had arrived.

German tanks crept steadily from north to south, toward Veghel. Lieutenant Bob Perdue, an assistant platoon leader in F Company, dismounted from a truck in the middle of town and, with the rest of the platoon, headed north, on a collision course with the enemy tanks. Before they knew it, they found themselves practically face-to-face with them, probably no more than fifty or one hundred yards away. "One tank was coming directly at me," Perdue wrote "[I]t fired . . . and destroyed a British ammunition truck to my right. The explosion knocked me uninjured to the ground." Perdue and many of the other troopers crawled for the cover of a nearby ditch. Calls went out for bazookamen. The ammunition truck burned fiercely, oily black smoke belching from the carcass. Ammo cooked off, and the crew of the truck scattered in every direction. One of the British soldiers slipped and slid his way into a muddy ditch alongside Staff Sergeant John Taylor, a squad leader in F Company. "He fell down beside me and when he got up . . . the rigging on his pack got hung up on my leg and he jerked me down." The two men worked for several seconds to untangle themselves.

As they did so, and the tanks kept approaching, there was a flurry of activity on the road behind them. A scratch group from Battery B, 81st Airborne Antitank Battalion, unhooked a fifty-seven-millimeter antitank gun from a jeep and wheeled it into place. They had driven all the way from Son to deal with the German attack on Veghel. The group consisted of Lieutenant Colonel X. B. Cox, the battalion commander, Captain Alphonse "Fonse" Gueymard, the battery commander, Corporal Rogie Roberts, Corporal William Bowyer, and Flight Officer Thomas Berry, a glider pilot who was on his way back to his unit's base in England and volunteered to help out. General McAuliffe had personally ordered them to the scene.

Ordinarily a fifty-seven-millimeter gun crew would dig their piece in or anchor it in some fashion to guard against recoil. In the excitement of the moment, though, this odds-and-ends crew simply set up the gun in the middle of the cobblestone street. The lead Mark V Panther was only one hundred yards away, and there was little time for worrying about such niceties. To Private First Class William True, an infantryman who was watching from the vantage point of a nearby ditch, the gunners looked incredibly vulnerable standing in the middle of the street, in full view of the enemy tank. "I was terribly impressed with the guts of those gunners . . . it seemed like their gun . . . was a mere pea-shooter . . . facing up to the much heavier firepower of the tank." Lieutenant Colonel Cox and Flight Officer Berry acted as ammo bearers. Captain Gueymard did the spotting.

Corporal Roberts acted as the gunner. He bent down and looked through the viewing scope. Smoke from the burning truck obscured his view. Someone nearby yelled, "Fire! Fire!"

"I'll fire when I can see it!" he barked back without taking his eye off the scope.

At last, the smoke cleared, and he saw the Mark V, impossibly close. "I quickly depressed the gun and fired," he recalled. "I hit the tank between the tracks where fire began to belch out. Smoke rose from the turret." Meanwhile, the unsecured gun recoiled violently and smashed Roberts in the knee, breaking his kneecap.

A pair of enemy crewmen leaped out of the tank and tried to run away. American infantrymen in the ditches cut them down with a wall of rifle and machine gun fire. "[They] were easy targets for our guys," Sergeant Russ Schwenk, who was close enough to the tank to "count the bolts on the tread," recalled.

Captain Gueymard ordered Roberts to fire more shots into the stricken Panther. But Roberts was in serious pain from his injury. "Captain, I can't move," he replied. Gueymard loaded the gun and fired two more rounds himself, both of which hit the Panther. Thirty-seven-millimeter antitank crews from the 327th Glider Infantry Regiment added more fire, as did a nearby British tank (the glider gunners and the tankers also claimed credit for the kill). Under the weight of all this fire, the other enemy tanks pulled back.

The incident set the tone for the Battle of Veghel. German tank and half-track crewmen were wary enough of American antitank opposition that they were reluctant to press their attacks aggressively for the town center. Still, the enemy armor roved in small groups, causing mayhem along the road and in parts of the town. With every passing moment, more 101st Airborne reinforcements arrived and expanded the scope of the fighting, until McAuliffe had the equivalent of a shaky perimeter around Veghel.

Perhaps the biggest threat to Allied control of the area occurred when elements of Kampfgruppe Huber managed to sideslip American opposition at Schijndel and converge on the main road bridge over the Zuid-

Willems Vaart Canal. They showered the bridge and its environs with deadly mortar and artillery fire. British antiaircraft crewmen and American troopers took cover together in ditches and buildings. McAuliffe had to personally circulate around and order these men back to their weapons. At the same time, he fed the newly arrived D Company, 506th Parachute Infantry Regiment, into the line to stave off the German push for the bridge. "The attack was broken up," one of the soldiers later recalled, mainly by "pumping mortars and . . . [firing] several bazooka rounds and rifle grenades. We got some forty Germans to surrender along with a disabled tank." Instead of continuing to push for the bridge, the Kampfgruppe Huber survivors swung to the south and cut the road from that direction. They ran right into the 1st Battalion, 327th Glider Infantry Regiment, as it was hurrying to Veghel. The glider soldiers drove the enemy soldiers away from the road into neighboring woods. They took about seventy prisoners and killed at least thirty-five German soldiers.

Late in the afternoon, British Typhoons swooped in and helped keep the Germans at bay. "We waved and hollered as they circled above the Germans through puffs of light flak," Private Webster later wrote. "One by one they peeled off and screamed down. Whoosh! they released the rockets under their wings. There was a wonderful sound of continuous booming. Several fires started to burn." The air strikes limited the mobility of the Germans. No tank commander in his right mind wanted to move on the roads or anywhere in the open while the planes were overhead. The air strikes were so effective that, in the estimation of one medic in Ballard's 2nd Battalion, "The British fighter planes probably saved us. Their rockets were pretty effective against the German tanks and half-tracks, and we were able to hold on."

By nighttime, the intensity of the fighting tapered off. Half of Taylor's division was now concentrated in the embattled Veghel perimeter and at Uden, a few miles to the north. Fighting raged in both towns, and along the road that connected them, for much of the next day, but the Germans could not capture the bridges. What they could—and did—do with seeming impunity was cut the road at various times, thus demonstrating the vulnerability of the entire Allied corridor (even as they wrecked the momentum of General Horrocks's attempts to rescue the 1st Airborne Division at Arnhem). In fact, the XXX Corps commander had to send the 32nd Guards Brigade to help Taylor keep the road open. "Though they eventually succeeded," Horrocks wrote, "the road was closed to all traffic for twenty-five very important hours." Not to mention the fact that the brigade was diverted from its original mission of assisting in the abortive British drive for Arnhem. Nor did the end of the Veghel crisis mean that the Germans were finished in their attempts to sever the Allied corridor.[2]

Located immediately on the opposite side of the Zuid-Willems Vaart Canal from Veghel, the village of Eerde was marked by a geographic oddity. The terrain beyond the little farm hamlet was honeycombed with sand dunes of every size and description. In gazing at the dunes, a newcomer might have been tempted to think he had happened upon a coastal beach rather than rich agricultural low country. "Those sand dunes were piles of dirt about 20 feet high and had 8 inch trees growing out of them," one paratrooper later wrote. The town itself comprised little more than a windmill, a cluster of homes, a schoolhouse, and a church.

While the Veghel battle was raging on September 23, Colonel Johnson had ordered his 1st and 3rd battalions to disengage from their fight in Schijndel and withdraw closer to the vital road. They had ended up in Eerde, with the 1st Battalion manning the forwardmost outpost positions among the dunes, looking across a no-man's-land bramble of trees toward German-held territory. The colonel established his headquarters in a compact brick farmhouse, whose occupants had only recently vacated their home. The staff worked on the crowded first floor, while gazing at family pictures of the young couple who owned the house. The second-floor attic was filled with trunks and apples, but the Americans seldom ventured up there for fear of shell fire. Staff officers took catnaps under the dining room table, while hoping (usually in vain) not to get stepped on by their fellow soldiers.

Although the Allies had managed to turn the 107th Panzer Brigade and Kampfgruppe Huber away from the Veghel perimeter and restore traffic along the road, the Germans had not given up their hopes of permanently cutting the corridor. To the west, they scraped together four understrength battalions, with support from artillery and tank destroyers, for a new attack on the morning of September 24. Two of the battalions were composed of paratroopers from the 6th Fallschirmjäger (Parachute) Regiment, a unit that had fought the 101st Airborne Division at Carentan, in Normandy. The Germans knew there were gaps in the Allied lines west of the road. Dozens of vehicles were still logjammed along the road itself. The Germans also knew that Eerde was occupied by the 501st. Though the Germans aimed to seize the main road bridge over the Zuid-Willems Vaart Canal, they unwisely chose to focus their attack on Eerde rather than bypassing it in favor of the road.

Shortly after first light, the enemy paratroopers appeared, like morning phantoms, among the dunes. Small-arms fire crackled in random crescendos, ebbing and flowing amid the sand and trees. Lieutenant Charles Howser's outpost platoon fell back, under intense fire, to warn the rest of the 1st Battalion of the impending German assault. Enemy artillery, mortar, and tank destroyer fire laced into the town. The shells pounded the church steeple and the area around Johnson's headquarters. "Shells were beginning to crash into the windmill," Lieutenant Critchell recalled. "Mortar fire was falling in the streets of the town." One of the enemy tank destroyers zeroed in on the windmill and, in the recollection of Sergeant Guy Sessions, "was methodically taking it apart brick by brick." At the other end of town, masonry from the church steeple crashed to the street below. Technician Fifth Grade Ray Lappegard, for one, was saddened to see the enemy shells eat away at the old church. The nuns of this church had given him a pitcher of hot tea and a rosary. He was a Lutheran, but this hardly mattered. The budding friendship with the nuns, and the parish priest, had made a deep impression on Lappegard and his buddies that "the battle we were in was one that had to be fought."

The Americans responded to the German bombardment with mortar fire. Captain Harry Howard and Technician Fourth Grade Earl Tyndall climbed the church steeple and braved the heavy enemy shelling to spot targets for the mortars. Colonel Johnson arranged for reinforcement from nine British tanks. As he stood in the street coordinating plans with a British liaison officer, a mortar shell whooshed in and exploded close by, hitting the British officer and slicing off part of Johnson's ear. Lieutenant Colonel Harry Kinnard, the 1st Battalion commander, was standing between them, but he escaped with only a concussion-related earache.

Moments later, an ammunition truck braked to a halt. Lieutenant Robert Schorsch, the 1st Battalion supply officer (S4), and a group of about half a dozen men trotted over to unload it. An enemy shell scored a direct hit on the truck, touching off the whole load of ammunition. Everyone in Schorsch's group was either killed or wounded. "Men were lying about; some were crawling; others were obviously dead," Captain Ian Hamilton, the commander of B Company, recalled. Hamilton saw his old friend Schorsch lying in a heap, trembling violently. "I grabbed him and pulled him to a sitting position, but he was bleeding from his nose and mouth and was trying to speak." He died within seconds.

Shortly thereafter, the British tanks arrived. Kinnard planned to combine them with his infantrymen to counterattack the enemy paratroopers in the dunes. The three leading Shermans, under the command of Lieutenant Roy Hooper, halted just short of the windmill, almost within sight of where the fighting was still raging among the dunes. Captain Robert Phillips, commander of C Company, expected them to keep rolling past the windmill to the scene of the heaviest fighting. He figured the tanks would lay down fire, while his troopers rooted out the enemy soldiers. Instead, the Shermans halted right where the enemy could see them. Captain Phillips approached Lieutenant Hooper and told him, in no uncertain terms, to keep moving before the Germans spotted him and opened fire. Hooper looked at Phillips, leaned over in his turret, and shook his head. "I can't go into an attack with you," he yelled, "until I get orders from my battalion commander."

Phillips's radioman, Technician Fourth Grade Frank Carpenter, saw the captain's face turn an angry shade of red. "You didn't talk to Captain Phillips that way," Carpenter said. "[He] was madder than a wet hen." As the two officers argued ineffectually, Carpenter sidled away, leaned against the side of the tank, and rested his heavy radio against it.

At the same instant, the crew of an enemy Jagdpanther spotted Hooper's tank and fired. The armor-piercing shell smashed into the Sherman just below the gun tube, flew right through the tank and out the rear. Flames shot from the Sherman. Carpenter looked up in time to see Hooper blown from the turret. "[He] flew through the air, falling down beside me, and rolled into a little ditch, screaming bloody murder. He'd been ripped open in the groin and one leg was almost off at the hip." As Hooper writhed in agony, he pointed at his stricken Sherman and yelled, "Save my men! Get them out! They'll burn to death!" Those were his last words.

In seconds, the enemy tank destroyer scored hits on the other Shermans, setting them afire, adding to the disaster. A few of the crewmen escaped from their tanks. The paratroopers braved the flames in an attempt to rescue the others. As Private First Class John Cipolla headed for one of the tanks, he saw a crewman emerge in flames. The man emitted horrible shrieks of pain as he fell to the pavement. "I rushed to the tank to help the others inside," Cipolla recalled. He began climbing onto the Sherman.

"Get the hell off that tank before you get blown off!" Captain Phillips ordered.

Just then, the ammunition inside the tank exploded, blowing Cipolla into the air. He landed on his butt several yards away, more shaken than hurt. The men inside were doomed. They burned to death as the Americans stood by helplessly. When the flames finally died down, Cipolla looked inside and saw "the charred remains of a man with his head the size of a baseball and shoulders as small as a doll." In a different tank, Technician Fifth Grade Joe Haller witnessed the horribly burned remains of another crewman. "The hands were up in the air as if reaching for the hatch cover."

After this horrifying fiasco, the British tankers refused to participate in the battle any further until the Americans cleared the dunes and a stretch of nearby railroad tracks. In effect, this meant that the paratroopers were on their own. Lieutenant Colonel Kinnard ordered an infantry-only attack against the German-held dunes. His A Company comprised the assault force, while C Company, the mortars, and a few artillery pieces lent fire support. Most of the troopers had not eaten a decent meal in four days. They were hungry and weary. But they did not hesitate for a moment. With almost reckless abandon, they left their foxholes and attacked the dunes, all the while employing the usual fire and maneuver tactics of the U.S. Army.

The fighting was personal. Small groups of troopers sprinted from dune to dune, killing enemy soldiers in foxholes and behind trees and embankments. In a few instances, they even clubbed them to death. Those who wished to surrender were hurriedly waved to the rear. Troopers from the company headquarters, including the first sergeant, ran back and forth from Eerde to the head of the advance, hauling badly needed ammunition. Lieutenant Sumpter Blackmon, one of the platoon leaders, marveled at the initiative and teamwork of the troopers all around him. "I saw one man throwing rocks into the scrub to one side of him . . . so as to attract enemy fire so as to locate gun positions," he said. "He got a line on the enemy fire position and knocked it out. I saw three men consult among themselves, then get their heads down and . . . charge an enemy mg [machine gun] twenty five yards away and manned by three enemy and destroy men and gun. That was the way the thing went all day."

A group of paratroopers neared a small hole defended by Private Eckart Schucany, a German soldier in the 6th Fallschirmjäger's 10th Company. He had camouflaged the hole with potato plants but to no avail. A pair of shots ripped into the position, barely missing him. He rustled around, trying to disguise the hole better, but that only attracted more American fire. "I immediately stopped, because surely the subsequent shot would have been the end of me," he said, "thus the cat-and-mouse game continued."

The Germans were losing ground, but they were fighting hard nonetheless. A group of them used the cover of ditches to close in and attack Private Carl Beck's machine gun position, throwing white phosphorous grenades at the American. "That's pretty wicked stuff," Beck said. The fighting was so ferocious that he fired ten boxes of ammunition at his attackers (five hundred rounds per box). "The ground looked like it had been plowed out [from the recoil of the gun] where I'd set up my machine gun 'cause they were kinda after me." The heavy fire blunted their counterattack. The direct fire of machine gunners like Beck and the mortar crews (most of whom were dug in behind the schoolhouse in Eerde) proved to be much more effective than the artillery, if only because they were more precision weapons. Most friendly artillery shells exploded too far behind the German positions to do the American attackers much good.

At the head of the American advance, German machine gun and rifle fire was so heavy that the soldiers were forced to hurl themselves as flat as possible lest they have their heads blown off. Private John Bleffer, a machine gunner, got up and ran to the left, where he could lay down effective fire. He loosed several long bursts of .30-caliber fire until the enemy bullets tapered off a bit. "Let's go!" Lieutenant Harry Mosier yelled.

"Every man sprang from the ground and started the assault," Lieutenant James Murphy later wrote. "All this time we were receiving a terrific amount of enemy machine gun, mortar and rifle fire." Still they kept going. In the face of such a fierce assault, some of the German troopers threw down their weapons and fled. Others fought to the death, sometimes in hand-to-hand combat. The battle degenerated into a brawl. Officers had little control of this intimate struggle. "I actually saw individual men and small groups of two or three charge machine gun emplacements and either destroy or chase the enemy forces from his positions," Murphy recalled. "The spirit and courage of the men was [sic] beyond anything I had ever imagined possible . . . the sheer guts and courage of every man terrorized the enemy . . . causing him to abandon his arms and flee or be annihilated. What we did in those moments we could scarcely remember afterward because we had no time to think. It was . . . almost foolish courage, and I doubt if any group of men could have held their ground against it."

The battle of the dunes raged on like this until the late afternoon, when the Americans finally succeeded in driving the enemy force away from Eerde. Thanks to the 501st Parachute Infantry Regiment, the town proved to be a complete dead end for the Germans. Nor did they ever come close to the bridge. Casualties from the battle were high on both sides. Company A alone lost thirty men, comprising about one-third of its strength. This included eight men dead, most of whom had been killed when a German tank shell exploded in their midst. Company C accounted for a dozen more U.S. casualties. The British, of course, had lost three tanks and several crewmen. The Germans probably lost at least fifty killed. The Americans captured twenty-six enemy paratroopers, wounded at least twice that number, and sent many more to flight.

Instead of renewing their efforts to take Eerde and the dunes, the Germans simply veered to the south (something they should have done in the first place), cut the road at Koevering, and shot up yet another convoy of British vehicles. In the estimation of Lieutenant Colonel Friedrich von der Heydte, commander of the 6th Fallschirmjäger Regiment, this attack was "the last serious attempt undertaken by the German forces to eliminate the corridor." It took the Allies another day and a half to chase them away and secure Hell's Highway for good.[3]

The Germans also put pressure on the Groesbeek heights, where the 82nd Airborne Division was still spread out along the ridges. At Devil's Hill (officially known as Hill 75.9), the highest spot in the whole area, isolated troopers from A Company, 508th Parachute Infantry Regiment, plus a couple squads from G Company, held out day after day against repeated enemy assaults. "[They] repulsed four attacks in company plus strength," a regimental report related. "Attacks were made from three and four sides at once. Food and ammunition were extremely short. The constant attacks and enemy infiltration allowed the men . . . very little sleep." In one attack, German paratroopers made it to within fifteen feet of the Americans before they were stopped. "The forest was full of bullets," one of the German survivors later recalled. "Down went comrades. I hadn't seen anything. I grasped the ground and sheltered in [a] hollow. I was terrified and crying."

Accurate artillery and mortar support helped keep the Americans on the hill alive. Every approach route to Devil's Hill was periodically under heavy shell fire. The hill itself comprised a sharp, wooded incline above a dirt track and open farmland. The troopers crouched low in heavily camouflaged foxholes and rifle pits. At night, men in neighboring foxholes tied empty cartridge bandoliers to one another in order stay awake. They subsisted on K rations and whatever local chickens they could catch. Small patrols managed to infiltrate in and out of the area, replenishing the ammo stocks, although, at one point, the riflemen were down to five rounds apiece. During one lull in the fighting, they laid their dead friends—eleven in all—faceup in a mass grave. They covered their faces with tablecloths they had scrounged from a nearby house and shoveled dirt over them.

The company commander, Captain Jonathan "Jock" Adams, set the determined tone, as did Lieutenant John Foley, one of his platoon leaders who had led the original American assault to seize the hill. They and their men had spent the early days of Market Garden fighting in the streets of Nijmegen (Adams and several others were isolated there for over two days). The company first sergeant, Frank Taylor, bucked up the spirits of the men by teaching them the words to a song called "I'll Walk Alone."

Another sergeant disseminated watches from captured Germans to his men. "I'm going to keep this watch as long as I live," one of the men solemnly told him. Through several subsequent enemy attacks, he was true to his word. Then one night, when he heard Germans forming for yet another night infiltration, he yanked the watch off his wrist and flung it into the darkness at them. "If you want the damn watch so bad, take it!"

His squad mates broke out into gales of laughter. "It was the kind of comic situation that helped us get through those trying times," one of them later said.

At last, on the evening of September 24–25, the rest of the division fought its way to the hill. Troopers from A Company, 504th Parachute Infantry Regiment, relieved the embattled survivors of the Devil's Hill battle. In all, the defenders had spent five days on the hill, cut off from friendly contact for the majority of that time.

Throughout that last week of September and early October, the fighting ebbed and flowed along the ridges. One particularly potent attack hit the 508th lines near Beek and Berg en Dal. "The enemy began intensive shelling of our forward, reserve and regimental command post areas," the regimental after-action report chronicled. "Light, medium and heavy artillery were employed. The enemy culminated an extremely heavy barrage with an infantry attack supported by armor." Erroneous rumors swirled that the Germans were attacking with sixteen thousand infantrymen and a hundred tanks. By now, the entire 82nd Airborne Division was in place. The 325th Glider Infantry Regiment had finally landed, more or less intact, on September 23 (the remainder of the 101st Airborne's glider echelons also arrived safely on the same day). These infantry reinforcements, in addition to British armor and a full complement of divisional and British artillery, helped General Gavin parry the enemy attacks. One artillery battalion alone fired 620 rounds. "It was one of the most successful defensive artillery barrages of the war," Captain Kim LeFever, one of the battery commanders, later claimed. "The Jerries massed in a wood's edge on which we had registered several times. Before they had cleared the woods, down roared thirty-six rounds of high explosives right on them. Horrible but effective." The German attack failed miserably.

Like General Taylor, who was defending Hell's Highway like a cavalryman in the Old West, Gavin knew that the best way to keep the enemy off balance along the heights was to order counterattacks of his own. Some of the most intense fighting raged around Mook. The Germans had tried very hard on September 20 to take the town and capture the nearby Heumen bridge (this enemy counterattack had occurred during the bold Waal crossing in Nijmegen). More inconclusive fighting followed in late September. The town was pulverized by artillery shells. By early October, the Heumen bridge was secure, but British engineers wanted to build a new bridge supply line across the Maas-Waal Canal at Mook. The Allies controlled the town, but the German lines were still just several hundred yards away from the bridge construction site. Gavin fed the 325th into Mook with orders to push the Germans back a few thousand more yards, into the Reichswald. The glider soldiers had just spent several days fighting an exhausting, inconclusive battle in the Kiekeberg woods, a jumbled bramble that rather resembled the Wilderness of Civil War infamy.

On the morning of October 2, the regiment's 1st and 3rd battalions were in place at Mook, ready for the attack. They were supported by British tanks and artillery. "Several British tanks stood along the road with engines idling like a far-distant thunderstorm," Staff Sergeant John Reynolds recalled. "A column of men silently moved along a hedgerow to the road and climbed on the rear of these armored giants." All around Reynolds, soldiers exchanged nervous grins or jibes. Many of them were haggard and bearded. Quite a few had not slept during the previous four or five days while they fought in the Kiekeberg woods. Few were enthusiastic about the job in front of them. The mood improved, though, when the men noticed a silent, tall figure walk past. An M1 Garand slung across his back, he was instantly recognizable. Up and down the line of soldiers, men nudged one another, pointed, and said, "General Jim's here." Reynolds, for one, never forgot "what a feeling of pride those words caused." The troopers smiled and greeted Gavin warmly. They did not take inspiration from his presence so much as solace. If he was here, perhaps the attack would not be so bad.

Moments later, under the cover of an early-morning fog, they rolled out of the town, onto the gentle plain beyond. At first, they made good progress against no resistance at all. Then gusts of wind blew the fog away. For the Americans, no fog meant no concealment. In the open fields, they made perfect targets for Germans who were holed up in stone houses and the woods beyond. "All hell broke loose," a regimental postbattle report said. "German artillery rained down from the skies. MG 34's [machine guns] opened up from the stone houses."

Terrified infantrymen frantically scattered and looked for cover. "The air screamed with death tokens," Staff Sergeant Reynolds recalled. "Clods of dirt and moss flew as though taking sides in the battle. Sand rained as the shells hit. Machine guns tic-tacked. My head started to pound as though it were a huge anvil continually swelling under the powerful blow of a mighty hammer. Blood appeared as though without cause on the faces and bodies of the men advancing beside you." Staff Sergeant Richard Wagner was taking cover in a ditch when he looked up and saw a bewildered cow wandering around, looking for safety. She tripped off a mine. "Her belly was full of holes and the blood was running out," he said. "She looked down at me as [if] to say, 'Please help me.' I love animals and this just about got me."

After the initial shock of the enemy fire wore off, a heavy blanket of Allied counterbattery artillery fire decreased the intensity of the enemy fire. The battle turned into a methodical effort to destroy every enemy-controlled stone house. Tanks pounded the windows with high-explosive shells and set fire to roofs with white phosphorous rounds. Infantrymen poured into the houses, killing or capturing German survivors. "It was a bitter, close-in fight for every house," one officer later wrote. This was how they spent most of the day. By nightfall they had their objectives. A tense night of shelling ensued. Throughout the day and night, the Allies had expended ten thousand artillery rounds. The troopers fully expected to renew their assault the next day. Instead they were relieved by British troops. Mook was finally secure. An uneasy equilibrium had descended over the Groesbeek heights.[4]

CHAPTER 14

Opheusden

The Germans were hardly reconciled to the loss of Nijmegen and its bridges. Even as Allied commanders managed to evacuate 2,398 British and Polish survivors (out of an original group of nine thousand 1st Airborne Division men who fought on the north bank of the Rhine) from the embattled perimeter at Oosterbeek, the Germans were planning countermoves of their own. The enemy still hoped to wreck the Nijmegen bridges and cut off the Allied bridgehead north of the Waal River. German artillerymen kept the bridges under periodic fire, and anyone who crossed went through the nerve-racking experience of wondering whether the enemy might score a lucky hit. Damage from the shells was limited, though. The Luftwaffe launched daily raids with every plane German air commanders could put in the air. Over the course of several days, a blend of twin-engine Heinkel bombers, Stuka dive-bombers, FW-190 fighters, and even brand-new jet aircraft all attacked the bridges. The Germans even launched pilotless planes, packed with explosives, in an effort to destroy the crossings. None of these efforts succeeded. Most of the bombs fell on the streets of Nijmegen, some as many as a mile or two away from their targets. Allied planes shot down forty-six German aircraft. In all, the Germans scored two hits on the railroad bridge and one on the road bridge. The Royal Engineers repaired the damage.

Having failed in their effort to destroy the bridges from the air, the Germans tried to wreck them with specially trained underwater demolition teams (known as "frogmen" in the lingo of the time). On the evening of September 28–29, two teams of frogmen from Marine-Einsatz-Kommando 65, comprising a total of twelve men, plunged into the Waal at Kommerdijk, five miles upstream from Nijmegen. They were clad in special wet suits, with swimming fins on their feet. Their weapons were specially fitted torpedo mines with timers. They planned to float downriver, attach the torpedoes to the bridge piers, set the timers, and then make their getaway as the bridges later exploded. One team of four was bound for the railroad bridge; the other eight men headed for the road bridge.

Both teams made it to their respective targets, right under the unwary noses of British soldiers whose job was to guard the vital bridges. The railroad team succeeded in placing their explosives on the center pier. The road bridge team had more difficulty. Their torpedoes banged against the pier, attracting nervous machine gun fire, and in the confusion of the moment, the German frogmen were not able to place their charges properly. The Germans floated away, several miles upriver. Ten were captured. Two managed to get away. Meanwhile, the center span of the railroad bridge exploded and crashed into the river, destroying the bridge. Only one torpedo charge exploded on the road bridge span, ripping a forty-foot hole in the side of the structure but otherwise leaving it intact. This was a very lucky break for the Allies. A Royal Navy diver disarmed the remaining torpedo charge, and engineers repaired the damage within a day. In the wake of this close call, the Allies guarded the road bridge with floodlights, antisubmarine netting, antitank guns, antiaircraft guns, and headlight-equipped riverboat patrols (all of which they should have done before). The Germans made no more such attempts on the road bridge.[1]

North of Nijmegen, the lines had stabilized by October along a finger of low land between the Lower (Neder) Rhine to the north and the Waal to the south that the Allies took to calling "the Island." The Germans controlled everything north of the Rhine, including a string of hills that were ideal for observation, while the Allies controlled much of the flat territory between the Rhine and the Waal. The western extreme of the Allied salient was only about three miles wide. "This area was flat and cut up by numerous ditches and canals," an American officer later wrote. "High ground across the Neder Rijn on the north made perfect observation for the Germans. No movement could take place during daylight hours. Apple orchards formed the only cover." Twenty-foot-high dikes ran parallel along both rivers. The Island was nothing more than a moist agricultural valley in between those dikes. A two-track railroad, built on a five-foot-high embankment, ran east to west, essentially bisecting the Island. "Opheusden, a small town of about one hundred brick buildings, lay between the Lower Rhine and the railroad," the 101st Airborne Division's official historian wrote. In early October, with the corridor around Veghel finally secured (partially due to the assistance of the British XII and VIII corps), the division boarded trucks bound for the Island. The 501st and 502nd parachute infantry regiments took up position along the Rhine, only a few miles from Arnhem. On October 3, the 506th Parachute Infantry Regiment relieved soldiers from the British 43rd Infantry Division and assumed responsibility for the western edges of the Island. Major Oliver Horton's 3rd Battalion of the 506th faced west, just outside of Opheusden, astride the railroad tracks. The 327th Glider Infantry Regiment was in divisional reserve.

Once the Germans had been foiled in their attempts to destroy the Nijmegen road bridge from the air and the water, they resolved to take it by land—a much more ambitious plan. They committed the newly reconstituted 363rd Volksgrenadier Division to seize the Island and take Nijmegen. The natural route for any such offensive would have been over the Arnhem road bridge, along the main road between the two cities. Ironically, though, after the failure of Market Garden, American planes had destroyed the Arnhem bridge. The Germans instead focused their offensive ten miles to the west, at the Island, where there were no bridges and

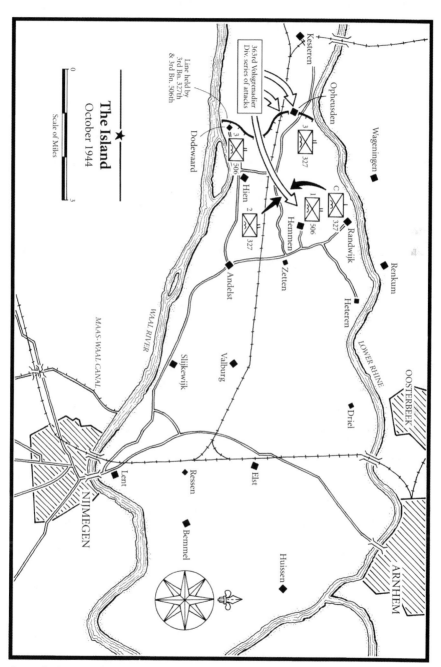

The Island
October 1944

Scale of Miles
0   3

363rd Volsgrenadier
Div. series of attacks

Line held by
3rd Bn. 327th
& 3rd Bn. 506th

Kesteren

Opheusden

3 327

3 506

3

Dodewaard

Hien

2 327

Wageningen

Hemmen

1 506

C 327

Randwijk

Zetten

Heteren

Renkum

Andelst

WAAL RIVER

MAAS-WAAL CANAL

Slijkewijk

Valburg

LOWER RHINE

Driel

OOSTERBEEK

Lent

Ressen

Elst

NIJMEGEN

Bemmel

Huissen

ARNHEM

the route of advance was much narrower. Here they could move the 363rd only piecemeal across the river by ferry, committing it to the attack in portions rather than the whole.

On October 5, just after 0600, their offensive began with a mix of heavy artillery fire and infantry assaults against Horton's forward foxholes. "After a severe artillery and mortar preparation, which knocked out two Company C.P.'s and destroyed communications, a German infantry regiment made a savage attack on Opheusden and along the railroad," a regimental report chronicled. Inside a schoolhouse that served as G Company's command post, Technician Fifth Grade Edward Vetch, a runner, was just taking off his boots for the first time since jumping into Holland, and had no sooner climbed into his sleeping bag when he heard the enemy artillery scream in "with a roar as thick as a hailstorm. At least six rounds hit us directly at once. The whole roof and part of one wall were blown in. I was in my sleeping bag along a wall and was pretty well buried under debris." Other soldiers managed to dig him out. Somehow he was not hurt. The company commander, Captain Joe Doughty, also survived the attack, although he was wounded. He ordered Vetch to check the forward lines at the edge of town. Just as the young runner arrived, the German infantrymen were attacking. "[They] were in the orchard directly in front and so close I could see the black boots through the branches. Everyone was firing continuously." As Vetch spoke with Lieutenant Eugene Rowe, the platoon leader, in the small cement building that served as his command post, the officer pulled out his pistol and fired it out the window. "A German soldier lurched out beside the building with blood gushing through his mouth."

A few minutes later, Vetch took the place of a dead machine gunner. The gunner had been firing so much that when Vetch picked up the gun, he burned his hand. Shaking off the pain, he set up the gun on the altar of the town church "with the roof blown off by the barrage. There was a small hole in the end facing the orchard." Vetch felt guilty about using the altar for such deadly purposes, but he had no other choice. The firing position was perfect. He leaned on the trigger and mowed down rows of German soldiers who were moving through the orchard outside.

Elsewhere in town, troopers from D Battery, 81st Airborne Antiaircraft Battalion, had set up .50-caliber machine guns to defend against enemy aircraft. Now they were using them against the German infantrymen, with devastating effect. The antiaircraft bullets tended to explode when they hit their respective targets. Red tracer rounds flew crazily in every direction. "First you see the enemy soldier," an awed gunner told Captain William Joe, the battery commander. "Then you see a white flash when a .50-caliber magnesium round hit; then you see this object (a man) fly backward." Artillery from attached British units and the 321st Glider Field Artillery Battalion added to the slaughter. The 321st alone fired 2,340 shells in the course of the day.

Still the determined Germans kept coming. There were so many of them, and their fire support was so heavy, that they simply overwhelmed the American defenders. Groups of Volksgrenadier soldiers overran or bypassed American foxholes. In one foxhole, Private First Class Leonard Schmidt and a buddy were leaning over a machine gun, firing at whatever Germans they could see, when his friend took a round through the skull. "It was like sitting and talking to somebody and, all of a sudden, you are by yourself," Schmidt said. "It was my first experience at seeing a buddy dead from that close and having to push his body off the gun so I could try to operate it."

Every trooper who could sit up and manipulate a weapon was needed to deal with the enemy tide. Engineers even fought as infantry. In one ditch just outside of town, Captain Donald Froemke, commander of B Company, 326th Engineers, stopped to ask an infantryman for directions to the nearest command post. A German shell screamed in and exploded at his feet. "The captain was blown about a hundred yards and was completely dismembered," Private First Class Thomas Fitzmaurice recalled.

Near the railroad station south of town, where H Company was fighting hard to ward off the attack, Major Horton arrived. The major was hoping to spot the German route of advance and arrange for artillery to saturate it. With First Lieutenant Robert Stroud, the company commander, in tow, he began working his way forward toward the railroad tracks. Private First Class Joe Harris saw the two officers and warned them that the enemy fire was heavy in that direction, but they ignored him. They stopped between a pair of houses in what amounted to no-man's-land and tried to spot the Germans. In seconds, mortar shells exploded all around them. "We immediately hit the ground," Stroud said. "After they stopped I got up, but Major Horton didn't. I turned him over and saw he was white and bubbling at the mouth." Stroud pulled the wounded major back in the direction of the company. Other soldiers left cover to help him. They managed to evacuate Horton but he died soon thereafter. A pair of medics placed his body on a jeep and began driving him to the rear, while dodging artillery shells all the way. They braked and swerved so much that one of the soldiers had to hang on to Horton's body to keep it from falling into the mud.

The Germans drove salients in the American lines, cut the railroad, and took over much of Opheusden. As the morning wore on and the periodic German attacks only intensified, Colonel Robert Sink, commander of the 506th, understood that he was dealing with more than a local attack. He reinforced the hard-pressed 3rd Battalion with his own 1st Battalion and the 5th Duke of Cornwall Light Infantry of the British Army's 43rd Infantry Division (Wessex), plus Shermans from a British tank squadron. These reinforcements braved heavy shell fire as they counterattacked the Germans.

By late afternoon and early evening, Opheusden itself had become a scene of nightmarish, close-quarters fighting. "Pandemonium reigned in Opheusden," Captain Bernard Ryan, a 3rd Battalion surgeon, later wrote. "The town was burning and shells were landing everywhere. One was as likely to encounter a German as an American." In fact, the Germans were all around the windmill that was serving as the battalion aid station. Even as American casualties streamed into the windmill shelter, wounded Germans did as well, but on their own, not as prisoners. At one point, an artillery shell scored a direct hit on the aid station, throwing Captain Ryan violently to the ground as he administered blood plasma to a wounded soldier. He got up, dusted himself off, and managed to free four wounded Germans who had been buried by debris. In the recollection of the captain they were "none the worse for the experience." One of the Germans, an officer, commented on the courage of the American soldiers and claimed that he never would have allowed the Russians to capture him. "He said we were apparently totally ignorant of the true concept of Communism," one sergeant who talked to him recalled.

All over town that night and the next day, fighting boiled from house to house, street to street. Behind one wall, Private Donald Burgett and several American soldiers were taking shelter from a German machine gun. Bullets cascaded up and down the street, bouncing off walls. To Burgett's chagrin, a pair of troopers kept popping their heads over the wall in an effort to see the enemy gunner's location. "Don't do that," Burgett warned. "That kraut is going to blow your heads off."

"Naw, he can't hit a damned thing," one of the men replied with a laugh.

Predictably, the next time the two men peeked over the wall, the German machine gunner loosed an accurate burst. "The two troopers' helmets flew into the air and brains spattered the ground behind them," Burgett wrote. "Both fell dead, the tops of their heads blown away." Burgett's squad spent hours trying to track the machine gunner down but never found him.

As Private Melvin "Ike" Iseneker's squad moved along another street, they came under accurate sniper fire. They ran for the cover of a nearby barn. Iseneker made it, but not his friend John Ivey. "[The] sniper hit him just under the left ribs," Iseneker said. "I hollered for the medic and he ran to John and was also hit." Other members of the squad spotted the sniper and either killed him or drove him off. "When another medic and I got to

[John] he was just gasping and couldn't talk." He died right there on the street.

Life and death seemingly hung on a random thread. Lieutenant Albert Hassenzahl noticed one of his bazooka teams across the street and summoned them to a doorway where he was taking cover from incoming rounds. Just as they arrived, a shell exploded right where they had been, gouging a huge crater in the ground. Their eyes widened and their complexions went pale. "The look they had on both of their faces I'll never forget as long as I live."[2]

In the morning, the Germans fed another regiment, along with some armor, into the attack around Opheusden. "Out of the morning mist the tanks came with supporting infantry," Staff Sergeant Charles Mitchell recalled. "The tanks were well camouflaged with leafy bushes and tree limbs," another infantryman recalled. Mitchell's B Company absorbed much of the brunt of the enemy push through an orchard and several tobacco fields along the railroad line. As always, artillery and mortar shells—from both sides—were exploding everywhere. One of Mitchell's squad leaders, Sergeant John Boitano, had prepared a sack of explosives he planned to throw on the tanks from the second-story window of a small house. A tree prevented him from unloading his homemade ordnance. At the prodding of Mitchell, he withdrew from the house. "The tanks fired directly at us and we fired back with everything we had, three bazookas and mortars," Private Gene Cook said. These weapons were enough to keep the tanks at a distance, but they did not destroy any of them.

The German tanks sprayed the Americans with machine gun and main gun fire. Enemy mortar shells and small-arms fire added to the danger. In one ditch, Corporal Charles Shoemaker watched in horror as a pair of shells exploded only a few feet away from Private First Class Duke Stewart. Back in England, before the jump, Stewart had predicted that he would either be dead or married by October 6. Now he lay dead in the ditch, on the exact day he had predicted, with no wedding ring on his finger. In the background, Shoemaker could hear the wails of animals that were caught in the cross fire. "The cattle were everywhere, confused like [us], and they didn't know where to go. If they got hit and didn't die right away, they lay there in agony and gave vent to it some way or another." To Shoemaker, their death groans almost sounded like human screams. Not far away, Corporal Henry Gogola and Private First Class Bill Arledge were hugging the ground as machine gun bullets from the tank buzzed overhead. A tank swiveled its turret in their direction and fired. "The ground shook like Jell-O," Gogola said. "I bounced up and was slammed back down." Gogola was okay, but the explosion tore much of Arledge's torso away. Gogola crawled to him and gave him a shot of morphine to make his final moments as comfortable as possible. "He was gone within a very short time. Another friend lost."

In the course of the day, under the weight of these kinds of attacks, the surviving infantrymen began to withdraw back into Opheusden. During the retreat, many of them had to cross the town sewage canal. Under fire all the way, they waded waist-deep through the noxious sludge and then climbed up the slippery slope. The odor they carried with them was indescribable. The situation in Opheusden was still chaotic. Neither side really controlled the town. Germans and Americans were likely to be everywhere and anywhere. "I remember going through 5 houses mostly basement window to window, then along a stone wall with sheds to crawl over, all the time being shot at," Private Cook wrote. All the while, he was bleeding from a shell fragment in his right leg.

German tanks loitered on the edges of the town and hurled main gun rounds at American-occupied houses. Sergeant Earl Patchin, a member of an artillery forward observation team from the 321st, was in a barn, manning a radio. He went outside for only the briefest of moments to relieve himself. "A shell landed only about 6 feet in front of me and exploded blowing me about 15 feet or more through the air," he wrote. "The medics were near and came to my assistance." His entire body was riddled with fragments. He ended up in the aid station, bandaged from his head to his boots. Private Iseneker was carrying a machine gun from one house to another when one of the tanks spotted him and fired. "The world flopped over. The tank shell hit so close to me all the schrapnel [*sic*] hit me in the legs . . . also ruptured my liver. I was on my back. I looked down and saw my left leg was broken between the knee and the hip and was twisted back under my left arm." A severed artery was gushing blood into his jump pants. Iseneker believed he was dying and he thought of a promise he had made to his mother that he would return home. Fortunately, a medic got to him, stanched the bleeding, and dragged him to the aid station.

Not far from the sewage canal, Sergeant Charles Weise dodged one near miss from a shell only to have another one explode close enough to send him bouncing off the ground. "Shrapnel entered my back, causing paralysis to my lower body and bleeding from a stomach wound," he said. He tried to crawl to safety. Sergeant Mitchell got to him, hoisted him onto his back, and carried him through the sewage canal, all the way to the aid station. Mitchell's pants were so inundated with human waste that he could not stand to wear them another minute. He took a pair of trousers off a dead trooper.

Artillery and tank shells continued to batter the windmill. Pieces of glass, timber, and metal whizzed in every direction, inflicting new wounds on many of the stricken soldiers. Weise was in terrible pain, drowsy from concussion, bleeding from the mouth, nose, and ears. He suspected that the medics had put him in the "dead pile" of men they expected to die. Corporal Don Patton, a buddy of Wiese's, was lying next to him, nursing a bad leg wound of his own. As the explosions reached a fever pitch, Patton clasped Weise's hand and began to pray. "It seemed like immediately the war stopped," Weise recalled. "We were not getting shelled. The medics stopped to listen. It was a very stirring moment in my life." It was too good to last. An artillery shell exploded just outside. A fragment tore a hole in the abdomen of First Lieutenant Cyrus Worrell, a physician who had once been an air force flight surgeon before volunteering for the airborne. Worrell staggered backward. A piece of his intestines bulged through the hole and he attempted to push it back in. The doctors laid him down, wet some gauze, and bound up his gruesome wound. He ended up losing several feet of intestine, but he lived.

That night, as Opheusden boiled with bitter fighting, the 327th Glider Infantry was on its way to help. Lieutenant Colonel Ray Allen, whose battalion was slated to reinforce the 506th, got into an argument with Colonel Sink over the wisdom of hanging on in Opheusden. Allen favored a general withdrawal to more defensible positions along the railroad tracks about half a mile southeast of the town. He figured that air strikes and artillery could then maul the Germans in the town and as they resumed their attacks to the east. Sink, whose regiment had already suffered about two hundred casualties, believed that any withdrawal from Opheusden represented a betrayal of his brave soldiers who had fought so hard for the town. Allen's view prevailed.

Under cover of darkness, the Americans began evacuating the town. The biggest problem was how to move the many wounded men who were lying on stretchers in the aid station and on the basement floors of neighboring houses. By that evening, there were 120 seriously wounded soldiers. About fifty of them could walk, so they made their way east, with some help from the medics. Major Louis Kent, the regimental surgeon, and Captain Joseph Warren, the 1st Battalion surgeon, arranged for carrying parties and transportation for the majority who were not ambulatory. German prisoners were even pressed into service as litter bearers.

The rest of the troopers who were able-bodied, but exhausted, filtered east all night long. Most had not slept in two or three days, and many were groggy from the concussion of near miss explosions. Companies were down to platoon size. Some platoons were led by sergeants or corporals. To the embattled survivors, the withdrawal was yet another endurance test. "It seemed like we marched all night long," Sergeant Don Brinninstool later commented. When they reached their respective destinations in and around an apple orchard, some still had the strength and discipline to dig foxholes, but many simply collapsed into ditches or haylofts and went to sleep. Lieutenant Patrick Sweeney, who had gone into Opheusden as the 1st Battalion supply officer but had been pressed into service as A Company's commander, came upon several men from another company who were sacked out underneath a tree. "I awakened them and told them to dig in. As I left them I could hear some very uncomplimentary remarks made about myself that could never be printed, but the soldiers got up and dug."

Private Donald Burgett had no option but to stay awake all night. At Colonel Sink's behest, Sweeney chose Burgett and four other men to serve as a rear guard for the entire unit. They were the sacrificial lambs. If the enemy attacked, they would be overwhelmed and destroyed, but they would warn the rest of the outfit. All night long they huddled together nervously over a pair of machine guns perched atop a culvert, listening for sounds of enemy movement. "It was so quiet I thought I could hear my own heartbeat," Burgett later wrote. "The silence gave way to a ringing in my ears that grew increasingly louder." They spoke haltingly to one another in whispers. At one point, they saw shapes of men moving past them. "It was an enemy patrol out searching for our positions." The Americans lay absolutely still until the patrol was gone. Finally, near dawn, the five men made their way back to their company. On the way there, they saw soldiers camped in small tents underneath trees along the road. They assumed they were British and waved at them. The soldiers waved back. Burgett and the four others uneventfully made it to A Company's new positions in the orchard. Like every other weary man in the battalion, they anticipated a day of rest and sustenance.

At almost the same moment, an odd convergence was taking place. Through sheer happenstance, the lead companies of the 327th had arrived in the darkness to a spot only a few hundred yards northwest of the 1st Battalion. Neither unit knew of the other's presence. Also, the Germans had moved up a new infantry battalion to renew their attack. During the night this outfit had sideslipped Opheusden and moved east behind the American lines. In fact, the men whom Burgett's group saw during the night were probably the lead scouts. The enemy battalion kept advancing against no resistance (according to their commander's later testimony, they were lost) and had ended up at the edge of the orchard, very close to where 1st Battalion had settled down. In fact, these were the men Burgett and his cohorts waved to as they returned to their company.

In the light of day, the two sides discovered each other. Men from both sides called ineffectually to the other to surrender. Soon shooting rang out. Troopers who had just drifted off to sleep suddenly heard the gut-wrenching sound of German machine guns and mortars. The Germans were in trouble, though. Most of them were in range and in sight of American weapons from both U.S. battalions. Soon they were in the cross fire of two well-sited American machine guns. Thirty-caliber bullets swept up and down the rows of German soldiers, hitting some, forcing others to scramble for cover underneath the trees. "The whole scene was like out of a movie where the 'bad guys' are easily seen," Private First Class Richard Turner said. "Some of us with rifles didn't even bother to fire them. The machine guns were doing too good a job and the rifles weren't needed." Other riflemen, like Private Burgett, were firing clip after clip. The air echoed with the unique pinging sounds of empty stripper clips ejecting from M1 Garands. "At that moment, the man in front of me, who was lying . . . behind a tree, was hit in the head," Burgett wrote. "I literally saw his head explode. Brains flew all over my face and arms. I tried to brush them off the best I could."

A couple hundred yards away, First Lieutenant Albert Hassenzahl was trying to figure out exactly what was going on. His C Company had gone into Opheusden with 118 men. At that point, he had been a platoon leader. Now only twenty-six remained, and they were under his command. Major James LaPrade, the 1st Battalion commander, materialized and ordered him to take what was left of his company to cut off the German route of retreat. "So we went along a ditch to flank them from an angle," Hassenzahl said. They arrived at an ideal spot from which to call in eighty-one-millimeter mortar fire. One of his NCOs, Sergeant Mariano

Sanchez, was blessed with outstanding eyesight and proved to be a perfect spotter. "He walked that eighty-one-millimeter mortar fire right into those woods," Hassenzahl said, "and you could see the explosions . . . and you could hear the cry of the krauts." When the fire lifted, the twenty-six men of C Company got up and charged into the trees. "We must have taken one hundred fifty prisoners."

Under the combined weight of the American firepower, the German will to fight deteriorated. When the shooting began to die down, a German soldier who was bleeding badly from a stump where his hand had once been got up and ran toward the American lines. "The blood was gushing like water from a garden hose," Lieutenant Sweeney said. Captain Warren, the doctor, boldly walked up to him, right into the German lines, and gave him first aid. Seemingly everyone stopped to watch, and that marked the end of the battle. The Americans killed sixty Germans, wounded thirty others, and captured 231 for the loss of two dead and five wounded. Among the prisoners was the battalion commander, who was clearly more concerned for the welfare of his wounded men than the loss of the battle. "Many wars are fought, won, or lost but men die only once," he told his captors. They found a map on him revealing that his mission had been to take the Nijmegen bridge. As Hassenzahl's men searched other prisoners, they found a fighting knife belonging to Captain Harold van Antwerp, who had been killed in Normandy. The knife even had Van Antwerp's name engraved on it. With no ceremony or deliberation, two C Company troopers took the prisoner into the woods and executed him.[3]

By the end of the day on October 7, the battle had entered a new phase. The 327th assumed primary responsibility for holding the front line, with most of the battered 506th in reserve. The Germans kept pouring in elements of the 363rd Volksgrenadier Division to launch more relentless attacks. The most violent enemy attack occurred late in the afternoon on October 9. After a quiet day, the Germans employed over one hundred artillery pieces to pound the U.S. lines. The barrage began at 1700 and lasted for nearly forty-five agonizing, terrifying minutes. "There were no distinguishing sounds, just an intense roar shaking my inner being," Private First Class Don Rich recalled. "I couldn't even hear myself think as my head was pounding. There was nothing to do but wait it out." In another foxhole, Private First Class George Mullins thought to himself, "How many eighty-eights [artillery pieces] do those krauts have?" He had fought in Normandy and all through this campaign, but he had never experienced shelling like this. British observers opined that it was the worst artillery fire they had seen since El Alamein. In a fifteen-minute period, some two thousand shells fell on C Company alone. "It was thought at the time that no human being could live through its intensity, yet the men remained under cover in their holes," one officer wrote. The men were indeed hunkered down in deep foxholes and gun pits, as well as the basements of sturdy brick houses. This provided the necessary cover from the damage wrought by each explosion. All but two soldiers in the company survived the pounding.

When the shelling tapered off, there was silence for a moment. Then the cries of wounded men could be heard, along with the menacing rumble of approaching enemy tanks. Two full enemy regiments assaulted. Eight tanks supported them. Now it was the turn of the Allied artillery to wreak havoc. With piercing shrieks, seventy-five- and 105-millimeter shells screamed in and exploded among the advancing German soldiers. In some instances, the Allied observers placed their rounds within seventy-five yards of the American lines. White phosphorous shells burst above groups of attacking Germans, burning them mercilessly. Their screams were so loud and so agonizing that they could be heard above the din of battle. Casualties among the Germans were devastating. Undaunted, they kept coming. An antitank gun destroyed one of the tanks. Elsewhere, a courageous machine gunner stood in a ditch and dueled with another one. "[He] fired so rapidly into the tank aperture that the tank had to turn around," Lieutenant Colonel Allen, who witnessed the incident, later said.

Yet another tank fired into the air raid shelter where Captain Walter Miller, commander of C Company, had placed his command post. "Every incident in my life flashed before me and I thought this was it," the captain later wrote. For some reason, the tank moved on instead of pumping more rounds into the shelter.

The enemy's advantage in numbers translated to a heavy volume of fire. Machine guns, mortars, and grenades raked the American positions. Private First Class Mullins soon found himself pinned down in his hole by such overwhelming fire. "I heard the enemy coming closer and closer with all the firepower that he could produce. Their machine guns, burp guns, and rifles were sending an endless stream of lead in our direction." Mullins quickly grew exasperated with his own helplessness. He decided that, if he was going to die, it would not happen while he was hiding in the bottom of his hole. He stood up and opened fire with a .30-caliber machine gun. "After a few bursts, I believe every man on that line began firing. Out in front, the enemy began screaming, yelling, and charging. Then a whistle blew for them to regroup and charge again." Mullins fired so many belts of ammunition that the gun overheated to the point that it would fire only one bullet at a time. Another company gunner fired so much that the heat from his gun began shooting off loaded rounds even without his pressing the trigger.

Overheated weapons were a common theme all along the line. Smoke poured from mortar tubes as gunners fired round after round. "The volume of fire laid down by our riflemen was so great that varnish was burned on many of the M-1 and BAR stocks," a unit after-action report said. In Captain Miller's company, several riflemen had to discard their weapons when the heat of their barrels became so intense that it scorched the wood and threatened to ignite their rifles. Grenades only added to the carnage. The captain estimated that his company alone discharged three hundred sixty-millimeter mortar shells, 11,280 rifle bullets, and ten thousand machine gun rounds. "The number of grenades thrown was so great that no accurate estimate could be made," he wrote. In order for the companies to maintain such a barrage, supply section soldiers made multiple trips from ammo dumps to the front lines, generally under heavy fire.

Against this wall of fire, the Germans kept coming, to the point of sheer desperation. "Enemy infantry continued to make suicidal attacks on our front throughout the remainder of the night," a regimental operations report said. "In one sector small groups of twelve to fifteen men made at least six mad attempts to penetrate our lines. All these fanatical attempts were repulsed by small arms fire. At times . . . the enemy advanced to within 10 yards of our front lines." Another soldier remembered their making it to within "arm's length." In a few instances, there was hand-to-hand fighting. More commonly, Germans were killed or wounded in front of the American holes, or waited for the shooting to calm down so they could surrender. In the end, the German attack was an unmitigated disaster. They suffered hundreds of casualties and gained nothing. "Not an inch of ground was lost," an officer on the 327th staff later wrote.

When the sun rose on October 10, the fatigued Americans beheld a tragic landscape of dead bodies and destroyed equipment. Private First Class Mullins found several dead Germans in front of his hole, including one who was "all decked out in battle gear with his finger frozen to the trigger of his automatic weapon, which was still pointed skyward." Another soldier had fired a bazooka round at an unseen enemy machine gunner during the night. In the morning, when he saw the young man's dismembered body, he felt anything but happy about it. "I was pretty shook up. This was the first time I knew that I had actually killed someone. I was sick and wanted to leave."

The Germans did not give up. For the next five days, they continued attacking, but none of their assaults were quite as powerful as this one. A few amounted to little more than aggressive patrols. Regardless, each time, the 327th repelled them. The cost was high. In most of the line companies, over the course of that week of combat, casualties ran at a 50 percent rate or higher. A few combat fatigue cases even surfaced. The cost for the Germans was much higher. The 363rd Volksgrenadier Division basically ceased to exist, and for no larger purpose. In the end, the Germans got nowhere at Opheusden. Nijmegen and the road bridge remained firmly in Allied hands. The Germans would never seriously challenge that control again. The 327th continued to hold the line, as did the entire 101st Airborne Division elsewhere on the Island. The ruined town of Opheusden became a heavily patrolled no-man's-land, infused with mines. This uneasy, gloomy fall stalemate stood as mute testimony—perhaps even a microcosm—of Market Garden's sad aftermath.[4]

CHAPTER 15

Stalemate

One October morning, General Lewis Brereton, the American commander of the First Allied Airborne Army, sat down at his expansive desk inside Sunninghill Park, the English mansion that served as his headquarters, opened his diary, and began to scrawl. Although he wrote primarily to chronicle his experiences, he had to admit that the diary was also an avenue in which to relieve his considerable frustrations. Those frustrations centered, in particular, on Market Garden. Though Brereton felt some professional excitement that the successful drops had proven the potency of airborne operations, in his heart he knew Market Garden overall was a dismal failure.

Brereton, like any other commander, did not like the idea of ceding control of his troops to another officer, especially for any appreciable length of time. As Brereton saw it, he had lent Field Marshal Montgomery the better part of his command, in return for no corresponding results. The 1st Airborne Division was destroyed, as was the Polish brigade. The 82nd and 101st airborne divisions were intact, but they had collectively suffered three thousand casualties by the end of September. Perhaps even worse, they were still in Holland, losing more men every day while Montgomery used them in a static, defensive role. For Brereton, this was unconscionable. It was bad enough that Market Garden had failed (something Montgomery still seemed loath to admit). Now, in the face of repeated requests, Montgomery refused to yield control of the two American airborne divisions. "The delay in the withdrawal," he wrote in the diary, "is causing me grave concern."

Airborne troopers were trained for quick-hitting offensive missions, not long campaigns. The divisions were designed to seize objectives and hold them until relieved by more substantial ground forces. They were not supposed to engage in sustained combat. Airborne replacements were scarce. They could not simply be fed into the front line to replace losses like in a regular infantry division. "They have to be specially trained," Brereton wrote. "Ordinary infantrymen cannot be used as replacements. They [airborne units] should come out quickly; otherwise their morale will be seriously dented. They resent remaining in the line after their initial job is finished." The inevitable result of all this was not just resentment—such feelings arguably grow out of all infantry frontline service. The more serious issue was that nearly all of the airborne companies on the line in Holland were significantly understrength and becoming more so by the day as they wasted away in static positions. "It is hard to find trained parachutists nowadays," Brigadier General Anthony McAuliffe echoed in an October letter to his wife, "and it is a shame to fritter them away in defensive action that can be handled by ordinary infantry." Yet, in the view of the American commanders, none of this seemed to matter at all to Monty.

In fact, Montgomery fully understood that the American airborne divisions were not well suited for protracted frontline combat, but he simply could not spare them. His Twenty-first Army Group was spread too thin. If he was to clear the Scheldt estuary and open up Antwerp, as Eisenhower apparently wanted, he needed every man to hold the Allied perimeter in Holland. Brereton understood this, but he did not like it one bit. When he finished his diary entry, he took his concerns straight to Eisenhower himself. "I must protest . . . the continued use of the eight two and one naught [sic] one divisions in Holland as ground troops," Brereton wrote in a carefully worded message. In the end, this protest note and several others like it amounted to nothing. Ike wanted the airborne divisions out of Holland, but he understood Montgomery's manpower situation. The supreme commander knew that the Twenty-first Army Group was too small for its responsibilities. He had already earmarked two new American divisions, the 7th Armored and the 104th Infantry, to help Montgomery. The 7th Armored Division, like all other armored divisions in the U.S. Army, was designed as a slashing offensive mobile force. But the field marshal was so desperate for troops to hold his line that he assigned the 7th Armored the defensive mission of holding a flank on the eastern side of the Allied salient in Holland. The 104th was scheduled to assist Monty's forces in clearing the Scheldt estuary. The two American airborne divisions stayed put, with no substantive interference from Ike.[1]

These high-level decisions of omission rather than commission consigned the troopers to a dreary fall of frontline duty. Throughout October and part of November, they manned stalemated forward positions on the Island, along the Waal River outside of Nijmegen and amid the Groesbeek heights. By and large, the conditions were poor. The weather turned cold and wet. Temperatures plummeted into the thirties and forties. Sheets of misty rain fell. "It started to rain . . . and it continued off and on," Sergeant Robert Rader wrote. "The fields and roads became quagmires of runny, sticky, gooey mud. We were wet everyday [sic]—our clothing, food, guns, equipment wet everyday." General McAuliffe wrote to his wife that "we all walk around with great gobs of mud adhering to our boots. The men up front are the ones who really suffer." Most of the combat troops lived in muddy, moldy, foul-smelling foxholes or dugouts. "The guys were living like animals in a hole, afraid to come out," Private First Class Don Rich commented. Many of the holes were dug into the sides of dikes or embankments. Another soldier recalled that "our foxholes and slit trenches filled with water, and our weapons picked up a rusty film unless they were cleaned daily." Sergeant Joseph Kissane wrote to his mother that "in one area every farmhouse is burnt to the ground and dead cattle everywhere. What with the rain, cold, and shelling, sleeping is difficult."

Opheusden, which, of course, had been the scene of so much fighting, was especially grim. Staff Sergeant Donald Pearson, an engineer platoon sergeant, thought of it as "the essence of death. The entire town proper was mined and booby-trapped by the Germans with only a few paths cleared. Dead bodies of civilians and Germans who had been killed probably weeks earlier lay about the area. Pigs, goats, and other farm animals, some with gaping wounds, wandered through the wreckage." To top it all off, the pancake-flat body of a British tank crewman lay on the main road. "Untold numbers of vehicles had run over his body until it was a flattened, unrecognizable mess." The mines and booby traps continued to cause casualties. "Many lost legs, arms and occasionally eyes," Captain Herbert Jacobs, a surgeon in the 327th Glider Infantry later wrote.

Under such static conditions, any movement during the day could be deadly, especially on the Island, the bulk of which was under direct observation by enemy observers on the north side of the Rhine. A man's foxhole was his home, perhaps even his world. Some ingenious souls, like Private Thomas Morrison, made elaborate improvements on their holes as the weeks dragged by. "I . . . made lamps out of C ration cans, cutting them in half and using candles," Morrison said. "Camouflaged parachutes covered my . . . foxhole, so at least I felt safe." He even improvised a drainage system to keep water out of the hole. Boredom and depression were common. The hours dragged by with excruciating stolidity. Sergeant Spencer Wurst, whose squad had fought so hard around the Nijmegen road bridge, was practically awestruck now by the isolation of the front lines. At night, he often stared into the blackness and brooded on the fact that there was nothing between the Germans and him. "The loneliness and vulnerability of a frontline soldier in a defensive position are almost impossible to describe: There is fatigue, physical discomfort, psychological distress—but above all you are conscious of being the point of the whole U.S. Army in your theater of operations."

The loneliest and most dangerous duty was to serve on an outpost forward of the main line, in no-man's-land. Sometimes outpost soldiers holed up in wrecked houses, but usually they just lay perfectly still in the mud all night long, listening and looking for any sign of the enemy. "Your imagination plays tricks on you," Sergeant Burt Christenson wrote. "A shadow of a bush you have been observing may suddenly take the form of a man. You may convince yourself that you recognize the silhouette of a German soldier," only to find out it was nothing more than a shrub, a tree, or an oversize rock.

Lucky troopers found shelter in abandoned or destroyed homes (most of the civilians had long since been evacuated from the frontline areas). One of Private Dwayne Burns's finest recollections was being issued a new pair of clean, dry socks in one such home. The fact that the socks were four sizes too large for his feet hardly mattered. "It's amazing what a little thing in life can do for jangled nerves," he said. Captain Louis Hauptfleisch, who was Colonel Tucker's adjutant in the 504th Parachute Infantry Regiment, spent many of his evenings in a house that served as the regimental command post. Several times, he had the opportunity to hear an Armed Forces broadcast of the World Series. "I was a St. Louis Browns fan," he said. As such, this was a truly special event for him, because it was the only time his team ever appeared in a World Series (though they lost to the crosstown St. Louis Cardinals). Corporal Mickey Graves, who worked for Hauptfleisch in the personnel section, fondly recalled the welcome distraction of listening to the Series. "The war and all that was taking place around us was completely forgotten for a short interval. We got a tremendous kick out of the cheers of the crowd and the American expressions and slang used by the broadcasters, which were now so foreign to our ears." Bathing was an especially desirable treat. The average trooper rotated off the line into Nijmegen for a five-minute shower and fresh clothing at least once or twice over the course of the two months in Holland. By the time they hit the water, some had not bathed in a month or more. As Sergeant Kissane stripped and showered, he discovered chigger bites up and down his arms. "They are similar to poison ivy in effect," he wrote in a letter home. The hot water offered welcome relief.[2]

Because the two divisions were under British command, the men often ate British rations. Bully beef, mutton, oxtail soup, and tea were common offerings. Few of the Americans found this fare appealing. Diarrhea was all too common. Captain John Harrell, an artilleryman in the 101st Airborne Division, found the mutton to be tough and stringy, but he especially disliked the powdered tea. "After you added water . . . it tasted gritty." The excess powder reminded him of "beach sand which would settle to the bottom of the canteen cup." In the opinion of Lieutenant William Kotary, the British food "was not particularly appetizing to the GIs, and an issue was never large enough of a particular main item to serve all our troops." The Americans were simply used to larger portions of food than their British allies. Sergeant Rader was stunned when his company received only two meals of the British food per day. "So in between you eat what?" he asked the supply people rhetorically.

The Americans especially despised the British Players cigarettes and yearned for their own domestic brands. When Lieutenant General Horrocks visited the line and asked whether there was anything he could do for his American charges, he was inundated with requests for American cigarettes and coffee instead of tea. The kindhearted British general promised to look into the problem. Within a day, large bags of coffee were delivered to many of the frontline units. "Where he got them, I don't know," Lieutenant Colonel Teddy Sanford, a battalion commander in the 325th Glider Infantry Regiment, said. Some outfits even began receiving American cigarettes. The only thing most of the Americans liked about the British provisions was the rum ration, but even that came in small, and infrequent, quantities.

Eventually, American K and C rations became more commonly available along the front lines (many were the U.S. soldiers who were surprised to find themselves suddenly enthusiastic about tearing into these previously disliked meals). Still, the young, hungry troopers were always looking to augment their diets with something—anything—different.

Foraging was as common as breathing. Anything and everything was fair game. Famished soldiers raided the kitchens, cellars, and barns of the Dutch, scrounging milk, buttermilk, meat, vegetables, fruit, candy, and even pickles. Technician Fifth Grade Joe Comer excitedly wrote home with a list of the food he had scrounged: "Chicken, veal, beef, pork, and even a duck that one of the boys shot on a pond nearby. All of that meat and no ration points to put out." First Sergeant Frank Taylor knew that his wife at home was dealing with such things as ration points and meat shortages, and he felt guilty when she wrote sympathetically, but ignorantly, that she could hardly eat for fear he was going hungry. "At the same time I was having chicken fried in butter, fresh eggs found in a crock of lime solution in a basement, pancakes gotten from a bombed-out store, fresh vegetables from a greenhouse, and fresh fruit from an orchard."

Private First Class Bill True and several of his buddies found some canned meat and vegetables in the cellar of an empty farmhouse. One of the men offered to cook it into a stew, but the only "pot" they could find was an old bedpan. They scrubbed the pan with concentrated GI soap and washed it out thoroughly. The cook spent an hour preparing the meal, enhancing it with potatoes and onions. When it was ready, he spooned portions of it into the mess kit of each man. True was the last to receive his share. Just as he tipped the bedpan over and poured the last remaining juices into his mess kit, a pair of British tankers arrived and stopped in their tracks, with their eyes practically bugging out. "Blimey, Yank," one of them guffawed, "if you chaps are that hard up we'd be happy to do a bit of reverse lend-lease to tide you over."

Elsewhere, in the midst of onerous frontline outpost duty, one company in the 508th Parachute Infantry Regiment managed to put together a minifeast to celebrate the birthday of a popular officer. "Bill Frickel cooked a pot of the best chicken soup—the chicken was 'liberated' from a farmer's yard," Sergeant Warren Brown wrote. "We obtained a five gallon can of jelly to spread on K ration biscuits . . . and we swapped some K rations with a farmer for some canned fruit." The jelly actually came from a factory in Elst, behind the German lines.

Sergeant William Tucker, a mortar observer in I Company of the 505th Parachute Infantry, was especially fortunate. He operated from an expansive, well-stocked farmhouse just a few hundred yards behind his company's forward positions. For some reason, the Germans never shot at the house. A generous supply of local cows, combined with copious amounts of food in the house, meant that he ate very well. He and his cohorts even ate at the long dining room table. "You could get up from the dining room dinner table, walk a few paces into the living room, and actually observe the German infantry outpost line," Tucker said. In spite of this, no dining room meal was ever disturbed by the enemy. One evening, Tucker even hosted Private First Class True, who was an old friend, and another soldier for a banquet of sorts. "A formal table had been set, with linen napkins, porcelain dinnerware, and silver cutlery," True wrote. They dined on steak that came from a local cow, and French-fried potatoes from the farmhouse cellar, and washed it down with an array of French wines, also from the cellar. For True, the experience of eating such a sumptuous, civilized meal only a stone's throw from the front lines was "surreal." Sergeant Tucker, who was an irrepressible sort, enjoyed seeing the amazed reaction of his friends. "They were two very surprised guys," he wrote.

Inside another farmhouse a few miles away, Private Dwayne Burns and his squad mates found a package of what looked like pancake mix. Under the sink in the kitchen, they found a dusty can that looked like maple syrup. They rummaged through the drawers, found a pan and some utensils. They heated up the house's woodstove, poured some mix in the pan, and cooked it. "Will miracles never cease?" he wrote. "There in the frying pan was the most beautiful pancake we had ever seen . . . golden brown with shades of light and dark brown mingled together." As the men feasted, Burns thought happily of Saturday morning pancake breakfasts at home when he was a child. The soldiers all ate their fill and even had quite a few flapjacks left over.

Sergeant Spencer Wurst's squad was not so fortunate. Near their fox-holes, they searched an abandoned store and found bags of what they assumed was flour (no one could read Dutch). But when the designated squad cook baked the powder into biscuits, they discovered they were made out of plaster of Paris. "Those biscuits were so rock-hard we probably could have used them as weapons," Wurst quipped.

At times, the Americans ate the meat of farm animals that were killed in the cross fire. Most commonly, though, they surreptitiously killed and butchered local farm animals themselves, using such euphemisms as "accidentally shot" or "liberated" to describe the process. The pig and cow population in the frontline areas declined noticeably. Every unit seemed to have a country boy or two who knew all about skinning carcasses and preparing meat. Even unschooled city boys often got into the act. Private Donald Burgett, a Detroit native, lured a pig into a barn, where his buddy smashed it over the head with a pump handle, killing it instantly. "We butchered it and boiled small chunks of pork in our helmets, which we filled with water and set over small fires," he wrote. Soon, other members of the platoon sniffed the aroma and asked to join in. "We wound up sharing the pork with the entire platoon. There weren't that many of us left, and the small pig fed us all with some left over."

Though officers commonly joined in such impromptu feasts, the Allied command as a whole frowned on the practice, partially for sanitary reasons, but mainly out of concern for Dutch property. Eventually, these concerns grew into a larger effort to prevent looting. No British or American commander wished to alienate their Dutch allies by stealing from them. Almost universally, the Americans held the Dutch in high regard. They admired their work ethic, the cleanliness of their towns and homes, along with their inherent friendliness. They were very grateful for the assistance of the Dutch resistance. Soldiers foraged for food because they were hungry young men and perceived that if they did not eat the food, it would go to waste.

Property was another matter, though. Holland's standard of living was among the highest in the world. The reality was that, in such a highly developed country, much could be wrecked. Homes, barns, windmills, furniture, vehicles, and valuables of every sort were inevitably destroyed in the fighting. Captain Neil Sweeney never forgot the acute grief of one Dutch farmer after British tanks demolished his family windmill in an effort to kill German artillery spotters. The windmill had apparently been in his family for many generations. "There was something about the old man rocking his head from side to side with the tears splashing on the floor, sobbing about his windmill, that made the whole business of war seem utterly incongruous," Sweeney later wrote.

If anything, the destruction was only magnified by the stalemate conditions, as civilians gravitated away from their homes or farms, and soldiers—who were far more concerned about surviving than preserving property—moved in on a semipermanent basis. They tended to appropriate such items as beds, pillows, couches, and other furniture for their own comfort. Sergeant Wurst actually saw British tanks "going down the road with overstuffed chairs on them, mounted so they wouldn't get in the way of the turret. Furniture and other civilian items were roped and tied down onto the decks." The muddy, dirty frontline conditions practically guaranteed that the soldiers would spread their filth into private homes. Soldiers soiled carpet, linens, and bedding.

The temptation to take valuables such as money, silver, china, and clothes was ever present. One airborne artilleryman helped himself to an entire silver service that a German general had been using in his headquarters. "I packed it all back in the case and carried it away with me when we left," he said. He hauled it around for weeks until it grew too heavy for him. "I finally dumped it in a ditch. I can laugh about it today but it wasn't funny at the time." Private First Class Warren Purcell used a bazooka in an attempt to blast open a safe that a group of soldiers had found inside a store. "I shot one bazooka round through that safe," he said. The bazooka rocket hardly put a dent in the safe, but it did plenty of damage to the building. "I have *never* seen so much dust and plaster come from one room. That round blew not only all the window glass out but the window sashes too. You could see all the wall studding and ceiling joists."

In at least one instance, American soldiers looted a bank vault. Private Tom Moseley, an 82nd Airborne soldier, guarded one battle-hardened paratrooper who was caught red-handed by his superiors stealing Dutch guilders from a bank. The man told Moseley that he had used a bazooka to blow the door off the vault. He took as many banknotes as he could carry and buried them somewhere nearby. "Tell me, where did you bury it?" Moseley asked him. "You or me or both of us may not get out of the battle alive. Someone ought to know where the loot is."

"If I don't get out of here alive, no one's gonna know," the soldier replied firmly, with a hint of menace in his eyes.

Technician Fifth Grade Ray Lappegard heard about a similar bank heist in the 101st Airborne and recalled that General Taylor "did visit our battalion on one occasion to inform us that this was not proper behavior with regard to our allies." In fact, as the weeks wore on and the potential for similar occurrences grew, Allied authorities from Eisenhower on down made it a priority to prevent looting in Holland. This had an effect. Platoon leaders and company commanders made it clear to their men that stealing Dutch property would be punishable by court-martial with heavy penalties, including hard labor or perhaps even execution. First Sergeant Carwood Lipton, whose E Company, 506th Parachute Infantry, would one day be immortalized in *Band of Brothers*, was called off the line one day and told to report to battalion. When he arrived, he found himself looking at "a very angry Dutch family and a contingent of irate officers. The Dutch family said that my men had looted their home and that they wanted me punished and wanted full payment for all they had lost." They could not have been more wrong. In fact, when Lipton and the other E Company soldiers had moved into the ornate house, they had been so respectful of the family's beautiful furnishings that they carefully packed up everything and stored it an adjacent building. When Lipton took them to the building and showed them that their property was safe and sound, "they were most apologetic and grateful."

Among the combat troops, the word spread that anyone who did not have a bill of sale for a civilian item would face a court-martial. Although there was clearly an element of bluff in the threats, they worked. "The warning . . . was repeated so many times that it convinced us Eisenhower was not kidding," one sergeant said, "and we started throwing away our civilian souvenirs." They also stopped any further looting.[3]

Like all the other commanders, General Gavin was happy to see the looting peter out. He was nowhere near as sanguine, though, about the protracted nature of his division's deployment in Holland. "The best offensive troops in the theater and here we sit in foxholes for two months," he wrote bitterly in his diary one chilly morning. True to form, he insisted on living in similar conditions to his soldiers, even though the fall weather was doing no good for his aching back. His command post was still in the woods, instead of a comfortable house, as was typical for most division headquarters. His only steady shelter was a tent, where he caught a few hours of sleep each night. "I have slept on the ground every night and am getting to the point where I don't believe that I could sleep in a bed," he wrote to his adolescent daughter. "My hole is about three feet away. I don't like to get into it unless I have to." In another letter, he told her that he and his men had become "quite accustomed to the cold and while it may be harmful to us in the long run, right now we just take it for granted."

His only concession to creature comfort was a sleeping bag he had had since Normandy. "Parachute officers had to set an example and learn to live like other troopers," he explained years later in his memoir. One day, Lieutenant General Miles Dempsey, the British Second Army commander, visited Gavin at his command post. When he shook hands with Gavin, he graciously said, "I'm proud to meet the commanding general of the finest division in the world today." Gavin modestly accepted this great compliment with a sincere thank-you. When Gavin showed Dempsey his command post, the British general was so surprised at how Spartan it was that, within a day, he sent Gavin a personal command trailer. "It was well equipped with a bunk, toilet facilities, battle maps on the wall—typical of the vans then in use by all the senior officers," Gavin wrote. He politely thanked Dempsey, but he refused to use it. The only time he ever darkened its door was for a brief party his staff threw for him when he was promoted to major general in the latter part of October.

As always, during the daily combat grind, he was determined to verify information himself rather than trust it at face value. That meant seeing things with his own eyes. With his trusty M1 Garand in hand, he visited the front lines and outposts frequently. He circulated around the division so much that many of his troopers grew used to seeing him at even the most forward positions. In one typical instance, Private First Class John Leh, an antitank crewman, was taking cover during a heavy firefight near the Reichswald. Enemy artillery was exploding in the trees, sending wood shards in every direction. Some of the brush caught fire. Bullets were zipping several feet overhead, and he was trying to find the courage to leave his foxhole and man his gun. He noticed a solitary figure, with a rifle slung over his shoulder, walking along a trail at the edge of the woods. "Doesn't that nut know he's right on the front lines?" Leh thought. Still the man kept coming until Leh could tell it was the general. "If he could walk around like that, I guessed that I could get out of my foxhole," Leh wrote. "What a guy . . . to be up [there] with us!" Gavin later told him that he had heard the artillery fire was heavy but wanted to see for himself what was actually going on. For Leh, the incident represented "an example of leadership I have tried to follow ever since."[4]

Gavin felt that such frontline visits comprised the bare minimum of good combat leadership. He knew that the troopers were stuck at the front, regardless of conditions; their commanders were obligated to be there with them. Day after day, danger lurked. There was constant concern that the Germans might stage another major attack, as they had done at Opheusden. Every Allied soldier at the front lines had to be on full alert for this possibility. There were plenty of lulls, but the shelling and sniping between the two sides seldom ceased for very long. At times, German planes even materialized for strafing runs. Artilleryman Bruce Barton and a buddy survived a close call from a pair of strafing Messerschmitts one day as they were walking from Nijmegen back to their unit. "I guess we are fated to live," the other soldier said to Barton. A couple days later, a heavy enemy artillery barrage pounded their battery positions. His friend was killed instantly. Barton somehow remained unscathed.

Even when the soldiers were behind the lines, in reserve, they were not completely safe from the ubiquitous enemy shells. One night, as the non-coms of Headquarters Company, 3rd Battalion, 501st Parachute Infantry Regiment, met in a schoolhouse while in reserve, an artillery shell exploded against a windowsill. At the moment of the blast, Technician Fifth Grade William Dellapenta was playing the piano not far from the window. He was killed instantly. Technician Fifth Grade Lappegard was "lifted up and thrown down by the concussion. I remember thinking that I was dead because the light had been blown out in the explosion." There were about twenty men in the room. Most of them fell all over one another as they ran for the door. Sergeant Desmond Jones was disoriented from the explosion, and deeply frightened, but he could hear someone moaning near him. He felt around in the darkness and found that the moans were coming from Technician Fifth Grade Walter Radel, who was badly wounded. Jones dragged him out of the room and called for help. "He was dying," Jones said. "As I held him in my lap and felt the life going out of him, I raised hell to get a doctor. They sent the chaplain, who gave him the last rites. I remember cussing him and pleading for a doctor." It was too late. Radel died in Jones's lap.

Private Joseph Hecht's platoon came under heavy fire one day as they moved along the Maas-Waal Canal. "The only place we could hide to prevent getting hit by the shrapnel was to jump into [a] three-foot-wide and six-feet-deep ditch." The ditch was mined. A soldier next to Hecht stepped on one of the mines and it shredded his legs. "All of us were terribly shook up. We lived with the scene for many days, and I see it today just as it was then."

A particularly intense and accurate shower of mortar shells landed among the frontline foxholes and destroyed the house that served as the command post for E Company, 504th Parachute Infantry, one bleak afternoon. The command group was wiped out. "I suffered a traumatic amputation of my right leg and a shattered left foot," Captain Walter van Poyck, who had helped take the Grave bridge, later wrote. The medics mistakenly gave him two shots of morphine, which could have killed him, but he survived. Two of his privates also lost legs, and two others died of their wounds. Three of his lieutenants had to be evacuated. In all, the company lost eleven men to the enemy mortars.

Judging by the accuracy of the German shelling, they probably had a well-placed observer somewhere near the E Company positions. Whether American, British, or German, observers were savvy, courageous, and often quite ruthless. On both sides, artillery and mortar observers found good vantage points, such as attics, barns, farmhouses, well-placed foxholes, or even thick rows of trees from which to spot targets. They knew the enemy's location and often they knew his personal habits. Sergeant Tucker, when he wasn't enjoying steak dinners at his company's farmhouse base, did so much spotting from the house's attic that he came to know the toilet habits of an individual German soldier. Each afternoon at 1500, the redheaded German would emerge from his foxhole to relieve himself. "There would be a flurry of dirt as he dug a little hole," Tucker wrote. "He would then unfasten his belt and put himself in a vulnerable position." Every observer in the area would call down fire on him. Somehow, the German would always make it back to his hole right before the American shells came in. Private Lud Labutka peered through binoculars one day and spotted a pair of Germans in no-man's-land, squatting with their pants down. He and the mortar sergeant waited until more enemy soldiers joined them and then called down sixty-millimeter fire on them. "They were all tree bursts, hitting those big fir trees. Those Germans scattered all over. You should have seen them run with their pants halfway up. I think it was the first time I'd laughed like that since I'd gotten over there [into combat]."

Snipers were, of course, even more accurate. Both sides had plenty of good shooters who killed or wounded any enemy soldiers they saw. On one occasion, the Germans infiltrated a sniper while they evacuated wounded men under a Red Cross flag. The German rifleman zeroed in on a sergeant who was observing targets for an eighty-one-millimeter mortar team and shot him in the head. The sergeant died within two hours. Corporal Earl Boling and three other soldiers helped carry the man's corpse to the rear. "We had to wait until dark to remove his body from the hole and [carry] him back. Each individual knelt down and each in his own way offered a prayer." Two of the men were Catholics, one was Jewish, and one was Protestant. "This I will always remember as a show of combined faiths all working and praying as one." The affected company unleashed snipers of its own and, according to the unit diary, "made the Jerries pull in their ears." Once the remains of dead soldiers were behind the lines, service troops (often African-American) loaded them in trucks and buried them in a temporary cemetery. One trooper even witnessed a truck full of dead bodies "with stiff legs sticking out the tailgate."

Nor were the commanders immune to becoming casualties. General Taylor got hit one day while he was checking the lines in what had been a quiet sector. Taylor was a courageous man, but he was not known as the type of general who related to enlisted men or valued their input all that much. At the frontline position, he ordered Corporal Richard Klein's mortar team to open fire at a distant tree stump "even though we cautioned him that it would draw fire. After it drew the anticipated artillery, he again, against our advice, left the safety of the stone watchtower we were in. That is when he got his Purple Heart, [a] shell fragment in the posterior." As Taylor recalled it, "A small German shell . . . exploded a few yards away, raising a cloud of dust and sending me rolling with a small fragment lodged in the *sitzplatz*." Taylor was especially amused at the reaction of one of the sergeants: "Joe, I think the krauts got the old man in the tail," he said to his buddy.

Colonel Howard "Jumpy" Johnson, commander of the 501st Parachute Infantry Regiment, was not quite so fortunate. The forty-one-year-old colonel was a hard-charging, larger-than-life commander, part martinet, part big brother to the men. He would chew a soldier out one second and offer him a helping hand the next. By the fall of 1944, he had become something of a legendary figure to his troopers. He seemed indestructible, almost in the Patton mold. "Everybody seemed to admire him," Private Ivan Ladany said. "All the old-timers talked about what a great guy he was."

Johnson did not believe that a senior officer should take cover from enemy fire, feeling it set a bad example for the men. As he visited the frontline positions of his D Company near a dike along the Neder Rhine one day to speak with a couple officers, they began taking some inaccurate artillery fire. Johnson hardly seemed to notice. Then a close one came in. The two officers with him heard the shell and took cover. Colonel Johnson was slow to hit the ground. Fragments ripped through his neck, shoulder, hip, and back. "A jeep was brought up and he was taken away on a stretcher," Private Bill Hayes, an eyewitness, later wrote. "As he . . . passed our position he looked bad." He had the waxy pallor so common to wounded men in shock. The colonel knew he was in bad shape. Several times, he asked officers around him to "take care of my boys." Major Francis Carel, the regimental surgeon, tried to save his life, but he died on the operating table. "The news went through our regiment like an electric shock," Lieutenant Laurence Critchell wrote. "He had been too alive, too vital, too much of a personality. He had been the personality of the regiment since the beginning. To outlive him seemed strange." Lieutenant Colonel Julian Ewell took command of the regiment.[5]

Most commonly that fall, frontline duty for the troopers meant patrolling, nearly always at night. Amid the stalemate, commanders were constantly thirsting for information on enemy dispositions, strength, and intentions. The only way to gather information, and maintain a sharp fighting edge, was to patrol. There were three types of patrols: contact patrols to establish links with a neighboring outfit; reconnaissance patrols to pinpoint the location of enemy positions; and combat patrols, to capture prisoners. A couple of the most successful patrols rescued 1st Airborne survivors and downed aviators from the north side of the Rhine, but such dramatic events were rare. In the main, patrolling was mundane, workaday stuff. All of it was dangerous, and nearly everyone below the rank of company commander participated in some sort of patrol at one time or another.

On patrol, troopers almost always eschewed helmets in favor of soft wool caps to reduce their silhouettes and promote better hearing. Some men blackened their faces. It was common practice to tape dog tags together to reduce their jangling. Troopers carried only essential weapons, ammo, and grenades. Many armed themselves with Thompson submachine guns, an ideal weapon for close contact. Patrols ranged in size from two men to platoon-size groups of about twenty. They were almost always led by a sergeant or a lieutenant. These small groups would roam the black nights along carefully chosen routes, braving mines, booby traps, and enemy discovery. Every minute was tense, almost pregnant with menace. The job required full concentration. Daydreaming could mean death. Any mistake, no matter how small, could lead to disaster. Needless to say, it was nerve-racking and dangerous work. No one could do it night after night. All good commanders made sure to rotate patrolling responsibilities fairly among their men.

Private Tom Moseley participated in a patrol to grab a German prisoner one blustery evening in late October. He led a group of eight men through a cabbage patch and began to worry about how much noise their pant legs were making as they swished past the mature cabbages. "Then we went up into some woods and we were climbing a hill," he said. "There was a barn there. All of a sudden flares went up. Bang, it was broad daylight. Three machine guns opened up right in front of me. The German tracers were red. Then the bastards started throwing hand grenades at me." One of the grenades exploded close enough to destroy his tommy gun and paralyze his right hand. He was fortunate to work his way out of range, back to the American lines, but he lost the middle finger on his right hand. No one else on the patrol was hurt.

Such firefights were hardly uncommon. Lieutenant Albert Hassenzahl led a three-man patrol one night that ran right into a German patrol along a railroad embankment (the Germans were, of course, doing just as much patrolling as the Allies). Hassenzahl came within a couple feet of the leading enemy soldier. "As soon as he saw me . . . I let him have a burst from [my] tommy gun. And then all hell broke loose. The other krauts and the other patrol members reacted and they were firing on top of the embankment. We were very, very lucky to get back to our own lines intact." The German soldier was probably killed. Hassenzahl got clipped on the lip by a bullet. Another millimeter in either direction and he probably would have been dead. "That's about as close as you can come, I guess," he later said.

Close calls were practically the norm. Lieutenant Harry Druener was leading a squad-size patrol one evening when his point man rounded the side of a haystack and literally found himself face-to-face with a German soldier who was leading his own patrol. "They were both so surprised they just looked at each other for a minute, and then the German turned and ran into the darkness, at which moment a firefight ensued. Miraculously, we sustained no casualties." Sergeant Bob Bowen led a patrol one evening that sideslipped a German listening post and proceeded to keep going, perilously close to an enemy-held house. The Americans saw several ghostly figures in the darkness and took cover in a canal. "A loud pop, a stream of rising light, a bursting flare," Bowen wrote. "It drifted down, swinging, lighting up everything. We froze, faces buried in water. Even though I was soaking wet and cold, sweat rolled down my spine." In training, soldiers had been taught to freeze when illuminated by a flare, even if they were standing up. This was because the human eye at night reacts to movement, and not necessarily objects or shapes. A few minutes after the flare burned out, a group of Germans walked right by the canal, no more than ten feet away, and then sat down to eat cookies. "I could hear their teeth crunching on them. We backed away and took cover in another canal." Bowen was lucky to make it to safety with all of his men.

Near Groesbeek, Private Hecht and a few other men on a reconnaissance patrol heard a radio crackling and tracked it by sound to an unguarded building. His sergeant ordered him and another man to crawl up to the house, look inside, and see what was there. "We . . . peered in. We observed six German officers standing around a large table studying what appeared to be a large map of the area. It was obvious that this was an important headquarters. On the floor above them, we could hear laughter, conversation, and the crackling of the radio." The patrol members made it back to their company and reported what they saw to their captain. As was so often the case with riflemen, Hecht never knew how the information was put to use, if at all.

Occasionally, the tension of a patrol was broken by a welcome moment of humor. Corporal Edward Mitchell and several other soldiers were patrolling along the Rhine one night when they heard odd noises emanating from a nearby house. "We figured we had ourselves a whole houseful of the most ignorant Germans in the whole German Army," he later wrote. They set up around the house and planned an attack. "As I kicked the door open expecting to see a lot of surprised Germans, [I] was met by two pigs just having themselves a grand old time. It was quite a relief . . . and sure seemed funny to us. Good eating, too, by the way."

By and large, though, the stalemate war was grim and unrelenting. Throughout that seemingly endless fall, the soldiers of the two airborne divisions persevered as best they could amid the cold, the rain, and the ever-present danger and privation. Patrols whittled away the strength of the rifle companies, but artillery and mortars inflicted most of the damage. Basically, the airborne divisions were bleeding away. By the second week of November, both divisions had suffered as many casualties during the dreary weeks of static warfare as they had during the Market Garden phase of their time in Holland (officially defined as September 17–26). Truly, September hope had turned into November despair.[6]

CHAPTER 16

Timberwolves

I n mid-October, even as the post–Market Garden stalemate unfolded, Field Marshal Montgomery finally got serious about clearing the Scheldt estuary. The Allied logistical situation was worsening by the day. Eisenhower was eager, almost to the point of desperation, to use Antwerp as a supply port. For that to happen, of course, the Scheldt had to be cleared. Throughout September and October, the supreme commander had mentioned Antwerp's importance in several communications with Montgomery, but he did not make it clear that Antwerp should enjoy top priority. Yet Ike also stressed the importance of breaching the Rhine and enveloping the Ruhr. These mixed signals gave Monty the excuse to remain fixated on his abortive push for the Rhine (Ike had, after all, given the go-ahead for Market Garden), much at the expense of Antwerp. "The trouble was that Eisenhower wanted the Saar, the Frankfurt area, the Ruhr, Antwerp, and the line of the Rhine," Montgomery later wrote in critiquing Eisenhower's broad-front strategy. "To get *all* these in one forward movement was impossible." Monty was quite right that these goals were too ambitious. But he did not understand—possibly because he had so little face-to-face contact with Ike during the fall—that the supreme commander envisioned a broad-front advance into Germany that would be fed by Antwerp. To Ike, Market Garden represented only a bridgehead over the Rhine, a stepping-stone into Germany, not a divergence from his overall strategy. He did not realize, until it was too late, that Market Garden could come only at the expense of his broad-front plan. Thus, when in October, Monty mildly complained by telegram to the supreme commander about the mixed signals he was getting, Ike finally responded with unequivocal language. "Let me assure you that nothing I may ever say or write with respect to future plans in our advance eastward is meant to indicate any lessening of the need for Antwerp, which I have always held as vital, and which has grown more pressing as we enter the bad weather period."

This spurred Montgomery into action, and not a moment too soon. Back in September, as he had planned Market Garden, he had thought the overstretched Canadian First Army could handle the task of clearing the Scheldt, even as he asked the Canadians to also take such Channel ports as Dunkirk and Calais. Just as Eisenhower was too ambitious in wanting so many objectives in Germany, Montgomery was far too optimistic in his belief that he could spend most of his resources on Market Garden while the manpower-impoverished Canadian formations took the Scheldt. As he himself later acknowledged, it was a tremendous oversight with profound consequences. "I must admit a bad mistake on my part. I underestimated the difficulties of opening up the approaches to Antwerp. I reckoned that the Canadian army could do it *while* we were going for the Ruhr. I was wrong." In fact, this colossal mistake allowed the better part of the German Fifteenth Army to escape potential encirclement in northern France and Belgium and instead fortify the Scheldt. The Germans seemed to have a stronger grasp of Antwerp's importance than their opponents. Right under the noses of the distracted Allies, they evacuated, mainly by rafts and boats, eighty-six thousand soldiers, six hundred artillery pieces, six thousand vehicles, and six thousand horses. Some of these men had ended up fighting against the 101st Airborne Division along Hell's Highway. The majority stayed at the Scheldt estuary and fortified it. They dug bunkers and firing pits, manned coastal guns, sowed tens of thousands of land mines, and infested the estuary waters with hundreds of naval mines.

By the middle of October, the Canadians were fighting hard to take the estuary, and dealing with miserable, wet weather and difficult terrain. "Much of the area was actually below sea level, comprising 'polder' land that had been reclaimed from the sea," a Canadian army study said. "It was only the large raised embankments (dikes) that kept the waters from flooding the flat low-lying land. The German defenders skillfully exploited these conditions" with a dizzying array of deep bunkers and guns dug into the sides of dikes. They also flooded much of it, thus limiting vehicular movement and routes of advance. The Canadians were making progress, but they were taking heavy casualties (many of whom could never be replaced by the all-volunteer Canadian military establishment), and they needed help. With Ike's directive in mind, Montgomery reinforced them with British, Polish, and American troops. Monty now had two new American divisions in his army group—the 7th Armored and the 104th Infantry. He assigned the 7th Armored Division to static duty holding the right flank of the Market Garden salient, ten miles east of Eindhoven, in a section of Holland known locally as the Peel Marshes. He sent the 104th Infantry Division to the Canadian First Army, with orders to assist in the taking of the Scheldt.[1]

The nickname of the 104th was the Timberwolves. The division patch featured a howling gray wolf against a forest green background. The 104th was a standard U.S. Army infantry division with three regiments, plus artillery, medics, quartermasters, engineers, and the like. The division had been activated in 1942 at desolate Camp Adair in Oregon. The unit was composed of draftees, veterans of Mediterranean battles, reservists, and, since early 1944, many thousands of young men who had been aviation cadets or members of the now defunct Army Specialized Training Program (ASTP). The ASTP had offered these nineteen- and twenty-year-olds the opportunity to go to college on the army's dime and learn militarily applicable skills, such as engineering or languages. By 1944, with the invasion of Europe looming, American leaders came to understand that they could not afford the luxury of the ASTP, so they abolished the program and reassigned most of its members to ground combat units. Thus, the

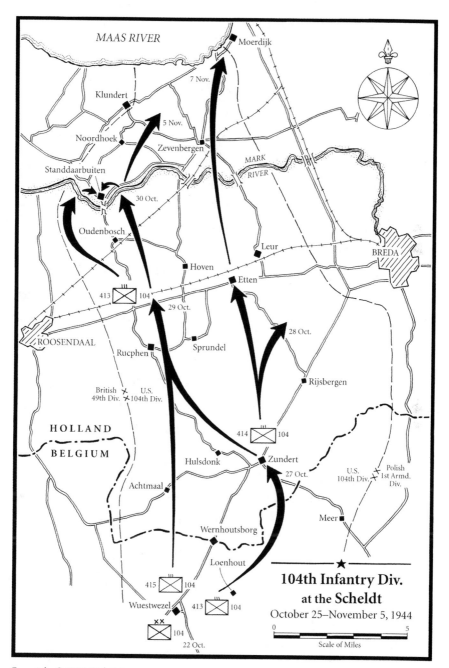

MAAS RIVER

Moerdijk

Klundert

7 Nov.

5 Nov.

Noordhoek

Zevenbergen

MARK
RIVER

Standdaarbuiten

30 Oct.

Oudenbosch

Leur

BREDA

Hoven

Etten

413 | 104

29 Oct.

ROOSENDAAL

Rucphen

Sprundel

28 Oct.

Rijsbergen

British
49th Div.

U.S.
104th Div.

HOLLAND

414 | 104

BELGIUM

Hulsdonk

Zundert

27 Oct.

U.S.
104th Div.

Polish
1st Armd.
Div.

Achtmaal

Meer

Wernhoutsborg

Loenhout

★

**104th Infantry Div.
at the Scheldt**

October 25–November 5, 1944

415 | 104

Wuestwezel

413 | 104

XX
| 104

0   5

22 Oct.

Scale of Miles

Timberwolves were a young division, with an average age somewhere around twenty-two. By the time they got to Europe in early September, they had endured many months of intensive infantry training, such as twenty-mile hikes, live fire exercises, night problems, maneuvers, calisthenics, instructions in infantry tactics, and plenty of time on the shooting range.

Their commander, fifty-six-year-old Major General Terry Allen, was one of the most battle-wise generals in the army. Allen was an old cavalryman. As the son of a colonel, he had grown up in the army. He was passionate, in equal parts, about the game of polo, a good nip of bourbon, and the welfare of his soldiers. In World War I, as a young major, he had commanded a battalion in the 90th Infantry Division and had been wounded three times. In 1942 and 1943, the general had led the legendary 1st Infantry Division in North Africa and Sicily. He had earned a reputation as a hard-driving, down-to-earth, tempestuous, profane general who worried more about getting results in battle than maintaining garrison-style discipline.

In the Mediterranean, even as the 1st Infantry Division (Big Red One) established a national reputation as one of the finest combat formations in the army, it became known for hard drinking, indiscipline, and an insular, almost surly contempt for the army hierarchy as a whole. The attitude could be summed up in an oft-expressed opinion among the division's enlisted men that the army consisted of "the Big Red One and ten million replacements." Allen's boss at the time, Omar Bradley, respected Allen's bravery and obvious favorable traits as a combat leader, but he had little use for him otherwise. Bradley came to believe that, instead of instilling proper discipline in the division, Allen stoked the resentful attitude of his men. When several of his infantrymen who were on leave in Oran got into a brawl with a group of military policemen, Allen supposedly said, "Once we've licked the Boche, we'll go back to Oran and beat up every MP in town." Bradley was never quite comfortable with the whiff of disrespect that emanated from the 1st Division. At the end of the Sicily campaign, he relieved Allen, under the guise that he was exhausted, and sent him home.

There was no possibility that such a successful fighting general would sit out the rest of the war. In the fall of 1943, he assumed command of the Timberwolves. He was the architect of the division's realistic, arduous training program, particularly its emphasis on night fighting. He immediately established a strong rapport with his troops. "They had an unusually high belief in themselves, and an unusually high combat esprit," he later wrote to a fellow general. Even before entering combat, the soldiers had formed a powerful bond with Allen, and some even came to idolize him. "I sensed that Gen. Allen saw us rather than merely looked at us," one of his riflemen later wrote. "It seemed obvious to me that he respected his Timberwolves and that the Timberwolves certainly respected him. That mutual respect was the core ingredient of our discipline and morale." Allen passionately believed that night attacks were the best way to seize objectives and minimize casualties. When the division arrived in France, Allen was deeply disappointed to learn that the Timberwolves would not enter combat immediately. The men spent several weeks sitting in Normandy, because the transportation and supplies necessary to sustain them at the front were instead used for Market Garden. So he was thrilled when, in late October, orders came to join the Canadians for the Scheldt campaign. The Timberwolves traveled across France by train and debarked near the Belgian–Dutch border. Here they waited for the final word to participate in the next attack.

On October 25, even as the rifle companies were relieving the British 49th Infantry Division in frontline positions, Montgomery made a personal visit to the 104th's command post at Hoogerheide. Allen, his staff officers, and most of his battalion and regimental commanders listened as Montgomery implored them to thrust forward, engage the enemy, and "drive him northward with all possible speed." The 104th would be part of the British I Corps, whose commander, Lieutenant General John Crocker, followed up Monty's pep talk with a speech of his own. "The Boche is softening all around, and we don't want to miss an opportunity."

The Timberwolves took their place between the 49th Infantry Division on the left (north) flank and the Polish 1st Armored Division on the right. The Americans were responsible for taking some twenty-two miles of wet low-country terrain from the Belgian border through Achtmaal, Zundert, and Oudenbosch, across the Mark River, and then a few more miles beyond to the Maas River. The width of the division front was about eight thousand yards. General Allen planned to employ all three of his infantry regiments at the same time, nearly shoulder-to-shoulder in the coming attack.

The terrain in this sector was, in the recollection of one officer, "flat with an imperceptible slope to the northwest. Under the sandy surface, impervious clay prevented standing water from draining and necessitated ditching not only of the roads but of the fields. Grain, sugar beets, turnips, and potatoes were grown where the ground was not too marshy. Elsewhere was rough pasture and small but numerous planting of pine woods in various stages of growth. Vehicular traffic was road-bound." The main roads were paved. Others were narrow and muddy, essentially little more than cow paths or, more cynically, quagmires in the waiting. "The buildings and steeples of numerous villages provided the only observation." The land was not only marshy; it was pool-table flat. The Germans would be able to see the Americans coming from miles away. But this twenty-two-mile stretch had to be taken as part of the larger mission to clear the Scheldt and open up Antwerp.[2]

Many of the Timberwolves had been training for combat and wondering what it would be like for more than two years. The natural result of all this anticipation was rookie jitters. "No matter how thorough the training, combat is a shock," Private Charles Dodd later wrote. "You finally realize that someone is actually trying to kill you." For Sergeant Felix McRan, an engineer, "The war that until now seemed so far away, suddenly had become very close and personal." A tense silence descended over most of the men, as if only now they realized the grim reality of why they were here. Like all soldiers entering combat for the first time, they had to get used to the sights, sounds, smells, and rhythm of the front lines. Senses were heightened to the utmost. Everything seemed new, exotic, and dangerous. "Nerves were on edge," Sergeant Roger Ries, a medic in D Company, 329th Medical Battalion, wrote. "Your brain was working overtime to think of a good joke or some funny happening. But try as you might, all you could think of were the coming events."

Even the experience of relieving the British under cover of darkness was somewhat surreal. As Private Dodd watched a line of British soldiers trudge to the rear, he was struck by the fact that "every fifth or sixth man had a teapot tied to the side of his pack." First Lieutenant Art Decker, the executive officer of L Company, 413th Infantry Regiment, coordinated the relief with one of the British company commanders. "He had such a cockney dialect that it was most difficult for me to understand him, and I worried whether I was learning what I needed to know during those stressful moments," he said. Decker tried hard to understand the captain, but he was never quite sure whether he really did. Private Bob Bilinsky and his buddies in G Company, 414th Infantry Regiment, were extremely nervous when they took over frontline foxholes previously occupied by a Scottish unit. Then, as the Scots marched off, a bagpiper began playing with a perfect cadence, and that melted the tension away. "At that moment . . . thoughts of war, and perhaps imminent enemy gunfire, diminished as we listened to the delightful bagpipe sounds that echoed about us," Bilinsky said. "More than a few of us smiled in appreciation of the moment."

As quietly as possible, the Timberwolves began occupying the frontline foxholes and ditches. The novelty of being at the front gave way to abject fear of the unknown. In the darkness of the night, everything seemed to portend danger. "Shots were fired at anything that moved or made any noise at all," Staff Sergeant Fred Dunham wrote. "Livestock and trees and bushes moving in the wind were certainly not safe that night!" The worst enemy for most of the soldiers was their vivid imagination. Sergeant Frank Perozzi and his foxhole buddy spent the night more or less quaking at the shadows around them. "Everything out forward in the dark seems to be enemy approaching & rustling leaves, stumps, water moving in a brook, small animals, even cows" caused alarm for them. One company history joked that "each cow must have been wearing a German helmet and must have had a swastika painted on its side." As was common at the front, shells periodically flew back and forth. The young American soldiers had to become attuned to what was outgoing and what was incoming. "Every few minutes we'd jump a mile as a British artillery unit would cut loose with a round or so, from the woods behind us," Sergeant David Malachowsky wrote to his parents. "Us 'greenies' were sure each shell was meant for us, and it took hours before we got accustomed to the blast of the guns and the eerie whining of the shells."

Gradually Malachowsky and his many thousands of divisional comrades got used to the combat environment in which they were immersed. Throughout the day and night on October 25 and 26, the 104th began to attack against varying levels of enemy resistance. "Even though we had never done it for blood, we had practiced the fundamentals of infantry in the attack so many times that it felt natural for us," Lieutenant Decker said. Riflemen advanced by fire and maneuver. Machine gunners and mortar crews covered them. Artillerymen and self-propelled gunners laid down well-planned barrages considerably ahead of the advancing troops, mainly against German-occupied houses or dugouts. The Germans responded with artillery, mortar, and machine gun fire of their own. "The Germans customarily dug in on the reverse slope of the dikes and set up positions in houses along the roads," a unit after-action report related. "They masked their mortars behind houses, making it extremely difficult to knock them out. Machine gunners set up in culverts, at road junctions, and in holes beside houses, as well as at each end of the drainage ditches."

When the Germans opened up on the attacking Americans, the usual chaos ensued. Units became mixed-up or got lost. Men were hit or scattered for cover. As always, the advance was carried out by small groups of frightened but determined—and often bewildered—men. When several squads from I Company, 413th Infantry Regiment, were pinned down in open ground by an enemy machine gun crew, Private First Class Beverly Tipton grabbed a BAR and sneaked up on the crew by using the cover of a small hedgerow. He advanced to within six feet of the German machine gunners and sprayed them with BAR fire, killing all of them. He even captured their gun. "Throughout the entire action . . . Private Tipton was subjected to direct, aimed fire from three enemy snipers," the citation for his Distinguished Service Cross said. The advance resumed.

In one ditch, Private First Class Bill Kortlander's squad was pinned down by heavy machine gun fire when artillery shells began to scream in ahead of them and behind them. This meant that German observers were finding their range (the usual GI term was "bracketed"). The shells exploded so close that Kortlander could see a white flash, feel the concussion, and hear the unique buzzing sound of fragments hurtling through the air. "The sound is like angry hornets swarming around their quarry," he wrote. Eventually, a shell scored a direct hit on the ditch. "I saw one of our sergeants stand up, his face blackened by the exploding shell, and then fall over." Cries for a medic rang out. Kortlander did not know what happened to the sergeant, and soon became involved with a group of five soldiers under the leadership of a lieutenant he did not know. The officer was convinced that the German artillery observer who was calling down such accurate fire was in a nearby farmhouse. He ordered the soldiers to fix bayonets and charge the house. "It never occurred to me that I would participate in a bayonet charge," Kortlander commented. "That was Civil War and WWI stuff!" He and the others expected to get mowed down by small-arms fire. Instead, they easily took the house and found only a badly wounded German officer lying in its courtyard. "His brain [was] oozing through his skull from a terrible head wound." He begged for water. Kortlander's first inclination was to give him a drink from his canteen but he hesitated for fear of running out. He wondered what would happen if he got wounded and could not take his sulfa pills for lack of water. He pondered for a few long moments what to do. "My choice—one that over sixty years later still saddens me—was to move on." This hardening process took place among many other Timberwolves. As Private George Delbene and his buddies crawled through one watery gully, "We had to go over the first two dead bodies of men from the company. That experience awakened us all to the tragedies of war." At that moment, in Delbene's opinion, they changed from "boys to fighting infantry soldiers."

Elsewhere, Private Raymond Potter, a rifleman, was advancing across a rutabaga field when his company came under grazing rifle and machine gun fire. Basically, this meant that the enemy bullets were coming in at thigh level or below, so low that some were thudding into the dirt. The Germans were engaging in one of their favorite tricks. They shot one gun high with tracer rounds, creating the impression among the Americans that they could simply go to ground to escape the bullets, while another gun, with no tracer rounds, fired low, along the ground. "I received a rifle bullet through my right leg about halfway between my ankle and knee," Potter recalled. "The bullet splintered the fibula and caused me to lose so much blood I passed out." A fellow soldier tied a makeshift tourniquet to his leg, preventing him from bleeding to death. But then the American company retreated. A German patrol later found Potter and took him prisoner.

Near Heilbloom, German mortars pounded Private Charles Dodd's company, forcing them to take shelter in ditches near a raised road. A mortar round exploded in the ditch. Dodd saw a man fly through the air like a rag doll and looked away. Already several men in his L Company, 413th Infantry Regiment, were dead. One had taken a round right in the heart. Another was shredded by mortar fragments. Many others were wounded, including Tech Sergeant Thorval Askeland, who had been hit in the hip by a twenty-millimeter bullet. "I could hear Glenn White screaming," Askeland said. "He had been hit in the stomach and was begging for anyone to come over and put him out of his misery. I don't know how long it took him to die." Askeland lay for hours, bleeding badly, before help got to him. Still the mortars kept coming in. Rumors spread that the Germans were about to launch a counterattack. "We were preparing to fix bayonets when we heard the rumble of tanks to our left rear." Two British Churchill tanks rolled into place. Captain Marshall Garth left cover and accessed the field phones on the back of each tank to direct their fire. The tank shells were devastating to the Germans and ruined any possibility of a counterattack. The Allied advance resumed. "The Limey tankers made a good impression with their aggressive attitude," a unit report later declared.[3]

The Germans were spread thinly enough that they did not have continuous defensive lines so much as well-placed strongpoints, along all necessary avenues of advance. Their goal was to make it as time-consuming and costly as possible for the Timberwolves to clean out each strongpoint. To fill the gaps, the Germans made extensive use of mines, booby traps, and carefully constructed roadblocks. When infantry soldiers took cover in ditches, they had to worry about hurling themselves atop mines. "You could see them if you looked but you had to be careful," Private James Wasilewski said, "because they just laid them right on top of the ground in the grass." Many of the open fields were also mined. It was a foregone conclusion that any viable road contained mines. There were wooden Schu mines, the size of an undersize shoe box, designed to blow off a man's foot or shatter his leg. The S-mines, or "Bouncing Betties," as the GIs called them, were buried with small igniter prongs emerging from the ground. When tripped, the mine popped out of the ground until it was about waist-high, when it exploded and scattered 350 steel balls. The largest of these impersonal killers was the Teller mine, which looked like an undersize manhole cover and could destroy a vehicle (what it could do to a man is best left unsaid).

In one typical instance, Sergeant Billie Henderson's company encountered a roadblock of felled trees. As artillery shells rained down, the troops bypassed the trees by taking to the surrounding fields. "Small foot mines welcomed them. Mean little weapons." In an instant, an explosion rang out "and a cry for help, and then a warning to stay away as there were more mines." A medic who attempted to reach the wounded man also tripped a mine. He lost a leg. Another time, the jeeps of the 415th Infantry Regiment Intelligence and Reconnaissance Platoon were leading a column of armored cars, trucks, and troops at the vanguard of the regimental advance when the lead jeep ran over a Teller mine. "There was a large explosion," Private First Class Duane Robey recalled. "Dirt flew overhead in a solid black ceiling and clattered through the trees on our right." Robey took cover from the falling debris. When the dust settled, he got up and investigated. The jeep was tipped over. The right rear wheel was gone, as was the radio. A box of grenades was strewn along the road—somehow none of them exploded. His platoon leader, Lieutenant Everett Pruitt, was "standing at the right side of the jeep with his clothes missing on his right side bleeding out of his mouth, ears, and nose. He did not know where he was." The driver was drenched with gasoline and groggy with concussion, but otherwise okay. A wounded sergeant in the backseat lay "crumpled like a piece of cloth." Medics took the three wounded men away. The men in the other I&R jeeps immediately fortified them with sandbags.

Engineers were in constant demand. They trudged along the roads, sometimes even ahead of the infantry, swinging and swaying their mine detectors. The detectors could reveal metallic mines, but they were no use in finding the wooden Schu mines. For that the engineers had to get down on their hands and knees and search with bayonets or probe gingerly with pitchforks. The plethora of trees that lined Holland's roads made perfect raw material for elaborate, often booby-trapped roadblocks. Sergeant Felix McRan and the men in his engineer squad had to dismantle one of these blocks at night, without the benefit of any light. "The trees were huge. We checked [them], removed a few charges in the limbs, and began to work. We winched with a truck, tugged, pulled, chopped, and the job went slow, impatiently slow. Somebody raised an ax, a limb fell, then a deafening explosion, a moan and a stumble in the dark. A booby trap." The stricken man was wounded in the face but he survived. McRan and the others were angry, but they finished the dangerous job "and internally everybody sighed deeply."

Private First Class Douglas Miller's outfit, C Company of the 329th Engineers, dealt with perhaps the most elaborate of all the roadblocks emplaced by the Germans. It had concrete blocks some five feet high and six feet thick. Tetrahedrons were chained and bolted to the concrete blocks. To top it off, the Germans had hidden Schu mines within and around the blocks. As the engineers worked in the shadows of late afternoon, one of the mines detonated and killed three men. The team waited until full daylight the next morning to finish the job and they found the surrounding mines. "We couldn't understand why the other mines didn't explode in a 'sympathy' detonation," Miller said. "Particularly disturbing was a pool of partly coagulated blood." A small terrier began sniffing at a nearby pile of dirt and touched off yet another mine. "The headless dog was blown several feet into the air." None of the men were hurt, though.

In spite of such terrifying obstacles, the advance was steady, though the 104th Infantry Division was paying a price. The dead either remained where they fell or were recovered by increasingly busy graves-registration teams. Casualties were already in three figures and counting. Men in the rifle companies were often inclined emotionally to pause and help their wounded buddies, but during training they had been taught to keep moving and let medics deal with the casualties. Frontline medics treated wounded men, but, in the chaos of so many firefights, it was often impossible to evacuate them to the rear in any timely manner. Battalion aid stations were generally located in houses only about a mile behind the fighting, but, under these circumstances, they might as well have been thousands of miles away. Wounded men often lay by themselves for hours, even days. As the fighting units kept moving, battalion medics and litter teams circulated around in their wake, looking for wounded soldiers. "We were trained to put splints on, stop the bleeding, give 'em a shot of morphine, and hope that somebody was gonna pick 'em up . . . and get 'em back to the aid station," Private First Class Paul Marshall, a medic in the 413th Infantry, recalled. "We'd . . . stop the bleeding . . . sit, hold their hand, try to give 'em a drink of water, and let 'em know they were gonna be picked up. That was the important thing, for guys to know that they'd be picked up soon." This gave them hope and encouraged them to hang on, even if they were in pain.

Just as often, the medics comprised two- or four-man litter teams that went out—normally at night—to pick up the wounded men and haul them to safety. This was a backbreaking, thankless job. It often meant carrying wounded soldiers through mud and rain, sometimes for miles. "Evacuation from the field was habitually by litter to a forward jeep collecting point, thence by jeep to the Aid Station," the after-action report of one medical unit explained. In one characteristic instance, Private First Class Harry Whitlatch and three other men stumbled through darkness to find a wounded, unconscious rifleman and then haul him arduously to the aid station. "It seemed like we encountered one fence after another, each of which was separated by shallow, water-filled ditches," he said. "It was exhausting for us; it would have been an absolute nightmare for that poor rifleman had he been fully conscious."

In most cases, the aid stations were busy places, rife with the trauma so inherent in caring for wounded young men. "Ambulance after ambulance painfully crawled along the bumpy cowpath in the blackness of the moonless night, to come to rest before the blacked out admission tent, already loaded with our wounded," Sergeant Malachowsky wrote his parents. "Tags were checked, completed and their wounds examined. Those needing further treatment were carried into surgery. The tired eyes, the dull, pale, dirt-smeared faces, the broken bodies, and the ever present red of their blood seeping through their clothes onto the litters gave us the incentive" to keep working hard.[4]

Conditions were rainy, chilly, wet, and muddy. Moisture seemed to infuse everything and everyone. A moldy green moss seemed to grow on everything. "We were wet all the time we were in Holland and never saw the sunshine," Private First Class Marshall said. The overcast skies and moist air made the temperature seem even colder than it actually was. "The weather was cold," Lieutenant Cecil Bolton, a platoon leader, said. "Sleety rain beat down on the troops, who went for days soaked to the skin and slimy with mud." It was almost impossible to get dry for any length of time. Soldiers scrounged for hay, straw, or even blankets to keep the bottoms of their respective foxholes dry, but nothing worked. "The water level . . . was just below the surface of the sod," one soldier wrote. "First we felt our feet becoming wet and then the foxhole was so full that it was impossible to have its protection." Private John Light got to the point where he realized it was out of the question to even dig a regular foxhole. "The best you could do was to remove the sod from your foxhole and pile it on the perimeter to form a little wall." This was the basic equivalent of stacking sandbags around a flat surface. It gave nowhere near as much protection as a belowground foxhole. "Even with this method you would usually get wet overnight from the water seeping in." Lieutenant Bolton found that the only place he and his men could dig in without being flooded out was the side of dikes "which were approximately fifteen feet high and twenty feet across."

To make matters worse, the land was honeycombed with canals of various sizes. Often the men had no choice but to wade through them. Private John Rheney stepped into one canal that looked like it contained only a few feet of water. "[It] turned out to be more than six feet of water and [I] promptly sank like a rock." As Rheney flailed under the water, his buddy Private Donald Clement, who was much taller and stronger, pulled him out. Clement was a Northerner; Rheney was a Southerner. When Clement pulled Rheney to safety, he wisecracked, "If I'd have known it was a Rebel, I'd have let you drown." Rheney smirked but said nothing. A day later, when they were moving through a canal while under wickedly accurate sniper fire, Clement the Northerner got hit in the helmet, was knocked unconscious, and fell into the water. Rheney helped pull him out of the canal and later told him that only a Yankee could have had a hard enough head to deflect a bullet. Private Light, like many other men, often tried to leap across the smaller canals, with mixed results. "You would make this great run, make a terrific leap, and then fall backward into the water because of the slope of the opposite bank."

Anyone who was unlucky enough to fall in was even more soaked than normal, and usually for days on end. Sickness and trench foot became common, siphoning off manpower from the rifle companies. "Trench foot, badly swollen feet, fungus infection were a part of everybody's life," one infantryman recalled. Private Light was shocked to take off his socks one day and see "my feet appeared to be covered with a green growthlike fungus." This was the early stages of trench foot. He combated it by changing his socks more often. This approach was at odds with a divisional order to the men not to remove their brogan-style combat boots lest their feet swell so much that they could no longer fit back into the boots. Light was correct. In most cases, when soldiers aired out their feet and changed socks regularly, they were better off than when they kept them encased for days, or weeks, in soggy boots.

By October 30, after five days of continuous operations, the division had pushed about fifteen miles to within sight of the Mark River and had liberated the sizable towns of Zundert and Oudenbosch. As had been the case during Market Garden, Dutch resistance groups were extremely helpful. In one instance, an operative provided Lieutenant Colonel Gerald Kelleher, commander of the 3rd Battalion, 415th Infantry Regiment, two volumes of maps, overlays, and extensive intelligence information on German dispositions in the Scheldt. The information was so valuable that General Allen eventually forwarded it up the chain of command to First Canadian Army headquarters. When Sergeant Parley Allred entered one Dutch home, he met a boy who immediately informed him that a nearby group of German soldiers wished to surrender. The boy led him to the correct building and even acted as an interpreter. "When the first one came out, he threw down his gun, discarded his rifle belt, threw down his helmet, and put on a stocking cap . . . and started to walk towards me. Sixteen more of them did the same thing."

As the Americans entered the various towns, joyous liberation scenes unfolded. In Oudenbosch, a picturesque village that was dominated by a nineteenth-century basilica, Captain William Dyer, a company commander, and his men were welcomed by black-frocked priests. The smiling clerics offered the Americans grapes, apples, and pitchers of cider. Soon, in Dyer's recollection, the sidewalks were jammed with "a wildly cheering throng . . . spilled over into the street; a crying, laughing throng that broke out long-hidden flags of orange and waved them as if making up for the last four years. Pitchers of hot milk, with butter floating on top, were brought out, and quickly finished before lines of soldiers began to move again." Seemingly out of nowhere, a black banner was strung across the street, with orange letters trumpeting, "Welcome, our Liberators."

On another street, as Private First Class Duane Robey and the soldiers of his Intelligence and Reconnaissance platoon dismounted their jeeps, civilians converged on them, "asking who we were; some were smiling, some were crying with joy." Others just stood to the side and watched quietly. At first, some of the Dutch thought that Robey and the other soldiers were French legionnaires. When the soldiers made it clear they were U.S. Army scouts, "They looked at us in awe and [with] great respect." As the troops of B Company, 414th Infantry Regiment, entered another small town, children and nuns lined up happily to greet them. "They were waving orange flags . . . and offering apples . . . as we went by," the company history said. Another unit history fondly recalled "the huge Dutch flags, the orange hats, sashes and streamers . . . which greeted the eye as far as the American lines reached." In another small town, Private First Class Dick Williams, an artilleryman, enjoyed the carnival atmosphere that ensued from the excitement of liberation. "People of all ages and both sexes were dressed in their best, scurrying everywhere. Everyone wore an orange hair ribbon, armband, buttons, or carried an orange flag to denote their loyalty to the royal house of Orange." He struck up a conversation with several girls, one of whom was excited at the possibility that her boyfriend in the Dutch resistance might now be able to make his way back to her. "It makes you feel pretty good to be cheered and befriended by the people," he wrote to friends at home. "You know you are doing something." Private Peter Branton had badly torn his pants on a wire fence. By the time his unit liberated Zundert, the torn trousers were literally flapping against his boots. A pair of young women offered to mend them. "As I sat in a chair, they kneeled on the floor and very carefully restored my pants to a more serviceable condition." He never forgot this kind act of friendship.[5]

By now, the 104th Infantry Division was in position at the Mark River, a few miles ahead of the British 49th Infantry Division on the left and the Polish 1st Armored Division on the right. The Mark was really just a large canal—about fifty feet wide and eight to ten feet deep, with a slow-moving current—but it was the last remaining obstacle before the Maas River. The Mark was also a natural defensive barrier for the retreating Germans. Rather than pausing the 104th while the others caught up, General Crocker ordered Allen to make a quick crossing of the Mark before the Germans could regroup, blow the main bridge at the town of Standdaarbuiten, and put up a strong defense. As it turned out, they did destroy the bridge, almost right in the faces of Lieutenant Colonel Kelleher's 3rd Battalion, 415th Infantry, as his soldiers were held up by an elaborate roadblock and machine gun nests about two hundred yards south of the river. Crocker was undeterred. He still wanted a crossing as soon as possible. The job went to the 1st Battalion, 415th Infantry Regiment. During the night, Canadian engineers trucked in canvas assault boats, similar to those used in September by Major Cook's paratroopers in Nijmegen.

For much of the night, as they huddled in wet holes near the Mark, the assault troops dealt with unrelenting artillery and mortar fire, not to mention the gut-wrenching anticipation of the river crossing. With the arrival of the boats, the men left their holes, plopped their weapons and equipment into their respective boats, and began hauling them to the river. "The plowed fields were soft and soggy, almost black mud," Private First Class Albert Siklosi later wrote. "At each step we sank ankle deep. That dropped the bottom of the canvas boats to minus ground clearance. So we slogged forward and came to the first irrigation ditch. Surprise! It was about 3 feet wide and, as we later found out after somebody fell in, about 6 feet deep! We shoved and tugged our way across." For much of the journey to the river's edge, Siklosi's group was under enemy fire, as were many others.

The commanders had hoped to pull off a night crossing, but by the time the boat teams made it to the riverbank, hours had passed. Thus, the sun was already rising by the time the battalion was finally ready to cross at 0630. The weather—perhaps fitting for Halloween morning—was windy and cold, with intermittent sheets of misty rain cascading onto everyone. Already the troops were under small-arms and mortar fire. One by one, each boat team splashed into the Mark River and began to paddle across. Some made it across with no problem. Others found themselves under heavy fire. "[They] crossed by clinging to the sides of the assault boats rather than risk the grazing machine gun fire," the regimental after-action report said.

In spite of the enemy opposition, most of the battalion succeeded in crossing the Mark River within only a few minutes. At this point, though, they walked into a disaster. Since they were the only Allied unit on the north side of the Mark, the Germans were able to concentrate most of their artillery, mortars, machine guns, and even tanks against the battalion. The Americans were soon pinned down amid the muddy fields, dikes, and ditches around Standdaarbuiten. Almost every open field was bordered by irrigation canals. "We dug foxholes and received a whale of a lot of fire," Private First Class Harold Zuercher recalled. "There was mortar fire coming in and it seemed like there was an observer who was able to call fire into our position." At one point, he retreated from a shell crater, only to watch as a mortar shell scored a direct hit on the very spot where he had just been. In fact, as Zuercher suspected, the Germans did have many observers dug into the dikes all around Standdaarbuiten. They probably also had spotters in the steeple of the town church. Well-positioned machine guns chattered from several buildings at the edge of the little river town (about seventy-five buildings, according to the estimate of Allied intelligence at the time). Snipers could hardly miss the Americans who were clustered in the muddy fields. "Quite a few men had already been hit or were shell-shocked all around us," Private First Class Ralph Bleier, a machine gunner, recalled.

Colonel John Cochran, the regimental commander, had planned to send his 2nd Battalion over the Mark right after the 1st. But so many boats were lost or destroyed during the crossing, and the situation on the north bank was so chaotic, that this was impossible. Basically, the unfortunate 1st Battalion was on its own, trapped on the wrong side of the river, right under the enemy's muzzles, with very little chance to escape. "There was no way to get vehicles across the river," an officer wrote. "81mm mortars could not function due to lack of observation, and constant counter battery fire, and the artillery was unable to lend its support because it was impossible to maintain wire communication. Radio communications had been eliminated by mortar fire and weather conditions made it impossible to attempt any air missions."

Cochran authorized a withdrawal, and some of the soldiers did manage to disengage, find boats, and make it back to the south bank. But for most of those who were pinned down in the open fields, it was too late. The Germans soon began attacking them with tanks and infantrymen. "Tanks . . . overran positions and fired into individual foxholes," one eyewitness wrote. Private First Class George Roxandich was taking cover in what amounted to a slit trench when he looked up and saw a tank drive up and open fire from a distance of only about seventy yards away. "One of the shots hit in back of me on the other side of the ditch, and the concussion of that knocked me out." A few minutes later, he awoke and began firing rifle grenades at the vehicle. The tank backed up a bit but kept firing. There were also German infantry soldiers around the tank. One of them climbed onto the turret and began talking to the commander. "I fired a shot at him. It happened to be a tracer bullet. It went right between him and the tank. I kept firing . . . until I ran out of shells [bullets]." The tank stopped firing and Private First Class Roxandich took shelter in a fairly deep foxhole, only to be later discovered and captured by a small group of German soldiers. Private First Class Zuercher, in the meantime, played dead while most of the Americans around him were captured. He lay as still as he could in a muddy puddle of water, with only his nose sticking out for air. When the Germans passed, he holed up in a building and managed to avoid capture.

After dark, Colonel Cochran sent patrols across the river to the north bank in hopes of salvaging what was left of the 1st Battalion. With the help of coordinated artillery fire, they succeeded in driving a wedge in the German line and forcing the tanks to retreat. They were then able to find and evacuate many soldiers from A and B companies. Still, the battalion was decimated. About sixty-six were wounded, and probably a like number dead. Over 120 were missing, most of whom ended up as prisoners of war (some sixty-five more hid out and subsisted on rutabagas, beets, and turnips until the Timberwolves rescued them a few days later). On the south bank, the survivors of the 1st Battalion went into division reserve. That grim evening of November 1, the battalion commander, Major Fred Needham, who had experienced the horror of the abortive crossing alongside his men, tried to cheer up his survivors. "Men, I want you to forget this little incident," he told them. "Consider this a reconnaissance in force." But few could think of it as anything other than what it was—a debacle.[6]

The 104th Division waited for a couple days while General Allen and his chastened Allied colleagues coordinated a better-conceived multidivision assault across the Mark, with the Timberwolves once again taking the lead role. Allen planned a two-prong attack. Just west of Standdaarbuiten, the 1st and 2nd battalions of the 413th Infantry Regiment were to cross the river and envelop the town from the west to the east. The 2nd Battalion of the 415th Infantry Regiment would cross at Standdaarbuiten and push through the town. To their right, the regiment's 3rd Battalion was to envelop east to west and join hands with the 413th beyond the village. The other regiment, the 414th, would feint and then provide fire support. The engineers were to assemble the assault boats and ferry the infantrymen across the Mark. Once that was done, they would concentrate their efforts on building temporary bridges. The crossing would, of course, take place at night.

Just after dark on November 2, the 104th's artillery battalions, plus several regiments of British artillery, comprising about 120 guns, began pounding Standdaarbuiten and its environs. "The sky was a dull, red glow that suddenly became long sheets of flame," Tech Sergeant Herbert Goins, an artilleryman, recalled. "I could see round after round of time fire bursting at a perfect height across the river." As the rounds exploded, great booming waves of concussion engulfed the whole area. The sky lit up with flashes almost as bright as day. "The preparation was so intense that it seemed like a continuous earthquake," Lieutenant Cecil Bolton wrote. "Time fire was bursting all over the fields and the sky was brilliantly lighted." Private First Class Tommy Boles, a rifleman in one of the assault companies, had a good vantage point near the river and was transfixed by the barrage. "The sky was a glorious red—balls of fire exploding in midair with a guttural, splitting sound—explosions on the ground throwing earth, rocks and hot steel in every direction." It reminded him of the Fourth of July, and the sight of it comforted him. Perhaps the assault would not be so bad after all. On the other side of the river, the Germans either took cover or got killed. Dutch civilians huddled in their basements even as their homes crashed down all around them or caught fire. "Every building . . . in the battle area were [sic] ablaze," Private First Class Robey recalled. "Everywhere there was . . . the sight and smell of burning."

As the bombardment went on, the infantrymen and engineers laboriously hauled their boats into position, battling mud and unseen canals at nearly every step. "It was not the mushy kind of mud, but more of a congealing consistency," Private First Class Theodore Sery, an engineer, remembered. "You walked on top of it and not through it, but with every step a layer of it would cling to the bottom of your boots. It would build up and only fall off by its own weight after three or four layers had accumulated. It made your feet feel like lead." Another soldier was deeply concerned that the gooey mud "would pull my shoes off, or that I would get completely stuck and be separated from the company." No such thing happened, though. He and the hundreds of other troops made it unscathed to the riverbank, although most were wet from wading through canals. Near the river, Lieutenant Bolton encountered a Dutch farmer, who asked him what they were doing. "We're going to kill some Boche," Bolton said. The farmer gave him a bottle of cognac. A few minutes later, Bolton passed the bottle around to the men in his platoon as they waited to board their boats.

At 2100, the crossing began, with very little interference from the Germans. "We eased the boat into the water and the men climbed in," Private First Class Daniel Ponzevic, an engineer, later wrote, "putting their rifles down and picking up the paddles. Then 'stroke, stroke, stroke' and we were across the river. The men quickly spread out along the raised road." Ponzevic and the other engineers went back for a new load of soldiers.

Both of the 413th Infantry battalions were on the north side within forty-five minutes, and the assault units of the 415th were across within the hour. The lead unit, K Company, cleared Standdaarbuiten house by house. Amid the maelstrom of flames and the tension of rooting out hidden Germans, the company's soldiers used the word "Kayo" to identify one another in the darkness. At one cluster of houses, Private First Class Charles Golden's platoon encountered a German machine gun. As the enemy gunners fired, white tracers streaked through the black night and flaming shadows. "Rifles, automatic rifles, and grenades spoke," Golden said. "On the right the Second Platoon . . . slashed their way into the houses. The Third, following the First, moved on through [a] sugar foundry, across [an] intersection and started slowly up the street toward the high-steepled church, blasting each house with grenades and rifle fire." When Dutch civilians emerged from their basements and saw the Americans, many of them asked, "Are you a Kayo?" By 2250, Standdaarbuiten was firmly in American hands. Only a few desultory rounds of German artillery continued to come in.

Around the many fields, dikes, and irrigation canals outside of town, the Timberwolves were also driving the Germans away and establishing a firm bridgehead. "The flashes of light from the firing and detonation of artillery, the sound of exploding rounds simultaneously with cries of pain and MEDIC followed immediately with sounds of wet chunks of soil and pieces of shrapnel that had not found flesh . . . was cacophonous," Private First Class Jim Henderson, an ammo bearer in a mortar platoon, wrote. His platoon leader, Lieutenant Jack Baldridge, was killed, and a man on his gun crew severely wounded in the back by shell fragments.

For many squads, the muddy terrain and canals were the greatest impediment. Other units, like Lieutenant Bolton's platoon, ran into determined resistance. "Tracer bullets were snapping about 4 feet off the ground," Bolton wrote. "105mm artillery fire was heavy and the Germans were checkerboarding the area with 120mm mortars, 81mm mortars and the small 51mm mortars." While taking cover among the ditches, Bolton's platoon members became hopelessly scattered and out of contact with one another. The lieutenant was hit in his legs by mortar fragments, but this hardly slowed him down. He waded through icy water and led numerous attacks on German machine gun nests, one of which was in a house. He shot several enemy soldiers with his carbine, killed more with white phosphorous grenades, and supervised a bazooka team that took out more Germans. At one point, he wielded the bazooka himself, firing it and destroying a self-propelled gun near a barn. He fired another bazooka rocket into the barn and was surprised to see a tank emerge "out of the barn up onto the dike and move to the rear. [I] did not even know a tank was inside the barn." Only when he was sure that the platoon had cleared the area of German resistance and his men were out of harm's way did Bolton think of seeking medical attention. On the way to the medics, a sniper shot him in the left shoulder, almost at the neck, badly wounding him. He earned the Medal of Honor for his leadership that night. "Lieutenant Bolton's heroic assaults in the face of vicious fire, his inspiring leadership and continued aggressiveness even though suffering from serious wounds, contributed in large measure to overcoming strong enemy resistance and made it possible for his battalion to reach its objective," his citation read. Privates First Class Martin Specht and Wallace Worley, who made up the bazooka team that worked with Bolton, earned Silver Stars.

By sunrise on November 3, German opposition in and around Standdaarbuiten was finished. The Timberwolves were across the Mark. The entire night action had cost the division twenty-three casualties. They had captured 148 POWs. Timberwolf and British engineers had succeeded in constructing a footbridge, a class-nine (meaning it could hold nine tons) bridge, and, by midday on November 3, they had constructed a class-forty Bailey bridge, suitable for armor. For a time, the Bailey bridge was under uncannily accurate enemy artillery fire. Undeterred, the engineers kept working. "They very calmly went about their job and didn't pay much attention to the enemy fire," Private First Class Charles Norris said. He was especially impressed with a British officer who walked around calmly smoking a pipe, inspecting the work. Brigadier General Bryant Moore, Allen's second in command, arrived and formed the opinion that the artillery fire was accurate because the Germans must have an observer nearby. He ordered patrols out to find the spotter. Sure enough, one patrol found a German officer and a sergeant concealed with a radio under the abutment of the destroyed Standdaarbuiten bridge, directing fire. The patrol shot and killed them, and the shelling ceased.

With the Allies firmly on the north side of the Mark River, German resistance in the 104th Infantry Division sector collapsed. For the next two days, the Timberwolves pursued the enemy remnants north for the few remaining miles until the Maas River. "As we moved over soft muddy ground we checked each house and barn in our path," one sergeant said. Seldom did they run into any opposition. At 1615 on November 5, advance patrols reached the Maas River. On the same day, General Allen received orders from the U.S. First Army. The division was being released from British control and was to report to the Aachen area as soon as possible. German resistance in the Scheldt was winding down, and the Americans were no longer needed in Holland.

By November 7, the Timberwolves had relocated to Aachen, Germany. The fighting in Holland had cost the division 1,426 casualties, including 313 killed and 103 missing (some of whom were captured in the ill-fated first Mark River crossing). Congratulatory thank-you letters from Montgomery, Crocker, and the Canadian commanders flowed in. General Allen disseminated copies of the letters among his regiments and wrote a personal letter of thanks to everyone in the division, concluding with his favorite motto: "Nothing in hell must stop the Timberwolves!" His survivors were, of course, forever marked by their combat experiences in the Scheldt campaign. "My men know the effects of war far more than you or I could ever visualize or even realize," Sergeant John Meier proudly wrote his parents in mid-November. "[T]o relate what they have done would take more ink than paper. They have shown the qualities that make our Army the best in the world."

The multinational Allied army finally cleared the Germans from the Scheldt by the end of the first week of November. However, it took the Royal Navy three more weeks to sweep the estuary waters clear of mines. At last, in early December, right on the eve of the Battle of the Bulge, supplies began flowing onto the docks of Antwerp.[7]

CHAPTER 17

Off the Line

Gradually, the days grew shorter and the winds blew chillier. The gloomy fall days portended the forlorn hardness of impending winter. And finally, in mid-November, orders came down from Montgomery's Twenty-first Army Group to release the two American airborne divisions in Holland back to the control of Brereton's First Allied Airborne Army. The 82nd Airborne Division left first, starting on November 13, the 101st Airborne Division two weeks later (just before the Germans flooded part of the Island by blowing a hole in one of the dikes).

From the Island all the way to Groesbeek, the exhausted, wet troopers left the line amid little fanfare. When soldiers from the Canadian 3rd Infantry Division relieved the 82nd Airborne on a rainy, dark night, the men of the two units conversed in low-key, easygoing tones, as if they had known one another for years. They swapped food, liquor, and cigarettes, but mostly they shared war stories. The Americans talked about Market Garden. The Canadians discussed their bitter fight to clear the Scheldt.

Nearly everyone was tired, marred in some way. Like many other troopers, Captain Adam Komosa had let his beard grow for several days. At some point, the heel of his left boot had come off, and he had bought a cane from a Dutchman to compensate for his inadequate footgear. As Komosa limped along with the assistance of the cane, he made eye contact with a similarly bearded Canadian captain who was sitting in a jeep. "Where you going, limey?" the Canadian captain asked with a wide smile.

431

Komosa smiled back, as if sharing an unspoken joke with a fellow North American.

Sergeant William Tucker was saddened by the haggard appearance of the Canadian soldiers with whom he conversed. "I will never forget how pathetic their situation was," Tucker said. Most of them had been fighting for months, with no respite in sight. "They . . . were really exhausted." Their ranks were so thin that they could occupy the former American positions with only half as many men. Tucker could not help but feel very sorry for them, and almost guilty at leaving them behind. He and the other weary 82nd Airborne troopers marched about twenty miles to Oss, where they set up tents and bivouacked for several days. Tucker was struck by how much different everyone looked after their two-month ordeal in Holland. "The guys seemed to look older and harder." They circulated around, looking to see which buddies in other units had survived. They renewed friendships with men they had not seen for weeks. "Although tired, we sat around until late at night rehashing the campaign," Sergeant Ross Carter, who had fought for several key bridges and participated in the Waal crossing, later wrote. "The different accounts of the same battle clarified many happenings which for the individual soldier in his foxhole had but a fragmentary meaning." On November 17, they boarded trucks that took them to French army barracks in Suippes and Sissone, about twenty miles outside of Rheims. "The British had given us a double ration of rum as a parting gift at Oss, but all of us were more than ready for champagne," quipped Sergeant Spencer Wurst, who had fought so hard in the Hunner Park. Aboard one truck, Corporal Mickey Graves thought morosely of the long, bloody fall he and the other soldiers of the 504th Parachute Infantry Regiment had spent in Holland. He decided that the operation had been "a glorious failure . . . despite all our accomplishments paid in blood, Arnhem was still in German hands, the Siegfried Line had not been turned, and the Germans seemed more firmly entrenched in their positions than ever."

Private Donald Burgett, like many other 101st Airborne troopers on the Island, actually left the front by boat to escape the German-inspired flooding. The boat, piloted by a Canadian engineer, took Burgett's squad to dry land. At a monastery, they enjoyed their first shower since leaving England. "Hot water was sprayed from holes drilled in pipes fastened to the ceiling." The water tapered off as the soldiers soaped themselves, and then came back on when they were ready to rinse. When they were finished, the men shaved and put on clean uniforms. Corporal Edward Mitchell and his cohorts in D Company, 506th Parachute Infantry Regiment, got paid when they were safely off the line. Naturally, this led to the outbreak of craps games. "All the small game winners eventually got into one big game and I was fortunate enough to be in this one." Scottish soldiers from the 51st (Highland) Infantry Division who were relieving them clustered around to watch the game. Soon some of the Scots grew curious and decided to get in on the action. "It all wound up with the Scotchmen broke, and me and a couple of my buddies walked away big winners."

The troopers boarded trucks and drove down Hell's Highway one final time, winding their way through and past the now familiar places— the Nijmegen road bridge, the Hunner Park, Grave, Veghel, St. Oedenrode, Son, and Eindhoven. Many of the troopers thought of the terrible battles they had fought in these places, and the numerous comrades they had lost. Staff Sergeant John Taylor, who saw heavy combat at both Veghel and Eindhoven, could not help but think of those troopers in his platoon who were missing. The platoon had jumped on September 17 with fifty men. Now only twelve were left. Among the thirty-eight platoon casualties, ten were dead, their remains buried somewhere in the hallowed soil of the temporary American cemetery at Molenhoek. In the bigger picture, the casualty numbers were equally sobering. In Holland, the 101st Airborne Division lost 3,792 killed, wounded, and missing; the 82nd Airborne suffered 3,344 casualties. In both divisions, about half the casualties were suffered during Market Garden in September, and about half during the fall stalemate.

Already, the Dutch were hard at work repairing streets, patching up buildings, and clearing rubble. When they saw the Americans, they paused from their work, raised their hands high with "V"-for-victory signs, and happily yelled, "September seventeen! September seventeen!" The Americans watched them with admiration, and soldiers smiled and waved with weary arms at their old friends. "At the first word that the American paratroopers were leaving Holland, the people lined the roads once again with orange flags and the little children came out to scream and wave," Lieutenant Laurence Critchell recalled. "Everywhere in the towns were the smiles of grateful people. Much of their land had been ruined but they were still grateful—grateful for freedom." The Americans were equally grateful to them for so many reasons—the valuable assistance of the Dutch resistance, the shelter of Dutch homes, the warm welcome of so many ordinary people, or perhaps just the friendly smile of a pretty girl. All had been morale boosters for men facing death; all of it had led to a strong bond of friendship that never abated. "They had aided us at every possible opportunity," Private Burgett wrote, "even to the point of giving their lives." Though the Dutch inhabitants of the Market Garden corridor faced the sad prospect of rebuilding their homes, their farms, and, for that matter, their lives, they were actually the lucky ones. The majority of Holland remained under German control, including, so tragically, Arnhem. The unfortunate Dutch citizens who lived in these areas faced yet another hard winter of occupation (their fifth), one that was to be marked by terrible privation and hunger. Not until April 1945 was Montgomery able to renew the offensive and liberate the rest of Holland.

As the 101st Airborne convoy wound its way out of Holland and headed for French army barracks at Mourmelon, some of the men struggled with diarrhea. There was, of course, no such thing as a bathroom break, so the affected had to improvise. In one instance, when a truck briefly halted in traffic somewhere near Brussels, a suffering trooper leaped out of the truck and hurried over to a slit trench by the side of the road. Only as he began to relieve himself did he notice that just beyond the slit trench was a soccer stadium. A game had just ended and hundreds of spectators were approaching. They noticed the lone soldier in the trench and gathered around to see what he was doing. Scores of them pointed at the embarrassed trooper and giggled. He had no choice but to put up with the indignity of the moment. "Somehow it seemed a fitting conclusion to our service under Monty," the platoon leader, Lieutenant William Sefton, later commented.

Indeed, in the bitter aftermath of Market Garden, the blame game began throughout the Allied world. Eisenhower distanced himself from the operation, affording it only a passing mention in his postwar writings. Like Sefton, most of the other American paratroopers blamed Montgomery for the failure of the operation. The field marshal did not help matters in a postwar memoir when he made the foolish (and intelligence-insulting) claim that the operation "was ninety percent successful." Such percentages meant nothing. If the operation did not succeed—and it clearly did not—then it failed. One cannot, after all, be 90 percent pregnant or 90 percent alive. One either is or is not, and such was the case with Market Garden. In any event, Montgomery remained an unrepentant advocate of Market Garden for the rest of his life. "If the operation had been properly backed from its inception, and given the aircraft, ground forces, and administrative resources necessary for the job," he once wrote, "it would have succeeded *in spite of* my mistakes." In his view, Market Garden was never given a full chance to succeed by Ike and the other power brokers at SHAEF.

Julian Cook and the 504th Parachute Infantry troopers who made the Waal crossing never quite forgave the Guards Armored Division and, to some extent, General Horrocks for not making a stronger push for Arnhem on the evening of September 20–21. In their opinion, the 1st Airborne Division died at Arnhem, and Market Garden went down in flames, because of an endemic lack of aggressiveness among the British ground forces. Many analysts, whether senior officers involved in the battle or latter-year historians, pointed to a slew of other factors, such as bad weather, the decision to drop the 1st Airborne Division too far away from its main objective, radio communication failures, the overextension of the 82nd Airborne Division, the destruction of the Son bridge, and the willful Allied tendency to underestimate German capabilities in September 1944, to the point of ignoring vital information on the presence of the two understrength panzer divisions near Arnhem. All of these were important factors in the tragedy of Market Garden. All contain an element of truth, but none explains the larger whole. The ultimate blame for the failure of Market Garden should properly go to Eisenhower, not Montgomery. The supreme commander was the one who sent mixed signals to his subordinates in the late summer and early fall of 1944 on grand strategy and objectives. He was distant from the battle areas and he did not communicate effectively with his commanders (an unusual failing for him, because, in general, he was an excellent communicator). More than any of that, though, Market Garden was his decision. If Montgomery was the architect who presented him with flawed building blueprints, Ike was still the one who ordered the misbegotten structure to be built, and with disastrous consequences. His was the ultimate responsibility.

Shortly after leaving Holland, General Gavin sat down at a typewriter in his office in Suippes to resume the correspondence he had neglected while in combat. "It is nice for a change to be away from the immediate range of the krauts," he wrote his daughter. "I now have a bed, a room with electric lights, and a bath." Such amenities were a given for most generals, but not for this young division commander who was still something of a rifleman at heart. For him, and for so many of his veteran troopers, the prospect of more battles lay ahead. Gavin and these stalwarts had already made four combat jumps together. It was natural for all of them to wonder how much longer their luck would hold out. "Many of them are banged up from combat and hardly fit mentally or physically for further parachute operations yet they have no other prospects," he confided to his diary. "It hardly seems right, there should be some other way out other than being killed or wounded." He empathized with them as only one of their own truly could. They were his men, his troopers, and he was proud of what they had done in Holland. They had fought their hearts out. They had taken key bridges. They had pulled off one of the boldest combat river crossings in the history of warfare. They had successfully defended a huge swath of territory against all comers. They had liberated thousands. Still, it had not been enough to guarantee the success of the larger operation.

Now, in the aftermath, their prospects for the future were admittedly grim, but at least they were still alive. His thoughts turned to those who were not so fortunate. By his count, 535 of his men had been killed in Holland; another 622 were missing, many of whom could be assumed dead. The numbers were nearly overwhelming to him, almost like an anvil weighing down his shoulders. What had it all been for? he wondered. The answers were elusive, not just for him but for his troopers too. He knew instinctively that, for many years to come, as long as they lived, Market Garden would remain at the forefront of their minds—a battle that they would rehash, refight, and discuss above all others. For Gavin, that session at the typewriter was only the first of many hours of thought, reflection, and erudition he would devote to Market Garden in the decades to come. Years later, after a lifetime of contemplation, he summed up the entire experience in one telling sentence: "The high hopes of the late summer of '44 faded with the first chill of an early winter."[1]

ACKNOWLEDGMENTS

September Hope has been a joy to write, a true journey like I've never experienced before. The research process was extensive and very challenging. Needless to say, the book you hold in your hands (or peruse on your electronic reader) would not exist without the tremendous help of a great many individuals, possibly even more than I can remember to thank, so I would like to apologize in advance for any omissions. Also, I'd like to take full responsibility for any errors I have made in this book.

I would like to thank the military archivists at the National Archives in College Park, Maryland, for helping me navigate their vast collection of World War II operational records. At the Library of Congress, Alexa Potter mined the sizable Veterans History Project collection and made many firsthand accounts from Market Garden veterans available to me. The U.S. Army Military History Institute in Carlisle, Pennsylvania, is one of the great archives in the world today. I appreciate the efforts of the institute's world-class staff to assist me during my extensive research visit. A special thank-you goes to Terry Foster for his personal wisdom and his willingness to go above and beyond the call of duty to find me everything I needed to see.

Cornelius Ryan, author of the great classic *A Bridge Too Far*, had the foresight to preserve all of his extensive research material and donate it to the Alden Library at Ohio University. Cancer cut this great writer's life short in the 1970s, so I never knew him personally, but this makes me no less thankful to him. The rich accumulation of questionnaires, diaries, letters, interview transcripts, memoirs, documents, and photographs (all numbering in the multiple thousands) that comprise the Ryan collection stand as an enduring monument to this greatest of all Market Garden historians. His modern-day kindred spirit is Doug McCabe, the knowledgeable curator of the remarkable Ryan collection. Doug has done a truly exceptional job of organizing all of this valuable material into many dozens of easily accessible boxes, with precise, time-saving finding aids. Thanks to him, my research visit to Athens was truly a pleasure. Not only did he do everything in his power to make the entire Ryan collection available to me, but he even arranged special access to the library for me so that I could work after hours and on weekends. Thank you, Doug!

My old friend Vivian Rogers Price and the folks at the Mighty Eighth Air Force Heritage Museum are also in a special category. The museum library and archive is a real treasure. If there is a better repository of first-hand accounts from American World War II aviators, I have yet to see it. I believe that the Eighth Air Force bombing and resupply missions in support of Market Garden have generally been overlooked by most historians. So my goal was to include this important part of the story. Without the archive, this would not have been possible. Vivian exhaustively searched the library's vast database of personal accounts for anything remotely connected to Market Garden. As a result, I was able to access a rich blend of fascinating stories. Another staff member at the museum, my friend Jerry McLaughlin, provided me with valuable information on the 435th Troop Carrier Group and referred me to several veterans of that unit.

In Holland, my good friend Jan Bos was kind enough to give my wife, Nancy, and me a guided tour of all the 82nd Airborne Division Market Garden battlefields. As a native of Nijmegen, Jan has been studying this topic for nearly four decades. He has interviewed veterans, corresponded with them, shown them the places where they fought, and he has conducted much original archival research himself. He is the author of a fine book on the 376th Parachute Field Artillery Battalion. All in all, I think it is fair to say that he is the most knowledgeable person in the world today on the 82nd Airborne experience in Holland. In multiple conversations, and much subsequent correspondence, Jan has been kind enough to share his vast expertise with me. This book would be much the poorer without his considerable input, and I am personally very grateful to him. Also, during our time in Holland, we were fortunate enough to spend time with another good friend, filmmaker Richard Lanni. Richard is the director, writer, and creative force behind several fine documentaries on the American combat experience in Europe during World War II, including one entitled *The Americans on Hell's Highway*. He invested several days of his valuable time to give us a detailed, worm's-eye tour of the 101st Airborne battle areas in Holland. He also made firsthand accounts from his own collection of veterans' interviews available to me, and facilitated cross-promotion of this book (as well as previous books I've written) on his vibrant blog.

My buddy Paul Clifford, a Vietnam veteran, went out of his way to provide me with a copy of a book his friend Ken McAuliffe prepared of Ken's uncle Anthony's letters. These fascinating letters gave me rare insight into the thinking of the 101st Airborne Division leadership during Market Garden. Cynthia Tinker, an old friend from the Center for the Study of War and Society in Tennessee, provided me with several interview transcripts from the center's excellent collection. John Warmington, the son of a 104th Infantry Division Timberwolf officer, gave me an enormous amount of useful material on the division's combat experiences in Holland during the fall of 1944. In addition, he lent me his personal copies of *Timberwolf Howl*, the division newsletter, many of which contained rare firsthand memoirs from veterans. Thank you, John. Also, thank you to Bill Jackson, longtime editor of the newsletter, for his efforts in putting me in touch with many veterans of the unit. The 82nd Airborne, 101st Airborne, and 104th Infantry Division associations were all very supportive of my efforts. Through these organizations, I was able to locate and talk to, or correspond with, many veterans. The same goes for the World War II

Glider Pilots Association. The glider pilots are truly a unique breed, and I was honored to get to know so many of them.

I am thankful for the significant financial assistance I received from Missouri University of Science and Technology to help offset travel costs. I am fortunate to receive the affirmation and inspiration of my colleagues in the department of history and political science at the university: Diana Ahmad, Mike Bruening, Petra DeWitt, Shannon Fogg, Pat Huber, Tseggai Isaac, Michael Meagher, Jeff Schramm, and Kate Sheppard. Robin Collier, our department secretary, took care of many travel details and once again showed what an exceptional professional and person she is. A special word of appreciation goes to Russ Buhite for nearly two decades of friendship and mentoring. I am eternally grateful to Larry Gragg, the chair of our department, for his fine leadership, professionalism, and everyday support. Three of my students contributed substantially to the research for this book. Stefan Dubois located many former glider pilots and put me in touch with them. Dustin Schroer, one of our finest history majors, served as my research assistant and was helpful to me in a myriad of ways. Most notably, he prepared an extensive, well-organized listing of veterans' accounts for me to consult at the Library of Congress. This focused my efforts and saved me a great deal of time. Thank you, Dustin. Roger Erisman, a former U.S. Army sergeant, pinpointed the Google Earth coordinates of several Market Garden battle sites, and this enhanced my knowledge significantly.

Several of my fellow military historians strengthened this book by acting as sounding boards or lending their own considerable expertise. Frank van Lunteren, a true expert on the 504th Parachute Infantry Regiment, clarified many factual matters for me on the unit's experiences in Holland. My friend Pat O'Donnell, one of our country's best combat historians, shared his savvy perspective on Market Garden with me. He was also kind enough to listen to my own ideas on the topic. The redoubtable Roger Cirillo, whose knowledge of the World War II U.S. Army is encyclopedic, shared his learned ideas and interpretations on the topic with me. Though Roger's views did not always mirror my own, this hardly mattered, because they influenced my thinking in important ways. Perhaps the highest compliment I can pay Roger is that I always learn something when talking or corresponding with him.

I would like to thank my editor, Brent Howard, for many contributions, large and small, to the betterment of *September Hope*. NAL/Caliber is very fortunate indeed to have an editor of his intellect and foresight. As an editor, he has mastered the fine art of extending a steady, yet nonintrusive, hand. To say I have enjoyed working with him would be an understatement of elephant-size proportions. My thanks also to eagle-eyed copy editor Tiffany Yates Martin for a fine job. Ted Chichak, my agent, is a constant source of inspiration and sustenance. I am very grateful to Ted for his wise counsel, his integrity, and his relentless pursuit of excellence. Without him, this book and so many others could never have happened.

The master cartographer who created the first-rate maps for *September Hope* is my old friend Rick Britton, whose prodigious talent is equaled only by his boundless decency as a human being. As always, working with Rick was a true pleasure. Many thanks to him for producing an unforgettable series of maps that strengthened this book immeasurably. Thank you to John Brueck and Jon Pennington for their input on the airborne perspective. Along those lines, I am grateful to Tommy McArdle, a former paratrooper and police officer, for making so much excellent 82nd Airborne historical material available to me.

A special word of thanks goes to my dear friend and fellow military historian Kevin Hymel, who opened his home to me for long periods of time while I was in Washington, D.C. Kevin also located many of the images that appear in the photo section. Perhaps most important, his friendship was a real bright spot for me during what could otherwise have been many lonely days and nights far away from home.

I am fortunate enough to count so many wonderful people among my true friends. Whether they know it or not, all of these individuals helped inspire or sustain me through the writing of this book: Sean Roarty, Mike Chopp, Thad O'Donnell, Dick Hyde, Don Patton, Stuart Hartzell, Conor Larkin McManus, Joe Carcagno, Ron Kurtz, Steve Loher, Steve Kutheis, John Villier, Chuck Hemann, Doug Kuberski, Tom Fleming, Steve Vincent, Harry and Jean Eisenmann, Bob Kaemmerlen, Big Davey Cohen, plus Roland and Ginny Merson.

Of course, the greatest support comes from my family. My in-laws, Ruth and Nelson Woody, have always treated me like their own son. For that I'm forever grateful. I'm also thankful for Ruth's incredible chocolate cake and Nelson's considerable wisdom in choosing a lifelong favorite baseball team. Thank you to David, Angee, and the girls, as well as Doug, Tonya, and the boys, along with Nancy and Charlie. My sister, Nancy, and my brother, Mike, are surprisingly tolerant of their kid brother's obvious obsession with the martial past. I would like to thank them both, plus my brother-in-law, John, for the countless ways they have supported me over the years. My nephew, Michael, and my nieces, Kelly and Erin, are a source of constant joy—and entertainment—to their uncle. Kelly, I'm sorry this book cost me a chance to see your high school graduation. I just hope that the end result will make it all somehow worth it. My parents, Mike and Mary Jane, are, quite simply, the greatest. Each book I write is like a payment toward a lifetime mortgage of gratitude for all they've given me. Perhaps that mortgage will be paid off someday, but I seriously doubt it. My final, and most special, word of thanks goes to my wife, Nancy, to whom I've dedicated *September Hope*. She is the inspiration and the cornerstone for me. She is the key to everything I do. Her daily love, understanding, and support make all else possible. I strive each day to be worthy of her love. Only she can know if I've succeeded. . . .

John C. McManus

St. Louis, MO

SELECT BIBLIOGRAPHY

Archives and Manuscript Collections

Athens, OH. Cornelius Ryan Bridge Too Far Collection, Mahn Center for Archives and Special Collections, Alden Library, Ohio University

Carlisle, PA. United States Army Military History Institute

College Park, MD. National Archives and Records Administration (II)

Columbia, MO. Western Historical Manuscript Collection, University of Missouri–Columbia

Knoxville, TN. University of Tennessee Special Collections Library (repository of the Center for the Study of War and Society)

New Orleans, LA. National World War II Museum

Savannah, GA. Mighty Eighth Air Force Heritage Museum Library

Washington, D.C. Library of Congress, Veterans History Project

Books

Ambrose, Stephen. *Band of Brothers*. New York: Simon & Schuster, 1992.

Ammerman, Gale. *An American Glider Pilot's Story*. Bennington, VT: Merriam Press, 2008.

Angier, J. Francis. *Ready or Not into the Wild Blue: The Aviation Career of a B-17 Bomber Pilot*. South Burlington, VT: Success Networks International, 2003.

Astor, Gerald. *Terrible Terry Allen: Combat General of World War II—The Life of an American Soldier*. New York: Ballantine Books, 2003.

Bando, Mark. *Vanguard of the Crusade: The 101st Airborne Division in World War II*. Bedford, PA: The Aberjona Press, 2003.

Bennett, David. *A Magnificent Disaster: The Failure of Market Garden, The Arnhem Operation September 1944*. Philadelphia and Newbury: Casemate, 2008.

Bennett, Ralph. *Ultra in the West: The Normandy Campaign, 1944–1945*. New York: Charles Scribner's Sons, 1979.

Blair, Clay. *Ridgway's Paratroopers: The American Airborne in World War II*. Garden City, NY: The Dial Press, 1985.

Bledsoe, Marvin. *Thunderbolt: Memoirs of a World War II Fighter Pilot.* New York: Van Nostrand Reinhold Company, 1982.

Booth, T. Michael, and Duncan, Spencer. *Paratrooper: The Life of Gen. James M. Gavin.* New York: Simon & Schuster, 1994.

Boroughs, Zig. *The Devil's Tale: Stories of the Red Devils of the 508 Parachute Infantry Regiment 82nd Airborne Division in World War Two.* College Park, GA: Static Line Books, 1992.

Bos, Jan. *Circle and the Fields of Little America: The History of the 376th Parachute Field Artillery Battalion, 82nd Airborne.* Baltimore, MD: Gateway Press, Inc., 1992.

Bowen, Robert. *Fighting with the Screaming Eagles: With the 101st Airborne Division from Normandy to Bastogne.* London: Greenhill Books, 2001.

Bradley, Omar. *A Soldier's Story.* New York: Henry Holt and Company, 1951.

———, and Clay Blair. *A General's Life.* New York: Simon & Schuster, 1983.

Brereton, Lewis. *The Brereton Diaries.* New York: William Morrow and Company, 1946.

Burgett, Donald. *The Road to Arnhem: A Screaming Eagle in Holland.* Novato, CA: Presidio Press, 1999.

Burriss, T. Moffatt. *Strike and Hold: A Memoir of the 82nd Airborne in World War II.* Washington, D.C.: Brassey's, 2000.

Butcher, Harry. *My Three Years with Eisenhower: The Personal Diary of Captain Harry C. Butcher, USNR.* New York: Simon & Schuster, 1946.

Carter, Ross. *Those Devils in Baggy Pants.* New York: New American Library, 1951.

Chandler, Alfred, editor. *The Papers of Dwight David Eisenhower, Volumes IV and V.* Baltimore and London: The Johns Hopkins Press, 1970.

Compton, Lynn "Buck," and Marcus Brotherton. *Call of Duty: My Life Before, During and After the Band of Brothers.* New York: Berkley Caliber, 2008.

Critchell, Laurence. *Four Stars of Hell.* New York: Jove Books, 1947.

D'Este, Carlo. *Eisenhower: A Soldier's Life.* New York: Henry Holt and Company, 2002.

Eisenhower, Dwight. *Crusade in Europe.* New York: Doubleday, 1948.

Fauntleroy, Barbara Gavin. *The General and His Daughter: The Wartime Letters of General James M. Gavin to his Daughter Barbara.* New York: Fordham University Press, 2007.

Gardner, Ian, and Roger Day. *Tonight We Die as Men: The Untold Story of Third Battalion, 506th Parachute Infantry Regiment from Toccoa to D-Day.* New York: Osprey Publishing, 2009.

Gavin, James. *Airborne Warfare.* Washington, D.C.: Infantry Journal Press, 1947.

———. *On to Berlin: A Fighting General's True Story of Combat in World War II.* New York: Bantam, 1979.

Grilley, Robert. *Return from Berlin: Eye of a Navigator.* Madison, WI: University of Wisconsin Press, 2003.

Guarnere, William, Edward Heffron, and Robyn Post. *Brothers in Battle, Best of Friends: Two WWII Paratroopers from the Original Band of Brothers Tell Their Story*. New York: Berkley Caliber, 2007.

Hoegh, Leo, and Howard Doyle. *Timberwolf Tracks: The History of the 104th Infantry Division, 1942–1945*. Washington, D.C.: Infantry Journal Press, 1946.

Holt, Tonie, and Valmai Holt. *Major and Mrs. Holt's Battlefield Guide: Operation Market Garden*. South Yorkshire, UK: Leo Cooper, 2001.

Horrocks, Sir Brian. *Corps Commander*. London: Sidgwick & Jackson, 1977.

Ingrisano, Michael. *Valor Without Arms: A History of the 316th Troop Carrier Group, 1942–1945*. Bennington, VT: Merriam Press, 2009.

Irwin, Will. *Abundance of Valor: Resistance, Survival and Liberation, 1944–1945*. New York: Ballantine Books, 2010.

Jordan, Jonathan. *Brothers, Rivals, Victors: Eisenhower, Patton, Bradley and the Partnership that Drove the Allied Conquest in Europe*. New York: NAL Caliber, 2011.

Kershaw, Robert. *It Never Snows in September: The German View of Market Garden and the Battle of Arnhem, September 1944*. Hersham, UK: Ian Allan Publishing, 2007.

Koskimaki, George. *Hell's Highway: A Chronicle of the 101st Airborne Division in the Holland Campaign*. New York: Ballantine Books, 2007.

Light, John. *An Infantryman Remembers World War II*. Shippensburg, PA: Beidel Printing House, Inc., 1997.

Lord, William. *History of the 508th Parachute Infantry*. Washington, D.C.: Infantry Journal Press, 1948.

Lynch, Tim. *Operation Market Garden: The Legend of the Waal Crossing*. Stroud, UK: The History Press, 2011.

MacDonald, Charles. *The U.S. Army in World War II: The Siegfried Line Campaign*. Washington, D.C.: Center of Military History, United States Army, 1993.

Marshall, S. L. A. *Battle at Best*. New York: Jove Books, 1989.

Margry, Karel, editor. *Operation Market Garden, Then and Now, Volumes 1 and 2*. Essex, UK: After the Battle Publishers, 2008.

McLaren, David. *Beware the Thunderbolt: The 56th Fighter Group in World War II*. Atglen, PA: Schiffer Military History, 1994.

Megellas, James. *All the Way to Berlin: A Paratrooper at War in Europe*. New York: Ballantine Books, 2003.

Montgomery, Field Marshal Bernard Law. *The Memoirs of Field Marshal the Viscount Montgomery*. Cleveland and New York: The World Publishing Company, 1958.

———. *Normandy to the Baltic*. London: Hutchinson and Company, 1946.

Moorehead, Alan. *Eclipse*. New York: Bantam, 1988.

Nordyke, Phil. *All American All the Way: The Combat History of the 82nd Airborne Division in World War II.* St. Paul, MN: Zenith Press, 2005.

———. *Four Stars of Valor: The Combat History of the 505th Parachute Infantry Regiment in World War II.* St. Paul, MN: Zenith Press, 2006.

O'Donnell, Patrick. *Beyond Valor: World War II's Ranger and Airborne Veterans Reveal the Heart of Combat.* New York: Free Press, 2001.

Pogue, Forrest. *The United States Army in World War II: The Supreme Command.* Washington, D.C.: Office of the Chief of Military History, 1954.

Possemato, Paul, William Johnston, and D. Michael Johnston. *Heroes and Teachers: Stories of Veterans Proud of Their Service in World War II and in the Los Angeles Unified School District.* Bloomington, IN: AuthorHouse, 2007.

Powell, Geoffrey. *The Devil's Birthday: The Bridges to Arnhem, 1944.* London: Buchan & Enright Publishers, 1984.

Rapport, Leonard, and Arthur Northwood. *Rendezvous with Destiny: A History of the 101st Airborne Division.* Nashville, TN: Battery Press, 1948.

Richlak, Jerry, editor. *Glide to Glory: Unedited Personal Stories from the Airborne Glidermen of World War II.* Chesterland, OH; Cedar House, 2002.

Ridgway, Matthew. *Soldier: The Memoirs of Matthew B. Ridgway.* New York: Harper and Brothers, 1956.

Ryan, Cornelius. *A Bridge Too Far.* New York: Touchstone, 1995.

Saunders, Tim. *Hell's Highway: U.S. 101st Airborne & Guards Armoured Division.* South Yorkshire, UK: Leo Cooper, 2001.

———. *Nijmegen: U.S. 82nd Airborne and Guards Armored Division.* South Yorkshire: Pen & Sword, 2001.

Sefton, G. William. *It Was My War: I'll Remember It the Way I Want To!* Manhattan, KS: Sunflower University Press, 1994.

Smith, Jack. *Mustangs & Unicorns: A History of the 359th Fighter Group.* Missoula, MT: Pictorial Histories Publishing Company, 1997.

Stacey, Colonel C. P. *The Canadian Army, 1939–1945: An Official Historical Summary.* Ottawa: King's Printer, 1948.

Taylor, Maxwell. *Swords into Plowshares.* New York: Da Capo, 1972.

Tedder, Arthur. *With Prejudice: The War Memoirs of Marshal of the Royal Air Force Lord Tedder.* London: Cassell, 1966.

True, William, and Deryck Tufts True. *The Cow Spoke French: The Story of Sgt. William True, American Paratrooper in World War II.* Bennington, VT: Merriam Press, 2002.

Tucker, William. *Parachute Soldier.* Harwichport, MA: International Airborne Books, 1994.

Warren, John. *Airborne Operations in World War II, European Theater.* Montgomery, AL: USAF Historical Division, 1956.

Webster, David Kenyon. *Parachute Infantry: An American Paratrooper's Memoir of D-Day and the Fall of the Third Reich.* New York: Delta Trade Paperbacks, 2002.

Wilmot, Chester. *The Struggle for Europe.* New York: Harper & Brothers, 1952.

Wolfe, Martin. *Green Light! A Troop Carrier Squadron's War from Normandy to the Rhine.* Washington, D.C.: Center for Air Force History, 1993.

Wurst, Spencer, and Gayle Wurst. *Descending from the Clouds: A Memoir of Combat in the 505 Parachute Infantry Regiment, 82nd Airborne Division.* Haverton, PA: Casemate, 2004.

NOTES

PROLOGUE: **Into the Blue Dutch Sky**

1. 82nd Airborne Division, plans and orders, Record Group 407, Entry 427, Box 11753, Folder 1, National Archives, College Park, MD; General James Gavin, letter to Captain John Westover, July 26, 1945, located in World War II Combat Interviews Collection, #171, microfiche copy of the entire collection in the author's possession (hereafter referred to as CI); General James Gavin, personal diary, September 14, 1944, James Gavin Papers, Box 10, Folder 2, United States Army Military History Institute (USAMHI), Carlisle, PA; James Gavin, letter to Cornelius Ryan, October 25, 1972, Box 101, Folder 9; Robert Wienecke, letter to Cornelius Ryan, May 14, 1968, Box 102, Folder 6, both in Cornelius Ryan Bridge Too Far Collection, Mahn Center for Archives and Special Collections (Mahn Center), Alden Library, Ohio University, Athens, OH; James Gavin, *On to Berlin: A Fighting General's True Story of Combat in World War II* (New York: Bantam, 1979), pp. 161–70; James Gavin, *Airborne Warfare* (Washington, D.C.: Infantry Journal Press, 1947), pp. 100–01; Cornelius Ryan, *A Bridge Too Far* (New York: Touchstone, 1995), p. 135; Tim Saunders, *Nijmegen: U.S. 82nd Airborne and Guards Armored Division* (South Yorkshire: Pen & Sword, 2001), pp. 27–29; Clay Blair, *Ridgway's Paratroopers: The American Airborne in World War II* (Garden City, NY: The Dial Press, 1985), pp. 49–51. The biographical aspects of General Gavin's life come from my perusal of his extensive collection of papers at the USAMHI and a general reading of T. Michael Booth and Duncan Spencer, *Paratrooper: The Life of Gen. James M. Gavin* (New York: Simon & Schuster, 1994).

CHAPTER 1: **A Big Idea**

1. 21st Army Group, "Operation Market Garden," RG407, Entry 427, Box 1377, Folder 4, National Archives; Bernard Law Montgomery, *The Memoirs of Field Marshal the Viscount Montgomery* (Cleveland and New York: The World Publishing Company, 1958), pp. 240–47; Alfred Chandler, editor, *The Papers of Dwight David Eisenhower, Volume IV* (Baltimore and London: The Johns Hopkins Press, 1970), pp. 2115–21; *The Papers of Dwight David Eisenhower, Volume V* (Baltimore and London: The Johns Hopkins Press, 1970), p. 166; Forrest Pogue, *The United States Army in World War II: The Supreme Command* (Washington, D.C.: Office of the Chief of Military History, 1954),

pp. 280–81; Chester Wilmot, *The Struggle for Europe* (New York: Harper & Brothers, 1952), pp. 488–90. For good information on Montgomery's life, see the multivolume biography by Nigel Hamilton.

2. General Dwight D. Eisenhower, comments, June 11, 1951, RG319, Entry 95, Box 5, Folder 7, Records of the Army Staff, Records of the Office of the Chief of Military History, "The Supreme Command," National Archives; Carlos D'Este, *Eisenhower: A Soldier's Life* (New York: Henry Holt and Company, 2002), pp. 304–05; 601–05; Dwight Eisenhower, *Crusade in Europe* (New York: Doubleday, 1948), pp. 304–06; Ryan, *Bridge Too Far*, pp. 74–78.

3. Air Chief Marshal Sir Arthur Tedder, notes from meeting, September 10, 1944, Box 5; Eisenhower notes, both at RG319, Records of the Army Staff, Records of the Chief of Military History, "The Supreme Command," National Archives; Arthur Tedder, *With Prejudice: The War Memoirs of Marshal of the Royal Air Force Lord Tedder* (London: Cassell, 1966), pp. 589–91; Karel Margry, editor, *Operation Market Garden, Then and Now* (Essex: After the Battle Publishers, 2008), p. 23; Wilmot, *Struggle for Europe*, pp. 489–90; Ryan, *Bridge Too Far*, pp. 82–88; Eisenhower, *Crusade in Europe*, pp. 306–07; D'Este, *Eisenhower*, pp. 605–06; Montgomery, *Memoirs*, pp. 246–47.

4. 21st Army Group, "Operation Market Garden"; Eisenhower, Tedder notes, all at National Archives; Charles B. MacDonald, "The Decision to Launch Operation Market-Garden," pp. 434–42, published in Chapter 19 of *Command Decisions* (Washington, D.C.: Office of the Chief of Military History, 1960); Charles B. MacDonald, *The U.S. Army in World War II: The Siegfried Line Campaign* (Washington, D.C.: Center of Military History, United States Army, 1993), pp. 120–22; Omar Bradley and Clair Blair, *A General's Life* (New York: Simon & Schuster, 1983), pp. 326–28; Wilmot, *Struggle for Europe*, pp. 488–92; Eisenhower, *Crusade in Europe*, pp. 306–07; Montgomery, *Memoirs*, pp. 246–48; Ryan, *Bridge Too Far*, pp. 88–89; Pogue, *Supreme Command*, pp. 281–84; D'Este, *Eisenhower*, pp. 611–13; Margry, *Operation Market Garden, Then and Now*, p. 18. Bradley, on page 328 of his autobiography, asserted that Eisenhower authorized Market Garden, in part, because he was mesmerized by the force of Montgomery's personality at the September 10 meeting. Because Bradley was not present at the meeting, and none of the participants mentioned any such factor, I have omitted this interpersonal element as a cause of Eisenhower's decision.

CHAPTER 2: **Plans and Schemes**

1. First Allied Airborne Army, Report on Operation Market Garden, Folder 1; AAR, Folder 4, both in RG407, Entry 427, Box 1563, National Archives; Brigadier General Floyd Parks, chief of staff, FAAA, diary and meeting notes, September 10, 1944, Floyd Parks Papers, Box 2, USAMHI; Lewis Brereton, *The Brereton Diaries* (New York: William Morrow and Company, 1946), p. 308; John Warren, *Airborne Operations in World War II, European Theater* (Montgomery, AL: USAF Historical Division, 1956), pp. 81–89; Margry, *Operation Market Garden, Then and Now*, pp. 14–15; The background informa-

tion on Brereton comes from research I did for a currently unpublished book called "Tipping the Balance: The United States in World War II"; Ryan, *Bridge Too Far*, pp. 112–13, 121–26; MacDonald, *The Siegfried Line Campaign*, pp. 127–31. Originally there was some thought of dropping the 101st Airborne at Arnhem, but, because the British 1st Airborne bases were geographically closer to the town and had already constructed a detailed sand table of it, they received the assignment.

2. IX Troop Carrier Command, AAR, RG407, Entry 427, Box 1564, Folder 3; First Allied Airborne Army, Report on Operation Market Garden; AAR, all at National Archives; Gavin diary, September 6, 1944; Parks, diary and meeting notes, both at USAMHI; Lieutenant Colonel Jack Norton, meeting notes, September 10, 1944, Box 100, Folder 3, Ryan Collection, Mahn Center; Brereton, *Brereton Diaries*, pp. 340–41; Margry, *Operation Market Garden, Then and Now*, pp. 14–15; Ryan, *Bridge Too Far*, pp. 124–26; Warren, *Airborne Operations in World War II*; Gavin, *Airborne Warfare*, pp. 72–74; Gavin, *On to Berlin*, pp. 159–60; Booth and Spencer, *Paratrooper*, pp. 150, 212–14.

3. First Allied Airborne Army, AAR, National Archives; Major General James Gavin, letter to General Smith, January 17, 1954, comments on "The Siegfried Line" by Charles MacDonald, James Gavin Papers, Box 15, Folder 7; Matthew Ridgway, letter to Cornelius Ryan, June 24, 1973, Matthew Ridgway Papers, Series 2, Retirement Correspondence, Box 44, Folder 17; Parks, diary and meeting notes; Gavin diary, September 14, 1944, all at USAMHI; Anthony McAuliffe, notes from interview with Cornelius Ryan, July 18, 1967, Box 96, Folder 9, Ryan Collection, Mahn Center; Ken McAuliffe, editor, "The WWII Letters of General Anthony McAuliffe," self-published, pp. 277–81, copy of the book provided to me courtesy of Ken McAuliffe, the general's nephew; Leonard Rapport and Arthur Northwood, *Rendezvous with Destiny: A History of the 101st Airborne Division* (Nashville, TN: Battery Press, 1948), pp. 263–65; Matthew Ridgway, *Soldier: The Memoirs of Matthew B. Ridgway* (New York: Harper and Brothers, 1956), p. 108; Brereton, *Brereton Diaries*, pp. 340–41; Ryan, *Bridge Too Far*, pp. 125–28; Gavin, *Airborne Warfare*, pp. 85–86; Warren, *Airborne Operations in World War II*, p. 89. Some accounts claim that General Taylor was present at the Sunninghill meeting, but he was not. The meeting notes include the name of every officer present, and Taylor is not listed. General McAuliffe, in his postwar interview, remembered standing in for him. General Gavin clearly recalled McAuliffe airing the 101st Airborne grievances, something that Taylor himself would have done had he been present.

4. 82nd Airborne Division, Market Garden field orders, Record Group 407, Entry 427, Box 11753, Folder 1; 101st Airborne Division, Market Garden field orders, Record Group 407, Entry 427, Box 11776, Folder 3; IX Troop Carrier Command, AAR, all at National Archives; Gavin diary, September 14, 1944; Parks diary, September 11–12, 1944, both at USAMHI; Norton meeting notes, September 11, 1944, Mahn Center; Warren, *Airborne Operations in World War II*, pp. 90–91; Gavin, *On to Berlin*, pp. 161–64; *Airborne Warfare*, pp. 86–92; Ryan, *Bridge Too Far*, pp. 134–36; Rapport and Northwood, *Rendezvous with Destiny*, pp. 263–65; Brereton, *Brereton Diaries*,

pp. 341–42; Margry, *Operation Market Garden, Then and Now*, p. 24. The Market Garden plans were, of course, more complex and detailed than I have outlined here. In the interest of clarity, I related them as simply as possible without bogging down in operational minutiae. For the purposes of this book, the most significant aspect of the British drop zone plan at Arnhem was the considerable distance they chose to land from their key objective, the city's main highway bridge.

5. Colonel James Duke, questionnaire, Box 107, Folder 9, Ryan Collection, Mahn Center; Chandler, *Papers of Dwight Eisenhower, Volume IV*, pp. 2133–35, 2143–49; Montgomery, *Memoirs*, pp. 247–51; Bradley, *General's Life*, pp. 327–28; MacDonald, *Siegfried Line Campaign*, pp. 128–29; Pogue, *Supreme Command*, pp. 283–84.

6. SHAEF Weekly Intelligence Summary, September 16, 1944, RG331, Entry 13, Box 45, Folder 8; Major General Bedell Smith, interview with S. L. A. Marshall, April 18, 1949, RG 319, Entry 95, Box 5, Folder 7, Records of the Office of the Chief of Military History, History Division, "The Siegfried Line," by Charles MacDonald; Brigadier General E. T. Williams, G2, Twenty-first Army Group, letter to Forrest Pogue, July 30, 1951; RG319, Entry 91, Box 6, Folder 8, Records of the Office of the Chief of Military History, History Division, "The Supreme Command," by Forrest Pogue, all at National Archives; Brian Urquhart, notes from interview with Frederic Kelly, January 24, 1967; letter to Major General Shan Hackett, September 1, 1959, both in Ryan Collection, Box 108, Folder 6, Mahn Center; Geoffrey Powell, *The Devil's Birthday: The Bridges to Arnhem, 1944* (London: Buchan & Enright Publishers, 1984), pp. 44–48; Ralph Bennett, *Ultra in the West: The Normandy Campaign, 1944–1945* (New York: Charles Scribner's Sons, 1979), pp. 151–55; Ryan, *Bridge Too Far*, pp. 157–60; D'Este, *Eisenhower*, pp. 613–15. Urquhart, of course, was way too junior to know about the supersecret Ultra. In general, only commanders and key staff officers at the army level and above knew about it. Strangely, and interestingly, the reconnaissance photographs have never been found. Montgomery, in his memoirs, was absolutely silent on Major Urquhart and the September 15 meeting with Bedell Smith.

CHAPTER 3: **Foreboding**

1. 506th Parachute Infantry Regiment, AAR, RG407, Entry 427, Box 11815, Folder 1; unit journal, September 14 and 15, 1944, Box 11816, Folder 6; S3 Journal, September 14 and 15, 1944, Box 11818, Folder 10; "DZ Europe: History of the 440th Troop Carrier Group," pp. 61–62, Box 13417, Folder 1, all at National Archives; Captain Derwood Cann, "The Operations of the Third Battalion, 506th Parachute Infantry Regiment (101st Airborne Division) at the Marshaling Area in England and Holland from 14–19 September 1944," pp. 6–10, copy in author's possession; Ian Gardner and Roger Day, *Tonight We Die as Men: The Untold Story of Third Battalion, 506th Parachute Infantry Regiment from Toccoa to D-Day* (New York: Osprey Publishing, 2009), pp. 323–31; Donald Burgett, *The Road to Arnhem: A Screaming Eagle in Holland* (Novato, CA: Presidio Press, 1999), pp. 11–12.

2. Supreme Headquarters Allied Expeditionary Force, Operation Market, Field Order #4, September 13, 1944, RG331, Entry 1, Box 75, Folder 3, National Archives; Charles Vest, questionnaire, Box 98, Folder 3; Captain Abner Blatt, letter to his wife, February 1945, Box 97, Folder 31; Delbert Jones, questionnaire, Box 97, Folder 53, all in Ryan Collection, Mahn Center; Cann, "Operations of the 3rd Battalion, 506th Parachute Infantry Regiment," p. 11; Ross Carter, *Those Devils in Baggy Pants* (New York: New American Library, 1951), pp. 131–33.

3. Donald Lassen, questionnaire, Box 104, Folder 57; William Tucker, questionnaire, Box 105, Folder 13; James Corcoran, questionnaire, Box 99, Folder 16; James Baugh, questionnaire, Box 106, Folder 2; Frank Castilione, questionnaire, Box 97, Folder 2; John Cipolla, questionnaire, Box 97, Folder 4; Frank Taylor, questionnaire, Box 105, Folder 39; Richard Klein, questionnaire, Box 97, Folder 11, all in Ryan Collection, Mahn Center; William Tucker, *Parachute Soldier* (Harwichport, MA: International Airborne Books, 1994), pp. 76–77; Gavin, *On to Berlin*, pp. 167–68.

4. William Mastrangelo, questionnaire, Box 104, Folder 64; Dan Zapalski, questionnaire, Box 98, Folder 7; Robert O'Connell, questionnaire, Box 97, Folder 16; Frank Carpenter, questionnaire, Box 96, Folder 20; Melvin Iseneker, questionnaire, Box 98, Folder 22; Jack Isaacs, questionnaire, Box 104, Folder 47; Tom Moseley, interview with the author, May 29, 2010.

5. Philip Nadler, questionnaire, Box 103, Folder 12; Warren Purcell, unpublished memoir, pp. 1–2, Box 97, Folder 18; James Blue, unpublished memoir, p. 1, Box 105, Folder 28; James Allardyce, letter to Heather Chapman, November 20, 1967, Box 105, Folder 25; Edward Wierzbowski, letter to Cornelius Ryan, February 20, 1969, Box 98, Folder 5, all in Ryan Collection, Mahn Center; Captain Jack Tallerday, "The Operations of the 505th Parachute Infantry Regiment (82nd Airborne Division) in the Airborne Landing and Battle of Groesbeek and Nijmegen, Holland, 17–23 September 1944," pp. 13–14, copy in author's possession; Cann, "The Operations of the 3rd Battalion, 506th Parachute Infantry Regiment," pp. 11–13; Corporal George "Mickey" Graves, unpublished diary, September 15, 1944, copy in author's possession courtesy of Mr. Tommy McArdle. I would like to pass along my great appreciation to Tommy for making this rare primary source document available to me; Gavin, *Airborne Warfare*, pp. 89–90.

6. IX Troop Carrier Command, AAR, National Archives; August Duva, questionnaire, Box 104, Folder 25; Patrick Mulloy, questionnaire, Box 106, Folder 14; Carl Kappel, questionnaire, Box 103, Folder 1; Tech Sergeant W. E. Wood, diary, September 15–17, 1944, Box 16, Folder 5; William Richmond, questionnaire, Box 107, Folder 17; Neal Beaver, questionnaire, Box 105, Folder 27, all in Ryan Collection, Mahn Center; "Red Devil Memories of World War II: Headquarters Company, 2nd Battalion, 508th Parachute Infantry Regiment," no pagination, Irving Shanley Collection, Box 1, USAMHI; Lieutenant Colonel Curtis Renfro, Combat Interview #226 (hereafter referred to as CI-226), entire collection in author's possession; "DZ Europe," p. 62. Lieu-

tenant Beaver was one of Lieutenant Colonel Mendez's company commanders. He witnessed the colonel's briefing and vividly recalled the details.

7. Dwayne Burns, unpublished memoir, p. 104, Dwight D. Eisenhower Center (EC), National World War II Museum, New Orleans, LA; Robert Neill, questionnaire, Box 97, Folder 14; Clark Fuller, questionnaire, Box 102, Folder 25; Walter van Poyck, questionnaire, Box 103, Folder 24; Wierzbowski letter, all in Ryan Collection, Mahn Center; Carl Kappel, "The Operations of Company 'H,' 504th Parachute Infantry (82nd Airborne Division), in the Invasion of Holland, 17–21 September 1944," pp. 12–14, copy in author's possession; Cann, "The Operations of the 3rd Battalion, 506th Parachute Infantry Regiment," p. 11; "Market Day: The Spirit Behind the 82nd Division," article found in undated 82nd Airborne Division newsletter; Graves diary, September 16, 1944; Burgett, *Road to Arnhem*, p. 12; Carter, *Those Devils in Baggy Pants*, p. 137.

8. Major General James Gavin, letter to Colonel Robert Weinecke, January 5, 1954, James Gavin Papers, Box 15, Folder 7, USAMHI; James Gavin, letter to Cornelius Ryan, November 18, 1966; James Gavin, letter to Cornelius Ryan, October 25, 1972, both in Box 101, Folder 9; Harry Bestebreurtje, notes from interview with Frederic Kelly, November 28–30, 1966, Box 101, Folder 7; Norton, meeting notes, September 16, 1944, all in Ryan collection, Mahn Center; Lieutenant General Frederick Browning, letter to Office of the Chief of Military History, United States Army, February 1955, Box 10, Folder 1; Brigadier General Roy Lindquist, letter to Colonel John Meade, September 9, 1955; Colonel Thomas Shanley, letter to Office of the Chief of Military History, United States Army, September 2, 1955, both of these letters in Box 10, Folder 4, all in RG319, Entry 95, Records of the Office of the Chief of Military History, History Division, "The Siegfried Line" by Charles MacDonald, National Archives; Gavin to Westover, CI-171; Gavin, "Airborne Army's First Test," p. 25; Gavin, *On to Berlin*, pp. 165–67; Ryan, *Bridge Too Far*, pp. 142–43.

9. First Allied Airborne Army, Weather Reports, September 17, 1944, RG331, Entry 256, Box 35, Folder 1; First Allied Airborne Army, AAR, both at National Archives; Parks diary, September 16, 1944, USAMHI.

CHAPTER 4: **Rumblings**

1. VIII Fighter Command, Mission Summaries, September 17, 1944, RG18, Entry 7A, Box 3295, Folder 6, National Archives; Eighth Air Force, Intelligence and Operation Summaries, September 17, 1944; Tech Sergeant John Dornick, diary, September 17, 1944, 2008.0507.0001, both located at Mighty Eighth Air Force Heritage Museum, Savannah, GA (hereafter referred to as Mighty Eighth Museum); Lieutenant Tom Prior, letter to "Dick," December 2, 1944, Box 28, Folder 2389, Western Historical Manuscript Collection (WHMC), University of Missouri, Columbia, MO; John Albanese, "Thoughts on Flak," located at www.486th.org; 457th Bomb Group, Mission Number 123, Nijmegen, Holland, summary, located at www.457thbombgroup.org;

J. Francis Angier, *Ready or Not into the Wild Blue: The Aviation Career of a B-17 Bomber Pilot* (South Burlington, VT: Success Networks International, 2003), p. 153; Warren, *Airborne Operations in World War II*, p. 100.

2. 92nd Bomb Group, Mission Records, September 17, 1944, Box 385, Folder 7; 94th Bomb Group, Mission Records, September 17, 1944, Box 513, Folder 3; 388th Bomb Group, Bombardier's Narrative, September 17, 1944, Box 1871, Folder 8; 447th Bomb Group, Mission Records, September 17, 1944, Box 2393, Folder 12; 452nd Bomb Group, Mission Records, September 17, 1944, Box 2535, Folder 2, all in RG18, Entry 7A, National Archives; Dr. P. C. Boeren, "The Last Air Raid Alarm," Box 118, Folder 9; Johanna Bremen, notes from interview with Frederic Kelly, November 16, 1966, Box 123, Folder 13; C. J. Rooyens, diary, September 17, 1944, Box 123, Folder 34, all in Ryan Collection, Mahn Center; Lieutenant William Duane, diary, September 17, 1944; Lieutenant Jim O'Connor, unpublished memoir/diary, September 17, 1944, both located on library shelves at Mighty Eighth Museum; Ryan, *Bridge Too Far*, pp. 206–08.

3. 401st Bomb Group, Mission Summary, September 17, 1944, Box 2197, Folder 19; 384th Bomb Group, Mission Records, September 17, 1944, Box 1707, Folder 8, both in RG18, Entry 7A, National Archives; 381st Bomb Group, War Diary, September 17, 1944, www.381st.org; 384th Bomb Group, Group Leader's Narratives, September 17, 1944, Box 70.2.1, Folder 1.1; 544th Bomb Squadron, History, September 1944, Box 70.2, Folder 2; 545th Bomb Squadron, History, September 1944, Box 70.2, Folder 2.1; 547th Bomb Squadron, History, September 1944, Box 70.2, Folder 2.3, all in RG403; 612th, 613th, 614th, and 615th, Histories, September 1944, library shelves; all material at Mighty Eighth Museum; Lieutenant Bill Frankhouser, diary, September 17, 1944, www.398th.org; Robert Grilley, *Return from Berlin: Eye of a Navigator* (Madison, WI: University of Wisconsin Press, 2003), pp. 78–79.

4. First Allied Airborne Army, AAR, National Archives; 614th Bomb Squadron, History, September 1944; 486th Bomb Group, Unit History; Staff Sergeant Raymon Ytuarte, diary, September 17, 1944, all on library shelves, Mighty Eighth Museum; Lieutenant Charles Mellis, diary, September 17, 1944, www.398th.org; James Talley, interview with Dr. Charles W. Johnson, June 5, 1990, MS1764, Box 17, Folder 47, Center for the Study of War and Society, University of Tennessee (hereafter referred to as CSWS); Warren, *Airborne Operations in World War II*, p. 100; Ryan, *Bridge Too Far*, pp. 187–88.

5. 53rd Troop Carrier Wing, AAR, RG18, Entry 7A, Box 3486, Folder 9; IX Troop Carrier Command, AAR; "DZ Europe," p. 64, all at National Archives; Colonel Maurice Beach, letter to Cornelius Ryan, February 18, 1968, Box 107, Folder 2; Cipolla questionnaire, both in Ryan Collection, Mahn Center; "Combat Record of the 504th Parachute Infantry Regiment," self-published, no pagination, at USAMHI; Cann, "The Operations of the 3rd Battalion, 506th Parachute Infantry Regiment," pp. 14–15; James Megellas, *All the Way to Berlin: A Paratrooper at War in Europe* (New York: Ballantine Books, 2003), pp. 104–05; Carter, *Those Devils in Baggy Pants*, p. 139; Burgett, *Road to Arnhem*, pp. 21–22.

6. Team Clarence, Personnel records, RG226, Entry 128, Box 10, Folder 21; Team Clarence, Records, London Historical Office, RG226, Entry 101, Box 1, Folder 8, both at National Archives; Hugo Olson, notes from interview with Frederic Kelly, June 3, 1968, Box 102, Folder 2; Leonard Tremble, questionnaire, Box 103, Folder 22; Thomas Furey, questionnaire, Box 104, Folder 35; Bestebreurtje interview notes, all in Ryan Collection, Mahn Center; Will Irwin, *Abundance of Valor: Resistance, Survival and Liberation, 1944–1945* (New York: Ballantine Books, 2010), p. 38; David Kenyon Webster, *Parachute Infantry: An American Paratrooper's Memoir of D-Day and the Fall of the Third Reich* (New York: Delta Trade Paperbacks, 2002), pp. 67–68.

7. William Addison, questionnaire, notes from interview with Cornelius Ryan, December 11, 1967, Box 102, Folder 8; Jack Carroll, questionnaire, Box 104, Folder 15; Samuel Carp, questionnaire, Box 97, Folder 36; Francis DeVasto, questionnaire, Box 97, Folder 42; George Hurtack, questionnaire, Box 98, Folder 21; Bob Piper, questionnaire, Box 104, Folder 77; James Megellas, questionnaire, Box 103, Folder 10; Ernest Murphy, questionnaire, Box 103, Folder 11, all in Ryan Collection, Mahn Center; 1st Battalion, 502nd Parachute Infantry Regiment, combat interview with Colonel S. L. A. Marshall and Captain John Westover, CI-226; Graves diary, September 17, 1944; Carter, *Those Devils in Baggy Pants*, p. 139. General Taylor rode with the 1st of the 502nd. For the record, the St. Louis Cardinals won the World Series in 1944.

8. John Foley, questionnaire, Box 106, Folder 41; John Holabird, questionnaire, notes from interview with Frederic Kelly, February 27, 1968, Box 106, Folder 10; Robert O'Connell, questionnaire, Box 97, Folder 16; Allardyce letter, Box 105, Folder 25; James Cadden, questionnaire, Box 98, Folder 12; Charles Mitchell, questionnaire, Box 98, Folder 30, all in Ryan Collection, Mahn Center; Burt Christenson, unpublished memoir, pp. 1, 7–9, Richard Winters Collection, Box 4, Folder 4, USAMHI; Burns, unpublished memoir, pp. 106–07, EC; "Combat Record of the 504th Parachute Infantry Regiment."

9. First Allied Airborne Army, AAR; IX Troop Carrier Command, AAR, both at National Archives; Ernest Blanchard, questionnaire, Box 104, Folder 7; Wood, diary, September 17, 1944, Box 16, Folder 5; Russell O'Neal, questionnaire, Box 104, Folder 74; Thomas Wilder, questionnaire, Box 99, Folder 1, all in Ryan Collection, Mahn Center; Sir Brian Horrocks, with Eversley Belfield and Major General H. Essame, *Corps Commander* (London: Sidgwick & Jackson, 1977), pp. 101–02; Carter, *Those Devils in Baggy Pants*, p. 140; Rapport and Northwood, *Rendezvous with Destiny*, pp. 268–69; Ryan, *Bridge Too Far*, pp. 211, 245; Margry, *Operation Market Garden, Then and Now*, pp. 208–11.

CHAPTER 5: **Drop Day**

1. VIII Fighter Command, Mission Report, September 17, 1944, RG18, Entry 7A, Box 3295, Folder 6; 364th Fighter Group, Mission Report, September 17, 1944, RG18, Entry 7A, Box 3248, Folder 5; 366th Fighter Group, Mission Report, September 17,

1944; "Manual for Fighter-Bomber Pilots," both in RG18, Entry 7A, Box 3447, Folders 5 and 3, respectively; First Allied Airborne Army, AAR, all in National Archives; Thomas Steger, questionnaire, William Breuer Collection, Box 1, Folder 4, USAMHI; Peter Dispenza, questionnaire, Box 104, Folder 24, Ryan Collection, Mahn Center; "The Blue Nosed Bastards of Bodney: A Commemorative History of the 352nd Fighter Group," self-published by the 352nd Fighter Group Association, p. 136, located on the library shelves of the Mighty Eighth Museum; David McLaren, *Beware the Thunderbolt: The 56th Fighter Group in World War II* (Atglen, PA: Schiffer Military History, 1994), p. 128; Marvin Bledsoe, *Thunderbolt: Memoirs of a World War II Fighter Pilot* (New York: Van Nostrand Reinhold Company, 1982), pp. 243–45; Warren, *Airborne Operations in World War II*, pp. 102–03, 107–09. At Wesel, far to the east of the Market Garden drop zones, American fighter pilots did encounter enemy fighter opposition, in two separate incidents. In both cases, the Germans attacked with fifteen planes. In one encounter, the 4th Fighter Group claimed to have shot down six for the loss of one American P-51 Mustang. In the other battle, the 361st Fighter Group destroyed one enemy plane with no American losses.

2. Captain Henry Keep, letter to mother, November 20, 1944, James Gavin Papers, Box 15, Folder 5; Steger, questionnaire, both at USAMHI; Robert Franco, questionnaire, Box 104, Folder 33; Charles Santasiero, unpublished memoir, pp. 4–5, Box 98, Folder 35; Blue, unpublished memoir, p. 4; Wood, diary, September 17, 1944, all in Ryan Collection, Mahn Center.

3. First Allied Airborne Army, AAR, National Archives; Otis Sampson, unpublished memoir, p. 3, Box 104, Folder 79; Jack Isaacs, questionnaire, Box 104, Folder 47; August Duva, questionnaire, Box 104, Folder 25, all in Ryan Collection, Mahn Center; Martin Wolfe, *Green Light! A Troop Carrier Squadron's War from Normandy to the Rhine* (Washington, D.C.: Center for Air Force History, 1993), p. 282; T. Moffatt Burriss, *Strike and Hold: A Memoir of the 82nd Airborne in World War II* (Washington, D.C.: Brassey's, 2000), p. 105; Carter, *Those Devils in Baggy Pants*, p. 140; Warren, *Airborne Operations in World War II*, pp. 102–03.

4. 82nd Airborne Division, Drop Zone Charts, RG407, Entry 427, Box 10397, Folder 2; 101st Airborne Division, Glider Statistics, RG407, Entry 427, Box 11753, Folder 11; 52nd Troop Carrier Wing, AAR, RG18, Entry 7A, Box 3486, Folder 9; First Allied Airborne Army, AAR; IX Troop Carrier Command, AAR, all at National Archives; Winston Carter, questionnaire, Box 104, Folder 16; Lawrence Dunlop, letter to Cornelius Ryan, November 15, 1974, Box 16, Folder 1; William Best, questionnaire, Box 97, Folder 30; Delbert Kuehl, questionnaire, Box 103, Folder 6; Jack Tallerday, questionnaire, Box 105, Folder 9; William Meddaugh, questionnaire, Box 104, Folder 69; George Doxzen, questionnaire, Box 98, Folder 15; Arthur Ferguson, questionnaire, Box 102, Folder 23; Virgil Carmichael, questionnaire, Box 102, Folder 16; Megellas questionnaire, all in Ryan Collection, Mahn Center; Paul Mullan, interview with Lieuten-

ant Colonel Louis Frasche, Paul Mullan Papers, Box 39, Folder 10; Virgil Carmichael, unpublished memoir, pp. 13–14, William Breuer Collection, Box 1, Folder 4, both at USAMHI; George Koskimaki, *Hell's Highway: A Chronicle of the 101st Airborne Division in the Holland Campaign* (New York: Ballantine Books, 2007), pp. 62–65; Burriss, *Strike and Hold*, pp. 105–06; Warren, *Airborne Operations in World War II*, pp. 102–12; Megellas, *All the Way to Berlin*, pp. 97–100; Rapport and Northwood, *Rendezvous with Destiny*, pp. 269–71; Margry, *Operation Market Garden, Then and Now*, p. 112; Joe Curreri, "Journey to Disaster, Market Garden: Shot Down Behind Enemy Lines," *Army*, November 2004; Frank van Lunteren, unpublished account of the downing of Lieutenant Rynkiewicz's plane. I would like to thank my friend Frank for kindly providing me a copy of his work. Of the thirty-five planes lost on September 17, five made it to base or an emergency landing field, but were so badly damaged that they had to be junked.

5. 505th Parachute Infantry Regiment, AAR, RG407, Entry 427, Box 10471, Folder 4; 506th Parachute Infantry Regiment, AAR, RG407, Entry 427, Box 11815, Folder 1; 504th Parachute Infantry Regiment, History, RG407, Entry 427, Box 10469, Folder 3; 508th Parachute Infantry Regiment, AAR, RG407, Entry 427, Box 17081, Folder 9; 101st Airborne Division, "Report on Men Who Returned with Planes," RG407, Entry 427, Box 11758, Folder 11; 82nd Airborne Division, drop zone charts; First Allied Airborne Army, "Report on Pathfinder Missions," RG331, Entry 256, Box 34, Folder 3; AAR; IX Troop Carrier Command, AAR, all at National Archives; "DZ Europe," pp. 65–66; Frank MacNees, questionnaire, Box 107, Folder 16; Lieutenant Colonel Charles Young, questionnaire, diary, September 17, 1944, Box 107, Folder 24; John Lindberg, questionnaire, Box 98, Folder 26; Beaver, Cadden questionnaire, all in Ryan Collection, Mahn Center; Donald Orcutt, unpublished memoir, pp. 3–5, William Breuer Collection, Box 1, Folder 4, USAMHI; 1st Battalion, 502nd Parachute Infantry Regiment, Combat Interview with Colonel S. L. A. Marshall and Captain John Westover, CI-226; 506th Parachute Infantry Regiment, combat interview with Colonel S. L. A. Marshall and Captain John Westover, CI-226; Michael Ingrisano, *Valor Without Arms: A History of the 316th Troop Carrier Group, 1942–1945* (Bennington, VT: Merriam Press, 2009), pp. 158–63; Warren, *Airborne Operations in World War II*, pp. 101–12; Gavin, *Airborne Warfare*, pp. 90–95. The terminology of the 101st Airborne drop zones can be confusing because of reversed letter designations. The troop carrier commanders, for instance, called the southern zone, where the 506th came down, B, and the zone to the north, where the 502nd landed, C. The airborne reversed this usage. To them, the northern zone was B and the southern zone C. I have elected to go with the troop carrier designations.

6. 505th Parachute Infantry Regiment, AAR, National Archives; Jakob Moll, unpublished memoir, pp. 1–3, Box 132, Folder 12; Nadler, Blanchard questionnaires, all in Ryan Collection, Mahn Center; Steger, questionnaire, USAMHI; Major Benjamin F. Delamater, "The Action of the 1st Battalion, 508th Parachute Infantry (82nd Air-

borne Division) in the Holland Invasion, 15–24, September 1944, Personal Experiences of the Battalion Executive Officer," pp. 6–8, copy of the paper in author's possession; Robert Kershaw, *It Never Snows in September: The German View of Market Garden and the Battle of Arnhem, September 1944* (Hersham, UK: Ian Allan Publishing, 2007), pp. 63–68; Spencer Wurst and Gayle Wurst, *Descending from the Clouds: A Memoir of Combat in the 505 Parachute Infantry Regiment, 82nd Airborne Division* (Haverton, PA: Casemate, 2004), pp. 170–71; Burgett, *Road to Arnhem*, pp. 30–31. The 506th Parachute Infantry Regiment's combat interview, CI-226, corroborates Burgett's recollection. According to the eyewitnesses who participated in the interview, the two men were struck by a crashing plane "and the prop cut them to pieces."

7. 505th Parachute Infantry Regiment, AAR, National Archives; James Coyle, questionnaire, Box 104, Folder 21; LeGrand Johnson, questionnaire, Box 97, Folder 52; Gus Bernardoni, questionnaire, Box 96, Folder 16; Desmond Jones, unpublished memoir, pp. 1–2, Box 97, Folder 7; Hanz Druener, questionnaire, Box 102, Folder 21; John McElfrish, questionnaire, Box 97, Folder 13; Guy Sessions, questionnaire, Box 97, Folder 24; Louis Hauptfleisch, questionnaire, Box 102, Folder 29; Blue, unpublished memoir, p. 5; Zapalski questionnaire, all in Ryan Collection, Mahn Center; Lieutenant General James Gavin, Conference with Army War College Faculty and Students, April 16, 1975, James Gavin Papers, Box 1, USAMHI; Wurst, *Descending from the Clouds*, p. 171; Webster, *Parachute Infantry*, pp. 68–69; Gavin, *On to Berlin*, pp. 169–70; Megellas, *All the Way to Berlin*, pp. 104–06.

8. 101st Airborne Division, Glider Statistics, RG407, Entry 427, Box 11753, Folder 11; 376th Parachute Field Artillery Battalion, History, RG407, Entry 427, Box 10459, Folder 3; 437th Troop Carrier Group, power pilot interrogation sheets, September 17, 1944, glider pilot interrogation sheets, September 17, 1944, in RG18, Entry 7A, Box 3491, Folders 1, 4, and 6, all at National Archives; Thomas Wilder, questionnaire, Box 99, Folder 1; John Harrell, questionnaire, Box 96, Folder 8, both in Ryan Collection, Mahn Center; Lieutenant James "Buck" Dawson, interview with Ervis Lewis, transcript in James Gavin Papers, Box 15, Folder 5; John McNally, "As Ever, John: The Letters of Colonel John V. McNally to His Sister, Margaret McNally Bierbaum, 1941–1946, self-published, 1985, pp. 51–53; Gavin AWC conference, all at USAMHI; Lieutenant Colonel Sidney Davis, Chief Signal Officer, 101st Airborne Division, combat interview with Major Jeremiah O'Sullivan, CI-226; John "Jack" Whipple, unpublished memoir, pp. 1–2, copy in author's possession courtesy of Mr. Whipple; Jan Bos, *Circle and the Fields of Little America: The History of the 376th Parachute Field Artillery Battalion, 82nd Airborne* (Baltimore, MD: Gateway Press, Inc., 1992), pp. 177–93; Warren, *Airborne Operations in World War II*, pp. 106–07, 111–12; Rapport and Northwood, *Rendezvous with Destiny*, pp. 269–71; Burgett, *Road to Arnhem*, pp. 33–34; Koskimaki, *Hell's Highway*, pp. 80–90; Gavin, *Airborne Warfare*, pp. 73–74, 103. I would like to thank Jan Bos for personally giving me a copy of his fine book.

9. Arie Bestebreurtje, letter to Cornelius Ryan, July 12, 1973; interview notes, Box 101, Folder 7, Ryan Collection, Mahn Center; Gavin, AWC Conference, USAMHI; Gavin, *On to Berlin*, pp. 170–72; Warren, *Airborne Warfare*, pp. 101–02; Ryan, *Bridge Too Far*, pp. 339–42, 394, 408; Margry, *Operation Market Garden, Then and Now*, pp. 146–47.

10. 505th Parachute Infantry Regiment, AAR, National Archives; James Kaiser, questionnaire, Box 104, Folder 51; Maria Josef Van Grotenhuis Van Onstein, questionnaire, Box 123, Folder 1; Dr. A. J. Henneman, notes from interview with Cornelius Ryan, December 7, 1967, Box 122, Folder 43; Wilhelmus Fischer, questionnaire, Box 126, Folder 39; Paul Nunan, questionnaire, Box 104, Folder 72; Thomas Horne, questionnaire, Box 105, Folder 30; Mattheas van Oorschot, diary, September 17, 1944, Box 127, Folder 7; Roy Nickrent, questionnaire, Box 97, Folder 66; Lieutenant Colonel Harold "Hank" Hannah, diary, September 17, 1944, Box 96, Folder 7; Wilhemina Ouweneel-Coppens, questionnaire, Box 126, Folder 9; James Howell, questionnaire, Box 97, Folder 49; Gerardus Otten, unpublished memoir, pp. 6–9, Box 126, Folder 21; Adrianus Marinus, questionnaire, Box 123, Folder 6, all in Ryan Collection, Mahn Center; Zig Boroughs, *The Devil's Tale: Stories of the Red Devils of the 508 Parachute Infantry Regiment 82nd Airborne Division in World War Two* (College Park, GA: Static Line Books, 1992), pp. 153–55. Henry McLean originally told this story of the Hotel de Groot and the cold beer in a letter to Jan Bos, the leading Dutch historian on the 82nd Airborne Division in Market Garden. Jan confirmed the story to me during a visit to the area in the summer of 2010.

CHAPTER 6: **Objectives**

1. 82nd Airborne Division, AAR, RG407, Entry 427, Box 11753, Folder 1; 504th Parachute Infantry Regiment, history, RG407, Entry 427, Box 10469, Folder 3, both at National Archives; John Westover, "The American Divisions in Operation Market," unpublished manuscript, Box 99, Folder 48; Frank Dietrich, questionnaire, Box 102, Folder 19; Mr. Van Haaren, Statement Regarding Maas-Waal Canal Bridge, Box 124, Folder 5, all in Ryan Collection, Mahn Center; Steger, questionnaire, USAMHI; 1st Battalion, 504th Parachute Infantry Regiment, combat interview; Company A, 1st Battalion, 504th Parachute Infantry Regiment, combat interview; Company B, 1st Battalion, 504th Parachute Infantry Regiment, combat interview; Company C, 504th Parachute Infantry Regiment, combat interview, all with Sergeant George Corporan and in CI-171; Tim Saunders, *Nijmegen*, pp. 49–55; Gavin, *On to Berlin*, pp. 174–76; Carter, *Those Devils in Baggy Pants*, pp. 141–42; Margry, *Operation Market Garden, Then and Now*, pp. 154–55. A patrol from the 505th Parachute Infantry Regiment helped take Bridge Number 7 on the evening of September 17.

2. 82nd Airborne division, daily history, September 17, 1944, RG407, Entry 427, Box 10397, Folder 2; AAR; 504th Parachute Infantry Regiment, S3 Journal, September 17, 1944, RG407, Entry 427, Box 10469, Folder 3, History, all at National Archives; 2nd Battalion, 504th Parachute Infantry Regiment, Unit Journal, September 17, 1944,

James Gavin Papers, Box 15, Folder 8; John Thompson, unpublished memoir, pp. 1–4, James Gavin Papers, Box 15, Folder 5, both at USAMHI; Edward Wellems, questionnaire, letter to Heather Chapman, March 8, 1968, Box 103, Folder 25; Edward van Poyck, questionnaire, notes from interview with Frederic Kelly, January 27, 1968, Box 103, Folder 24; Petrus Nefkens, Grave resident, questionnaire, Box 122, Folder 42, all in Ryan Collection, Mahn Center; Major Edward Wellems, CO, 2nd Battalion, 504th Parachute Infantry Regiment, combat interview; Company E, 504th Parachute Infantry Regiment, combat interview, both with Major Jeremiah O'Sullivan, CI-171; John "Jocko" Thompson entry, www.baseballreference.com; Saunders, *Nijmegen*, pp. 38–40; Margry, *Operation Market Garden, Then and Now*, pp. 154–55; personal survey of Grave bridge combat site, July 2010.

3. 82nd Airborne Division, daily history, September 17, 1944; AAR; 504th Parachute Infantry Regiment, S3 Journal, September 17, 1944, History, all at National Archives; Captain Victor Campana, D Company, 504th Parachute Infantry Regiment, statement on the taking of Grave bridge; First Lieutenant Stuart McCash, narrative history of the capture of the Grave bridge, both in James Gavin Papers, Box 15, Folder 4; Joseph Watts, World War II questionnaire #10767, 504th Parachute Infantry Regiment Material, Box 1; 2nd Battalion, 504th Parachute Infantry Regiment, unit journal, September 17, 1944, all at USAMHI; Second Lieutenant John Scheaffer, Silver Star Citation, Box 103, Folder 16; Leo Hart, questionnaire, notes from interview with Frederic Kelly, January 29, 1968 and March 11, 1968, Box 102, Folder 28; Nadler questionnaire, notes from interview with Frederic Kelly, December 7, 1967, and March 1, 1968, Box 103, Folder 12; Wellems letter; Van Poyck questionnaire, interview notes, all in Ryan Collection, Mahn Center; Company D, 504th Parachute Infantry Regiment, combat interview; Company F, 504th Parachute Infantry Regiment, combat interview, both with Sergeant George Corporan; Wellems combat interview, E Company combat interview, all in CI-171; Moseley interview with the author; Saunders, *Nijmegen*, pp. 41–44; Margry, *Operation Market Garden, Then and Now*, pp. 154–55; personal survey of Grave bridge combat site; Frank van Lunteren, e-mail to the author, January 9, 2011. I would like to personally thank Frank, a Dutch historian and expert on the 504th Parachute Infantry in Market Garden, for providing me with excellent information on the time and manner of Lieutenant Files's death. In 2004, during a special ceremony on the sixtieth anniversary of the battle, the Grave bridge was commissioned the John S. Thompson Bridge. He had died in 1988 but his widow and several veterans were in attendance. Thompson never did pitch for the Red Sox, although he did make it to the big leagues with the Philadelphia Phillies between 1948 and 1951.

4. 101st Airborne Division, AAR; history both in RG407, Entry 427, Box 11753, Folders 3 and 4; 326th Airborne Engineer Battalion, AAR, RG407, Entry 427, Box 11794, Folder 1; 506th Parachute Infantry Regiment, AAR; unit journal, September 17, 1944; S1 Journal, September 17, 1944; S3 Journal, September 17, 1944, all at National Archives; Charles Shoemaker, questionnaire, notes from telephone conversation with Cor-

nelius Ryan, March 1, 1968, Box 98, Folder 37, in Ryan Collection, Mahn Center; Captain Richard Winters, diary, September 17, 1944, Richard Winters Collection, Box 1, Folder 6, USAMHI; Albert Hassenzahl, oral history, Albert Hassenzahl Collection, #5222, Veterans History Project, American Folklife Center, Library of Congress, Washington, D.C.; Gene Cook, unpublished memoir, pp. 1–3, copy in author's possession courtesy of Mr. Cook; 506th Parachute Infantry Regiment, combat interview with Lieutenant Colonel S. L. A. Marshall and Captain John Westover, CI-226; 2nd Battalion, 506th Parachute Infantry Regiment, combat interview with Captain John Westover, CI-226; William Guarnere, Edward Heffron, and Robyn Post, *Brothers in Battle, Best of Friends: Two WWII Paratroopers from the Original Band of Brothers Tell Their Story* (New York: Berkley Caliber, 2007), pp. 106–07; Tim Saunders, *Hell's Highway: U.S. 101st Airborne & Guards Armoured Division* (South Yorkshire, UK: Leo Cooper, 2001), pp. 87–92; Koskimaki, *Hell's Highway*, pp. 113–24; Burgett, *Road to Arnhem*, pp. 35–43; Webster, *Parachute Infantry*, pp. 70–77; Rapport and Northwood, *Rendezvous with Destiny*, pp. 271–75; Margry, *Operation Market Garden, Then and Now*, pp. 116–19; personal survey of Son bridge combat site, July 2010. By nightfall on September 17, the Americans began using the sanatorium as a hospital. Accounts differ as to how many eighty-eights the Germans had along the canal. Some claim it was two, others three. For this reason, I have deliberately made no attempt to stipulate a specific number, although I personally think there were three. A couple records claim that, in Son, the Germans had two eighty-eights, but all the soldier accounts agree that there was just one, next to the boys' school. There was actually another gun across the canal that was apparently not dug in or sighted to face a ground attack. The Germans never used it.

5. 501st Parachute Infantry Regiment, Summary of Events, RG407, Entry 427, Box 17058, Folder 7; 502nd Parachute Infantry Regiment, plans and intelligence, Operation Market, RG407, Entry 427, Box 11814, Folder 6; S3 Journal, September 17, 1944, RG407, Entry 427, Box 11812, Folder 3; Colonel S. L. A. Marshall and Captain John Westover, "502nd Parachute Infantry at Best, 17–19, September 1944," Battalion and Small Unit Study #6, RG407, Entry 427, Box 11810, Folder 5; 101st Airborne Division, history, all at National Archives; Major General Walter Poppe, "Second Commitment of the 59th Infantry Division in Holland, 18 September to 25 November 1944," pp. 14–15, Foreign Military Studies, Box 20, B-149, USAMHI; Robert Jones, questionnaire, Box 97, Folder 54; William Craig, questionnaire, Box 97, Folder 40; General Kurt Student, "The Student Report," pp. 9–12, Foreign Military Studies, B-717; Student, notes from interview with Cornelius Ryan, October 18, 1967, both in Box 131, Folder 7; Wierzbowski letter, all in Ryan Collection, Mahn Center; Corporal Arthur Evans, H Company, 502nd Parachute Infantry Regiment, interview with Captain John Westover, CI-226; www.battleatbest.com; S. L. A. Marshall, *Battle at Best* (New York: Jove Books, 1989), pp. 3–13; Koskimaki, *Hell's Highway*, pp. 157–59; Rapport and Northwood, *Rendezvous with Destiny*, pp. 283–85; Margry, *Operation Market Garden, Then and Now*, pp. 172–73; Kershaw, *It Never Snows in September*, pp. 116–17; personal

survey of Best bridge combat site, July 2010. General Taylor originally earmarked just one platoon from H Company to nab the Best bridges. Lieutenant Colonel Cole later requested, and received, permission to send all of the company to do the job.

6. 502nd Parachute Infantry Regiment, S3 Journal, September 17, 1944; Marshall and Westover, "502nd Parachute Infantry at Best," both at National Archives; Captain Abner Blatt, letter to wife, February 1945, Box 97, Folder 31; Wierzbowski letter, both in Ryan Collection, Mahn Center; www.battleatbest.com; Marshall, *Battle at Best*, pp. 13–21; Koskimaki, *Hell's Highway*, pp. 159–61; Rapport and Northwood, *Rendezvous with Destiny*, pp. 285–87; Saunders, *Hell's Highway*, pp. 106–09; personal survey of Best bridge combat site.

7. 82nd Airborne Division, AAR; G2 Journal, September 17, 1944, RG407, Entry 427, Box 10409, Folder 3; 508th Parachute Infantry Regiment, AAR; unit journal, September 17, 1944, both in RG407, Entry 427, Box 17081, Folder 9; Colonel Shields Warren, letter and comments to Colonel Meade, July 5, 1955, RG319, Entry 95, Box 10, Folder 4, records of the Office of the Chief of Military History; "The Siegfried Line," by Charles B. MacDonald; Lindquist, Shanley letters, all at National Archives; Lieutenant General James Gavin, comments on "The Siegfried Line" by Charles B. MacDonald, January 17, 1954, James Gavin Papers, Box 15, Folder 7; Lieutenant Colonel Shields Warren, narrative of events, September 17–21, 1944; Captain Jonathan Adams, "The Holland Operation," both in James Gavin Papers, Box 15, Folder 4; "Red Devil Memories of World War II," all at USAMHI; James Gavin, notes from interview with Cornelius Ryan and Frederic Kelly, January 20, 1967, Box 101, Folder 10; Norton, meeting notes, September 16, 1944, both in Ryan Collection, Mahn Center; Colonel Roy Lindquist, answers to historian's questions; Gavin letter to Westover, both in CI-171; Delamater, "The Action of the 1st Battalion, 508th Parachute Infantry," pp. 9–10; William Lord, *History of the 508th Parachute Infantry* (Washington, D.C.: Infantry Journal Press, 1948), pp. 43–44; Gavin, *On to Berlin*, pp. 178–79; *Airborne Warfare*, pp. 164–65; Boroughs, *The Devil's Tale*, pp. 157–58; Margry, *Operation Market Garden, Then and Now*, p. 164; multiple conversations with Jan Bos; personal survey of Nijmegen battle sites, July 2010. Lieutenant Weaver's patrol returned to the 1st Battalion lines outside of Nijmegen on the morning of September 18. Captain Graham, the liaison officer, claimed that, in the late afternoon of September 17, General Gavin became angry when he found out that Colonel Lindquist had not already pushed for the Nijmegen bridge on his own initiative. With Graham in tow, Gavin hopped in his jeep, went to the 508th command post, and said to Lindquist, "I told you to move with speed." The general then told him in no uncertain terms to take the bridge immediately.

8. 82nd Airborne Division, AAR; G2 Journal, September 17, 1944; 508th Parachute Infantry Regiment, AAR; unit journal, September 17, 1944; Warren letter and comments, all at National Archives; Warren, narrative of events; Adams, "The Holland Operation," both at USAMHI; Private Walker's account is in "We Served Proudly: The Men of HQ Company," self-published, pp. 135–36, George Stoeckert Collection, #50621, LOC; 10th

SS Panzer Division, daily diary, September 17, 1944, Box 130, Folder 11; Frank Taylor, questionnaire, Box 105, Folder 39; Martijn Deinum, diary, September 17, 1944, Box 123, Folder 17; Boeren, "The Last Air Raid Alarm"; Blue, unpublished memoir, pp. 6–10; Allardyce letter; all in Ryan Collection, Mahn Center; Major Jonathan Adams, letter to Major Ben Delamater, April 7, 1947, attached to Delamater, "The Action of the 1st Battalion, 508th Parachute Infantry"; Kershaw, *It Never Snows in September*, pp. 99–101; MacDonald, *The Siegfried Line*, p. 164; Boroughs, *The Devil's Tale*, pp. 159–68; Gavin, *On to Berlin*, pp. 179–80; *Airborne Warfare*, pp. 164–65; Saunders, *Nijmegen*, pp. 124–33; Margry, *Operation Market Garden, Then and Now*, p. 164; Jan Bos, e-mail to the author, January 18, 2011; multiple conversations with Jan Bos; personal survey of Nijmegen battle sites. In spite of the fact that several sources claim that the Adams patrol got to the Belvedere, literally right next to the road bridge, Captain Adams explicitly stated that at no time was his patrol within sight of that particular bridge.

CHAPTER 7: **Frenzy**

1. 82nd Airborne Division, AAR; 504th Parachute Infantry Regiment, S3 Journal, September 18, 1944, both at National Archives; 2nd Battalion, 504th Parachute Infantry Regiment, Unit Journal, September 18, 1944, USAMHI; Johannes Barten, Grave resident, interview notes, Box 122, Folder 40; Nefkens, interview notes; Van Poyck, questionnaire, interview notes; Nadler, interview notes, all in Ryan Collection, Mahn Center; Moseley interview; Wellems combat interview; Companies E and F combat interviews, all in CI-171; Margry, *Operation Market Garden, Then and Now*, pp. 158–59.

2. 82nd Airborne Division, AAR; 508th Parachute Infantry Regiment, AAR; unit journal, September 18, 1944; 504th Parachute Infantry Regiment, S3 Journal, September 18, 1944, all at National Archives; sworn statements regarding the capture of Bridge Number 10 from Colonel Roy Lindquist, Major Otho Holmes, Lieutenant Lloyd Polette, Lieutenant Jean Trahin, Sergeant George Fairman, Sergeant Seale, James Gavin Papers, Box 15, Folder 5, USAMHI; Boroughs, *Devil's Tale*, pp. 170–74; Gavin, *On to Berlin*, p. 175; Lord, *History of the 508th Parachute Infantry*, p. 47; Saunders, *Nijmegen*, pp. 55–58; Carter, *Those Devils in Baggy Pants*, pp. 142–43; Margry, *Operation Market Garden, Then and Now*, p. 289.

3. 82nd Airborne Division, AAR; 508th Parachute Infantry, AAR; unit journal, September 18, 1944; Warren letter and comments, all at National Archives; Warren, narrative of events, USAMHI; First Lieutenant Howard Greenawalt, statement, Box 105, Folder 24; Glen Vantrease, questionnaire, Box 105, Folder 40; Agardus "Gas" Leegsma, letter to James Blue, April 27, 1963, Box 105, Folder 28; questionnaire, notes from interview with Cornelius Ryan, November 22, 1967, unpublished memoir, p. 1, Box 123, Folder 24; Glen Vantrease, questionnaire, Box 105, Folder 40, all in Ryan Collection, Mahn Center; Delamater, "The Action of the 1st Battalion, 508th Parachute Infantry," pp. 9–11; Boroughs, *The Devil's Tale*, pp. 163–65, 177–81; Saunders, *Nijmegen*, pp. 133–35; Ker-

shaw, *It Never Snows in September*, pp. 139–41; Lord, *History of the 508th Parachute Infantry*, p. 46; Gavin, *On to Berlin*, p. 180.

4. 82nd Airborne Division, chief of staff journal, September 18, 1944, RG407, Entry 427, Box 10399, Folder 2; G2 Journal, September 18, 1944, AAR; 508th Parachute Infantry Regiment, AAR; unit journal, September 18, 1944; Team Clarence records; Warren, letter and comments; Shanley letter, all at National Archives; Warren, record of events; Gavin, comments on "The Siegfried Line," both at USAMHI; Major General James Gavin, letter to Nijmegen burgomaster, March 8, 1947, Box 101, Folder 10; Woodrow Millsaps, questionnaire and unpublished memoir, pp. 4–6, Box 105, Folder 34; Allardyce letter; Arie Bestebreurtje, correspondence and notes from interview, all in Ryan Collection, Mahn Center; Gavin, letter to Westover, CI-171; Gavin, *On to Berlin*, pp. 182–85; Kershaw, *It Never Snows in September*, pp. 139–41; Boroughs, *The Devil's Tale*, pp. 167–68; Saunders, *Nijmegen*, pp. 133–35; Blair, *Ridgway's Paratroopers*, pp. 556–57. When Gavin spoke with Bestebreurtje, the Dutch captain related the report about the demolition controls in the post office. Gavin addressed this with Warren during their meeting, and the battalion commander told him about the Adams patrol. Over the course of the general's life, he gave several accounts of his actions on September 18. In some, he said that he met with Warren before Bestebreurtje, but in others he described it exactly the other way around. After pondering this and sifting through all the evidence, I believe that the general first met with Lindquist, then Bestebreurtje, and then Warren. Given the realities of geography, the battle situation, and command customs, this would have been the most logical sequence, so my description reflects this belief.

5. 101st Airborne Division, daily history, casualties, RG407, Entry 427, Box 11753, Folder 11; 2nd Battalion, 502nd Parachute Infantry Regiment, unit journal, September 18, 1944, RG407, Entry 427, Box 11810, Folder 7; 101st Airborne Division, AAR; History; Marshall and Westover, "502nd Parachute Infantry at Best"; 502nd Parachute Infantry Regiment, S3 Journal, September 18, 1944, all at National Archives; Richard Beranty, "Don't Ever Call Me Chicken," article manuscript in Lud Labutka Collection, #43785, LOC; "Between the Lines and Beyond: Letters of a 101st Airborne Division Paratrooper," by Guy Whidden, Julia Whidden, and K. Bradley Whidden, self-published, 2009, pp. 307–11, located at USAMHI; Bernard McKearney, questionnaire, Silver Star citation, Box 97, Folder 62; LeGrand Johnson, questionnaire; Vest, questionnaire, all in Ryan Collection, Mahn Center; www.battleatbest.com; Rapport and Northwood, *Rendezvous with Destiny*, pp. 289–91; Kershaw, *It Never Snows in September*, pp. 117–18; Marshall, *Battle at Best*, pp. 22–24; Koskimaki, *Hell's Highway*, pp. 172–77; Saunders, *Hell's Highway*, pp. 110–11; personal survey of Best battle site, July 2010. The 2nd Battalion linked up with the 3rd Battalion late in the day. I would like to thank Dick Beranty for directing me to his fine article.

6. 101st Airborne Division, AAR; history; Marshall and Westover, "502nd Parachute Infantry at Best"; 502nd Parachute Infantry Regiment, S3 Journal, September 18,

1944; daily history, casualties, all at National Archives; Blatt letter; John Fitzgerald, questionnaire, Box 97, Folder 44; Charles Olson, questionnaire, Box 97, Folder 67; John Brandt, questionnaire, Box 97, Folder 33, all in Ryan Collection, Mahn Center; www .battleatbest.com; www.battledetectives.com, Battle Study #10; Rapport and Northwood, *Rendezvous with Destiny*, pp. 291–92; Marshall, *Battle at Best*, pp. 23–26; Koskimaki, *Hell's Highway*, pp. 168–71; Saunders, *Hell's Highway*, p. 112; personal survey of battle site. Lieutenant Watson later admitted to army historians that he could not bring himself to utter the phrase "Cole is dead." Most accounts claim that the kill shot came from a building about one hundred yards away. The Battle Detective study determined that, in 1944, only one house was standing in the area and it was 350 yards away, well within the range of a good sniper. Cole earned the Medal of Honor for bravery in Normandy. On September 18, 2009, a monument was unveiled at the site of the colonel's death. He is buried in the American cemetery at Margraten, Holland.

7. Marshall and Westover, "502nd Parachute Infantry at Best"; 502nd Parachute Infantry Regiment, S3 Journal, September 18, 1944; Wierzbowski letter, Ryan Collection, Mahn Center; www.battleatbest.com; Rapport and Northwood, *Rendezvous with Destiny*, pp. 293–96; Marshall, *Battle at Best*, pp. 26–30; Koskimaki, *Hell's Highway*, pp. 164–65; personal survey of battle site.

8. 101st Airborne Division, AAR; history; 506th Parachute Infantry Regiment, AAR; daily history; unit journal, September 18, 1944; S1 Journal, September 18, 1944; S2 Journal, September 18, 1944; S3 Journal, September 18, 1944, all at National Archives; John Taylor, unpublished memoir, pp. 46–48, Richard Winters Collection, Box 6, Folder 3; Winters diary, September 18, 1944, both at USAMHI; Charles Santasiero, unpublished memoir, pp. 8–11, Box 98, Folder 35; Helena Wolfensberger, questionnaire, Box 127, Folder 29; Jack Grace, questionnaire, Box 98, Folder 17, all in Ryan Collection, Mahn Center; Staff Sergeant John Taylor, combat interview with Captain John Westover, CI-226; 506th Parachute Infantry Regiment Combat Interview, CI-226; www.battledetectives.com, Case File numbers 1 and 2; Cann, "Operations of the 3rd Battalion, 506th Parachute Infantry Regiment," pp. 17–20; Patrick O'Donnell, *Beyond Valor: World War II's Ranger and Airborne Veterans Reveal the Heart of Combat* (New York: Free Press, 2001), pp. 210–12; Stephen Ambrose, *Band of Brothers* (New York: Simon & Schuster, 1992), p. 127; Lynn "Buck" Compton with Marcus Brotherton, *Call of Duty: My Life Before, During and After the Band of Brothers* (New York: Berkley Caliber, 2008), pp. 128–30; Paul Possemato, William Johnston, and D. Michael Johnston, *Heroes and Teachers: Stories of Veterans Proud of Their Service in World War II and in the Los Angeles Unified School District* (Bloomington, IN: AuthorHouse, 2007), pp. 41–42; Rapport and Northwood, *Rendezvous with Destiny*, pp. 301–05; Koskimaki, *Hell's Highway*, pp. 125–42; Margry, *Operation Market Garden, Then and Now*, pp. 230–35. Panovich returned home and became a teacher in the Los Angeles Unified School District. Brewer recovered from his wounds and returned to Easy Company.

9. 506th Parachute Infantry Regiment, AAR; daily history; unit journal, September 18,

1944; S1 Journal, September 18, 1944; S2 Journal, September 18, 1944; S3 Journal, September 18, 1944, all at National Archives; Taylor, unpublished memoir, p. 49, USAMHI; Lawrence Davidson, Box 98, Folder 14; Maria Van Dijk, questionnaire, Box 122, Folder 22; Joop Muselaars, questionnaire, Box 122, Folder 29; Jan Peter Boyens, questionnaire, Box 122, Folder 15; Elmer Gilbertson, questionnaire, Box 98, Folder 16; Joke Lathouwers, diary, September 18, 1944, Box 122, Folder 20; Lindberg questionnaire; Santasiero, unpublished memoir, pp. 11–12, all in Ryan Collection, Mahn Center; 506th Parachute Infantry, Taylor combat interviews; Koskimaki, *Hell's Highway*, pp. 143–48; Burgett, *Road to Arnhem*, pp. 51–52; Guarnere, Heffron, and Post, *Brothers in Battle, Best of Friends*, p. 111; Rapport and Northwood, *Rendezvous with Destiny*, pp. 305–06; Webster, *Parachute Infantry*, pp. 82–83; Margry, *Operation Market Garden, Then and Now*, pp. 236–47; Saunders, *Hell's Highway*, pp. 78–81.

CHAPTER 8: **Landing Zones**

1. 2nd Air Division, mission summary, September 18, 1944, RG18, Entry 7A, Box 2297, Folder 8; 65th Fighter Wing, mission report, September 18, 1944, RG18, Entry 7A, Box 3295, Folder 7; 359th Fighter Group, mission report, September 18, 1944, RG18, Entry 7A, Box 3392, Folder 22; IX Troop Carrier Command, AAR; 52nd Troop Carrier Wing, AAR, all at National Archives; Paul Tisdale, questionnaire, Box 107, Folder 20; James Fox, notes from interview with Heather Chapman, November 2, 1967, Box 107, Folder 10; James Hopkins, questionnaire, notes from interview with Frederic Kelly, no date, Box 107, Folder 13; Frederick Gilliam, questionnaire, Box 197, Folder 12; Ralph Smith, questionnaire, Box 97, Folder 25; Adam Komosa, unpublished memoir, pp. 8–9, Box 103, Folder 5, all in Ryan Collection, Mahn Center; Abe Friedman, interview with the author, May 11, 2010; Don Rich and Kevin Brooks, "Ordinary Eagle: One Soldier's Role in Glider Operations of the 101st Airborne Division During World War II," p. 120, unpublished manuscript under consideration by Texas A&M University Press (I served as a manuscript reviewer); Jack Merrick, letter to the author, June 18, 2010, and unpublished memoir, pp. 1–2, in author's possession courtesy of Mr. Merrick; Fred Lunde, e-mail to the author, June 4, 2010; Gale Ammerman, *An American Glider Pilot's Story* (Bennington, VT: Merriam Press, 2008), pp. 159–60; Warren, *Airborne Operations in World War II*, pp. 117–21; Margry, *Operation Market Garden, Then and Now*, pp. 262; 276; Ryan, *Bridge Too Far*, pp. 364–66.

2. 505th Parachute Infantry Regiment, S4 Journal, September 18, 1944, RG407, Entry 427, Box 10471, Folder 4; S3 Journal, September 18, 1944; AAR, all at National Archives; Major General Helmuth Reinhardt, "Commitment of the 406th Division Against the Allied Air Landing at Nijmegen in September 1944," Foreign Military Studies, Box 74, Folders C-085 and C-085a; Colonel William Ekman, letter to Major General James Gavin, January 22, 1954, James Gavin Papers, Box 15, Folder 7; Gavin, comments on "The Siegfried Line"; Allen Langdon, "Ready: The History of the 505th Parachute Infantry Regiment, 82nd Airborne Division, World War II," self-published,

p. 96, all at USAMHI; Arthur "Dutch" Schultz, letter to Cornelius Ryan, October 28, 1966, Box 105, Folder 2; Richard Brownlee, questionnaire, Box 104, Folder 12; Gus Sanders, questionnaire, Box 104, Folder 80; Sergeant William Bennett, questionnaire, diary, September 18, 1944, Box 104, Folder 5; Francis Dwyer, questionnaire, Box 104, Folder 26; Olson interview; Tallerday questionnaire, all in Ryan Collection, Mahn Center; Tallerday, "Operations of the 505th Parachute Infantry Regiment," pp. 17–19; personal survey of Landing Zone N, July 2010; Gavin, *On to Berlin*, pp. 184–85; MacDonald, *The Siegfried Line*, pp. 166–67; Kershaw, *It Never Snows in September*, pp. 120–22; Margry, *Operation Market Garden, Then and Now*, pp. 283–85.

3. 508th Parachute Infantry Regiment, AAR; unit journal, September 18, 1944; Warren letter and comments, all at National Archives; Warren, narrative of events; Gavin, comments on "The Siegfried Line"; Reinhardt, "Commitment of the 406th Division," all at USAMHI; Blue, unpublished memoir, pp. 10–11; Millsaps, questionnaire and unpublished memoir, pp. 6–7; Allardyce letter, all in Ryan Collection, Mahn Center; Delamater, "Action of the 1st Battalion, 508th Parachute Infantry," pp. 11–15; personal survey of Landing Zone T, July 2010; Lewis Milkovics, "'The Devils Have Landed': With the Fighting U.S. Airborne," self-published, 1993, pp. 89–90, copy in author's possession; Boroughs, *Devil's Tale*, pp. 183–85; Kershaw, *It Never Snows in September*, pp. 121–24; Gavin, *On to Berlin*, pp. 185–86; Saunders, *Nijmegen*, pp. 97–101; Margry, *Operation Market Garden, Then and Now*, pp. 280–81; MacDonald, *The Siegfried Line Campaign*, pp. 166–67; O'Donnell, *Beyond Valor*, pp. 214–15.

4. VIII Fighter Command, mission report, September 18, 1944, RG18, Entry 7A, Box 3295, Folder 7; 65th Fighter Wing, mission report, September 18, 1944; 359th Fighter Group, mission report, September 18, 1944, 313th Troop Carrier Group, AAR, mission reports, September 18, 1944, RG18, Entry 7A, Box 3486, Folder 8; 82nd Airborne Division, drop zone maps, charts, RG407, Entry 427, Box 10397, Folder 2; IX Troop Carrier Command, AAR; 52nd Troop Carrier Wing, all at National Archives; "DZ Europe," pp. 67–69; Gilliam questionnaire, both in Ryan Collection, Mahn Center; Dawson interview, USAMHI; Lieutenant J. W. McAlister, diary, September 18, 1944, RG403, Box 9, Folder 17; 20th Fighter Group, intelligence bulletin, September 18, 1944, RG403, Box 66, both at Mighty Eighth Museum; Morris Johnson, unpublished memoir, pp. 1–3, copy in author's possession courtesy of Mr. Johnson; Lunde e-mail; personal survey of landing zones T and N, July 2010; Jack Smith, *Mustangs & Unicorns: A History of the 359th Fighter Group* (Missoula, MT: Pictorial Histories Publishing Company, 1997), pp. 109–10; Bledsoe, *Thunderbolt*, pp. 246–50; Gavin, *On to Berlin*, pp. 185–86; *Airborne Warfare*, pp. 108–09; Bos, *Circle and the Fields of Little America*, pp. 198–99; Margry, *Operation Market Garden, Then and Now*, pp. 281–84; Warren, *Airborne Operations in World War II*, pp. 120–23; Ingrisano, *Valor Without Arms*, pp. 164–83.

5. 327th Glider Infantry Regiment, AAR, report on glider landings, and glider statistics, RG407, Entry 427, Box 11753, Folder 11; report on disposition of gliders, RG407, Entry 427, Box 11809, Folder 1; S1 Journal, September 18, 1944, RG407, Entry 427,

Box 11808, Folder 1; 3rd Battalion, 327th Glider Infantry Regiment (hereafter known as 1st Battalion, 401st Glider Infantry Regiment), AAR, RG407, Entry 427, Box 11806, Folder 3; 437th Troop Carrier Group, Power Pilot Interrogation Sheets, September 18, 1944, RG18, Entry 7A, Box 3491, Folder 7; glider pilot interrogation sheets, September 18, 1944, RG18, Entry 7A, Boxes 3491 and 3492, Folders 1, 3, and 10; IX Troop Carrier Command, AAR; 101st Airborne Division, glider statistics, all at National Archives; Walter Cronkite, letter to Cornelius Ryan, September 13, 1967, Box 96, Folder 6; Tisdale questionnaire; McAuliffe, interview notes, all in Ryan Collection, Mahn Center; Alvin Karges, interview with Tom Swope, August 4, 2002, Alvin Karges Collection, #2218, LOC; 327th Glider Infantry Regiment, combat interview with Lieutenant John Westover, CI-226; 1st Battalion, 401st Glider Infantry Regiment, combat interview with Lieutenant John Westover, CI-226; Captain Robert Evans, "The Operations of Company G, 327th Glider Infantry Regiment (101st Airborne Division) in Holland, 18 September–15 October (Personal Experience of a Company Commander)," pp. 8–10, copy in author's possession; USAF Historical Division, "Brief History of the 434th Troop Carrier Group," copy in author's possession; Phillip Rawlins, "Red Light, Green Light Geronimo: A History of the 77th Troop Carrier Squadron, 435th Troop Carrier Group in World War II," self-published, 1993, pp. 84–86, copy in author's possession courtesy of Mr. Jerry McLaughlin; Rich, "Ordinary Eagle," pp. 120–22; McAuliffe, editor, "WWII Letters," pp. 285–87; Flight Officer Shelton Rimer, letter to wife, no date, copy in author's possession courtesy of Mrs. Dorothy Rimer; Merrick, unpublished memoir, pp. 2–3; personal survey of Landing Zone W, July 2010; Robert Bowen, *Fighting with the Screaming Eagles: With the 101st Airborne Division from Normandy to Bastogne* (London: Greenhill Books, 2001), pp. 85–87; Rapport and Northwood, *Rendezvous with Destiny*, pp. 299–301; Margry, *Operation Market Garden, Then and Now*, pp. 262–71; Koskimaki, *Hell's Highway*, pp. 94–99; Warren, *Airborne Operations in World War II*, pp. 118–20.

6. 82nd Airborne Division, Operation Market Garden, Lessons Learned; chief of staff journal, September 18, 1944, RG407, Entry 427, Box 10399, Folder 2; 307th Airborne Engineer Battalion, AAR and S1 Journal, September 18, 1944, RG407, Entry 427, Box 10454, Folder 4; 319th Glider Field Artillery Battalion, history, unit journal, September 18, 1944, RG407, Entry 427, Box 10455, Folder 3; 320th Glider Field Artillery Battalion, history, unit journal, September 18, 1944, RG407, Entry 427, Box 10457, Folders 8 and 10; 456th Parachute Field Artillery Battalion, history, unit journal, September 18, 1944, RG407, Entry 427, Box 10463, Folder 1; 101st Airborne Division, glider statistics; 327th Glider Infantry Regiment, report on glider landings; Glider Statistics, S1 Journal, September 18, 1944; IX Troop Carrier Command, AAR; 52nd Troop Carrier Wing, AAR; 313th Troop Carrier Mission Report; 437th Troop Carrier Group, Interrogations, all at National Archives; Tisdale, questionnaire, Ryan Collection, Mahn Center; Gavin, *On to Berlin*, pp. 185–86; Rapport and Northwood, *Rendezvous with Destiny*, pp. 299–301; Wolfe, *Green Light!*, pp. 325–37; Warren, *Airborne Operations in*

World War II, pp. 118–23. Gavin's comments were in the Lessons Learned and the IX Troop Carrier Command AAR. Interestingly, General Taylor disagreed with Gavin's assessment of glider pilots on the ground. He felt that their level of training was fine and that there was no need to meld them with airborne units. The comments on the suitability of glider pilots for combat as infantry soldiers are purely my opinion.

7. 364th Fighter Group, mission reports, September 18, 1944; RG18, Entry 7A, Box 3428, Folder 5; 392nd Bomb Group, information on downed crew from September 18, 1944, Mission, RG18, Entry 7A, Box 2087, Folder 10; 448th Bomb Group, briefing information for September 18, 1944, mission, RG18, Entry 7A, Box 2470, Folder 7; 491st Bomb Group, mission records, September 18, 1944, RG18, Entry 7A, Box 3065, Folder 4; 2nd Air Division, mission summary, September 18, 1944; VIII Fighter Command, mission report, September 18, 1944; 65th Fighter Wing, mission report, September 18, 1944, all at National Archives; Eighth Air Force, intelligence and operation summaries, September 18, 1944; 20th Fighter Group, unit history; 68th Bombardment Squadron, 44th Bomb Group, unit history; 506th Bomb Squadron, unit history; Staff Sergeant Warren McPherson, diary, September 18, 1944; 392nd Bomb Group, crew diaries, recollections of September 18, 1944, mission; Manny Abrams, unpublished memoir, pp. 8–10; 446th Bomb Group, unit history; 489th Bomb Group, unit history; 491st Bomb Group, unit history; Roy Grimm, "Memories of Twining's Crew," all on library shelves of Mighty Eighth Air Force Museum; Dawson interview, USAMHI; Komosa, unpublished memoir, pp. 15–16; Gilliam questionnaire, both in Ryan Collection, Mahn Center; F. C. "Hap" Chandler, interview with the author, May 12, 2010; For information on the disposition of Sewell's crew, I relied partially on www.b24net/missions/macr; Headquarters, 2nd Bombardment Division, "Target Victory," September 23, 1944, pp. 1–7, copy in author's possession courtesy of Dr. Vivian Rogers Price; Graves diary, September 18, 1944; personal survey of drop zones, July 2010; Warren, *Airborne Operations in World War II*, pp. 123–25.

CHAPTER 9: **Euphoria and Desperation**

1. 82nd Airborne Division, chief of staff journal, September 19, 1944, National Archives; Gavin, AWC Conference; comments on "The Siegfried Line," both at USAMHI; James Gavin letter to Cornelius Ryan, October 2, 1973, Box 101, Folder 9; Allan Adair, notes from interview with Frederic Kelly, April 6, 1967, Box 114, Folder 38; Edward Goulburn, unpublished memoir, pp. 2–3, Box 115, Folder 3; Megellas questionnaire; Gavin interview notes, all in Ryan Collection, Mahn Center; personal survey of Grave/Oversasselt linkup area, July 2010; Megellas, *All the Way to Berlin*, p. 109; Gavin, *On to Berlin*, pp. 186–88; Ryan, *Bridge Too Far*, pp. 410–13; Saunders, *Nijmegen*, pp. 135–36; Margry, *Operation Market Garden, Then and Now, Volume 2*, pp. 330–48.

2. 1st Battalion, 327th Glider Infantry Regiment, AAR, statistics, RG407, Entry 427, Box 11753, Folder 11; S2 Journal, September 19, 1944, RG407, Entry 427, Box 11807, Folder 9; 101st Airborne Division, history; 327th Glider Infantry Regiment, AAR,

statistics; 502nd Parachute Infantry Regiment, S2 Journal, September 19, 1944; S3 Journal, September 19, 1944, Marshall and Westover, "502nd Parachute Infantry at Best," all at National Archives; 101st Airborne Division, G2 Periodic Report, September 19, 1944, CI-226; 1st Battalion, 327th Glider Infantry Regiment, combat interview with Lieutenant John Westover, CI-226; 1st Battalion, 327th Infantry Regiment, history of the Holland campaign, CI-226; 2nd Battalion, 327th Glider Infantry Regiment, combat interview with Lieutenant John Westover, CI-226; 2nd Battalion, 327th Glider Infantry Regiment, history of the Holland Campaign, CI-226; 1st Battalion, 401st Parachute Infantry, 327th Glider Infantry, combat interviews; Poppe, "2nd Commitment of the 59th Infantry Division," p. 5, USAMHI; Wierzbowski letter, Ryan Collection, Mahn Center; Evans, "The Operations of Company G, 327th Glider Infantry," pp. 10–17; Rich, "Ordinary Eagle," pp. 127–29; www.battleatbest.com; personal survey of Best battle site; Rapport and Northwood, *Rendezvous with Destiny*, pp. 306–14; Koskimaki, *Hell's Highway*, pp. 179–91; Marshall, *Battle at Best*, pp. 30–42; Saunders, *Hell's Highway*, pp. 112–22; Margry, *Operation Market Garden, Then and Now*, pp. 376–81. At least two of Wierzbowski's men evaded the Germans after the capitulation of the platoon, while several other badly wounded soldiers remained, at least for the time being, in the German hospital.

3. 101st Airborne Division Reconnaissance Platoon, diary, September 19, 1944; 81st Airborne Antiaircraft Battalion, AAR, both in RG407, Entry 427, Box 11753, Folder 11; 101st Airborne Division, history; 327th Glider Infantry Regiment, AAR; 1st Battalion, 327th Glider Infantry Regiment, AAR; 326th Airborne Engineer Battalion, AAR, all at National Archives; General Hans Reinhardt, "LXXXVIII Corps, (6 June–21 December, 1944)," pp. 28–29, Foreign Military Studies, Box 32, B-343, USAMHI; Shoemaker, questionnaire, notes from telephone conversation, Ryan Collection, Mahn Center; 1st Battalion, 327th Glider Infantry Regiment, 327th Glider Infantry Regiment, combat interviews, CI-226; McAuliffe, editor, "WWII Letters," pp. 287–90; personal survey of Son battle site, July 2010; Kershaw, *It Never Snows in September*, pp. 118–19, 144–47; Koskimaki, *Hell's Highway*, pp. 293–302; Rapport and Northwood, *Rendezvous with Destiny*, pp. 314–18; Saunders, *Hell's Highway*, pp. 94–101; Margry, *Operation Market Garden, Then and Now*, pp. 390–93. During the fighting, the Germans actually got their hands on McAuliffe's jeep and pushed it into the canal.

4. 82nd Airborne Division, AAR; chief of staff journal, September 19, 1944; 505th Parachute Infantry Regiment, S2 Journal, September 19, 1944; S3 Journal, September 19, 1944; Benjamin Vandervoort, unpublished memoir, pp. 3–5, James Gavin Papers, Box 15, Folder 5; George Jacobus, editor, "Echoes of the Warriors: Personal Experiences of Enlisted Men and Officers of E Company of the 505th Parachute Infantry Regiment, 82nd Airborne Division in World War II," self-published, pp. 349, 369–70; Langdon, "Ready," pp. 97–98, all at USAMHI; H. F. Stanley, unpublished memoir, p. 2, Box 102, Folder 17; Robert Steele, unpublished memoir, pp. 2–3, Box 115, Folder 31; A. G. "Tony" Heywood, questionnaire, notes from interview with Frederic Kelly, December

4, 1967, Box 115, Folder 7; Tim Smith, notes from interview with Frederic Kelly, no date, Box 115, Folder 29; Robbert Smulders, notes from interview with Frederic Kelly, no date, Box 123, Folder 36; Gerardus Groothuijsse, statement, Box 124, Folder 6; Bestebreurtje, correspondence and interview notes; Goulburn, unpublished memoir, pp. 2–5; Franco, questionnaire, all in Ryan Collection, Mahn Center; personal survey of post office and railroad bridge battle sites, July 2010; Gavin, *On to Berlin*, pp. 187–91; Ryan, *Bridge Too Far*, pp. 428–30; Saunders, *Nijmegen*, pp. 135–42; Margry, *Operation Market Garden, Then and Now*, pp. 349–53, 358–62; Wurst, *Descending from the Clouds*, pp. 175–76. Heywood and Smith opened fire on the strafing German plane.

5. 82nd Airborne Division, AAR; chief of staff journal, September 19, 1944; 505th Parachute Infantry Regiment, S2 Journal, September 19, 1944; S3 Journal, September 19, 1944, all at National Archives; Otis Sampson, unpublished memoir, pp. 7–9, James Gavin Papers, Box 15, Folder 5; Vandervoort, unpublished memoir, pp. 3–8; Jacobus, "Echoes of the Warriors," pp. 349–53, 369–70; Langdon, "Ready," pp. 97–98, all at USAMHI; Earl Boling, questionnaire, Box 104, Folder 9; James Keenan, questionnaire, Box 104, Folder 53; Pat O'Hagan, questionnaire, notes from interview with Heather Chapman, January 22 and February 19, 1968, Box 104, Folder 73; Otis Sampson, questionnaire, Box 104, Folder 79; Spencer Wurst, questionnaire, notes from interview with Frederic Kelly, March 14, 1968, Box 105, Folder 21; Meddaugh questionnaire; 10th SS Panzer Division daily diary, September 19, 1944; Lassen questionnaire; Bestebreurtje, correspondence and interview notes; Goulburn, unpublished memoir, pp. 2–7; Franco, questionnaire, all in Ryan Collection, Mahn Center; Captain John Phillips, "Operations of the 3rd Platoon, Company 'E,' 505th Parachute Infantry Regiment (82nd Airborne Division) in the Seizure of the Nijmegen Bridge, 19–20 September 1944, Personal Experiences of a Platoon Leader," pp. 9–16, copy in author's possession; personal survey of Nijmegen road bridge site and surrounding blocks, July 2010; Gerard Thuring et al., "Market Garden: Waal Crossing, 20 September 1944, Nijmegen, Holland," self-published by Groesbeek Liberation Museum, 1992, pp. 25–34, copy in author's possession; Phil Nordyke, *Four Stars of Valor: The Combat History of the 505th Parachute Infantry Regiment in World War II* (St. Paul, MN: Zenith Press, 2006), pp. 272–74; Kershaw, *It Never Snows in September*, pp. 137–42; Saunders, *Nijmegen*, pp. 136–39; Margry, *Operation Market Garden, Then and Now*, pp. 350–62; Wurst, *Descending from the Clouds*, pp. 177–80.

6. 82nd Airborne Division, AAR; chief of staff journal, September 19, 1944, both at National Archives; Lieutenant General James Gavin (retired), speech in Nijmegen on fortieth anniversary of Waal River crossing, James Gavin Papers, Box 37, Folder 4; Gavin, oral history; Conference with AWC faculty and students; comments on "The Siegfried Line," all at USAMHI; Brian Horrocks, letter to James Gavin, August 3, 1975, Box 2, Folder 2; Horrocks, interview notes; Gavin, letters to Ryan; Adair, interview notes, all in Ryan Collection at Mahn Center; Horrocks, *Corps Commander*, pp. 109–12; Gavin, *On to Berlin*, pp. 187–90; Saunders, *Nijmegen*, pp. 143–44; Margry, *Operation Market*

Garden, Then and Now, p. 489; Ryan, *Bridge Too Far*, pp. 431–33. Horrocks claimed in his memoirs that he came up with the idea of the river crossing and persuaded Gavin to do it. All other sources are unanimous that it was Gavin's concept and that he proposed it to his British colleagues. Ryan's account of the Malden meeting takes place inside the Malden schoolhouse and included several other officers, including Colonel Reuben Tucker, commander of the 504th. I believe Ryan was in error on this. Gavin, in multiple sources, was adamant that the meeting took place outside. He never mentioned Tucker's presence; nor did Tucker do so in any of his recollections. Moreover, when Gavin dispensed orders to the 504th, he did it through Lieutenant Colonel Warren Williams, Tucker's executive officer. He never would have done this if Tucker had been at the meeting.

CHAPTER 10: **Resolve**

1. 82nd Airborne Division, AAR, National Archives; Jacobus, "Echoes of the Warriors," p. 370, USAMHI; Sister Symons Disithee, diary, September 19–20, 1944, Box 123, Folder 39; John Keller, questionnaire, Box 104, Folder 54; William McMandon, questionnaire, Box 104, Folder 68; Albertus Uijen, diary, September 19, 1944, Box 124, Folder 1; Carroll questionnaire; Boling questionnaire; Deinum diary, September 19, 1944; Steele, unpublished memoir, pp. 2–3; Wurst questionnaire, interview notes, all in Ryan Collection, Mahn Center; Phillips, "Operations of the 3rd Platoon, Company E," pp. 11–13; Alan Moorehead, *Eclipse* (New York: Bantam, 1988), pp. 207–09; Brereton, *Brereton Diaries*, pp. 349–50; Ridgway, *Soldier*, pp. 109–10; Wurst, *Descending from the Clouds*, pp. 182–84; Saunders, *Hell's Highway*, pp. 101–03; Margry, *Operation Market Garden, Then and Now*, pp. 395–401.

2. 82nd Airborne Division, AAR; G2 Journal, September 20, 1944; 307th Airborne Engineer Battalion, AAR, all at National Archives; 3rd Battalion, 504th Parachute Infantry Regiment, unit journal, September 20, 1944, William Breuer Collection, Box 1, Folder 4; Carmichael, unpublished memoir, pp. 20–21; Gavin, comments on "The Siegfried Line," all at USAMHI; Julian Cook, questionnaire, letter to Cornelius Ryan, November 21, 1967, notes from interview with Cornelius Ryan, February 25, 1968, Box 102, Folder 17; Gavin interview; Gavin, notes from conversation with Cornelius Ryan, September 27, 1973, both in Box 101, Folder 10; Reuben Tucker, unpublished memoir, p. 1, Box 103, Folder 23; John Holabird, questionnaire, interview notes, all in Ryan Collection, Mahn Center; Colonel Reuben Tucker, combat interview, CI–171; 3rd Battalion, 504th Parachute Infantry Regiment, Combat Interview, CI-171; Thuring et al., "Market Garden: Waal Crossing," pp. 20–21; Gavin, *On to Berlin*, p. 190.

3. 82nd Airborne Division, AAR, National Archives; Gavin, AWC Conference; Comments on "The Siegfried Line," both at USAMHI; Gavin letter, October 2, 1973; interview; Tucker, unpublished memoir, p. 1; Hugo Olson, letter to Cornelius Ryan, June 3, 1968; interview notes, both in Box 102, Folder 2, all in Ryan Collection, Mahn Center; Tucker, 3rd Battalion, 504th Parachute Infantry Regiment, combat interviews; Gavin,

On to Berlin, pp. 190–91; Ryan, *Bridge Too Far*, pp. 456–58; Margry, *Operation Market Garden, Then and Now*, pp. 488–92; Rapport and Northwood, *Rendezvous with Destiny*, pp. 323–27.

4. 82nd Airborne Division, AAR, National Archives; 3rd Battalion, 504th Parachute Infantry, unit journal, September 20, 1944; Keep letter; Carmichael, unpublished memoir, p. 24, all at USAMHI; Robert Tallon, questionnaire, notes from interview with Frederic Kelly, March 6, 1968, Box 103, Folder 20; Moffatt Burriss, notes from interview with Cornelius Ryan, December 11, 1967, Box 102, Folder 14; Giles Vandeleur, notes from interview with Frederic Kelly, August 10, 1967, Box 115, Folder 36; Henry Keep, notes from interview with Frederic Kelly, December 5, 1967, Box 103, Folder 2; Cook, interview notes; Kappel questionnaire, notes from interview with Frederic Kelly, February 29, 1968, Box 103, Folder 1; Tucker, unpublished memoir, pp. 1–2, all in Ryan Collection, Mahn Center; 3rd Battalion, 504th Parachute Infantry Regiment, combat interview; Burriss, *Strike and Hold*, pp. 108–11; Ryan, *Bridge Too Far*, pp. 458–59; Bos, *Circle and the Fields of Little America*, pp. 208–09.

5. 2nd Battalion, 504th Parachute Infantry Regiment, Unit Journal, September 20, 1944; Carmichael, unpublished memoir, pp. 24–27, both at USAMHI; Richard LaRiviere, questionnaire, notes from interview with Frederic Kelly, March 23, 1968, Box 103, Folder 7; Tom MacLeod, notes from interviews with Frederic Kelly, December 11, 1967, and March 1, 1968, Box 106, Folder 13; Dunlop letter, Kuehl questionnaire, Megellas questionnaire; Cook questionnaire, interview notes; Carmichael questionnaire; Druener questionnaire, all in Ryan Collection, Mahn Center; Thuring, "Market Garden: Waal Crossing," pp. 45–48; Megellas, *All the Way to Berlin*, pp. 114–15; Burriss, *Strike and Hold*, pp. 111, 116; O'Donnell, *Beyond Valor*, p. 216. Colonel Tucker did not know that Chaplain Kuehl planned to cross the Waal with the first wave. Had the commander found out, he would have forbidden Kuehl from going, so the young chaplain pointedly avoided the colonel throughout the day.

6. 82nd Airborne Division, AAR; chief of staff journal, September 20, 1944; G2 Journal, September 20, 1944; 505th Parachute Infantry Regiment, AAR, all at National Archives; Gavin, oral history; Gavin, AWC conference; Gavin, comments on "The Siegfried Line"; Gavin speech on Waal crossing; James Gavin, letter to Matthew Ridgway, June 23, 1981, Matthew Ridgway Papers, Series 2, Retirement Correspondence, Box 36, Folder 15, all at USAMHI; General Eugen Meindl, "II Parachute Corps," Box 129, Folder 15; James Gavin, letters to Hugo Olson, July 10, 1973, Box 102, Folder 6; April 18, 1968, Box 102, Folder 17; Wienecke questionnaire, letter; Gavin, all correspondence with Ryan; interview, all in Ryan Collection, Mahn Center; Gavin, *On to Berlin*, pp. 192–94; Kershaw, *It Never Snows in September*, pp. 189–91. Cook later told Cornelius Ryan that Gavin left the Waal crossing site because he did not really believe in the mission there. This contention was a source of considerable irritation for the retired general, so he went to great lengths to document his actions on September 20 and explain his decision-making process. Olson, the general's aide, vo-

ciferously disagreed with Cook, as did every former member of the staff who addressed the issue.

7. 82nd Airborne Division, AAR; 505th Parachute Infantry Regiment, AAR; S2 Journal, September 20, 1944; S3 Journal, September 20, 1944; 456th Parachute Field Artillery Battalion, history, all at National Archives; Lieutenant General Matthew Ridgway, letter to Major General James Gavin, October 5, 1944, and Major General James Gavin, letter to Lieutenant General Matthew Ridgway, October 6, 1944, both in James Gavin Papers, Box 25, Folder 2; Matthew Ridgway, letters to James Gavin, July 3, 1973, and August 31, 1974; James Gavin, letters to Matthew Ridgway, June 27, 1973, September 3, 1974, and June 23, 1981, all in Matthew Ridgway Papers, Series 2, retirement correspondence, Box 44, Folder 17; Ridgway, letter to Ryan; Gavin diary, October 8, 1944; Langdon "Ready," pp. 98–99; Ekman letter, all at USAMHI; Elmo Jones, questionnaire, Box 104, Folder 50; Robert Yeiter, questionnaire, Box 105, Folder 23; Kenneth Truax, questionnaire, diary, September 20, 1944, Box 105, Folder 12, all in Ryan Collection, Mahn Center; 1st Battalion, 505th Parachute Infantry Regiment, combat interview with Sergeant George Corporan, CI-171; Company B, 505th Parachute Infantry Regiment, combat interview with Major Jeremiah O'Sullivan, CI-171; Margry, *Operation Market Garden, Then and Now*, pp. 508–11; Kershaw, *It Never Snows in September*, pp. 190–92; Gavin, *On to Berlin*, p. 193; Ridgway, *Soldier*, pp. 110–11.

8. 82nd Airborne Division, AAR; 505th Parachute Infantry Regiment, AAR; 508th Parachute Infantry Regiment, unit journal, September 19–20, 1944, all at National Archives; James Gavin, notes on leadership, James Gavin Papers, Box 10, Folder 3; Gavin, oral history; AWC conference; comments on "The Siegfried Line"; Ekman letter; 508th Parachute Infantry Regiment, AAR, all at USAMHI; James Gavin, letter to William Ekman, June 28, 1973; James Gavin, letter to Louis Mendez, June 28, 1973; James Gavin, letter to Kathy Ryan, April 21, 1975, all in Box 2, Folder 2; John Brickley, letter to James Blue regarding "Devil's Hill," February 6, 1962, Box 105, Folder 28; Gavin, all correspondence with Cornelius Ryan; interview; Foley questionnaire; Olson letter, interview; Wienecke questionnaire, letter, all in Ryan Collection, Mahn Center; 1st Battalion, 505th Parachute Infantry Regiment, and B Company, 505th Parachute Infantry Regiment, combat interviews; Delamater, "Action of the 1st Battalion, 508th Parachute Infantry Regiment," pp. 15–20; Gavin, *On to Berlin*, pp. 193–95; Margry, *Operation Market Garden, Then and Now*, pp. 512–15; Kershaw, *It Never Snows in September*, pp. 189–92; Saunders, *Nijmegen*, pp. 68–75, 110–17. One of the B Company soldiers killed in the fighting at Mook was Private John W. O'Daniel, son of Major General John O'Daniel, commander of the 3rd Infantry Division.

CHAPTER 11: Resolution

1. 82nd Airborne Division, AAR; 505th Parachute Infantry Regiment, AAR, both at National Archives; Gavin, oral history; Jacobus, "Echoes of the Warriors," pp. 321–22, 336–51, 370; Adams, "The Holland Operation"; Langdon, "Ready," pp. 99–100, all at

USAMHI; Robert Dwyer, questionnaire, Box 104, Folder 27; Deinum diary, September 20, 1944; Meddaugh questionnaire; Boling questionnaire; Sampson questionnaire; 10th Panzer Division, daily diary, September 20, 1944, all in Ryan Collection, Mahn Center; Phillips, "Operations of 3rd Platoon, Company E," pp. 17–19; Adams letter; Kershaw, *It Never Snows in September*, pp. 192–93.

2. 82nd Airborne Division, AAR; 505th Parachute Infantry Regiment, AAR; S2 Journal, September 20, 1944; S3 Journal, September 20, 1944, all at National Archives; Vandervoort, unpublished memoir, pp. 10–13; Jacobus, "Echoes of the Warriors," pp. 336–51, 370; Langdon, "Ready," pp. 99–100, all at USAMHI; Wayne Galvin, questionnaire, Box 104, Folder 36; Goulburn, unpublished memoir, pp. 8–9; Stanley, unpublished memoir, pp. 3–4; Wurst questionnaire, interview, citation; Bestebreurtje interview; 10th SS Panzer Division, daily diary, September 20, 1944, all in Ryan Collection, Mahn Center; Phillips, "Operations of 3rd Platoon, Company E," pp. 17–22; Margry, *Operation Market Garden, Then and Now*, pp. 494–99; Saunders, *Nijmegen*, pp. 160–71; Wurst, *Descending from the Clouds*, pp. 189–92; Kershaw, *It Never Snows in September*, pp. 192–93.

3. 82nd Airborne Division, AAR; 504th Parachute Infantry Regiment, history; S3 Journal, September 20, 1944; 307th Airborne Engineer Battalion, AAR; 376th Parachute Field Artillery Battalion, history; unit journal, September 20, 1944, all at National Archives; 3rd Battalion, 504th Parachute Infantry Regiment, unit journal, September 20, 1944; Keep letter, both at USAMHI; Walter Hughes, unpublished memoir, pp. 1–2, Walter Hughes Collection, #38545, LOC; Tallon questionnaire, interview notes; Kuehl questionnaire; Keep interview notes; MacLeod interviews; Cook interview notes; Holabird questionnaire, interview notes, all in Ryan Collection, Mahn Center; 3rd Battalion, 504th Parachute Infantry Regiment, combat interview, CI-171; Company H, 504th Parachute Infantry Regiment, combat interview, CI-171; Kappel, "The Operations of Company H," p. 28; Thuring, "Market Garden Waal Crossing," pp. 10–11, 28–29; Burriss, *Strike and Hold*, pp. 111–13; Megellas, *All the Way to Berlin*, pp. 116–17; Margry, *Operation Market Garden, Then and Now*, pp. 490–91; Bos, *Circle and the Fields of Little America*, pp. 206–10, 214; Ryan, *A Bridge Too Far*, pp. 460–61; MGM Pictures, *A Bridge Too Far*, feature film, 1977. This movie is a valuable source, because the filmmakers reenacted the Waal crossing at the actual site with similar boats. Among the various accounts of the Waal crossing, there is a distressing dissimilarity in the times listed for the arrival of the boats, the fire support, and the start of the crossing. I believe that the best sources for the actual timing of these important events are the original unit records and combat interviews. This is because they were compiled during or, at the latest, immediately after the action, when such facts were fresh in the minds of the participants. My account thus reflects this belief.

4. 82nd Airborne Division, AAR; 504th Parachute Infantry Regiment, history; S3 Journal, September 20, 1944; 307th Airborne Engineer Battalion, AAR; 376th Parachute Field Artillery Battalion, history; unit journal, September 20, 1944, all at National

Archives; Delbert Kuehl, World War II questionnaire #4377; 3rd Battalion, 504th Parachute Infantry Regiment, unit journal, September 20, 1944; Keep letter, all at USAMHI; Jan van Gent, diary, September 20, 1944, Box 123, Folder 21; Hyman Shapiro, notes from interview with Frederic Kelly, March 10, 1968, Box 106, Folder 52; Kenneth Nicoll, questionnaire, Box 103, Folder 13; Bill Chennell, notes from interview with Frederic Kelly, August 21, 1967, Box 114, Folder 47; John Gorman, questionnaire, notes from interview with Frederic Kelly, October 30, 1967, Box 115, Folder 2; Edward Tyler, questionnaire, notes from interview with Frederic Kelly, September 29, 1967, Box 115, Folder 33; Matthew Kantala, questionnaire, notes from telephone conversation with Frederic Kelly, February 28, 1968, Box 102, Folder 30; Herbert Keith, questionnaire, notes from interview with Frederic Kelly, March 1, 1968, Box 103, Folder 3; Leonard Tremble, questionnaire, Box 103, Folder 22; Albert Tarbell, questionnaire, notes from telephone conversation with Frederic Kelly, February 27, 1968, Box 103, Folder 21; Tallon questionnaire, interview notes; Fuller questionnaire, Murphy questionnaire; Mulloy questionnaire, interview notes; Dunlop letter; Colonel Reuben Tucker, letter to the burgomaster of Nijmegen, February 21, 1947, unpublished memoir, pp. 1–2; Kuehl questionnaire; Cook questionnaire, letters, interview notes; Kappel questionnaire, interview notes; Megellas questionnaire; Burriss, interview notes, all in Ryan Collection, Mahn Center; 3rd Battalion, 504th Parachute Infantry; H Company, 504th Parachute Infantry, combat interviews; Kappel, "The Operations of Company H," pp. 28–29; Thuring, "Market Garden Waal Crossing," pp. 50–52, 94–95; Megellas, *All the Way to Berlin*, pp. 117–25; Burriss, *Strike and Hold*, pp. 113–17, 140–41; O'Donnell, *Beyond Valor*, pp. 216–17; personal survey of crossing site, July 2010.

5. 82nd Airborne Division, AAR; 504th Parachute Infantry Regiment, history; S3 Journal, September 20, 1944; 307th Airborne Engineer Battalion, AAR; 376th Parachute Field Artillery Battalion, history; unit journal, September 20, 1944, all at National Archives; 3rd Battalion, 504th Parachute Infantry Regiment, unit journal, September 20, 1944; Keep letter, both at USAMHI; Jack Bommer, questionnaire, notes from interview with Heather Chapman, January 26, 1968, letter to Heather Chapman, January 30, 1968, Box 102, Folder 12; Dietrich questionnaire; Shapiro interview notes; Dunlop letter; Fuller questionnaire; LaRiviere questionnaire, interview notes; Carmichael questionnaire; Burris interview notes; Megellas questionnaire, all in Ryan Collection, Mahn Center; Hughes, unpublished memoir, pp. 1–2, LOC; Kappel, "The Operations of Company H," pp. 28–30; Thomas Pitt, interview with Thomas Pitt Jr., located at www .thedropzone.com; Company A, 1st Battalion, 504th Parachute Infantry Regiment, combat interview; Company B, 1st Battalion, 504th Parachute Infantry Regiment, combat interview; Company C, 1st Battalion, 504th Parachute Infantry Regiment, combat interview with Sergeant George Corporan; Company G, 3rd Battalion, 504th Parachute Infantry Regiment, combat interview with Sergeant George Corporan; Colonel Reuben Tucker, combat interview; Company H, 504th Parachute Infantry Regiment, combat interview; 3rd Battalion, 504th Parachute Infantry Regiment, combat interview, all in

CI-171; Graves diary, September 20, 1944; Thuring, "Market Garden Waal Crossing," pp. 50–55; Megellas, *All the Way to Berlin*, pp. 124–27; Burriss, *Strike and Hold*, pp. 114–15; Kershaw, *It Never Snows in September*, pp. 196–98; Carter, *Devils in Baggy Pants*, pp. 147–48; personal survey of crossing site, July 2010.

6. 82nd Airborne Division, AAR; 504th Parachute Infantry Regiment, history; S3 Journal, September 20, 1944; 307th Airborne Engineer Battalion, AAR; 376th Parachute Field Artillery Battalion, history; unit journal, September 20, 1944, all at National Archives; Edward Sims, unpublished memoir, pp. 2–3, World War II questionnaire #6056; 3rd Battalion, 504th Parachute Infantry Regiment, unit journal, September 20, 1944; Mullan interview, all at USAMHI; Kappel, "The Operations of Company H," pp. 33–34; A, B, C, G, H companies, 504th Parachute Infantry, combat interviews; 3rd Battalion, 504th Parachute Infantry Regiment, combat interview, all in CI–171; Colonel Fullreide, Hermann Göring Division, diary, September 27, 1944, Box 131, Folder 20; Allan McClain, questionnaire, notes from interview with Frederic Kelly, January 29, 1968, Box 103, Folder 9; 10th SS Panzer Division, daily diary, September 20, 1944; Megellas questionnaire; Dunlop letter; Tarbell questionnaire, conversation notes; Kappel questionnaire, interview notes; Tallon questionnaire; LaRiviere interview notes; Gorman interview notes; Tyler interview notes, all in Ryan Collection, Mahn Center; Megellas, *All the Way to Berlin*, pp. 127–31; Bos, *Circle and the Fields of Little America*, pp. 212–15; Kershaw, *It Never Snows in September*, pp. 197–200; Burriss, *Strike and Hold*, p. 141; personal survey of crossing site, Fort Hof van Holland, railroad bridge, July 2010.

7. 82nd Airborne Division, AAR; 504th Parachute Infantry Regiment, history; S3 Journal, September 20, 1944; 307th Airborne Engineer Battalion, AAR; 376th Parachute Field Artillery Battalion, history; unit journal, September 20, 1944, all at National Archives; 3rd Battalion, 504th Parachute Infantry Regiment, unit journal, September 20, 1944, USAMHI; H Company, 3rd Battalion, 504th Parachute Infantry combat interviews; Peter Robinson, notes from interview with Frederic Kelly, September 19, 1967; Guardsman Leslie Johnson, letter to parents, circa 1944, both in Box 115, Folder 22; A. G. "Tony" Jones, questionnaire, unpublished memoir, pp. 110–11, notes from interview with Frederic Kelly, September 13, 1967, Box 115, Folder 12; Benjamin Vandervoort, letter to Frederic Kelly, March 28, 1969, Box 105, Folder 14; Heinz Harmel, notes from interviews with Cornelius Ryan, November 2, 22, December 6, 1967, Box 130, Folder 12; 10th SS Panzer Division, daily diary, September 20, 1944; Goulburn, unpublished memoir, pp. 9–10; Burriss interview notes; LaRiviere interview notes; Dunlop letter, all in Ryan Collection, Mahn Center; Burriss, *Strike and Hold*, pp. 122–23; Megellas, *All the Way to Berlin*, p. 134; Saunders, *Nijmegen*, pp. 173–76; Ryan, *Bridge Too Far*, pp. 471–75; Kershaw, *It Never Snows in September*, pp. 200–01; Margry, *Operation Market Garden, Then and Now*, pp. 500–05; Richard Lanni, director, *The Americans on Hell's Highway*, documentary, circa 2010 (in the documentary, Lanni conducted an insightful interview with Moffatt Burriss); personal survey of

Nijmegen road bridge and surrounding area, July 2010. The Americans and British later bickered over who was the first to capture the bridge. In my opinion, this was a foolish and unnecessary argument and really quite beside the point. The plan, after all, called for the American paratroopers to take the north end of the bridge while the British tanks took the south end. This is exactly what happened. Plain and simple, the taking of the bridge was an *Allied* achievement.

8. Major General Orlando Ward, letter to Colonel A. L. Van den Berge, September 17, 1951; Colonel A. L. Van den Berge, letter to Colonel Stewart; September 21, 1951; Dr. L. de Jong, comments on "The Siegfried Line" manuscript, September 22, 1956; Arie Bestebreurtje, letter to Charles MacDonald, October 25, 1956, all in RG319, Entry 95, Box 10, Folders 1 and 4, Office of the Chief of Military History, History Division; "The Siegfried Line" by Charles MacDonald; 82nd Airborne Division, AAR, all at National Archives; James Gavin, letter to William Breuer, October 6, 1982, James Gavin Papers, Box 28, Folder 4; James Gavin, letter to T. Moffatt Burriss, January 15, 1979; T. Moffatt Burriss, letter to James Gavin, February 8, 1979, both in James Gavin Papers, Box 15, Folder 8; Gavin speech on Waal crossing; Gavin, comments on "The Siegfried Line," all at USAMHI; General Hans Albin Rauter, statement on Nijmegen bridge, October 10, 1948, Box 130, Folder 1; Jones questionnaire, unpublished memoir, pp. 110–12; Bestebreurtje interview notes; Gavin interview notes; Kappel interview notes, all in Ryan Collection, Mahn Center; MacDonald, *The Siegfried Line*, pp. 183–84; Ryan, *Bridge Too Far*, p. 474; Margry, *Operation Market Garden, Then and Now*, pp. 363, 503–07. Today, a video at the National Liberation Museum in Groesbeek presents the Jan van Hoof story as established fact. I personally view this as unconscionable and ahistorical. Rauter was tried for a litany of war crimes and executed in 1949.

9. 82nd Airborne Division, AAR, National Archives; Gavin, oral history; AWC conference, both at USAMHI; Father William Peterse, unpublished memoir, pp. 3–4, Box 123, Folder 30; A. D. Demetras, letter to Cornelius Ryan, October 23, 1970, Box 102, Folder 18; Bommer questionnaire; LaRiviere interview notes; Burriss interview notes; Megellas questionnaire; Gavin, letters to Ryan, Olson; interview notes; Vandeleur interview notes; Adair interview notes; Harmel interview notes; Gorman interview notes, all in Ryan Collection, Mahn Center; Pitt interview, www.thedropzone.com; Hughes, unpublished memoir, pp. 3–4, LOC; H Company, 504th Parachute Infantry; 3rd Battalion, 504th Parachute Infantry; Tucker, combat interviews; Lieutenant Colonel Roger Cirillo (USA, Ret.), e-mails to author August 21, 24, 2010; MGM, *Bridge Too Far*; Lanni, *The Americans on Hell's Highway* documentary; Tonie and Valmai Holt, *Major and Mrs. Holt's Battlefield Guide: Operation Market Garden* (South Yorkshire, UK: Leo Cooper, 2001), pp. 177–84; David Bennett, *A Magnificent Disaster: The Failure of Market Garden, the Arnhem Operation, September 1944* (Philadelphia and Newbury: Casemate, 2008), pp. 121–25; Megellas, *All the Way to Berlin*, pp. 135–37; Burriss, *Strike and Hold*, pp. 123–24; Ryan, *Bridge Too Far*, pp. 477–79; Margry, *Operation Market Garden, Then and Now*, pp. 500–07; MacDonald, *The Siegfried Line*, pp. 184–86;

Gavin, *On to Berlin*, pp. 200–02; Horrocks, *Corps Commander*, pp. 116–18; Saunders, *Nijmegen*, pp. 186–90; Rapport and Northwood, *Rendezvous with Destiny*, pp. 323–42. After the war, Carrington entered politics and eventually became foreign secretary under Margaret Thatcher. He denied that Burriss had ever threatened to kill him, but Burriss himself and several of his men confirmed that he did. Gavin, for most of his life, contended that, had Ridgway been in charge of the operation, the Allies would have gotten to Arnhem, perhaps even a day or two before September 20. Interestingly, in a 1954 letter to the Office of the Chief of Military History, Gavin placed ultimate blame for the failure to link up at Arnhem on Eisenhower. Gavin believed that Ike should have reinforced Market Garden with another corps or two and that this might have led to success. This argument of Gavin's was, in political terms, somewhat courageous because, in 1954, he was still an active-duty army officer and Eisenhower was president.

CHAPTER 12: **Self-Deception**

1. Lieutenant General Omar Bradley, letter to General Dwight Eisenhower, September 21, 1944; Lieutenant General Omar Bradley, letters to Lieutenant General Courtney Hodges and Lieutenant General George Patton, September 23, 1944, Clay and Joan Blair Collection, Bradley Files, Box 34, Folder 2; Major Chester Hanson, diary, September 22 and 23, 1944, Box 31; Brigadier General Raymond Moses, Supply Officer (G4), Twelfth Army Group, Memorandum of Conference with General Bradley, September 23, 1944; personal diary, September 21–24, 1944, Raymond Moses Collection, Box 1, Folders 4 and 5, all at USAMHI; Jonathan Jordan, *Brothers, Rivals, Victors: Eisenhower, Patton, Bradley and the Partnership that Drove the Allied Conquest in Europe* (New York: NAL Caliber, 2011), pp. 407–08; Harry Butcher, *My Three Years with Eisenhower: The Personal Diary of Captain Harry C. Butcher, USNR* (New York: Simon & Schuster, 1946), pp. 671–76; Omar Bradley, *A Soldier's Story* (New York: Henry Holt and Company, 1951), pp. 422–23; Bradley, *General's Life*, pp. 252–54; Tedder, *With Prejudice*, pp. 594–98; Pogue, *Supreme Command*, pp. 294–96; D'Este, *Soldier's Life*, pp. 619–20; Eisenhower, *Crusade in Europe*, pp. 310–12; Montgomery, *Memoirs*, pp. 253–54; Chandler, editor, *Papers of Dwight Eisenhower, Volume IV*, pp. 2175–76, 2183–86, 2215–16, *Volume V*, p. 167. Montgomery did not quite get everything he wanted at the September 22 meeting. In addition to asking for Eisenhower to halt the other armies and divert all supplies to the Twenty-first Army Group, Montgomery— through de Guingand—requested that the U.S. First Army be placed under his direct command. Knowing this would have been unthinkable to American public opinion, Eisenhower turned him down. Bradley, for one, was immensely relieved, because this would have gutted his army group.

CHAPTER 13: **Road Killing and Ridge Holding**

1. S. L. A. Marshall, "Operation Market," RG407, Entry 427, Box 11753, Folder 1; 101st Airborne Division, AAR; history; 501st Parachute Infantry Regiment, summary of

events; 101st Airborne Division Reconnaissance Platoon, diary, September 22, 1944, all at National Archives; S. L. A. Marshall, "Parachute Battalion in Holland," Small Unit Study No. 1; Poppe, "2nd Commitment of the 59th Infantry Division," pp. 6–7, both at USAMHI; Darwin Clippinger, transcript of interview with Fran Foley, July 11, 2003, Darwin Clippinger Collection, #14878, LOC; 101st Airborne Division, G2 Periodic Report, September 22, 1944; Order of Battle Report for September 22, 1944, both in CI-226A; Rich, "Ordinary Eagle," pp. 134–38; Neill questionnaire; Otten diary, September 22, 1944, both in Ryan Collection, Mahn Center; Laurence Critchell, *Four Stars of Hell* (New York: Jove Books, 1947), p. 123; Maxwell Taylor, *Swords into Plowshares* (New York: Da Capo, 1972), pp. 90–91; Saunders, *Hell's Highway*, pp. 157–68; Koskimaki, *Hell's Highway*, pp. 251–58, 313–18; Rapport and Northwood, *Rendezvous with Destiny*, pp. 345–54; Kershaw, *It Never Snows in September*, pp. 252–57; Margry, *Operation Market Garden, Then and Now*, pp. 537–40; Bowen, *Fighting with the Screaming Eagles*, p. 114; Webster, *Parachute Infantry*, p. 99.

2. 506th Parachute Infantry Regiment, AAR, RG407, Entry 427, Box 11815, Folder 1; unit journal, RG407, Entry 427, Box 11816, Folder 6; 321st Glider Field Artillery Battalion, AAR, RG407, Entry 427, Box 11753, Folder 11; 907th Glider Field Artillery Battalion, AAR, RG407, Entry 427, Box 11804, Folder 2; 101st Airborne Division, AAR; history; 501st Parachute Infantry Regiment, summary of events, all at National Archives; John Taylor, unpublished memoir, pp. 50–51; Bill Brown, "Fighting Fox Company," pp. 103–10, both in Richard Winters Collection, Box 6, Folders 3 and 5, USAMHI; Wayne Walton, unpublished biography, pp. 10–11, Wayne Walton Collection, #39155, LOC; X. B. Cox, questionnaire, Box 98, Folder 56; Walter Miller, unpublished memoir, pp. 4–5, Box 98, Folder 50, both in Ryan Collection, Mahn Center; 1st and 2nd battalions, 327th Glider Infantry Regiment, combat interviews with Westover, 1st Battalion, 401st Glider Infantry Regiment, combat interview with Westover, all in CI-226A; Major Robert Kemm, "Operations of the 101st Airborne Division in the Airborne Invasion of the Netherlands (Personal Participation—Battalion Executive of an Airborne AA/AT Battalion," pp. 17–19, copy in author's possession; Robert Perdue, "Battle at Veghel Revisited," *After the Battle*, Number 127, pp. 32–39; William True and Deryck Tufts True, *The Cow Spoke French: The Story of Sgt. William True, American Paratrooper in World War II* (Bennington, VT: Merriam Press, 2002), pp. 102–04; Koskimaki, *Hell's Highway*, pp. 320–32; Margry, *Operation Market Garden, Then and Now*, pp. 541–51; Kershaw, *It Never Snows in September*, pp. 256–62; Rapport and Northwood, *Rendezvous with Destiny*, pp. 354–61; Webster, *Parachute Infantry*, p. 99; Horrocks, *Corps Commander*, p. 121.

3. 321st Glider Field Artillery Battalion, history; S3 Journal, September 24, 1944, both in RG407, Entry 427, Box 11795, Folder 10; AAR; 101st Airborne Division, AAR; 501st Parachute Infantry Regiment, summary of events; also "Battle of the Sand Dunes," located in the same box and folder; 81st Airborne Antitank Battalion, AAR; Marshall, "Operation Market," all at National Archives; Marshall, "Parachute

Battalion in Holland," USAMHI; Lieutenant Colonel Friedrich von der Heydte, "6th Falschirmjäger Regiment in the Action against U.S. Paratroopers in the Netherlands in September 1944," pp. 7–11, Box 131, Folder 25; Friedrich von der Heydte, letter to Major General James Gavin, January 30, 1954, Box 2, Folder 2; Robert Phillips, questionnaire, letter to Heather Chapman, August 24, 1967, Box 97, Folder 17; Ray Lappegard, questionnaire, Box 97, Folder 12; Cippola questionnaire, all in Ryan Collection, Mahn Center; Critchell, *Four Stars of Hell*, pp. 134–44; Koskimaki, *Hell's Highway*, pp. 260–71; Saunders, *Hell's Highway*, pp. 186–200; Kershaw, *It Never Snows in September*, pp. 280–87; Rapport and Northwood, *Rendezvous with Destiny*, pp. 362–74; Margry, *Operation Market Garden, Then and Now*, pp. 552–63; Beck and Schucany were quoted in Lanni, *The Americans on Hell's Highway*. Richard Lanni was kind enough to provide me with a transcript of the Schucany interview. Personal survey of Eerde and the remnants of the sand dune battle area, July 2010.

4. 325th Glider Infantry Regiment, history; S2/S3 Journal, September 27–October 3, 1944, both in RG407, Entry 427, Box 10466, Folder 2; 508th Parachute Infantry Regiment, AAR; unit journal, September 21–30, 1944; 505th Parachute Infantry Regiment, AAR; 319th Glider Field Artillery Battalion, history; 320th Glider Field Artillery Battalion, history; 376th Parachute Field Artillery Battalion, history; 456th Parachute Field Artillery Battalion, history, all at National Archives; Teddy Sanford, oral history, Teddy Sanford Papers, Box 1; Staff Sergeant John Reynolds, transcript of radio interview regarding the Battle of Mook, October 1–3, 1944, James Gavin Papers, Box 15, Folder 5; Langdon, "Ready," pp. 101–02, all at USAMHI; Richard Wagner, questionnaire, Box 106, Folder 34; Brickley letter; Foley, questionnaire, Taylor, questionnaire, all in Ryan Collection, Mahn Center; Delamater, "Action of the 1st Battalion, 508th Parachute Infantry," pp. 20–23; 325th Glider Infantry Regiment, combat interview, CI-171; Jerry Richlak, editor, *Glide to Glory: Unedited Personal Stories from the Airborne Glidermen of World War II* (Chesterland, OH; Cedar House, 2002), pp. 281–82; Bos, *Circle and the Fields of Little America*, p. 241; Saunders, *Nijmegen*, pp. 75–78, 114–18; Margry, *Operation Market Garden, Then and Now*, pp. 710–11; Boroughs, *Devil's Tale*, pp. 197–201; MacDonald, *The Siegfried Line*, pp. 192–93; personal survey of Devil's Hill and Mook, July 2010. Sanford was the commander of 1st Battalion, 325th Glider Infantry. His unit bore the brunt of the Mook attack.

CHAPTER 14: **Opheusden**

1. Warren, *Airborne Operations in World War II*, p. 146; MacDonald, *The Siegfried Line*, pp. 202–03; Margry, *Operation Market Garden, Then and Now*, pp. 704–07.

2. 327th Glider Infantry, Presidential Unit Citation information, RG407, Entry 427, Box 11807, Folder 8; Regiment 506th Parachute Infantry Regiment, Unit Citation, RG407, Entry 427, Box 11796, Folder 3; AAR; unit journal, October 5 and 6, 1944; S2 Journal, October 5 and 6, 1944; S3 Journal, October 5 and 6, 1944; 101st Airborne Division, AAR; 326th Airborne Engineer Battalion, AAR; 321st Glider Field Artillery

Battalion, AAR; S3 Journal, October 5 and 6, 1944; 81st Airborne Antiaircraft Battalion, AAR, all at National Archives; Hassenzahl, oral history, LOC; Iseneker, questionnaire; Mitchell, questionnaire, both in Ryan Collection, Mahn Center; Mark Bando, *Vanguard of the Crusade: The 101st Airborne Division in World War II* (Bedford, PA: The Aberjona Press, 2003), pp. 191–93; Rapport and Northwood, *Rendezvous with Destiny*, pp. 384–87; Koskimaki, *Hell's Highway*, pp. 434–45; Saunders, *Hell's Highway*, pp. 167–77; Burgett, *Road to Arnhem*, pp. 106–13; personal survey of Opheusden battle area, July 2010.

3. 101st Airborne Division, AAR; 506th Parachute Infantry Regiment, AAR; Unit Citation; unit journal, October 6 and 7, 1944; S2 Journal, October 6 and 7, 1944; S3 Journal, October 6 and 7, 1944; 327th Glider Infantry Regiment, Presidential Unit Citation information; 321st Glider Field Artillery Battalion, AAR; 81st Airborne Antiaircraft Battalion, AAR, all at National Archives; Earl Patchin, unpublished memoir, pp. 3–4, Earl Patchin Collection, #50458; Hassenzahl, oral history, both at LOC; Patrick Sweeney, unpublished memoir, pp. 4–6, Box 98, Folder 40; Shoemaker, questionnaire, telephone conversation notes; Iseneker, questionnaire, all in Ryan Collection, Mahn Center; 1st Battalion, 327th Glider Infantry Regiment; 2nd Battalion, 327th Glider Infantry Regiment; 1st Battalion, 401st Glider Infantry Regiment, combat interviews, CI-226A; Cook, unpublished memoir, pp. 6–8; Rapport and Northwood, *Rendezvous with Destiny*, pp. 387–93; Koskimaki, *Hell's Highway*, pp. 446–61; Bando, *Vanguard of the Crusade*, p. 194; Burgett, *Road to Arnhem*, pp. 119–41; personal survey of Opheusden battle area, July 2010. The Americans were stunned to see the British battalion form up and attack across an open field, right into the muzzles of German guns. The result was a needless slaughter. Numerous American witnesses compared the tragedy to something out of the Civil War.

4. 2nd Battalion, 327th Glider Infantry Regiment, "Battle of Opheusden with Company Accounts," RG407, Entry 427, Box 11808, Folder 12; 1st Battalion, 401st Glider Infantry Regiment, "Battle of Opheusden with Company Accounts," RG407, Entry 427, Box 11808, Folder 16; 327th Glider Infantry Regiment, Presidential Unit Citation information; AAR; S1 Journal, October 7–15, 1944; S2 Journal and Periodic Reports, October 7–15, 1944; S3 Periodic Reports and Tactical Operations, October 7–15; 1st Battalion, 327th Glider Infantry Regiment, AAR; 2nd Battalion, 327th Glider Infantry Regiment, AAR; 1st Battalion, 401st Glider Infantry Regiment, history, all at National Archives; Walter Miller, questionnaire, unpublished memoir, pp. 5–15, Box 98, Folder 50; Ray Allen, questionnaire, Box 99, Folder 10, both in Ryan Collection, Mahn Center; 1st Battalion, 327th Glider Infantry Regiment; 2nd Battalion, 327th Glider Infantry Regiment; 1st Battalion, 401st Glider Infantry Regiment, combat interviews, CI-226A; Rich, "Ordinary Eagle," pp. 147–52; Rapport and Northwood, *Rendezvous with Destiny*, pp. 394–96; Koskimaki, *Hell's Highway*, pp. 461–66; MacDonald, *Siegfried Line*, pp. 202–03. In previous books, I have pointed out the complete fallaciousness of S. L. A. Marshall's contention that only 15 to 20 percent of American riflemen in World

War II ever fired their weapons. The 327th Glider Infantry Regiment's experiences at Opheusden are yet another example of how incorrect Marshall's arguments were.

CHAPTER 15: **Stalemate**

1. SHAEF, G3 memo on release of the U.S. airborne divisions, October 4, 1944; Allied Expeditionary Air Forces, operation memo on release of U.S. airborne divisions, September 28, 1944, both in RG331, Entry 1, Box 75, Folder 6; Lieutenant General Lewis Brereton, message to General Dwight Eisenhower on release of U.S. airborne divisions, October 8, 1944, RG331, Entry 256, Box 34, Folder 3, all at National Archives; McAuliffe, editor, "WWII Letters," p. 292; Brereton, *Brereton Diaries*, pp. 361, 367–68; Chandler, editor, *Papers of Dwight Eisenhower, Volume IV*, pp. 2222–25; MacDonald, *Siegfried Line*, pp. 203–05. The pragmatic but shortsighted use of airborne divisions in protracted defensive combat was not new. The same thing had happened at Salerno, Anzio, and Normandy. It would soon happen again in the Battle of the Bulge.

2. Robert Rader, unpublished memoir, pp. 4–5, Box 12, Folder 9; Christenson, unpublished memoir, p. 5, Box 4, Folder 4, both in Richard Winters Collection, USAMHI; Burns, unpublished memoir, p. 118, EC; Donald Pearson, questionnaire, letter to Heather Chapman, August 28, 1967, Box 99, Folder 8; Herbert Jacobs, questionnaire, Box 98, Folder 47; Joseph Kissane, questionnaire, notes from interview with Heather Chapman, November 30, 1967, letters to mother, October 1, 15, 1944, May 16, 1945, Box 105, Folder 32; Thomas Morrison, questionnaire, Box 99, Folder 38; Hauptfleisch, notes from interview with Frederic Kelly, January 12, 1968, and phone conversation with Frederic Kelly, February 26, 1968, Box 102, Folder 29, all in Ryan Collection, Mahn Center; McAuliffe, editor, "WWII Letters," p. 294; Rich, "Ordinary Eagle," p. 163; Graves diary, October 4, 1944; Bowen, *Fighting with the Screaming Eagles*, p. 150; Wurst, *Descending from the Clouds*, pp. 210–11.

3. Carwood Lipton, unpublished memoir, pp. 11–12, Box 9, Folder 7, Richard Winters Collection; Rader, unpublished memoir, p. 4; Sanford, oral history, all at USAMHI; Joseph Comer, letter to Edith Rogers, November 21, 1944, Joseph Comer Collection, #57958; "We Served Proudly," p. 79, both at LOC; Burns, unpublished memoir, pp. 120–21, EC; William Kotary, questionnaire, Box 106, Folder 30; Neil Sweeney, questionnaire, Box 98, Folder 2; Arthur Parker, questionnaire, Box 98, Folder 56; Harrell, questionnaire, letter; Taylor, questionnaire; Tucker, questionnaire, letter; Purcell, unpublished memoir, pp. 6–8; Lappegard, questionnaire, all in Ryan Collection, Mahn Center; Moseley interview; True, *The Cow Spoke French*, pp. 111–12; Tucker, *Parachute Soldier*, pp. 97–101; Wurst, *Descending from the Clouds*, pp. 205–07; Burgett, *Road to Arnhem*, pp. 155–56.

4. John Leh, unpublished memoir, pp. 4–5, World War II Survey #6101; Gavin diary, November 1, 1944; Gavin, notes on leadership, all at USAMHI; James "Buck" Dawson, letter to Cornelius Ryan, March 5, 1973, Box 101, Folder 9; Olson interview notes, letter, all in Ryan Collection, Mahn Center; Barbara Gavin Fauntleroy, *The General and*

His Daughter: The Wartime Letters of General James M. Gavin to His Daughter Barbara (New York: Fordham University Press, 2007), pp. 137–40; Booth and Spencer, *Paratrooper*, p. 241; Gavin, *On to Berlin*, pp. 204–09. Dawson overheard Dempsey's "finest division in the world" comment and wrote it down for posterity.

5. 101st Airborne Division, AAR; 501st Parachute Infantry Regiment, summary of events, both at National Archives; Jacobus, "Echoes of the Warriors," pp. 374–76; 2nd Battalion, 504th Parachute Infantry Regiment, unit journal, October 1944, both at USAMHI; Ivan Ladany, oral history, EC; Bruce Barton, unpublished memoir, pp. 77–78, Bruce Barton Collection, #10953; Beranty, "Don't Call Me Chicken," both at LOC; Desmond Jones, unpublished memoir, pp. 6–7; Lappegard, questionnaire; Van Poyck, questionnaire, interview notes; Tucker, questionnaire, letter; Boling, questionnaire; Allardyce letter; Klein, questionnaire, all in Ryan Collection, Mahn Center; William Hayes, unpublished memoir, pp. 104–05, copy in author's possession courtesy of Mr. Hayes; Joseph Hecht, "Living History: A Story of Personal Experiences While a Member of the 82nd Airborne Division in WWII," *The Static Line*, December 2002, p. 32; Phil Nordyke, *All American All the Way: The Combat History of the 82nd Airborne Division in World War II* (St. Paul, MN: Zenith Press, 2005), pp. 581–84; Taylor, *Swords and Plowshares*, pp. 93–95; Koskimaki, *Hell's Highway*, pp. 418–20, 484–85; Tucker, *Parachute Soldier*, p. 97; Bando, *Vanguard of the Crusade*, pp. 202–03; Critchell, *Four Stars of Hell*, pp. 163–65; Rapport and Northwood, *Rendezvous with Destiny*, pp. 397–400. Walter Van Poyck had a bittersweet postwar life. He spent two years recovering from his wounds in army hospitals, but ended up getting married and enjoying a highly successful career as a business executive. However, his wife died in 1956 of carbon monoxide poisoning while having coffee with neighbors. Van Poyck himself died in 1973. His son and namesake grew into a hardened criminal who eventually was convicted of armed robbery and murder. As of this writing, he is on death row in Florida. For more on this tragic story, see Meg Laughlin's article "Death Row Prisoner Ponders Life in Memoir" in the January 4, 2004, edition of *The Miami Herald*. Van Poyck writes a regular blog from prison and is currently appealing his sentence.

6. First Allied Airborne Army, AAR; 101st Airborne Division, AAR; 508th Parachute Infantry Regiment, AAR; 504th Parachute Infantry Regiment, AAR, all at National Archives; Langdon, "Ready," p. 102, at USAMHI; Hassenzahl, oral history, LOC; Edward Mitchell, questionnaire, Box 98, Folder 31; Dreuner, questionnaire, both in Ryan Collection, Mahn Center; Moseley interview; Hecht, "Living History," p. 32; Bowen, *Fighting with the Screaming Eagles*, pp. 145–47; Koskimaki, *Hell's Highway*, pp. 475–80, 492–508; Rapport and Northwood, *Rendezvous with Destiny*, pp. 399–413; MacDonald, *Siegfried Line*, pp. 205–06.

CHAPTER 16: Timberwolves

1. 21st Army Group, "The Clearing of the Scheldt Estuary, October–November 1944," RG407, Entry 427, Box 1376, Folder 2; General Gustav von Zengen, "Fifteenth Army,"

RG549, Entry 2202, Foreign Military Studies, Box 32, B-343, both at National Archives; Canadian Army, "The Clearing of the Scheldt Estuary and the Liberation of Walcheren, 2 October–7 November," pp. 2–6, copy in author's possession; Colonel C. P. Stacey, *The Canadian Army, 1939–1945: An Official Historical Summary* (Ottawa: King's Printer, 1948), pp. 220–35; Field Marshal Bernard Montgomery, *Normandy to the Baltic* (London: Hutchinson and Company, 1946), pp. 153–68; Montgomery, *Memoirs*, pp. 253–56, 266; Chandler, editor, *Papers of Dwight Eisenhower, Volume IV*, pp. 2215–17, 2221–25; MacDonald, *Siegfried Line*, pp. 207–15. For more information on the 7th Armored Division's battle in the Peel Marshes, see pages 231–48 of MacDonald's fine study.

2. 104th Infantry Division, AAR, October 1944, RG407, Entry 427, Box 11946, Folder 6; "Holland After Action Report," RG407, Entry 427, Box 11946, Folder 7; Major General Terry Allen, letter to Major General John Stokes, April 26, 1956, RG319, Entry 95, Box 10, Folder 3, records of the Office of the Chief of Military History, History Division, "The Siegfried Line" by Charles MacDonald, all at National Archives; Leo Hoegh and Howard Doyle, *Timberwolf Tracks: The History of the 104th Infantry Division, 1942–1945* (Washington, D.C.: Infantry Journal Press, 1946), pp. 3–52, 61–63; Gerald Astor, *Terrible Terry Allen: Combat General of World War II—The Life of an American Soldier* (New York: Ballantine Books, 2003), pp. 185–91, 218–29, 236–48; Bradley, *Soldier's Story*, pp. 100, 110–11; Bradley, *General's Life*, pp. 136, 158, 171–73, 195. My statements on the Timberwolves' high esteem for Terry Allen are drawn primarily from dozens of soldiers' firsthand accounts, plus some personal interviews, all of which would be too numerous to cite. I found no negative comments about Allen.

3. 413th Infantry Regiment, history, RG407, Entry 427, Box 11995, Folder 10; AAR, October–November 1944, RG407, Entry 427, Box 11995, Folder 12; 414th Infantry Regiment, history, RG407, Entry 427, Box 12000, Folder 7; AAR, October–November 1944, RG407, Entry 427, Box 12000, Folder 3; 415th Infantry Regiment, history, RG407, Entry 427, Box 12006, Folder 1; AAR, October–November 1944, RG407, Entry 427, Box 12006, Folder 3; 104th Infantry Division, AAR, October 1944; Holland after-action report, all at National Archives; L Company, 413th Infantry Regiment, company history, Robert Doerr Papers, Box 1, Folder 14; Frank Perozzi, questionnaire, World War II Survey #7968, Box 3; B Company, 414th Infantry Regiment, company history, self-published, all at USAMHI; Art Decker, "I Company's Baptism of Fire," *Timberwolf Howl*, March 2008, p. 4; Raymond Potter, "Eight Days in Holland— 6 Months a Prisoner," *Timberwolf Howl*, January 2003, p. 13; Bob Bilinsky, unpublished memoir; Charles Dodd, diary, October 26, 1944, both located at www.104infdiv. org; "Combat History, 413th Infantry Regiment"; "Combat History, 415th Infantry Regiment," copies in my possession courtesy of Mr. John Warmington; Fred Dunham, unpublished memoir, p. 15, copy in my possession courtesy of Mr. Sonny Dunham; Bill Kortlander, e-mail to author, February 17, 2010; Hoegh and Doyle, *Timberwolf Tracks*, pp. 56–66.

4. 329th Engineer Combat Battalion, AAR, RG407, Entry 427, Box 11992, Folder 6; 329th Medical Battalion, AAR, November 1944, RG407, Entry 427, Box 12009, Folder 10; 413th Infantry Regiment, medics, history, RG407, Entry 427, Box 11999, Folder 5; AAR; history; 414th Infantry Regiment, AAR; history; 415th Infantry Regiment, AAR; history; 104th Infantry Division, AAR; Holland after-action report, all at National Archives; Billie Henderson, questionnaire, World War II Survey #4683, Box 3, Folder 8; Duane Robey, unpublished memoir, pp. 37, 48, located in library stacks at USAMHI; James Wasilewski, interview with Stuart Wasilewski, June 15, 2008, James Wasilewski Collection #60618; Walter Walko, interview with Tom Swope, September 13, 2001, Walter Walko Collection #463, both at LOC; Douglas Miller, unpublished memoir; Harry Whitlach, unpublished memoir; Duane Robey, unpublished memoir, all at www.104infdiv.org; "Combat History of the 413th Infantry Regiment," "History of the 329th Engineer Battalion," both in author's possession courtesy of Mr. John Warmington; Paul Marshall, interview with the author, February 5, 2010; Hugh Daly, unpublished memoir, pp. 57–58, copy in author's possession courtesy of Mr. Daly; Hoegh and Doyle, *Timberwolf Tracks*, pp. 57–73. Walko and Daly were members of Robey's I&R platoon. Their accounts corroborated the details of Robey's memoir.

5. 104th Infantry Division, Holland after-action report; 413th Infantry Regiment, medics, history, both at National Archives; L Company, 413th Infantry, company history; B Company, 414th Infantry, company history; Robey, unpublished memoir, pp. 63–64, all at USAMHI; John Rheney, unpublished memoir; Parley Allred, unpublished memoir; Dick Williams, unpublished memoir, all at www.104infdiv.org; Cecil Bolton, "Operations of the Weapons Platoon, Company 'E,' 413th Infantry Regiment (104th Infantry Division) Night River Crossing of Mark River, Holland, 2d November 1944, Personal Experiences of a Platoon Leader," p. 5, copy in author's possession; "Combat History of the 413th Infantry"; Marshall interview; Peter Branton, "Zundert Revisited," *Timberwolf Howl*, June 2003, p. 13; John Light, *An Infantryman Remembers World War II* (Shippensburg, PA: Beidel Printing House, Inc., 1997), pp. 66–67; Hoegh and Doyle, *Timberwolf Tracks*, pp. 70–75; personal survey of Oudenbosch, July 2010.

6. 415th Infantry Regiment, unit journal, October 30–November 1, 1944, RG407, Entry 427, Box 12006, Folder 1; AAR; history; 104th Infantry Division, AAR; Holland after-action report, all at National Archives; John Wade, unpublished memoir, 22–23, John Wade Papers, Box 1, Folder 1, USAMHI; Harold Zuercher, unpublished memoir; George Roxandich, unpublished memoir; Eugene Traiteler, unpublished memoir, all at www.104infdiv.org; "Combat History of the 415th Infantry"; "Night Operations: A Report of Night Operations as Executed by the 104th (Timberwolf) Infantry Division," *Military Review*, January 1946, pp. 56–57; Albert Siklosi, "The Mark River Crossing," *Timberwolf Howl*, January 2002, pp. 10–12; Ralph Bleier, "The First Crossing of the Mark River," *Timberwolf Howl*, June 2007, pp. 12–13; Hoegh and Doyle,

Timberwolf Tracks, pp. 75–80; MacDonald, *Siegfried Line*, pp. 224–25; personal survey of Mark River crossing site and Standdaarbuiten, July 2010.

7. 104th Infantry Division Artillery, AAR, RG407, Entry 427, Box 11991, Folder 1; 386th Field Artillery Battalion, history, RG407, Entry 427, Box 11993, Folder 9; 387th Field Artillery Battalion, history, RG407, Entry 427, Box 11994, Folder 8; 929th Field Artillery Battalion, history, RG407, Entry 427, Box 11994, Folder 8; 104th Infantry Division, Holland after-action report; 413th Infantry Regiment, history; AAR, October–November, 1944, unit journal, November 2–5, 1944; 414th Infantry Regiment, history; 415th Infantry Regiment, history; AAR, November, 1944; unit journal, November 2–5, 1944; 329th Engineer Combat Battalion, AAR, all at National Archives; Robey, unpublished memoir, p. 68; L Company, 413th Infantry Regiment, company history, both at USAMHI; Sergeant John Meier, letter to parents, November 14, 1944, WHMC; Theodore Sery, unpublished memoir, www.104infdiv.org; "Combat History of the 413th Infantry"; "Combat History of the 415th Infantry"; "History of the 329th Engineer Battalion"; "The Clearing of the Scheldt Estuary," pp. 15–16; Bolton, "Operations of the Weapons Platoon," pp. 7–19; "Night Operations," pp. 56–57; Daniel Ponzevic, "The Lieutenant's Shovel," *Timberwolf Howl*, June 2004, pp. 12–13; Jim Henderson, "Crossing the Mark River," *Timberwolf Howl*, June 2006, p. 12; Charles Norris, unpublished memoir, pp. 187–88, copy in author's possession courtesy of Mr. Norris; Hoegh and Doyle, *Timberwolf Tracks*, pp. 79–102; MacDonald, *Siegfried Line*, pp. 225–30; Astor, *Terrible Terry Allen*, pp. 264–66; Stacey, *The Canadian Army*, pp. 227–29; personal survey of Standdaarbuiten and Mark River crossing site, July 2010. Another factor in opening up Antwerp was the V weapons, Hitler's early-generation rockets. He hurled twelve hundred of them at the Antwerp area, killing twenty-nine hundred civilians and wounding 5,433 others. These terror weapons could not, and did not, prevent the Allies from using the port facilities, but they incited plenty of fear among anyone in the vicinity of the city. Many Timberwolves recalled seeing the rockets flying overhead, on the way to Antwerp or other targets.

CHAPTER 17: **Off the Line**

1. 101st Airborne Division, "Operation Noah" evacuation plan for the Island, RG407, Entry 427, Box 11753, Folder 5; AAR; First Allied Airborne Army, AAR, all at National Archives; John Taylor, unpublished memoir, p. 67; Gavin diary, November 18, 21, 1944, both at USAMHI; Komosa, unpublished memoir, p. 28; William Tucker, questionnaire; Edward Mitchell, questionnaire; Gavin, letter to Ryan, February 21, 1973, all in Ryan Collection, Mahn Center; Graves diary, November 15, 1944; G. William Sefton, *It Was My War: I'll Remember It the Way I Want To!* (Manhattan, KS: Sunflower University Press, 1994), pp. 141–44; Fauntleroy, *The General and His Daughter*, pp. 140–41; Tucker, *Parachute Soldier*, p. 103; MacDonald, *The Siegfried Line*, pp. 204–06; Burgett, *Road to Arnhem*, pp. 158–60; Carter, *Those Devils in Baggy Pants*, pp. 169–70; Rapport and Northwood, *Rendezvous with Destiny*, p. 420; Wurst, *Descending from*

the Clouds, p. 212; Bando, *Vanguard of the Crusade*, pp. 208–09; Nordyke, *All American, All the Way*, pp. 584–85; Montgomery, *Normandy to the Baltic*, pp. 148–49; *Memoirs*, pp. 256–57, 265–67; Critchell, *Four Stars of Hell*, pp. 194–95; Gavin, *On to Berlin*, pp. 210–11, 219. The Canadians ended up spending significantly more time in the Groesbeek area than the Americans. For that reason, the locals today have a far better recollection of them than of the 82nd Airborne troopers.

INDEX

John C. McManus earned a PhD in American History and Military History from the University of Tennessee, where he served as assistant director of the Center for the Study of War and Society, helping oversee a project collecting the firsthand stories of American veterans of World War II. He is currently associate professor of U.S. military history at Missouri University of Science and Technology, where he teaches courses on the Civil War, World War II, Vietnam, U.S. Military History, and Modern American Combat Experience. He also currently serves as the official historian for the United States Army's Seventh Infantry Regiment.

CONNECT ONLINE

www.johncmcmanus.com

Printed in the United States
by Baker & Taylor Publisher Services